MANAGERIAL ACCOUNTING FOR BUSINESS DECISIONS

Second Edition

Ray Proctor

With contributions from
Nigel Burton and Adrian Pierce

FT Prentice Hall
FINANCIAL TIMES

An imprint of **Pearson Education**
Harlow, England • London • New York • Boston • San Francisco • Toronto
Sydney • Tokyo • Singapore • Hong Kong • Seoul • Taipei • New Delhi
Cape Town • Madrid • Mexico City • Amsterdam • Munich • Paris • Milan

Pearson Education Limited
Edinburgh Gate
Harlow
Essex CM20 2JE
England

and Associated Companies throughout the world

Visit us on the World Wide Web at:
www.pearsoned.co.uk

First published 2002
Second edition published 2006

© Pearson Education Limited 2002, 2006

ISBN: 978-0-273-68155-7

British Library Cataloguing-in-Publication Data
A catalogue record for this book is available from the British Library

Library of Congress Cataloging-in-Publication Data
A catalog record for this book is available from the Library of Congress

10 9 8 7 6 5 4 3
09 08 07

Typeset in 10.5/12.5pt Minion by 35
Printed in Malaysia, KHL

MANAGERIAL ACCOUNTING FOR BUSINESS DECISIONS

One Week Loan

I dedicate this book to my wife, Sara, who has endured many periods of solitude during its writing, with little or no complaint. Without her support, the book would not have reached completion. I welcome this opportunity to thank her publicly.

Contents

Part 4
PRODUCT COSTING AND PRICING   217

Part 5
BUDGETARY CONTROL   331

15 Using budgets to control   Diss!
     operations   364

Part 6
STRATEGY IMPLEMENTATION AND
PERFORMANCE MANAGEMENT   393

16 Strategic management
   accounting and performance
   indicators   394

17 Business performance
   management   413

Supporting resources

Visit **www.pearsoned.co.uk/proctor** to find valuable online resources

For instructors
- Solutions to the end of chapter questions posed in the text
- Complete downloadable Instructor's Manual
- PowerPoint slides that can be downloaded and used as OHTs

For more information please contact your local Pearson Education sales representative or visit **www.pearsoned.co.uk/proctor**

Preface to the first edition

Rationale

Is there really a need for yet another book on management accounting? There are many texts currently available on this subject. They tend to fall into one of two categories. First, those aimed at students aiming to become qualified accountants and, second, those aimed at students of business and management who do not intend to be accountants.

This book falls firmly into the second category. But the question still remains, is another book of this type needed? As an experienced teacher of business and management students, I believe it is. My justification is as follows.

Management accounting books for business and management students go into less technical detail than those aimed at professional accountancy students. This is sensible and I also take this approach. However, in my opinion, this only goes partway to fulfilling these students' needs. They also need to know the practicalities of how the techniques are actually used in business. Without this, they will end up as foundation-level accountancy students instead of what they wish to be, i.e. effective business managers.

Management emphasis

The reluctance of some students to embrace management accounting has arisen due to the emphasis being misplaced on accounting rather than management. All too often, assessment of students has tested mathematical proficiency rather than ability to apply appropriate techniques to business situations. This book is different in that it has a **strong management approach**. This is especially evident in the 'Manager's point of view' section of each chapter and in Chapter 14 on not-for-profit organisations. These unique features use actual examples from the world of business to place the theory into its practical context. Their objective is to remind students that management accounting is a means to an end and not an end in itself.

Market

This introductory book is particularly suitable for students of business and management who have no previous knowledge of management accounting. Provided this condition applies, it is suitable for both undergraduate and MBA students. It is also relevant and useful to practising managers.

Many readers will work in the service sector rather than manufacturing so I have used examples from the service sector wherever I can to reflect this. I also include a chapter highlighting managerial accounting in the 'not-for-profit' sector in order to make the book more relevant for those students working in it.

Accounting and managerial accounting

Accounting is not about numbers; it is about organisations, what they do and the things they use. Sales, equipment, remuneration, purchases, debtors, owners' investments and many other items all fall within this description. In order to express the relationships between them, they are all measured in the same units. These units are the currency used by the organisation. In the UK this unit is usually the pound sterling, in the USA it is the dollar, etc.

The numbers are merely the medium through which the value of these things, and changes to them, are expressed. When a credit sale changes stock into a debtor, all three items are measured in the same units. A sale of £80 may change stock valued at £50 into a debtor of £80. Competence at arithmetic is very useful in accountancy, knowledge of higher mathematics is less so. The ability to estimate answers mentally is very valuable as this enables a check to be performed on the broad accuracy of the detailed calculations. These estimates give ballpark figures approximating to the accurate answers and, for some purposes, are sufficient in themselves.

Financial accounting is essentially orientated towards the past. Its rules are intended to ensure that the statements of performance for a financial year, and the position at the end of that year, give a true and fair view of the organisation. Financial accounts can only be completed after the financial year has ended.

Management accounting is orientated towards the future. It is primarily concerned with the provision of information to managers to help them plan, evaluate and control activities. It is essentially a service function; a means to an end rather than an end in itself. Managerial accounting also fits this description but the use of the word 'managerial' emphasises the service role. This may seem obvious but, for much of the twentieth century, management accounting was used mainly to serve the needs of financial accounting rather than to assist managers in their tasks. (This theme is discussed further in Chapter 13 on strategic management accounting.) **Managerial accounting is about improving the future performance of organisations**.

Structure of the book

The structure of this book is summarised by the table of contents. It is split into six parts preceded by a preface and followed by a glossary and an index. Each chapter starts with a detailed list of contents, an introduction and a list of learning objectives to give the reader a framework for their study. The main topics are then discussed in a logical order. Often there is an illustration of how each technique is applied, followed by an invitation to the reader to attempt a similar question to test their understanding. Answers to these self-assessment questions are given at the end of each chapter.

One important feature appearing in each chapter is the section on the limitations of the techniques discussed. It is very important for you to appreciate that these techniques are financial models of business activity and that no model can ever be as rich as the reality it attempts to represent. In simple terms, the answers produced by the calculations are approximations and not exactitudes. An answer given to five decimal places may be very precise but that does not mean to say that it is accurate! Due to the assumptions built into the models, all the decimal places, and even some numbers to the left of the decimal point, may be worthless as well as misleading.

Next comes 'the manager's point of view'. These sections are written by Nigel Burton, who has spent over 20 years as a high-level manager in the chemical industry (he is also a qualified accountant). He writes from a practical point of view, giving many insights – born of his extensive experience – into the ways managers can use accounting techniques to their advantage. The chapters on not-for-profit organisations and working capital management are written by Adrian Pierce, who is also a qualified accountant and has practised his profession for more than 15 years in various businesses. At the time of writing, he holds a senior management position in a multi-million pound not-for-profit organisation. His experience offers a particularly relevant outlook on the extra dimensions of this type of organisation. The whole of Chapter 18 is a 'not-for-profit manager's point of view'.

After this section is a 'summary' of the main points covered by the chapter. This is to help the reader review the material and make connections between the various items discussed. This is similar to the complete picture emerging from the correct placing of all the pieces of a jigsaw. (It can also serve the useful function of a summary 'revision list' for examinations.)

Following this, the chapter is concluded by a section concerning assessment. First, an extensive case study is presented (the answer is given in the Lecturer's Guide). These cases are holistic in that they attempt to bring together many of the different aspects discussed within the chapter. They are suitable for either individual students or groups of students. It is impossible to be exact but these case studies are unlikely to take less than two hours to complete.

Next, the answers are given to the self-assessment questions contained within the chapter. Finally, several additional questions are presented for extra practice. The answers to some of these are given at the end of the book. The answers to the remaining questions are given in the Lecturer's Guide, which will also contain masters of overhead transparencies, etc. Supplementary material can be downloaded from http://www.booksites.net/proctor

In summary, each chapter:

- sets the context;
- introduces the subject;
- specifies the learning objectives;
- explains the principles in easy steps;
- encourages the reader to practise the techniques immediately;
- explains the limitations of the financial models;

- gives the manager's point of view;
- gives a summary of the main points;
- has a comprehensive case study;
- gives answers to self-assessment questions;
- has additional practice questions.

Advice to readers

Much thought was given by the author to the order of the contents. The topics are presented in a logical sequence but not a unique one. Any chapter can be studied without reference to other chapters but they are easier to understand in the light of the other chapters in the same part. For example, the two chapters on budgets are best read consecutively and the five chapters on costing and pricing are best read in conjunction with each other. The order in which Parts 2, 3, 4, 5 and 6 are read is not so important.

I strongly recommend that you attempt the self-assessment questions as you come across them. This gives an active, rather than passive, understanding of the subject matter and aids comprehension of the following sections. It is easy to believe you understand what you have just read, but attempting these questions will test this and reinforce your understanding of the subject matter.

Writing style

The writing style attempts to be concise and unambiguous. The overriding objective is **clarity**. Diagrams, many of them original, are included wherever they can aid understanding. Explanations are kept as simple as possible in order not to confuse. Intermediate steps in the solutions to questions have been included to ensure students can follow them. However, unnecessary algebra has been omitted in favour of a common-business-sense approach. My experience is that students appreciate this approach and learn faster. Much of the text is purposely written in a 'conversational' style to engage readers and put them at their ease. It is consistently practical in its approach, often referring to real situations.

Objective of the book

The objective of this book is to make you a better manager by enabling you to understand and apply managerial accounting techniques effectively. By knowing the assumptions and approximations on which these financial models are constructed, you will be aware of their limitations and the danger of applying their results without wider consideration of their business context. Most business decisions are too important to leave to the accountants. Use the information provided by them as a starting point for your deliberations, not as a prescribed course of action.

Organisational activities are not scientifically deterministic. If they were, there would be little or no need for managers. Managing is more of an art than a science. Information provided by accountants is important but it is not sufficient in itself. You also need a good intuitive feeling for how your customers, suppliers, markets and regulatory environment will behave in different situations. This comes from experience rather than academic learning. However, if I did not believe that the contents of this book could help you be a better manager, I would not have made the effort to write it. I wish you success in your management careers.

Preface to the second edition

It is pleasing to note that when a sample of lecturers from a variety of different institutions was asked what they thought of the first edition of this book, they all said they liked it. However, they all were of the opinion that it would benefit from the addition of other topics. Of course, their ideas about what this content should be differed from person to person. Where there was some consensus of opinion, I have written new material to covers these areas.

Some of the existing chapters have new sections such as 'annuities' in capital investment appraisal and 'sales mix effects' in variable costing and breakeven analysis. Also, some new self-assessment questions, end-of-chapter questions and case studies have been added. But the major additions are the following four new chapters:

Chapter 3   Ratio analysis and financial management
Chapter 4   Working capital management
Chapter 13   Divisional performance and transfer pricing
Chapter 17   Business performance management

Chapters 3 and 4 form the new 'Part 2' entitled 'Financial management'.

I sincerely hope users of this book find these useful as much thought and effort has gone into their creation. This is an appropriate place to record my thanks, once again, to my co-authors, Nigel Burton and Adrian Pierce. Nigel has written new 'Manager's point of view' sections for each of the four new chapters. As usual, these are not only authoritative and knowledgeable, but also interesting and informative – no mean feat when writing about accountancy!

Adrian has co-authored the new chapter on working capital management. I contributed some of the theoretical content but he has written the majority of the text, including many practical aspects of the day-to-day 'juggling' of working capital which is unavoidable when organisations do not have sufficient cash to enable their operations to run smoothly. Ability in these areas can literally mean the difference between life and death for a business. I know of no one more skilled than Adrian in this field and thank him for taking some of his valuable time to share his knowledge with us.

However, I personally accept full responsibility for the complete contents of this second edition. Every single piece of text is there because I want it to be; any errors are mine. I hope these are few and far between but please let me know if you find any. Indeed, I welcome and encourage feedback. I hope you find the book improved and useful.

About the authors

Ray Proctor started his career as an auditor. He then worked as a management accountant for a UK subsidiary of a multinational company in the food business. After this he became the accountant for a touring caravan manufacturer where his role embraced all aspects of financial and management accounting. On leaving this firm, he and his wife started their own business manufacturing and selling weaving equipment. At the same time as this venture, he began to teach accounting on a part-time basis. He was encouraged to qualify as a teacher and, upon achieving this objective, became a full-time teacher in further education. Having established himself in this role, he gained a Warwick University MBA by distance learning in his spare time. He then moved into higher education, joining the staff of Coventry University in 1996, where he currently holds the position of senior lecturer in accounting. Currently, he also acts as a tutor on the Management Accounting module of the Warwick University MBA. In addition to his accounting and management experience in the commercial world, he has more than 20 years' experience of teaching accounting.

Nigel Burton qualified as a chartered accountant in 1976 with a London firm, Tansley Witt & Co. After two years of post-qualification experience, he opted for a life in industry, and became financial accountant of the UK subsidiary of a large American chemical corporation. Here he remained for the next 21 years. His initial stint as financial accountant was followed by a three-year term in a European financial capacity, before becoming chief accountant, and then financial director, in the UK. He was appointed managing director after a reorganisation in 1992, and in 1996 assumed additional responsibility for one of the European business groups. His extensive experience of life in a manufacturing environment has been seen from not only the financial, but also the administrative and business perspectives. Throughout this period, he has been fully involved in the management of change within his organisation, reflecting the rapid technological and managerial advances taking place in the business world. He is, therefore, admirably placed to comment on the contribution that managerial accounting can make to a company's development.

Adrian Pierce also started his career as an auditor in a 'Big Six' audit firm, before becoming the accountant for a small UK manufacturing company in the outdoor leisure industry. He began as assistant management accountant but soon progressed to the all-embracing role of company accountant. In this senior position, he gained valuable management experience in addition to developing his financial and management accounting abilities. Also, during this time, he qualified as a chartered management accountant. He remained with this company for several years, during which it experienced sustained growth in a fiercely competitive market. He then moved on to become the financial accountant for a high-profile public-sector organisation. After a couple of years he was also appointed as company secretary. As part of this multiple role, he has gained much experience in the submission of claims to key funding partners. This particular activity has given him significant insight into the extra dimensions of not-for-profit organisations. He currently occupies a senior management role in a not-for-profit organisation and has more than 15 years' experience of accounting and management.

Acknowledgements

I would like to take this opportunity to thank my co-writers, Nigel Burton and Adrian Pierce, for their encouragement, enthusiasm and willingness to share their experience with the rest of us. This book would be significantly lacking without their contributions. I find their writing interesting, insightful and helpful; I have learned more than a little from them. I will be surprised if readers of this book do not form the same opinion.

I would like to thank the staff of Pearson Education, the publishers of this book. In particular, I would like to thank my original acquisitions editor, Paula Harris, for her belief in this text and in me. I would also like to thank the acquisitions editor, Jacqueline Senior, and the editorial manager, Alison Stanford, for guiding me through the last year or so of this project. They, and their assistants, have always been helpful and courteous to me, a first-time author who did not 'know the ropes'.

My colleagues at Coventry University also deserve my thanks for their advice, constructive criticism and help with the end-of-chapter questions and cases, particularly David Blight, Steward Hughes, John Panther, Keith Redhead, Graham Sara and Stan Smith. My thanks also go to Bob Evans and Jeff Clowes for reviewing certain sections of the text.

Thanks also to my wife, Sara, and my sister, Rita, for help with proofreading, indexing, scanning and administration. My students also deserve my thanks for the searching questions they have asked me over the years, challenging my understanding and helping me to learn more about my subject. The 2000/2001 cohort deserve a particular mention as they helped to 'debug' draft chapters of the book.

For the second edition I would like to thank my editor Matthew Smith, Mary Lince and their colleagues at Pearson Education. I would also like to thank those of my friends who helped with the arduous task of proofreading.

Finally, I would like to thank the Chartered Institute of Management Accountants for allowing me to reproduce definitions from *Management Accounting Official Terminology* to construct an authoritative glossary and recent articles from their monthly magazine as part of Chapter 19 on current issues. These articles give different points of view on contentious issues currently under debate. They enable the reader to appreciate these views easily without having to go to the trouble of first gathering the information.

Publisher's acknowledgements

We are grateful to the following for permission to reproduce copyright material:

Figure 4.4, from Watson D. and Head A. (2004) *Corporate Finance – Principles and Practice,* 3rd edition, Pearson Education Ltd; Figure 8.7, Atrill P. and McLaney E. (1994) *Management Accounting: An Active Learning Approach,* Blackwell Publications Ltd; Figures 10.1, 10.2 and 16.5 from Kaplan R. S. and Cooper R. (1998) *Cost and Effect: Using Integrated Cost Systems to Drive Profitability and Performance,* Harvard Business School Press; Figure 17.1, from Hartle F. (1995) *Re-engineering The Performance Management Process,* Kogan Page, copyright F. Hartle; Figure 17.2, from Torrington D. and Hall L. (2004) *Human Resource Management,* 6th edition, Pearson Education Ltd.

Guardian Newspapers Limited for extracts from 'Waiting-time figures "rigged"' by Gaby Hinsliff published in *The Observer* 1st August 2004 © Guardian Newspapers Limited 2004 and 'Break out of the budget cycle' by Simon Caulkin published in *The Observer* 20th July 2003 © Guardian Newspapers Limited 2003.

In some instances, we have been unable to trace the owners of copyright material, and we would appreciate any information that would enable us to do so.

FOUNDATIONS

Part 1 comprises:

Part 1 covers the basic information that will help readers understand the rest of the book. An understanding of the different ways in which costs can behave when the volume of activity changes is of fundamental importance to managers. Cost control will always be an important managerial activity.

Just as important is the need for managers to have a clear understanding of the difference between profit and cash. Many companies that go into liquidation are profitable! They cease to trade because they have run out of cash. Cash is the life-blood of organisations. Without it, they cannot function and pursue their objectives. The information in the rest of this book will be of little use to you if your business fails to survive. Understanding the difference between profit and cash is fundamentally important.

Chapter contents

- Introduction
- Learning objectives
- Types of business
- Product and period costs
- Variable and fixed costs
- Analysis of semi-variable costs into their fixed and variable elements
- Absorption costs: direct and indirect
- Comparison of alternative cost analyses
- Cost analysis by activity
- Relevant and irrelevant costs
- Summary
- Further reading
- Answers to self-assessment questions

Introduction

As a manager, you might find yourself asking your accountant for the cost of one of your products. The answer you expect to be given is probably a specific amount of money, e.g. £49.55. If your accountant replies 'Why do you want to know?' you may think he (or she) is being unnecessarily awkward and assume that he is in a bad mood for some reason or other. However, the accountant's reply is actually very sensible, even though it would have been better for him to reply 'The answer depends on why you want to know.' At first, this may seem very strange to you but a product has several different costs, each of which serves a different purpose. As you will see in the next few chapters of this book, there are several different costing systems in existence, each giving a different answer to your original question.

The absorption costing system gives the absorption cost, the variable costing system gives the variable cost and the activity-based costing system gives the activity-based cost. They all give the correct cost in the context of their own system. Each system is a financial model based on its own rules and assumptions. Different rules and assumptions result in different numerical answers. For example, the product in question may have an absorption cost of £49.55, a variable cost of £20.95 and an activity-based cost of £142.00. **Each of these three answers is correct.**

The word 'cost' is a general word and is often used in a general sense. However, when a manager asks an accountant for the cost of a product, the manager usually has a specific purpose in mind. The reason why the accountant replied 'Why do you want to know?' is that he wanted to determine the manager's specific purpose so that he could give the right answer. He was actually trying to be helpful rather than awkward! In this chapter, we will look at the different ways in which costs can behave and see how some of these form the bases of the different costing systems.

Learning objectives

Having worked through this chapter you should be able to:
- explain the difference between manufacturing, trading and providing services;
- explain the difference between product and period costs;
- explain the difference between variable and fixed costs;
- explain what semi-variable costs and stepped fixed costs are;
- find fixed and variable elements of semi-variable costs using the high–low method;
- draw a scattergraph based on periodic cost and output data and interpret it;
- explain **in outline** what regression analysis is;
- explain the difference between direct and indirect costs;
- compare variable cost analysis with absorption cost analysis;
- explain the basis for analysing activity-based costs;
- say what relevant costs are used for.

Types of business

There are three main categories of businesses: manufacturers, traders and service businesses. Manufacturers make the goods they sell by converting raw materials into finished products. Traders buy in goods and sell them without altering them in any significant way (they may be repackaged and re-presented). Service businesses create intangible products – for example, banks, accountants, lawyers, financial advisers, freight companies, railways, theatrical agents, education and training institutions. So costs can be described as manufacturing costs, trading costs or service costs.

It is worth noting that the type of organisation affects the format of the financial accounts. Gross profit is meaningful for a manufacturer or trader but much less so for a service business. Production accounts (to calculate the cost of production) are essential for manufacturers but not applicable to traders or service businesses. However, it is wise not to be too pedantic about this as services tend to be mainly intangible but often include minor tangible items such as chequebooks, sets of accounts, property deeds, share certificates, bills of lading, rail tickets, contracts of employment and degree certificates. In these cases you would probably agree that gross profit is inappropriate.

On the other hand, manufacturers often include a small service element in their products. When you buy a new car, the first two services may be free of charge and there may be a three-year warranty. The price of a new computer usually includes the right to use a selection of software applications for word processing, spreadsheets, databases, etc.

But what about pubs, restaurants and clubs? Are they manufacturers, traders or service providers? The answer is, of course, that they can be all three. The meals are created

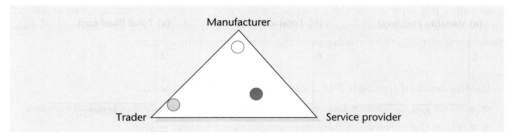

Figure 1.1 **Business orientations**

on the premises, the drinks are bought in and waiting at table, pouring drinks, etc., are pure services. The same applies to residential health clubs and activity holidays where you learn to produce something tangible such as a painting or a piece of pottery.

Figure 1.1 illustrates the relationship between these different types of organisation. The darker-coloured circle shows the approximate position of a restaurant. The empty circle represents firms such as furniture makers and the lighter-coloured circle could represent a national chain of off-licences.

Product and period costs

There are two ways of including costs in the profit and loss account. First, they can be included as part of the production cost of the products made. The production cost of all goods sold in the period gives the total *cost of sales* figure, which is deducted from *sales revenue* to give *gross profit*. Closing stock of finished goods is also valued at production cost. This is how production costs of goods unsold at the year-end are carried forward to the year in which they are sold. (This complies with the accounting rule/concept of realisation.) These costs are known as *product costs*.

Second, the full amount of non-production overheads for marketing, administration, etc., appears directly in the profit and loss account of the period in which they were incurred. No attempt is made to apportion them to different financial years. These costs are known as *period costs*.

Product and period costs will be discussed further in Chapter 11, 'Comparison of profits under absorption and variable costing'.

Variable and fixed costs

Variable costs

These are costs which vary **in total** with a measure of activity – for example, the total cost of raw materials increases as output increases (see Figure 1.2b). Take the example of a business making furniture – if the number of chairs produced doubles then the cost of raw materials also doubles.

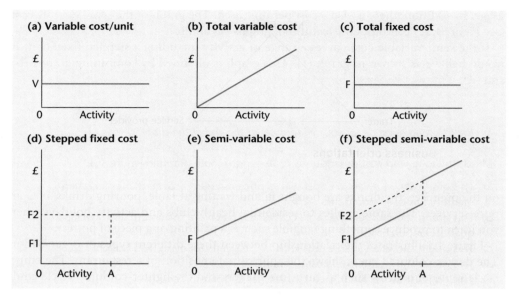

Figure 1.2 **Patterns of variable and fixed cost behaviour**

Fixed costs

These are costs incurred for a period of time, which, within a given range of production and/or sales activity, do not change (see Figure 1.2c). Continuing the furniture-making example above, if the number of chairs produced doubles, the business rates on the premises do **not** change.

Note that variable costs can be calculated per unit of output but that fixed costs refer to the business as a whole. Variable costing assumes that the variable cost **per unit** stays the same over a range of activity (see Figure 1.2a). This means that **total** variable costs increase linearly with activity (see Figure 1.2b).

Great care must be taken if *fixed cost per unit* is used in calculations. This measure will change every time the number of units changes, i.e. fixed cost per unit is **not** fixed!

Stepped fixed costs

When a certain level of production and/or sales activity is reached, there is a sudden increase in fixed costs from F1 to F2 (see Figure 1.2d). For example, when output increases significantly, it may be necessary to put on an extra work shift. This occurs at activity level A and entails extra costs for items such as supervision, security, heating and lighting, etc.

Semi-variable costs

Although there are several costs which are either purely variable or purely fixed, many costs are semi-variable. The utilities, such as telephone and electricity, often have a fixed cost element such as line rental or a standing charge which has to be paid irrespective of usage. In addition, there is also a cost per unit used. The graph of the semi-variable cost (see Figure 1.2e) combines the features of graphs (b) and (c).

If the semi-variable cost covers a range of activity including a stepped fixed cost, it would behave as shown in graph (f). This graph is obtained by combining graphs (b) and (d).

Self-assessment question S1.1

Try the following question for yourself (answer at the end of the chapter).

Match the following cost descriptions to the appropriate graph in Figure 1.3.

a) This graph shows a variable cost with a price discount activated after a certain quantity has been purchased.
b) This graph shows a semi-variable cost which reaches a maximum at a specified quantity of purchases.
c) This graph shows a variable cost with 10 free units for every 100 bought.
d) This graph shows the fixed cost per unit.
e) This graph shows a variable cost which has a minimum charge.
f) This graph shows the variable cost of a scarce item. When local supplies have been exhausted, it has to be purchased abroad, entailing extra transport costs.

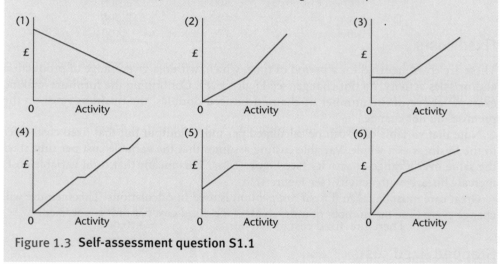

Figure 1.3 Self-assessment question S1.1

Analysis of semi-variable costs into their fixed and variable elements

It is not just the utilities that have semi-variable costs. Many other costs, such as security and maintenance, also follow this pattern. Often, only the **total** amounts of these semi-variable costs are known and the fixed and variable elements have to be worked out mathematically. Three alternative ways of doing this are shown below.

Month	Output (units)	Maintenance cost (£)
1	586	12,340
2	503	11,949
3	600	12,400
4	579	12,298
5	550	12,075
6	500	12,000

Figure 1.4 **Monthly maintenance costs**

The high–low method

Figure 1.4 shows the machine maintenance costs and the output level of products for the first six monthly periods of the year.

Only two sets of monthly information are used, one from the highest-output month (month 3 = 600 units) and the other from the lowest-output month (month 6 = 500 units).

	Highest (month 3)	600 units	£12,400
Less:	Lowest (month 6)	500 units	£12,000
	Difference	100 units	£400

Since both the £12,400 and the £12,000 include the fixed cost element, this is eliminated by the subtraction and the £400 difference is due solely to the variable cost of the 100 units difference.

Variable cost per unit produced = £400/100 units = £4/unit

Using this in month 6:

$$\text{Variable cost of 500 units} = 500 \times £4 = £2,000$$
$$\text{Total cost of 500 units} = £12,000$$
$$\text{Therefore, fixed cost of 500 units} = £10,000$$

These cost elements can be checked by applying them to the other month used, month 3:

$$\text{Variable cost of 600 units} = 600 \times £4 = £2,400$$
$$\text{Fixed cost of 600 units} = £10,000$$
$$\text{Therefore, total cost of 600 units} = £12,400$$

This shows the calculations to be correct. However, if any of the other months **not** used in the calculation is chosen to test the results, it will probably not work! This is because the high–low method uses the information from only two months. It ignores all the other information. It assumes that the relationship between the cost and production output is a linear one, i.e. if all the monthly points were plotted on a graph, they would all be points on the same straight line. In fact, this is not so, as you can probably see from Figure 1.4. For instance, month 2 has a higher output (503 units) than month 6 (500 units) but a lower maintenance cost.

It can be seen that the high–low method is a fairly crude way of estimating the fixed and variable cost elements of a semi-variable cost. However, its advantage is that it is easy to understand and easy to calculate.

Scattergraphs

If the monthly information shown above (in the high–low method) was plotted on a graph it would look like Figure 1.5.

The line of best fit is drawn on the graph by eye. The intersection of this line and the vertical cost axis gives the fixed cost element. This is **read** from the graph and should be close to £10,000.

The slope of the line,

$$\frac{\text{change in cost}}{\text{change in output}} = \frac{2{,}384}{600} = \pounds\textbf{3.97}$$

gives the variable cost per unit. You may remember the equation for a straight line is

$$y = a + bx$$

where a is the intersection with the vertical axis and b is the slope of the line. In this context, the fixed cost is a and the variable cost per unit is b.

The disadvantage of this method is that drawing the line of best fit by eye is subjective and different individuals will produce slightly different lines. However, it does have the advantage of using all the available information and, like the high–low method, a scattergraph will give a workable estimate and is easy to understand.

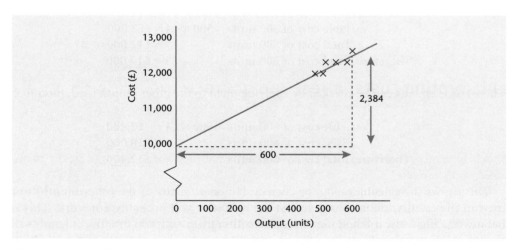

Figure 1.5 **A scattergraph**

Regression analysis

This method is similar to the scattergraph but the line of best fit is not drawn by eye. The equation for the line is calculated by a statistical technique called *regression analysis*. It is sometimes known as *least squares regression*. It is more precise than the other two methods but it is much more complex mathematically. The technique of regression analysis is not covered by this book. It is sufficient for you to know of its existence and availability if needed.

The most important thing to remember is that, although it is more precise than the high–low and scattergraph methods, it still only gives an estimate of the fixed and variable cost elements. The extra complexity involved may not be worth the improvement in accuracy gained.

Self-assessment question S1.2

Try the following question for yourself (answer at the end of the chapter).

As the manager of an Indian restaurant with a take-away service, you have been asked to prepare a detailed budget for next year. To help you with this, you need to know the fixed and variable cost elements of your delivery cost to customers' homes.

The following information is available from the monthly accounts. Calculate the fixed and variable cost elements using the *high–low* method.

Month	No. of deliveries	Total delivery cost (£)
July	403	662.70
August	291	561.90
September	348	613.20
October	364	627.60
November	521	768.90
December	387	648.30

Absorption costs: direct and indirect

Direct cost

This is expenditure which can be economically identified with, and specifically **measured** in, a product.

Consider an advertising agency specialising in the production of television adverts. The cost of hiring a celebrity to appear in one such advert is a measurable direct cost of that advert. Similarly, if the company is a furniture manufacturer, the cost of materials used to make a chair and the pay of the operative assembling it are measurable direct costs of that chair.

Indirect cost (or overhead)

This is expenditure which **cannot** be economically identified with, and specifically **measured** in, a product.

There are many, many different overheads including expenses such as the supervisor's pay, depreciation of fixed assets, business rates and insurance. Somehow, a proportion of these non-measurable expenses has to be included in the total product cost. Absorption costing is one way of doing this. It is based on the assumption that costs can be analysed into their 'direct' and 'indirect' components. For each product, the direct cost is measured but the indirect cost is estimated.

Absorption cost = direct cost + indirect cost

The estimates of indirect costs are usually based on some connection or correlation between the cost and a measure such as machine hours used, direct labour hours used or total cost of direct materials used. Absorption costing is the subject of Chapter 9.

Comparison of alternative cost analyses

Variable costing analyses total costs into fixed and variable components. Absorption costing analyses total costs into direct and indirect components. In itself, this is not problematical as these two systems of costing, variable and absorption, are independent financial models. However, it is not unusual to be confused by these terms and how they interrelate. The aim of Figure 1.6 is to clarify these relationships.

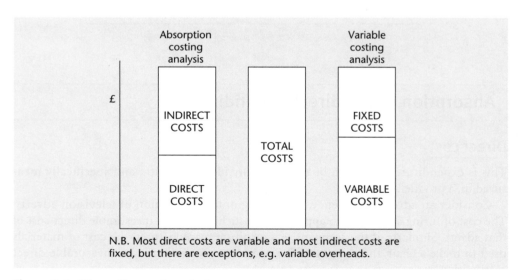

N.B. Most direct costs are variable and most indirect costs are fixed, but there are exceptions, e.g. variable overheads.

Figure 1.6 **Alternative cost analysis**

Cost analysis by activity

This analysis is based on the principle that costs are **caused** by activities and that activities are caused by products or services. The activity-based cost of a product is a result of determining the costs of all the activities caused by that product. This principle is fundamentally different from the correlation principle used in absorption costing.

Activities are identified and their costs calculated before being attached to products via a measure of the activity called a *cost driver*. Activity-based costing gives significantly more accurate product costs than absorption costing but it has difficulties of its own and does not give 100% accurate costs. This subject is discussed at length in Chapter 10.

Relevant and irrelevant costs

This analysis of costs is very useful in decision making. In brief, it differentiates between those costs which affect a decision (i.e. relevant costs) and those that do not (irrelevant costs). This approach to decision making is discussed further in Chapter 7.

Summary

- Each product can have several different costs.
- The cost of a product depends on the purpose for which this information is required.
- Business types can be divided into three categories: manufacturing, trading and providing services.
- Period costs are written off to the profit and loss account of the period for which they were incurred.
- Product costs are built into the production cost of manufactured items and are accounted for by either the cost of sales figure for the year in which they were incurred or carried forward to the next period in the closing stock valuation figure.
- Total cost can be analysed into variable and fixed cost elements.
- Semi-variable costs have both variable and fixed cost elements.
- Fixed costs are stable only up to a certain level of activity; above this, they step up to a higher level.
- There are three ways of analysing semi-variable costs into their fixed and variable components: the high–low method, scattergraphs and regression analysis.
- Total cost can be analysed into direct and indirect cost elements.
- Costs can be analysed causally according to production activities and activities can be analysed causally by products.
- As an aid to decision making, costs can be analysed into relevant and irrelevant types.
- Direct and indirect costs are similar to, but different from, variable and fixed costs.

Further reading

Anderson, M. C., Banker, R. D. and Janakiraman, S. N. (2003) 'Are selling, general, and administrative costs "sticky"?', *Journal of Accounting Research*, Vol. 41, Issue 1, March.

Drury, C. (2004) *Management and Cost Accounting*, 6th edition, Thomson Learning, London. See chapter 'An introduction to cost terms and concepts'.

Horngren, C., Bhimani, A., Datar, S. and Foster, G. (2002) *Management and Cost Accounting*, Prentice Hall Europe, Harlow. See chapter 'Determining how costs behave'.

Liu, L. and Robinson, J. (2002) 'Double measure', *Financial Management (CIMA)*, October.

Upchurch, A. (2003) *Management Accounting, Principles and Practice*, 2nd edition, Financial Times/Prentice Hall, Harlow. See chapter 'Cost estimation'.

Weetman, P. (2002) *Management Accounting, an Introduction*, 3rd edition, Financial Times/Prentice Hall, Harlow. See chapter 'Classification of costs'.

Answers to self-assessment questions

S1.1. Cost behaviour graphs

a) Graph 6
b) Graph 5
c) Graph 4
d) Graph 1
e) Graph 3
f) Graph 2

S1.2. Indian take-away delivery costs

Only two sets of monthly information are used, one from the highest-activity month (November = 521 deliveries) and the other from the lowest-activity month (August = 291 deliveries).

	Highest (November)	521 deliveries	£768.90
Less:	Lowest (August)	291 deliveries	£561.90
	Difference	230 deliveries	£207.00

Variable cost per delivery = £207.00/230 = **£0.90/delivery**

Using this in November:

Variable cost of deliveries = 521 × £0.90 = £468.90
Total cost of 521 deliveries = £768.90
Therefore, Fixed cost of 521 deliveries = £300.00

These cost elements can be checked by applying them to the other month used, August:

$$\text{Variable cost of 291 deliveries} = 291 \times £0.90 = £261.90$$
$$\text{Fixed cost of 291 deliveries} \qquad = \underline{£300.00}$$
$$\text{Therefore, Total cost of 291 deliveries} \qquad = \underline{\underline{£561.90}}$$

CHAPTER 2 | The difference between profit and cash

Chapter contents

Introduction

There are many people, including some business people, who think that profit is the same thing as cash. They use the two words interchangeably, believing there to be no difference in their meaning. They are mistaken.

Profit is not the same as cash

As a manager, it is vital that you understand this. If you do not, studying the many other useful topics in this book may prove to be a waste of time!

Cash is the money that individuals and organisations use to exchange things of value. It consists of bank notes, coins and bank account balances.

Profit is the excess of income over expenditure (incurred to produce that income) in a specified period of time. There are many accounting rules, principles and concepts governing the way profit is calculated. They can be very complex (because business is very complex) and are sometimes controversial.

MG Rover, which collapsed in April 2005, is a good example of a complex organisation. The holding company, Phoenix Venture Holdings (PVH), was at the top of a web of 15 or so other companies which were connected to each other in complicated ways. Some of these immediately went into administration when the Shanghai Automotive Industry Corporation (SAIC) of China pulled out of talks to buy a significant part of the UK operation, but others remained trading as solvent entities. In the emotional aftermath of the collapse which resulted in many thousands of people losing their jobs, it was reported in the press that there was a possible 'black hole' in PVH's accounts into which £452 million of cash had disappeared. This figure was the difference between the £1,563 million paid into the company since it started in 2000 and the £1,111 million of capital expenditure and losses during most of that period. This so-called black hole is pure speculation as its calculation mixes together cash flows and profit/losses; these are fundamentally different concepts and cannot be combined in this way. Its creators either do not understand this difference or are mischievously ignoring it.

You may have heard of 'creative accounting' where profits shown by audited company accounts have been manipulated (usually increased) by the dubious, but legal, application of accounting rules. Every few years there is a major court case to test whether a company has gone too far and broken the rules rather than just bent them. This situation is partly due to the way in which the world of business is constantly changing, while the rules lag behind until suitably amended.

One result of creative accounting over the years is that many people do not now trust reported profit figures as much as they used to. They are aware that there are many ways in which profit figures can be manipulated. Also, they acknowledge that to understand published accounts fully, a high degree of accounting knowledge is needed.

Take the example of a new road haulage firm that has bought a small fleet of lorries for £500,000. Reducing balance depreciation at 40% a year will give a depreciation charge of £200,000 (£500,000 × 40%). This gives a net profit of £50,000 (see Figure 2.1a). However, if the owner had told his bank that first-year profits would be in the region of £100,000, he might decide to change the depreciation method to straight line over five years. This would give a depreciation charge of £100,000 (£500,000/5) and a profit of £150,000 (see Figure 2.1b). Note that for exactly the same set of business transactions in the year, two different **legitimate** profits have been produced without breaking any accounting rules! This example of creative accounting (which can be extremely complex) has been kept very simple in order to illustrate the point.

a) Reducing balance depreciation at 40% p.a.

	£
Sales revenue	640,000
Depreciation (500,000 × 40%)	200,000
All other expenses	390,000
Total expenses	590,000
Net profit	**50,000**

b) Straight line depreciation over 5 years

	£
Sales revenue	640,000
Depreciation (500,000/5)	100,000
All other expenses	390,000
Total expenses	490,000
Net profit	**150,000**

Note: No physical change but profits tripled!

Figure 2.1 **Creative accounting in a road haulage firm**

The published accounts contain three major statements: the balance sheet, the profit and loss account and the cash flow statement. Many professional people who use accounts in their work now believe that the cash flow statement is just as important as the profit and loss account, if not more so. They know that, although profits can be manipulated, cash cannot.

Every figure making up the balance sheet totals is subject, to some extent, to subjective opinion, **except cash**. Cash can be, and is, counted and verified for audit purposes. The 'Pizza Wagon' example below illustrates the difference between profit and cash and shows just how critical this difference can be. It can be literally a matter of life or death for a business.

<table>
<tr><td>

Learning objectives

</td><td>

Having worked through this chapter you should be able to:

- define what is meant by 'cash';
- define what is meant by 'profit';
- explain the importance of cash flow statements;
- convert profits into cash flows (and vice versa);
- reconcile total profit to total cash flow over the lifetime of a business;
- explain the importance of understanding the difference between profit and cash.

</td></tr>
</table>

Illustrative example: The Pizza Wagon

Olive Napoloni has recently lost her job as a result of her employer going into liquidation and ceasing to trade. She is approaching her 57th birthday but will not be able to access her private pension until she is 60 in three years' time. Because Olive is an active woman with a positive attitude to life, she wants to work for the next three years but in a different way from her last 30 years of office work.

Over the years she has helped a friend run a local business providing the catering for one-off events such as weddings and anniversary parties. She enjoys the catering business but would like to work outdoors and to have the opportunity of meeting new people as well. After much careful thought, she decides to start a business of her own offering a mobile catering facility at outdoor events such as pop festivals, fairs and sporting events. She has always been able to make good pizzas and decides to capitalise on this strength. Her business will be called 'The Pizza Wagon' and will be run from a specially converted parcel van.

The final cost of this van, including all alterations, has been quoted at £19,500. However, after three years' heavy use she believes it will not be worth very much and, to be on the safe side, decides to assume it will be worth nothing at all. Her preliminary costings show that the ingredients for one good-sized pizza will be £1.00 and she decides to sell them for £4.00 each. Her budgeted accounts for the three financial years and for the three-year period as a whole are as follows.

	Year 1	Year 2	Year 3	3-year period
No. of pizzas sold	15,000	20,000	25,000	60,000
	£	£	£	£
Sales revenue	60,000	80,000	100,000	240,000
Cost of ingredients	15,000	20,000	25,000	60,000
Gross profit	45,000	60,000	75,000	180,000
Van depreciation	6,500	6,500	6,500	19,500
Van running costs	9,000	9,000	9,000	27,000
Site fees	11,000	14,000	19,000	44,000
Advertising	5,000	4,000	4,000	13,000
Administration	3,500	3,500	3,500	10,500
Total overheads	35,000	37,000	42,000	114,000
Net profit	10,000	23,000	33,000	66,000

Olive is very pleased with these projections, especially as she will avoid making a loss in her first year and need not bother asking her bank for a loan to pay herself a salary. Although the £10,000 in year 1 is only about two-thirds of what she is earning now, she believes she will be able to manage on that for one year if she is very careful with her personal expenditure.

However, because she has no track record in business, she is unable to buy her van on credit terms and has to pay the full £19,500 at the start of her first year of trading. Fortunately, she has been able to arrange an overdraft facility to cover this and other business costs by pledging her home as security. She knows it will be a hard three years but is pleased to be in a position to give this new venture a try.

Unfortunately there is a major flaw in Olive's logic. Can you see what it is?

She is assuming that the profit and the net cash inflow for The Pizza Wagon are the same thing. But there is one legitimate item on the budgeted accounts which does not translate into an equivalent cash movement. The sales revenue figures mean cash inflows of those amounts. The cost of ingredients and the overhead expenses translate into cash outflows with the exception of one item, **depreciation**.

Depreciation is a non-cash expense. In Olive's case, the accounts show straight-line depreciation over three years with a zero residual value for the van. Because she has to pay for it in full at the beginning, the cash outflow for the van in year 1 is £19,500 not £6,500. The cash outflow is £13,000 more than the depreciation for year 1, so the profit of £10,000 translates into a net cash **outflow** of £3,000 (see below).

Olive will not receive £10,000 in cash in year 1. In fact, during that year she will have to put **an extra £3,000** into her business. And what is she going to live on? How is she going to pay for her food, electricity, clothes, etc.? She may or may not be able to arrange a loan from some source to cover the £13,000 difference and provide her with adequate living expenses. But unless she understands the difference between profit and cash her business and personal life will turn into a financial disaster!

Having looked carefully at year 1, let us consider what happens in years 2 and 3. The depreciation in these years (correctly shown in the accounts) does not translate into any cash flows at all. The financial effect of this is shown below.

	Year 1	Year 2	Year 3	3-year period
	£	£	£	£
Net profit	10,000	23,000	33,000	66,000
Adjustment	−13,000	+6,500	+6,500	–
Net cash flow	−3,000	+29,500	+39,500	+66,000

So it is not all bad news for Olive. Although her cash flow is negative in year 1, in years 2 and 3 it is not only positive but greater than she expected. The figures show a timing difference between profit and cash. Timing differences are what the accruals accounting concept is all about. Accruals and prepayments are part of this jigsaw and so are provisions such as depreciation and doubtful debts. The above example has been kept very simple in order to illustrate the principle involved. However, in practice detailed cash budgets must be prepared and monitored for the business to survive. Many, many, many **profitable** businesses have had to cease trading due to insufficient cash resources. Lack of cash is one – if not the major – reason for business insolvency.

The lifetime view

Remember that business is about money, i.e. cash. Profit, on the other hand, is the result of an arbitrary set of rules set by people in government, accountancy associations and committees. It is an intangible concept. The financial year is, to some extent, an irrelevant time period imposed upon businesses. Companies are not created specifically to trade for exactly one year. The vast majority of them wish to trade continuously into the future and would be very happy to prepare published audited accounts only every few years instead of every year. Some businesses, like The Pizza Wagon above, are created for a specific purpose and have a set life span. These organisations tend to view financial years as artificial divisions of their existence. They are much more interested in the outcome of the project over its whole life than its annual profits.

Looking at The Pizza Wagon figures above, you can see that **over the whole lifetime of a business, the total of profit exactly equals the total of cash** (£66,000 in this case). This principle is just as true for the many continuing businesses all around us even though it is far from obvious.

Self-assessment question S2.1

Try the following question for yourself (answer at the end of the chapter).

The Bourton Trading Company existed for four years only before being wound up. Its financial record is shown below in the form of summary annual profit and loss accounts.

	Year 1	Year 2	Year 3	Year 4
	£000	£000	£000	£000
Sales revenue	400	375	440	380
Cost of sales	225	200	250	220
Gross profit	175	175	190	160

Increase/(decrease) in doubtful debt provision	20	(5)	(5)	(10)
Training expenses	–	3	4	13
Inf'n system depreciation	10	10	10	10
Other administ'n expenses	45	40	45	50
Co. vehicle depreciation	40	32	26	22
Marketing expenses	25	30	40	35
Bank interest	35	25	30	20
Total overheads	175	135	150	140
Net profit	0	40	40	20

Notes:

1 £10,000 of the £40,000 marketing expenses in year 3 were actually paid in year 2 in order to secure advertising space for a campaign run early in year 3.
2 In order to help the business establish itself, the bank allowed it to defer the payment of 40% of the interest charges it incurred in year 1 until year 2. The profit and loss accounts show the full amounts of interest incurred in each year.
3 In order to get the best discounts, the company always bought its fixed assets for cash with a lump-sum payment.
4 The information system cost £40,000 and was obsolete and worthless when the company closed.
5 The company vehicles cost £140,000 in total. At the end of year 4 they were sold for £20,000 cash.

Tasks:

a) Calculate the net cash flow for each of the four years.
b) Compare the total of profit to the net cash flow for the four-year period as a whole.

The manager's point of view

It is an enduring fact of life that you never have enough money to do everything you want. This is as true of companies as it is of individuals. Cash is a company's most precious resource and its stewardship in the best interests of the business is central to the art of management.

Every company has to re-invest in order to survive. If a company were to pay out 100% of its profits in dividends, it would run out of cash in short order. Even a static business will need to spend on renovating or renewing old plant, training replacement staff, and seeking out new customers to replace those that inevitably get lost. Standing still is never an option. And if your company has to change, it may as well become bigger and stronger.

All companies therefore pursue the holy grail of growth. Even Olive in the above example is expecting her little business to show some impressive expansion. Growth demands injections of cash in many different areas: new product developments, new plant on which to manufacture them, new markets into which to sell them, broader infrastructure to support the growing business, and increased working capital to allow the company to operate on a day-to-day basis. It may be several years before even profitable ventures reach the stage of cash-generation rather than cash-consumption.

In the 1980s, our company was one of a number developing components for use in airbag safety systems for motor cars. Here was a product, which, if successful, would quickly become a standard part in every new car. Even with strong competition, the opportunities were clearly enormous. Within just a few years, sales went from zero to multiples of millions. The real challenge to management was to ensure that the plant capacity and administrative infrastructure were continuously upgraded in advance of the ever-growing demand. This meant that every penny generated, together with a good deal of additional outside financing, was ploughed back into the business, and the shareholders, sitting on a hugely profitable venture, saw plenty of capital growth, but precious little cash return in their dividends.

This was, of course, an exceptional circumstance, yet I doubt if there are many companies whose profit projections do not anticipate continuous future growth. How often do we see the 'hockey-stick' graph of a company's projected performance, where actual profits in recent years have remained flat, but future projections show a sharply upward trend? Managers would be accused of, at best, lack of ambition, and at worst, lack of competence, if their input was not expected to bring improved company results. But how many companies actually achieve these forecasts? If a business fails to make its expected profits, the first casualty may well be cash flow. Budgets are often set as targets, designed to stretch sales efforts and encourage cost savings. Truly realistic estimates might indicate a need for rather higher cash requirements.

So it is easy to overestimate the amount of cash which will become available. Take capital projects for example. In a large, diverse organisation, there is always competition between the various businesses for the available capital funds. Senior management will support those projects which give both the greatest rate of return and the quickest payback on their investment. There is pressure on those preparing the supporting documentation to ensure that their project looks attractive, so optimistic salesmen are likely to over-pitch the sales forecasts, while over-confident engineers underestimate the total costs of construction. The result is that the project is far less profitable than forecast, takes much longer to pay back the investment, and in the worst circumstances, could pull the entire company down. A business obtaining capital funds on such an unsound basis will almost certainly come unstuck. Every capital investment is, to some degree, a gamble, but the risks can be minimised if a realistic approach to the cash-flow requirements is taken.

Perhaps the most common source of liquidity problems today is the failure of management to control working capital, i.e. stocks and debtors, less creditors. This represents the amount of cash needed to oil the wheels of the business, as opposed to investment in capital projects, and is an area which can swallow up large chunks of cash, if it is not properly managed. In fact, it is so frequently neglected, particularly by smaller companies, that the topic warrants a chapter of its own in this book (see Chapter 4).

Sometimes there are external factors which can have a dramatic impact on cash flow. In the early 1970s, a huge increase in the price of oil led to unprecedented levels of inflation, which drove many companies towards insolvency. With inflation in excess of 20% a year, much of the cash generated was needed simply to keep the company standing still. It required 20% more cash than in the previous year to purchase replacement stock, pay the employees wages, or repair a piece of plant.

These increases could, of course, be recovered in selling prices, but this was usually too late, as the many of the higher costs would be incurred well before the customer had paid up. Any company which was unable to keep pace with the ever increasing cash requirement had to make up the difference through borrowings, which, in turn, hurt profits with continually rising interest costs. During this period, cash generation, rather than profit, became the critical factor to the survival of many companies.

Accounts based on historical costs ceased to give a sufficiently accurate picture of a company's health, so the concept of 'Current Cost Accounting' was introduced. This required balance sheet items to be revalued at their replacement cost, in order to give a better view of the company's solvency, and its ability to continue trading on a going-concern basis. This is why the cash flow statement is of such importance. The company may be full of clever people, all pursuing excellent projects which push the overall profits higher and higher, but the sum of their efforts might be bankruptcy. Therefore a wise manager will always keep an eye on the cash implication of everything he (or she) does.

Finally, a comment on creative accountancy: it is certainly true that there are many different ways of accounting for business activities. Over the years I have had many dis-cussions with the auditors over depreciation rates, accruals, levels of bad debt and obsolete stock reserves, and provisions for other identifiable expenses. There are many areas in a set of accounts where judgement must be applied. But I have never argued for an **increase** in profit unless the underlying circumstances clearly supported it. The prudence concept should be the guiding star for accountants. To anticipate profits, i.e. to take in sales too early, or to underprovide for expenses, is dangerous, irresponsible, unprofessional, does no service to the business, and will get you fired! To be conserva-tive, however, would be regarded as prudent, pragmatic and farsighted. All businesses have to cope with unexpected items of expenditure, such as a bad debt, major repair, exchange loss, etc., and in my experience, managing directors expect their accoun-tants to hold a few 'pots of money', i.e. conservative provisions, which can be released to offset unexpected hits to profit.

The rule is therefore: Keep some provisions up your sleeve for a rainy day, but never, ever, conceal your losses.

Summary

- Cash consists of notes, coins and bank balances.
- Profit is an intangible concept measured by the application of accounting rules.
- Cash is not the same as profit.
- Annual accounts contain many timing differences.
- Timing differences include non-cash expenses, provisions, accruals, prepayments.
- Profits can be manipulated, cash cannot.
- The cash flow figures are at least as important as the profit and loss figures.
- Understanding the difference between profit and cash is vital.
- Many profitable businesses have ceased trading due to lack of cash.
- Over the complete lifetime of a business, total profits equal total net cash flow.

Further reading

Arnold, J. and Turley, S. (1996) *Accounting for Management Decisions*, 3rd edition, Financial Times/Prentice Hall, London. See Chapter 2, 'Accounting and decision making', *section 2.5*: 'The issue of measurement'.

Harrison, W. and Horngren, C. (2001) *Financial Accounting*, 4th edition, Prentice Hall, Englewood Cliffs, NJ. See Chapter 3, 'Accrual accounting and the financial statements', *section*: 'Accrual-basis accounting versus cash-basis accounting'.

Weetman, P. (2002) *Financial Accounting, an Introduction*, 3rd edition, Financial Times/ Prentice Hall, Harlow. See chapter 'Who needs accounting', *supplement*: 'Introduction to the terminology of business transactions'.

Answer to self-assessment question

S2.1. The Bourton Trading company

a) Calculate the net cash flow for each of the four years.

	Year 1 £000	Year 2 £000	Year 3 £000	Year 4 £000
Net profit	0	40	40	20
Increase/(decrease) adjustments:				
1. Doubtful debt provision	20	(5)	(5)	(10)
2. Prepaid advertising	–	(10)	10	–
3. Deferred bank interest	14	(14)	–	–
4. Inf'n system depreciation	(30)	10	10	10
5. Co. vehicle depreciation	(100)	32	26	42
Cash in/(out) flow	(96)	53	81	62

Note: The £42,000 vehicle depreciation adjustment in year 4 consists of the £22,000 depreciation charge plus the £20,000 cash received for the sale of the vehicles.

b) Compare the total of profit to the net cash flow for the four-year period as a whole.

Year	Profit	Cash flow
1	0	(96)
2	40	53
3	40	81
4	20	62
Total	100	100

FINANCIAL MANAGEMENT

Part 2

Part 2 comprises:

Chapter 3   Ratio analysis and financial management
Chapter 4   Working capital management

Part 2 is about creating a financial 'infrastructure' within which business activities can flourish. These activities include developing, making, buying, selling and delivering products and services to customers. They do not happen in a vacuum; for example, manufacturers must have sufficient cash resources to fund their purchases of raw materials whilst waiting for their credit customers to pay up. The amount of interest paid on short- and long-term finance should not be so great that it puts a strain on the working capital. A healthy gross profit margin can be erased by allowing the over-heads to get out of control.

A wise company will monitor the effects of trading on its own financial infrastructure. It may also take a pro-active approach to designing this infrastructure in order to improve its profitability. Note that it is possible to enlarge profits in this non-trading way. A company that reduces the amount of money tied up in working capital will pay less interest on its overdraft or have surplus funds to invest elsewhere. Actively managing a company's financial infrastructure is a 'second string' to its profit-making bow.

CHAPTER 3

Ratio analysis and financial management

Chapter contents

Introduction

All companies produce an annual set of accounts consisting of a balance sheet, profit and loss account and a cash flow statement. Most of these companies also produce interim sets of accounts during the year, usually on a monthly or quarterly basis. These interim accounts are called 'management accounts' and are not available to people outside the company. As their name implies, they are for the company's managers only, enabling them to monitor progress on a regular basis. To do this, ratio analysis can be used.

Managers need to know how well they are performing now to enable them to make their businesses perform better in the future. They need to know the baseline from which their performance as a manager will be measured. An awareness of the current business performance and position will help them to focus their efforts. The analysis of the financial statements enables current performance to be evaluated and this evaluation can be used to determine future action.

Having worked through this chapter you should be able to:

- evaluate a company's financial position by calculating appropriate liquidity ratios;
- determine a company's financial structure by calculating appropriate gearing ratios;
- evaluate a company's profitability by calculating appropriate profitability ratios;
- evaluate a company's management of working capital by calculating appropriate management efficiency ratios;
- explain the limitations of ratio analysis in evaluating business performance and position.

Financial statements and ratio analysis

The balance sheet is a 'position' statement; it summarises the financial position at the year-end. The profit and loss account is a 'performance' statement; it tells the story of the year's activities. The cash flow statement also tells a performance story, that of where the cash has come from and how it has been used. Accounts are historical in nature; they describe what has happened and where the business was at the end of a financial period. Sets of accounts are notoriously difficult to understand but, fortunately, the technique of ratio analysis is available to help.

A mathematical ratio compares one (or more) numbers to each other. For example, the gradient of a road may be expressed as '1:4', meaning that for every 4 metres you travel horizontally, you will go up (or down) 1 metre. This is the vertical change compared to the horizontal change. It can also be expressed as a percentage: 1:4 is equivalent to 25%.

If we define a ratio as the comparison of two numbers, how many different ratios can be calculated from a single set of accounts? The answer could easily be *over 1 million!* But almost all of these comparisons are meaningless. For example, what use would it be to compare the cost of new fixed assets purchased to the amount of year-end debtors, or the value of debentures to the provision for obsolete stock?

However, there are a few ratios that **are** meaningful; these are the ones that create the additional information that helps us understand how the business has been performing. An example of this would be the 'profit margin' (which is usually expressed as a percentage). If the profit divided by the sales revenue equals 12%, this can be interpreted as the company making a profit *on average* of 12 pence for every pound of sales it achieves. This average figure gives business managers an estimate of how much profit they will make when selling different amounts of products. A basic set of no more than 20 ratios will enable you to interpret the accounts of a business.

When these ratios have been calculated, they can be compared *to each other* in three different ways to tell us three different things. Continuing the example used above, the *actual* profit margin can be compared to the profit margin calculated from the *budgeted* figures. This tells us if the business is as profitable as it was planned to be. Second, this year's actual profit margin can be compared to the profit margins of competitors for the

Devah plc: Balance sheet as at 31 December

(All figures in £m)	Cost	Depn	2006 NBV	Cost	Depn	2005 NBV
Fixed Assets:						
Land & buildings	860	0	860	780	0	780
Equipment	540	220	320	440	150	290
	1,400	220	1,180	1,220	150	1,070
Current assets:						
Stocks	530			382		
Debtors	156			102		
Cash at bank	0			30		
		686			514	
Less: Current Liabilities:						
Creditors	312			242		
Tax due	44			58		
Dividends due	54			60		
Overdraft	18			0		
		428			360	
Net current assets			258			154
Net total assets			1,438			1,224
Less: Debentures (10%)			500			400
			938			824
Financed by:						
Ordinary shares of £1		700			600	
Retained earnings		238			224	
			938			824

Devah plc: Profit and loss accounts for y/e 31 December

(All figures in £m)		2006		2005
Sales		3,646		3,136
Cost of sales		2,482		2,068
Gross profit		**1,164**		**1,068**
Admin & marketing expenses	1,002		884	
Debenture interest	50		40	
		1,052		924
Profit before tax		**112**		**144**
Taxation		44		58
Profit after tax		**68**		**86**
Dividends		54		60
Retained profit for the year		**14**		**26**

Figure 3.1 **The accounts of Devah plc**

same time period or thereabouts (usually only possible for annual published accounts). This type of 'industry' comparison is a form of 'benchmarking', identifying best practice in order to emulate it. Third, the actual profit margin for this year can be compared to the equivalent figure for previous years. This may exhibit a trend or it may show fluctuating margins over the years. (Be careful about extrapolating any identified trend into the future as this assumes that neither the business environment nor the internal processes will change.) The following sections of this chapter use ratios in the third of these three ways, comparing them to the equivalent figure for previous years.

To learn how financial statements are interpreted, a simplified set of accounts for a firm called Devah plc will be used – see Figure 3.1. If a real set of accounts were used, the wealth of detail would detract from the understanding of basic principles. In published annual reports, the accounts cover about five pages and the notes to the accounts can cover up to 20 pages or more!

Performance ratios: profitability

Performance is about how well the company has been doing. Is it producing a lot of profit or only a little? Is the annual profit improving, deteriorating or staying about the same? To get a feeling for this, it is not a bad idea to compare profits for recent years. But which profit figure should be used? If you look at Devah's accounts, you will see that there are several different profits shown: gross profit, profit before tax, profit after tax and profit retained after dividends. (In reality it gets even more complicated due to items like 'profit before extraordinary activities'.) The answer depends on why you are carrying out your analysis; in other words, it depends on your 'point of view'. If you are a shareholder, you may be most interested in the 'profit before dividends' as that is what is left for you after the banks and the Inland Revenue have taken the interest and tax due to them. If you are a manager, you are probably most interested in the profits arising from manufacturing and trading activities. This is normally referred to as the 'operating profit' and is defined as the 'profit before interest and tax' (PBIT). As this book is about management, the analysis of performance will be from the manager's point of view.

Figure 3.2 refers to Devah plc; profits are shown for the five most recent years along with the annual changes. Also shown is a list of profits in a standardised form which sets the profit for the most recent year at 100 and all other profits as a percentage of this. This can be useful for comparison purposes. To help get an idea as to the trend (if any), it is a good idea to create a graph of the profits. This type of information is communicated so much better by a graph than by a series of numbers.

It is also worthwhile repeating this exercise for sales revenue; Figure 3.3 illustrates this. Be aware that changes in revenue can be caused by changes in volume, changes in price or, more usually, a combination of both. (Unless there has been a significant change in the profit margin percentage, it is not worth doing a similar analysis of sales *volume* as this will give the same picture. Additionally, this may be distorted by changes in sales mix for multi-product firms and it would be impossible to do for competitors as the necessary information would be confidential.)

An alternative is to display both operating profit and sales revenue on the same chart, but a single scale causes some loss of clarity (see Figure 3.4).

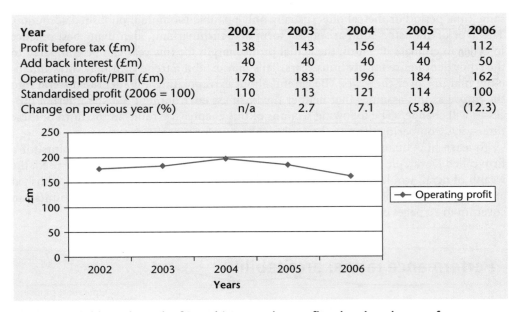

Year	2002	2003	2004	2005	2006
Profit before tax (£m)	138	143	156	144	112
Add back interest (£m)	40	40	40	40	50
Operating profit/PBIT (£m)	178	183	196	184	162
Standardised profit (2006 = 100)	110	113	121	114	100
Change on previous year (%)	n/a	2.7	7.1	(5.8)	(12.3)

Figure 3.2 Table and graph of Devah's operating profits showing changes from previous years

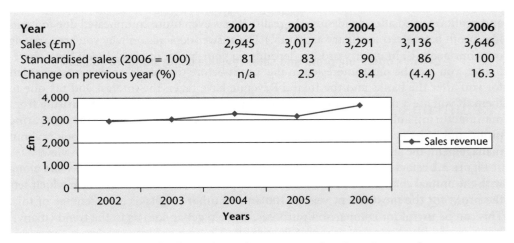

Year	2002	2003	2004	2005	2006
Sales (£m)	2,945	3,017	3,291	3,136	3,646
Standardised sales (2006 = 100)	81	83	90	86	100
Change on previous year (%)	n/a	2.5	8.4	(4.4)	16.3

Figure 3.3 Table and graph of Devah's sales revenue showing changes from previous years

However, a more informative comparison of these two items is given by using their standardised values, taking 2006 as 100 (see Figure 3.5).

The first three of these graphs indicates how the company is performing in absolute terms but the fourth displays the situation in relative terms. This 'relative' approach (showing how one item behaves relative to another) is continued below by looking at three important ratios, return on capital employed, profit margin and asset utilisation.

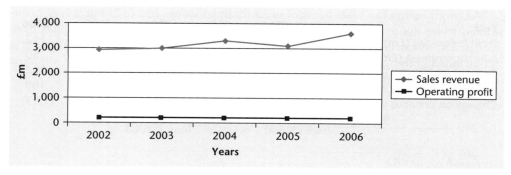

Figure 3.4 **Devah's operating profit and sales revenue**

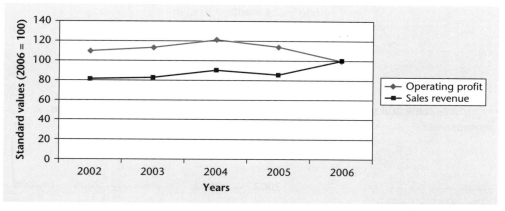

Figure 3.5 **Devah's operating profit and sales revenue using standard values**

Return on capital employed (ROCE)

If you put money into a savings account, you expect it to earn interest; if you invest money in a business, you also expect it to earn a return for you. The return on capital employed ratio is expressed as a percentage and tells you the rate at which the business is earning profit relative to the amount of money invested.

$$\text{ROCE} = \frac{\text{operating profit}}{\text{total capital employed}}$$

$$= \frac{\text{operating profit}}{\text{share capital} + \text{reserves} + \text{loan capital}}$$

But what is meant by 'operating profit' and where is it found? A brief examination of Devah's profit and loss account shows that four of its ten lines are labelled as 'profit', so which one is the operating profit? Actually, none of them are; of the four choices, 'net profit before tax' is the nearest. The calculation and payment of taxation and dividends are obviously not a direct part of a business's trading activities.

'Net profit before tax' takes account of all trading income and costs but it is not considered to be the precise definition of 'operating profit' because 'interest' has been deducted in its calculation. 'Interest' is the cost of borrowing rather than trading so it is not included in the 'operating profit' which is defined as 'profit before interest' or, more commonly, 'profit before interest and tax'. So,

$$\text{ROCE} = \frac{\text{profit before interest and tax}}{\text{share capital} + \text{reserves} + \text{loan capital}}$$

For Devah plc (2005):

$$\text{ROCE} = \frac{(144 + 40)}{600 + 224 + 400} = \frac{184}{1{,}224} = 15.0\%$$

Self-assessment question S3.1	Try the following question for yourself (answer at the end of the chapter). Calculate the ROCE ratio for Devah plc for 2006 and comment on your findings.

Profit margin

The profit margin expresses the operating profit as a percentage of sales revenue. It can be thought of as the amount of profit for every £100 of sales.

$$\text{Profit margin} = \frac{\text{operating profit}}{\text{sales revenue}}$$

For Devah plc (2005):

$$\text{Profit margin} = \frac{184}{3{,}136} = 5.87\%$$

This means that, on average, it makes £5.87 operating profit on every £100 of sales turnover.

Self-assessment question S3.2	Try the following question for yourself (answer at the end of the chapter). Calculate the profit margin for Devah plc for 2006 and comment on your findings.

Asset utilisation

This ratio indicates how efficiently the assets of the business are being used to generate sales.

$$\text{Asset utilisation} = \frac{\text{sales revenue}}{\text{net total assets}}$$

Another way of expressing the same idea would be to measure how efficiently managers are using the total capital employed in the business to generate sales.

$$\text{Capital utilisation} = \frac{\text{sales revenue}}{\text{total capital employed}}$$

These two ratios will have identical answers because the value of 'net total assets' is always equal to the value of 'total capital employed'. This equality is the fundamental basis of the balance sheet; it is why it balances!

For Devah plc (2005):

$$\text{Asset utilisation} = \frac{\text{sales revenue}}{\text{net total assets}} = \frac{3,136}{1,224} = 2.56 \text{ times}$$

The managers are using the assets to create 2.6 times their value in sales revenue.

Try the following question for yourself (answer at the end of the chapter).

Calculate the asset utilisation ratio for Devah plc for 2006 and comment on your findings.

Self-assessment question S3.3

Relationship between the three ratios

At this point, it is useful to look at the relationship between the three profitability ratios examined so far. The ROCE is the profitability ratio of primary importance but it can be analysed into its two constituent parts as shown below:

$$\frac{\text{operating profit}}{\text{total capital employed}} = \frac{\text{operating profit}}{\text{sales revenue}} \times \frac{\text{sales revenue}}{\text{total capital employed}}$$

$$\frac{\text{operating profit}}{\text{total capital employed}} = \frac{\text{operating profit}}{\text{sales revenue}} \times \frac{\text{sales revenue}}{\text{net total assets}}$$

$$\text{ROCE} = \text{profit margin} \times \text{asset utilisation}$$

For Devah plc (2005):

$$15.03\% = 5.87\% \times 2.56 \text{ times}$$

Self-assessment question S3.4

Try the following question for yourself (answer at the end of the chapter).

Check that this relationship holds good for Devah plc for 2006. (You will probably need to use two decimal places to be sure the arithmetic is consistent.)

The relationship merits further discussion:

$$\text{ROCE} = \text{profit margin} \times \text{asset utilisation}$$

Obviously, ROCE will be high if both the profit margin and asset utilisation ratios are high. Also, it will be middle range if both the profit margin and asset utilisation ratios are middle range (as for Devah plc above). But a middle-range ROCE can also come from a high profit margin combined with a low utilisation of assets or a low profit margin combined with a high utilisation of assets:

$$\text{(A) high profit margin} \times \text{low asset utilisation} = \text{mid-range ROCE}$$
$$20\% \times 0.8 \text{ times} = 16\%$$

$$\text{(B) low profit margin} \times \text{high asset utilisation} = \text{mid-range ROCE}$$
$$2.5\% \times 6.0 \text{ times} = 15\%$$

Example (A) could be a business with relatively few premium-priced sales at the top end of the quality market whereas example (B) could be a 'pile-them-high–sell-them-cheap' business. These are two well-known business strategies.

Gross margin and cost control

If the ratio analysis shows that the profit margin has gone down, it means that the amount of operating profit has reduced relative to the amount of sales revenue. One possible cause of this is that costs are increasing, indicating a need for management attention.

But which costs should be investigated – the direct ones or the overheads? One way to find out is to calculate the 'gross profit margin' and compare it to that of last period. This ratio shows whether the direct costs (such as raw materials) are under control.

$$\text{Gross margin} = \frac{\text{gross profit}}{\text{sales revenue}} = \frac{(\text{sales revenue} - \text{direct cost of sales})}{\text{sales revenue}}$$

A decrease in gross margin indicates that direct costs are increasing at a greater rate than sales revenue. An investigation should reveal whether corrective action is possible. For example, if raw material prices have increased, it may be possible to change suppliers. On the other hand, if the increase has been caused by a worldwide increase in oil prices, there may not be any remedy.

Alternatively, if the gross margin is holding steady or improving, any decrease in profit margin will be due to an increase in overhead costs. This can be quantified by calculating either of the following ratios:

$$\frac{\text{overheads}}{\text{sales revenue}} \text{ or } \frac{\text{overheads}}{\text{total costs}}$$

Either of these will indicate any disproportionate increase in overhead costs. As the sales revenue figure is easier to find, the first ratio is recommended. Note that because operating profit is before the deduction of interest, the figure for total overheads should not include any interest costs.

For Devah plc (2005):

$$\text{gross margin} = \frac{1,068}{3,136} = 34.1\%$$

$$\frac{\text{overheads}}{\text{sales revenue}} = \frac{884}{3,136} = 28.2\%$$

Cost control is an important management task necessary to maintain and improve business performance.

Self-assessment question S3.5

Try the following question for yourself (answer at the end of the chapter).

Self-assessment question S3.2 shows the following profit margins: 2005 = 5.87%, 2006 = 4.44%. Explain this decline in performance by calculating the gross margin and overheads/revenue ratios for Devah plc for 2006.

Performance ratios: working capital

All businesses need to control their working capital; the importance of this is discussed at length in the chapter on working capital elsewhere in this book. Appropriate control will result in the overall value of working capital being kept to a minimum. In turn, this will have a positive effect on the primary ratio, ROCE; the smaller the total capital employed (including working capital) the greater the ratio. So, minimising working capital will improve profitability provided that any reductions do not affect sales revenue in any way.

Working capital is formally known as 'net current assets' (current assets minus current liabilities) and the management of each of its constituents can be assessed by the use of an appropriate ratio. However, the critical asset of 'cash' will be discussed further on in this chapter in the section on liquidity ratios. Stock, debtors and creditors will now be examined. The constituent ratios are:

- stock turnover period;
- debtors collection period;
- creditors payment period.

Stock turnover ratio

This ratio gives the average amount of time for which stock is held before being sold. (A more descriptive title is 'stock-holding period'.)

$$\text{Stock turnover} = \frac{\text{year-end stock}}{\text{average daily cost of sales}}$$

To be more precise, this formula estimates the amount of time the year-end stock will take to sell. It can only be an estimate because it uses the *average* daily cost of sales. It is unlikely to give a very accurate answer but it may give a reasonable indication of the stock-holding period, depending on the degree of seasonality of the sales. (For example, if the financial year-end occurs during a peak selling time, this ratio will overestimate the length of the stock turnover period.) Note that the answer to this formula will be a number of *days*; if the average cost of sales were expressed in weeks, the answer would also be given in weeks etc. In order to calculate the stock turnover, the average daily cost of sales is needed but this information is not given in the accounts. Only the annual cost of sales is given; this is divided by 365 to give a daily average and the formula changes as follows.

$$\text{Stock turnover} = \frac{\text{year-end stock}}{\text{annual cost of sales}/365}$$

Mathematically, this is the same as

$$\text{Stock turnover} = \frac{\text{year-end stock}}{\text{annual cost of sales}} \times 365$$

For Devah plc (2005):

$$\text{Stock turnover} = \frac{382}{2,068} \times 365 = 67 \text{ days}$$

This indicates that the company's money is tied up in stocks for just over two months. If this is longer than in the last period, stock control is deteriorating, but if it is shorter, it is improving.

Try the following question for yourself (answer at the end of the chapter).

Calculate the stock turnover ratio for Devah plc for 2006 and comment on your findings.

So far in this section, it has been assumed that the business being analysed is a retail trading business. These organisations buy products and resell them with little or no conversion work. But if the business manufactures the products it sells, the above formula for the stock turnover ratio needs adjusting. This is because manufacturers have three types of stock rather than just one: raw materials, work-in-progress and finished goods. Three formulae are now needed.

$$\text{Raw materials turnover} = \frac{\text{year-end stock of RM}}{\text{annual cost of RM used}} \times 365$$

$$\text{Work-in-progress turnover} = \frac{\text{year-end W-i-P}}{\text{annual cost of production}} \times 365$$

$$\text{Finished goods turnover} = \frac{\text{year-end stock of FG}}{\text{annual cost of sales}} \times 365$$

These show the average length of time that cash is tied up in raw materials, work-in-progress and finished goods stock respectively. If you work for a manufacturing business and are analysing its accounts, you should be able to access the values of the three different types of stock. But if you are analysing another manufacturer, possibly a competitor, it is very unlikely that you will able to do this. Accounts published in the public domain usually show just a single figure for the value of stocks. In this case, the best you can do is to calculate a single 'stock turnover' period; for a manufacturer this will be an average across the three different types of stock and will lack the detail available from internal management accounts.

Debtor collection period

When stock is sold, either cash is received immediately or, if the customer is given a period of credit in which to pay, a debtor is created.

$$\text{Debtor collection period} = \frac{\text{year-end debtors}}{\text{average daily credit sales}}$$

Again, the daily figure is not available but the annual one is (provided the sales turnover figure in the profit and loss account is assumed to consist totally of credit sales). So the daily amount can be calculated as above and the formula becomes

$$\text{Debtor collection period} = \frac{\text{year-end debtors}}{\text{annual credit sales}} \times 365$$

This gives an estimate of how long it will take for the year-end debtors to pay up.

For Devah plc (2005):

$$\text{Debtor collection period} = \frac{102}{3,136} \times 365 = \textbf{12 days}$$

This indicates that the company's money is tied up in debtors for nearly two weeks. If this is longer than in the last period, credit control is deteriorating, but if it is shorter, it is improving.

Self-assessment question S3.7	*Try the following question for yourself (answer at the end of the chapter).* Calculate the debtor collection period for Devah plc for 2006 and comment on your findings.

Creditor payment period

This ratio is a mirror image of the debtor collection period, 'the other side of the same coin'. Businesses usually buy their supplies from other businesses on credit terms, paying for items many days after they have received them. This time, they are freeing up their money for the length of time they take to pay. This works in favour of their liquidity rather than against it (as for stock and debtors).

$$\text{Creditor payment period} = \frac{\text{year-end creditors}}{\text{average daily credit purchases}}$$

Once again, the daily amount is not usually available so the 'divide the annual by 365' device is employed. But there is a bigger problem here. Published sets of accounts do not show 'purchases' for any period of time; the nearest they get to it is the figure for the annual cost of sales. However, if the figures for the opening and closing stocks are known, the amount of the purchases can be calculated by using the following relationship:

$$\text{Cost of sales} = \text{opening stock} + \text{purchases} - \text{closing stock}$$

So,

$$\text{Purchases} = \text{cost of sales} + \text{closing stock} - \text{opening stock}$$

Of course, if you are analysing the accounts of the company you work for, you should have access to the annual total of purchases.

For Devah plc (2005):

Devah's accounts at the beginning of this chapter contain sufficient information to calculate the creditor payment period for 2006 but not for 2005. For the purpose of this illustration, it will be assumed that the stock at the start of 2005 had a value of £290 million.

$$\text{Purchases} = \text{cost of sales} + \text{closing stock} - \text{opening stock}$$
$$= 2{,}068 + 382 - 290$$
$$= 2{,}160$$

$$\text{Creditor payment period} = \frac{\text{year-end creditors}}{\text{average daily credit purchases}}$$

$$= \frac{242}{2{,}160} \times 365$$

$$= 41 \text{ days}$$

This indicates that the company is using its supplier's money for about six weeks. If this is shorter than in the last period, control is deteriorating, but if it is longer, it is improving.

Try the following question for yourself (answer at the end of the chapter).

Calculate the creditor payment period for Devah plc for 2006 and comment on your findings.

Self-assessment question S3.8

The cash cycle

The above three ratios can be combined to give the average length of time it takes for the business to get back the cash it spends on the purchase of stock. This period is called the 'cash cycle' and is illustrated in Figure 4.10 in the chapter on working capital management. It is defined as follows:

Cash cycle = (stock turnover – creditor payment period) + debtor collection period

Notice that the bracketed term above represents the length of time money is tied up in stock. For example, if stock is held for 10 weeks and suppliers are paid 6 weeks after goods are received, money would be tied up in stock for 4 weeks.

For Devah plc (2005):

$$\text{Cash cycle} = (67 \text{ days} - 41 \text{ days}) + 12 \text{ days}$$
$$= 26 \text{ days} + 12 \text{ days}$$
$$= 38 \text{ days}$$

(In the case of a manufacturing organisation, the stock turnover period consists of the three types of stock turnover as explained a few pages above.)

The shorter the cash cycle, the less cash is needed by the business; the smaller amount is compensated for by its faster 'velocity of circulation'. The longer the cycle, the more cash is needed by the business. When cash is a scarce resource (which is the case for many businesses) it is vital that it is managed efficiently. The most common cause for organisations going out of business is insufficient cash; this is despite the fact that most of them were making profits at the time of their demise!

Self-assessment question S3.9

Try the following question for yourself (answer at the end of the chapter).

Calculate the cash cycle for Devah plc for 2006 and comment on your findings.

Position ratios: liquidity

It is important to consider whether the business is likely to survive in the immediate future. As the key to survival is having an adequate amount of cash, it is important to know the liquidity position of the business. The following two liquidity ratios will be calculated for Devah plc:

$$\text{Current ratio} = \frac{\text{current assets}}{\text{current liabilities}}$$

$$\text{Liquid ratio} = \frac{\text{liquid assets}}{\text{current liabilities}}$$

The current ratio shows how many times the current liabilities are covered by the current assets and is usually expressed in the form of a mathematical ratio. For example, a ratio of 1.5:1.0 can be interpreted as the current liabilities being covered one-and-a-half times. This means that there is £1.50 of current assets to pay for every £1.00 of current liability.

The liquid ratio (often called the acid test ratio) is a *sharper* measure of liquidity in that it seeks to exclude any current assets that are not very liquid. For many businesses, 'stock' would come under this heading as it may yet have to be converted into saleable goods, stored and sold on credit terms before it could be described as liquid. In this case, the formula would be

$$\text{Liquid ratio} = \frac{\text{current assets} - \text{stock}}{\text{current liabilities}}$$

However, in some businesses, stock could reasonably be considered to be liquid. This would be so where the stock-holding period is similar to or less than the debtors collection period.

For Devah plc (2005):

$$\text{Current ratio} = \frac{\text{current assets}}{\text{current liabilities}} = \frac{514}{360} = 1.4{:}1.0$$

$$\text{Liquid ratio} = \frac{\text{current assets} - \text{stock}}{\text{current liabilities}} = \frac{514 - 382}{360} = 0.4{:}1.0$$

Try the following question for yourself (answer at the end of the chapter).

Calculate the current and liquid ratios for Devah plc for 2006 and comment on them.

Self-assessment question S3.10

Position ratios: gearing/capital structure

A different aspect of position is that of how the business is financed at the end of the accounting period. Where has the money to run the business come from? Who has provided the capital employed?

There are three basic sources of company funds: shareholders (who own the business), lenders (like banks) and profits retained within the business. As the profits ultimately belong to the shareholders, there are really only two sources: owners and non-owners. (Non-owners are sometimes referred to as 'third parties' to differentiate them from the company itself and the company's owners.) The 'gearing' ratio examines the relationship between these two sources of funds and its implications. It is commonly expressed in two different ways:

$$\text{Gearing} = \frac{\text{funds from third parties}}{\text{total funds}}$$

$$= \frac{\text{funds from third parties}}{\text{shareholder funds} + \text{funds from third parties}}$$

$$= \frac{\text{loan capital}}{(\text{shareholder capital} + \text{reserves}) + \text{loan capital}}$$

This is calculated as a percentage and identifies the proportion of total funds provided by non-owners. A ratio of 75% means that 75% of funds are provided from 'outside' the company and 25% from 'inside'; the higher the percentage, the higher the gearing.

Alternatively,

$$\text{Gearing} = \frac{\text{funds from third parties}}{\text{shareholder funds}}$$

$$= \frac{\text{loan capital}}{\text{shareholder capital} + \text{reserves}}$$

This alternative ratio is a direct comparison of the amounts provided by the two sources and is expressed simply as a number. A ratio of 3.0 means that third parties provide £3 of funds for every £1 provided by shareholders. This describes the identical financial structure as in the 75% ratio shown above. So, a business with a gearing of 3.0 has the same financial structure as one with a gearing of 75%.

For Devah plc (2005):

$$\text{Gearing} = \frac{\text{loan capital}}{\text{shareholder capital} + \text{reserves} + \text{loan capital}}$$

$$= \frac{400}{600 + 224 + 400} = \frac{400}{1,224}$$

$$= 32.7\%$$

Self-assessment question S3.11

Try the following question for yourself (answer at the end of the chapter).

Calculate the gearing ratio for Devah plc for 2006 and comment on your answer.

The basic idea of 'gearing' is to transform an input into a higher or lower output. Consider a business which has exactly half its £2 million of funds provided by shareholders and half by a bank in the form of a £1 million debenture bearing interest at the rate of 10% a year. The business is producing a return of 15% a year on its total capital employed. The £1 million provided by the bank is earning a return to the company of £150,000 a year but the company is paying only £100,000 of this to the bank in interest. The other £50,000 earned by the loan goes to the shareholders. Their own £1 million capital is earning £150,000 and they also get £50,000 return on the loan capital. So they get a total return of £200,000 on an investment of £1 million; this is a return of 20%. In effect, their investment is *geared up* to 20%. (Of course, all shareholders' earnings are subject to tax but, for the sake of clarity, we will ignore taxation in this explanation.)

Unfortunately, gearing is not always advantageous to the shareholder. If the company's trading activities are earning at a rate greater than it is paying on its loans, the shareholder benefits. However, when the company is earning at a rate less than it is paying on its loans, the shareholder suffers. For example, if the loan in the above case was subject to interest at 25% a year (instead of 10%), the shareholder would get a return of only 5%. (The company's activities produce a return of 15% on £2 million = £300,000. The bank receives 25% of £1 million = £250,000 in interest. This leaves only £50,000 for the shareholders, which is a return of 5% on their investment of £1 million.)

Gearing is a 'two-edged sword' – it cuts both ways! It amplifies the return to the shareholders irrespective of whether that return is positive or negative relative to its rate of earning. The consensus of opinion is that it is advantageous to shareholders to have some level of gearing in their company but that too much gearing is a bad thing; the higher the gearing, the greater the risk. The Channel Tunnel Company (Eurotunnel) is a prime example of a very highly geared company; at one time its ratio was approximately 99%! For every £1 provided by shareholders, a consortium of banks provided around

£99 in loans. In order to reduce this, some debt has been converted to share capital but it is still very highly geared.

At the time of writing (May 2005) Eurotunnel's creditors were being asked to write off £4 billion out of their total £6.4 billion debt! Not surprisingly, they refused. However, the company faces a liquidity crisis in 2006 when interest payments become more onerous and guaranteed minimum payments received from rail operators cease. Furthermore, in 2007, Eurotunnel is due to repay some of the capital to the creditor banks. But this will be impossible without further financial restructuring and the company will become bankrupt; hence the request to write off £4 billion of debt.

At the very least, huge amounts of debt will have to be converted into new share capital to reduce drastically the amount of interest paid annually. One way or the other, the creditors will be hit badly in the short term. However, in the long term, Eurotunnel could be a viable company. It already makes a healthy operating profit but this is turned into a loss by the enormous amount of interest paid out. The accounting firm Deloitte recently reported that Eurotunnel would be a viable business provided its debt was no more than about £2 billion, so the ostentatious request for £4 billion to be written off by the creditors was not as crazy as it first seemed.

This is a prime example of a company with far too much gearing, causing the shareholders to suffer. Because interest has to be paid before dividends can be declared, the shareholders have had very little, if any, return on their investment in recent years. A financial restructuring in the near future is inevitable in order to correct this situation.

Try the following question for yourself (answer at the end of the chapter).

Self-assessment question S3.12

Devah's ROCE is 15.0% for 2005 (see above); this is greater than the interest rate of 10.0% on its debenture. For this year, the return on shareholders' funds (ROSF) is 17.5% (ignoring taxation).

$$\text{ROSF} = \frac{\text{profit before tax}}{\text{total shareholders' funds}} = \frac{144}{824} = 17.5\%$$

Suppose the debenture had been for £400 million more and the ordinary share capital for £400 million less. The 10% debenture would have been for £800 million (instead of £400 million), the ordinary share capital would have totalled £200 million (instead of £600 million) and the gearing ratio would have doubled from 32.7% (see above) to 65.4% as follows:

$$\text{Gearing} = \frac{800}{200 + 224 + 800} = \frac{800}{1,224} = 65.4\%$$

What effect would this have had on the ROSF?

Although it is useful for a manager to have a good understanding of gearing and its effects on shareholders, the manager will be more directly concerned with the business's ability to pay the required amounts of interest on the loans (as well as the repayment of the loan capital itself) when they become due. The 'interest cover' ratio gives some insight into this; its objective is to calculate the number of times the interest on third-party loans can be paid for by the operating profit. This gives an idea of the sensitivity and criticality of these payments. A company whose operating profit is only 1.5 times as big as the amount of interest due would be much more concerned than one whose profit was 7.5 times as big. (Third-party loans are also known as 'debt capital', 'long-term indebtedness' or just 'debt'; this can be confusing until you get used to it.)

$$\text{Interest cover} = \frac{\text{operating profit}}{\text{interest payable}}$$

If the operating profit is £5.5 million and the interest on loan capital is £500,000, the interest is covered '11 times'.

Consider a company with no third-party loans (i.e. zero gearing) which has made a 'profit before tax' of £1 million. If, instead of zero gearing, part of that company's finance had been provided by a £2 million 10% debenture, its 'profit before tax' would have been £800,000 (£1,000,000 profit − £200,000 interest). 'Profit before tax' depends on both the trading performance and the financial structure of the company. 'Profit before interest' depends only on the trading activities and can correctly be described as 'operating profit'.

For Devah plc (2005):

$$\text{Interest cover} = \frac{\text{profit before tax} + \text{interest}}{\text{interest}} = \frac{144 + 40}{40} = 4.6 \text{ times}$$

Whether this is considered to be good or bad depends on the volatility of profits. Small variations on this would not concern a stable company but if profits fluctuate violently from one year to the next, 4.6 could easily turn into 1.6 and that would cause concern.

Self-assessment question S3.13	*Try the following question for yourself (answer at the end of the chapter).* Calculate the interest cover ratio for Devah plc for 2006 and comment on your answer.

Limitations of ratio analysis

The introduction to this chapter stressed that managers need to know the current position of the business in order to measure future improvements. Ratio analysis enables this position to be established – but how accurate is the picture it paints? This is not an easy question to answer; each of the following factors impact on the reliability of the analysis.

Financial scandals such as Enron, Worldcom and Parmalat are evidence that annual accounts are sometimes nearer to fiction than fact, even when they have been given a clean bill of health by their auditors! Creative accounting is alive and well in the twenty-first century. **Ratios are only as good as the data they use.**

Normal application of accounting conventions can sometimes give misleading information. For example, when inflation is significant, the historic cost convention means that the value of assets on the balance sheet may seriously understate the total of resources being used by the company and, therefore, the amount of capital it employs.

When two competing companies are compared, it is assumed that they have adopted identical accounting policies. It is unlikely that this is absolutely true, which means that like is not being compared to like and the comparison is invalid to some extent. For example, one company may use straight-line depreciation whilst the other uses the reducing-balance method. If they had exactly the same assets purchased for the same money at the same time, it would mean that they had different amounts of capital employed. The fact that no two businesses are ever exactly alike weakens the comparative analysis approach.

Ratio analysis is sometimes used to predict future performance. This assumes that neither the business environment nor the internal processes of the business will change significantly for the period being forecast. However, due to the accelerating rate of change, this assumption is becoming less and less reliable with the passing of time. It is increasingly risky to assume past performance to be a good indicator of future performance.

Ratios may be able to quantify **what** has happened but they often offer no explanation as to **why** it has happened. Also, ratios can only provide information on those aspects of business that can be expressed in numbers. They cannot throw any light on important factors such as 'intellectual capital' or 'employee goodwill'.

The manager's point of view

A set of accounts can, at first, seem nothing more than a dry statement of financial data. If you do not have a detailed knowledge of the company, which will always be the case unless the business is your own, you will need to apply ratio analysis to this data, in an attempt to throw a little light on the reality behind the figures. In your own company, of course, you will already be fully conversant with the background, but ratio analysis can still perform a key, if somewhat different, role.

The single most important ratio, by far, is the Return on Capital Employed. Nothing else really matters. Is your company making good use of the money invested in it, or would the shareholders be better off investing elsewhere, or, indeed, leaving the money sitting securely in the bank? A satisfactory ROCE will show an acceptable performance in comparison with previous years, a return which contrasts favourably with rival companies, and a profit sufficiently large to compensate shareholders for the perceived risks they are taking. If the ROCE is running at the right level, and the company's cash position is adequate, it hardly matters what else the accounts may be telling you. All the other ratios are aids which can help you keep the ROCE on track.

In my company, the ROCE became an issue only once a year, during the budget preparation. The worldwide corporation had a target ROCE of 20%, and we were all under pressure to edge up our own individual performances, to enable this global target to be achieved. Our own ROCE in the UK was already in excess of this, which helped to compensate for the younger businesses elsewhere which still fell some way short. There was no question of our being able to rest on our laurels, though, and at budget time, the impact of our own proposals on the global position was closely scrutinised. The usual detailed budget discussions were held, followed by endless tweaking, until we had honed it down to a set of figures which we all felt were achievable, and which met the requirements of profits growth, profit margins and ROCE. This process may have included some other ratio checks, but with a satisfactory ROCE target, we could now set out to achieve the individual budget numbers, in the knowledge that they would automatically lead to the desired statistics.

During the year, we tended to use only three financial ratios. The first was Direct Profit Margin, i.e. net sales, less direct costs of material, labour and overhead, expressed as a percentage of net sales. This was potentially the most variable item in the income statement. You cannot control the customers. They may buy more or less than you anticipated, or buy different products at different times, thereby changing the mix; you may not get the price increase you were hoping for, or suffer from cost increases which you cannot recover in time. All these will have an impact on the Direct Profit Margin. However, if you can achieve the budgeted target here, you know you will have a good chance of achieving both the Net Profit and ROCE targets, as all the other items in the accounts are more or less within the company's control. Concentration on the profit margin will instantly highlight variations from the expected pattern, and allow you to take early remedial action. If the variations produce a higher profit margin than planned, you can look forward to the excess falling straight through to the bottom line, assuming that overheads are kept under control.

The other two ratios used on a regular basis were Debtor Collection Period and the Stock Turnover Period. These were used in setting up the balance sheet budget at the beginning of the year, and were usually set at the same level, or slightly tighter, than the actual performance in the previous year. In this way, they were used as targets for the credit and stock control functions, and, as investment in Working Capital is an important element of Total Capital Employed, a good performance here could have a positive impact on the ROCE achievement. They were monitored on a monthly basis, and were considered sufficiently important to warrant inclusion in our company's list of key performance indicators.

Ratio analysis is perhaps a more valuable tool when investigating companies with which you are considering entering into trading commitments. You will need to examine the accounts of not only new customers, to ensure that they are sufficiently financially sound to pay their future bills, but also new vendors, to check that they are viable companies who will be able to meet their supply obligations over the longer term.

The contents of a company's annual accounts are prescribed by a series of Companies Acts introduced over many decades, which have required ever greater disclosure of company activities. In return for the comfortable safety net of limited liability, companies are required to place specified information in the public domain, for the benefit of potential trading partners. Yet the accounts can still fall frustratingly short of divulging the full picture.

The more financial detail a company makes available, the better you will be able to judge its performance. But at the same time, any information which helps you, as a prospective partner, will also be of considerable interest to the company's competitors. Consequently, there is a great temptation for companies to obey the letter and, for the most part, the spirit of the law, but in such a way as to reveal as little really useful information as possible. For example, a geographical analysis of sales provides an interesting snapshot of a company's business, but knowledge of a company's market penetration could be invaluable to competitors. My company used to overcome this particular problem in its accounts by aggregating the numbers for completely different businesses within our chemicals portfolio, rendering them impenetrable to competitors.

Extensive ratio analysis, however, can reveal information which is not immediately apparent. Accounts, and particularly the Notes to the Accounts, are full of nuggets of information, which can add unexpected colour to a drab set of numbers. You may wish to calculate sales and profit per employee, compare capital spending with depreciation, or dividends with profit. When looked at over a period of years, this information can be very revealing. It may not prove anything conclusively, but such trends may shed light on the direction the company is travelling, and flag up potential problems down the line.

Conversely, steady trends in the right direction may reflect the competence of the company's management, and allow you to enter into financial arrangements with the company in greater confidence. History, of course, is no guarantee of future success, but a good track record is as good a reassurance as one can expect in business.

Whilst the dissection of published accounts can yield interesting facts, this, too, will usually stop short of giving you the complete picture, so some educated guesswork is usually necessary. But in doing this, some further caveats should be borne in mind. Companies can play the same sort of games with published accounts as we saw with budgets. This is known as window dressing, and is normally resorted to by unsound companies desperate to show their financial position at the year-end in the best possible light. This can take the form of anything from convoluted schemes for off-balance-sheet financing to simply delaying the payment of creditors. Running stocks down to artificially low levels and conducting major purges on outstanding debts are other common year-end tactics. These will tend to improve the company's apparent cash position, so it is important to consider the balance sheet and notes in total, instead of focusing just on a single item like cash.

You should also bear in mind that the accounts you are looking at may be considerably out of date. Companies can submit their accounts up to 10 months after their year-end. The latest accounts available therefore will probably relate to the year before last. So, in the absence of current information, you may have to rely on historical trends to predict the future.

Finally, always remember to check the audit report. Although current audit reports are heavily hedged around by disclaimers as to the extent and purpose of their work, the auditors' final view that the accounts show a true and fair view is still a source of comfort. A qualified audit report should set all the alarm bells ringing. After all, the basic purpose of using published accounts is to look for indications of anything that might be going wrong with the company. So, any warning signs, whether explicit in the audit report, or emerging from your ratio analysis, should make you stop and think, 'Is this a risk I am prepared to accept?'

Summary

- Ratios can compare actual performance to budget.
- Ratios can compare a business to its competitors.
- Ratios can compare one year to previous years.
- Business performance can be evaluated by profitability ratios.
- ROCE can be analysed into profit margin and asset utilisation.
- Management performance can be evaluated by working capital ratios.

- The cash cycle is the combination of the stock, debtors and creditors ratios.
- Liquidity ratios evaluate financial position and indicate survival chances.
- Gearing ratios show what proportion of finance is provided by third parties.
- Gearing can amplify the returns to shareholders, both positive and negative.
- The interest cover ratio highlights the criticality of interest payments.
- Ratios are only as good as the accounts they use.
- Accounting conventions and policies can distort intercompany comparisons.
- Trends revealed by ratio analysis must be extrapolated with great care.
- Ratios tell you what has happened but not why it has happened.

Summary table of ratio formulae

a) *Profitability:*

$$\text{Return on capital employed, ROCE} = \frac{\text{profit before interest and tax}}{\text{shareholder capital} + \text{reserves} + \text{loan capital}}$$

$$= \frac{\text{profit before interest and tax}}{\text{fixed assets} + \text{current assets} - \text{current liabilities}}$$

$$\text{Profit margin} = \frac{\text{profit before interest and tax}}{\text{sales}}$$

$$\text{Asset utilisation} = \frac{\text{sales}}{\text{fixed assets} + \text{current assets} - \text{current liabilities}}$$

$$\text{Gross profit margin} = \frac{\text{gross profit}}{\text{sales}}$$

b) *Working capital control:*

$$\text{Stock turnover} = \frac{\text{year-end stock}}{\text{average daily cost of sales}}$$

$$\text{Debtor collection period} = \frac{\text{year-end debtors}}{\text{average daily credit sales}}$$

$$\text{Creditor payment period} = \frac{\text{year-end creditors}}{\text{average daily credit purchases}}$$

c) *Liquidity:*

$$\text{Current ratio} = \frac{\text{current assets}}{\text{current liabilities}}$$

$$\text{Liquid ratio} = \frac{\text{current assets} - \text{stock}}{\text{current liabilities}}$$

d) *Capital structure:*

$$\text{Gearing} = \frac{\text{loan capital}}{\text{shareholder capital} + \text{reserves} + \text{loan capital}}$$

$$\text{Interest cover} = \frac{\text{profit before interest and tax}}{\text{interest payable}}$$

Further reading

Atrill, P. and McLaney, E. (2004) *Accounting and Finance for Non-Specialists*, 4th edition, Pearson Education, Harlow. See Chapter 6, 'Analysing and interpreting financial statements'.

Halkos, G. E. and Salamouris, D. S. (2004) 'Efficiency measurement of the Greek commercial banks with the use of financial ratios: a data envelopment analysis approach', *Management Accounting Research*, Vol. 15, Issue 2, June.

Horngren, C., Sundem, G. and Stratton, W. (2005) *Introduction to Management Accounting*, 13th edition, Pearson Education, Englewood Cliffs, NJ. See Chapter 17, 'Understanding and analysing consolidated financial statements'.

Answers to self-assessment questions

S3.1. For Devah plc (2006)

$$\text{ROCE} = \frac{\text{profit before interest and tax}}{\text{share capital} + \text{reserves} + \text{loan capital}}$$

$$= \frac{(112 + 50)}{700 + 238 + 500} = \frac{162}{1,438} = 11.3\%$$

This shows that there has been a very sharp drop in the ROCE from 15.0% to 11.3%, a fall of about one-quarter. It is imperative for management to find out why this has occurred and, if possible, to correct this trend over the coming year.

S3.2. For Devah plc (2006)

$$\text{Profit margin} = \frac{162}{3,646} = 4.44\%$$

This shows that the profit margin has reduced by about a quarter, from 5.87% to 4.44%. This is a significant change and should be corrected if possible.

S3.3. For Devah plc (2006)

$$\text{Asset utilisation} = \frac{\text{sales revenue}}{\text{net total assets}} = \frac{3,646}{1,438} = 2.54 \text{ times}$$

This shows that there has been no significant change in the utilisation of assets (2005 = 2.56 times).

S3.4. For Devah plc (2006)

$$\text{ROCE} = \text{profit margin} \times \text{asset utilisation}$$
$$11.3\% = 4.44\% \times 2.54 \text{ times}$$

This confirms the accuracy of the calculations and it also shows that the drastic fall in ROCE is almost entirely due to the fall in the profit margin.

S3.5. For Devah plc

		2006	2005
Profit margin	=	4.44%	5.87%
Gross margin $= \dfrac{1,164}{3,646}$	=	31.93%	34.06%
$\dfrac{\text{Overheads}}{\text{Sales revenue}} = \dfrac{1,002}{3,646}$	=	27.48%	28.19%

This shows that the overheads are a smaller proportion of sales revenue in 2006 than they were in 2005, indicating that they have been well controlled. However, the gross margin has declined from 34% to 32%, indicating that there has been a disproportionate increase in the direct cost of sales. So management attention should be focused on direct costs rather than overheads.

S3.6. For Devah plc (2006)

$$\text{Stock turnover} = \frac{530}{2,482} \times 365 = 78 \text{ days}$$

This shows that the management of stock has worsened over the year; stock days have increased from 67 to 78, a deterioration of 16%.

S3.7. For Devah plc (2006)

$$\text{Debtor collection period} = \frac{156}{3,646} \times 365 = \textbf{16 days}$$

This shows that the management function of 'credit control' is being performed much less well than last year. Debtor days have increased by one-third, from 12 to 16.

S3.8. For Devah plc (2006)

$$\begin{aligned}
\text{Purchases} &= \text{cost of sales} + \text{closing stock} - \text{opening stock} \\
&= 2,482 + 530 - 382 \\
&= 2,630
\end{aligned}$$

$$\text{Creditor payment period} = \frac{\text{year-end creditors}}{\text{average daily credit purchases}}$$

$$= \frac{312}{2,630} \times 365$$

$$= \textbf{43 days}$$

This shows a very slight improvement in creditor days, from 41 to 43.

S3.9. For Devah plc (2006)

$$\begin{aligned}
\text{Cash cycle} &= (\text{stock turnover} - \text{creditor payment period}) + \text{debtor collection period} \\
&= (78 \text{ days} - 43 \text{ days}) + 16 \text{ days} \\
&= 35 \text{ days} + 16 \text{ days} \\
&= \textbf{51 days}
\end{aligned}$$

This shows that the cash cycle has increased by about one-third over the year, from 38 days to 51 days. This significant deterioration indicates inefficient management of working capital. It is important for this trend to be reversed as soon as possible.

S3.10. For Devah plc (2006)

$$\text{Current ratio} = \frac{\text{current assets}}{\text{current liabilities}} = \frac{686}{428} = \textbf{1.6:1.0}$$

$$\text{Liquid ratio} = \frac{\text{current assets} - \text{stock}}{\text{current liabilities}} = \frac{686 - 530}{428} = \textbf{0.4:1.0}$$

This shows that although the current ratio has improved slightly compared to last year, the liquid ratio has not changed.

S3.11. For Devah plc (2006)

$$\text{Gearing} = \frac{\text{loan capital}}{\text{shareholder capital} + \text{reserves} + \text{loan capital}}$$

$$= \frac{500}{700 + 238 + 500} = \frac{500}{1,438} = 35\%$$

This shows that there has been a slight increase (of two percentage points) in gearing compared to the previous year.

S3.12. For Devah plc (2005)

	£m	£m
Gross profit		1,068
Admin & marketing expenses	884	
Debenture interest @ 10%	80	
		964
Profit before tax		104

$$\text{ROSF} = \frac{\text{PBT}}{\text{TSF}} = \frac{104}{200 + 224} = \frac{104}{424} = 24.5\%$$

The doubling of the gearing has increased the ROSF from 17.5% to 24.5%. (Although this is a very significant increase, note that the ROSF has not doubled.) In this case, the shareholders are considerably wealthier due to the increase in gearing.

S3.13. For Devah plc (2006)

$$\text{Interest cover} = \frac{\text{profit before tax} + \text{interest}}{\text{interest}} = \frac{112 + 50}{50} = 3.2 \text{ times}$$

Although this does not represent any imminent danger, the interest cover has reduced by about a quarter to 3.2 times (from 4.6 times). Further borrowing will worsen this position.

JRP Ltd

This case study shows how ratio analysis can be used by managers to help them improve the performance of their business.

JRP Ltd is a large wholesaler of electrical goods formed four years ago by the amalgamation of two smaller companies. Extracts from its annual accounts are shown below.

Early in year 4, one of JRP's most important suppliers insisted that all future deliveries should be paid for on or before delivery. As a result of this, JRP decided not to use this supplier and to source its goods elsewhere.

Management were aware that sales were significantly down in year 4 and had taken the prudent step of drastically reducing JRP's overheads. Staffing levels had been reduced at each of the depots and in every department at head office, including marketing and accounting. Due to cost cutting, JRP's 'quarterly' catalogue, from which most of its sales originate, had been revised only once during the year.

The accounts section lost one-third of their staff and could not keep up with the demand for information. They usually produced management accounts on a quarterly basis but the last set produced was for the first quarter and these were not completed until the middle of month 5. The chief accountant made a positive decision to concentrate on cash management in order to keep the business afloat.

Early in the year, the chief accountant realised that the company was going to breach its overdraft limit of £110,000. He approached JRP's bank who agreed to increase this to £120,000. But just before the end of the year, he had no choice but to ask the bank for a further increase of £25,000. Very reluctantly, the bank agreed to this, but **only** on a temporary basis for three months.

As soon as the accounts for year 4 were approved by the auditors, the management team held a meeting to discuss the results. They were aware that, due mainly to a downturn in the house-building market, year 3 had been disappointing compared to year 2. It had been assumed that its results would be worse than those of the previous year but when the pre-tax loss of £40,000 was announced, the directors were shocked.

It seemed to them that the drastic cost-cutting exercise of last year had been in vain. They could not see any other overheads that could be reduced without directly harming the business – all the fat had been dispensed with. In fact, they knew that there were certain areas which were in desperate need of more money being spent on them rather than less. They realised that immediate remedial action was necessary, but they did not know what to do or where to start.

Task:

Analyse the company's performance and advise management on the action it should take to restore this to the levels achieved in previous years.

(Assume that the stock at the start of year 1 was valued at £50,000.)

Extracts from profit and loss account (all figures in £000)

	Year 1	Year 2	Year 3	Year 4
Sales	1,090	1,950	1,480	1,040
Cost of sales	650	1,190	899	748
Gross profit	440	760	581	292
Admin & marketing costs	375	654	509	320
Debenture interest	10	10	12	12
Profit before tax	55	96	60	−40
Taxation	15	38	18	0
Profit after tax	40	58	42	−40
Dividends	20	30	20	0
Retained profit for the year	20	28	22	−40

Extracts from balance sheet (all figures in £000)

	Year 1	Year 2	Year 3	Year 4
Net fixed assets	**280**	**290**	**340**	**270**
Current assets – stock	60	115	135	160
– debtors	210	393	385	265
Total	**270**	**508**	**520**	**425**
Current liabilities – creditors	55	240	297	165
– overdraft	100	107	105	140
– dividends	10	15	10	0
– taxation	15	38	18	0
Total	**180**	**400**	**430**	**305**
Net current assets	**90**	**108**	**90**	**120**
Total net assets	**370**	**398**	**430**	**390**
Debentures	50	50	60	60
Total	*320*	*348*	*370*	*330*
Financed by:				
Share capital	300	300	300	300
Retained earnings	20	48	70	30
Shareholders' funds	*320*	*348*	*370*	*330*

Questions

An asterisk * on a question number indicates that the answer is given at the end of the book. Answers to the other questions are given in the Lecturer's Guide.

Q3.1* Panther plc

Tasks:

1. Calculate the profitability ratios for each of the three years.
2. Calculate the working capital ratios for each of the three years.
3. Calculate the liquidity ratios for each of the three years.
4. Calculate the capital structure ratios for each of the three years.
5. Interpret your findings by describing the company's trading history over the three-year period and evaluate its performance.

Profit and loss accounts for year ended 31 December (*all figures in £m*)

	2007	2006	2005
Sales	23,093	17,931	14,345
Cost of sales	17,394	14,572	11,358
Gross profit	5,699	3,359	2,987
Indirect costs	4,172	2,522	2,224
Debenture interest	93	59	44
Profit before tax	1,434	778	719
Taxation	410	278	241
Profit after tax	1,024	500	478
Dividends	477	229	172
Retained profit for the year	547	271	306

Balance sheet as at 31 December (*all figures in £m*)

	2007	2006	2005
Fixed assets (NBV)	5,100	4,458	4,678
Current assets:			
Stocks	2,850	2,177	1,790
Debtors	2,711	2,260	2,356
	5,561	4,437	4,146
Less current liabilities:			
Creditors	3,216	2,980	2,474
Tax due	540	278	241
Dividends due	368	133	92
Overdraft	491	605	1,447
	4,615	3,996	4,254
Net current assets	946	441	−108
Net total assets	6,046	4,899	4,570

	2007	2006	2005
Less debentures	1,564	964	906
	4,482	**3,935**	**3,664**
Financed by:			
Share capital	2,666	2,666	2,666
Retained earnings	1,816	1,269	998
	4,482	**3,935**	**3,664**

(Assume opening stock for 2005 = 1,689.)

Q3.2* The Wholesale Textile Company Limited

The annual accounts of the Wholesale Textile Company Limited have been summarised for 2005 and 2006 as follows:

	2005 £	2005 £	2006 £	2006 £
Sales				
Cash	60,000		64,000	
Credit	540,000	600,000	684,000	748,000
Cost of sales		472,000		596,000
Gross profit		128,000		152,000
Expenses				
Warehousing		26,000		28,000
Transport		12,000		20,000
Administration		38,000		38,000
Selling		22,000		28,000
Debenture interest		–		4,000
		98,000		118,000
Net profit		**30,000**		**34,000**

	31 December 2005 £	31 December 2005 £	31 December 2006 £	31 December 2006 £
Fixed assets (net book value)		60,000		80,000
Current assets				
Stock	120,000		188,000	
Debtors	100,000		164,000	
Cash	20,000	240,000	14,000	366,000
Less current liabilities				
Trade creditors		100,000		152,000
Net current assets		140,000		214,000
		200,000		294,000
Less: Debenture		–		60,000
		200,000		**234,000**
Financed by:				
Share Capital		150,000		150,000
Reserves and undistributed profit		50,000		84,000
		200,000		**234,000**

You are informed that:

1 All sales were from stocks in the company's warehouse.
2 The range of merchandise was not changed and buying prices remained steady throughout the two years.
3 Budgeted total sales for 2006 were £780,000.
4 The debenture loan was received in 1 January 2006, and additional fixed assets were purchased on that date.

Task:

Perform a ratio analysis to assist the management of the company to measure the efficiency of its operation, including its use of capital. Your answer should name the ratios and give the figures (calculated to one decimal place) for 2005 and 2006. Discuss possible reasons for changes in the ratios over the period. (Ratios relating to capital employed should be based on the capital at the year-end. Ignore taxation.)

Q3.3* Chonky Ltd

Chonky Ltd is a private company manufacturing and supplying spares to the motor trade. The following is a summary of the results of the business for the last four years together with year-end balance sheets.

Summary trading and profit and loss accounts (£000)

	2005		2006		2007		2008	
Cash sales	280		340		450		500	
Credit sales	120		160		350		500	
Total sales		400		500		800		1,000
Opening stock	20		24		26		74	
Purchases	244		307		568		732	
	264		331		594		806	
Less closing stock	24		26		74		126	
Cost of goods sold		240		305		520		680
Gross profit		160		195		280		320
Operating expenses	120		144		210		260	
Depreciation on plant	10		11		12		14	
Debenture interest	–		–		3		6	
		130		155		225		280
Net profit before tax		30		40		55		40
Taxation		12		15		21		16
Net profit after tax		18		25		34		24
Proposed dividend		8		10		14		12
Retained profit		10		15		20		12

Balance sheets as at 31 December (£000)

	2005		2006		2007		2008
Freehold property		100		100		140		140
Plant less depreciation		50		66		70		92
Fixed assets		150		166		210		232
Stocks in hand		24		26		74		126
Debtors		11		15		35		54
Investments		10		10		2		–
Cash at bank		12		14		–		–
Total assets		207		231		231		412
Creditors	22		26		50		92	
Proposed dividend	8		10		14		12	
Taxation accrued	12		15		21		16	
Bank overdraft	–		–		6		20	
Current liabilities		42		51		91		140
Net total assets		165		180		230		272
Less: Debentures		–		–		30		60
		165		180		200		212
Financed by:								
Ordinary shares		100		100		100		100
Retained earnings		65		80		100		112
		165		180		200		212

Note: There were no sales of fixed assets during the four-year period.

Task:

Comment on Chonky's liquidity, capital structure, profitability and working capital management during the four-year period. (State any assumptions you make.)

Q3.4 Digby plc

The following are extracts from the profit and loss accounts and balance sheets of Digby plc:

Profit and loss account (£m)

	2006	2005	2004
Sales	3,000	2,000	1,000
Cost of goods sold	1,950	1,240	600
Gross profit	1,050	760	400
Operating expenses	760	590	330
Debenture interest	16	13	8
Net profit before tax	274	157	62
Taxation	96	55	22
Profit after tax	178	102	40
Preference dividend	10	10	10
Equity dividend	60	30	10
Retained profit	108	62	20

Balance sheet at 31 December (£m)

	2006	2005	2004
Fixed assets	330	302	250
Stock	250	170	120
Debtors	190	140	80
Cash	20	10	20
Liabilities < 12 months	140	110	70
Net capital employed	650	512	400
Less Debentures 10%	160	130	80
Net assets employed	490	382	320
Financed by:			
Equity capital	200	200	200
Retained profits	190	82	20
Preference shares	100	100	100
	490	382	320

Task:

Comment on Digby's liquidity, capital structure, profitability and working capital management during the three-year period. (State any assumptions you make.)

Q3.5 Shoes Limited

Shoes Limited has operated in the retail sector for the past eight years. A summary of its financial statements for the year just ended is given below:

Trading and profit and loss account

	£000
Sales	1,200
Cost of sales	740
Gross profit	460
Expenses	390
Interest	12
Net profit	**58**

Balance sheet

	£000	£000
Fixed assets (at WDV)		700
Current assets:		
Stock	240	
Debtors	10	
	250	
Less current liabilities:		
Creditors	50	
Taxation	14	
Dividends	35	
Bank overdraft	14	
	113	

Net current assets	137
Net total assets	837
Debentures	98
	739
Financed by:	
Equity capital	100
Reserves	639
	739

Task:

You are required to calculate the following ratios and, by comparing them to the industry averages shown below, comment upon the financial state of the company, particularly with regard to liquidity, profitability and working capital management. (Assume the opening stock for the year was £220,000 and that only 20% of sales are made on credit terms.)

	Industry average
1 ROCE	9.5%
2 Gross profit margin	55%
3 Net profit margin	8%
4 Asset utilisation	1.6 times
5 Stock turnover period	87 days
6 Debtors collection period	7 days
7 Creditor payment period	46 days
8 Current ratio	1.5:1.0
9 Liquid ratio	0.3:1.0

Chapter contents

Introduction

All businesses need resources to function. Some resources are of a long-term nature (buildings, machinery, vehicles, etc.) whilst others are short term (stocks, debtors, cash, etc.). This chapter concentrates on the short-term resources used for conducting day-to-day business operations; these are normally referred to jointly as the *working capital* of the business. Just because these resources are short term, it does not mean that they are small compared to their long-term equivalents. Typically, the investment in working capital is between 40% and 60% of the total investment in the business.

Working capital consists of cash and other items that can be quickly converted into cash or cash equivalents. Of course, businesses also have short-term liabilities which are normally paid for with these short-term assets. An example of this is a payment out of the business's bank account to a supplier of raw materials. Cash is the asset which typifies working capital for most managers as it is the most easily applied of its components; in other words, it is the most 'liquid'. It is worth pointing out that 'cash' usually means the combination of 'cash-in-hand' and 'cash-at-bank'. Cash can be thought of as being 100.0% liquid and cash-at-bank as 99.9% liquid; in practical terms, they are both as instantaneously applicable as each other.

The majority of businesses also have stock, debtors and creditors and these are often larger in amount than their cash balance, especially when the business is running a bank overdraft. (Overdrafts are actually a liability rather than an asset as they are money owing by the business to the bank.) Of course, there are exceptions – supermarkets, for example, would have a far larger amount of cash than debtors, though their creditors may well be of a similar size to 'non-cash' businesses in different economic sectors.

The control and management of working capital directly influences an organisation's ability to survive. To illustrate this, consider the fact that many organisations that go out of business are profitable! The reason they can no longer function is that they have run out of cash; if they cannot pay their creditors on time they are not going to receive any further supplies on credit terms. If they cannot get their supplies, they cannot produce their goods and services; if they cannot do this, they have nothing to sell! If they have nothing to sell, their cash position will deteriorate rapidly and everything will soon grind to a halt. If you were employed by such a company, how long would you continue to work for no pay?

<table>
<tr><td>

Learning objectives

</td><td>

Having worked through this chapter you should be able to:

- define working capital;
- calculate economic order quantities for stock;
- rank stock items according to the ABC system;
- discuss the just-in-time system of stock control;
- explain 'buffer stock' and 'consignment stock';
- describe how computers can improve stock control;
- explain the importance of regular physical stock counts;
- list the advantages and disadvantages of holding stock;
- describe a standard credit control system;
- explain 'factoring' and 'invoice discounting';
- decide if debt insurance is appropriate;
- discuss alternative policies for dealing with multi-currency debts;
- evaluate the issuing of self-billing invoices to customers;
- define 'cash' and 'liquid funds';
- appreciate the fundamental importance of operating cash budgets;
- understand the concept of 'dynamic cash flow';
- compare leasing and buying fixed assets;
- describe the difference between an operating and a finance lease;
- explain the advantage of depositing 'surplus' cash overnight;
- describe the usefulness of 'small-firms loan guarantees';
- explain the importance of good supplier relationships;
- explain when alternative suppliers should be used;
- decide whether 'self-billing' for suppliers is justified;
- compare and contrast the working capital cycle with the cash cycle;
- define 'overtrading' and 'overcapitalisation';
- appreciate the limitations of various techniques used to control working capital.

</td></tr>
</table>

Definition of working capital

If you look at a balance sheet, you will see that working capital has a section of its own where each of its components is itemised. It will look similar to Figure 4.1.

Notice that the current assets are shown in the order of reverse liquidity with the most liquid being shown last. (This is traditional and the balance sheet would still balance if the order was changed.) Stock sold on credit terms creates debtors and these debts have to be collected to convert the asset into cash. So stock is the least liquid of the current assets with debtors coming between stock and cash.

All these items can, and should be, controlled. However, due to their nature, managers do not usually spend time trying to control 'prepayments' and 'accruals'. Prepayments are very similar to debtors; debtors are *money* owed to the business whereas prepayments are usually *services* owed to the business. An example would be an annual insurance premium for cover commencing one-third of the way through a financial year. At the year-end, the invoice for the full 12 months would have been entered in the accounting records but there would still be four months of insurance cover (the service) owing to the business. (One way of 'controlling' this is to pay by instalments; this action is also a good example of cash control which is discussed later in the chapter.)

Similarly, accruals are amounts owed for goods or services received in the year which have not been recorded in the books of account at the year-end. This is usually due to the appropriate invoices not having been received from the supplier so an estimate of the cost involved has to be made. If the year-end is 31 December and the last invoice from the electricity supplier was for the quarter ended 30 November, the next invoice would not be due until early March of the following year. As the accounts would normally have to be produced and audited by then, the creation of an accrual for the electricity used in December is essential. So managers spend much more of their time chasing debtors and fending off creditors than trying to control prepayments and accruals.

Current assets
Stock
Debtors
Prepayments
Cash (in hand and at bank)

Less: Creditors due in less than 12 months (*current liabilities*)
Creditors
Accruals

Equals: Net current assets (*also known as* **working capital**)

Figure 4.1 **Balance sheet extract showing the structure of working capital**

Objectives of working capital management

There are two main objectives of working capital management:

1 To maintain sufficient liquidity for the business to function effectively and efficiently.
2 To improve the profitability of the business.

Unfortunately, these objectives tend to conflict with one another. The greater the amount of working capital, the more likely the business is to run smoothly, but this will reduce its profitability. Consider the effect on the *return on capital employed* ratio:

$$\text{ROCE} = \frac{\text{operating profit}}{\text{total capital employed}}$$

$$= \frac{\text{operating profit}}{\text{fixed capital} + \text{working capital} + \text{loan capital}}$$

Any increase in working capital will increase the denominator of the fraction which will result in a smaller ROCE. The interrelationship of ratios is shown in Figure 4.2.

Those businesses which choose actively to reduce the amount of working capital in order to improve profitability can be described as 'pro-active'; those that do not employ this strategy, as 'passive'. The effects are shown in Figure 4.3.

If the firm is performing well and is 'cash rich', it may maintain a high level of working capital (almost by default) which helps the trading operations to run smoothly. On the other hand, if it is undergoing a survival crisis and desperately short of cash, it may have no choice but to operate with an inadequate amount of working capital investment. This leads to turbulent day-to-day operations causing management and accounts staff much extra work. However, provided nothing goes wrong, it will improve the ROCE percentage. The necessary 'juggling' of resources has the potential for upsetting both

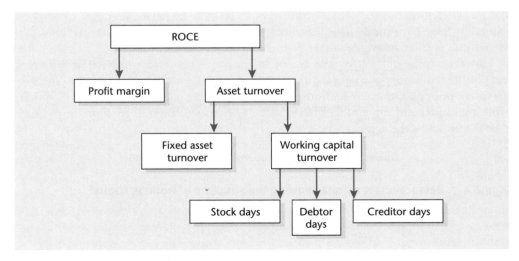

Figure 4.2 **The interrelationships of ratios**

Summarised balance sheet		
	Passive	Pro-active
	£m	£m
Net fixed assets	80	80
Working capital	45	40
Total net assets	125	120
Total capital employed (TCE)	125	120
Profitability calculations:		
PBIT	12	12
ROCE (= PBIT/TCE)	9.6%	10.0%

Figure 4.3 **Effect of working capital size on profitability**

suppliers and customers as well as the bank manager; a vicious circle may ensue, causing things to worsen continually to the point of insolvency.

Effect of working capital financing policies on profitability

It makes sense to finance fixed assets by long-term funds as this matches up the life spans of the two entities. This implies that working capital (a.k.a. net *current* assets) should be financed by short-term funds. However, a little thought will show that a certain amount of working capital is continuously needed on a long-term basis. The total of working capital will fluctuate between a minimum and a maximum amount. The 'minimum' amount is needed on a permanent basis but amounts above this are temporary in nature. Therefore, it is logical and consistent to finance the permanent part of working capital by long-term funds. This leaves only the temporary part to be financed by short-term funds such as an overdraft (see Figure 4.4a – the *matching* policy).

However, some businesses will decide to adopt the low-risk approach of financing part of the temporary working capital with long-term funds (see Figure 4.4b – the *conservative* policy). Others will choose the high-risk approach of financing all of their working capital and some of their fixed assets (permanent capital) by short-term funds (see Figure 4.4c – the *aggressive* policy).

The 'risk' referred to above comes from the uncertainty of interest rates payable when rolling over short-term funds on a regular basis compared to the fixed rates of interest available on long-term finance. Compare the renewal of a one-year short-term loan for 10 consecutive years (at rates as yet unknown) with a single 10-year loan at one fixed rate of interest. Because there is less risk and uncertainty associated with long-term loans, they tend to cost more than short-term ones. Thus, adoption of an aggressive policy should result in less interest being paid which will improve profitability *after interest*.

However, the conservative policy carries a risk of a different type as part of the temporary working capital is financed by the more expensive long-term funds. If there is a

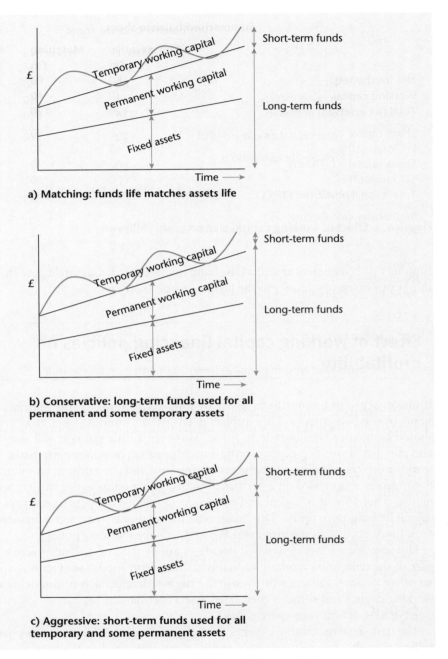

Figure 4.4 Three alternative policies for financing working capital
Source: Based on D. Watson and A. Head (2004) *Corporate Finance – Principles and Practice,* 3rd edition, Financial Times/Prentice Hall, Harlow

reduction in the amount of working capital needed in total, the short-term element will be reduced and it will cost more to fund as more interest will be paid proportionately. The long-term finance element cannot be adjusted until it is due for renewal, which may be several years into the future.

Summarised balance sheet

	Conservative £m	Matching £m	Aggressive £m
Net fixed assets	80	80	80
Working capital	40	40	40
Total net assets	120	120	120
Share capital	60	60	60
L-T loans (10%)	40	30	20
Share capital + L-T loans	100	90	80
S-T funds (7%)	20	30	40
Total capital employed (TCE)	120	120	120
Profitability calculations:			
PBIT	12	12	12
Interest @ 10%	4.0	3.0	2.0
Interest @ 7%	1.4	2.1	2.8
Total interest	5.4	5.1	4.8
Profit before tax (= PBIT − total interest)	6.6	6.9	7.2
PBT/TCE	*5.5%*	*5.8%*	*6.0%*
NB: ROCE (= PBIT/TCE)	*10.0%*	*10.0%*	*10.0%*

Figure 4.5 Impact of working capital financing choice on profitability

Note that these terms should only be used for companies in the same line of business. It is not valid to say that the working capital policy of a retailing organisation is aggressive compared to that of an engineering company.

If the provision of both long- and short-term funds cost the same (i.e. bore the same rate of interest), there would be no 'financing' effect on profitability. However, long-term funds, such as debentures, tend to cost more than short-term ones so the choice of funding will have an impact on profitability *after interest* (sometimes called 'profit before tax'). This is illustrated by Figure 4.5.

After considering working capital as a single entity, the management of each of its individual components will now be discussed in detail.

Stock

Economic order quantity (EOQ)

Holding goods in stock has a cost: if a business did not need stock it would not need to pay for a storekeeper or storage facilities. The less stock it holds, the less it costs to store it. This argument points towards ordering small quantities on a frequent basis, say every week. However, this means a very active 'purchase ordering' department with lots of work to do. If larger orders were placed less frequently, fewer resources would be needed to run the purchasing section. This illustrates the dilemma between the cost of holding stock and the cost of ordering it. So is there a happy medium? Is there a specific ordering quantity for each stock item which will keep the combination of these costs to a minimum? Traditional theory says there is such a quantity and calls it the 'economic order quantity'.

If

$$h = \text{holding cost of one unit for one year}$$
$$d = \text{annual demand in units}$$
$$p = \text{average cost of making one purchase order}$$

then

$$EOQ = \sqrt{(2pd/h)}$$

(This formula can be derived from first principles by the use of calculus but it is not necessary to be able to do this in order to use it!)

For example, if

$$h = £5$$
$$d = 50,000 \text{ units}$$
$$p = £200$$

then

$$EOQ = \sqrt{(2 \times 200 \times 50,000/5)}$$
$$= \sqrt{(20,000,000/5)}$$
$$= \sqrt{4,000,000}$$
$$= 2,000 \text{ units}$$

So, it would be most economical if this particular stock item was ordered in quantities of 2,000 units.

Self-assessment question S4.1

Try the following question for yourself (answer at the end of the chapter).

What is the EOQ for a stock item whose annual demand is 45,000 units if the holding cost of one unit is £10 a year and the average cost of placing a single order is £1,000?

It should be pointed out that the EOQ is of limited practical use. First, consider the difficulty in calculating the three numbers involved. Any calculation of the holding cost of stock (h) or the cost of making a purchase order (p) involves many estimations and averages as this information is not readily available. Also, annual demand is a forecast rather than a certainty. This formula will give a precise mathematical answer but its result should be treated very much as an estimate rather than an accurate figure. (This concept is known as 'spurious accuracy'.) For the EOQ to be genuinely useful, the business would have to be in a very stable economic environment where the predictability of transactions is high. In the twenty-first century, there are very few businesses with an environment like this.

The ABC ranking system of stock control

A traditional method of classifying stock is known as the *ABC system*. This method of control offers management a tool for sorting stock into three broad categories (in terms of their monetary value) to help concentrate resources on the higher-value items. This is a sensible approach as it is not efficient to spend a lot of time on the maintenance of minor stock items at the expense of securing and maintaining stocks critical to your products. For example, if you were making wheel braces for the motor vehicle industry, sandpaper would be a grade 'C' item but high-grade steel would be grade 'A'.

Figure 4.6 shows the majority of stock items being of low value (C), a smaller mid-range group of medium-value items (B) and a smaller still proportion of high-value stock items (A). This classification provides a simple tool managers can apply to make the most efficient use of their resources according to the relative value of stock elements.

Although the ABC stock ranking system is a useful management tool, it is not without its problems. For example, there is often a grey area as to where to draw meaningful monetary boundaries for classification, or finding that items regularly move from one category to another as a result of constant price changes in the marketplace.

As an extension to the ABC method, or perhaps as an alternative to it, a business may find it beneficial to think more in terms of *customer-critical stock*. This looks at those items of stock which are critical in enabling it to make its most important sales. Management have a responsibility to protect and develop sales relationships wherever possible. To this end, a view must be taken on which of their customers are most important and attention paid to the delivery requirements set down by them. This focuses management attention on the quantity, quality, cost and availability of component

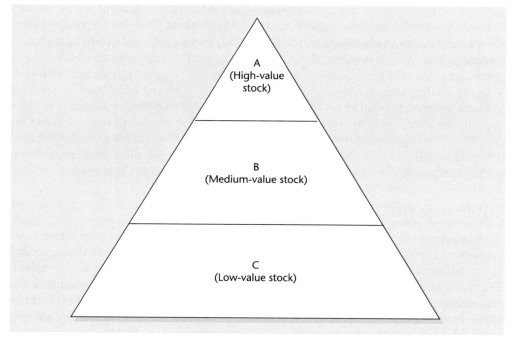

Figure 4.6 The ABC system of stock control

stocks required to meet the customer delivery targets. As a result potential stock-outs of critical stock may be identified at an early stage and action can be taken by management to avoid them.

Suppose your business supplied, amongst other items, a tyre pressure valve to a manufacturer of agricultural tractors; this component is a very small and inexpensive part of the tractor but its absence would prevent the completion of vehicle sales. The valve would be a low-value category C item but lack of attention to maintaining adequate stocks may result in the termination of an important supplier–customer relationship. By applying the ABC method alone, a supplier may easily run into a stock-out position through failure to address the reorder levels of what is a relatively low-value item, resulting in a full production line stoppage at the customer's premises. The potential contractual compensation charges for causing a delay in a customer's multi-thousand-pound vehicle production is far greater than the cost of correct procurement of the necessary numbers of tyre pressure valves in the first place!

So it can be seen that a relatively low-value stock item can have a major influence on the supplier–customer relationship, whether it represents the sole range of product supplied to that customer or whether it forms only a small but critical part of an existing customer product range. Sales managers and company directors will not thank their stock controllers if their sophisticated stock control system fails to ensure delivery of the **complete** customer order due to the unavailability of the smallest of parts!

Another concept linked to the idea of customer-critical stock provision is that of 'supplier ratings'. By giving your suppliers a rating in accordance with the importance of the quality of their products to your business, you can improve your own quality standards. The supplier rating is not based on the kudos or reputation of your supplier but on the importance of the supplied product to the quality of your own products. This idea is particularly important in quality/safety-controlled industries such as the motor vehicles industry where, for example, a quality standard such as ISOTS16949 (developed from the motor industry's QS9000 standard and BS5750) may be required of you by your customers and by you of your suppliers. The idea behind this recognised standard is to ensure specified minimum levels of quality are met. The accounting manager can work with the quality manager in ascribing a grade (from 1 = most important to 5 = least important) to each supplier on its master record, thereby helping to ensure it is given appropriate attention in accordance with its grading. Stock-outs of key stock components can then be avoided through simple actions such as ensuring that all 'priority' accounts are paid on time. Additionally, more internal attention and control procedures, such as random quality checks, can be applied to the higher-grade suppliers.

Just-in-time (JIT)

This approach to stock control is often used due to the highly competitive cost-orientated environment in which businesses now operate. It requires dialogue and appreciation of the timeliness of deliveries on the part of both supplier and recipient. The main principle of JIT is the reduction in required stock-holding levels due to the guaranteed delivery of stock at the time it is needed for production. Although JIT can be applied to most repetitive production processes, it is most suitable for those businesses with high predictability of demand which use predetermined supply-chain scheduling.

The process can be applied externally in defining the supplier–customer delivery mechanism or internally by considering each subdivision within a production process as an 'internal supplier/internal customer unit' within the same organisation. The goal of JIT is the delivery of the exact amount required, on time, to specification and within cost. Such is the power of control available with this system that customers may require more than one delivery in a day.

It is the supplier's responsibility to ensure that the appropriate product is available to the customer exactly when required. The supplier may also use a JIT system in its own supply chain, thereby reducing its stock-holding costs, freeing up of space for alternative use and reducing insurance premiums due to lower stock levels. The principle of JIT, although now widely adopted in industry, has been used on individual projects as long ago as the construction of the Empire State Building, New York, in 1930. Due to the limited storage space on the building site, the 60,000 tons of steel girders had to be delivered in small batches when they were needed by the construction workers. It would have been impossible to store them all without demolishing several adjacent buildings! In this sense, JIT can be seen as part of a project management procurement approach.

The JIT principle uses a stock reorder system known as the 'Kanban' or two-bin system. Two 'bins' (any device for storing a small amount of stock) are used, both full at the start of the production activity. The contents of bin 'A' are reordered immediately it becomes empty, for delivery just before bin 'B' becomes empty. This is a simple but effective method of stock control as the empty bin itself acts as the trigger for stock replenishment. JIT applications range from ones as simple as this to highly sophisticated electronic versions controlled by spreadsheets or bespoke software which take account of minimum stock levels, anticipated lead times and appropriate reorder levels.

Consider the scenario of a fish and chip shop; the opening of its last drum of frying oil can be used as a trigger to place an order for another drum to avoid running out of stock. However, the chip shop would probably require a higher level of 'buffer' stock so as not to run out completely if it experienced an unexpected increase in sales. It may prefer to have a stock of two drums of oil rather than one; this would be a three-bin system with the third oil drum being the 'buffer stock' bin.

Buffer stock and consignment stock

When buffer stock is held internally, the holder incurs the cost of ownership. Alternatively, your suppliers may be persuaded to hold a comfortable level of 'reserve' stock to assist you in calling off purchase requirements quickly, so avoiding costly delays arising from stock-outs and delivery lead times. The benefit to the purchaser is that less working capital is tied up in stock and the benefit to the supplier is a guaranteed sale immediately the stock is required. In this situation, a supplier may be able to minimise its risk by retaining stocks in a semi-finished state from which it could effect last-minute finishing operations to convert them to the required specification. At the same time, this approach will minimise its own stock-holding costs.

The term *buffer stock* is not to be confused with *consignment stock* (also known as *factored goods*) which refers to stock held at your premises that does not belong to you. An example of this is 'sale-or-return' goods which allow you to sell on the stock to a third party as 'agent' for the supplier. Alternatively, the consignment stock may be on your premises to enable you to work on the goods before they are returned to the supplier. In these circumstances, the stock remains the property of the supplier and is not part of your working capital. Of course, practicalities such as insurance and duty-of-care requirements have to be considered, but working capital is not directly affected as no cash resources are tied up in stock. It is effectively stock that may be returned, with or without further processing, if unsold by the purchaser.

Computers and stock control

Computers can be a great help in controlling stock; the greater the number of stock items, the greater the potential benefits. Supermarkets typically carry more than 50,000 different stock items and would find it almost impossible to control their stock without the help of sophisticated information systems. When customers pay for their purchases at the checkout, the details of every item they buy are used to update the theoretical quantities remaining in stock. This is done by the electronic point of sale system (EPOS), an integrated information system with many different functions. When the stock level reaches the preset reorder level, a 'reorder' instruction is generated automatically; some systems also automatically send an order to the supplier for replacement goods. Provided that reorder levels are reviewed from time to time in the light of historical purchasing data, such systems are very effective in the retail environment. A periodic physical stock check will also be necessary to adjust the computer stock to that physically present as 'shrinkage' may occur, e.g. through theft.

Computers can also be very useful to manufacturers. The information system called *material requirements planning* creates a list of all the components needed to meet a given production schedule and this is used to ensure adequate stocks are available when needed. This system is particularly useful where the product is complex, such as vehicles or jet engines. There are also many other less sophisticated systems, within a wide price range, that help to control stock. Businesses should be careful to choose one with an appropriate capability, at a reasonable price. Sometimes, for small businesses, a chalk mark on a wall in the stores can be more effective than a computerised stock control system.

Physical stock counts

Although physically checking the amount of stock held is a very basic procedure, businesses avoid this aspect of stock control at their peril. It is essential that stock is counted (and examined) on a regular basis. This should be at least once a year but, preferably, more frequently. For example, all important, high-value items (category A items) could be counted every month and other items only counted every three months on a rotational basis. The reason that stock counts are so important is that the condition and existence of the stock directly affect its value and its value affects profits on a pound-for-pound basis. Stock is subject to damage, deterioration, theft and obsolescence. As it is often a significant item on the balance sheet, an incorrect stock value may give a misleading impression of the business's performance. Physically counting the stock is an important and necessary reality-check for any business.

Advantages and disadvantages of holding stock

The arguments in favour of holding and not holding stock are considered below but, ultimately, management must decide what level of stock-holding best suits its production processes and market conditions.

The advantages are:

- minimised risk of stock-outs and consequential lost sales due to inability to supply demand;
- reduced order costs as able to purchase less often;
- ability to benefit from quantity discounts for buying in bulk;
- reduced set-up costs as a result of ability to perform longer production runs;
- potential 'investment' value, in cases of likelihood of the purchase price increasing in the near future;
- ability to maintain the continuity of supply to own customers.

The disadvantages are:

- higher demands on physical space requirements;
- increased costs of insurance and other storage costs;
- greater risk of damage, deterioration, theft and obsolescence;
- missing out on possible future price reductions;
- internal 'systems' costs such as recording and maintaining stock records;
- tying up money in working capital!

As can be seen, there is no quick solution that will suit every business and consideration of the above factors will have to be given before a decision is made. With regard to the type of stock (see 'customer-critical stock' above) the optimal level held is likely to vary depending on the nature of the stock items and their importance to the business. Stock represents money which cannot be used elsewhere in the business; it is important that no more than is necessary is tied up in this way.

Debtors

Debtors result from selling goods or services on credit. They are often called 'trade debtors' but this narrow definition would not include debts arising as a result of, for example, the sale of fixed assets, investments or even a whole business. Trade debt is likely to be more liquid than non-trade debt as it is usually dealt with according to widely accepted, standardised terms of trading as opposed to being tightly defined in specific, legal transactions of which payment may form only one of many conditions to be met. There is also the benefit of being able to put pressure on trade debtors to pay by temporarily withholding supplies (known as putting them 'on stop') – an option clearly not available in the case of a one-off sale of a fixed asset.

Standard credit control

Debtors are created by a business granting credit to its customers; so the activity of collecting debts is known as 'credit control'. Most businesses operate a standard credit control system similar to the one shown in Figure 4.7.

The quality of the debts receivable should be regularly reviewed, at least every time a set of accounts is prepared and preferably on a monthly basis. The usual way of doing this is by analysing them according to their age. Figure 4.8 shows a simplified example of

Step	Action
1	Grant credit status on the basis of bank and trade references, published accounts, visits to customer's premises or by using a professional credit-rating agency
2	Determine an appropriate credit period – this is usually in accordance with the company's standard terms of trading, say 30 days
3	Send a monthly statement to customers reminding them how much they owe and when it is due
4	If money not received by due date, send a first 'reminder' letter
5	If money still not received after another week, phone debtor asking for payment
6	If money still not received after another week, send second 'reminder' letter
7	If money still not received after another week, phone again
8	If money still not received after another week, send final letter threatening legal action
9	When debt is two months overdue, put it in the hands of a solicitor or professional collection agency

Figure 4.7 **An example of a standard credit control process**

a typical age analysis. Hanwing Co. appears to be a good customer although it disputes the £500 which is several months old. Pitson Ltd seems to be a reasonable customer although it is a slow payer which exceeds its 30-day credit limit. Jewse Ltd presents a real danger as it has exceeded its credit period by one month and two months and has not taken delivery of any items in the most recent month. Is it still trading? Priority should be given to recovering these debts as soon as possible. The oldest part of £14,500 should be put into the solicitor's hands if this has not already been done. Although its debt is not as old, Contro Inc. is overdue for the large amount of £54,500 and should also be chased as a priority. This should be put into the solicitor's hands without hesitation at the appropriate time. Quinit Ltd appears to have ceased trading with the business and is in dispute over an old debt of £125; this may have to be written off as solicitors' fees to collect it would probably exceed this amount. The £30,000 owed by Wim & Co. should already be with the solicitors for legal action. It is a large amount and is over three months old.

Collecting debts is a time-consuming activity so it is worthwhile thinking about ways of encouraging prompt payment. One well-known method is to offer a discount for

Customer	Total Debt	1–30 days	31–60 days	61–90 days	More than 90 days
	£	£	£	£	£
Hanwing Co.	80,500	80,000			500
Pitson Ltd	145,000	95,000	50,000		
Jewse Ltd	31,000		16,500	14,500	
Contro Inc.	54,500		54,500		
Quinit Ltd	125				125
Wim & Co.	30,000				30,000
Totals	341,125	175,000	121,000	14,500	30,625

Figure 4.8 **A debtors age analysis**

early settlement. For example, a discount of 5% could be offered to customers who pay on receipt of goods or services. An invoice of £1,000 could be cleared by a cheque for £950 sent to the supplier on the same day as the goods were received. The supplier may be very happy to suffer the £50 discount in order to improve the cash flow of the business. The theoretical cost of this can be calculated. If the supplier is operating on an overdraft bearing 12% a year interest, the early receipt of the £950 will save it £9.50 (£950 × 12% × 1/12). But the cost of this saving is £50 so the transaction seems very bad from the company's point of view, resulting in a deficit of £40.50 (50.00 − 9.50).

However, this theoretical comparison does not tell the whole story. Whilst debts exist, there is always a chance that they will go bad and not be collectable; money in the bank has a definite advantage over the promise of money in the future. More importantly, if the business is desperate for cash to ensure its survival (a situation not as unusual as you might think) the £40.50 may be worth every penny.

Factoring and invoice discounting

Normally, businesses perform their own credit control, from invoicing to collection of cash. However, there are alternatives and these may suit certain businesses which can more profitably invest their time and resources elsewhere. For example, a company may decide to outsource its invoicing in circumstances where the large volume of transactions makes it profitable to do so. This can be done as a single service, or it can also involve the sale of the debts arising from the invoices; this is known as *factoring*. The originating company would receive an immediate cash injection equal to the value of the debt sold less the fee charged by the factoring company. The arrangement may be *factoring with recourse*, where the purchaser of the debt has the right to resell it back to the originating company if the debt cannot be recovered within a certain predetermined time period. Alternatively, it may be *factoring without recourse*, where the purchaser of the debt has no come-back on the seller and so must pursue the debtor until ultimately the debt is paid or written off. The second of these two options is likely to be more expensive to the original vendor of debt as the risk is higher to the purchaser. Both methods offer an immediate injection of cash into the originator's working capital thereby allowing the earlier reinvestment of resources into the business. However, it will be fairly obvious to the debtor that it now owes money to a third party and not the original supplier of the goods.

Another option is for a company to sell its debts receivable but continue to collect the debts itself. This is known as *invoice discounting* and also provides the company with the benefit of an immediate cash injection, typically set at 75% of the total invoiced value. It also eventually receives the 'balance' of 25% less the deduction of an operational percentage and other small charges levied by the finance company. In this case, the discounting provider would typically protect itself from bad debt in two ways: first, by applying individual 'capping limits' to the credit covered on more risky debtors; and second, by operating an overall 'retention' comprised of not only the 25% not yet paid, but also a percentage of the overall book debt calculated with respect to its ageing.

Invoice discounting is done on a 'confidential' basis leaving the purchaser totally unaware of the fact that the seller has raised cash through the sale of its debts to a third party. In practice, the only clue is that a new bank account will suddenly appear as the one into which payments have to be made; this is often explained as necessary for 'administrative purposes'. The perceived benefit to the selling company of the 'confidential' route is that its customers know of no change of ownership of the debt and, correspondingly, of no external debt financing, which could be perceived as a weakening in the position of a company's finance structure.

In addition, where the primary seller–buyer relationship is split via the use of a separate third party, the purchaser's loyalty and goodwill towards its supplier can easily be reduced. For example, when dealing with a separate body in terms of payment, it becomes easier to distance the accounts payable function from the purchasing department in order to 'stretch' an otherwise tightly controlled relationship, as the vendor has no immediate incentive to chase in the debt. Consequently, although likely to be slightly more expensive, it may be preferable to choose the 'confidential invoice discounting' route as opposed to an otherwise transparent sale of debt route such as factoring.

Debt insurance

Sometimes, to safeguard its asset, a company will choose to insure some or all of the amounts owing by its trade debtors. This may arise where security is required for a bank loan giving the bank 'first charge' on its current assets. To cover itself as much as possible, the bank may insist that the company insures its debts receivable. Even without this external influence, a manager may decide that to insure the company's trade debt is a wise decision. Of course, in practice this would depend upon the perceived risk of non-payment; a company with a 'blue-chip' customer base may perceive the risk to be so low as not to merit any such form of insurance. This situation would effectively leave the seller in a position of managing the risk internally or 'self-insuring' its debt. This option is often adopted by large suppliers with good credit control systems and a wide statistical spread of customer debt.

As with all control systems, management should periodically review the policy in use, its appropriateness and its effectiveness, as circumstances can quickly change in the business environment. A mixed policy may also be appropriate, such as deciding to insure only the overseas debt when considering the associated costs and benefits. It is usually far easier and cheaper to recover debts from businesses based in the same country as the seller, either directly or through solicitors, than it would be for a foreign-based debt. The decision to insure the debts receivable should be taken in the light of the costs of doing so.

Multi-currency debts

In the worldwide marketplace of today, it is not unusual for a company to have some of its debts in a foreign currency. One policy for dealing with these is for it to invoice everything in its own currency, thereby eliminating all exchange risk. The reduction of exchange risk resulting from this inflexible policy must be compared to the reduction in potential trading opportunities where customers are not prepared to be invoiced in this currency. Less extreme policies must address whether the company is going to collect the debt itself or use overseas agents. It may choose to have multi-currency bank accounts or simply have the debt payments converted into its home currency; it must decide how to manage its cash balances through multi-currency treasury management.

Of course, a potential benefit of invoicing in a foreign currency, especially a common one such as the euro or US dollar, is that the paid debt provides a readily available pool of funds (free of conversion costs) from which to pay your own foreign currency creditors. This makes the whole process simple and quick and is especially beneficial for the smaller organisation which does not have its own dedicated treasury department. The 'opportunistic' value of holding cash can be vital; it may be that a business deal can be clinched simply by having the funds readily available in the right currency at the right time.

Self-billing invoices

In some circumstances a business may encounter a situation where its customers raise their **own** form of invoice for goods supplied to them. To do this, the customer has to be in a very strong bargaining position as the vendor usually has to spend more than the usual amount of time reconciling the account on a regular basis. The name given to these customer-created documents varies, with some customers raising 'self-billing invoices' and others raising 'credit notes'.

The process involves the customer receiving goods from the supplier and then raising its own (self-billed) invoice as recognition of the debt in respect of the goods/service supplied. By doing this, the customer controls the invoicing process from start to finish and avoids any discrepancies between goods received and goods invoiced **as recorded in their books of account**. When the supplier's invoices are received, they are usually filed for reference if needed but not used to generate entries on the seller's account.

With regard to 'invoice discounting' and 'debt factoring' activities mentioned earlier, for the sake of simplicity, the banks will often agree to recognise a vendor's own invoices rather than the customer's self-billed invoices. The larger the customer and more stable the trading relationship, the more likely the bank is to accept these customers on the same terms as 'normal' ones. However, this gesture of 'goodwill' from the banks is often accompanied by a small reduction in the amount of the cash advance they offer on the debt.

Cash

'Cash' usually means the combination of 'cash-in-hand' and 'cash-at-bank'. Cash in the form of notes and coins can be thought of as being 100.0% liquid and bank current accounts as 99.9% liquid; in practical terms, they are both as easily convertible as each other. (There are also numerous types of investment or deposit accounts whose liquidity is inversely proportional to their notice periods. Any notice period of more than a week or so would indicate that the asset should be listed as a short-term investment rather than cash.) Cash is the most liquid of funds due to its inherent portable nature: it can usually be used to secure purchases of all types. It is so readily acceptable because it can be reused by the recipient without any difficulty.

However, there are exceptions to the universal acceptability of cash: for example, where the physical volume of notes and coins would be large enough to cause concern to the recipient over its security. Imagine paying for a new car in this way! This would be an obvious opportunity to make use of the bank account and pay by cheque. More importantly, in a period of unstable inflation where the value of money itself was rapidly falling, it would be preferable to be paid in a more stable medium such as gold. Foreign currency deposits are relatively common in today's global business environment. With the growth of desktop computer banking, these are becoming more common and are almost as easy to use as the 'home' currency.

As stated in the introduction to this chapter, businesses need cash to survive; if they cannot pay their creditors on time they are not going to receive any further supplies on credit. If they cannot get their supplies, they cannot produce their goods and services; if they cannot do this, they have nothing to sell! If they have nothing to sell, their cash position will deteriorate rapidly and everything will soon grind to a halt.

Cash budgets

Using cash budgets to manage cash actively is one of the most important tasks performed by finance managers. It is especially important for start-up businesses and those that find themselves struggling to build up or maintain working capital in a difficult competitive marketplace. Of course, there are longer-term matters that are of equal significance in the battle to survive and grow, such as ensuring costs are driven down and sales levels achieved, but none is as time critical to a business's survival as the effective short-term management of cash. Businesses do not suddenly go under as a result of poor profit margins; they cease trading due to a lack of cash and the resulting inability to pay their debts.

No cash means no more credit from suppliers and no access to goods/services needed for the production process. A creditor is not usually interested in its customers' profit margins but it is very interested in their ability to pay their debts. However, in the case of an unpaid debt of sufficient minimum value, it can go to the extreme of petitioning the courts for a winding-up order in the event of continued non-payment.

Cash budgets are used to monitor cash flow on a regular basis, usually monthly, weekly or daily. However, in the event of a cash crisis, the monitoring can be done on an hourly basis to deal with events and changes occurring throughout the day (see 'Dynamic cash flow' below). An important point to realise is that, whereas budgets for revenue, expenses and profits are usually subject to variance analysis (see Chapter 15) on a monthly, historical basis, the cash budget will normally be used much more frequently on a pro-active, 'real-time' basis. Although time consuming, this task may be partly devolved to junior staff by giving them control over expenditure within reasonable preset limits and tasking them to produce regular summaries for senior management. (The creation and use of cash budgets is also covered in Chapter 14.)

Dynamic cash flow

Sometimes, if credit is not available, it may be necessary to spend more cash than planned in order to generate extra sales which, in turn, generate extra cash. This extra cash generated may be essential to the company's survival. For example, it may be that unless a business fulfils its predetermined sales obligations to another business it will lose a vital long-term contract. The only way to ensure the contracted sales are completed in time may be to find cash urgently to source a component critical to the completion of the output. This may sound extreme but, in practice, it can come this 'close to the wire'. (The concept is embodied in the saying, 'You have to speculate to accumulate'.)

One real-life scenario of key cash management which illustrates the critical nature of the timing of cash flows is not knowing until the very morning of pay day whether sufficient funds will be in the company's bank account to meet the payroll bill. Another example is having an aircraft full of passengers sat on the runway, with its passengers blissfully unaware that the holiday company is frantically sourcing cash to pay for the fuel in advance of the aircraft taking off.

Usually, the only people aware of the critical nature of the cash and working capital position are those on the inside of the business. Obviously, whilst not wishing to lie overtly about its cash position, it would be counter-productive for a business voluntarily to alert external creditors to its short-term cash crisis. The impression given should be analogous to that of the proverbial swan gliding smoothly over the water whilst, under the surface and unseen, its legs are paddling like mad.

On a 'real-time' basis, cash management is necessary to cope with the constantly changing business environment – 'do we pay company A and produce product X or shall we pay companies B and C in order to source the product needed to keep customer Z supplied?' Cash controllers must be willing to adapt their thinking continually as these decisions directly affect the performance of the business. In today's competitive world, managers should **expect** to have to alter their cash flow plans. The ever-shortening time frame for budget planning is leading to a JIT approach to management decision making.

Another key element in the effective management of cash and working capital is that of communication between managers. For example, a seemingly minor action such as paying a supplier of machine parts on time may avoid a production line stoppage. Not only do unexpected events, such as the appearance of a new niche market, present opportunities to generate extra cash, but they can also have a 'multiplier' effect by the immediate reinvestment of that cash in subsequent cash-generating projects.

It is useful to think of cash as the lubrication of the machinery of business itself; the machinery needs constant maintenance and must not be allowed to stop!

Purchase of fixed assets: lease or buy?

From time to time, businesses need to purchase fixed assets such as buildings, vehicles and computer systems. This raises the question of how they will pay for them. If they are 'cash rich', they can pay with cash; alternatively, they may decide to pay by raising a loan from their bank or even to issue some new shares if the asset is very expensive. But if the business is short of cash it may make more sense to *hire* the asset and pay a monthly rent rather than buy it outright for the full purchase price. This type of arrangement is usually done through a 'lease'; the *owner* of the asset is called the 'lessor' and the *user* is called the 'lessee'. A lease is a legal contract by which the lessor retains ownership but allows the lessee to use the asset for a specified period of time in return for a series of rental payments on specific dates.

There are two common types of lease, an *operating* lease and a *finance* (or *capital*) lease. *Operating leases* are where the user hires the asset for a given purpose and returns it when that purpose has been fulfilled. This is the same idea as people hiring tools, such as concrete mixers, from a plant hire company for a specific job and returning them when it is finished. The lessor bears the maintenance costs of the asset. Alternatively, a *finance lease* is where the user acts as though it also owns the asset; the hire period is usually equivalent to its economic lifetime and the user may bear the maintenance costs. With a finance lease, the lessee pays for the asset by instalments over its lifetime, which is better for the company's cash flow than paying its total cost at the date of acquisition.

Leasing is very useful to businesses which have liquidity problems or find it difficult to raise loans; they are also flexible with mid-term cancellation options. Operating leases also have the advantages of minimising asset obsolescence and avoiding maintenance costs. They also create 'off-balance-sheet' finance (see below) but finance leases do not.

If a company buys its fixed assets, they appear on the balance sheet under that heading. On the other hand, if it hires its fixed assets on operating leases, they do not appear on the balance sheet. The leasing costs are shown as overheads on the profit and loss account but no entry is made on the balance sheet as the assets are not owned by the business. One of the advantages of this off-balance-sheet finance is that it makes the company's financial performance look better; the return on capital employed (ROCE) ratio will increase as the asset base will be smaller. Also, by not borrowing large sums to purchase fixed assets, the business avoids increasing its gearing ratio.

However, where the hire contract is judged to be a finance lease, International Accounting Standard 17 (IAS 17) requires that the assets and their related finance are shown on the balance sheet (as fixed assets and long-term liabilities) as though they were owned by the business. The aim is to prevent showing a distorted picture to the users of published accounts due to the inclusion of misleading information.

Figure 4.9 shows the effect on its ROCE of a company using an operating lease instead of a cash purchase for 25% of its fixed assets. Note that leasing £20 million of fixed assets means that the cash balance is £20 million higher than it would otherwise have been. The only difference between the two scenarios is the lease/purchase decision; in all other respects, trading is identical but ROCE has increased by nearly one-third from 11.1% to 14.4%!

	Cash Purchase		Operating Lease	
	£m	£m	£m	£m
BALANCE SHEET				
Fixed assets	80		60	
Net current assets	30		50	
Total capital employed		110		110
Less: long-term loans		20		20
		90		**90**
Share capital and reserves		**90**		**90**
PROFIT and LOSS				
Gross profit		60		60
Depreciation	20		15	
Lease payments	–		2	
Other overheads	30		30	
		50		47
Operating profit		**10**		**13**
ROCE		**9.1%**		**11.8%**

Figure 4.9 **The effect of an operating lease on ROCE**

Try the following question for yourself (answer at the end of the chapter).

The extract below from the accounts for Akro's first year of trading shows that the business owns £300 million of fixed assets. If Akro had hired one-third of these on operating leases instead of purchasing them, how would this affect its ROCE? Assume that the depreciation charge would reduce by one-third and that the annual leasing costs would be £10 million.

Akro Ltd

	Cash £m	Purchase £m
BALANCE SHEET		
Fixed assets	300	
Net current assets	70	
		370
Less: Long-term loans	50	
		320
Share capital and reserves		**320**
PROFIT and LOSS		
Gross profit		
Depreciation	45	
Lease payments	–	
Other overheads	235	
		280
Operating profit		**40**
ROCE		**12.5%**

Surplus cash and overnight deposits

An organisation may find itself in a situation where it regularly has large cash funds available surplus to its immediate requirements, on either a long- or short-term basis. In such circumstances, it may be possible to gain access to higher than normal rates of interest by investing these funds in the 'overnight money markets'. The idea is that by pooling together, many individual organisations can lend/invest very large sums of money on the money markets, thereby gaining access to higher than normal rates of return. This can be done for periods as short as one day or even less! It would be done through an intermediary, such as a bank, which would charge a commission or fee for its brokering role.

The funds required are usually large amounts; typically, a minimum balance of £100,000 may be required to gain entry-level rates, with stepped rate increases available for sums above £500,000. The likely participants are large corporations with access to abnormally large, if constantly turning over, sources of cash, such as supermarkets. However, large charities or other project-based organisations with access to project management funding can also benefit from such opportunities. It is the duty of the financial manager to investigate the possibility of benefiting from higher interest rates in such circumstances.

Small-Firms Loan Guarantee (SFLG)

Small firms may be able to raise cash by getting the UK government to guarantee the greater part of a bank loan otherwise not available. The access to 'normal' loans may not be as great for smaller companies as for larger ones because they have a relatively small asset base to offer as security to the lender. The SFLG scheme enables commercial lenders to make loans that, using their standard risk assessment methods, they would not normally make.

The government recognises that smaller businesses may never reach their full potential if not given some form of assistance in their early growth stage. This assistance aims to promote the spirit of entrepreneurship and lead to potential increased employment and further spending in the community once successful growth has occurred.

Of course, not all loans will be paid back due to business failure. However, a business must provide a rigorous business plan and financial forecasts in the normal manner in order for it to recommended by its bank to the Department for Trade and Industry (DTI) for an SFLG loan. This will eliminate those ventures thought to be too risky or ill-thought-out and leave a pool of projects which will have a statistical mix of 'stars' and 'wipe-outs' in terms of their future success.

Typically, the government will support 80% of the loan by underwriting it; the bank will provide 100% of the loan but only be exposed to a 20% risk. Hence the borrower is happy that it has gained access to a source of funds potentially not otherwise available and the lender is a lot more comfortable as the risk is reduced to losing only 20% of the total amount. The downside to the borrower is the initial barrage of 'red-tape' at the application stage and the continuing extra administration due to additional reporting requirements. Also, additional covenants, such as increases in the current asset ratios and the maintaining of minimum levels of funding from shareholders, may be introduced.

Businesses ignore the fundamentally important task of cash control at their peril. At best, they may be unable to take advantage of unexpected opportunities due to lack of available cash and, at worst, they could go out of business.

Creditors

Credit and the supplier relationship

When businesses first start to trade, they are very unlikely to be offered credit by their suppliers. Before this happens, they have to establish a 'track record' of cash on delivery in order to convince suppliers, and their credit insurers, of their reliability and trustworthiness. Trading on credit terms is not an automatic right; it must be earned. And once it has been earned, it must be maintained.

The establishment of good supplier relationships is an important part of an effective supply chain. This involves 'give-and-take' when things do not go exactly to plan; tolerance and a constructive approach to putting things right build the relationship over time.

Accepting a delivery schedule change, proposed at short notice by a supplier, may help when you ask the supplier, at a future date, to allow you an extra month's credit for a particular payment.

This example illustrates how creditors can be used to manage working capital. Taking longer to pay creditors increases the amount of cash available. However, the relationship should not be put under too much strain or it may break down altogether.

Great care must be taken to avoid suppliers putting a 'stop' on deliveries as the consequences of a stock-out can be extremely serious. For example, the non-payment of a supplier's invoice for £8,000 could result in the non-delivery of a vital stock item. This, in turn, could cause a production line stoppage costing the manufacturer £60,000 a day!

Communication is fundamentally important in avoiding such a breakdown. The supplier may refuse your request for an extra month's credit but may suggest weekly stage payments instead. This kind of compromise is common in day-to-day dealings between businesses. Ideally, the purchaser–supplier relationship should be viewed as a partnership by both sides; after all, they both stand to gain from it.

Alternative suppliers

One strategy for managing a continuous flow of materials is for a business to source stock items from at least two different suppliers. If, for any reason, one of the suppliers cannot deliver as planned, the other supplier(s) can be asked to increase its delivery quantities to meet the shortfall. By buying identical goods from multiple sources, the purchaser is able to manage the risk of stock-outs. This approach is particularly useful to businesses which use JIT stock control or something close to it.

Self-billing

If, as a purchaser, you consider that the invoices received from your supplier contain too many errors, you may decide to 'self-bill' this creditor (self-billing is discussed above, under 'Debtors'). This consists of raising your own 'invoices' for goods received and using them to dictate your payment schedule to this particular supplier. For this to be successful, you need to be the 'senior' partner in the relationship, otherwise you may find yourself having to find an alternative supplier.

Early-settlement discounts

If a business is in the happy position of having more than an adequate amount of cash available, it could choose to take advantage of any early-settlement discounts offered by suppliers. Of course, it should first calculate whether it is worthwhile to do so. Suppose a supplier is offering a 2.5% discount for payment on or before delivery as an alternative to the normal credit period of one month. The discount on goods invoiced at £1,000 is £25 (£1,000 × 2.5%). If the buyer is operating on an overdraft bearing interest at 12% a year, the early payment will cost it £10 (£1,000 × 12% × 1/12). So, in this case, the discount should be taken as it will save the buyer £15. Of course, it will also cost the supplier £15 (assuming it also operated on an overdraft at 12% a year). As discussed above under 'Debtors', the reason a supplier is willing to suffer this cost is to ensure an adequate supply of cash flows into its business.

Self-assessment question S4.3

Try the following question for yourself (answer at the end of the chapter).

A business, which operates an overdraft at 15% a year, is about to receive goods costing £18,000 from one of its regular suppliers. Is it worth taking advantage of a 2.5% cash discount offered for cash on delivery if the supplier's normal trading terms are 'payment two months after delivery'?

Cycles and ratios

The 'operating cycle' is the average time (usually measured in days) for raw materials and/or products for resale to be received into stock, converted into output, the output sold and the money received. The period from receiving stock to that stock being sold, possibly in a converted form, is known as the 'stock-holding' or 'stock turnover' period.

The 'cash cycle' is the average number of days between the time the purchased stocks are paid for and the time the sales revenue is received. The cash cycle may be reduced by maximising the time taken to pay creditors (creditor days); the operating cycle can be reduced by minimising the stock-holding and production times and minimising the debt collection period. These cycles are illustrated in Figure 4.10 and the methods for calculating the periods involved are given in the chapter on financial statement analysis.

In today's competitive world, reducing the average time for which cash is tied up, i.e. the cash cycle, is a key management task. Usually, the first step in achieving this is to extend the creditors payment period as this is the easiest to achieve. However, when doing this, due consideration must be given to the supplier–customer relationship (as well as government and business regulations concerning interest charges and creditor protection). If the supplier feels it is being unduly taken advantage of, it may refuse to supply further goods until overdue payments have been made. Even worse, if the creditor thinks that the extended non-payment is a sign of deteriorating liquidity, it may impose more stringent terms of trading; for example, it could insist on being paid in advance for future supplies.

The other side of the same coin is to tighten up on credit control to reduce the debtors collection period. Giving debtors more frequent reminders may do the trick, at least with some of them. But the manager's opposite number in the customer's business probably knows the game just as well because they both play the same game. This highlights the 'two-faced' nature of working capital management, chasing debtors for earlier payment whilst taking longer to pay creditors. It is not unknown for managers to have two lists, one giving excuses for late payment to creditors and the other listing the counter-arguments to the same points! For example, the creditor payment list may include 'the cheque signatory is ill and absent from work at the moment' and the credit control list may state 'all businesses should anticipate this occurrence and have deputy signatories'.

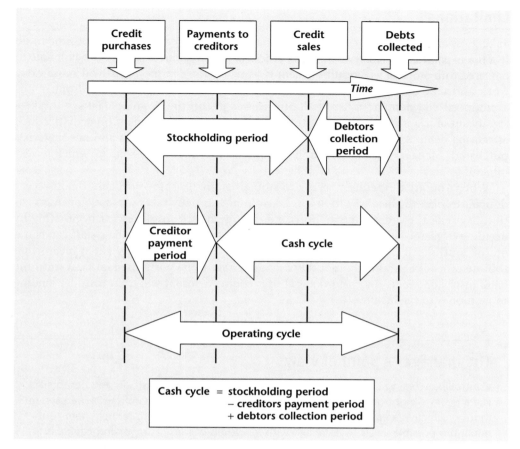

Figure 4.10 **The operating and cash cycles**

Overtrading and overcapitalisation

Overtrading occurs when a business has insufficient working capital to support its trading activities. This is often associated with rapid expansion of trading such as when the economy is recovering from a recession. More sales means more money tied up in stock and production, more debtors and more overheads. Increased trading activity requires increased working capital. Unfortunately, ignorance of this can, and does, lead to businesses being wound up even though they are making profits. This can be seen as 'a problem of success' but it is crucial that working capital is expanded at the same time as sales: **the bigger the engine, the more lubrication it requires!**

At the other end of the scale, a business may have too much working capital. Whilst not as serious as overtrading, this *overcapitalisation* means that the business is not making the best use of its money. Too much stock, debtors and cash mean that excessive funds are tied up in short-term assets when they could be used to finance long-term projects such as opening another branch of the business or developing a new version of an existing project. Overcapitalisation is evidenced by excessive liquidity ratios and stock-holding periods.

Limitations

Taking capital management as a whole, a major limitation can be the lack of time to do it. This is particularly true when the business is having a cash crisis. Not being able to pay creditors on time will result in them chasing up their money. This will cause extra work and take up extra time. For example, an officer of the court may appear unannounced and demand a list of all business assets on the premises. This will take a significant amount of management time which would be better spent on activities such as chasing debtors to improve cash flow so that creditors can be paid and raw materials purchased. Managers in this situation find themselves in a 'vicious circle' which is very difficult to break.

'When you are desperately trying to stop alligators biting your backside, it is very difficult to plan the best way to drain the swamp.' It usually takes some major intervention to break these destructive loops, e.g. a large injection of new cash, possibly by deciding to factor your debtors. The workload on accountants and their staff can spiral out of control. All the unscheduled work done to keep the company afloat means that routine tasks like producing monthly accounts have to be postponed, at least until the bank insists on seeing an up-to-date set of accounts before it will even consider lending more money to the business!

The manager's point of view

Controlling working capital is a bit like going to the gym. Excess stocks and debtors act like a heavy weight on a company, locking up cash which might otherwise be used in more productive areas. Stocks and debtors need constant work to reduce them to the minimum possible levels. A company with low levels of non-cash working capital is fit, lean and healthy, with cash in the bank providing flexibility and opportunity. It is probably true to say that, in most companies, working capital does not receive the attention it deserves, as management prefer to focus on profit generation. Yet this is an area which can cripple a business perhaps more quickly than any other.

Firstly, let us consider stocks. The difficulty here is that nearly everyone in the company wants a high level of stock-on-hand. Sales people want product available to sell off the shelf, as quick delivery times will give them an edge over the competition. Production staff like high levels of both raw materials and finished goods, so that they can plan their production schedules with the greatest efficiency. The purchasing department, too, like the keener prices that bulk-buying offers, together with the reduced risk of panic buying to avoid stock-outs. On the other side of the scales sit the accountants, whose interests are in keeping to a minimum the amount of cash locked up in stock. I once asked a salesman to specify the sales department's optimum stock levels for finished products; he produced a requirement which was four times the existing level, a financial impossibility for the company. These conflicting positions can lead to some interesting discussions. Management must put all the variables into a pot, and come up with a stock-holding policy which strikes an acceptable mean between the various demands. Then the position needs to be watched on a continuous basis, as each element is constantly variable, and the policy can swiftly become out-of-date.

I advocate a strict write-off policy for ageing stock. My company's products generally had a long shelf life, and could have remained in a saleable state in our warehouse for years. However, in order to ensure that our book stocks did not become over-burdened with slow- or non-moving items, we made a provision against anything which had not moved for a year. This length of time will of course vary considerably from company to company, depending on its type of product, but the important thing is to place a time limit so that all old stock is ultimately dealt with. Then there is the question of physically disposing of the stock. It may seem extravagant to dispose of perfectly good saleable stock when a customer for it may appear at any time. As a chemical company, disposal of the stock was also an expensive operation. But the danger is that the warehouse will become clogged with obsolete material, increasing stock-holding costs, and reducing efficiency. The long-awaited customer may never appear. Better, in my view, to take the hit for producing unwanted stock, and keep the company lean.

Debtors can lead to similar problems. It is always very tempting to offer the customer extended credit terms as a final incentive. This is especially attractive to sales people, as the cost will be lost somewhere in interest charges, and therefore well outside their own area of responsibility. Once again, cash tied up for lengthy periods in debtors acts like dead weight upon the company.

Credit control is a vital function, and it always surprises me that many companies, even quite large ones, do not have a dedicated credit control function. In our company, the credit controller carried considerable power. He was required to approve all new business, and to sanction all business which exceeded existing credit limits. This naturally led to disagreements with the sales department, resolved through an appeals process, which led ultimately to the managing director's office.

Of course, his principal activity was the timely collection of debts. We did send out statements and reminder letters, but in my view, these were of limited value, as reluctant payers came to recognise the pattern, and wait until the second reminder before paying up. We also avoided the use of discounts for prompt payment; customers will tend to take these anyway, whether they pay on time or not, leaving you with the problem of collecting irritatingly small balances which may not be worth chasing. A far more effective approach was to build a working relationship with the customer's payables department. This frequently allowed us to expedite payments, probably at the expense of other, less rigorous, suppliers. Another productive strategy was to ensure close liaison between credit control and sales people on the status of outstanding debts, so that the appropriate pressure could be applied during sales negotiations.

The credit controller's ultimate weapon was to place a stop on all business with a customer who had overdue balances, an extremely effective method of recovering outstanding amounts. It is a fallacy to believe that strict application of credit terms will frighten customers away. Invariably the reaction of a purchaser who is prevented from placing an order is to give an earful to the accounting department for failing to pay invoices on time. I do not believe we lost a single customer as a result of our strong credit control policy.

We once took over a company which had a six-figure debt with its principal customer, representing around 18 months' trading. On investigation, we found that this customer had minimal capital employed, and no loans or overdrafts. We were financing its entire operation, on an interest-free basis. With a certain amount of encouragement and threat from us, the customer managed to bring its business on to a more conventional financial footing and paid off its outstanding debt to us over the next few months. Thereafter, we traded with the customer on a normal and completely satisfactory basis.

In some industries, and in some parts of the world, extended credit terms are simply a fact of business life. We used to trade on 180-day terms with customers in the Middle East and South America. Such lengthy credit periods are a concern, as so much time will pass before you get any inkling of any bad debt problems. You may even have made further shipments to the customer in the meantime. There are ways of laying off the risks through insurance or factoring without recourse, but these are expensive. They may, however, be essential if the debt is of critical importance to your company. Until we had established a satisfactory track record with a customer, we preferred to operate with a confirmed letter of credit, where a bank guarantees the debt on the basis of the bank's knowledge of the customer's financial soundness. Thereafter, we would operate on open account, and I'm pleased to say that our bad debt experience was negligible.

On the other side of the coin, you can always improve cash flow by delaying payments to creditors. We tried this only once, when our finance director embarked on a project to reduce the company's interest costs. Our overdraft balances certainly decreased, but the action generated a huge number of telephone calls from irate suppliers. Our purchasers found that they were on the defensive when trying to negotiate prices, and at times were unable to obtain material at all, putting production schedules at risk. Failure to pay on time damages the reputation of the company, and raises the suspicion that the company may be heading into financial difficulties. All in all, it was a disastrous experiment, and is not to be recommended.

So, even without manipulating creditors, there is plenty of mileage in the control of stocks and debtors to release valuable amounts of cash back into the business.

Summary

- Working capital consists of current assets and current liabilities.
- Working capital objectives and policies should be clear and explicit.
- Working capital policy can be conservative, matching or aggressive.
- Conservative policy is low risk; aggressive policy is high risk.
- Conservative policy reduces profit; aggressive policy increases it.
- Cash is the only 100% liquid asset.
- The most economic quantity for ordering stock can be calculated.
- Stock items can be ranked according to their monetary value and more attention can be paid to high-value stocks.
- Low-value 'customer-critical' stock items can be vital to the maintenance of good customer relations.
- Suppliers can also be ranked according to the criticality of the quality of their products to your business.
- Stock-holdings can be kept to a minimum by adopting a 'just-in-time' approach to supplies of raw material stocks.
- Persuading suppliers to hold stocks until you need them minimises your investment in stock; buffer stocks are also minimised.

- 'Consignment stock' is not owned by you although it is physically on your premises.

- Stock items can be reordered automatically by using a computerised stock control system (e.g. EPOS).

- The cost of using computerised stock control systems needs to be carefully evaluated.

- Regular physical stock counts are essential for verifying the quantity and quality of stock.

- Holding stocks has both advantages and disadvantages.

- The amount of money owed to the company by customers can be controlled by a systematic 'credit control' process.

- The total debtors figure can be analysed by customer and by age to help prioritise debts for collection.

- When companies are short of cash, they should be prepared to pay (e.g. offer cash discounts) to ensure that debts are collected promptly.

- Debts can be sold or 'factored' to another company which specialises in their collection; customers may or may not be aware of the situation.

- 'Invoice discounting' is similar but the original company continues to perform its debt collection activities on behalf of the new owners of the debt; debtors are totally unaware of the situation.

- Debts can be insured, if thought appropriate, on a piecemeal basis if required.

- Companies should have policies regarding foreign debts, e.g. the currency in which debts should be paid and the country where they should be paid.

- Very powerful customers may issue their own 'self-billing' invoices and use them in their books of account instead of the invoices issued by the selling company; you have to accept this if you want their business.

- Businesses will not survive if they do not have adequate amounts of cash, no matter how profitable they are.

- Monthly cash budgets are a good way of monitoring cash; in a crisis, they can be done weekly or daily.

- 'Dynamic cash flow' describes cash paid out in order to ensure a greater amount of cash flows in soon afterwards.

- Operating leases are where a user hires an asset for a given purpose and returns it when that purpose has been fulfilled.

- A finance lease is where a user acts as though it also owns the asset; the hire period is usually equivalent to its economic lifetime and the user may bear the maintenance costs. With a finance lease, the lessee pays for the asset by instalments over its lifetime, which is better for the company's cash flow than paying its total cost on acquisition.

- Large sums of surplus cash can be invested overnight to earn extra interest.

- The UK government's Small-Firms Loan Guarantee scheme enables commercial lenders to make loans that, using their standard risk assessment methods, they would not normally make.
- Relationships with suppliers/creditors are very important. Trading on credit terms is not an automatic right; it must be earned and maintained.
- By buying identical goods from more than one supplier, the purchaser is able to manage the risk of stock-outs.
- If you are in a very strong position as a customer, you may decide to 'self-bill' your supplier.
- If a business has an adequate amount of cash available, it could choose to take advantage of any early-settlement discounts offered by suppliers.
- The 'working capital cycle' is the average time (usually measured in days) for raw materials and/or products for resale to be received into stock, converted into output, the output sold and the money received. The working capital cycle can be reduced by minimising the stock-holding and production times and minimising the debt collection period.
- The period from receiving stock to that stock being sold, maybe in a converted form, is known as the 'stock-holding' or 'stock turnover' period.
- The 'cash cycle' is the average number of days between the time the purchased stocks/products are paid for and the time the final sales revenue is received. The cash cycle may be reduced by maximising the time taken to pay creditors (creditor days).
- Overtrading occurs when a business has insufficient working capital to support its trading activities.
- Overcapitalisation occurs when a business has too much working capital. Too much stock, debtors and cash mean that excessive funds are tied up in short-term assets when they could be used to finance long-term projects such as opening another branch of the business or developing a new version of an existing project.

Further reading

Antanies, J. (2002) 'Recognising the effects of uncertainty to achieve working capital efficiency', *Pulp & Paper*, July.

Arnold, G. (2005) *Corporate Financial Management*, 3rd edition, Financial Times/Prentice Hall, Harlow. See Chapter 13.

Atrill, P. and McLaney, E. (2004) *Management Accounting for Decision Makers*, 4th edition, Financial Times/Prentice Hall, Harlow. See Chapter 9, 'Managing working capital'.

Bridge, M. and Moss, I. (2003) 'COSO back in the limelight', *Perspectives on financial services*, April.

Committee of Sponsoring Organizations of the Treadway Commission (COSO) (1994), *Internal Control-Integrated Framework*, COSO, New York.

Cotis, L. (2004) 'Lean working capital management', *Business Credit*, January.

Deloof, M. (2003) 'Does working capital management affect profitability of Belgian firms?', *Journal of Business Finance & Accounting*, Vol. 30, Issue 3/4, April.

Hall, C. (2002) 'Total working capital management', *Treasury and Cash Management*, November/December.

Howorth, C. and Westhead, P. (2003) 'The focus of working capital management in UK small firms', *Management Accounting Research*, Vol. 14, Issue 2, June.

Pike, R. and Neale, B. (2002) *Corporate Finance and Investment*, 4th edition, Prentice Hall International, Harlow.

Samuels, J., Wilkes, F. and Brayshaw, R. (1999) *Financial Management and Decision Making*, International Business Press. See Chapter 18, 'Management of debtors and inventory'.

Stokes, J. R. (2005) 'Dynamic cash discounts when sales volume is stochastic', *Quarterly Review of Economics & Finance*, Vol. 45, Issue 1, February.

Watson, D. and Head, A. (2004) *Corporate Finance – Principles and Practice*, 3rd edition, Financial Times/Prentice Hall, Harlow.

http://www.coso.org/index.htm

http://www.planware.org/workcap.htm#1

http://www.sbap.org/resources/CashFlowManagement.pdf

http://www.treasury.govt.nz/publicsector/workingcapital/deptworkingcapital.pdf

Answers to self-assessment questions

S4.1

Here

$$h = £10$$
$$d = 45,000 \text{ units}$$
$$p = £1,000$$

so

$$
\begin{aligned}
\text{EOQ} &= \sqrt{(2 \times 1,000 \times 45,000/10)} \\
&= \sqrt{(90,000,000/10)} \\
&= \sqrt{9,000,000} \\
&= \textbf{3,000 units}
\end{aligned}
$$

So, it would be most economical if this particular stock item was ordered in quantities of 3,000.

S4.2 Akro Ltd

	Cash £m	Purchase £m	Operating £m	Lease £m
BALANCE SHEET				
Fixed assets	300		200	
Net current assets	70		170	
		370		370
Less: Long-term loans	50		50	
		320		320
Share capital and reserves		320		320
PROFIT and LOSS				
Gross profit				
Depreciation	45		30	
Lease payments	–		10	
Other overheads	235		235	
		280		275
Operating profit		40		45
ROCE		12.5%		14.1%

Note that even though none of the trading activities changed due to the lease, the ROCE has improved significantly, implying that the business is performing better. Indeed, the reduction in overhead cost shows that the business is performing better (in a financial sense) but it should not be assumed that its trading performance has improved.

S4.3

$$\text{Saving:} \quad \text{discount} = £18{,}000 \times 2.5\% = £450$$
$$\text{Cost:} \quad \text{interest} = £18{,}000 \times 15.0\% \times 2/12 = \underline{£450}$$
$$\text{Net saving} = \underline{0}$$

The cash discount offers no financial advantage.

Kindorm Limited

Kindorm Limited manufactures a variety of metal and plastic fasteners for other businesses. Its summarised accounts for 2006 are shown below. In 2007, it plans to increase its sales turnover by 20% by extending the length of time it allows its customers to pay. The average credit period will increase by 14 days. Administration and marketing costs are expected to rise by 10% but debenture interest will be unchanged at £50,000. Annual taxation will be £75,000 and dividends will total £80,000, both payable in full in 2008.

It expects the cost of goods sold and the value of year-end creditors also to increase by 20%. At the same time, it intends to improve its stock control and reduce the length of time for which stock is held. This should enable it to limit the increase in the value of stock to 10%. Any additional necessary expansion in working capital is to be provided by the overdraft. The current overdraft limit of £25,000 was only recently negotiated and the bank is unlikely to welcome any request for a further increase without the provision of additional security. However, all the available security has been set against the debenture.

All Kindorm's purchases and sales are made on credit terms. No new issue or redemption of share capital or debentures is expected in 2007. The annual accounts for 2006 are shown below.

Kindorm Limited: Balance sheet as at 31 December 2006

	£000 Cost	£000 Depn	£000 NBV
Fixed assets:			
Land and buildings	860	0	860
Equipment	540	220	320
	1,400	220	1,180
Current assets:			
Stocks	530		
Debtors	156		
Cash-at-bank	0		
		686	
Less: Current liabilities:			
Creditors	312		
Tax due	44		
Dividends due	54		
Overdraft	18		

	£000 Cost	£000 Depn	£000 NBV
Net current assets			258
Net total assets			1,438
Less debentures			500
			938
Financed by:			
Ordinary shares of £1		700	
Retained earnings		238	
			938

Kindorm Limited: Profit and loss account for y/e 31 December 2006

	£000	£000
Sales		3,646
Cost of sales		2,482
Gross profit		1,164
Admin and marketing expenses	1,002	
Debenture interest	50	
		1,052
Profit before tax		112
Taxation		44
Profit after tax		68
Dividends		54
Retained profit for the year		14

Tasks:

(You are advised to work to the nearest £000 in your calculations.)

A. Calculate the size of the resulting overdraft at the end of 2007 (assume the current ratio remains the same as it was in 2006).

(15 marks)

B. Calculate the length of the cash cycle at the end of 2007 and compare it to 2006 (assume the value of stock at the end of 2005 was £382,000).

(15 marks)

C. Calculate the operating profit and the retained profit 2007.

(15 marks)

D. Calculate the profitability ratios for 2006 and 2007.

(15 marks)

E. Evaluate Kindorm's expansion strategy and advise it regarding any actions it needs to take to ensure its success.

(40 marks)
(Total 100 marks)

Theory questions on working capital management (answers to be found in the text)

A. Stock:

1 Create a numerical example to explain how the economic order quantity for stock can be calculated.
2 Describe the 'ABC ranking system' of stock control and the concept of 'customer-critical stock'; discuss how these could conflict.
3 Explain the part played by 'kanbans' in JIT stock control systems.
4 Summarise the advantages and disadvantages of holding stock.

B. Debtors:

1 Outline the steps followed by a standard credit control process.
2 Explain what is meant by a 'debtors age analysis' and describe how it is used.
3 Explain the difference between 'factoring' and 'invoice discounting'.
4 How do 'self-billing invoices' work?

C. Cash:

1 'Cash flow is more important than profit for the survival of a business.' Explain this statement and describe how cash budgets can be used to avoid insolvency.
2 Describe the concept of 'dynamic cash flow' by giving an example.
3 Explain the difference between an 'operating lease' and a 'finance lease'. Give four advantages of operating leases to a business.
4 What is the objective of 'small-firms loan guarantees'? Briefly describe how they work.

D. Creditors and cycles:

1 Explain how a good relationship with its trade creditors can help a business to perform well.
2 How would you decide whether or not to accept an early-settlement discount from a supplier? Give an example to illustrate your answer.
3 Draw a 'timeline' diagram to illustrate the relationships between the working capital cycle, cash cycle, creditor payment period, debtor collection period and stock-holding period.
4 Describe and compare 'overtrading' and 'overcapitalisation'.

Questions

An asterisk * on a question number indicates that the answer is given at the end of the book. Answers to the other questions are given in the Lecturer's Guide.

Q4.1* Worthy Limited

It is 30 January 2007 and Worthy Limited's board of directors is meeting to discuss the 2006 accounts (summarised below together with those of 2005). Worthy Limited is a manufacturing business and all its sales and purchases are made on credit terms. During 2006, it adopted an expansion strategy led by an across-the-board reduction in its selling prices. Its overdraft limit is £1.6 million but, towards the end of 2006, the bank reluctantly agreed to increase this to £2.0 million on a temporary basis. The directors are due to meet their bank next week to present a report analysing the causes of the cash shortage and outlining the action they intend to take in order to improve the situation. It is very likely that the bank will give notice that the temporary overdraft extension will be terminated in the near future. (Worthy's stock at 1 June 2004 was £230,000.)

	2005 £000	2006 £000
P & L A/C for year ended 31 May		
Sales revenue	3,000	4,600
Cost of sales	(1,650)	(2,700)
Gross profit	1,350	1,900
Distribution costs	(300)	(450)
Administrative expenses	(700)	(950)
Profit before taxation	350	500
Taxation	(75)	(85)
Profit after taxation	275	415
Dividends	(80)	(80)
Transferred to reserves	195	335
Balance sheets at 31 May		
Fixed assets at cost	2,300	3,000
Less: Accumulated depreciation	250	300
	2,050	2,700
Current assets:		
Stocks	370	1,200
Trade debtors	440	810
Cash	80	140
	890	2,150
Current liabilities:		
Bank overdraft	(900)	(1,950)
Trade creditors	(450)	(950)
Taxation	(75)	(100)
Dividend	(80)	(80)
	1,505	3,080
Net current assets	(615)	(930)
Net total assets	1,435	1,770
Financed by:		
Share capital	200	200
Profit and loss account	1,235	1,570
Total capital employed	1,435	1,770

Task:

Prepare a report for the board of directors of Worthy Limited examining the financial performance of the company during the two-year period to 31 May 2006. The report should also include advice as to how the company could reduce its overdraft to below the original limit of £1.6 million.

Q4.2* BKZ Limited

BKZ Limited is a new company about to launch its business-to-business service on the Internet. The launch will take place in April and it hopes to achieve monthly sales of £100,000 in only four months! Most of its sales will be on credit terms and, based on their experience, its directors expect customers to pay as follows: 30% in the month of sale, 50% one month after sale, 15% two months after sale with 5% lost as bad debts.

BKZ does not carry any stock and it intends to pay all its expenses in the month they are incurred. At the beginning of April, after paying for its fixed assets, it will have a positive bank balance of only £2,000. However, its bank has agreed to give it an overdraft (secured against its assets) with a limit of £40,000.

An extract from its budget for the first six months of trading is shown below (all figures in £000). Depreciation of £13,000 a month is included in the expenses figures.

Month	April	May	June	July	August	September
Sales	20	40	60	100	100	100
Expenses	63	53	57	63	63	63

Tasks:

1 Based on the information given above, what will the overdraft be at the end of each month? Comment on your answer.
2 The financial director suggests offering a cash discount of 10% to customers paying on the day of sale. He believes this will be sufficient to attract many customers who would otherwise pay after one month. Customers are now expected to pay as follows: 60% in the month of sale, 20% one month after sale, 15% two months after sale with 5% lost as bad debts. What will the overdraft be at the end of each month? Advise BKZ on how it could manage its working capital to solve its problems.

Q4.3* Rogers Motor Parts

Vic Rogers is a sole trader running a vehicle parts business for the motor trade. All his sales are on credit terms. During 2005, he reduced his selling prices in order to increase the volume of sales. His objective was to make his business bigger, stronger and more profitable. To facilitate this expansion, he had to build an extra storeroom and purchase more storage bins. However, during 2005, he was surprised that he had to ask his bank for an overdraft. He was originally granted £5,000 but had to apply for a further £5,000 a few months later. The bank reluctantly agreed to his request but made it clear that they would not consider any further increase until 2007. They also insisted that the whole £10,000 overdraft was secured against his private residence. But even with this facility, some of his suppliers are very unhappy with the length of time Vic is taking to pay them. At the moment, he is relying heavily on their goodwill for continued supplies of stock items.

Summarised balance sheets as at 31 December 2004 and 2005 (£000s)

		2005		2004
Fixed assets at net book value		43		33
Current assets:				
Stock	18		7	
Debtors	36		12	
Bank	0		1	
Current liabilities:				
Creditors	37		15	
Overdraft	10		0	
Working capital		7		5
Net total assets		**50**		**38**
Owner's capital:				
Opening balance	38		21	
Annual profit	35		30	
Less: Drawings	23		13	
Total capital employed		**50**		**38**

Trading results for the years to 31 December 2004 and 2005 (£000s)

	2005	2004
Sales	200	120
Cost of sales	150	80
Gross profit	50	40
Overheads	15	10
Net profit	35	30

Tasks:

1 Calculate the following ratios for both years:
   - Percentage mark-up on cost of sales
   - Gross profit margin
   - Return on capital employed
   - Debtor collection period
   - Stock turnover days
   - Creditors payment period (stock at 1 January 2004 = £5,000)
   - Current ratio
   - Liquid ratio.
2 Discuss how the profitability and liquidity have been affected by the increase in sales and advise Vic on the running of his business in 2006.

Q4.4 Alborg Co. Ltd

The Alborg Company Limited manufactures and sells doors and window frames to the building trade. It has been expanding rapidly over the last two years, experiencing an annual growth rate of 25%. The board is looking at the draft results for 2007 together with a forecast for 2008 (see below). Although the company wishes to continue growing rapidly, it is uncertain whether it will be able to finance this due to the size of the fore-cast overdraft.

The overdraft at the end of 2007 is £245,000 compared to a positive bank balance of £25,000 one year earlier when the overdraft limit was £125,000. During 2007, the bank had agreed a temporary increase to £250,000 but has now written to say that this increase can no longer be allowed, and must be reduced to £125,000 by the end of March 2008, i.e. within the next three months.

The board observes from the forecast that, without corrective action, the predicted overdraft in 12 months' time will be £605,000. Currently there are no alternative sources of finance available and the board is now considering how it might resolve the problem.

Income statements for y/e 31 December

	2006 £000		2007 £000		2008 forecast £000	
Sales		2,000		2,500		3,000
Costs:						
Materials used	750		950		1,125	
Other production costs	500		600		700	
Depreciation	200		300		400	
Cost of goods sold	1,450		1,850		2,225	
Admin and selling	100	1,550	150	2,000	200	2,425
Profit before tax		450		500		575
Taxation		125		150		200
Profit after tax		325		350		375
Dividends		195		210		225
Retained profit		130		140		150

Balance sheets at 31 December

	2006			2007			2008		
Fixed assets (net book value)		1,000			1,200			1,475	
Current assets									
Stocks: Raw materials	175			275			375		
Finished goods	325			475			575		
Debtors	150			225			375		
Bank	25			0			0		
	675			975			1,325		
Less: Current liabilities:									
Trade creditors	150			225			275		
Tax due	125			150			200		
Dividends due	195			210			225		
Overdraft	0	470	205	245	830	145	605	1,305	20
			1,205			1,345			1,495
Financed by:									
Issued share capital			500			500			500
Retained profits			705			845			995
			1,205			1,345			1,495

Tasks:

1 Using a cash flow statement for 2007, explain why the cash position has deteriorated during that year.
2 Comment on the company's management of working capital by examining the operating and cash cycles for all three years and suggest ways in which the company might improve its working capital position. (You are aware that the 2006 position is typical of the industry in which Alborg operates.)
3 By looking at your suggestions to improve working capital and at the expected cash flow over the next three months, advise the company how (if at all) the overdraft can be reduced to £125,000 by the end of March 2008.

Q4.5 Charlesworth plc

Charlesworth plc distributes tiles to the building trade. The vast majority of these tiles are purchased in Eastern Europe and South-East Asia. It has been quite successful since it was set up 10 years ago with sales growing, on average, at the rate of 10% a year.

Amy Backson has recently taken over as managing director to oversee a planned expansion of about 20% in the coming year. Amy is satisfied that the expansion can be managed from a logistical point of view as £11 million is planned to be spent on new vehicles and warehousing facilities. The old vehicles being replaced will be sold at auction and are expected to raise £250,000 which is also their net book value at the end of the current year. (The £21 million forecast for expenses includes £5 million for depreciation.)

However, the first draft of the forecast for next year is causing some concern as it predicts a substantial overdraft. The summarised accounts of Charlesworth plc have just been completed in draft form for the current year together with a forecast for next year (see below). Amy has been told by the bank that the overdraft limit has just been doubled to £1 million but no further increases will be granted for the foreseeable future. Charlesworth pays interest at 10% a year on its overdraft and loans.

Amy wants to have these matters discussed at the board meeting next week and has asked you for some help in preparing the necessary figures setting out some options.

Balance sheets as at 31 December (£000)

	Current year			Next year's forecast	
Fixed assets (at NBV)		30,000			35,750
Stocks	8,000		12,000		
Debtors	8,000		11,000		
Bank	300		0		
	16,300		23,000		
Creditors	2,900		3,500		
Overdraft	0		5,800		
Tax due	3,000		2,500		
Dividends due	4,000	9,900	4,200	16,000	
Working capital		6,400			7,000
		36,400			42,750
Less: Loan @ 10%		4,000			7,000
		32,400			35,750

	Current year			Next year's forecast	
Financed by:					
Share capital	10,000			10,000	
Reserves	22,400	32,400		25,750	35,750

Profit and loss accounts for year ended 31 December (£000)

		Current year		Next year's forecast	
Sales		52,000			61,000
Opening stock	5,000			8,000	
Purchases	30,000			33,000	
	35,000			41,000	
Less: Closing stock	8,000			12,000	
Cost of goods sold		27,000			29,000
Gross profit		25,000			32,000
Less:					
Expenses	17,000			21,000	
Interest – O/D	0			250	
Interest – loan	400	17,400		700	21,950
Net profit		7,600			10,050
Tax		3,000			2,500
Profit after tax		4,600			7,550
Dividends		4,000			4,200
Retained in year		600			3,350

Tasks:

1 Create a cash flow statement for next year explaining why the cash position deteriorates during that year.

2 Comment on the company's management of working capital by examining the operating and cash cycles for both years and suggest ways in which the company might improve its working capital position.

3 In what other ways could Charlesworth achieve its planned expansion whilst not breaching the overdraft limit of £1 million?

DECISION MAKING

Part 3

When Henry Mintzberg performed his analysis of what managers actually spent their time doing, he found that making decisions did not take up very much of their time. However, when managers do have to make decisions, it is important that they get them right. Management accounting is a source of help on these occasions.

Some decisions will have an immediate, short-term effect but others will impact on the business for many years to come. Contribution analysis (Chapters 5 and 6) is a simple yet powerful technique to help you make correct decisions. Basically, it concentrates on the costs and revenues that will change because of the decision and ignores those that will not. If absorption costing were used in these situations, the wrong decision would often be made as it takes account of **all** the costs associated with the product, whether or not they will change. Relevant costing continues along the same lines as contribution analysis but widens the scope of consideration to include the indirect effects of decisions as well as the direct ones. For example, if a decision to cease production of one particular product meant that 10 employees would become redundant, the redundancy pay arising (say £100,000) would be included as a cost arising from the decision. Chapters 5, 6 and 7 should be read in sequence as they reflect increasing degrees of reality.

Capital investment appraisal concerns decisions which will affect company performance for many years. Essentially, they are about deciding which fixed assets to buy. The more expensive the fixed assets, the more relevant the use of capital investment appraisal techniques. Typically, large sums of money are tied up for long periods of time. Make the wrong decision and either you will have to live with it for a long time or it will be **very** expensive to correct. Although there are many qualitative factors to consider, any help from management accounting techniques is very welcome when such important decisions have to be made.

CHAPTER 5

Variable costing and breakeven analysis

Chapter contents

Introduction

Sometimes there are ways of doing things which are so simple they seem almost too easy, too good to be true. Variable costing is one of these. But do not be fooled by its simplicity – it is a very powerful technique. It is used mainly for short-term decision making and calculating the effect of production and sales levels on profitability. Short-term decision making is the subject of the next chapter. This chapter concentrates on the relationship between profit and activity (i.e. production and sales), commonly known as breakeven analysis.

At some point in your life you will probably think seriously about starting your own business. If the type of business you have in mind involves providing the same item for many different customers, breakeven analysis will be very useful to you. Suppose you decide to open a driving school, offering lessons to learner drivers. After much careful thought you will be able to estimate your total annual cost. Dividing this amount by the number of lessons (**estimated conservatively**) will give you the cost per lesson. But what are you going to charge your customers for each lesson? How do you know if you will make a profit or a loss? And how much is it likely to be? These are very important questions for anyone going into business on their own. Breakeven analysis is the financial model designed to answer these questions.

Note: Variable costing is also known as *marginal costing* and *cost–volume–profit (CVP) analysis*.

Having worked through this chapter you should be able to:
- **differentiate between variable and fixed costs;**
- **define contribution;**
- **explain the relationship between contribution, fixed costs and net profit;**
- **calculate contribution;**
- **calculate breakeven point;**
- **draw traditional and contribution breakeven charts;**
- **define and calculate the margin of safety;**
- **evaluate different cost structures in terms of their operational gearing;**
- **calculate the activity level to produce a target profit;**
- **draw and use a profit–volume chart;**
- **discuss the assumptions and limitations of breakeven analysis.**

Learning objectives

Cost behaviour

This section is a brief revision of Chapter 2. Variable costing is based on the difference between fixed and variable costs, which are defined as follows and illustrated in Figure 5.1.

Variable costs – Costs which vary with output (e.g. raw materials)
Fixed costs – Costs which do not change when output changes (e.g. business rates)
Semi-variable costs – Costs which are partly fixed and partly variable (e.g. telephone)

Although there are several costs which are either purely variable or purely fixed, many costs are semi-variable. The utilities, such as telephone and electricity, often have a fixed cost element, such as line rental or a standing charge, which has to be paid irrespective

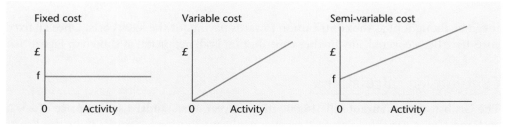

Figure 5.1 **Patterns of cost behaviour**

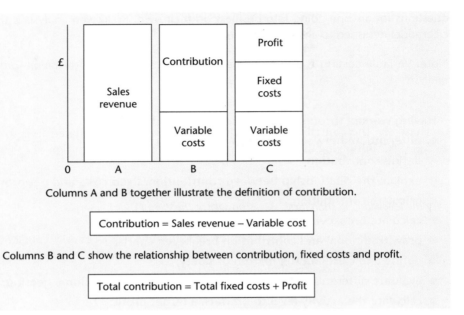

Columns A and B together illustrate the definition of contribution.

Contribution = Sales revenue – Variable cost

Columns B and C show the relationship between contribution, fixed costs and profit.

Total contribution = Total fixed costs + Profit

Figure 5.2 **Contribution relationships**

of usage. In addition, there is also a cost per unit used. The graph of the semi-variable cost combines the features of the other two graphs. Sometimes, only the total amounts of semi-variable costs are known for successive periods and the fixed and variable elements have to be worked out. (One way of doing this is the 'high–low method' as detailed in Chapter 1, on cost behaviour.)

Contribution

In the introduction to this chapter, it was pointed out that ignoring fixed costs is sometimes the correct thing to do. As fixed costs cannot be changed **in the short term**, there is no point considering them for short-term decision making. This approach results in something that is like 'profit' but is not 'profit'. To avoid confusion, this new entity is called 'contribution'.

Contribution is defined as the excess of sales revenue over the variable costs.

It can be thought of as the contribution towards paying for the fixed costs. Once all fixed costs have been covered, any further contribution is all net profit, as shown in Figure 5.2.

Contribution calculations

The Grubsteaks restaurant sells 18,000 meals a year at a standard selling price of £5. If each meal has a variable cost of £2, what annual contribution is earned? If the fixed costs are £30,000 in total, what is the net profit?

$$£$$
$$\text{Sales revenue} = 90,000 \quad (18,000 \times £5)$$
$$\text{Variable costs} = \underline{36,000} \quad (18,000 \times £2)$$
$$\text{Contribution} = 54,000$$
$$\text{Fixed costs} = \underline{30,000}$$
$$\text{Net profit} = \underline{\underline{24,000}}$$

Alternatively, the contribution per unit could have been calculated first to give £3 ($= £5 - £2$). Multiplying this by 18,000 meals gives the total contribution of £54,000.

Self-assessment question S5.1

Try the following question for yourself (answer at the end of the chapter).

The Good Health drinks tent at a local horse-race meeting sells all its drinks at £2.50 each. The variable cost of each drink is £1.00 and the fixed cost for the one-day event is £2,700. If 4,000 drinks are sold in the day, what is (a) the total contribution, and (b) the net profit?

Breakeven point

Definition and calculation

The total contribution increases as more units are sold. A point will come when the total contribution is just enough to cover the fixed costs. At this precise level of sales, all the costs have been covered and the next unit sold will produce the first profits for the business. This critical point, where the business makes neither a profit nor a loss, is known as the *breakeven point* (BEP). This is a useful concept for planning and control purposes.

At BEP, Total contribution = total fixed costs

Continuing with the example used above: the Grubsteaks restaurant sells 18,000 meals a year at a standard selling price of £5 and a variable cost of £2 with fixed costs of £30,000; how many meals will it need to sell to break even?

Let breakeven occur when N meals have been sold; in other words, when N lots of unit contributions have been received.

$$\text{Total contribution} = \text{total fixed costs}$$
$$N \times \text{unit contribution} = \text{total fixed costs}$$
$$N \times (5 - 2) = 30,000$$
$$N = 30,000/3$$
$$N = \textbf{10,000 meals}$$

The relationship between costs and revenues can be illustrated graphically by *breakeven charts*. Figure 5.3 gives the basic structure; this is then added to in two alternative ways

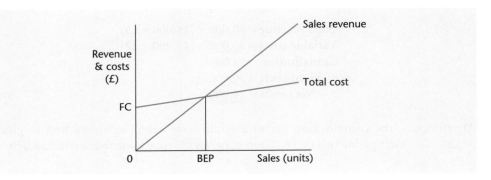

Figure 5.3 **Fundamental structure**

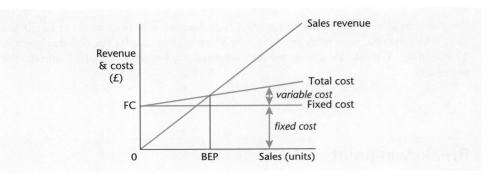

Figure 5.4 **Traditional breakeven chart**

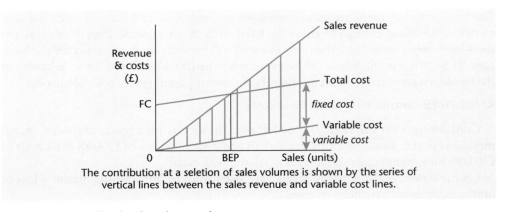

The contribution at a seletion of sales volumes is shown by the series of
vertical lines between the sales revenue and variable cost lines.

Figure 5.5 **Contribution breakeven chart**

in Figures 5.4 and 5.5. It is these two alternatives that are normally seen and used
in practice.

Figure 5.4 shows the total cost broken down into its fixed and variable elements.

Figure 5.5 also shows the fixed and variable elements, but with their positions
reversed. This enables the contribution to be clearly illustrated by the shaded area. (This
is not possible on the traditional breakeven chart.)

Try the following question for yourself (answer at the end of the chapter).

Continuing with S5.1 above: the Good Health drinks tent at a local horse-race meeting sells all its drinks at £2.50 each. The variable cost of each drink is £1.00 and the fixed cost for the one-day event is £2,700. How many drinks does it need to sell to break even?

Graphical representation

The restaurant example used above can be illustrated by the chart in Figure 5.6.

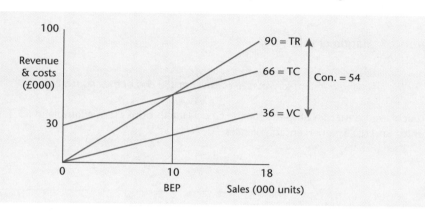

Figure 5.6 **Contribution breakeven chart for the Grubsteaks restaurant**

Try the following question for yourself (answer at the end of the chapter).

Using your answers from S5.1 and S5.2 above, draw a contribution breakeven chart (to scale) for the Good Health drinks tent.

Margin of safety

This is a measure of the amount by which sales can fall before profit turns to loss, i.e. the excess of actual sales over breakeven sales. This can be expressed as a number of units or as a percentage of sales and is illustrated by Figure 5.7.
For the Grubsteaks restaurant example:

$$
\begin{aligned}
\text{Actual number of meals sold} &= 18,000 \\
\text{Breakeven level of sales} &= \underline{10,000} \\
\text{Margin of safety} &= \underline{\ 8,000}\ \textbf{meals}
\end{aligned}
$$

$$
\text{or,}\quad \frac{\text{Margin of safety in units}}{\text{Actual sales in units}} \times 100 = \frac{8,000}{18,000} \times 100 = \textbf{44\% of sales}
$$

So sales could fall by 44% before losses occurred.

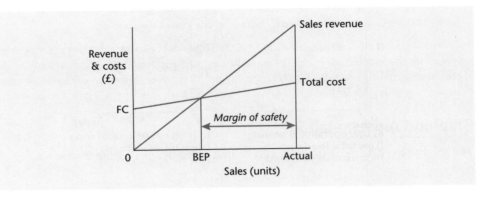

Figure 5.7 **Margin of safety**

Try the following question for yourself (answer at the end of the chapter).

Calculate the margin of safety for the Good Health drinks tent example in S5.3, (a) in units, and (b) as a percentage of sales.

Operational gearing

Operational gearing describes the relationship between fixed costs and total costs. The greater the amount of fixed costs, expressed as a percentage of total costs, the greater the operational gearing. The greater the operational gearing, the greater is the effect of changes in sales volume on contribution and profit. The following formula expresses this numerically:

$$\text{Operational gearing} = \frac{\text{change in contribution or profit}}{\text{change in output}}$$

Consider the following situation where two separate businesses make and sell the same item at the same price. They both make cardboard 'outer' boxes to contain, for example, 48 packets of cereal. These large outers are used to transport large volumes of goods around the country.

Business A keeps fixed costs to a minimum but has a high proportion of variable costs. It uses simple bending and gluing devices operated by 12 employees and buys in large sheets of ready-made cardboard as its raw material. On the other hand, business B has invested heavily in automated machinery whose first process is to make its own cardboard sheet. This needs only two people to operate but causes a much larger amount of depreciation (i.e. fixed cost) than in business A. Its raw material is shredded recycled paper and other fibres which are much cheaper to buy than ready-made cardboard. Consequently, business B has a much higher proportion of fixed costs than variable costs compared to A. (See Figure 5.8 and notice the change in slope of the total cost line.)

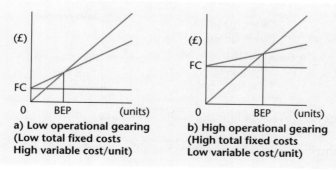

Figure 5.8 **Operational gearing**

As an example, for one outer:

	A £	B £
Selling price	5	5
Variable cost	3	1
Contribution	2	4
Annual fixed cost	£100,000	£300,000

If there is a new order for 3,000 outers the profit will increase by £6,000 (3,000 × £2) for business A but by £12,000 (3,000 × £4) for business B. B will do better than A.

However, if a customer decides to purchase its outers elsewhere and cancels an order for 3,000 outers, the profit will decrease by £6,000 (3,000 × £2) for business A but by £12,000 (3,000 × £4) for business B. This time, A will do better than B.

The greater the operational gearing, the greater is the effect of changes in sales volume on profit. In other words, the greater the operational gearing, the greater the risk.

When starting a new business, and sales are not very predictable, low operational gearing is preferable to high operational gearing. Low gearing means that there are fewer fixed costs to be covered before reaching profitability. This strategy helps to minimise risk.

On the other hand, as shown in the above example, provided the business is making profits, high gearing gives a greater increase in profit for each extra item sold.

Activity levels for target profits

Another useful calculation is to determine the number of items that has to be sold to achieve a given net profit. Figure 5.2 at the start of this chapter illustrates the following relationship:

Total contribution = total fixed costs + profit

If the unit contribution, the total fixed cost and the target profit are known, the activity level can be calculated. Suppose you were given the following information:

	£/unit
Direct materials	4
Direct labour	7
Variable overhead	3
Selling price	24
Total fixed cost	£5,000

How many items need to be sold for the business to make a profit of £10,000?

$$\text{Unit contribution} = \text{sales revenue} - \text{variable costs} = 24 - (4 + 7 + 3) = 10$$

Let the number of items needed $= N$.

$$\text{Total contribution} = \text{total fixed costs} + \text{profit}$$
$$N \times 10 = 5{,}000 + 10{,}000$$
$$10N = 15{,}000$$
$$N = 1{,}500$$

1,500 items need to be sold to achieve a profit of £10,000.

Self-assessment question S5.5

Try the following question for yourself (answer at the end of the chapter).

A new style of electric bass guitar is about to be launched by a well-known instrument company. The materials for each guitar total £25 and 2.5 hours of labour (paid at £12/hour) are needed to assemble one. Variable overheads are charged at £2/labour hour and the associated fixed costs are £600 per month. If the selling price is set at £160, how many guitars need to be sold to achieve an annual profit of £20,000?

Profit–volume relationships

Sometimes it is preferable to bypass the details of sales and costs and compare profit directly with the volume of activity. The profit–volume chart shown in Figure 5.9 has the same horizontal axis as the breakeven chart but the vertical axis is for profit only. The breakeven point is where the profit line crosses the horizontal axis.

In order to draw a profit–volume graph, two points are needed to determine the position of the profit line. One of these points is easy to find. When activity is zero, the loss being made is exactly equal to the total of fixed costs. For the other point, a calculation is needed. The following relationship is used (see Figure 5.2):

$$\text{Total contribution} = \text{total fixed costs} + \text{profit}$$

Assuming the total of fixed costs is given, the amount of profit can be calculated for a chosen activity level if the total contribution at that level can be found.

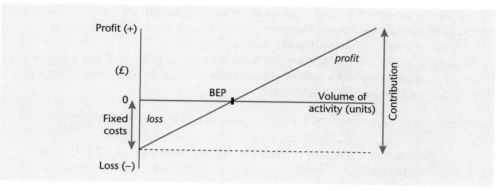

Figure 5.9 **Profit–volume chart**

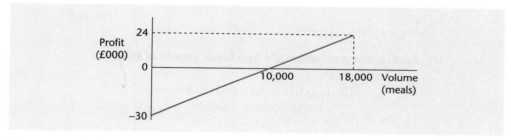

Figure 5.10 **Profit–volume chart for the Grubsteaks restaurant**

The Grubsteaks restaurant example earlier in this chapter showed the application of this formula. At the activity level of 18,000 meals a year the profit was calculated to be £24,000 (see Figure 5.10).

The advantage of the profit–volume chart over the breakeven chart is that the profit can be determined for any level of activity with the range of the graph. This is done simply by reading the graph.

Try the following question for yourself (answer at the end of the chapter).

Using the answer to S5.1, draw a profit–volume graph for the Good Health drinks tent. From this graph, **read** the profit for sales of (a) 1,200 drinks and (b) 2,500 drinks.

Self-assessment question S5.6

Effect of alternative sales mixes

The vast majority of businesses sell more than one product and many of these sell lots of different products. As different products tend to have different unit contributions and no one knows for sure the sales mix that will occur in the next period, it is impossible to determine the breakeven level of output for the whole business. Different sales mixes will have different breakeven points. However, if the sales mix tends not to change much, it is possible to make an estimate with some degree of reliability.

Consider a business with just two products, As and Bs. Product B has a higher price and unit contribution, but a lower volume, than product A. The current sales mix is three As are sold for every B (A:B = 3:1).

Product	A	B	Total
Sales price	10	18	
Variable cost	4	9	
Unit contribution	6	9	
Quantities	30,000	10,000	40,000
Total contribution	180,000	90,000	270,000
Total fixed costs			148,500
Profit			121,500

To calculate the breakeven point, let N = number of Bs sold at BEP:

$$\text{Total contribution} = \text{total fixed cost}$$
$$3N(6) + N(9) = 148,500$$
$$27N = 148,500$$
$$N = 5,500$$
At BEP, 16,500 As and 5,500 Bs are sold (22,000 units in total)

But if the sales mix is changed to 2:1 (= A:B),

$$\text{Total contribution} = \text{total fixed cost}$$
$$2N(6) + N(9) = 148,500$$
$$21N = 148,500$$
$$N = 7,071$$
At BEP, 14,142 As and 7,071 Bs are sold (21,243 units in total)

Note that this is 757 items less in total than the previous sales mix.

What if the original volume was sold in total (40,000 units) but in the new sales mix of 2:1?

Product	A	B	Total
Sales price	10	18	
Variable cost	4	9	
Unit contribution	6	9	
Quantities	26,667	13,333	40,000
Total contribution	160,002	119,998	280,000
Total fixed costs			148,500
Profit			131,500

Note that this is £10,000 greater than with the original sales mix.

Self-assessment question S5.7

Try the following question for yourself (answer at the end of the chapter).

Hoffman Limited makes and sells only two types of portable cooking stove, the Lightweight (L) and the Megarange (M). The Megarange is more sophisticated and sells for more than twice as much as the Lightweight which is very popular. Consequently, nine Ls are sold for every M. The selling prices for Ls and Ms respectively are £8.20 and £19.40; their variable costs are £3.70 and £10.90. The budget for next year shows 50,000 stoves sold altogether with fixed overheads costing £150,000 in total.
    For next year, calculate:

1 Profit if sales mix remains L:M = 9:1.
2 Breakeven point if sales mix remains L:M = 9:1.
3 Breakeven point if sales mix becomes L:M = 15:1.
4 Profit if sales mix becomes L:M = 15:1.

Limitations of variable costing

The relationship between sales income and quantity sold may not be linear. Beyond a certain point, it may be necessary to reduce the selling price in order to achieve further sales. The previously straight sales revenue line starts to curve beyond this point. (See Figure 5.11.)

The relationship between total costs and quantity produced may not be linear. The greater the quantity of units produced, the lower may be the price per unit of materials purchased. The straight total cost line also turns into a curve. (See Figure 5.11.)

Contribution analysis can be unreliable outside the relevant range (the range of activity levels for which the curves approximate to straight lines). At very high (close to maximum capacity) and very low activity levels, costs and revenues may not be representative of normal values (see Figure 5.11).

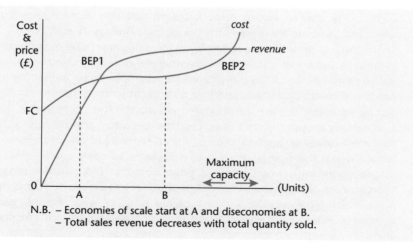

N.B. – Economies of scale start at A and diseconomies at B.
      – Total sales revenue decreases with total quantity sold.

Figure 5.11 **Economists' cost–volume graph**

Breakeven analysis is not very useful for multi-product businesses as different breakeven points are produced for different sales mixes. Because different products have different unit contributions, different sales mixes for the same overall activity will have different breakeven points.

It is difficult to measure activity for 'jobbing' businesses, where every item produced is different. Breakeven calculations and charts are applicable to firms which make large volumes of the same product. They are of no use to firms which make only one or a few of each item. This would include civil engineering firms producing public buildings and boatyards producing to customer specification only.

It is assumed that all the items made are sold, i.e. there is no increase or decrease in stock levels over the period. But stock levels may change over a financial period. When this is the case, the production activity will not be the same as the sales activity. Which of these two activity levels should be used for breakeven purposes? As breakeven is based on contribution (sales revenue – variable cost) the sales activity level should be used. 'Variable cost' is the variable cost of the items sold, not the items made.

The manager's point of view

Breakeven analysis can provide vital financial information, particularly for small, relatively simple companies. It also has a role to play in larger, more complex organisations, although its potential applications tend to be limited. In all companies, however, it can help managers to understand the cost/price/volume relationships in their businesses.

The main use of breakeven analysis in single-product companies is to calculate the number of items to be sold before a profit can be made. Most small businesses know exactly where this point is, and it becomes one of the driving forces of the business. Once this point is reached, managers know that they are starting to generate profit. A small businessman of my acquaintance reckons that he works on Mondays to pay the taxman, Tuesdays to pay the VAT man, Wednesday and Thursday to pay his suppliers, and only starts working for himself on Friday. He knows nothing about accounting, and his logic may be slightly suspect, but his little joke demonstrates that, even if he doesn't realise it, he has grasped the principles of breakeven analysis!

The same basic technique is employed for various purposes in large companies. It is commonly used, in conjunction with other measurements, in capital appraisals. All formal proposals for capital projects will be accompanied by supporting financial data, which will inevitably demonstrate that a satisfactory rate of return and payback period can be expected. But are the numbers reasonable? It is possible that the underlying assumptions about projected sales, capital expenditure and operating costs are all at their most optimistic limits, and could spell disaster if just one of them failed to materialise. To test the figures, therefore, it is useful to carry out a sensitivity analysis, calculating the impact on the rate of return of, say, a 10% reduction in sales, or a 20% overspend in capital expenditure. One of the key calculations here is the breakeven point, which represents the 'least acceptable' position. What level of inaccuracy in the numbers will bring the project down to its breakeven level? This neatly puts all the alternative scenarios into context and allows management to assess the robustness of the proposed figures.

Some years ago, breakeven principles played an important part in another type of major project, this time the sale of a business. We were instructed by our American parent company to shed a particular product line, and achieve a specified net gain for the company. The matter was greatly complicated when the favoured purchaser decided to buy only the trading assets, i.e. customer lists, product know-how, and working capital, but not the fixed assets, i.e. land, buildings and plant. As a result, we were obliged to close down the factory, leading to significant expenditure which had not been envisaged when the sale of the business had first been authorised. This included decommissioning of the plant, building demolition, environmental testing, land remediation, and redundancy, among many others. Against these we had several unforeseen items of revenue, such as sale of plant and the disposal of the land. Our job was to ensure that the ultimate sale of the land covered all the net expenditure, leaving the American parent company with the profit it expected from the sale of the business. We used a breakeven model to monitor progress on this project, initially using esti-mated figures, and replacing them with the actual numbers as they became confirmed. In this way we were able to monitor constantly the proceeds required from the sale of the land to break even, and keep an eye on the property market to see if this level was achievable. Unfortunately, when we were ready to sell, the property market was in a slump, so we retained the land for a further five years until the market had recovered sufficiently to enable us to reach our breakeven point.

These examples will hopefully illustrate that breakeven principles can be used in a variety of different ways, even if the determination of sales volume, especially in small companies, remains its most common application. However, in large companies, the breakeven point of individual items is rather muddied by the multiplicity of products being sold; if you sell more of Product A than you expected, thus recovering a higher level of overhead, the breakeven point on Product B may go down. That is why we found ourselves concentrating more on the overall level of marginal income being gen-erated by groups of products, and the contribution that they made towards fixed costs. The concept of contribution is a useful way of focusing on profit, and analysing the elements which are causing you to over- or underachieve the profit target. By increasing volume, or by changing the mix of sales towards the higher margin pro-ducts, more marginal income will be generated. This additional contribution should fall straight through to the bottom line profit, assuming that the fixed costs remain fixed. In practice, of course, they rarely do. There are always spending variances to be man-aged, but this merely demonstrates another opportunity for effective profit generation. If you can reduce the level of fixed costs, at the same time as increasing marginal income, the gearing effect on the profit line can be significant.

Finally, the concept of contribution can sometimes show expenditure in a startling light. For instance, how big a deal do your American salespeople have to make, in order to pay for the managing director's first-class flight to New York to sign the final contract? The contribution calculation will tell you this, although you may not wish to point it out to the MD! Perhaps a more relevant question is: 'Will the contribution gen-erated by the New York sale cover all the costs associated with it, and still leave a satisfactory profit?' Consider not only the variable costs of materials, labour, variable overhead and freight, but also other related costs, such as warehousing, export docu-mentation, currency risks from $ invoicing, extended credit terms and bank charges, as well as the cost of customer visits and technical support. The MD's visit could be the final straw which pushes this piece of business into loss!

Summary

- Costs can be analysed into variable and fixed.
- Contribution is sales revenue minus variable cost, either per unit or in total.
- Total contribution equals total fixed cost plus profit.
- At breakeven point (profit = 0) total contribution equals total fixed cost.
- There are two types of breakeven charts, traditional and contribution.
- The margin of safety shows how far above breakeven point a firm is operating.
- Operational gearing affects the amount of profit due to changes in sales volume.
- Activity levels can be calculated for target profits.
- The profit–volume chart is an alternative to the breakeven chart.

Further reading

Horngren, C. T. (2004) 'Management accounting: some comments', *Journal of Management Accounting Research*, Vol. 16.

Horngren, C., Bhimani, A., Datar, S. and Foster, G. (2002) *Management and Cost Accounting*, 2nd edition, Prentice Hall Europe, Harlow. See Chapter 8, 'Cost–volume–profit relationships'.

Upchurch, A. (2003) *Management Accounting, Principles and Practice*, 2nd edition, Financial Times/Prentice Hall, Harlow. See Chapter 6, 'Cost/volume/profit analysis'.

Weetman, P. (2002) *Management Accounting, an Introduction*, 3rd edition, Financial Times/Prentice Hall, Harlow. See chapter 'Profit measurement and short-term decision making'.

Answers to self-assessment questions

S5.1. Good Health drinks tent

$$£$$

Sales revenue = 2.50/unit
Variable costs = <u>1.00</u>/unit
Unit contribution = 1.50/unit
Number of units = <u>4,000</u>
Total contribution = 6,000
Fixed costs = <u>2,700</u>
Net profit = <u>3,300</u>

a) Total contribution = £6,000
b) Net profit = £3,300

S5.2. Good Health drinks tent

Let BEP occur when B drinks have been sold.

$$\text{Total contribution} = \text{total fixed costs}$$
$$\text{B} \times \text{unit contribution} = \text{total fixed costs}$$
$$\text{B} \times (2.50 - 1.00) = 2,700$$
$$\text{B} = 2,700/1.50$$
$$\textbf{Breakeven point, B} = \textbf{1,800 drinks}$$

S5.3. Contribution breakeven chart for the drinks tent

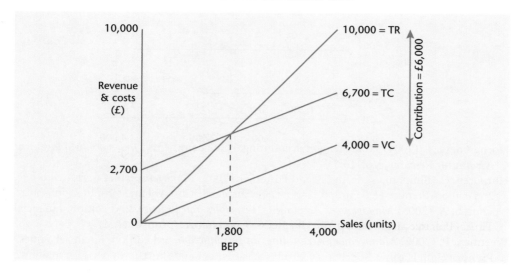

S5.4. For the Good Health drinks tent example

a) Actual number of drinks sold = 4,000
Breakeven level of sales = 1,800
Margin of safety = 2,200 drinks

b) $\dfrac{\text{Margin of safety in units}}{\text{Actual sales in units}} \times 100 = \dfrac{2,200}{4,000} \times 100 = 55\%$

So sales could fall by 55% before losses occurred.

S5.5. Variable costs

Materials	25	
Labour	30	(2.5 × 12)
Overheads	5	(2.5 × 2)
Total	60	
Sales price	160	
Unit contribution	100	

Let the number of items needed $= N$

Total contribution = total fixed costs + profit

$$N \times 100 = (600 \times 12) + 20,000$$
$$N = 27,200/100$$
$$N = 272$$

So, 272 bass guitars need to be sold to create a net profit of £20,000.

S5.6. Profit–volume chart for the Good Health drinks tent

a) If 1,200 drinks are sold, a **loss** of £900 would occur.

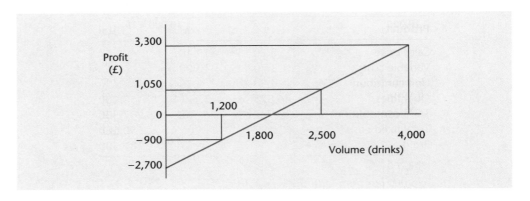

b) If 2,500 drinks are sold, a **profit** of £1,050 would occur.

S5.7. Hoffman Ltd

The current sales mix is 9 Ls are sold for every M (L:M = 9:1).

Product	L	M	Total
Sales price	8.20	19.40	
Variable cost	3.70	10.90	
Unit contribution	4.50	8.50	
Quantities	45,000	5,000	50,000
Total contribution	202,500	42,500	245,000
Total fixed costs			150,000
Profit			95,000

To calculate the breakeven point, let $N =$ number of Bs sold at BEP:

Total contribution = total fixed cost

$$9N(4.50) + N(8.50) = 150,000$$
$$49N = 150,000$$
$$N = 3,061$$

At BEP: 27,549 Ls and 3,062 Ms are sold (30,611 stoves in total)

But if the sales mix changed to 15:1 (= L:M),

$$\text{Total contribution} = \text{total fixed cost}$$
$$15N(4.50) + N(8.50) = 150,000$$
$$76N = 150,000$$
$$N = 1,974$$

At BEP: 29,610 Ls and 1,974 Ms are sold (31,584 stoves in total)

Note that this is 973 stoves more in total than the previous sales mix.

What if the original volume was sold in total (50,000 stoves) but in the new sales mix of 15:1?

Product	L	M	Total
Sales price	8.20	19.40	
Variable cost	3.70	10.90	
Unit contribution	4.50	8.50	
Quantities	46,875	3,125	50,000
Total contribution	210,937	26,563	237,500
Total fixed costs			150,000
Profit			87,500

Note that this is £8,000 less than with the original sales mix.

The Hutton Vinification Company

HVC Ltd is based in north Somerset and has a financial year starting on 1 August. It produces wine from bulk grape juice bought from vineyards in southern England. In 2006/07 it made and sold 90,000 litres of wine in standard-sized 750 millilitre bottles to customers located throughout the UK. The maximum annual output of its plant is estimated to be 98,000 litres. Demand has grown steadily over the last 10 years in step with increased interest in, and knowledge of, wine in the UK. Home market production has been encouraged by the recent gradual warming of the climate.

However, the number of complaints received by HVC Ltd has risen sharply over the last two years and if nothing is done to correct this, sales and profits are expected to fall next year. The directors attribute the complaints to the difficulty in controlling the quality of the 'must' (bought-in grape juice). The managing director has suggested that it would be easier to control the quality of harvested grapes rather than processed must. This means that HVC Ltd would have to acquire wine-pressing equipment to process the purchased grapes. Despite the extra temporary labour involved in pressing the grapes, the resulting self-pressed must is expected to have a variable cost equal to only 60% of bought-in must. The necessary grape-pressing machinery will cost £440,000 and will last 10 years before being scrapped (at zero value).

The managing director's remuneration is £42,000 p.a. and the sales director's is £38,000 p.a. In addition to the two directors, HVC Ltd has five full-time employees, whose pay in 2006/07 totalled £89,000. This included £25,000 annual salary for the production manager and basic annual pay of £10,000 for each of four operatives. This remuneration is considered to be a fixed cost but the remainder, which was earned as overtime by the four operatives, is considered to be a variable cost.

The total cost of must purchased in 2006/07 was £45,000. The average cost of the bottle, cork and label is £0.20 a bottle and delivery costs average £0.10 a bottle. HVC Ltd has a policy of having zero stocks at the end of July (this is also the company's financial year-end). Apart from a negligible amount, it has managed to achieve this for the last few years.

With effect from 1 August 2007 the directors will be entitled to a profit-related bonus dependent on the annual increase in net profit. Naturally, they are both very keen to earn a good bonus. With this in mind, the managing director has analysed the costs for 2006/07 (which was a typical year) as follows:

Fixed costs	£	Variable costs	£
Salaries and wages	145,000	Must	45,000
Depreciation	88,000	Overtime pay	24,000
Production costs	47,000	Bottle, cork and label	24,000
Selling costs	33,000	Delivery	12,000
Administration costs	29,000		£105,000
Interest	8,000		
	£350,000		

The sales director is not entirely convinced that the managing director's idea is the best solution. She thinks it would be better to go further south than at present, into central France, in order to purchase better-quality must. She believes that the effect of this would be to increase the must cost by 25% but this would be more than covered by her proposed 5% increase in the sales price.

HVC Ltd: Profit and loss account for y/e 31 July 2007

	£000	£000
Sales		504
Must	45	
Operatives' wages	64	
Bottles, corks and labels	24	
Production depreciation	53	
Other production costs	47	
Manufacturing costs of goods sold		233
Gross profit		271
Salaries	105	
Depreciation	35	
Selling costs	33	
Delivery costs	12	
Administration costs	29	
Bank interest	8	
Total overheads		222
Net profit		49

Tasks:

1 For 2006/07:
  a) Calculate the breakeven point in litres.
  b) Calculate the net profit if HVC Ltd had made and sold 95,000 litres.
  c) How many litres would have to be sold to increase net profit by 50%?

(20 marks)

2 If the MD's plan to buy and press grapes (instead of purchasing grape must) is put into operation for 2007/08 and output increases to 95,000 litres and the selling price increases by 5%:
  a) What would the revised breakeven point be?
  b) What would the revised profit be?

(20 marks)

3 Alternatively, if the sales director's plan to buy better-quality grape must is put into operation for 2007/08 and output increases to 95,000 litres and the selling price increases by 5%:
   a) What would the revised breakeven point be?
   b) What would the revised profit be?

(20 marks)

4 Evaluate the directors' plans and recommend a course of action for 2007/08. You may wish to use chart(s) to illustrate your answer.

(40 marks)

(Total 100 marks)

The Muesli Company

The Muesli Company (TMC) is a small business which makes and sells muesli. It was started two years ago by Rosemary Helms on the basis of her family's liking for the homemade mixture of cereals, nuts and dried fruits she had created for personal consumption. When a new farm shop opened nearby, she enquired if it would be interested in selling her muesli. The shop agreed to give it a try and found that it sold sufficient quantities to justify a permanent place in the shop. Rosemary now has five outlets and is considering selling her muesli on the Internet.

The business has reached a point where decisions have to be made concerning product type and distribution channel. The original recipe used nine different ingredients which were sourced from supermarkets and local shops. However, in recent months, Rosemary has created a new simplified recipe which uses only organic ingredients. Her idea is to appeal to the growing health food market which is willing to pay premium prices for organic foods. However, she has discovered that if she wishes to use the word 'organic' on the label, she must register with the Soil Association and pay an annual fee of £440. As the business is just starting up, she is undecided as to whether this cost is worthwhile. She could continue with the current labels (omitting the word 'organic') whilst still using the organic ingredients to improve the taste.

Whilst searching for organic materials, she discovered a wholesaler based 25 miles (40 km) away which delivers direct to its customers. The minimum quantities purchased are much higher but the prices are significantly lower than local shops. Rosemary now saves time and effort by using this supplier for all her ingredients. The supplier has pointed out that she could get even better prices if she ordered in greater quantities (about five times what she orders now). Although she is tempted by these low prices, she does not think the volume of sales justifies this.

Her son, who is something of a computer expert, has suggested creating a website to sell the muesli over the Internet. She is not too sure about this but is investigating the possibility and thinking about the consequences. How much would it cost to set up? What would the minimum delivery size have to be? How much extra would customers be prepared to pay for postage and packing? Could she cope if demand surged? How much would she need to sell to break even? Are there any 'hidden' costs?

In a two-and-a-half-hour session, she makes 12 kg of muesli. The product is packed in individual 500 g bags and special scales are needed to ensure the weight is accurate. (To ensure no bag is underweight, each one is slightly overfilled.) The Internet orders would be for a 'parcel' of seven bags. She thinks the website would last for about five years before a complete overhaul would be necessary. Although it is a few years old, she could use her present computer, but she would need to purchase broadband access. The current selling price is £2.00 a bag to her retail outlets who sell it to their customers for £3.00 a bag. For the Internet business, direct to the consumer, she thinks she will charge £21.00 a parcel (7 bags @ £3.00).

Whilst doing this exercise, Rosemary realises that she does not know what her current breakeven point is and decides to calculate it. Also, it will serve as a useful comparison to the proposed Internet business. She does not use a computer for the local farm shop business and she uses her own car to deliver orders. It is difficult to be precise but she estimates that her average delivery is 12 bags, takes one hour and costs her £1.80 in petrol. She has recently purchased the scales and bag-sealing machine. Her costs are shown below.

For all sales:	£
Cereals	0.20/500 g bag
Nuts	0.45/500 g bag
Dried fruits	0.50/500 g bag
Plastic bags and sealing tape	0.01/500 g bag
Labels	0.05/500 g bag
Bag-sealing machine	45.00
Weighing scales	235.00

For Internet sales only:	
Creation of website	250.00
Maintenance of website	50.00 per month
Internet payment company charges	30.00 per month
Broadband access	20.00 per month
Packing materials	0.42/parcel of 3.5 to 4.0 kg
Postage	7.21/parcel of 3.5 to 4.0 kg

At the moment she is only selling about 12 bags a week and wants to expand in order to create more income. Her objective is to make a profit of approximately £10,000 a year by working no more than 20 hours a week for 50 weeks a year on her muesli business.

Tasks:

Without the use of 'organic' labels – Soil Association fee not paid:

1 Calculate the breakeven point of her current 'farm shop' business (in numbers of bags). Assume all sales are through farm shops and Internet sales are zero.

(15 marks)

2 If Internet sales caused the volume to increase sufficiently, the bulk purchase of edible ingredients would be justified, giving a 25% saving on current costs. Calculate the breakeven point (in numbers of bags) if this was so. Assume all sales are over the Internet and farm shop sales are zero.

(15 marks)

3 Assuming the 25% bulk saving was in operation, how many bags would Rosemary need to sell in order to make a profit of £10,000 a year? Assume all sales are over the Internet and farm shop sales are zero.

(15 marks)

With the use of 'organic' labels only – Soil Association fee paid:

4 Repeat task 1.

(5 marks)

5 Repeat task 2.

(5 marks)

6 Repeat task 3.

(5 marks)

General

7 Advise Rosemary about the possible expansion of her business to achieve her desired level of profit.

(40 marks)
(Total 100 marks)

Questions

An asterisk * on a question number indicates that the answer is given at the end of the book. Answers to the other questions are given in the Lecturer's Guide.

Q5.1* Bodgit Ltd

Bodgit Ltd makes 200 wooden kitchen chairs every month and sells them for £50 each. Fixed monthly overheads are £3,000 and the standard cost of one chair is as follows:

	£
Materials	15
Direct labour	8
Variable overheads	7

Tasks:

1 Calculate for one month:
   a) the variable cost of one chair
   b) the breakeven point
   c) the profit if 200 chairs are sold
   d) the number of chairs sold to give a profit of £4,000.
2 In an attempt to boost sales, Bodgit plans to reduce the selling price to £48, improve the quality by spending 20% more on materials and increase its advertising by £1,000 a month.
      Calculate:
   a) the new breakeven point
   b) the profit if 350 chairs are sold
   c) the margin of safety (expressed as a % of sales) if 350 chairs are sold
   d) the number of chairs sold to give a profit of £4,000.
3 Explain why your answers to the above questions should be seen as estimates rather than exact answers.

Q5.2* Concord Toy Company

The Concord Toy Company has two separate strategic business units. A draft plan, incorporating a target return on capital employed (ROCE) of 20% per annum, has been created by the managing director. Aware that the toy industry is a volatile one, the board of directors wishes to review the flexibility of the profit forecast shown by the plan. In preparation for the board meeting to discuss the plan, certain questions have been posed for each operating unit (see below).

Operating Unit 1 – novelty pens

This unit produces novelty pens. Most of these are based on popular cartoon characters. Variable costs are taken as raw materials and royalties. All other costs are assumed to be fixed in the short term. The following forecasts have been made:

Selling price per pen	£2
Variable cost per pen	£1.50
Sales revenue	£800,000
Average capital employed	£300,000

Within the output range 300,000 to the maximum capacity of 450,000 pens, the fixed costs are £150,000.

Operating Unit 2 – dolls' accessories

This unit produces three main products – a doll's buggy, a doll's scooter and a doll's personal stereo. In the past, the company has exported most of its products but in its drive to develop home sales, it has recently obtained a contract to supply a national chain store. The store's toy buyer has requested the company to supply a doll's convertible car in addition to its existing products.

Forecast accounts

Product	Buggy	Scooter	Personal stereo	Total
Selling price	£20	£10	£10	
Unit sales (000)	100	100	100	
Sales (£000)	2,000	1,000	1,000	4,000
Variable costs (£000)	600	200	400	1,200
Contribution (£000)	1,400	800	600	2,800
Fixed costs (£000)	700	700	700	2,100
Profit/loss (£000)	700	100	(100)	700

Fixed costs are apportioned on the basis of unit sales. The average capital employed is estimated at £3.6 million. To make a doll's convertible car would require new plant, financed in full by a bank loan.

Tasks re Unit 1:

1 What is the breakeven point in sales volume and value?
2 What is the margin of safety shown by the forecast?
3 Will the operating unit achieve a 20% return on capital employed?
4 What will be the profit if production output increases to maximum capacity? Qualify your answer.
5 How many pens must be sold to make a profit of £60,000?
6 What actions can be taken to improve profitability?

Tasks re Unit 2:

1 Will this operating unit achieve a 20% return on capital employed on the existing sales forecast?
2 If the sales mix remains at equal volumes of the three products, what is the breakeven point in sales volume and value?
3 What will the operating profit be if the sales volume on each product falls
   a) 10% below forecast?
   b) 20% below forecast?
4 Should Concord stop producing and selling the personal stereo?

5   Should the selling price of the personal stereo be increased to £12 to cover the full costs?
6   What further information is required to decide whether or not to make a doll's convertible car?

Q5.3* Rover's 'last chance saloon'

The following comments were broadcast on a television news programme in the first week of February 1999:

> *Rover's future depends on the success of their latest model, codename R75. They intend to attract buyers away from Audi and Volvo to what they describe as the best car they have ever built. They claim to have paid more attention to detail than ever before on this upmarket saloon car. This may be why the launch has been put back from autumn 1998 to the summer of 1999.*
>
> *Selling prices will be a crucial element in their battle for market share and are expected to range from £18,000 to £26,000. Rover say they need to sell 140,000 cars a year to break even and acknowledge that this is a significant challenge. However, this is one test they cannot afford to fail. It is no coincidence that the R75 has been nicknamed 'the last chance saloon'!*

Investigation

Assume:

The retail selling price is £22,000 (average of £18,000 and £26,000)
The trade selling price is 75% of the retail price
The total cost is 80% of the trade selling price
The variable cost is X% of the total cost

Tasks:

1   Calculate the total fixed costs for the R75 project if X is
    a)   50%
    b)   65%
    c)   80%.
    As well as an annual total, express your answers in £/day.
2   Assuming the variable cost is 65% of total cost, how many R75s need to be sold for profit to be £100 million?
3   If 200,000 R75s were sold in the year, assuming the variable cost is 65% of total cost, how much profit would they make?
4   If the total capital employed on the R75 project is £10,000 million and Rover's owners wanted a 20% return on capital employed (ROCE), how many cars would have to be sold?

Q5.4 · SACCUS

SACCUS is a local charity which decides to hold an outdoors fund-raising event in mid-summer. The secretary has a connection with an entertainments company which puts on musical laser light shows for the public. For charities, it charges a reduced rate of

£375 all-inclusive. The venue would be provided free of charge by a local farmer. A barbecue would be put on and the food and drink would be included in the ticket price. It is estimated that the food would cost £2 a head and the drink £1 a head. Also, a special licence for the sale of alcohol would be needed at a cost of £25. Based on the experience of similar events, SACCUS expects to sell 500 tickets at £5 each.

However, the treasurer (who has a degree in business studies) is a little concerned about this plan and proposes an alternative. She suggests hiring a nationally known West Indian steel band at their special rate of £100 plus £50 transport costs. The ticket price would remain at £5 and food would be provided as before. However, no drink would be provided, the audience being invited to bring their own. The number of people attending is expected to be half that for the laser show.

Tasks:

1 Advise SACCUS as to which event it should stage.
2 Illustrate your answer by sketching a contribution breakeven chart for each event.

Q5.5 Royal Hotel

Jim Culf is the manager of the Royal Hotel, Bigtown-on-Sea. In anticipation of preparing next year's budget, he has analysed his recent costs and income. His findings are summarised below.

	£/week
Staff salaries	2,000
Head office charge	400
Depreciation of equipment and fittings	875
Heating	425

For each guest the average variable cost of food, drink, linen and sundries totals £100 per week. Jim considers all other overheads to be semi-variable and has produced the following data from his records:

Week no.	Occupancy (no. of guests)	Other overheads (£)
13	75	7,050
14	94	8,200
15	70	6,980
16	61	6,500
17	57	6,350
18	83	7,590
19	85	7,700

The average price charged for a week's stay is £240 per guest. Since it is a seaside hotel, the vast majority of its customers stay for either one or two weeks at a time.

Tasks:

1 Calculate the average number of guests needed each week to avoid making a loss.

2 The hotel can accommodate a maximum of 120 people. How much is the weekly profit if the average occupancy level is
   a) 70%?
   b) 80%?
   c) 90%?
3 Jim has been invited by an international tour company to quote a competitive price for a group of 20 Japanese tourists who wish to stay in the area for two weeks. They are due to arrive in 10 days' time.
   a) Calculate the lowest price Jim can quote if he is to avoid making a loss on the tour. (Assume that the hotel is currently 70% booked for the two weeks in question.)
   b) If Jim wants to make a profit of £2,000 from this tour, what price should he quote?

Q5.6 Hughes Healthfoods

Hughes Healthfoods makes and sells two types of diet supplement, Slim Quick (SQ) and Healthy Living (HL). It has a single production line on which the two products are made alternately in batches. Some details from next year's budget are shown below:

Product	Unit selling price (£)	Unit variable cost (£)	Annual sales volume (units)
SQ	5.00	2.00	800,000
HL	9.00	4.00	200,000

The annual total fixed cost is £2.9 million and the production facility has an absolute maximum capacity of 1.1 million units a year.

Tasks:

1 Calculate the budgeted profit.
2 Determine the breakeven point. (Assume the budgeted sales mix is stable throughout the year.)
3 Is it possible for the business to double its profit whilst maintaining the budgeted sales mix?
4 Is it possible for the business to double its profit if the budgeted sales mix changed to two SQs being sold for every HL?

Short-term decisions using variable costing

Chapter contents

Introduction

Suppose you were a director of a well-known international passenger airline whose main route was London–New York. You operate this route with a fleet of several large aircraft, each with a capacity to carry 450 passengers. However, due to the number of competitors flying the same route, there is much surplus capacity and your aircraft often fly with more than 100 of their seats empty. Your standard return fare is £500, which is based on the total cost of £400 per available seat plus a 25% profit margin. The £400 total cost includes items such as depreciation of aircraft, fuel, on-board food and drink for passengers, rent of airport facilities, staff pay, training and administration costs.

Unexpectedly, a well-known holiday company offers to purchase 50 seats on every one of your flights for the next six weeks but is only willing to pay £100 a seat – only one-quarter of the total cost! What would your response be? Would you, politely but firmly, inform the holiday company that its offer is far too low or would you accept gladly and get the contract signed as soon as possible?

To solve this problem, you need to think about how your net income would change if you accepted the offer. Obviously, your revenue would increase by £100 for each of the 50 seats. But what about your costs? Which of the costs listed in the previous paragraph would increase? Most of them would not change at all! Only the cost of the on-board food and drink for passengers would increase. If this costs £10 per person, you would be increasing your net income by £90 a seat or £4,500 per return flight. If there were 100 flights during the six-week period, the net income from the contract would be

£450,000. This is the case even though each seat is sold at £300 less than total cost. This is because most of the costs are 'fixed' and only the food and drink are 'variable' (see Chapter 1 on cost behaviour if you do not understand this). Your positive decision to accept the offer is based on your knowledge of variable costing and your company is nearly half a million pounds better off because of it! An understanding of variable costing will enable you to make similar, good, profitable decisions in your business career.

Note: This use of variable costing for short-term decision making is also known as *contribution analysis*.

Learning objectives

Having worked through this chapter you should be able to:
- **advise whether or not to cease certain activities;**
- **advise on the order of production when one of the resources used is scarce;**
- **advise whether or not to accept one-off contracts;**
- **advise whether to produce or buy in components used in your products;**
- **discuss the limitations of decision making using variable costing.**

Cessation of activities

The previous chapter dealt with the application of variable costing to breakeven analysis. We will now concentrate on commercial decision making in the short term, i.e. the immediate future. This aspect of variable costing is also known as *contribution analysis*. Four typical situations will be considered.

The first situation is where a financial analysis shows that a product line or profit centre is making a net loss and a proposal is made to close it down. A contribution analysis is performed to confirm or deny this course of action.

Provided the selling price of a product is greater than its variable cost, each sale will create a positive contribution towards the organisation's fixed costs. This is so even when the product is making a net loss. Cessation of that product would mean that fewer of the fixed costs were covered **and the loss would be greater than before**. Remember that fixed costs are, by definition, costs which do not change with the level of activity, even if that level falls to zero. In other words, fixed costs cannot be eliminated **in the short term**.

Take the example of the Top Ski Holiday Company, which offers specialist skiing holidays in Norway, Spain and Italy. A financial analysis of last season in which 3,000 holidays were sold (1,000 for each country) shows the following:

	Norway	Italy	Spain	Total
	£000			
Total cost	950	700	450	2,100
Sales revenue	700	650	800	2,150
Net profit	(250)	(50)	350	50

The company would like to increase its selling prices but believes this to be unwise as its competitors are offering very similarly priced holidays in those countries. Alternatively, it has been suggested that if the Norwegian and Italian holidays for next season were withdrawn (starting in the near future) Top Ski would increase its profits from £50,000 to £350,000 by eliminating the losses for those two countries. This is based on the reasonable assumption that 1,000 holidays will continue to be sold for Spain.

A more detailed examination of the financial analysis reveals that the total fixed costs for last season were £600,000. These were for items such as brochures, advertising, directors' salaries and head office administration costs. These fixed costs were spread evenly over all the holidays. As 3,000 holidays had been sold, fixed costs of £200 (£600,000/3,000) were absorbed into each holiday. A contribution analysis of the above figures reveals the following:

| | | £000 | | | |
		Norway	Italy	Spain	All
	Total cost	950	700	450	2,100
Less:	Total fixed costs	200	200	200	600
	Variable cost	750	500	250	1,500
	Sales revenue	700	650	800	2,150
	Contribution	(50)	150	550	650
Less:	Total fixed costs				600
	Net profit				50

If the Norwegian and Italian holidays did cease, the analysis would change as follows:

| | | £000 | | | |
		Norway	Italy	Spain	All
	Contribution	0	0	550	550
Less:	Total fixed costs				600
	Net profit/(Loss)				(50)

So, instead of the profit increasing by £300,000, it would actually decrease by £100,000 to give a net **loss** of £50,000. The situation would be much worse than if no action had been taken and the Norwegian and Italian holidays sold as before.

The contribution analysis shows that although the Italian holidays are making a loss, they are still making a positive contribution to the company's fixed costs. However, the Norwegian holidays are making a negative rather than positive contribution. Every time one of these is sold the company loses money it otherwise would not lose. Thus, it does seem a good idea to cease the Norwegian holidays.

If this happened and the Italian holidays continued, the analysis would be as follows:

| | | £000 | | | |
		Norway	Italy	Spain	All
	Contribution	0	150	550	700
Less:	Total fixed costs				600
	Net profit				100

The rule is, in order to improve profitability, cease activities with negative contributions. (This assumes that these negative contributions cannot be made positive in the short term.)

Of course, **in the long term**, maybe the fixed costs could be reduced or maybe an alternative holiday venue could be found. In the long term **anything** is possible. However, for short-term decisions, the correct course of action comes from a contribution analysis. Although a sudden cessation of the Norwegian and Italian holidays seemed a reasonable proposition at first sight, it would have been a disaster for Top Ski Holidays if they had both been withdrawn.

From a business point of view, other aspects of the situation should always be taken into account. In particular, are the products interrelated? Consider a company selling three products: a basic food processor, a grating attachment and a coffee grinding attachment. Suppose the company stops making the coffee grinder because the accounting system shows that it is making a loss while the other two items are making a profit. Those potential customers who would have bought the processor and the grinder will not now do so. As the products are interdependent, sales of related items will be lost. Suppose it was the processor making the loss instead of the grinder. Anyone suggesting that production of the processor should cease should be asking themselves if they are in the right job.

Self-assessment question S6.1

Try the following question for yourself (answer at the end of the chapter).

The V&A Group is made up of four operating subsidiaries: A, B, C and D. Its corporate accounting system has produced the following figures which show the group has made a loss of £1,000. Analyse them and state which operations (if any) you would recommend for closure in order to return the group to profitability.
Summarised profit and loss accounts for last year (£000):

	A	B	C	D	Group
Sales	180	420	500	900	2,000
Raw materials	41	95	202	370	708
Direct labour	62	89	37	105	293
Direct cost	103	184	239	475	1,001
Gross profit	77	236	261	425	999
Total overheads	90	210	250	450	1,000
Net profit	(13)	26	11	(25)	(1)

Note: Fixed overheads have been apportioned according to the amount of sales revenue from each operation. Overheads are considered to be 90% variable and 10% fixed.

Tasks:

a) State which operations you recommend closing and why.
b) What would the group's profit be if your recommendations were actioned?
c) What would the group's profit be if A and D were closed?

Scarce resources

The usual factor limiting an organisation's activities is the number of products it can sell. However, occasionally, a shortage of something it uses in its operations means that it cannot sell as many items as it otherwise would have. The item in short supply is known as a *scarce resource*. It is usually either a raw material or a particular type of specialised labour. For example, if there were an unforeseen shortage of crude oil due to some international dispute, the refining companies would not be able to make as much petrol as they could normally sell. In this case, in order to maximise profits, they would concentrate on the products which gave them the largest amount of contribution per barrel of oil.

The highest contribution might come from high-octane kerosene for jet engines. When the refining companies had produced all the aviation fuel that they could sell, they would concentrate on the product with the next-highest contribution per barrel, which might be unleaded petrol for cars. If there were any crude oil left after this, they would choose the next-highest-contribution product, and so on. In this way, they would ensure that they made the best use of every barrel of crude oil, i.e. every unit of their scarce resource. Here is a numerical example.

The following information has been extracted from the budget of Lonestar Petroleum:

	Contribution per 000 litres (£)	Barrels of crude per 000 litres	Sales forecast for month 5 (000 litres)	Quantity required (barrels)
Unleaded petrol	15.00	4.0	35,000	140,000
Diesel	12.00	3.0	18,000	54,000
Kerosene	20.00	4.0	8,000	32,000
Paraffin	8.00	5.0	7,000	35,000
				261,000

Due to an unexpected worldwide shortage of oil, the quota of crude oil available to Lonestar for month 5 has been set at 200,000 barrels.

Obviously, Lonestar will not be able to make all it planned to in month 5; it is 61,000 barrels short. One answer is to cut back production of all products pro rata but this would not maximise its profits. As crude oil is scarce, it needs to maximise the profit from each barrel. This is done by producing the highest-contribution-per-barrel product first, then the next-highest, etc. **Lonestar needs to put its products into order according to their *contribution per unit of scarce resource* and produce in this order.**

Care must be exercised here for the contributions shown in the budget information are per thousand litres of finished product, not per unit of scarce resource which is a barrel of crude oil. To solve the problem, the contributions per barrel of crude oil must be calculated for each of the four products.

	Contribution per 000 litres (£)	Order	Barrels of crude per 000 litres	Contribution per barrel (£)	Order
Kerosene	20.00	1	4.0	20/4 = 5.00	1
Unleaded petrol	15.00	2	4.0	15/4 = 3.75	3
Diesel	12.00	3	3.0	12/3 = 4.00	2
Paraffin	8.00	4	5.0	8/5 = 1.60	4

So, the order of production would be kerosene, diesel, unleaded petrol and paraffin, until the quota of crude oil was all used up. Production in this new order gives the following results:

	Order	Quantity required (barrels)	Cumulative quantity (barrels)	Actual quantity (barrels)	Contribution/ barrel (£)	Total contribution (£)
Kerosene	1	32,000	32,000	32,000	5.00	160,000
Diesel	2	54,000	86,000	54,000	4.00	216,000
Unleaded petrol	3	140,000	226,000	114,000	3.75	427,500
Paraffin	4	35,000	261,000	–		–
		261,000		200,000		803,500

It is clear from the cumulative column that not all the unleaded petrol and none of the paraffin will be able to be produced. The total contribution for month 5 is £803,500. After the kerosene has been produced in full, any other order of production will give a smaller total contribution (and so a smaller profit). To prove this, the following table shows the result of producing in the incorrect order of contribution per thousand litres of output:

	Order	Quantity required (barrels)	Cumulative quantity (barrels)	Actual quantity (barrels)	Contribution/ barrel (£)	Total contribution (£)
Kerosene	1	32,000	32,000	32,000	5.00	160,000
Unleaded petrol	2	140,000	172,000	140,000	3.75	525,000
Diesel	3	54,000	226,000	28,000	4.00	112,000
Paraffin	4	35,000	261,000	–		–
		261,000		200,000		797,000

This total contribution is £6,500 lower than before.

The decision-making rule here is to produce in the order of the highest **contribution per unit of scarce resource** until it is used up.

From a business point of view, other aspects of the situation should always be taken into account. Are the sales of the products related? Would the lack of paraffin cause any customers to purchase their petrol or diesel elsewhere? These are not easy questions to answer but in-depth knowledge of the customers should go a long way in arriving at the correct answers.

*Self-assessment
question S6.2*

Try the following question for yourself (answer at the end of the chapter).

Your company manufactures three products, Alpha, Beta and Gamma. The following information refers to next month:

	Alpha	Beta	Gamma
Sales demand (units)	50	150	200
Raw materials/unit	£100	£150	£80
Direct labour hours/unit	5	10	2
Fixed overheads/unit	£30	£60	£12

Direct labour is paid at £3.00 per hour. Variable overhead is equal to 10% of the cost of materials. Fixed overheads are attached to the products at the rate of 200% of the total direct labour cost. The selling price is calculated by doubling the prime cost (= total direct cost).

Tasks:

1 Calculate the contribution per unit for each product and rank them.
2 Using the ranking from the previous answer, prepare a forecast of the profit for each product and in total for next month if only 1,650 direct labour hours are available.
3 Calculate the contribution per direct labour hour for each product and rank them.
4 Using the ranking from the previous answer, prepare a forecast of the profit for each product and in total for next month if only 1,650 direct labour hours are available.
5 Quantify the difference between the answers to 2. and 4. and comment on your findings.

One-off contracts

Occasionally, in addition to their 'normal' business, organisations are offered work which is of a 'one-off' nature. Take the example of Goodtime Holiday Centre plc (GHC) whose normal business is to provide package holidays in the UK at its custom-built holiday village in Cornwall. All accommodation, meals and entertainment are included in the holiday price, which averages £350 per person per week. The centre can accommodate a maximum of approximately 500 people and holidays are offered between the beginning of May and the end of September. The winter months are taken up with maintenance and new projects. GHC has been approached by an international charity to provide a one-week holiday for 500 refugee children during the last week of April. The charity is willing to pay a total of £50,000 (£100 per child). In deciding whether to accept the offer, GHC must bear in mind its duty to its shareholders to maximise their wealth.

The following information is from GHC's management accounting system and is used to determine its holiday prices.

Annual costs	£000	£000
Marketing and advertising	600	
Depreciation of equipment, vehicles, etc.	538	
Administration staff (permanent)	132	
Insurance	80	
Local rates	90	
		1,440
Holiday season* costs		
Other staff (temporary)	470	
Food and drink	310	
Other holiday running costs	120	
		900
Total		2,340

* The holiday season lasts for 20 weeks.

The total cost of providing one week's holiday = £2,340,000/20 = £117,000
The price for one week's holiday offered by the charity = 500 × £100 = £50,000
It may appear that acceptance of the proposition will lead to a loss of = £67,000

However, before a decision is made, GHC should calculate the **contribution** arising from this one-off proposal.

Variable costs of special holiday:

	£000	
Other staff (temporary)	470	
Food and drink	310	
Other holiday running costs	120	
	£000	
Total variable costs for 20 weeks	900	
Total variable costs for 1 week	45	(900/20)
Total sales revenue from the charity	50	
Contribution for the special holiday week	+ 5	(50 – 45)

GHC should accept the offer because **profit will increase by £5,000.**

This positive contribution means that GHC will not be £67,000 worse off by agreeing to the special holiday but will, in fact, be **£5,000 better off.** This is because the remaining costs of £1,440,000 are **fixed** and will occur whether the special holiday goes ahead or not. If the fixed costs do not affect the financial outcome, they should not be used to make the decision. The fixed costs are absorbed into, and recovered by, the sales revenue from the 'normal holidays'.

The decision-making rule for one-off propositions is that **they should be accepted if they have a positive contribution and rejected if they do not.**

From a business point of view, other aspects of the situation should always be taken into account. For example, if the contract is a trial for a possible much larger order to follow, it should be made clear to the customer that the price is also a one-off and will not be sustainable in the long term. Also, any possible effects on normal sales should be considered. If a regular customer finds out that you have produced and sold a very similar product to the one it purchases from you but at a lower price for someone else, the customer may insist on renegotiating the price. The customer may even place future orders with a competitor.

Self-assessment question S6.3

Try the following question for yourself (answer at the end of the chapter).

a) Abacus Inc. is a small one-product firm which plans to make and sell 1,000 ornamental abacuses a year at a price of $250 each. How much profit does Abacus expect to make in a year if the standard cost of one abacus is as follows?

	$/unit
Materials	100
Direct labour	25
Variable overheads	20
Variable cost	145
Fixed cost (based on a budget of 1,000)	75
Total cost	220

b) An export order is received for 200 abacuses modified by the addition of some semi-precious stones. The effect of this is a 30% increase in the cost of materials and a 40% increase in the cost of direct labour. Also, special export insurance will cost $5 for each modified abacus shipped. However, the customer is not willing to pay more than $44,000 in total for this large order. Should Abacus Inc. accept this order?

Make or buy

Products and services are often made up of several component parts. A CD-player consists of an amplifier, motor, speakers, laser and casing. A holiday may consist of travel, accommodation, courier, food and drink. Businesses have a choice of creating these components themselves or buying them in from outside. Some very successful companies buy a significant proportion of their components from 'outside' companies. The world-leaders in aero engines, Rolls-Royce, buy in about 75% of parts included in their turbine-driven engines, enabling it to concentrate on the technology-critical areas. When reviewing their costs, organisations should compare the cost of making each component to that of buying it in. Sometimes, they are offered the chance of buying a component instead of making it. How should they decide?

Take the example of a meals-on-wheels service run by a local authority. It provides 100,000 meals a year from kitchens also used to prepare school dinners. Its costings for the meals-on-wheels service are as follows:

	£
Depreciation of kitchen equipment*	20,000
Depreciation of delivery vehicles	30,000
Catering staff wages*	30,000
Drivers' wages	90,000
Food and drink	50,000
Vehicle running costs	80,000
Total cost	300,000

* Based on proportion of total time used for meals-on-wheels.

An independent firm of caterers has offered to cook all the meals on its own premises and provide them to the authority for £0.90 each.

The cost of preparing the meals is

	£
Depreciation of kitchen equipment	20,000
Catering staff wages	30,000
Food and drink	50,000
Total cost	100,000

As 100,000 meals are provided a year, each one costs £1.00 (£100,000/100,000). This is £0.10 more than the price being offered by the outside caterers, whose offer looks very attractive in this light. However, in order to make the best decision, the **variable** costs should be determined as they will be the only ones that change if the offer is accepted.

Assuming the number of part-time catering staff and the hours they work can be easily adjusted, the variable cost of meals-on-wheels is

	£
Catering staff wages	30,000
Food and drink	50,000
Total variable cost	80,000

As 100,000 meals are provided a year, each one has a variable cost of £0.80 (£80,000/100,000). The fixed cost of kitchen depreciation will now have to be borne in full by the school dinners.

If the authority accepts the offer, it will be £10,000 worse off than before. This is because the offer price is £0.10 greater than the variable cost per meal. So the authority should not accept the offer.

The decision rule for make-or-buy situations is that **a component should be bought in only if its price is below the variable cost of producing it.**

From a business point of view, other aspects of the situation should always be taken into account. Will the supply of components be adequate and reliable? Will the quality of components be satisfactory? Will the price of components escalate in future? How easy would it be to start making the components again if the buying-in arrangement goes wrong?

Self-assessment
question S6.4

Try the following question for yourself (answer at the end of the chapter).

Vendco manufactures a variety of vending machines which have a number of common components. As part of a cost review, Vendco has found an external supplier who will supply it with one of these parts (which has a standard cost of £90 – see below) for £75.

	£
Direct labour	25
Direct materials	30
Variable overheads	5
Fixed overhead	30
Standard cost	90

Advise Vendco whether it should continue to make this part or to buy it in at £75.

Limitations of short-term decision making using variable costing

All the above decision-making techniques have been used strictly within the confines of the variable costing model. This is the accounting part of decision making. It provides a good basis for solving the problem. However, do not forget that making decisions is essentially a management function. The role of accountancy is to provide good information to help managers make the right decisions. Remember, the reality of the situation being faced is always more complex than the assumptions from which the financial model is constructed.

The next chapter, on relevant costing, builds on what you have learnt in this chapter. It, also, is about making decisions but its context is widened to include any other effects caused by those decisions. For example, your contribution analysis may indicate that you should stop making one of your products. However, this may cause a significant number of redundancies to be made at a cost of hundreds of thousands of pounds. Whereas the variable costing model would not take this into account, relevant costing would include the redundancy costs because its boundary of cause and effect is so much wider. To find out more, have a look at the next chapter.

The manager's point of view

Like most manufacturing concerns, my chemical company carried out periodic business reviews to consider withdrawing products which were no longer generating a satisfactory profit. There are many reasons why profitability might be in decline on individual items – perhaps a mature product has reached the end of its natural life, and been superseded by new technology, or fierce competition from Far Eastern suppliers has caused prices to fall to uneconomic levels. Management had to decide whether there was any course of action which would bring these products back into profitability, or whether they should be terminated, to allow the company to concentrate its resources on the newer, more profitable products.

The decision often hinged on the impact of a product's withdrawal on the recovery of fixed overhead. If a product is making a marginal loss (i.e. its variable cost is greater than its selling price) and therefore making no contribution to fixed overhead, the decision is simple. But if the product is making a marginal profit, although not enough to cover all the overheads attributed to it by the costing system, the decision is rather more complicated. If it is terminated, and there is no accompanying reduction in fixed overhead, the contribution will be lost and the company will be worse off. The fixed overhead attributed to the product will simply be reallocated to the next product. This may then become unprofitable as well, and be terminated in its turn, and so it goes on, until the domino effect wipes out the business! In the short term, fixed overheads cannot easily be reduced, so it may well be wise to persevere with the product until longer-term actions can be taken.

In this situation, variable costing is clearly crucial in preventing you from making inappropriate short-term decisions, although you will still have uncovered a problem which needs resolution in the longer term, probably by fixed overhead reductions. The decision to terminate a product is a long-term issue, which will change the future shape of the business. However, variable costing is also valuable in assessing the appropriateness of temporary actions, as a situation in our chemical factory demonstrates.

One of our plants made a high-volume product for use in the paper industry. The plant had been built in the 1970s, and despite one or two capacity improvements, the demand had grown so much by the late 1980s that we were unable to cope, even with continuous shift working. At this point, we were faced with two options: we could increase capacity by building a second plant, or we could concentrate our existing resources on the most profitable pieces of business. An analysis of the business showed that some of the sales generated a relatively low marginal income, and that by eliminating these and accepting only the higher margin business, the profitability of the group would continue to rise.

This strategy was successful in the short term, and profitability improved. But it was an unsatisfactory way to run a business. Nobody likes to turn away business. It alienates the customer and sends them to the competition. The rejected business may have been at a lower margin, but it was still making a reasonable contribution to profit. The problem was that, at the time, there was insufficient business available to justify the cost of building a new plant. Fortunately, this changed over a period of time, and the growth in demand of both high- and low-margin business reached a point where the numbers started to add up. Accordingly, a new plant was built, doubling the capacity.

Now we had another problem. We had too much capacity for the present demand, and our sales projections showed that we would not be able to fill the plant for several years. At this point we had an enquiry from a large paper company, which needed a volume of product which roughly equated to 30% of our new plant's capacity. The margin on this product was lower than we would normally have accepted, but after much debate, we concluded that it did indeed make a positive contribution towards both fixed overheads and labour, which would otherwise have remained idle. We therefore accepted the business.

Such decisions are not as easy to make as they may seem. There are both quantifiable and unquantifiable issues to take into account. For instance, how fixed is the labour? If we do not accept this business, can we switch the labour on to cheaper single shifts, or is the volume of other business sufficient to require continuous shift-working anyway? What is the impact on the cover provided by other departments, such as maintenance, quality control or the canteen? What about the level of raw material and finished goods stocks that will be needed, with the consequent warehousing and interest costs? Are we happy that the product costs on which we are basing this significant decision are sufficiently accurate in the first place? We certainly do not want to discover too late that the new business is actually draining profit from the company. And there are also the less quantifiable issues to consider, such as the extent of management input required, or the impact on the company's ability to accept unexpected, but more profitable orders that may arise in the near future.

Once you have decided that it is in your company's interests to accept low-margin business, it is imperative that all parties are fully aware of the implications. Our American parent used marginal income percentage as one of the key measurements of our group's performance. The inclusion of a substantial piece of low-margin business naturally caused the marginal income percentage to decline, so it was important to ensure that the parent understood both the rationale and the effect of it, and that, if we chose not to do the business the following year, the parent would understand the reasons for a fluctuating sales line.

Such business should always be regarded as a one-off, separate piece of business which is outside the normal course of the company's activities. The business does not cover its share of the overheads, and is therefore technically unprofitable. We only consider accepting it when the overheads are already covered by other more profitable business. If there were a temptation to repeat this low-margin business year after year, perhaps a more advantageous course of action for the company would be to pursue a reduction in the level of fixed overheads.

There is also a risk in accepting low-margin business, in that it might encourage salespeople to chase more and more of it. After all, isn't any sale with a positive marginal income making a contribution towards overhead? Well, maybe, if you are a supermarket, where high sales volumes may well compensate for low margins and be sufficient to generate a satisfactory return. In manufacturing companies, however, capacity constraints will tend to limit the opportunity for substantial volume increases, so primary concentration on high-margin business is essential.

Summary

- Cease activities only if there is a negative contribution.
- Produce in the order of 'contribution per unit of scarce resource'.
- Decide whether to accept one-off contracts on the basis of their contribution.
- Buy in components if their price is less than the variable cost of manufacturing.
- Do not forget to take into account the factors outside the variable costing model. (The next chapter looks at this in greater depth.)

Further reading

Horngren, C., Bhimani, A., Datar, S. and Foster, G. (2002) *Management and Cost Accounting*, 2nd edition, Prentice Hall Europe, Harlow. See Chapter 8, 'Cost–volume–profit relationships'.

Upchurch, A. (2003) *Management Accounting, Principles and Practice*, 2nd edition, Financial Times/Prentice Hall, Harlow. See chapter 'Cost/volume/profit analysis'.

Weetman, P. (2002) *Management Accounting, an Introduction*, 3rd edition, Financial Times/Prentice Hall, Harlow. See chapter 'Profit measurement and short-term decision making'.

Answers to self-assessment questions

S6.1. V&A Group

	A	B	C	D	Group
Total overheads	90	210	250	450	1,000
Variable overheads (90%)	81	189	225	405	900
Fixed overheads (10%)	9	21	25	45	100
Variable costs					
Raw materials + direct labour	103	184	239	475	1,001
Add: Variable overheads	81	189	225	405	900
Variable costs	184	373	464	880	1,901
Sales income	180	420	500	900	2,000
Contribution	(4)	47	36	20	99

(a) Close factory A only

If A is closed:

	A	B	C	D	Group
Contribution	–	47	36	20	103
Less: Fixed costs					100
(b) Net profit					3

If A and D are closed:

	A	B	C	D	Group
Contribution	–	47	36	–	83
Less: Fixed costs					100
(c) Net loss					(17)

S6.2. Alpha, Beta, Gamma

	Alpha	Beta	Gamma	Total
Direct costs:				
Raw materials	100	150	80	
Direct labour	15	30	6	
Prime cost	115	180	86	
Variable overhead	10	15	8	
Variable cost	125	195	94	
Fixed overhead	30	60	12	
Total cost/unit	155	255	106	
Fixed overhead/unit	30	60	12	
Sales demand (units)	50	150	200	
Total fixed overhead	1,500	9,000	2,400	12,900

1	Alpha	Beta	Gamma	
Selling price	230	360	172	(200% of prime cost)
Variable cost	125	195	94	
Contribution/unit	**105**	**165**	**78**	
Ranking	**2**	**1**	**3**	

2	Alpha	Beta	Gamma	Total
Labour hours/unit	5	10	2	
No. of labour hours	150	1,500	–	1,650
No. of units sold	30	150	–	
Contribution/unit	105	165	78	
Total contribution	3,150	24,750	–	27,900
Less: Fixed costs				12,900
Net profit				**£15,000**

3			
Contribution/unit	105	165	78
Labour hours/unit	5	10	2
Contribution/labour hour	**21.0**	**16.5**	**39.0**
Ranking	**2**	**3**	**1**

4				Total
Labour hours/unit	5	10	2	
No. of labour hours	250	1,000	400	1,650
No. of units sold	50	100	200	
Contribution/unit	105	165	78	
Total contribution	5,250	16,500	15,600	37,350
Less: Fixed costs				12,900
Net profit				**£24,450**

5 Using the contribution per direct labour hour ranking gives £9,450 more profit than the contribution per unit ranking. So, using the contribution per unit of scarce resource does give the highest profit.

S6.3. Abacus Inc.

(a) Normal activity

	$
Sales price	250
Variable cost	145
Contribution	105/unit

$$\text{Total contribution} = 1,000 \times \$105 = 105,000$$
$$\text{Less: Fixed costs} = 1,000 \times \$75 = 75,000$$
Net profit $= \$30,000$

(b) Export order

	$
Materials	130 ($100 + 30%)
Direct labour	35 ($25 + 40%)
Variable overheads	20
Export insurance	5
Variable cost	190/unit
Sales price	220 ($44,000/200)
Contribution	+30/unit

Total contribution $= + \$6,000$ (200 × $30)

Recommend acceptance of the export order as it has a positive contribution.

S6.4. Vendco

Compare the relevant variable costs of manufacture with the buying-in cost. Remember that fixed overheads will still have to be paid for in the short term so these are irrelevant to the decision.

	£
Variable production costs	
Direct labour	25
Direct materials	30
Variable overheads	5
Total	60
Buy-in price	75

Therefore, buying in is not recommended (in the short term).

Sara Wray Enterprises

Sara Wray lives in the Cotswolds, an area of outstanding natural beauty in central–southwest England. She started her working life as a teacher of French and art but, after several years, she gave this up to have a family. As her children grew older, she went back to work on a part-time basis, not as a teacher but as an administrator of a local art gallery. Her children are now adults with jobs of their own and Sara is the driving force behind a successful business offering language tuition and cultural holidays to non-UK residents.

Her business actually started seven years ago when she decided to gain a Teaching English as a Foreign Language (TEFL) qualification. Having achieved this, she provided English language tuition to foreign students in the summer months. Two students would come to stay in her home at any one time, receiving formal tuition in the morning and going out for visits to local places of interest in the afternoon and evenings with Sara. During her first summer season, she had a total of nine students, eight staying for two weeks and one staying for one month. This was a total of 20 student-weeks' tuition. She established a good reputation and the number of students grew each year.

After a few years, Sara branched out by offering one-week Tours of the Cotswolds for groups of approximately 16 adults without any formal language tuition element. Her success with these tours is based on her organisational ability and her experience of arranging local trips for her language students. As well as general tours, she now offers two special-ised ones: English Gardens and Arts and Crafts. Sara still sees her English language courses as the basis of her operations as many of her tours include some people who have been students of hers or have been recommended by them. However, most of her tour cus-tomers come from her advertisements in France, Holland, Germany, Italy and Spain.

Current demand for her TEFL courses is such that she now employs seven other qualified teachers, each taking two students at a time. The students live in the teachers' homes and are taught there in the mornings but join together for the visits and eat out together each evening at a different venue. For these outings, Sara hires an 18-seater minibus and driver for her 12-week season (mid-June to mid-September). Her non-tuition tours start in May and finish in October but do not take place every week. These tour customers stay in local hotels which are block-booked in advance by Sara. She hires the same type of minibus and driver for her tour parties and she also hires a guide to accompany them.

Up to now, there has been no difficulty finding guides of the right quality. Unfortunately, her regular garden tour guide, Rose, is about to move to Paris due to her partner's unexpected relocation and will no longer be available to guide these tours. However, one of the TEFL teachers, Mary, is also an expert gardener and has volunteered her services as garden tour guide. As Mary speaks reasonably good French, Spanish and German, she would be an ideal choice for this job. But the two planned garden tours are scheduled to take place during the TEFL season and Sara would have to find a replacement teacher for those weeks. Most of the other good TEFL teachers living in the area have contracted with the many English language schools based in nearby Oxford and Sara is finding it impossible to find a suitable replacement. As the season is just about to start, it looks as though Sara will have to cancel either two teacher-weeks of English tuition or two one-week garden tours. She is unsure whether to use Mary as a TEFL teacher or a garden tour guide.

Whilst she is pondering this dilemma, Sara receives a letter from one of her previous students, Michael, who lives in Munich. Michael wants Sara to arrange a one-week 'Beer and Brewing' tour to include five beer-related visits for himself and 15 of his friends. When he was brushing up his English last year with Sara, he was very impressed with several local beers he tasted in the Cotswold area. He is offering to pay Sara £5,600 (16 @ £350 per person) for local accommodation, food, transport, brewery visit fees and knowledgeable guide. He will organise the travel between Munich and the Cotswolds.

Sara's friend, David, is a member of the Campaign for Real Ale (CamRA) and says that he would be willing to give up a week of his holidays to guide this tour for £500. Sara estimates admission fees at £650 and other costs the same as for a general or gardens tour. She does not see any reason why this tour should not go ahead. The only thing concerning her is that the price offered seems so low that the tour will make a loss. The lowest cost of her other tours is £6,000 (see below). She thinks she will probably have to contact Michael and refuse his offer.

As well as all this, she notices that the financial analysis prepared by her accountant shows that, although the general and gardens tours are profitable, the arts and crafts tours are making a loss (see below). Although they are more costly to run, she is reluctant to drop them but, on the other hand, does not want to run any of her activities at a loss. She is reluctant to increase her prices as she is aware of a firm in nearby Oxford which offers very similar arts tours at the price of £385 per person.

Sara wants to increase her profit next year by at least £3,000 by expanding either the English teaching or the tours but she is unsure what she needs to do to achieve this.

Financial analysis of TEFL activities

Maximum activity for season is 8 teachers for 12 weeks = 96 teacher-weeks
Each teacher has two students each week. Each student pays £400/week
Fixed costs (minibus hire, insurance, advertising, etc.) for TEFL total £19,200

For one teacher-week	£
2 hours' tuition/day for 5 days = 10 h @ £15/h =	150
Agent's commission, 2 students @ £25 =	50
Accommodation, 5 nights @ £20 × 2 students =	200
Evening meals, £5 × 2 students × 5 days =	50
Admission fees, £5 × 2 students × 5 days =	50
Total variable cost =	500
Fixed cost (£19,200/12 weeks/8 teachers) =	200
Total cost =	700
Sales revenue (2 @ £400) =	800
Net profit =	100

Financial analysis of tour activities

Tours planned: 3 general, 2 gardens and 2 arts and crafts
Maximum of 16 per tour, each person paying £400
Fixed costs (administration, insurance, advertising, etc.) for tours totals £12,810

Per tour (16 people)	General/Gardens £	Arts and Crafts £
Minibus and driver	800	800
Guide fees	350	500
Hotel, bed, breakfast & evening meal	2,620	2,620
Admission fees	400	800
Total variable costs	4,170	4,720
Fixed costs	1,830	1,830
Total cost	6,000	6,550
Sales revenue (16 × £400)	6,400	6,400
Net profit	400	(150)

Tasks:

Advise Sara on the decisions facing her:

1   Is it better to use Mary as a garden tour guide or English teacher for two weeks?

(25 marks)

2   Should she decline Michael's offer of £5,600 for a Beer and Brewing tour?

(25 marks)

3   Should she stop offering the Arts and Crafts tours?

(25 marks)

4   Next year, should she expand the English teaching or the tours?

(25 marks)
(Total 100 marks)

Questions

An asterisk * on a question number indicates that the answer is given at the end of the book. Answers to the other questions are given in the Lecturer's Guide.

Q6.1* Burgabar Corporation

Burgabar Corporation owns and operates a range of fast food outlets throughout the East End of London. A summary of next year's budget (before head office costs are taken into account) is given below:

Branch	Sales revenue £	Variable costs £	Salaries & wages £	Fixed costs £
West Ham	100,000	20,000	32,000	30,000
Hackney	120,000	24,000	32,000	30,000
Forest Gate	120,000	24,000	34,000	32,000
Mile End	140,000	28,000	34,000	34,000

The administrative head office of Burgabar Corporation is at Epping. Its running costs of £96,000 a year are apportioned to branches on the basis of sales revenue.

Concern is being expressed about the West Ham branch as it is showing a loss (after head office costs have been deducted). One director has suggested that the branch is closed as soon as possible and a new branch opened, possibly in the Ilford area. However, it would take approximately 12 months to open a new branch. The closure of the West Ham branch would reduce head office costs by £10,000 p.a. with immediate effect. Also, although West Ham's salaries and wages bill would disappear immediately, redundancy pay of £8,000 would be payable.

Task:

Advise the directors of Burgabar Corporation.

Q6.2* Profoot Ltd

Profoot currently makes and sells two types of protective shoe, model P1 and model P2.

	P1	P2
Annual sales demand (pairs)	14,000	10,000
Selling price	£40	£40
Variable costs per pair:		
Materials	£15	£15
Labour – Machining (£8/hour)	£2	£2
– Assembly (£7/hour)	£3.50	£3.50
– Packing (£6/hour)	£0.50	£0.50

Annual total fixed costs are currently £300,000.

For the next financial year, Profoot intends to keep model P1 as it is but to upgrade model P2 by the use of better materials. The materials cost for P2 is expected to be £20 a pair (an increase of £5 a pair) and its new selling price will be £50 a pair. Also, the amount of time spent machining P2s will double and the cost of this will increase to £4 a pair.

Also, next year, Profoot intends to introduce the PDL, a top-of-the-range model with a selling price of £65. Labour costs for machining will be £4 a pair, assembly £7 a pair and packing £0.50 a pair. Materials will cost £32.50 a pair.

Demand for the P1, P2 and PDL next year is predicted to be 14,000, 7,000 and 5,000 pairs respectively. Annual fixed costs are expected to increase by 2% next year.

Tasks:

1 Calculate the annual net profit for the current year.
2 Calculate the annual net profit for next year assuming the predicted demand is met in full.
3 If the maximum number of machine hours available next year is 8,500, create a production plan to maximise net profit. (Clearly show the quantity of each model produced and calculate the net profit.)
4 Profoot could purchase an additional machine costing £420,000 which would last for 10 years and have no residual value at the end of that period. This machine could be used for a maximum of 1,750 hours a year. How would the purchase of this machine affect next year's net profit?

Q6.3* King & Co.

The current annual budget for King & Co., makers of baseball caps, is summarised as follows:

	£000
Sales (1 million caps @ £5 each)	5,000
Less manufacturing cost of caps sold	3,000
Gross margin	2,000
Less sales and administration expenses	1,500
Operating income	500

King's fixed manufacturing costs were £2.0 million and its fixed sales and administration costs were £1.0 million. Sales commission of 5% of sales is included in the sales and administration expenses. It is approaching the end of the current financial year and looks as though it will exceed its budgetary targets.

King's has just been asked by its local first division football club to make a special order of 50,000 caps in the club colours to celebrate their promotion to the Premier league; they are willing to pay £4 a cap. However, a special badge of the club's emblem would have to be made for each cap.

Even though King & Co. has the necessary capacity to produce the order, the managing director has decided to reject the club's offer of £200,000 for the 50,000 caps. He explained his decision by saying, 'The club's offer is too low. I know we would save the sales commission but the badges alone will cost twice as much as that, and it costs us £4.50 to make our ordinary caps. I'm willing to cut our usual 10% profit margin to 5%, or even less, to get this order but I'm not prepared to do it for nothing and I'm certainly not prepared to make a loss on the deal.'

Task:

Comment on the managing director's decision.

Q6.4 Parfumier Jean-Paul

Jean-Paul Cie (J-P) is a world-famous haute-couture fashion house based in Paris. It also manufactures a range of perfumes, all made from secret recipes. Only one ingredient called 'maylarnge', a mixing agent, is used in all their products. Maylarnge is obtained from SML Laboratoire in Brussels and the quantity used varies with the particular perfume recipe.

Due to temporary processing difficulties, SML have informed J-P that it can supply only €13,100 worth of maylarnge over the next three months.

The budget below relates to the quarter in question under normal circumstances. The shortage of the mixing agent means that the budget will have to be revised.

Perfume	Passion	Entice	Magique	Exotique
Sales volume (50 ml bottles)	6,000	5,500	6,500	4,500
Variable costs per bottle	€	€	€	€
Maylarnge	1.00	0.80	1.20	0.60
Ingredients (as per recipe)	2.00	3.10	2.60	1.90
Selling price	12.90	15.70	16.10	14.50

Fixed costs for the quarter amount to €133,300 (including all wages and salaries).

Tasks:

1 What would the quarter's profit be if there was no shortage of maylarnge?
2 Calculate the profit for this period of shortage if the perfumes were manufactured in the order of their contribution per bottle until they ran out of maylarnge.
3 Calculate the revised sales budget and profit assuming J-P wishes to maximise its profit for this period of shortage.

Q6.5 MPB Ltd

Marie and Peter Bridge run a business manufacturing and selling sets of the popular French game, boules. The boules are turned from aluminium, packaged in a neat carrying case and sold for £22 a set. The raw materials cost £8 a set and each set takes 20 minutes of turning by skilled operatives who are paid £9.00 an hour. The fixed costs of the business are £480,000 a year. This year, they plan to produce 80,000 sets.

Tasks:

1 Calculate:
    a) the variable cost of a set of boules;
    b) the absorption cost of a set of boules;
    c) the breakeven point;
    d) the profit or loss if 80,000 sets are sold.

2 A large French champagne house has asked MPB Ltd if it will produce 5,000 boule sets for a worldwide promotion. Each set has to be engraved with the French company's logo and the carrying case must bear its brand name. The extra work involved in this will cost £2.50 a set. It has offered to pay a total of £75,000 for the order. Should MPB accept this offer?

3 A Chinese company has proposed to MPB that it should manufacture the finished boule sets in China and supply them to MPB for £14 delivered. This price would apply to the first 50,000 sets, but after this it would reduce to £10 a set. MPB appreciates that this would change its function to trading only and it would be able to eliminate its manufacturing facilities, saving £180,000 a year.

a) Advise MPB whether or not it should accept this proposition.

b) List the points MPB should consider carefully before accepting this proposition.

Q6.6

BBQ Limited manufactures two types of barbecue – the Deluxe BBQ and the Standard BBQ. Both undergo similar production processes and use similar materials and types of labour. However, a shortage of direct labour has been identified and this is limiting the company's ability to produce the required number of barbecues for the year ending 31 May 2002. Labour capacity is limited to 235,000 labour hours for the year ending 31 May 2002 and this is insufficient to meet total sales demand.

BBQ Limited has stated that the standard selling price and standard prime cost for each barbecue for the forthcoming year are as follows:

	Deluxe BBQ	Standard BBQ
Selling price	£100	£50
Direct material	£50	£11
Direct labour (rate £5 per hour)	£25	£20
Estimated sales demand (units)	10,000	50,000

It has been company policy to absorb production overheads on a labour hour basis. The budgeted information for the year ending 31 May 2002 is as follows:

Fixed production overhead	£188,000
Variable production overhead	£2 per direct labour hour

Non-production costs for the year ending 31 May 2002 are estimated to be:

Selling and distribution overhead:

Variable	10% of selling price
Fixed	£35,000

Administrative overhead:

Fixed	£50,000

Required:

a) Calculate the production plan that will maximise profit for the year ending 31 May 2002.

(7 marks)

b) Based on the production plan that you have recommended in part (a), present a profit statement for the year ending 31 May 2002 in a marginal costing format.

(9 marks)

c) Discuss two problems that may arise as a result of your recommended production plan.

(4 marks)

d) Explain why the contribution concept is used in limiting factor decisions.

(5 marks)

(Total = 25 marks)

CIMA Foundation: Management Accounting Fundamentals, May 2001

Short-term decisions using relevant costing

Chapter contents

Introduction

Managers should take decisions that result in maximum benefit for the organisation **as a whole**. This means taking into account **indirect** effects as well as the direct ones. Suppose that a lawn mower manufacturer decides to buy in a particular component, e.g. the motor, instead of making it, the justification being that the £15 purchase price of the motor is less than its £17 variable cost of manufacture. If the company uses 10,000 motors a year then the annual saving should be £20,000.

This looks like a good decision. But suppose that one indirect effect of this was to make five jobs redundant in the motor production section. If the average redundancy pay was £12,000, it would take three years before the total redundancy pay of £60,000 was covered by the savings made!

The point is that **all** the known quantifiable effects of a decision should be part of the analysis, not just the obvious ones. Relevant costing is particularly appropriate for managers as they are more likely to be aware of the indirect effects than the accountants. This applies even more so to the consideration of the qualitative factors involved. The voice of the manager should be paramount in these decisions.

Having worked through this chapter you should be able to:

- **describe relevant costing;**
- **distinguish between relevant and irrelevant costs;**
- **identify avoidable costs, opportunity costs, sunk costs, committed costs, non-cash costs and opportunity benefits;**
- **quantify the relevant cost of decisions;**
- **discuss the importance of qualitative factors;**
- **give good advice based on relevant costing.**

Definition of relevant cost/revenue

Relevant costs/revenues have three criteria. They are **always**:

- **avoidable** – they are caused by a positive decision and would not happen if the decision were negative;
- **future** – costs/revenues that have already happened cannot be altered by a decision not yet taken;
- **cash** – the net change in cash (not profit) is used to measure the decision's effects.

All three criteria must be fulfilled. If only one or two criteria are met, the cost/revenue is not relevant.

Types of relevant cost

The two main types of relevant costs are *avoidable costs* and *opportunity costs*.

Avoidable costs

These will only be incurred if a certain course of action is followed, otherwise they will not occur. If a positive decision means that a new lorry will be purchased for £22,000 then a negative decision means that expenditure of £22,000 will be **avoided**.

Opportunity costs

These are a measure of the net cash **benefit** foregone from the next most desirable alternative course of action. Even though these do not appear on the profit and loss account, they are real and relevant for decision making.

For example, if some **scarce** specialised labour (like a high-level relational database programmer) is reassigned due to a positive decision, the opportunity cost will be the net cash benefit sacrificed due to the discontinuation of the programmer's current assignment. If there are plenty of these programmers in the organisation the opportunity cost will not arise as both projects can be performed at the same time.

Types of irrelevant cost

The three main types of irrelevant costs are sunk costs, committed costs and non-cash costs.

Sunk costs

These relate to the proposal under consideration but are incurred **prior** to the decision being made. A good example is the cost of market research undertaken to help make decisions about a new product. Sunk costs are also known as 'past costs'.

Committed costs

These are costs that have not been paid at the time of making the decision but a legal obligation exists to pay them at some time in the future; for example, lease payments of premises for the project under consideration if that lease is already in existence but the premises are currently unoccupied. As the lease payments must be made whether the decision is positive or negative, these costs are also called 'common costs'. (They are common to both the 'yes' and 'no' decision as to whether the project goes ahead or not.)

Non-cash costs

The most usual example of these is the depreciation charged in the profit and loss account. Depreciation is a legitimate cost; indeed the net profit figure would be incorrect if depreciation had not been deducted from gross profit together with the other overheads. However, depreciation does **not** cause any movement of cash and therefore cannot be a relevant cost.

An example of relevant costing

Frank Jeffery Limited is a manufacturer of reproduction antique furniture. Three months ago it tendered for a one-off order from English Heritage to make a copy of a four-poster bed that was once slept in by Queen Elizabeth I. The cost of preparing this tender was estimated to be £250. The specification would use 5 cubic metres ('cubes') of English oak, a timber in regular use in the factory. Its current price is £400 a cube. There are three cubes in stock at the moment, which were bought in at £375 a cube.

Business is good and the factory is working at full capacity. To make the bed would need three skilled craftworkers for two weeks each. The company operates a 40-hour week and pays skilled craftworkers at the rate of £10 per hour. It is estimated that the normal work lost due to this order would produce a net cash contribution for the company totalling £3,000.

The machinery involved would depreciate by £400 in the two weeks and the cost of electricity to run the machines would be £80. The machines would be in continual use whether or not the tender was successful. Fixed production overheads are absorbed at the rate of £25 per direct labour hour.

One month ago, a new advanced type of hand-held router was purchased at the cost of £750 as it would be very useful if the bid was selected by English Heritage. (This was a bargain introductory offer for last month only; its price is now £899.) The company's policy is to write off in full hand tools costing less than £1,000 to the profit and loss account in the year of purchase.

What is the relevant cost to Frank Jeffery Limited of making the four-poster bed?

Solution

Item	Avoidable	Future	Cash	Note	Amount	Relevant
Tender preparation			X	1		–
English oak	X	X	X	2	5 cubes × £400	2,000
Craftworker's pay		X	X	3		–
Cash contribution lost	X	X	X	4		3,000
Machine depreciation		X		5		–
Machine electricity		X	X	6		–
Fixed production overhead		X		7		–
New router			X	8		–
					Relevant cost	**£5,000**

Notes:

1 Sunk cost.
2 As oak is in regular use, 5 cubes will need to be replaced at the current price.
3 Craftworkers are assumed to be permanent employees paid on a time basis.
4 Opportunity cost of next best alternative.
5 Depreciation is not a **cash** cost. It is a book entry not causing any cash to flow.
6 Common cost. The machines will be running irrespective of the tender.
7 Overhead absorption is a book entry. It does not change the overheads **incurred**.
8 Sunk cost.

Self-assessment
question S7.1

Try the following question for yourself (answer at the end of the chapter).

Welgrow Ltd is a manufacturer of garden seed compost. At the moment, it makes six different types and is considering adding a new basic compost to its range. Initially, it will make a batch of 10,000 kg and has listed the following costs involved.

1 Exclusive use of the company's mixing machine will be needed for one week. The depreciation of this machine is included as a production overhead at £520 per year.
2 The trial batch will need 7,000 kg of vermiculite. Welgrow does not use this material and does not have any of it in stock at present; its market price is £1.00 per kg.

3   Several years ago Welgrow bought a large quantity of black sand at £0.10 per kg for a special project. A left-over surplus of 3,000 kg is currently in stock as it has proved impossible to resell. Welgrow has no alternative use for this surplus other than as an ingredient in the new compost.

4   To ensure successful marketing of this new product at the right time, a contract for advertising space with a total cost of £500 has been signed. A deposit of 20% has been paid and the balance is due one month before launch next spring.

5   An aluminium storage bin, which was due to have been offered for sale at the realistic price of £100, will be used for the new compost.

Consider each item and state why you think it is relevant or not. Calculate the relevant cost to Welgrow of the decision to go ahead. Also, calculate the breakeven selling price of the new compost.

Opportunity benefits

These benefits, or savings, may be created by taking a positive decision to go ahead with a project. For example, some redundancy costs which were about to be incurred may be avoided by going ahead.

The avoidance or prevention of a cash cost is equivalent to cash income.

Opportunity benefits are relevant to the decision and must be taken into account.

Relevant cost of materials

The relevant cost of a material is not what it cost to buy it in the first place, i.e. a sunk or committed cost. If a material is in regular use, its relevant cost is its **replacement** cost. This is the **future, avoidable, cash flow** caused by the decision to use it.

But if the material was already owned and would not be replaced if used (i.e. it was not in regular use) its relevant cost is the **greater** of:

a) its current realisable value (i.e. the amount received from selling it) and
b) the value obtained from alternative uses.

You should recognise this as its opportunity cost.

Example of the relevant cost of materials

Birch Brothers is a low-volume, high-specification bicycle manufacturer based in South Yorkshire. It has been requested to quote for producing a special pedal-powered vehicle for promoting bicycle use in the UK. The vehicle has four pedalling positions at the front and four at the rear. In between these is a three-dimensional platform structure for advertising the various benefits of cycling. It is approximately the size of a small lorry.

Birch Brothers is currently short of work and is operating at well below its maximum capacity. Unfounded rumours of possible redundancies are circulating among the 20-strong workforce and morale is not good. No additional labour or overtime would be needed to build this 'promotional platform'. This order would provide some very welcome work for the business.

However, the contract would need the following materials:

a) New materials not normally used, e.g. a trailer chassis for the central advertising platform. These would total £5,000.
b) Materials currently in regular use and in stock, e.g. wheels, pedals, etc. These have a book value of £1,780 but would cost £2,000 to buy now.
c) 80 metres of stainless steel tube: Birch Brothers has 60 metres of this disused item in stock left over from a discontinued model. This stock has a resale value of £500 but it is planned to use it all for an export order commencing in four months' time in place of a very similar specification tube which would cost £12.50 a metre. The current price of stainless steel tube is £20 a metre.
d) 95 square metres of aluminium sheet: it has just this amount in stock. It was left over from the manufacture of a batch of bike-trailers, a product that was unsuccessful for the company. Birch Brothers has tried reselling these sheets but not a single buyer was found. The sheeting is taking up a lot of workshop space and it was decided last week to pay £200 to have it removed in the near future.
e) 8 sets of brakes: the company has 20 sets of old-fashioned brakes that are perfectly functional although there is no demand for them. The original cost of these was £12 a set. Whatever is left of this stock item will be thrown in the bin at the financial year-end stocktake.

Solution

Item	Avoidable	Future	Cash	Note	Amount	Relevant
a) New materials	X	X	X	1	£5,000	5,000
b) Regular materials	X	X	X	2	£2,000	2,000
c) 60 m st. steel tube	X	X	X	3	60 m × £12.50	750
d) 20 m st. steel tube	X	X	X	4	20 m × £20	400
e) Aluminium sheet	X	X	X	5	£200	(200)
f) Old-fashion. brakes				6		–
					Relevant cost	**£7,950**

Notes:
1 At current buying-in market price (= replacement cost).
2 At replacement cost.
3 First 60 metres at opportunity cost (= cost saved by use for export order).
4 Next 20 metres need to be bought in (at current replacement price).
5 This is an opportunity **benefit**. By using the sheeting, the company is saving the cost of its disposal.
6 No cash flows of any sort are caused by using these brakes.

Note also that there are no relevant labour costs. The labour force would be paid whether the contract is obtained or not. This is a common cost.

Try the following question for yourself (answer at the end of the chapter).

Self-assessment question S7.2

Tilly Ltd has been approached by a customer who wants a special job done and is willing to pay £20,000 for it. The job would require the following materials:

Material	Total units required	Units in stock	Book value of units in stock (£/unit)	Realisable value (£/unit)	Replacement cost (£/unit)
A	1,000	0	–	–	6
B	1,000	600	2	2.5	5
C	1,000	700	3	2.5	4
D	200	200	4	6	9
E	500	500	5	–	–

Material B is regularly used by Tilly Ltd in the manufacture of its standard products.

Materials C and D are specialist materials, in stock due to previous overbuying. No other use can be found for material C. However, the stock of material D could be used in another job as a substitute for 300 units of material M. Tilly has no stock of material M at present but it can be purchased locally at £5 a unit.

Since the stock of material E was acquired, its sale has been banned by the government (although previously acquired stocks are allowed to be used up). It is a toxic chemical and Tilly is expecting to pay £500 in the near future for its safe disposal as it has no other use for it.

Task:

To help Tilly Ltd decide whether or not to accept the job, calculate the relevant cost of materials needed.

Qualitative factors

Although relevant costing is a numerical or quantitative analysis technique, only a poor manager would ignore the non-numerical or qualitative factors involved in a decision. These are just as important, if not more so, and should be given serious consideration before the decision is made.

Take the case of an advertising agency that currently handles the Mars UK account being offered the chance to pitch for the business of Cadbury's Chocolate. Before doing so, it should think very carefully about the reaction of Mars UK to its acting for a major competitor. Would Mars UK see it as a conflict of interests and take its business elsewhere?

Although no **definite** numerical answers are attainable in such cases, organisations should be aware of the possible risks involved and act accordingly.

Limitations of decision making using relevant costing

The context of relevant costing is broader than that of variable costing (discussed in the last chapter). This lack of artificial boundaries makes it much more realistic. It also makes it more useful, as decisions usually have indirect consequences which should be included in the decision-making process. The main limitation of relevant costing is the difficulty in foreseeing all the indirect consequences arising from the decision in question.

Take the example used in the 'Limitations' section of the previous chapter on variable costing. This described the decision, based on an analysis of product contributions, to cease manufacturing one of several products. The indirect consequence of multiple redundancies and associated payments occurring had been foreseen and taken into account in the cessation decision. However, it may be that the dropping of that particular product would enhance the market's perception of the company as the product was considered to be outmoded and unattractive. Cessation may improve the 'positioning' of the company in the eyes of its customers and sales may increase accordingly. This particular indirect effect is much more difficult to foresee than the ensuing redundancies but its consequences are just as real.

This emphasises the point that making decisions is essentially a management, rather than an accounting, function. The role of accountancy is to provide good information to assist managers make the right decisions. But the manager always has a limited time frame in which to make the decision. During that short time, it is impossible to foresee **all** the consequences of the decision. Even when you have made the best decision you possibly could, events may yet overtake you. Being aware of this will make you a wiser and better manager.

The manager's point of view

Business decisions need to be taken in the round, giving thought to all the relevant factors and potential consequences of any actions taken. The decisions based on variable costing, as discussed in Chapter 6, would in practice never be taken on the arithmetic alone, but on their total impact on the business. While some of this will be quantifiable, much of it will not, and will require the input of judgement, inspiration and informed guesswork. Nevertheless, the starting point for most decisions remains the arithmetic. The way in which the quantifiable factors are handled in practice is perhaps best illustrated by the Capital Investment Appraisal procedures adopted by our company.

In every capital investment decision, the fundamental issue is: What is the total impact on my business of making this investment? To answer this question from a financial standpoint, we have to compare the consequences of making the investment with the consequences of not making it. Our capital appraisal model required a 'Before Case', which consisted of a 10-year income statement showing the results which would be expected if no capital investment was made, and an 'After Case', which showed the forecast position after the investment had been made. The 'Before Case' might, for example, see a flat sales line due to capacity constraints, or perhaps a declining sales line if perseverance with the old plant results in increased downtime for maintenance. Perhaps the old plant has been condemned for environmental reasons, so without the investment sales will be reduced to nil, and redundancies will ensue. All the costs and quantifiable implications of refusing the investment are considered here, including committed costs and opportunity costs, the latter being opportunities which would have been seized but for the project.

The 'After Case', on the other hand, might reflect continued sales growth arising from increased capacity, or reduced marginal costs due to more process automation, larger batch sizes or higher yields. Also shown here are the expected fixed overheads following the investment, including any changes to areas such as selling and administration. In producing these two sets of figures, the principles of relevant costing are regularly utilised. Is a particular cost directly attributable to the project, or would we have incurred it anyway? Many costs will be incurred regardless of the project, and therefore will appear in both Cases.

Then, by deducting the 'Before Case' numbers from the 'After Case' numbers, we arrive at the 'Incremental Case'. This represents exactly the expected impact of the initial investment on each line of the income statement for each of the next 10 years, i.e. the net increase in sales, the net reduction in marginal costs, the additional selling expenses, and so on. From this basic data, we can calculate both the rate of return and the number of years needed to pay back the initial investment, two of the key indicators used by management to assess the viability of the project.

This Capital Investment Appraisal procedure neatly captures and displays the quantifiable elements of an investment decision. These elements may tell a good financial story, but it may well be non-quantifiable issues which cause management ultimately to approve or reject the investment proposal. Another example from my chemical business illustrates the kind of issues which may have an influence on the decision.

One of our products had been used for many years by both the petroleum and plastics industries. It had always been profitable, not least because none of our competitors had quite managed to duplicate it, despite the fact that the patents had expired many years previously. Cheaper, but inferior, alternatives had become available on the market, but our business maintained its competitive edge.

The plant, and the technology on which it was based, was some 40 years old. Over the years, there had been many repairs and part replacements, but eventually the time came when a number of considerations, among them environmental concerns, brought us to the point when substantial changes were necessary. Failure to improve the environmental performance was ultimately likely to result in the plant's closure, although the timescales involved in this were indeterminate. We were also aware that the demand for the product from the petroleum companies might decline at some stage in the future as alternative technologies became available, although sales to the plastics industry were likely to continue. The timing of any decline was again largely a matter of guesswork.

Our options were: (a) to do nothing, and subcontract manufacturing when the plant was closed; (b) to patch up the plant once again, with a view to temporarily satisfying the environmental concerns, until such time as the petroleum business died a natural death, then sub-contract; or (c) to build a new plant, incorporating state-of-the-art technology. The financial implications of each of these scenarios were reasonably easy to establish. The 'Before Case' represented option (a), and included the costs of closing down and decommissioning the plant, as well as the redundancy costs of surplus staff. It also reflected the additional cost of buying in the material from a sub-contractor, for which role the most likely candidates were in India and China. Our first 'After Case' scenario (option (b)) was clearly the cheapest, but would provide us with only a short-term solution to our environmental problems. If the petroleum business did not decline within 5 years, a further patching-up project would almost certainly be required. Moreover, if the product turned out to have a much longer life than we anticipated, we might end up putting up a new plant anyway. Our second 'After Case' scenario (option (c)) was a high-cost, high-risk strategy, because if the petroleum demand turned out to be short term, we could find ourselves left with a relatively new but largely redundant plant. It would, however, solve all our environmental issues at a stroke.

Interestingly, neither of the capital investment scenarios (options (b) and (c)) produced a satisfactory Incremental Case when compared against option (a). This was not because either of the proposals themselves were non-viable, but because the cost of contracting out manufacture turned out, rather unexpectedly, to be much less than expected. The additional cost of buying in from a sub-contractor was substantially offset by overhead and labour savings, so a satisfactory level of profitability could more or less be maintained without any capital investment. The financial advantages offered by the two 'After Case' scenarios were therefore relatively small, and did not appear to justify the capital outlays. The financial arguments clearly pointed towards sub-contracting as a solution to our plant problem, but here the non-quantifiable aspects came into play. Did we really want to divulge our company secrets to a third party? Could we trust any confidentiality agreement signed by the sub-contractor? Was it worth the risk? After all, the product might yet have many years of life left with the petroleum industry and would anyway still be in demand from the plastics companies.

So we had to balance the risks of losing control of our know-how, and then possibly finding our business under threat from our own product coming in cheaply from the East, against the possibility of a white elephant of a plant if the petroleum companies converted in the near future. After much deliberation, we decided to carry out the full plant renewal (option (c)). Our 'Before Case' was changed to reflect our new assumption that we would lose business to the Eastern threat, and on this basis the figures showed an acceptable return and payback period. Now, several years later, the petroleum companies are still using the product, the capital outlay has already been paid back and the environmental problems are a thing of the past. There is still talk that the petroleum companies may soon discontinue their use of the product, but the new plant has already justified its existence.

So our gamble has paid off, but we hit upon the right solution not because we followed the direction pointed out by the financial information, but because we took our decision in the light of wider business considerations. The financials, however, built up on relevant costing principles, provided an essential basis for further decision making. Sound financials, plus informed judgement, experience, and a little bit of luck, can minimise risk, and bring you to the correct conclusion.

Summary

- Relevant costing is a financial model to aid managers with decision making.
- Its objective is to maximise future net cash inflows to the business.
- It considers the indirect, as well as direct, effects of decisions.
- Its method is to identify the relevant costs and benefits **caused by** the decision.
- Relevant costs are avoidable **and** future **and** cash.
- The two types of relevant cost are *avoidable* and *opportunity* costs.
- The three types of irrelevant cost are *sunk*, *committed* and *non-cash* costs.
- Opportunity benefits must be taken into account.
- Qualitative factors are important and should be seriously considered.
- Relevant costing is more realistic than variable costing but it is not perfect.

Further reading

Balakrishnan, R. and Sivaramakrishnan, K. (2002) 'A critical overview of the use of full-cost data for planning and pricing', *Journal of Management Accounting Research*, Vol. 14.

Drury, C. (2004) *Management and Cost Accounting*, 6th edition, Thomson Learning, London. See chapter 'Measuring relevant costs and revenues for decision making'.

Horngren, C., Bhimani, A., Datar, S. and Foster, G. (2002) *Management and Cost Accounting*, 2nd edition, Prentice Hall Europe, Harlow. See chapter 'Revenues, costs and the decision process'.

Upchurch, A. (2003) *Management Accounting, Principles and Practice*, 2nd edition, Financial Times/Prentice Hall, Harlow. See chapter 'Relevant costs and benefits for decision making'.

Answers to self-assessment questions

S7.1. Welgrow Ltd

Item	Avoidable	Future	Cash	Note	Amount	Relevant
1 Mixing machine		X		1		–
2 Vermiculite	X	X	X	2	7,000 @ £1	7,000
3 Black sand				3		–
4 Advertising space			X	4		–
5 Storage bin	X	X	X	5		100
					Relevant cost	£7,100

For the batch of 10,000 kg, the breakeven selling price is **£0.71 per kg**.

Notes:
1 Depreciation is a non-cash expense.
2 Vermiculite needs to be bought in at replacement cost.
3 Sunk cost with no alternative use.
4 The 20% deposit is sunk and the 80% remainder is committed.
5 Opportunity cost.

S7.2. Tilly Ltd

Item	Avoidable	Future	Cash	Note	Amount	Relevant
Material A	X	X	X	1	1,000 × £6	6,000
Material B	X	X	X	2	1,000 × £5	5,000
Material C	X	X	X	3	700 × £2.50	1,750
Material C	X	X	X	4	300 × £4	1,200
Material D (200 units)	X	X	X	5	300 × £5	1,500
Material E	X	X	X	6	£500	(500)
					Relevant cost	£14,950

Notes:
1 All 1,000 units need buying in at replacement cost.
2 600 units from stock need replacing and 400 need buying at replacement cost.
3 Opportunity cost = resale value.
4 Remaining 300 units bought in at replacement cost.
5 Opportunity cost is greatest of resale value of £1,200 (200 × 6) and saving the purchase of 300 units of M, £1,500 (300 × £5).
6 Opportunity **benefit**: using the stock of E in production avoids disposal costs of £500.

Roverco plc manufactures and markets a house-cleaning robot. At present, it is in the middle of a project to develop a voice-controlled robot from a laboratory prototype. The prototype was built from a patent which the company acquired for £50,000. The inventor agreed to accept payment in five equal instalments, three of which have now been paid.

At a recent board meeting, it was revealed that sales of Roverco's standard product had taken an unforeseen downturn and that this would have a knock-on effect on profitability and liquidity. This situation is partly due to increased competition from Housemouse Ltd, a dynamic new entrant to the market which specialises in the application of the very latest technology to its products. Also, Roverco's two long-established rivals, Cleanbot plc and Nomess plc, have been competing on price for the last year or so. Roverco decided against joining in the price war, hoping that it would soon be over. However, the market has responded positively to the price reductions, with increased orders going to Cleanbot and Nomess, causing Roverco to lose market share.

During the meeting, there was a heated discussion concerning the voice-controlled robot project. The project manager presented a financial statement (shown below) and reported that progress was slower than expected due to snags with the voice-recognition system. In connection with this, he recommends that a specialist electronic engineer is employed for the duration of the project, which he estimates will now continue for the next 18 months. The salary would be £28,000 p.a. on a fixed-term contract basis. Without this additional appointment, it is very doubtful that the project will be completed.

Project manager's financial statement

		£
Costs to date		42,000
Estimated costs for completion of project:		
Final payment for patent	20,000	
Gross salaries of two development engineers	75,000	
Gross salary of new engineer	42,000	
Materials and equipment (including M4411)	19,000	
Overheads	65,000	
		221,000
Total cost of project		263,000
Budgeted cost of project		218,000
Requested increase in budget		45,000

Following this, the finance director shocked the meeting into silence by proposing that the project be abandoned. She justified this course of action by pointing out that Roverco's share price had been falling slowly but steadily for the last three months and that in her regular meeting with share analysts from the big City firms, scheduled for next month, she feels it would be wise to issue a profits warning. The effect of this would be a steeper fall in the share price which, in turn, would make the company more vulnerable to a takeover bid. However, to avoid this, she believes the downwards profit trend can be quickly reversed by abandoning the voice-controlled project and putting the savings of £191,000 into price cuts on the existing product range.

The chairman is not sure what to do. He postpones the discussion for one week and asks you for advice. You ascertain the following information:

1 Market research costing £35,000 was commissioned for the project. This predicted that the optimum price/volume relationship was a selling price of £999, creating sales of 6,000 robots a year. The product life cycle was estimated as four years, at which point a major redesign would be needed to remain competitive.

2 Roverco's accountant has estimated that the new production facility fixed assets for the voice-controlled robot will cost £900,000 and will have a resale value of £400,000 after four years. Other fixed overhead costs of £340,000 p.a. will be incurred; these are caused solely by this product and include depreciation of £90,000 p.a. for the production facility. The variable cost of producing each robot will be £917.

3 A special miniature hydraulic mechanism will be used in the robot's production. Roverco has a stock of 9,000 of these left over from a previous product. They were originally bought at a 'bargain price' of £9 each (the current market price is £15 which is included in the £917 total variable cost). They could probably be sold as a job lot for £45,000. Roverco has no other use for these items.

4 If the project is abandoned, two development engineers will have to be made redundant at a cost to Roverco of £18,000 each.

5 Some specialised voice-control testing equipment could be sold for £8,500 in its present condition, or for £2,500 at the end of the project. The rest of the equipment has no resale value.

6 A £6,000 order (order no. M4411) for bespoke electronic components was placed last month for delivery in two months' time; three months' credit is normally allowed by the supplier. A legal contract was signed for this order which Roverco is not able to cancel.

7 The project overheads of £65,000 include £15,000 for depreciation of the buildings used for product development and a general administration charge of £3,000 (nominally for services from the rest of the company). They also include £17,000 as a proportion of the project manager's pay.

Task:

Identify the relevant cash flows and advise the chairman whether, on purely financial grounds, the project should continue or be abandoned. Support your calculations with clear statements as to why particular items have been included or excluded and state any assumptions that you make.

Questions

An asterisk * on a question number indicates that the answer is given at the end of the book. Answers to the other questions are given in the Lecturer's Guide.

Q7.1* Burton Brothers

Burton Brothers manufactures machine tools for metal-based industries. One of its customers, Wey Ltd, has placed a £590,000 order for a machine, including £10,000 for delivery and installation. Wey paid a deposit of £180,000 and has since paid instalments totalling £150,000. Unfortunately, Burton Brothers has received a letter from a solicitor informing it that Wey Ltd has gone into liquidation and is unlikely to be able to pay any of its debts. This project has incurred the following costs to date:

	£
Engineering design	70,000
Materials	129,000
Direct labour (760 hours @ £10/h)	7,600
Production overheads (760 hours @ £88/dlh)	66,880
	273,480

The production overheads are all fixed costs and it is company policy to absorb them on the basis of direct labour hours (dlh).

Another customer, Bridge & Co., has expressed an interest in the machine, provided some additions are made to the specification, and is willing to pay a price of £400,000. To complete the machine to the original specification, it is estimated that a further 2,000 direct labour hours (at £10/hour) and a further £204,000 of materials will be needed. Contracts for £24,000 of these materials have already been signed but no money has yet been paid. The contract provides for a cancellation fee of £6,000 provided cancellation is confirmed in the next 11 days. These materials are components made especially to order for this machine and have no other use or value. The rest of the materials are in regular use by Burton Brothers. Twenty-five per cent of the £204,000 of materials are currently in the stores.

The additions requested by Bridge & Co. will need a further £45,000 of materials and 400 hours of direct labour. Some of these additional materials, which have an estimated purchase price of £13,500, could be replaced by similar material currently in the stores. This was left over from a previous contract and has no other use. It originally cost £9,500, which is its current stock valuation, but if it were to be sold on the open market, it would fetch £12,000.

Burton Brothers is itself in a precarious position as it has no new orders on its books. If this job is abandoned, its direct workforce will be put on standby, which means they will be sent home and paid a rate of £4 an hour to retain their services. However, if this were to happen, the directors believe that some of these skilled workers would find permanent work elsewhere and would leave the company.

If no customer is found for the machine, it will be sent for scrap; this is expected to produce £6,000 income.

Task:

Burton Brothers is unsure whether or not to accept the offer from Bridge & Co. Consider each of the above items and advise the company accordingly.

Q7.2* Eezikum

Eezikum is a duo of rap artists currently touring the UK. They still have 11 venues remaining when they are asked to fill in at short notice on a tour of the USA, starting in two days' time. They will be the first act on stage to warm up the audience in preparation for the big American star whose tour it is. They know that this could establish them in the lucrative North American market but are not sure of the financial implications. There is a cancellation fee of £10,000 for each abandoned concert. Each time they perform in the UK they are paid a fee of £15,000 and their out-of-pocket expenses amount to £2,500. At present, they have no future work commitments once the UK tour is over.

If they join the tour of the USA, they will need to buy new equipment compatible with the American electricity supply and safety standards. The cost of this is estimated at £100,000 but it could be sold for £40,000 at the end of the nine-month tour, on their return to the UK. The money is not a problem as they currently have more than £1 million in a deposit account earning interest of 12% a year.

The US tour consists of 125 performances, each paying fees of £10,000 and having associated out-of-pocket expenses of £2,000. The airfare for the whole entourage, including a considerable amount of luggage, is £14,500 each way. Additional health insurance will cost £6,000 for the duration of the tour. Travel insurance is £9,000 (three-quarters of their existing annual worldwide policy, which carries a premium of £12,000).

Task:

Calculate the relevant benefit/cost of accepting the US tour.

Q7.3* Carbotest Corporation

Carbotest Corporation manufactures equipment to test for the presence of carbon monoxide in confined spaces. It has just been offered a contract to build some specialised monitoring equipment to test for the presence of carbon dioxide in the freight containers of lorries and railway wagons. The contract offers to pay £152,000 for 1,000 sets of testing equipment, which must be delivered in six months' time. Carbotest has looked into this opportunity and has produced the following information.

Materials

The contract will need 40,000 components which Carbotest does not currently use; these cost £3 each. However, it could use up old stock of 5,000 components that it recently tried to sell without success. But £1 will need to be spent on each of them to make them into suitable replacements for 5,000 of the 40,000 components needed. This old stock originally cost £20,000 but now has a scrap value of only £1,000. Each testing set also needs a carrying harness identical to those used for the carbon monoxide testing equipment. Carbotest has 600 of these currently in stock, valued at their cost price of £8 each. The suppliers of this harness have just increased their price to £9, which Carbotest will have to pay for future orders.

Labour

The contract will use five skilled operatives full time for six months. These operatives are paid £1,400 a month gross and are presently employed on the carbon-monoxide-testing production. They will have to be redeployed from this work to the new contract. Their combined output for the six-month period is estimated to have a sales revenue of £60,000, a variable cost of £48,000 and to absorb £8,000 of fixed overheads. It is thought that one of the factory supervisors (currently with a light workload) could manage the project for 50% of his time. His annual gross pay is £24,000. Carbotest is working at full capacity and has enough orders to keep it busy for 15 months.

Machinery

Three years ago, Carbotest bought a machine for a similar project, which had to be abandoned after two years. It cost £25,000 and was estimated to have a useful life of five years, with a zero residual value. (Carbotest uses the straight-line method of depreciation for all its fixed assets.) The machine has been 'mothballed' for the last 12 months and has been stored out of the way. Carbotest was just about to advertise it for sale at the very reasonable price of £5,000. It is thought that this intensive contract will effectively wear it out. To meet the six-month deadline, Carbotest plans to lease an identical machine for six months at a cost of £500 a month.

Accommodation

Employees have to park their cars on the road outside the factory. As the company is located in a busy area, this is often difficult, with cars having to be parked some distance away. Carbotest is just about to convert a rough piece of land in one corner of its site into an employees' car park. It hired a professional firm of surveyors to obtain planning permission for this and their invoice for £2,200 has recently been received but not yet paid. The cost of building the car park is £28,000. But if the contract is accepted, this land will have to be used for a temporary building to house the necessary machinery. The construction of this building will cost £8,000 and when the contract is completed, it will be demolished at a cost of £2,000. The car park will then go ahead.

Fixed overheads

Carbotest's absorption costing system attaches fixed overheads to production on a machine hour basis. The contract is expected to absorb £10,000 of fixed overhead.

Tasks:

State whether each of the above items is relevant or irrelevant to Carbotest's acceptance of the contract and explain your reasoning. Advise it whether or not to accept the contract. Discuss any other factors the company should take into consideration when making this decision.

Q7.4 Murray Polls

Murray Polls Limited recently contracted to conduct an opinion poll concerning global warming and its causes. Its costing for this job is shown below:

		£
Planning	100 hours @ £12	1,200
Questioning	800 hours @ £7	5,600
Travel and subsistence		4,800
Telephone	30,000 minutes @ £0.02/min	600
Analysis of results & report	60 hours @ £12	720
Fixed overheads	800 hours @ £25	20,000
Total cost		32,920
Profit @ 20% mark-up		6,584
Price to client		£39,504

(Overheads are absorbed on the basis of questioning hours.)

The client paid a deposit of £5,000 and contracted to pay the remainder within one month of receiving the report. Unfortunately, Murray has just been informed that its client has gone into liquidation and is not expected to be able to meet any of its debts.

At this point, Murray has completed all the planning and 75% of the questioning; travel and subsistence so far total £3,700 and 50% of the telephoning has been completed. No analysis has yet been done. If the poll is abandoned, two of the ten researchers involved will have to be paid a cancellation fee of £200 each.

The managing director of Murray immediately suspends all work on the contract and decides to attend an international conference on the environment, taking place in Stockholm next week. He is hopeful of finding another client for this project as he will be able to offer the completed poll and report at a greatly reduced price. His airfares, hotel bills and out-of-pocket expenses for the five-day Stockholm trip are expected to be £2,200. His rate of pay works out at £400 a day.

Task:

Calculate the lowest price the managing director can quote without making his firm worse off and advise him accordingly. State your reasons for including or excluding the above factors in your calculation.

Q7.5 Eldave Advertising Agency

The Eldave Advertising Agency has been working on a campaign for Greenpoint Leisure Limited for the last four months. The campaign is for Greenpoint's eco-friendly holidays in South America and uses both TV and Sunday paper magazines. The adverts have almost been completed and the campaign launch date is in six weeks' time. The estimated cost of completion is £2,400 (two people @ £400/week for three weeks). Greenpoint has signed a contract to pay Eldave £50,000 (for advert production) plus media space at cost.

Eldave has just received a letter from a firm of solicitors stating that Greenpoint has ceased trading with immediate effect and that its creditors are unlikely to receive any of the money they are owed. Fortunately, Eldave has received a non-returnable deposit of £25,000 (50% of the production fee) from Greenpoint but a summary of its account reveals an overall balance owing of £61,000 for work to date. This includes a general fixed overheads charge of £6,000 apportioned on the basis of total direct cost.

In order to minimise Eldave's losses, Eloise Thompson, the partner in charge of the Greenpoint account, has contacted three other travel firms specialising in the South American market. She has shown them the adverts and tried to persuade them to take over the work-in-progress for the special price of £25,000. One of these three, Trek Hols Limited, has offered £12,000 for the appropriately modified and completed adverts on condition that the campaign starts in two weeks' time.

Eldave has provisionally booked advertising space for eight consecutive weeks starting in six weeks' time. The cost of this is £30,000 a week, for which it has paid £12,000 (a 5% non-returnable deposit included in the £61,000). It has also booked a one-quarter-page colour space in the *Independent on Sunday* magazine for the same eight weeks. Each of these spaces costs £9,000 but, although a contract has been signed, no money has yet been paid (not included in the £61,000). The contract allows for a 50% reduction if cancellation occurs less than four weeks before publication. This reduction increases to 75% if cancellation occurs more than four weeks before publication. Although Trek Hols is happy to take over Greenpoint's media slots, it also wants the same weekly coverage for the four weeks immediately prior to the original launch date. Trek Hols insists the campaign must start in two weeks' time and agrees to pay for all the media space in full, at cost.

In order to complete the adverts for launch in two weeks' time, Eldave will have to redeploy two of its employees (gross pay £400 a week each) for one and a half weeks, at the end of which the adverts will be delivered to the media. As a result of this, the job these two are currently doing will be one and a half weeks late and Eldave will incur a financial penalty of '£1,000 a week or part-week'.

Tasks:

Identify the **relevant costs and income** and advise Eldave as to whether it should accept Trek Hols' offer. Your calculations must clearly show the reasons why each of the above items has been included or excluded. State any assumptions you make.

Q7.6 MOV plc

MOV plc produces custom-built sensors. Each sensor has a standard circuit board (SCB) in it. The current average contribution from a sensor is £400. MOV plc's business is steadily expanding and in the year just ending (2001/2002), the company will have produced 55,000 sensors. The demand for MOV plc's sensors is predicted to grow over the next 3 years:

Year	Units
2002/03	58,000
2003/04	62,000
2004/05	65,000

The production of sensors is limited by the number of SCBs the company can produce. The present production level of 55,000 SCBs is the maximum that can be produced without overtime working. Overtime could increase annual output to 60,500, allowing production of sensors to also increase to 60,500. However, the variable cost of SCBs produced in overtime would increase by £75 per unit.

Because of the pressure on capacity, the company is considering having the SCBs manufactured by another company, CIR plc. This company is very reliable and produces products of good quality. CIR plc has quoted a price of £116 per SCB, for orders greater than 50,000 units a year.

MOV plc's own costs per SCB are predicted to be:

	£	
Direct material	28	
Direct labour	40	
Variable overhead	20	(based on labour cost)
Fixed overhead	24	(Based on labour cost and output of 55,000 units)
Total cost	112	

The fixed overheads directly attributable to SCBs are £250,000 a year; these costs will be avoided If SCBs are not produced. If more than 59,000 units are produced, SCBs' fixed overheads will increase by £130,000.

In addition to the above overheads, MOV plc's fixed overheads are predicted to be:

Sensor production in units:	54,001 to 59,000	59,001 to 64,000	64,001 to 70,000
Fixed overhead:	£2,600,000	£2,900,000	£3,100,000

MOV plc currently holds a stock of 3,500 SCBs but the production manager feels that a stock of 8,000 should be held if they are bought-in; this would increase stockholding costs by £10,000 a year. A purchasing officer, who is paid £20,000 a year, spends 50% of her time on SCB duties. If the SCBs are bought-in, a liaison officer will have to be employed at a salary of £30,000 in order to liase with CIR plc and monitor the quality and supply of SCBs. At present, 88 staff are involved in the production of SCBs at an average salary of £25,000 a year: if the SCBs were purchased, 72 of these staff would be made redundant at an average cost of £4,000 per employee.

The SCB department, which occupies an area of 240 × 120 square metres at the far end of the factory, could be rented out, at a rent of £45 per square metre a year. However, if the SCBs were to be bought-in, for the first year only MOV plc would need the space to store the increased stock caused by outsourcing, until the main stockroom had been reorganised and refurbished. From 2003/04, the space could be rented out; this would limit the annual production of sensors to 60,500 units. Alternatively the space could be used for the production of sensors, allowing annual output to increase to 70,000 units if required.

Required:

a) Critically discuss the validity of the following statement. It was produced by Jim Elliot, the company's accountant, to show the gain for the coming year (2002/03) if the SCBs were to be bought-in.

Saving in:	£
Manufacturing staff – salaries saved: 72 staff × £25,000	1,800,000
Purchasing officer – time saved	10,000
Placing orders for SCB materials: 1,000 orders × £20 per order	20,000
Transport costs for raw materials for SCBs	45,000
Cost saved	1,875,000
Additional cost per SCB: (£116 – £112) × 58,000 units	232,000
Net gain if SCBs purchased	1,643,000

(10 marks)

b) i) Produce detailed calculations that show which course of action is the best financial option for the three years under consideration. (Ignore the time value of money.)

(12 marks)

ii) Advise the company of the long-term advantages and disadvantages of buying in SCBs.

(3 marks)

(Total = 25 marks)

CIMA Intermediate: Management Accounting – Decision Making, May 2002

CHAPTER 8

Capital investment appraisal for long-term decisions

Chapter contents

Introduction

Imagine that you are a director of a large business which urgently needs to replace one of its large old machines. Preliminary investigation has narrowed down your choice to two alternatives.

The first machine costs £3.2 million, is guaranteed for three years, is four times as productive as the present machine and can be sold back to its supplier for £0.5 million after five years. The second machine costs £2.5 million, is guaranteed for one year, is three times as productive as the present machine and cannot be sold back to its supplier. How do you decide which machine is the best one to buy?

Capital investment appraisal is the decision-making process used by businesses to decide which fixed assets to purchase. Vehicles, machines and buildings can be very expensive so it is important to make the best decision possible from the information available at the time.

Correcting a bad capital investment decision can be very costly. Consider a company that has a choice between buying a large piece of plant from either Atlas Ltd or Tyrell & Co. If it spends £3.2 million on an Atlas machine and three months later finds out it would have been better to buy a Tyrell machine, correcting this decision will entail significant extra costs. For a start, the Atlas machine will now be second-hand and will have lost value. There may not be a ready market for this type of machine and the price will have to be reduced further to sell it. Also, there is the cost of uninstalling and removing it. And how about the lost production caused by this change?

Because of the importance of these long-term decisions, managers normally seek help from their management accountants. Over the years several methods for determining the best choice have been established. This chapter looks at the four most popular of these (see Figure 8.1). Note that one uses profits but all the others use cash flows.

For each of these methods it is necessary to **estimate** future profits or cash flows arising from the new investments. However, when we do this, we usually get it wrong. The quality of the investment decision will depend on the quality of these estimates. You may think it is not worth bothering if the answers will probably involve such significant errors, but the alternative is to make these decisions by tossing a coin. It is better to attempt some analysis than none at all. Often, the objective is to choose between alternative fixed assets. As the same assumptions are made for each alternative, the results become more valid.

Having worked through this chapter you should be able to:

Learning objectives

- calculate the accounting rate of return (ARR);
- convert profits to cash flows;
- justify the exclusion of working capital from cash flows;
- reconcile cash flows with profits over the lifetime of a project;
- calculate the payback period (PBP);
- discount future cash flows to today's values;
- calculate the net present value (NPV);
- calculate the internal rate of return (IRR);
- discuss the limitations of the four methods;
- compare NPV to IRR;
- criticise the discounted payback approach;
- discuss the choice of available methods;
- appreciate the usefulness of sensitivity analysis in managing risk;
- explain why the financing decision is excluded from the investment decision;
- discuss the importance of relevant qualitative factors.

Method	Base
Accounting rate of return (ARR)	Profits
Payback period (PBP)	Cash flows
Net present value (NPV)	Discounted cash flows
Internal rate of return (IRR)	Discounted cash flows

Figure 8.1 **Summary of capital investment appraisal methods**

Method 1: accounting rate of return (ARR)

The ARR attempts to express the return on the investment as an annual percentage of the cost of that investment. This is similar to comparing interest-bearing bank and building society accounts with each other when deciding where to invest your money. Businesses using this method usually set a minimum threshold rate which must be equalled or exceeded by the ARR. For example, a company may be earning an average of 18% a year from all its current activities. It may use this as a threshold or target rate for any new investments. If the calculations for a possible new investment showed its ARR to be only 15%, the investment would not go ahead. This is because if it were adopted it would **reduce** the 18% currently achieved by the company as a whole. On the other hand, if the potential ARR was 20%, the investment would be considered further.

If Maniff plc (threshold ARR = 24%) had to choose between machines M1 (ARR = 29%), M2 (ARR = 22%) and M3 (ARR = 33%), it would disregard M2 and further consider M1 and M3. If ARR was the only technique it used, it would choose M3 as it produces the greatest return on investment (i.e. the greatest profitability).

Unfortunately, there are several ways of calculating ARR. However, as there is very little to choose between them, we will use the least complicated. The formula used in this book is as follows (see Figure 8.2):

$$ARR = \frac{\text{average annual profit}}{\text{initial investment}} \times 100$$

(Note that sometimes the **average** investment is used instead of the **initial** investment.)

Cost of capital project = £200,000   Profit in Year 1 = £43,000
Profit in Year 2 = £56,000
Profit in Year 3 = £41,000
Profit in Year 4 = £20,000

$$ARR = \frac{(43,000 + 56,000 + 41,000 + 20,000)/4}{200,000} \times 100$$

$$= \frac{160,000/4}{200,000} \times 100 = \textbf{20\%}$$

Figure 8.2 **Example of an ARR calculation**

Self-assessment question S8.1

Try the following question for yourself (answer at the end of the chapter).

You have the chance to open a manicure parlour in your local shopping centre at an initial cost of £25,000. For each manicure, the sales price will be £10 and the direct cost £6. The annual total of indirect costs (i.e. overheads) is estimated to be £16,000. Market research has estimated demand for manicures to be

Year 1	5,000 units
Year 2	6,000 units
Year 3	7,000 units
Year 4	8,000 units
Year 5	6,500 units

What is the ARR for the project?

Limitations of ARR

One reservation concerning profit-based ARR is that profits can vary much more than cash flows. Remember that the profit figure depends on many subjective estimates such as depreciation, stock valuation and provision for doubtful debts. On the other hand, the cash figure is theoretically measurable and therefore more objective. Thus, the ARR tends to be less reliable than the cash-flow-based methods.

Converting profits to cash flows

Having considered ARR, we will now look at the other three methods. These are all based on the relevant cash flows (not profits). A relevant cash flow is one **caused by the project**. If a cash flow will still occur whether we go ahead or not, it is not caused by the project, and so it is not relevant to our decision. Exclude irrelevant cash flows from your calculations.

Very often the starting point in these calculations is a profit and loss account rather than a cash flow forecast. In this case the first thing we have to do is to convert the profits to cash flows. This is done by **adding back any non-cash expenses** to the net profit. The most common of these is depreciation, see Figure 8.3. (If you are not sure about this, have a look at Chapter 2 on the difference between profit and cash.)

Self-assessment question S8.2

Try the following question for yourself (answer at the end of the chapter).

A building company is considering branching out into the mobile crane hire business. It is thinking of buying a 42 tonne model similar to ones it has often hired in the past. This will cost £190,000 and should last for nine years, after which time it will have an estimated scrap value of £10,000. The profits from this venture are expected to be as shown below. Calculate the associated cash flows.

Year	Profit(£)	Year	Profit(£)	Year	Profit(£)
1	10,000	4	30,000	7	30,000
2	18,000	5	35,000	8	20,000
3	24,000	6	38,000	9	10,000

A company is considering launching a new product requiring the purchase of new plant and machinery costing £5.5 million. The additional profits resulting directly from this five-year project are as follows:

Year	Profit/(Loss)
1	(0.5)
2	1.0
3	4.0
4	5.0
5	2.0

The company uses straight line depreciation and expects to be able to sell the plant for £0.5 million at the end of the project. What are the project's cash flows?

Answer

$$\text{Annual depreciation charge} = \frac{\text{Fall in value over project's lifetime}}{\text{Lifetime in years}}$$

$$= \frac{£(5.5 - 0.5)\text{m}}{5} = £1.0\text{m a year}$$

Year	Profit/(Loss)	Annual depreciation	Other items	Cash in/(out)flow
0	0.0	0.0	(5.5) plant purchase	(5.5)
1	(0.5)	1.0	0.0	0.5
2	1.0	1.0	0.0	2.0
3	4.0	1.0	0.0	5.0
4	5.0	1.0	0.0	6.0
5	2.0	1.0	0.5 sale of scrap	3.5
	11.5			11.5

N.B. 'Year 0' is the equivalent of *now*, i.e. the start of the project.

Figure 8.3 **Example of converting profits to cash flows**

Reconciliation of cash flows with profits

Over the whole lifetime of a project, the total of profits will equal the total of cash flows. (Note that this is **not** true for any one year within the lifetime.) This enables you to check the accuracy of your cash flow calculations. Look back at Figure 8.3 to check this; the lifetime total is £11.5 million.

Note: Beware of situations where fixed assets are sold for more or less than their written-down value. This will give a 'profit or loss on disposal' which must be included in the profit of the disposal year for the above statement to be true.

Method 2: payback period (PBP)

This calculates how long it will take for the business to recover the initial **cash** outflow to purchase the fixed asset. The answers are given in units of time, usually years. If the investment decision were a choice between several alternative capital projects, the one with the shortest PBP would be recommended. Most people agree that uncertainty increases the further you go into the future. Thus, choosing the project with the shortest PBP is a way of minimising risk. An example of a PBP calculation is shown in Figure 8.4.

Note that we have assumed the cash to flow **evenly** throughout the year. For example, an annual net cash flow of £120,000 is assumed to occur at the rate of £10,000 a month. In reality, this is most unlikely, especially for seasonal businesses. However, unless we can forecast more accurately, this is the assumption we have to make.

Initial cash outflow (i.e. project cost) = £240,000

Year	Net cash in £	Cumulative £	
1	93,000	93,000	
2	107,000	200,000	Payback not reached
3	120,000	320,000	Payback occurs in year 3
4	80,000	400,000	

$$PBP = 2 + \frac{\text{amount still needed}}{\text{total inflow in payback year}}$$

$$PBP = 2 + \frac{(240,000 - 200,000)}{120,000}$$

$$= 2 + \frac{40,000}{120,000}$$

$$= \textbf{2.33 years}$$

$or = \textbf{2 years 4 months}$ (0.33 years × 12 months/year = 4 months)

Figure 8.4 **Example of a payback period calculation**

Try the following question for yourself (answer at the end of the chapter).

*Self-assessment
question S8.3*

Calculate the payback period for the manicure parlour project in S8.1 if the only non-cash expense included in the annual fixed costs was depreciation of £2,000.

Limitations of PBP

One limitation of this technique is that it takes no account of the cash flows occurring after the payback point has been reached. Project A in Swindon may be chosen in preference to project B in Oxford because it has a shorter PBP. But the total of net cash inflows over the projects' lifetimes may be much greater for project B than for project A.

Thus, choosing project A may be the wrong decision for the business. It depends on how risky the project is perceived to be. If it is thought to be a high-risk investment, then project A may be the best decision after all as it is more likely to recover its initial cost. One reason for the relative popularity of the PBP method is that many business decisions are considerably risky. Another reason is that the concept is easy to understand.

Discounting cash flows

The time value of money

If I were to offer you either £900 now **or** £900 in 12 months' time, which would you choose? I suspect you would choose the £900 now.

Alternatively, if I were to offer to give you either £900 now **or** £945 in 12 months from now, which would you choose? This is a more difficult choice. To help you with your decision, you are told that the bank interest rate is currently 5% a year. If you accepted the £900 now and invested it for 12 months at 5% a year, it would be worth £945 in a year's time. This implies that the two alternatives are really the same, provided interest rates remain constant for the year.

The significance of this is that the value of money changes with time because it is possible to invest and earn interest on it over a period. Check your understanding of this by considering the following question.

If the interest rate changed to 3% a year and I offered you either £945 in 12 months' time or £900 now, which would you choose? The answer is that £900 invested now at 3% gives £927 in 12 months' time. So, on this occasion, it is worth waiting for the £945.

A sum of money **now** has a greater value than the same sum in a year's time because it can be invested for that year to earn interest.

Thus, £1 in one year is NOT worth the same as £1 in another year.

This concept is known as the 'time value of money'.

When looking at cash flows over a number of years, **to be sure of comparing like with like**, future amounts should be reduced by the business's interest or 'cost of capital' rate. In simple terms, it can be thought of as the overall rate of interest applying to a business. It is also referred to as the *discount rate*. The discounted cash flow technique is

All future cash flows should be discounted to *present values*.

Compounding and discounting

Compounding is the effect of repeatedly adding interest earned to the lump sum invested so that interest will be paid on larger and larger amounts as time passes (see Figure 8.5).

What is the value of £751 invested at 10% p.a. for 3 years?
(To increase a number by 10%, multiply it by the decimal 1.10)

Year 1   £751 × 1.10 = £826
Year 2   £826 × 1.10 = £909
Year 3   £909 × 1.10 = £1,000

The answer is £1,000.

Figure 8.5 **Example of a compounding calculation**

Try the following question for yourself (answer at the end of the chapter).

If £500 is invested at 7.5% p.a. compound, how much is it worth at the end of four years?

Self-assessment question S8.4

Discounting can be viewed as the opposite process to compounding (see Figure 8.7). If the interest rate was 10% p.a. (as in Figure 8.5), instead of multiplying by 1.10, you divide by 1.10 (see Figure 8.6).

An alternative method of obtaining discount factors is to use a present value table. These show the factors for different discount rates for a number of years. Their disadvantage is that they may not include the rate or the number of years you wish to use. A present value table has been included at the end of this chapter. Practise using it by finding the factor for year 9 at a discount rate of 17%. You should find 0.243. Now try finding the factor for year 18 at a discount rate of 12.5%.

Try the following question for yourself (answer at the end of the chapter).

Discount the cash flows of the manicure parlour (see answer to S8.3) to the present time using a rate of 3% p.a. What is the total of these present values?

Self-assessment question S8.5

You own a machine which will produce a cash income of £1,000 p.a. for each of the next three years. What is the present value of this income stream if the discount rate is 10% p.a.?

Year	Cash	10% Discount factor	Present value
1	1,000	1.0000/1.10 = 0.9091	909
2	1,000	0.9091/1.10 = 0.8264	826
3	1,000	0.8264/1.10 = 0.7513	751
		Total present value =	£2,486

Figure 8.6 **Example of a discounting calculation**

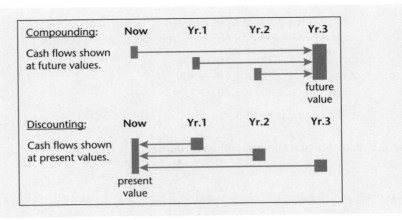

Figure 8.7 Diagrammatic illustration of compounding and discounting
Source: After P. Atrill and E. McLaney (1994) *Management Accounting: An Active Learning Approach*, Blackwell, Oxford

Method 3: net present value (NPV)

The NPV is the *sum total* of all the present values of all the cash flows caused by the project (see Figure 8.8).

NPV calculation procedure

1 Calculate the annual **net cash flows** (inflows are positive, outflows are negative).
2 Determine the discount rate.
3 Discount future cash flows to present values (calculate the factors or use PV tables).
4 Combine all the annual PVs to give the NPV for the whole project period.

A vending machine costs £2,500. It will produce positive net cash inflows of £1,000 a year for each of the next 3 years (residual value = nil). What is the NPV if the discount rate is 10% p.a.?

Year	Cash in/(out)	10% discount factors	Present value
0	(2,500)	1.0000	(2,500)
1	1,000	1.0000/1.10 = 0.9091	909
2	1,000	0.9091/1.10 = 0.8264	826
3	1,000	0.8264/1.10 = 0.7513	<u>751</u>
			NPV = £(<u>14</u>)

Figure 8.8 Example of an NPV calculation

Interpreting the results

- If NPV is positive, accept the project.
- If NPV is negative, reject the project.
- If several projects are being considered of which only one can be accepted (mutually exclusive projects) accept the project with highest positive NPV.

Try the following question for yourself (answer at the end of the chapter).

You are considering investing in production facilities for a new product with an estimated life span of four years. The fixed assets will cost £49,500 and the net cash inflows will be £20,000 for each of the first two years and £10,000 for each of the last two years. If the company's cost of capital is 10% p.a., what is the NPV of the project? Would you recommend going ahead? (Use three decimal places for your PV factors.)

Annuities

When projects have a long lifetime and their net cash flows are the same each year, the concept of an annuity can be used to make the NPV calculation easier. An 'annuity' is defined as a fixed periodic (e.g. annual) cash flow which continues for a defined period of time (or until a specified event occurs). Consider the following example.

Eastshore Airport is considering installing 50 'iris-recognition' devices to improve its security. These devices will cost a total of £2,500,000 and will have the effect of making 25 jobs redundant. The annual cost of each of these employees is £22,000. Fifteen of them will be redeployed and the average redundancy payment for the others is estimated at £30,000 each.

It is thought that these devices will have an effective life of 20 years before being replaced with more up-to-date technology. Their collective residual value in 20 years' time will be £250,000. Annual running costs will be £1,000 per device for the first half of their life but this will increase to £3,000 for the second half due to the increase in maintenance required.

Assuming Eastshore's cost of capital is 15% a year, calculate the NPV of this project. (Use the annuities present value table to determine the appropriate discount factors.)

Answer (£000)

	Years 1–10		Years 11–20	
Annual savings	25 × 22 =	550	25 × 22 =	550
Less annual running costs	50 × 1 =	50	50 × 3 =	150
Net annual savings		500		400

Determine the discount factors needed by reading the annuities table at the end of this chapter. A single factor can be used for years 1 to 10 as the annual savings (equal to relevant income) are £500,000; this is a 10-year annuity. Look at the 15% column and read off the factor of 5.019 for year 10. (Check this by adding up the 10 annual factors in the 'normal' single-value table for years 1 to 10.)

For years 11 to 20, the factor cannot just be read from the table as this would also include years 1 to 10. To obtain the correct factor, in the 15% column, deduct the 10-year factor from the 20-year factor, $6.259 - 5.019 = 1.240$.

	Year	Cash in/(out)	15% factors	Present values
Equipment	0	(2,500)	1.000	(2,500.00)
Redundancy	0	(300)	1.000	(300.00)
Net savings	1–10	500	5.019	2,509.50
Net savings	11–20	400	1.240	496.00
Residual value	20	250	0.061	15.25
				NPV = 220.75

Note that 18 lines of calculation are avoided by making use of the annuity factors.

Self-assessment question S8.7

Try the following question for yourself (answer at the end of the chapter).

The New English Wine Company is considering automating its operations by investing in some new bottling plant. It has a choice of two machines, A and B. Machine A costs £40,000 and will have a residual value at the end of its 10-year life of £1,000. Machine B costs £20,000 and will have a residual value at the end of its 10-year life of £500. Machine A will save £10,000 a year in labour costs but machine B will only save £6,000 a year. If the company's cost of capital is 20% a year, which machine would you advise the company to buy?

Limitations of NPV

For NPV calculations, all cash flows (except for the initial project cost outflows) are assumed to occur **on the last day of the year**. This is due to discounting being the opposite of compounding **once a year**. In reality, cash flows throughout the year, not just at its end. This is a weakness of the model.

A further weakness is that the cost of capital is assumed to remain constant over the whole lifetime of the project. The longer the time period involved, the less likely this is to be true.

Method 4: internal rate of return (IRR)

The IRR is the average annual rate of return that the project is expected to produce; it is calculated using cash flows adjusted for the time value of money. It is expressed as a percentage and is determined by calculating the discount rate that gives the project an NPV of zero.

A project costs £28,000 and produces net cash flows as shown. What is the IRR?

Year	Cash inflow	60% factor	PV	61% factor	PV
0	(28,000)	1.0000	(28,000)	1.0000	(28,000)
1	18,000	0.6250	11,250	0.6211	11,180
2	21,000	0.3910	8,211	0.3858	8,102
3	24,000	0.2440	5,856	0.2396	5,750
4	18,000	0.1530	2,754	0.1488	2,679
			71		(289)

IRR = 60% + [71/(71 + 289) × 1%] = 60% + [71/360]% = 60.2%

60%	IRR	gap = 1%	61%
+71	0	gap = 360	(289)

Figure 8.9 **Example of an IRR calculation**

When organisations use IRR to evaluate capital investment proposals they set a threshold or 'hurdle' rate (usually equal to or higher than their ROCE). This is the minimum acceptable IRR for the project to go ahead. In theory, this threshold is set equal to the organisation's cost of capital or discount rate. In other words, the cash **generated** by the project must be at least equal to the cost of financing the project. In practice, to allow for risk and inherent approximation in the IRR calculations, it may be set at a rate greater than the cost of capital.

If several mutually exclusive projects are being considered, the one with the greatest IRR is chosen. An example of an IRR calculation is shown in Figure 8.9. This mathematical technique is known as *interpolation*.

Procedure for calculating the IRR

1 Perform the NPV process using your best guess of the discount rate which will give an NPV of zero.
2 If your NPV is positive, repeat the process using a higher discount rate in order to give a negative NPV. (If the first NPV is negative, try a lower rate to find a positive NPV.)
3 When you have one positive and one negative NPV, use interpolation to find the rate giving NPV = 0.

Note: This is an **iterative** technique using **trial and error**. Most spreadsheets and some calculators have dedicated functions to calculate PV, NPV and IRR but they do the calculations using the same method.

Try the following question for yourself (answer at the end of the chapter).

Find the IRR of the project detailed in S8.6.

Self-assessment question S8.8

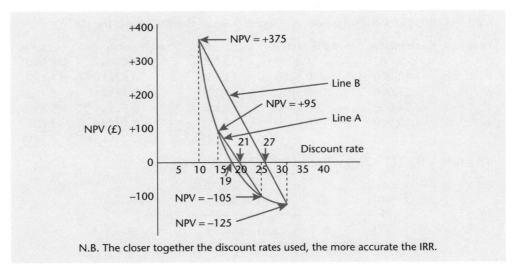

N.B. The closer together the discount rates used, the more accurate the IRR.

Figure 8.10 **Effect of discount rate choice**

Inherent approximation

Interpolation assumes that the NPV changes linearly with the discount rate. Mathematically, this is not true because the relationship is correctly represented by a curve rather than a straight line. Figure 8.10 illustrates this as follows.

Line B interpolates between NPVs of +375 (at 10%) and −125 (at 30%) and gives an IRR of 27%.

Line A interpolates between NPVs of +95 (at 15%) and −105 (at 25%) and gives an IRR of 21%.

The actual IRR is 19%.

Limitations of IRR

Consider two alternative projects, one in Sheffield and the other in Lincoln. The Sheffield project may have an IRR of 25% and the Lincoln project may have an IRR of 50%, so the Lincoln project would be chosen. But which project produces most money? (25% of £800,000 is greater than 50% of £300,000!) IRR is a **relative** measure. (In contrast, NPV is an **absolute** measure giving monetary answers rather than percentages.)

Also, due to the mathematics involved, if any of the cash flows after year 0 are net outflows, there may be **more than one value** of the IRR. (This is similar to the square root of 9 having two answers, +3 and −3.)

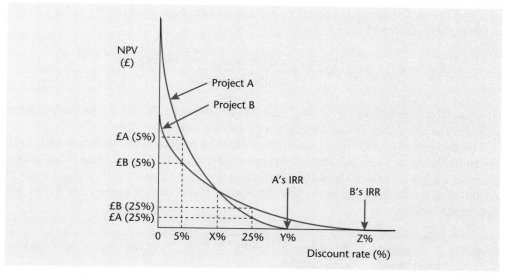

Figure 8.11 **Mutually exclusive projects**

Comparing NPV to IRR

Suppose a business has a choice between the Arundel project (A) and the Brighton project (B), what guidance can it gain from calculating their NPVs and IRRs? Assuming that they have different cash flows, the situation is represented in Figure 8.11 as follows:

● The Brighton project has the higher IRR (Z%).
● At a discount rate of 25%, Brighton has a higher NPV than Arundel.
● At a discount rate of 5%, Arundel has a higher NPV than Brighton.

To the right of the crossover point (X%), IRR and NPV will both recommend adopting the Brighton project. However, to the left of this point, IRR and NPV will conflict and recommend different projects.

Note: If the IRR decision conflicts with the NPV, the NPV decision should be used as it is technically more sound. Remember that IRR is a **relative** measure but NPV is an **absolute** measure (see 'Limitations of IRR' above).

Capital rationing and the profitability index

At any point in time, an organisation may have identified several projects in which it is worthwhile investing as they each have a positive NPV. Unfortunately, it may not be able to raise sufficient funds to invest in all of them. This situation is referred to as 'capital rationing' and the problem it poses is how the business decides in which of the available projects to invest.

A good way of approaching this decision is to calculate the 'profitability index' of each project. This is defined by the formula

$$PI = \frac{\text{present value of future cash inflows}}{\text{initial investment}}$$

This is effectively a 'benefit to cost' ratio. (The present value of future cash inflows excludes the initial investment, year 0 in NPV calculations.)

The decision rule is for the company to accept the projects with the greatest PIs until the funds run out. (This assumes all PIs are greater than 1.0, which means they have a positive NPV.) Consider the following example of a company with a maximum of £200,000 of funds to invest in the five different projects shown in the table below (all figures are in £000).

Project	Initial investment	PV of future cash inflows	NPV	PI	PI ranking	NPV ranking
A	78	105	27	1.35	2	3
B	55	70	15	1.27	3	4
C	200	250	50	1.25	4	1
D	66	94	28	1.42	1	2
E	72	79	7	1.10	5	5

If projects are ranked according to the size of their NPVs, only project C is able to be undertaken, which has a total NPV of £50,000.

NPV ranking	Project	Initial investment	NPV
1	C	200	50
Total		200	50

But if projects are ranked according to their PIs, projects D, A and B would be undertaken and the resulting NPV would increase by 40% to £70,000.

PI ranking	Project	Initial investment	NPV
1	D	66	28
2	A	78	27
3	B	55	15
Total		199	70

A suboptimal result is normally obtained when projects are ranked in the order of their absolute NPVs. This is because the largest projects tend to be selected due to their high individual NPVs. However, their combined NPV is usually lower than that of those projects selected by their PI ranking.

Self-assessment
question S8.9

Try the following question for yourself (answer at the end of the chapter).

Invest Quest plc has a maximum of £700 million to invest in new capital projects. Advise which of the following five projects should be chosen. (All figures are in £m.)

Project	Initial investment	PV of future cash inflows
A	185	269
B	197	260
C	81	137
D	210	299
E	282	352

Discounted payback period?

It may have occurred to you that it is possible to discount the cash flows used in payback calculations. The effect of this is to lengthen the period and so show more caution in the estimate of the time needed for the project to pay for itself.

At first sight this approach may seem an improvement on the basic PBP. However, the simplicity of PBP, which is one of its main attractions, is significantly diminished by it. Also, as PBP concentrates on the early years of a project, the benefit of discounting is limited.

More importantly, PBP assumes cash to flow evenly throughout each year but discounting assumes the annual cash flow to occur on the last day of the financial year. These two **contradictory assumptions** render this financial model theoretically unsound and its use inadvisable.

Choice of method

Having four methods of appraising capital investments at your disposal, how do you choose which one to use? Fortunately, you do not have to answer this question because you do not have to use only one method. Indeed, it is preferable to employ a variety of approaches to see how much consensus they produce. After all, each method tells you something different.

ARR tells you the percentage profit return on your investment. PBP tells you how long it will take to recoup your initial investment. NPV tells you the current cash value of the project measured in today's money. IRR tells you the average annual growth rate of your cash investment. As a starting point to your final discussion and recommendation, it is helpful to create a summary table of the results from all the methods employed. This makes the comparison of the findings relatively easy.

However, it is important not to overlook the limitations of the techniques you have used. Will the assumptions of the various methods impinge more on some projects than others or is the effect likely to be the same for all of them?

Finally, you should think more as a manager than an accountant. There will always be some qualitative factors to consider. Factors such as the availability of skilled labour, the ease of distribution to the market and the enhancement of the product range should not be ignored.

Sensitivity analysis

Whatever methods are chosen, sensitivity analysis can be used to evaluate the risk from each of the factors involved in the project. Once the non-starters have been eliminated and only the possible projects remain, each factor can be analysed to see how much it would need to change before the project would no longer be viable. Even where one single project has been chosen, it is wise to perform a sensitivity analysis to identify the factors which need to change least to cast doubt on the viability of the project. Sensitivity analysis is illustrated in the following example.

The Freeway Driving School is considering expanding its operations by employing one further instructor and car. The car will cost £15,000 (including the addition of dual controls), will be used for three years and then scrapped (for zero value). Fixed costs such as insurance, vehicle licence duty, servicing, etc., will be £4,600 a year and the annual cost of the instructor is £20,000. Instructors are expected to give a maximum of six lessons a day for five days a week and to work for 50 weeks a year. However, it is estimated that the take-up rate for lessons will be 90% of the maximum, i.e. 27 lessons a week ($5 \times 6 \times 90\%$). The selling price of each lesson is £32 and the petrol cost is £5. Freeway has calculated that its cost of capital is 12.5% p.a. Calculate the NPV of this three-year project and perform a sensitivity analysis to identify the relative sensitivity of the factors involved.

Suggested solution

Income	= 50 weeks × 27 lessons × £32/lesson	= £43,200
Variable cost	= 50 weeks × 27 lessons × £5/lesson	= £6,750
Fixed cost	= £4,600 (ins., etc.) + £20,000 (salary)	= £24,600
Total cost	= £24,600 + £6,750	= £31,350

NPV calculation

Year	Cash in	Cash out	Net cash flow	12.5% discount factors	Present value
0	0	15,000	−15,000	1.0000	−15,000
1	43,200	31,350	11,850	0.8889	10,533
2	43,200	31,350	11,850	0.7901	9,363
3	43,200	31,350	11,850	0.7023	8,323
					NPV = 13,219

If all assumptions prove to be correct, NPV = £13,219.

Sensitivity analysis – weeks worked per year

Year	Cash in	Cash out	Net cash flow	12.5% discount factors	Present value
0	0	15,000	−15,000	1.0000	−15,000
1	37,584	31,350	6,234	0.8889	5,541
2	37,584	31,350	6,234	0.7901	4,926
3	37,584	31,350	6,234	0.7023	4,378
					NPV = −155

Weeks worked per year can fall to 43.5 (−13%) before NPV ≤ 0 (43.5 × [30 × 90%] × £32 = £37,584).

Sensitivity analysis – take-up rate

Year	Cash in	Cash out	Net cash flow	12.5% discount factors	Present value
0	0	15,000	−15,000	1.0000	−15,000
1	37,440	31,350	6,090	0.8889	5,413
2	37,440	31,350	6,090	0.7901	4,812
3	37,440	31,350	6,090	0.7023	4,277
					NPV = −498

Take-up rate can fall to 78% (−13%) before NPV ≤ 0 (50 × [30 × 78%] × £32 = £37,440).

Sensitivity analysis – lesson price

Year	Cash in	Cash out	Net cash flow	12.5% discount factors	Present value
0	0	15,000	−15,000	1.0000	−15,000
1	37,800	31,350	6,450	0.8889	5,733
2	37,800	31,350	6,450	0.7901	5,096
3	37,800	31,350	6,450	0.7023	4,530
					NPV = 360

Lesson price can fall to £28 (−13%) before NPV ≤ 0 (50 × [30 × 90%] × £28 = £37,800).

Sensitivity analysis – petrol cost

Year	Cash in	Cash out	Net cash flow	12.5% discount factors	Present value
0	0	15,000	−15,000	1.0000	−15,000
1	43,200	36,750	6,450	0.8889	5,733
2	43,200	36,750	6,450	0.7901	5,096
3	43,200	36,750	6,450	0.7023	4,530
					NPV = 360

Petrol cost can increase to £9 a lesson (+80%) before NPV ≤ 0 (50 × [30 × 90%] × £9 = £12,150 plus fixed costs of £24,600 = £36,750).

Sensitivity analysis – fixed costs

Year	Cash in	Cash out	Net cash flow	12.5% discount factors	Present value
0	0	15,000	−15,000	1.0000	−15,000
1	43,200	36,750	6,450	0.8889	5,733
2	43,200	36,750	6,450	0.7901	5,096
3	43,200	36,750	6,450	0.7023	4,530
					NPV = 360

Fixed costs can increase by £5,400 (+22%) before NPV ≤ 0 (£6,750 + £24,600 + £5,400 = £36,750).

Sensitivity analysis – Discount rate

Year	Cash in	Cash out	Net cash flow	60.0% discount factors	Present value
0	0	15,000	−15,000	1.0000	−15,000
1	43,200	31,350	11,850	0.6250	7,406
2	43,200	31,350	11,850	0.3906	4,629
3	43,200	31,350	11,850	0.2441	2,893
					NPV = −72

Discount rate can increase to 60% (+500%) before NPV ≤ 0.

Note that depreciation was **not** included in the calculations as it does **not** cause any movement of cash. (NPV uses only cash flows.)

Summary table of changes needed to produce a negative NPV
(Most sensitive factors listed first)

Factor	Change
Weeks needed	−13%
Take-up rate	−13%
Lesson price	−13%
Fixed costs	+22%
Petrol cost	+80%
Discount rate	+500%

Findings

Taking each factor in isolation, the analysis shows that the three most sensitive factors are weeks worked, take-up rate and lesson price. A 13% reduction in any of these will produce a negative NPV. Next, a 17% increase in fixed costs or an 80% increase in petrol costs will have the same effect. Finally, the discount rate will need to increase by 500% to produce a negative NPV.

The financing decision

Project loans and interest payments

Obtaining a bank loan is one way of financing a capital investment project. All the cash flows associated with the loan (initial sum, interest payments and final repayment of sum) should be **excluded** from the cash flows used in capital investment appraisal. This is because the decision on how to finance a project is separate from the decision on whether or not to accept the project. The decision to accept a project or not should be made first. Only if this is positive will the choice of finance need to be made. (The financing decision is outside the scope of this book.)

If interest charges are not eliminated from the cash flows before they are discounted, double counting will occur. This is because the discounting process automatically allows for the time value of money, which is firmly based on the ability of money to earn interest.

To eliminate the effect of interest from the calculations, the annual interest charges (as well as the depreciation charges) are added back to profits to give the **cash flows before interest**.

Note: Concerning the subsection 'Reconciliation of cash flows with profits' we looked at earlier in this chapter, the position is modified as follows. **Over the whole lifetime of a project**, the total of profits (**before interest**) will equal the total of cash flows (**ignoring loans, interest and repayments**). (Note that this is not true for any one year within the project's lifetime.)

Qualitative factors

The management accountant's role is to provide the calculations and a recommendation. The manager's role is to apply experience and knowledge of the industry, weigh up the risks involved and make the decision. The work of the management accountant is important but it is only the starting point of the appraisal process. Other factors, many of which are not numerically quantifiable but still affect the decision, should be taken into account. Remember, the final decision should be a management decision, not an accounting one.

Limitations of capital investment appraisal techniques

The limitations of the four techniques have already been discussed at the end of each of their sections. However, it is worth pointing out that all capital investment appraisals are only as good as the forecasts of profit or cash flow on which they are based. The long-term nature of capital investment appraisal compounds this weakness. The further into the future the forecast goes, the less reliable it becomes.

Also, these techniques cannot tell companies when, and in what, they should be investing. For example, the oil company Shell announced record profits of £9.8 billion in 2004, an all-time record for a European company! But Shell's stated total of oil reserves was only 9 years which compared badly to its rivals BP and Exxon which had each identified sufficient oil to keep them in business for the next 14 years. This was an excellent opportunity to plough as much of the 'excess' profit as possible back into the company to finance increased exploration activities or research into alternative energy sources. After all, if it did not find any more oil or develop new products, it would be out of business in less than 10 years. However, Shell decided that it would spend its 'windfall' profits on paying a one-off special dividend to shareholders and buying back its own shares on the stock market in order to keep its share price high rather than invest in its long-term future.

The manager's point of view

Capital investment decisions are among the most challenging issues faced by management. The sums of money involved can be very large, and the decision to invest or not to invest can have a profound influence on the future of the business. Large projects are often turning points in the life of a company. Success can raise the business on to a new plane. Failure can bring it down altogether. Moreover, the decision has to be taken largely on the basis of estimates of what might happen in the future. Different assumptions about future circumstances will lead to different patterns of projected profits and cash flow. Management has to decide on the most likely outcome of the project, and ensure that the proposed level of capital expenditure is compatible with this outcome. Capital appraisal techniques are designed to rationalise all the relevant information and present management with a reasonable comparison between the options available.

Preparing a capital expenditure proposal is an iterative process. It is rather like budgeting. All the contributors to the process – the engineer, salesperson, raw material purchaser, production and technical representatives, etc. – draw up proposals relating to their areas, but without seeing the overall picture. As in budgeting, therefore, everyone starts by specifying their requirements with their own particular agendas in mind, whilst preparing to make concessions only if it is found that the figures do not ultimately add up. For instance, engineers will tend, perhaps rightly, to aim in the first instance for state-of-the-art technology, as they feel this will keep the company in the forefront of the industry. Salespeople, being optimistic by nature, may have a tendency to overestimate what their talents can achieve, so their projected sales levels may appear to support the high capital expenditure proposals. A decision to go for expensive plant under these circumstances would be very tempting, but it may be based on a false assumption of future cash flows and could in fact be quite the wrong option for the company.

A similar pattern of optimism and aspiration is likely to be repeated throughout the departments involved, so that, when all the figures are put together for the first time, the initial view may be completely distorted. It is likely to be quite different from the final article when the iterative process is complete. Every number in the financial statements must be challenged. Are the proposed sales volumes reasonable? Will the competition bring a better product to the market during the life span of the project?

Are the proposed selling prices supportable? Will the increased capacity in the market-place, created by the project itself, have an impact on prices? And so on. For every question asked, there will be a variety of inconclusive answers, more like statements of probabilities. But every discussion will give you a better feel for the robustness of a particular number. In the end, you can only go with one set of figures, but it is useful to bear in mind the best-case and worst-case scenarios, so that you develop an understanding of the risks inherent in the project.

Throughout the iterative process, the capital appraisal techniques outlined in this chapter provide a common point of comparison between the different financial scenarios which each set of circumstances throws up. They will help you to answer critical questions such as: 'Will the business support a full replacement of the plant, or is refurbishment the more viable option?' and 'Is it worth going for the expense of a bigger expansion now, so that we do not have to put up with the upheaval of a further expansion project in three, five or ten years' time?' The internal rate of return calculation takes into account the cash flows for the whole of a project's life span, and reduces it to a single figure which can be compared not only with alternative options, but also with the company's required benchmark.

Cash is a scarce commodity for many companies, so the payback period is also a critical measurement. If we make the capital investment today, how many years of cash inflow will it take to get our money back? In other words, how soon will we be making a genuine profit on our investment? If the profit arrives a long way into the future, we could be better off by simply keeping our funds on deposit. At the very least, we should consider alternative projects which give a quicker return.

For some years, my corporation's strategy had been aimed at raising the company's overall return on capital employed to 20%, a high target, but an attainable one for a speciality chemical business. In order to achieve this, the company set a minimum IRR of 20% and a maximum payback period of three years for all capital expenditure proposals. Any project with better returns than these had a good chance of success. Since it was a multinational corporation, however, competition for capital funds was always intense. If we submitted our project at a time when other subsidiaries were putting forward even better proposals, we could find ourselves being either turned down or deferred. There was always a temptation, therefore, to go forward with optimistic figures, and while optimism is fine, there is always the risk that it may spill over into fantasy land, with disaster following closely behind.

One of our fellow-subsidiaries had proposed a major expansion to one of its plants. The engineers determined that the capital cost would be $9.6 million. This included a number of specific pieces of plant for which firm quotations had been obtained, but the majority of it was based on estimates. In view of these uncertainties, it is common to add a general contingency into the cost, usually amounting to 10%. This contingency, at $960,000, was therefore completely non-specific. Yet this amount alone was larger than most other capital projects routinely undertaken by the subsidiary, all of which were subjected to the normal, detailed capital appraisal scrutiny. Much concern was expressed at the time over how this amount was to be controlled, but the engineers insisted that it represented only a buffer amount, and very little of it would actually be used. However, due to inaccurate estimating in the first place, and inadequate control during the installation process, especially over sub-contractors, the actual capital cost of the project spiralled, finally amounting not to $9.6 million, but $12.3 million. If this level of cost had been incorporated into the original financial appraisal, the IRR and payback would have been insufficient, and the project would never have been approved. As it was, the problem emerged too late for any remedial action to be taken. The business group concerned was left to carry an enormous burden, which severely inhibited its profitability for several years, and might well have caused the business to collapse.

This story demonstrates how critical the capital appraisal process can be to the well-being of the business. It will result in the business making a substantial commitment, not only in terms of capital, which can be significant, but also in respect of its future, strategic direction. Once the decision is made, the die is cast. It is critical, therefore, that the optimism inherent in capital proposals is tempered with a good dose of realism, or at least an element of conservatism. This is where the sensitivity analyses described earlier play an important part. They will demonstrate the robustness of the project if specific estimates, such as capital cost or sales levels, prove to be inaccurate.

When the project is approved and under way, it is also important that all the managers contributing to the appraisal process are held to account for their commitments. Post-completion audits are a good way to focus their minds. These can take place at any time in the life of a project, but usually occur after a period of several years, when the pattern of the business has been established. Although the threat of audit can sharpen the minds of managers, the disadvantage is that they happen so far after the event that any problems unearthed will almost certainly be beyond rectification. There is no substitute therefore for detailed analysis and testing of the basic assumptions underlying the capital appraisal, followed by close control of the project at every stage of its development. The potential risk to the business of unsound assumptions is simply too great to permit the slightest lack of rigour in the management review process.

Summary

- There are four alternative ways of appraising large investments in fixed (or capital) assets: ARR, PBP, NPV and IRR.

- They all use cash flow except ARR, which uses profit.

- Cash flows can be calculated by adding back depreciation to profits.

- Due to the long time periods involved, it is appropriate to discount future cash flows to present values for NPV and IRR.

- Discounting is the opposite process to the compounding of interest.

- Several methods should be used to aid decision making as each one considers a different aspect of the project.

- Each method is based on assumptions and has its limitations.

- The interpolation process for calculating IRR contains inherent approximations.

- It is possible for the NPV and IRR decisions to contradict each other. If this occurs, it is preferable to use the NPV recommendation.

- Sensitivity analysis helps to identify the major risk factors.

- The cash flows arising from the financing decision should **not** be included in the calculations.

- The final decision should take account of qualitative factors as well as the quantitative results of the methods used.

- Each method has its own limitations/weaknesses.

- All capital investment appraisal is limited by the inaccuracy of the cash flow/profit forecasts used.

Further reading

Atkinson, A., Banker, R., Kaplan, R. and Young, S. (2001) *Management Accounting*, 3rd edition, Prentice Hall, Harlow. See chapter 'Using management accounting information for investment decisions'.

Borgonovo, E. and Peccati, L. (2004) 'Sensitivity analysis in investment project evaluation', *International Journal of Production Economics*, Vol. 90, Issue 1, July.

Boston, J. (2002) 'Purer speculation', *Financial Management* (CIMA), March.

Cohn, E. (2003) 'Benefit-cost analysis: a pedagogical note', *Public Finance Review*, Vol. 31, Issue 5, September.

Horngren, C., Bhimani, A., Datar, S. and Foster, G. (2002) *Management and Cost Accounting*, 2nd edition, Prentice Hall Europe, Harlow. See Chapter 13, 'Capital investment decisions'.

Otley, D. (1987) *Accounting Control and Organisational Behaviour*, Heinemann Professional, Oxford. See Chapter 8, 'Capital budgeting'.

Pogue, M. (2004) 'Investment appraisal: a new approach', *Managerial Auditing Journal*, Vol. 19, Issue 4, April.

Upchurch, A. (2003) *Management Accounting, Principles and Practice*, 2nd edition, Financial Times/Prentice Hall, Harlow. See chapter 'Capital investment appraisal'.

Weetman, P. (2002) *Management Accounting, an Introduction*, 3rd edition, Financial Times/ Prentice Hall, Harlow. See chapter 'Capital budgeting'.

Answers to self-assessment questions

S8.1

Year	Units	Profit before fixed costs	Fixed costs	Net profit
1	5,000	20,000	16,000	4,000
2	6,000	24,000	16,000	8,000
3	7,000	28,000	16,000	12,000
4	8,000	32,000	16,000	16,000
5	6,500	26,000	16,000	10,000

$$\text{ARR} = \frac{(4 + 8 + 12 + 16 + 10)/5}{25} \times 100 = \frac{10}{25} \times 100 = 40\%$$

S8.2

$$\text{Annual depreciation charge} = \frac{\text{fall in value over project's lifetime}}{\text{lifetime in years}}$$

$$= \frac{(190,000 - 10,000)}{9} = £20,000$$

(Figures shown in £000)

Year	Profit/(Loss)	Annual depreciation	Other items	Cash flow in/(out)
0	0	0	buy crane (190)	(190)
1	10	20	0	30
2	18	20	0	38
3	24	20	0	44
4	30	20	0	50
5	35	20	0	55
6	38	20	0	58
7	30	20	0	50
8	20	20	0	40
9	10	20	sell scrap 10	40
	215			**215**

S8.3

Year	Profit	Depreciation	Cash flow	Cumulative
1	4,000	2,000	6,000	6,000
2	8,000	2,000	10,000	16,000
3	12,000	2,000	14,000	30,000
4	16,000	2,000	18,000	48,000
5	10,000	2,000	12,000	60,000

$$\text{Payback period} = 2 + \frac{(25 - 16)}{14} = 2 + \frac{9}{14} = 2.64 \text{ years} = \textbf{2 years 8 months}$$

S8.4

£500 invested for 4 years at 7.5% p.a. compound:

Year	Amount	Factor	Total
	£		£
1	500.00	1.075	537.50
2	537.50	1.075	577.81
3	577.81	1.075	621.15
4	621.15	1.075	**£667.73**

S8.5

Discounting cash flows at 3% p.a.:

Year	Cash flow	3% discount factor	Present value
	£		£
1	6,000	1/1.03 = 0.97087	5,825
2	10,000	0.97087/1.03 = 0.94260	9,426
3	14,000	0.94260/1.03 = 0.91514	12,812
4	18,000	0.91514/1.03 = 0.88849	15,993
5	12,000	0.88849/1.03 = 0.86261	10,351
	£60,000		Total **£54,407**

S8.6

Year	Cash in/(out)	10% factors	Present value
0	(49,500)	1.000	(49,500)
1	20,000	0.909	18,180
2	20,000	0.826	16,520
3	10,000	0.751	7,510
4	10,000	0.683	6,830
			NPV (460)

Recommendation: Do **not** go ahead with project.

S8.7

Machine A

Year	Cash in/(out)	20% factor	Present value
	£		£
0	(40,000)	1.000	(40,000)
1–10	10,000	4.192	41,920
10	1,000	0.162	162
			NPV = 2,082

Machine B

Year	Cash in/(out) £	20% factor	Present value £
0	(20,000)	1.000	(20,000)
1–10	6,000	4.192	25,152
10	500	0.162	81
			NPV = 5,233

Machine B appears to be a much better investment than machine A.

S8.8

Year	Cash in/(out)	10% factor	PV	9% factor	PV
0	(49,500)	1.000	(49,500)	1.000	(49,500)
1	20,000	0.909	18,180	0.917	18,340
2	20,000	0.826	16,520	0.842	16,840
3	10,000	0.751	7,510	0.772	7,720
4	10,000	0.683	6,830	0.708	7,080
			NPV = (460)		NPV = 480

By interpolation:

$$\text{IRR} = 9\% + \frac{480}{(480 + 460)} \times 1\% = 9.51\%$$

```
9%              9.51%              10%
 └────────────────┼────────────────┘
+480               0               (460)
```

S8.9

Calculate the NPV, PI and rankings for all projects.

Project	Initial investment	PV of future cash inflows	NPV	PI	PI ranking	NPV ranking
A	185	269	84	1.45	2	2
B	197	260	63	1.32	4	4
C	81	137	56	1.69	1	5
D	210	299	89	1.42	3	1
E	282	352	70	1.25	5	3

If projects are ranked according to the size of their NPVs, projects D, A and E are undertaken, giving a total NPV of £243 million.

NPV ranking	Project	Initial investment	NPV
1	D	210	89
2	A	185	84
3	E	282	70
Total		677	243

But if projects are ranked according to their PIs, projects C, A, D and B would be undertaken and the resulting NPV would increase by £49 million to £292 million.

PI ranking	Project	Initial investment	NPV
1	C	81	56
2	A	185	84
3	D	210	89
4	B	197	63
		673	292

Based on the figures alone, IQ plc should consider investing in projects A, B, C and D.

Nufone

Nufone plc is considering the launch of a new product, the latest in its range of mobile phones. Its major selling point is a modified microwave technology which will significantly improve the quality of the voice output and the robustness of the connection. Its inventor has approached Nufone plc with a view to selling it the patent and has given the company one week before he offers it elsewhere. The patent will cost £5 million. The profit estimates below are based on a market research survey for a similar concept which Nufone commissioned four months ago from an independent bureau.

If the project goes ahead, a new factory will have to be built at a cost of £2 million plus £6 million for machinery. The company is currently negotiating for a suitable site on which to build; it expects to have to pay £3 million for it. Nufone plc's depreciation policy is to use the equal instalment (straight-line) method with residual values always assumed to be zero. Patents are decreased in value (amortised) in the same way but land is not depreciated. It is assumed the patent will have no value in 10 years' time.

It is estimated that the product will have a life of 10 years, at the end of which time it will be obsolete. It is also assumed that the factory building will then be demolished. The cost of the demolition will be exactly covered by the sale proceeds of the 10-year-old machinery. Also, the land will be sold for an estimated £3 million.

The financing of the project will be assisted by a bank loan, which will incur interest of £300,000 p.a., payable in arrears at the end of each year. The working capital (stock, debtors and creditors) needed to run this project is estimated to be £1.2 million.

The profits shown below are **after** charging depreciation, interest on the bank loan and launch costs (£1.5 million, all in year 1).

Year	Profit/(Loss) £m	Year	Profit/(Loss) £m
1	(2.3)	6	10.0
2	1.5	7	8.0
3	6.0	8	6.0
4	8.0	9	4.0
5	10.0	10	2.0

(The project detailed above will be known as project T.)

Having seen the above project proposal from the technical director, the financial director suggests that they should lease an existing factory instead of building one. She estimates that the lease will cost £1.4 million to purchase (payable in advance) followed by 10 annual payments of £800,000 (payable in arrears). The machinery will still have to be purchased as before. (This alternative project will be known as project F.)

The sales director has come up with a third alternative. This is to go ahead with a new design of phone with a modified casing. In this case it would not be necessary to purchase the patent. As less new technology is involved, the production could take place in the present factory by putting on a night shift. However, £4 million would still need to be spent on new machinery, although the bank loan would be unnecessary. Working capital would be reduced to £0.8 million. The profits from this phone, after charging depreciation on the new machinery, are estimated as follows:

Year	Profit/(Loss) £m	Year	Profit/(Loss) £m
1	2.1	6	2.6
2	3.6	7	2.6
3	3.6	8	1.6
4	3.6	9	1.6
5	2.6	10	0.6

(This alternative project will be known as project S.)

Notes:

1 Nufone plc's cost of capital (or discount rate) is 12.5% p.a.
2 Work to the nearest £000 when performing your calculations.
3 You are expected to use a word processor and a spreadsheet for this assignment.
4 When performing your calculations, **show your workings** and do not use the dedicated functions for PV, NPV and IRR provided by spreadsheets and some calculators.

Tasks:

1 For each of the three alternatives, calculate the following:
   a) the cash flows
   b) the accounting rate of return (using the initial cost)
   c) the payback period
   d) the net present value
   e) the internal rate of return (using the 'interpolation' method).

(50%)

2 **On no more than two sides of A4 paper**, create an executive summary report for Nufone plc's board of directors, appraising the capital investment decision facing them. Justify any recommendations you make and discuss any reservations you have concerning the application and interpretation of the techniques used. *(Any work in excess of the first two pages will be ignored.)*

(50%)
(Total 100%)

The Private Healthcare Group (PHG) was started nine years ago by three doctors previously employed by the National Health Service. It is based in the East Midlands and specialises in cosmetic surgery; 91% of its clients come from the UK and 9% from overseas.

It is considering opening a new clinic in the Coventry area to treat medical problems connected with obesity. This business unit will be known as the 'Coventry Obesity Clinic'. It has been predicted that the number of obese people in the UK will more than double in the next few years and, although public awareness of obesity and its causes is growing fast, PHG believes that a significant market is opening up for it to serve.

An initial feasibility study has been carried out and several alternative ways forward have been identified. The two most likely are to erect a new building and to convert an existing one. The conversion is likely to be cheaper to build but more expensive to run.

The study was based on a clinic with a capacity of 20 beds open for business seven days a week. A new building would be operational for 50 weeks a year but a converted building for only 48 weeks a year due to the additional amount of building maintenance work needed on a regular basis. Any improvement work thought necessary could also be carried out during this shutdown period.

However, the fee to be charged to the clients (on a daily basis) and the occupancy rate are more difficult to determine due to the price elasticity of demand. The results of a market research report, commissioned as part of the feasibility study, are shown below in table A. It makes predictions for bed occupancy rates at various fee levels.

PHG thinks that the considerable entry barriers, such as high initial building costs, will result in a relatively low competitive environment for about five years. The NHS is likely to be offering at least some of these treatments by then. PHG will probably sell the business after five years and pursue other more profitable avenues. PHG has calculated that its accounting rate of return for the group was 21.4% in the previous financial year.

The cost of building the clinic from scratch is estimated at £6.0 million. An existing building, suitable for conversion, has been identified and is on the market at £3.0 million but a further £2.2 million would need to be spent to convert it to meet the clinic's building specification. In addition to this, in both cases, specialised medical equipment would need to be purchased and installed at a cost of £2.8 million. PHG has been professionally advised that the resale value of the new building in five years' time will probably be 10% lower than its initial cost. However, the same advisers stated that the converted building should maintain its value of £5.2 million over the same period.

PHG's policy on depreciation is to use the straight-line method, buildings over 25 years and equipment (including vehicles) over 5 years. The variable costs, such as food and drink, are estimated to be £40 per client per day. A schedule of fixed costs is currently being drawn up by the group accountant and will be available soon.

The chief executive officer of PHG has decided to ask for some calculations to be done regarding this project. He is particularly concerned about the reliability and inherent uncertainty in answers resulting from the application of accounting techniques having had his fingers burned in a similar situation a few years earlier.

As most of the funding for this project would be provided by a debenture, PHG estimates that the cost of capital for the obesity clinic project will be 16.5% a year.

The specialised medical equipment will have no value at the end of the five-year period. An analysis of fixed costs other than depreciation is shown below in table B.

Table A: Market research data

Daily fee (£)	Annual Occupancy rate (%)
500	94
600	91
700	82
800	77
900	67
1000	55

Table B: Annual Fixed costs other than depreciation

Item	New build (£)	Conversion (£)
Medical salaries	1,320,000	1,320,000
Admin salaries	170,000	170,000
Building maintenance	50,000	120,000
Heat, light and air-conditioning	70,000	100,000

Tasks:

1 Calculate the annual operating contribution and profit for each of the price/occupancy rate combinations in the market research report.

(30 marks)

2 Calculate the first year's return on capital employed for (a) a new building, and (b) a converted building. (Use **initial** capital employed.) Use the price/occupancy rate combination which gives the maximum profit in each case.

(8 marks)

3 Calculate the payback period of the project for (a) a new building, and (b) a converted building. Use the price/occupancy rate combination which gives the maximum profit in each case.

(8 marks)

4 Calculate the net present value (NPV) of the project for (a) a new building, and (b) a converted building. Use the price/occupancy rate combination which gives the maximum profit in each case.

(30 marks)

5 Explain what is meant by an 'NPV sensitivity analysis'. For the new building option only, calculate the **approximate** sensitivity of the advised end value of the building after five years.

(8 marks)

6 Advise the PHG directors on proceeding with the obesity clinic.

(16 marks)
(Total 100 marks)

Questions

An asterisk * on a question number indicates that the answer is given at the end of the book. Answers to the other questions are given in the Lecturer's Guide.

Q8.1* Frynas & Co.

Frynas & Co. is considering buying a mobile drilling rig to expand the range of services it provides for the water, gas and oil industries. The rig would cost £620,000 and last for four years, at the end of which it would be sold for £20,000. The estimated profits for each of the four years are shown below. (The company uses the straight-line method of calculating depreciation. Its latest set of accounts showed its return on capital employed to be 11.1%.)

Year	Profit/(Loss) £
1	(50,000)
2	50,000
3	150,000
4	50,000

Tasks:

1 Calculate and comment on the accounting rate of return (using the initial investment).
2 Calculate the payback period.
3 Calculate the net present value if Frynas's cost of capital is 10.0%.
4 Calculate the internal rate of return.
5 Comment on your findings.

Q8.2* Binley Blades Limited

Binley Blades specialises in the manufacture of rotor blades for helicopters. It has just spent £50,000 developing a new type of blade based on a mixture of carbon fibre and naturally occurring resins. These blades can stand 80% more stress than the company's standard blades but will cost approximately 50% more to manufacture. It now has to decide whether to go ahead and build a new production facility for its new blades. Unfortunately, the net present value analysis (reproduced below) indicates that it would be most unwise to go ahead with this project.

Year	0	1	2	3	4	5
COSTS (£000)						
Plant & equipment	2,000	0	0	0	0	0
Research & development	0	10	10	10	10	10
Materials usage	0	500	500	500	500	500
Direct labour	0	200	200	200	200	200

Year	0	1	2	3	4	5
Indirect labour	0	20	20	20	20	20
Working capital	150	0	0	0	0	0
Depreciation	0	200	200	200	200	200
Production overheads	0	40	40	40	40	40
Sales & administration overheads	0	60	60	60	60	60
Finance overhead	0	200	200	200	200	200
Total costs	2,150	1,230	1,230	1,230	1,230	1,230
REVENUES (£000)						
Sales revenue	0	1,450	1,450	1,450	1,450	1,450
Disposal of plant & equipment	0	0	0	0	0	1,000
Total revenue	0	1,450	1,450	1,450	1,450	2,450
NET TOTAL REVENUE	−2,150	220	220	220	220	1,220
10% discount factors	1	0.9	0.8	0.7	0.6	0.5
Present values	−2,150	198	176	154	132	610
NET PRESENT VALUE	**−880**					

Notes:

1 It is company policy to write off research and development costs over the lifetime of the product.

2 It is company policy to use straight-line depreciation over 10 years, with a zero residual value, for plant and equipment.

3 The company is currently developing an even stronger blade which uses a very different technology. Binley thinks it will take a further five years before it is ready for production. Thus, Binley considers that the carbon fibre/resin project will have a life of five years, at the end of which the plant and equipment will be sold off at 25% of their original cost.

4 The necessary plant and equipment will be purchased for £2 million, financed in full by a bank loan for this amount, bearing interest at 10% a year (shown above as 'Finance overhead').

5 The working capital consists of carbon fibre and resin material stocks.

6 Only half of the indirect labour costs will actually be caused by this project. The other half is a redistribution from standard blade production.

7 Only 12.5% of the production overheads will actually be caused by this project. The remainder is a redistribution from standard blade production.

8 Binley believes that its current marketing and administration departments will be able to cope with any increased workloads. The overheads shown are a redistribution from standard blade production.

Task:

Redraft the above schedule, correcting any mistakes you find. Comment briefly on your results.

Q8.3* Stobo plc

Stobo plc is a well-known national chain of high-street chemists. Its traditional markets of pharmaceuticals and beauty products are becoming increasingly competitive due to the aggressive entry of certain supermarkets. To counter this, it is considering expanding its services to the public. It plans to make more effective use of some of its retail space and storerooms by introducing some sort of personal healthcare service. A few stores have been chosen in specially selected locations for a five-year pilot scheme. Stobo intends to choose one of the three following alternative possibilities:

SR   Stress relief, including aromatherapy, massage and reflexology
OHC   Oral hygiene and chiropody
PF   Personal fitness using multigym equipment

Each of these would involve an initial cash outlay on appropriate equipment and the employment of specialist personnel. Market research and a financial analysis have been carried out for each alternative; an extract of the findings is shown below.

(All figures in £000)	SR	OHC	PF
Initial cash outlay	44	40	44
Net cash flow:			
Year 1	16	8	12
Year 2	14	10	12
Year 3	12	12	12
Year 4	10	14	12
Year 5	8	16	12
	60	60	60
Internal rate of return	13%	13%	11%

Tasks:

1 Calculate the payback period for each alternative.
2 Calculate the net present value of each alternative if Stobo's cost of capital is 10%.
3 Advise Stobo which of the three alternatives it should concentrate on.

Q8.4 Fiesole Limited

Fiesole Limited is considering the selection of one of a pair of mutually exclusive capital investment projects. Both would involve the purchase of machinery with a life of five years. Fiesole uses the straight-line method for calculating depreciation and its cost of capital is 15% per year.

Project 1 would generate annual net cash inflows of £400,000; the machinery would cost £1,112,000 and have a scrap value of £112,000.

Project 2 would generate annual net cash inflows of £1,000,000; the machinery would cost £3,232,000 and have a scrap value of £602,000.

Tasks:

1 For each project, calculate:
   a) the accountancy rate of return (using the initial investment)
   b) the payback period
   c) the net present value.
2 State which project, if any, you would recommend for acceptance. Give your reasons.

Q8.5 The Adaptor Company

The Adaptor Company has recently invested £40,000 in a market research survey to determine the demand for its new product, the AdaptAll. The bill for this survey has not yet been paid. Adaptor is encouraged by the survey and now has to decide whether or not to go ahead.

The AdaptAll cost £50,000 to develop and if it goes ahead will need a further £10,000 spending on packaging development before it can be put on the market. The equipment needed to produce it will cost £180,000.

The product will only have a four-year life. In years 1 and 2, annual sales will be 30,000 units, falling to 20,000 units in year 3 and 10,000 units in year 4. The selling price will be £12 per unit.

The costs of producing the AdaptAll are as follows:

Materials – One unit of AdaptAll requires one unit of raw material. The company has 15,000 units of material in stock. This material originally cost £2 per unit but could be sold immediately for £3 per unit. The material could not be used by The Adaptor Company for any other of its products. If the AdaptAll project does not go ahead, the material will be sold. The current market price of material is £4 per unit.

Labour costs are £2 for each AdaptAll.

Fixed overheads – The company will need to rent a new factory unit to produce the AdaptAll, at a cost of £50,000 per annum. It does not advertise its products individually but sends out a company catalogue every two months with details of all its products. The catalogue incorporates details of all existing and new products, including the AdaptAll. The catalogue costs £1,000,000 per annum to produce and distribute, and it is company policy to allocate an equal share of this cost to each of its products. AdaptAll will therefore bear its share, amounting to £10,000 a year.

Variable overheads amount to £1 for each AdaptAll.

At the end of the four years the machinery will be sold for £20,000. The company uses straight-line depreciation for all its assets.

The company has a cost of capital of 10%, although projects are normally expected to achieve an IRR hurdle rate of at least 20%.

Tasks:

1 Calculate the net present value (NPV) of the AdaptAll project.
2 Estimate the effect on NPV of a reduction in sales volume of 10% per year, and use this to assess the % fall in volume that will reduce the NPV to zero.
3 Advise the company on whether or not it should proceed with the AdaptAll project, raising any other issues you feel should be considered in the decision. Your advice should incorporate comments on the use of the 20% hurdle rate as a decision rule.

Q8.6 MN plc

MN plc has a rolling programme of investment decisions. One of these investment decisions is to consider mutually exclusive investments A, B and C. The following information has been produced by the investment manager.

	Investment decision A £	Investment decision B £	Investment decision C £
Initial investment	105,000	187,000	245,000
Cash inflow for A: years 1 to 3	48,000		
Cash inflow for B: years 1 to 6		48,000	
Cash inflow for C: years 1 to 9			48,000
Net present value (NPV) at 10% each year	14,376	22,040	31,432
Ranking	3rd	2nd	1st
Internal rate of return (IRR)	17.5%	14%	13%
Ranking	1st	2nd	3rd

Required:

a) Prepare a report for the management of MN plc which includes:
   - a graph showing the sensitivity of the three investments to changes in the cost of capital;
   - an explanation of the reasons for differences between NPV and IRR rankings – use investment A to illustrate the points you make;
   - a brief summary which gives MN plc's management advice on which project should be selected.

(18 marks)

b) One of the directors has suggested using payback to assess the investments. Explain to him the advantages and disadvantages of using payback methods over IRR and NPV. Use the figures above to illustrate your answer.

(7 marks)
(Total = 25 marks)

CIMA Intermediate: Management Accounting – Decision Making, November 2001

Q8.7 CAF plc

CAF plc is a large multinational organisation that manufactures a range of highly engineered products/components for the aircraft and vehicle industries. The directors are considering the future of one of the company's factories in the UK which manufactures product A. Product A is coming to the end of its life but another 2 years' production is planned. This is expected to produce a net cash inflow of £3 million next year and £2.3 million in the product's final year.

Product AA

CAF plc has already decided to replace product A with product AA which will be ready to go into production in two years' time. Product AA is expected to have a life of 8 years. It could be made either at the UK factory under consideration or in an Eastern

European factory owned by CAF plc. The UK factory is located closer to the markets and therefore if product AA is made in Eastern Europe, the company will incur extra transport costs of £10 per unit. Production costs will be the same in both countries. Product AA will require additional equipment and staff will need training; this will cost £6 million at either location. 200,000 units of product AA will be made each year and each unit will generate a net cash inflow of £25 before extra transport costs. If product AA is made in the UK, the factory will be closed and sold at the end of the product's life.

Product X

Now, however, the directors are considering a further possibility: product X could be produced at the UK factory and product AA at the Eastern European factory. Product X must be introduced in one year's time and will remain in production for three years. If it is introduced, the manufacture of product A will have to cease a year earlier than planned. If this happened, output of product A would be increased by 12.5% to maximum capacity next year, its last year, to build stock prior to the product's withdrawal. The existing staff would be transferred to product X.

The equipment needed to make product X would cost £4 million. 50,000 units of product X would be made in its first year; after that, production would rise to 75,000 units a year. Product X would earn a net cash flow of £70 per unit. After three years' production of product X, the UK factory would be closed and sold. (Product AA would not be transferred back to the factory in the UK at that stage; production would continue at the Eastern European site.)

Sale of factory

It is expected that the UK factory could be sold for £5.5 million at any time between the beginning of year 2 and the end of year 10. If the factory is sold, CAF plc will make redundancy payments of £2 million and the sale of equipment will raise £350,000.

CAF plc's cost of capital is 5% each year.

Required:

a) Prepare calculations that show which of the three options is financially the best.

(15 marks)

b) The directors of CAF plc are unsure whether their estimates are correct. Calculate and discuss the sensitivity of your choice of option in (a) to:
   i) changes in transport costs;

   (3 marks)

   ii) changes in the selling price of the factory.

   (3 marks)

c) Briefly discuss the business issues that should be considered before relocating to another country.

(4 marks)
(Total = 25 marks)

CIMA Intermediate: Management Accounting – Decision Making, May 2002

Present value factor table

The following table is used to calculate the present value of an amount received a number of years in the future, discounted at a given percentage rate.

Example 1: at the discount rate of 5%, a sum of £1 received in 25 years' time is currently worth £0.295
Example 2: at the discount rate of 5%, a sum of £1,000 received in 25 years' time is currently worth £295.00.

Discount rate / Years	1%	2%	3%	4%	5%	6%	7%	8%	9%	10%	11%	12%	13%	14%	15%	16%	17%	18%	19%	20%
1	0.990	0.980	0.971	0.962	0.952	0.943	0.935	0.926	0.917	0.909	0.901	0.893	0.885	0.877	0.870	0.862	0.855	0.847	0.840	0.833
2	0.980	0.961	0.943	0.925	0.907	0.890	0.873	0.857	0.842	0.826	0.812	0.797	0.783	0.769	0.756	0.743	0.731	0.718	0.706	0.694
3	0.971	0.942	0.915	0.889	0.864	0.840	0.816	0.794	0.772	0.751	0.731	0.712	0.693	0.675	0.658	0.641	0.624	0.609	0.593	0.579
4	0.961	0.924	0.888	0.855	0.823	0.792	0.763	0.735	0.708	0.683	0.659	0.636	0.613	0.592	0.572	0.552	0.534	0.516	0.499	0.482
5	0.951	0.906	0.863	0.822	0.784	0.747	0.713	0.681	0.650	0.621	0.593	0.567	0.543	0.519	0.497	0.476	0.456	0.437	0.419	0.402
6	0.942	0.888	0.837	0.790	0.746	0.705	0.666	0.630	0.596	0.564	0.535	0.507	0.480	0.456	0.432	0.410	0.390	0.370	0.352	0.335
7	0.933	0.871	0.813	0.760	0.711	0.665	0.623	0.583	0.547	0.513	0.482	0.452	0.425	0.400	0.376	0.354	0.333	0.314	0.296	0.279
8	0.923	0.853	0.789	0.731	0.677	0.627	0.582	0.540	0.502	0.467	0.434	0.404	0.376	0.351	0.327	0.305	0.285	0.266	0.249	0.233
9	0.914	0.837	0.766	0.703	0.645	0.592	0.544	0.500	0.460	0.424	0.391	0.361	0.333	0.308	0.284	0.263	0.243	0.225	0.209	0.194
10	0.905	0.820	0.744	0.676	0.614	0.558	0.508	0.463	0.422	0.386	0.352	0.322	0.295	0.270	0.247	0.227	0.208	0.191	0.176	0.162
11	0.896	0.804	0.722	0.650	0.585	0.527	0.475	0.429	0.388	0.350	0.317	0.287	0.261	0.237	0.215	0.195	0.178	0.162	0.148	0.135
12	0.887	0.788	0.701	0.625	0.557	0.497	0.444	0.397	0.356	0.319	0.286	0.257	0.231	0.208	0.187	0.168	0.152	0.137	0.124	0.112
13	0.879	0.773	0.681	0.601	0.530	0.469	0.415	0.368	0.326	0.290	0.258	0.229	0.204	0.182	0.163	0.145	0.130	0.116	0.104	0.093
14	0.870	0.758	0.661	0.577	0.505	0.442	0.388	0.340	0.299	0.263	0.232	0.205	0.181	0.160	0.141	0.125	0.111	0.099	0.088	0.078
15	0.861	0.743	0.642	0.555	0.481	0.417	0.362	0.315	0.275	0.239	0.209	0.183	0.160	0.140	0.123	0.108	0.095	0.084	0.074	0.065
16	0.853	0.728	0.623	0.534	0.458	0.394	0.339	0.292	0.252	0.218	0.188	0.163	0.141	0.123	0.107	0.093	0.081	0.071	0.062	0.054
17	0.844	0.714	0.605	0.513	0.436	0.371	0.317	0.270	0.231	0.198	0.170	0.146	0.125	0.108	0.093	0.080	0.069	0.060	0.052	0.045
18	0.836	0.700	0.587	0.494	0.416	0.350	0.296	0.250	0.212	0.180	0.153	0.130	0.111	0.095	0.081	0.069	0.059	0.051	0.044	0.038
19	0.828	0.686	0.570	0.475	0.396	0.331	0.277	0.232	0.194	0.164	0.138	0.116	0.098	0.083	0.070	0.060	0.051	0.043	0.037	0.031
20	0.820	0.673	0.554	0.456	0.377	0.312	0.258	0.215	0.178	0.149	0.124	0.104	0.087	0.073	0.061	0.051	0.043	0.037	0.031	0.026
21	0.811	0.660	0.538	0.439	0.359	0.294	0.242	0.199	0.164	0.135	0.112	0.093	0.077	0.064	0.053	0.044	0.037	0.031	0.026	0.022
22	0.803	0.647	0.522	0.422	0.342	0.278	0.226	0.184	0.150	0.123	0.101	0.083	0.068	0.056	0.046	0.038	0.032	0.026	0.022	0.018
23	0.795	0.634	0.507	0.406	0.326	0.262	0.211	0.170	0.138	0.112	0.091	0.074	0.060	0.049	0.040	0.033	0.027	0.022	0.018	0.015
24	0.788	0.622	0.492	0.390	0.310	0.247	0.197	0.158	0.126	0.102	0.082	0.066	0.053	0.043	0.035	0.028	0.023	0.019	0.015	0.013
25	0.780	0.610	0.478	0.375	0.295	0.233	0.184	0.146	0.116	0.092	0.074	0.059	0.047	0.038	0.030	0.024	0.020	0.016	0.013	0.010

Cumulative present value factor table (annuities)

The following table is used to calculate the present value of future, consecutive, equal, annual amounts, all discounted at the same percentage rate.

Example 1: at the discount rate of 5%, a sum of £1 received each year for 25 years is currently worth £14.094.
Example 2: at the discount rate of 5%, a sum of £1,000 received each year for 25 years is currently worth £14,094.00.

Discount rate Years	1%	2%	3%	4%	5%	6%	7%	8%	9%	10%	11%	12%	13%	14%	15%	16%	17%	18%	19%	20%
1	0.990	0.980	0.971	0.962	0.952	0.943	0.935	0.926	0.917	0.909	0.901	0.893	0.885	0.877	0.870	0.862	0.855	0.847	0.840	0.833
2	1.970	1.942	1.913	1.886	1.859	1.833	1.808	1.783	1.759	1.736	1.713	1.690	1.668	1.647	1.626	1.605	1.585	1.566	1.547	1.528
3	2.941	2.884	2.829	2.775	2.723	2.673	2.624	2.577	2.531	2.487	2.444	2.402	2.361	2.322	2.283	2.246	2.210	2.174	2.140	2.106
4	3.902	3.808	3.717	3.630	3.546	3.465	3.387	3.312	3.240	3.170	3.102	3.037	2.974	2.914	2.855	2.798	2.743	2.690	2.639	2.589
5	4.853	4.713	4.580	4.452	4.329	4.212	4.100	3.993	3.890	3.791	3.696	3.605	3.517	3.433	3.352	3.274	3.199	3.127	3.058	2.991
6	5.795	5.601	5.417	5.242	5.076	4.917	4.767	4.623	4.486	4.355	4.231	4.111	3.998	3.889	3.784	3.685	3.589	3.498	3.410	3.326
7	6.728	6.472	6.230	6.002	5.786	5.582	5.389	5.206	5.033	4.868	4.712	4.564	4.423	4.288	4.160	4.039	3.922	3.812	3.706	3.605
8	7.652	7.325	7.020	6.733	6.463	6.210	5.971	5.747	5.535	5.335	5.146	4.968	4.799	4.639	4.487	4.344	4.207	4.078	3.954	3.837
9	8.566	8.162	7.786	7.435	7.108	6.802	6.515	6.247	5.995	5.759	5.537	5.328	5.132	4.946	4.772	4.607	4.451	4.303	4.163	4.031
10	9.471	8.983	8.530	8.111	7.722	7.360	7.024	6.710	6.418	6.145	5.889	5.650	5.426	5.216	5.019	4.833	4.659	4.494	4.339	4.192
11	10.368	9.787	9.253	8.760	8.306	7.887	7.499	7.139	6.805	6.495	6.207	5.938	5.687	5.453	5.234	5.029	4.836	4.656	4.486	4.327
12	11.255	10.575	9.954	9.385	8.863	8.384	7.943	7.536	7.161	6.814	6.492	6.194	5.918	5.660	5.421	5.197	4.988	4.793	4.611	4.439
13	12.134	11.348	10.635	9.986	9.394	8.853	8.358	7.904	7.487	7.103	6.750	6.424	6.122	5.842	5.583	5.342	5.118	4.910	4.715	4.533
14	13.004	12.106	11.296	10.563	9.899	9.295	8.745	8.244	7.786	7.367	6.982	6.628	6.302	6.002	5.724	5.468	5.229	5.008	4.802	4.611
15	13.865	12.849	11.938	11.118	10.380	9.712	9.108	8.559	8.061	7.606	7.191	6.811	6.462	6.142	5.847	5.575	5.324	5.092	4.876	4.675
16	14.718	13.578	12.561	11.652	10.838	10.106	9.447	8.851	8.313	7.824	7.379	6.974	6.604	6.265	5.954	5.668	5.405	5.162	4.938	4.730
17	15.562	14.292	13.166	12.166	11.274	10.477	9.763	9.122	8.544	8.022	7.549	7.120	6.729	6.373	6.047	5.749	5.475	5.222	4.990	4.775
18	16.398	14.992	13.754	12.659	11.690	10.828	10.059	9.372	8.756	8.201	7.702	7.250	6.840	6.467	6.128	5.818	5.534	5.273	5.033	4.812
19	17.226	15.678	14.324	13.134	12.085	11.158	10.336	9.604	8.950	8.365	7.839	7.366	6.938	6.550	6.198	5.877	5.584	5.316	5.070	4.843
20	18.046	16.351	14.877	13.590	12.462	11.470	10.594	9.818	9.129	8.514	7.963	7.469	7.025	6.623	6.259	5.929	5.628	5.353	5.101	4.870
21	18.857	17.011	15.415	14.029	12.821	11.764	10.836	10.017	9.292	8.649	8.075	7.562	7.102	6.687	6.312	5.973	5.665	5.384	5.127	4.891
22	19.660	17.658	15.937	14.451	13.163	12.042	11.061	10.201	9.442	8.772	8.176	7.645	7.170	6.743	6.359	6.011	5.696	5.410	5.149	4.909
23	20.456	18.292	16.444	14.857	13.489	12.303	11.272	10.371	9.580	8.883	8.266	7.718	7.230	6.792	6.399	6.044	5.723	5.432	5.167	4.925
24	21.243	18.914	16.936	15.247	13.799	12.550	11.469	10.529	9.707	8.985	8.348	7.784	7.283	6.835	6.434	6.073	5.746	5.451	5.182	4.937
25	22.023	19.523	17.413	15.622	14.094	12.783	11.654	10.675	9.823	9.077	8.422	7.843	7.330	6.873	6.464	6.097	5.766	5.467	5.195	4.948

PRODUCT COSTING AND PRICING

Part 4

Part 4 comprises:

There are four major reasons why it is essential to know the cost of your products. First, they are an essential prerequisite for the creation of the financial accounts. The profit and loss account needs a valuation of the opening stock and the cost of sales. The balance sheet must show the value of closing stock. This is based on the production or buying-in cost of the business's products or services.

Second, every so often managers have to make decisions regarding products and activities. For example, a customer may ask you to produce some non-standard items on a one-off basis but at a lower price than your normal selling price. In order to decide whether to accept, you need to be aware of the different product cost models and which one will help you make the right decision.

Third, in order to control costs, you need accurate information as to how much your products actually cost. If you do not know how much something costs, how do you know if you are paying too much or too little for it? Marketing and selling are vital business activities but profits created by them will soon disappear if costs are not kept under control.

The fourth reason is to avoid setting your selling prices too low. The last chapter in Part 2 describes the various ways in which prices can be set. This is another crucial management task. If prices are set too high, demand will fall and profits will reduce or disappear completely. If prices are set too low, sales revenue may not be sufficient to cover costs and losses will occur rather than profits. To avoid this happening, you need to know what your costs are.

Also, there is the problem of how to set the selling price of goods sold by one division of a company to another division of the same company. The buying division will want it to be as low as possible but the selling division will want it to be as high as possible! These intra-group prices are known as 'transfer prices' and there are several different ways of calculating them. Group directors at head office need to be very careful about their choices in these matters as there is much scope for demotivating divisional managers and so diminishing overall group profits. Thus, transfer pricing is inextricably linked to the management of divisional performance.

Many large organisations adopt divisionalised structures in order to keep control over a business that may be involved in many different products and services in many different countries. However, divisionalisation implies a significant degree of autonomy being given to each business unit and, therefore, a lack of head office control. The question is, 'how much authority should be delegated to ensure optimal performance?' Then there is the problem of how divisional performance should be evaluated. Which of the alternative measures should be used?

Product costs using absorption costing

Chapter contents

Introduction

At some stage in your career, you may find yourself responsible for controlling costs. The object of this exercise is to minimise the costs of your products, which should enable you to keep their selling prices competitive. Hopefully, the result of this will be increased numbers of items sold and good levels of profit. Cost control is an important activity for all organisations. So how is it achieved?

The first step is fundamental. In order to control a cost, you have to have an accurate measurement of it, i.e. you need to know exactly how much the cost is. Without this information your task is impossible.

Another good reason for determining product costs is that, from time to time, you may be required to make decisions concerning your products. For example, if you do not know the cost of a product when setting its selling price, you may unknowingly set the price lower than cost. The obvious consequence of this is that you will trade at a loss rather than at a profit.

A further important reason for knowing your product costs is that they are used to value the cost of sales and stock in the periodic accounts of organisations. Indeed, the ninth statement of standard accounting practice (SSAP 9) prescribes that production and stock must be valued at the 'absorption' production cost for accounts which are accessible to owners and other interested people **outside** the organisation. In effect, if this is not done, the Companies Act is being broken and the company is acting illegally and should expect to suffer the adverse consequences.

Note: This chapter applies to those organisations which perform work on their raw materials to convert them into finished products. It does not apply to merchanting or trading companies which buy at one price and sell for a higher price without changing the products in any way.

Having worked through this chapter you should be able to:
- explain the difference between direct and indirect costs;
- list the constituent parts of an absorption cost;
- allocate and apportion overheads to cost centres;
- calculate overhead absorption rates using a variety of different bases;
- use overhead absorption rates to attach overheads to products.

Direct and indirect costs

(This section first appears in Chapter 1 but is repeated here for your convenience.) The absorption cost of a product is based on the assumption that costs can be analysed into their 'direct' and 'indirect' components which are defined as follows.

Direct cost

This is expenditure which can be economically identified with, and specifically measured in respect to, a relevant cost object or product. Consider an advertising agency specialising in the production of television adverts. The cost of hiring a celebrity to appear in one such advert is a measurable direct cost of that advert. Similarly, if the company is a furniture manufacturer, the cost of materials used to make a chair and the pay of the operative assembling it are measurable direct costs of that chair.

Indirect cost (or overhead)

This is expenditure on labour, materials or services which cannot be economically identified with a specific saleable cost unit or product. There are many, many different overheads, including supervisors' pay, depreciation of fixed assets, business rates and insurance. Remember,

$$\text{Total absorption cost} = \text{direct cost} + \text{indirect cost}$$

Try the following question for yourself (answer at the end of the chapter).

Macframe Limited makes photograph frames and sells them to national retail chains. The following costs are incurred in connection with its manufacturing process. Decide whether each cost is direct or indirect and give your reasons.

1 Picture frame moulding.
2 Pay of assembly department's supervisor.
3 Heating oil used for cutting department.
4 Pay of employees assembling frames.
5 Dab of glue put in each corner joint of frame.

The absorption cost of products

The way the product cost is determined in absorption costing is illustrated in Figure 9.1. This shows that as well as the total of direct costs (prime cost) the production overheads are included in the production cost (in accordance with SSAP 9). Stock of finished goods is unsold production so it is logical to value it at production cost. Note that all other overheads, although part of the total cost, are excluded from the production cost. These other overheads are treated as 'period' costs and are listed in the profit and loss account as deductions from the gross profit.

The objective of absorption costing is to ensure that both the direct and indirect costs of production are included in the production cost. The CIMA *Management Accounting*

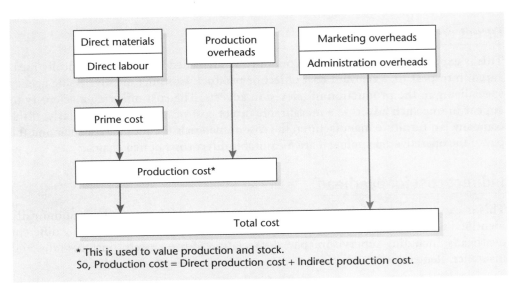

* This is used to value production and stock.
So, Production cost = Direct production cost + Indirect production cost.

Figure 9.1 **Outline of the absorption costing system**

Official Terminology (2000) describes absorption costing as 'a method of costing that, in addition to direct costs, assigns . . . production overhead costs to cost units by means of . . . overhead absorption rates'.

Determining the direct production costs is relatively simple as the amount of them in each product can be measured. But how do we know how much of the production director's pay, depreciation of equipment, etc., to include in the cost of a specific product or service? These indirect costs cannot be measured so there has to be some other mechanism for attaching them to products. This is achieved by allocation, apportionment and absorption of overheads.

Attaching overheads to products

Allocation

This is the assigning of **whole** items of cost, or revenue, to a single cost unit or centre. For example, in a company making furniture, an invoice for 50 kilograms of sausage meat can be safely allocated **in total** to the canteen cost centre. However, if the company produced processed foods, further investigation would be necessary. If the sausage meat was an ingredient of one of the company's products, it would be a direct cost and not an overhead.

Apportionment

This is the spreading of costs or revenues over two or more cost centres or units. For example, the invoice total for flu injections for all employees should be spread over all the cost centres in the organisation. But how is this done? In this particular case, the total could be spread in the same ratio as the number of people in each cost centre. For example, if the invoice was £500 for 500 people, the dispatch cost centre with 12 employees would receive twice the amount (£12) apportioned to the site security cost centre employing six people (£6).

An apportionment base should have a logical connection to the nature of the overhead concerned. It should have a rationality of some kind but it need not give as 'accurate' an answer as the flu injection example above. Costs can be apportioned in a 'fair' way to cost centres by means of physical or financial units. For example:

Costs	Basis of apportionment
Personnel department	Number of employees
Business rates	Area
Heating and lighting	Area **or** volume
Insurance	Net book value **or** cost of assets
Maintenance	Number of machines
Central stores	Value of production **or** number of stores issues
Production planning	Value of production

Absorption

This is the attaching of overheads to products or services by means of overhead absorption rates (OARs) using some measure of activity. For example,

£/direct labour hour   % of total labour cost
£/machine hour   % of prime cost

Overhead attachment procedure (Illustrated in Figure 9.2)

Step 1

Allocate or apportion the overheads to the production and service cost centres (by reasonable bases of apportionment).

Step 2

The total cost of the service centres is apportioned first to other service centres which use their service, and second to the production centres so that all overheads end up in production centres.

Step 3

The total amount of each production centre is divided by some measure of activity (e.g. machine hours) to derive the overhead absorption rate (OAR).

Note that production overheads are absorbed only from production cost centres or departments. All service centre overheads must be transferred into production cost

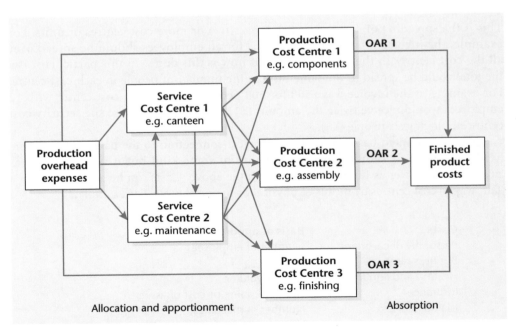

Figure 9.2 **Production overhead attachment**

centres. Where service cost centres service each other, the easiest way of dealing with this is to determine the order in which it happens and transfer the costs in that order. It may not exactly reflect reality but, unless the overheads involved are a very large proportion of total overheads, it will do the job. Remember that the nature of apportionment leads to estimates rather than perfect 'accuracy'.

Single- and multi-product companies

To illustrate these two alternative scenarios, a fork-lift truck driver's pay of £200/week is used as an example of a production overhead.

Single-product company

If a factory makes only one product, and makes 40 of them each week, the overhead absorption rate is

$$\text{OAR} = \frac{\text{estimated pay for period}}{\text{number of items made}} = \frac{200}{40} = £5/\text{unit}$$

Multi-product company

If a factory makes several different products, a different method is needed to absorb overheads into each product **on an equitable basis**. One way of doing this is to use the number of direct labour hours (dlh) for each type of product. Suppose a company makes two products, G and K, each G taking 10 dlh and each K taking 25 dlh to make.

$$\text{If estimated weekly production} = 30 \times \text{product G @ 10 dlh each} = \underline{300} \text{ dlh}$$
$$4 \times \text{product K @ 25 dlh each} = \underline{100} \text{ dlh}$$
$$\underline{\underline{400}} \text{ dlh}$$

$$\text{OAR} = \frac{\text{estimated pay for period}}{\text{output in dlh}} = \frac{£200}{400 \text{ dlh}} = £0.50/\text{dlh}$$

Each G would have £5 (10 dlh × £0.50/dlh) and each K would have £12.50 (25 dlh × £0.50/dlh) of the fork-lift truck driver's pay attached to it.

This approach is then extended to include all overheads. If these totalled £6,000 a week, then

$$\text{OAR} = \frac{\text{estimated total overhead cost for period}}{\text{output in dlh}} = \frac{£6,000}{400} = £15/\text{dlh}$$

In a machine-intensive, automated manufacturing environment, machine hours would probably be used instead of direct labour hours. (Remember that other factors may be used for OARs, such as multiples of the material cost or wages cost.)

Example of overhead attachment

Maykit Ltd manufactures plastic chairs. It has two production departments (Moulding and Assembly) and one service department (Canteen). The following information is taken from this year's budget:

	Moulding	Assembly	Canteen
Direct labour hours	10,000	50,000	–
Machine hours	15,000	5,000	–
Direct labour pay (£)	100,000	200,000	–
Indirect labour pay (£)	3,030	5,220	4,000

Fixed factory overheads (per year)

	£
Rent and rates	15,000
Depreciation of machinery (straight line)	7,200
Heat and light	4,800
Protective clothing	6,500

Other information

	Moulding	Assembly	Canteen
Number of employees	2	8	3
Area (square metres)	3,000	5,000	2,000
Cost of machinery (£)	60,000	36,000	24,000

Tasks:

1 Calculate the total overhead cost for each department.
2 Attach the service department overhead to the production departments.
3 Calculate the most appropriate overhead absorption rate for each production department.
4 What value of production overheads would be absorbed by a batch of chairs taking 2 machine hours to mould and 3 direct labour hours to assemble?

Solution to Maykit Ltd

Apportionment of rent and rates (total cost £15,000):

Most rational basis of apportionment is 'area'. Total area = 10,000 sq. m.

	Moulding	Assembly	Canteen	Total
Proportion	$\dfrac{3,000}{10,000}$	$\dfrac{5,000}{10,000}$	$\dfrac{2,000}{10,000}$	$\dfrac{10,000}{10,000}$
	= 3/10	= 5/10	= 2/10	= 10/10
Overhead cost	£15,000	£15,000	£15,000	£15,000
Apportionment	£4,500	£7,500	£3,000	£15,000

Apportionment of protective clothing (total cost £6,500):

Most **rational** basis of apportionment is 'number of employees' = 13.

	Moulding	Assembly	Canteen	Total
Proportion	2/13	8/13	3/13	13/13
Overhead cost	£6,500	£6,500	£6,500	£6,500
Apportionment	**£1,000**	**£4,000**	**£1,500**	**£6,500**

1.

	Moulding	Assembly	Canteen	Total
Indirect pay	3,030	5,220	4,000	12,250
Rent and rates (area)	4,500	7,500	3,000	15,000
Depreciation of machinery (cost)	3,600	2,160	1,440	7,200
Heat and light (area)	1,440	2,400	960	4,800
Protective clothing (employees)	1,000	4,000	1,500	6,500
Total overhead cost	**13,570**	**21,280**	**10,900**	**45,750**

2.

	Moulding	Assembly	Canteen	Total
Canteen overheads (employees)	2,180	8,720	(10,900)	–
Service overhead attachment	**15,750**	**30,000**	**–**	**45,750**

3.

	Moulding	Assembly
Machine hours	15,000	–
Direct labour hours	–	50,000
OAR	$\dfrac{15,750}{15,000}$	$\dfrac{30,000}{50,000}$
	= **£1.05/mh**	= **£0.60/dlh**

4. Batch of chairs

	Moulding	Assembly	
	2 mh	3 dlh	
Batch overhead	**£2.10**	**£1.80**	**Total £3.90**

Try the following question for yourself (answer at the end of the chapter).

Self-assessment question S9.2

Cayten Limited produces domestic robots to perform household chores. Its manufacturing facilities consist of three production departments and two service departments. The following information is taken from the company's current annual budget.

	Production cost centres			Service cost centres	
	PA	PB	PC	SD	SE
Indirect labour (£)	80,850	87,750	36,600	45,900	42,400
Direct labour (£)	100,000	110,000	140,000		
Direct labour hours (dlh)	90,000	120,000	90,000		
Machine hours (mh)	80,000	90,000	75,000		

Production overheads	£
Business rates	8,000
Electricity to run machines	6,000
Heating and lighting	4,800
Insurance for machinery ('like for like' policy)	2,700
Depreciation of machinery (straight line over 10 years)	19,000
Total	40,500

The following information relates to the cost centres:

	PA	PB	PC	SD	SE
Number of employees	20	35	25	12	8
Original cost of machinery (£)	60,000	70,000	40,000	20,000	–
Machinery written-down value (£)	20,000	40,000	25,000	5,000	–
Machinery power rating (joules)	350	450	250	150	–
Floor area (square metres)	12,000	8,000	5,000	3,000	4,000

Required:

a) Calculate the total overhead for each cost centre.

b) Reassign service cost centre overheads to production cost centres on the following basis:

	PA	PB	PC
SD	30%	50%	20%
SE	25%	40%	35%

c) Calculate an overhead absorption rate for each production cost centre using the following bases:

PA	machine hour basis
PB	direct labour hour basis
PC	percentage of direct pay

d) Calculate the total of production overheads absorbed by an order requiring the following resources:

	PA	PB	PC
Machine hours	7,000	2,100	900
Direct labour hours	600	9,800	2,000
Direct wages (£)	2,700	45,000	11,600

Limitations of absorption costing

Absorption costing is approximately a hundred years old. It was devised for a manufacturing era whose products relied upon direct labour much more than they do today. Volume production in the twenty-first century is based on computer-controlled automatic machinery. Compare a car production line from the 1930s to one 70 years later and the difference is quite astonishing. From a distance, the old line would look something like an ant's nest, with men scurrying about doing all kinds of job. The machinery used by them consisted to a great extent of hand-tools such as screwdrivers and spanners. The latest lines are often quite devoid of people apart from the occasional machine minder. The robotic machinery being overseen probably cost millions of pounds, which causes a commensurately large amount of depreciation (a production overhead). The trend over the last 50 years has been an increase in the importance of overheads. The proportion of overheads in the total production cost is far greater now than it was in the past.

Absorption costing was not designed for the modern automated technological environment. Overhead absorption rates are a crude device for attaching overheads to products. The absorption costing system is mathematically sound and ensures that all the production overheads are absorbed by all the production. In the days when overheads were only a small part of the total costs, it did not matter that it was not particularly accurate. Today, when overheads often represent well over 50% of total costs, it does matter. Fortunately, activity-based costing now exists to fill that gap. Having said all this, many businesses still use absorption costing. Like many aspects of business life, there is a reluctance to change from a tried-and-tested system to something new. However, the pressures of competitive marketplaces will drive the change. Absorption costing will be used less and less as time passes.

The manager's point of view

Conclusion

No single costing system is ever likely to provide the perfect answer to a company's costing requirements. However, all systems, by providing views of the business from different angles, will produce some information of greater or lesser value to management. In certain circumstances, absorption costing may indeed prove to be the best available solution, although its inherent drawbacks will render it inappropriate for many companies.

Absorption costing is essentially simple and is therefore best suited to companies with simple processes. Consider, for example, a paint blending operation, consisting of a wide range of end products being produced on a number of standard blending machines. The blending process is simple, identical for each product, and unlikely to require significant levels of overhead. In this case, the simple spreading of overhead across all products, on a volume (i.e. number of units produced) or machine hours basis, may be perfectly adequate, particularly as overhead is likely to be a relatively small component of the overall product cost.

As companies become more complex, the simple principles of absorption costing may give a distorted picture of product costs. If our paint blender were to decide to backward-integrate into paint manufacture, and, at the same time, diversify into paint can production, its previous practice of spreading overhead simply across products would clearly no longer be valid. It would need to introduce more sophistication into its costing system to match the needs of the more complicated business. As complexity grows, the problems with absorption costing become more apparent.

Imagine a large manufacturing company, with multiple production cost centres, each producing a range of products, by differing processes, on various items of plant. The absorption costing system first requires the allocation of expenses to cost centres. Consider electricity. How many companies can accurately attribute electricity usage to individual production areas, as opposed to equipment in the maintenance department, or heating in the offices, or lighting in the factory yard? Larger companies may have it all metered, but most will need to determine some kind of apportionment. This may apply not only to utilities like electricity, but also to other items such as supervisors' salaries where the supervisors work in more than one cost centre. This is a general problem, and not necessarily specific to the absorption costing method, but it does introduce a measure of inaccuracy which absorption costing compounds.

Then the service centre costs have to be reapportioned to production cost centres. These costs, which may include maintenance, quality control, waste treatment, general factory expenses, etc., can be relatively high, so the basis of apportionment is critical. Take the cost of maintaining machinery: 'number of machines' or 'machine hours' may be a reasonable basis, but the likelihood is that Machine A is continually breaking down, while Machine B runs perfectly smoothly. Some processes place much greater physical demands on the equipment than others. For example, a very corrosive process will wear out the equipment much more quickly than a non-corrosive process. So, perhaps actual time spent on these machines by the maintenance department in the past may be a better basis for reapportioning service centre costs – though not of course if the attention given to Machine A has finally fixed a long-running problem! Similar issues surround the allocation of all service departments, and have the potential to cause major distortions.

Finally, a basis is needed to attribute production cost centres to products. These cost centres now include the reapportioned service department costs, so the numbers are significant. The use of direct labour hours as a basis is very common, but this too can be troublesome. For instance, it does not take proper account of Product C, which requires a large amount of machine time (e.g. for cooling, drying or processing) but with minimum labour input. The use of direct labour hours will seriously undercost this product. On the other hand, using machine hours may substantially undercost Product D, which requires constant supervision throughout its production cycle and consequently uses a disproportionate amount of departmental resource.

A great deal of care is required in identifying the most appropriate bases of apportionment, but a similar amount of attention needs to be given to the flaws inherent in these bases. In arriving at the final cost of our products, we have had to resort to apportionments at every level. This raises some awkward questions. First, does the final product cost contain the correct overall charge for electricity? Answer: We have no idea! Second, is the product cost correct? Answer: We do not know! Third, what level of confidence do we have in the accuracy of the product cost? Answer: We are not sure!

The key to cost apportionment is to ensure that the bases are agreed and accepted as valid by all sides. For organisational reasons, many companies divide their products into logical groupings, or product lines, each with its own business manager. Each product line has its own sales department and production cost centre, but factory management and general administration remain centralised. The apportionment of overheads will have a direct impact on the profitability of individual product lines. And in a competitive world, where demands from senior management for higher returns grow ever louder, the two options available to the business manager are either to increase sales or to cut costs. The easiest way for a business manager to increase profits at a stroke is to convince the accountant that the overhead apportionments are unfair, and that some of the costs should consequently be transferred to other product lines. In my experience, this has proved to be a recurring cause of irritation, argument and management time consumption. For this reason it is essential that the cost apportionment bases are defensible. However, this is not an easy position to achieve in a conventional absorption costing environment.

Finally, while considering the impact of overhead apportionments on the profits of individual business groups, there is another area of legitimate concern for managers. In a single-business-group company, indirect expenses, such as the factory manager's salary, security and business rates, are genuinely fixed costs which do not change as sales levels grow. In a two-business-group company, these expenses will be apportioned between the businesses on the basis of, say, direct labour hours. Similarly, non-production expenses, such as general administration, will also have an arbitrary basis, perhaps sales or volume. If the two businesses grow at the same rate, the proportion of costs assigned to each will remain the same from year to year. But suppose one business ran into trouble, and its sales halved. This would result in a switch of overhead from the failing business to the successful business. Through no fault of its own, and without any increase in the overall level of expenses, the successful business will suffer a substantial increase in its fixed costs. Is this fair? I think not. It seems to me that the failing group should suffer the full impact on profits of its reduced income.

The same situation exists if the sales of the successful business forge ahead. If its apportionment of overhead were to go up proportionately, it would be tantamount to treating fixed costs as variable! Some reapportionment may well be desirable over time, but this could perhaps best be achieved by small changes over a number of years. Business group managers, and indeed all other users of financial information, are looking for consistency, fairness and clarity. Nothing is more frustrating than finding the impact of one's sales achievements being eroded by the blind application of accounting principles, which may be mathematically correct, but logically flawed. Senior managers judge businesses on their ability to produce consistent profit growth over a number of years, and the accounting principles adopted should serve to support this objective. Absorption accounting may do the job for you, but always be aware of its limitations, and treat the results with a due measure of caution.

My purpose here is not to devalue absorption costing as a valid accounting tool, but merely to highlight the potential pitfalls. These difficulties are evident in any accounting system which requires a measure of apportionment. But absorption costing can compound the margin of error through its broadbrush approach, to the point that the information provided is so inaccurate that it risks leading management into making erroneous decisions.

Summary

- The absorption cost is the sum of the direct and indirect costs.
- Absorption costing treats production overheads as product costs.
- Overheads are assigned to cost centres via allocation and apportionment.
- Apportionment uses bases which are rational but not necessarily accurate.
- Service cost centre totals are reapportioned to production cost centres.
- Overheads are absorbed into production costs via overhead absorption rates.
- Overhead absorption rates are usually different for each production cost centre.
- Absorption costing is becoming less relevant to advanced technological production.

Further reading

Atkinson, A., Banker, R., Kaplan, R. and Young, S. (2001) *Management Accounting*, 3rd edition, Prentice Hall, Harlow. See chapter 'Traditional cost management systems'.

Drury, C. and Tayles, M. (2005) 'Explicating the design of overhead absorption procedures in UK organizations', *British Accounting Review*, Vol. 37, Issue 1, March.

Johnson, H. and Kaplan, R. (1987) *Relevance Lost, the Rise and Fall of Management Accounting*, Harvard Business School Press, Boston, MA. This provides a fascinating history of traditional cost accounting and states the case for a new direction.

Lucas, M. (2000) 'The reality of product costing', *Management Accounting*, February.

Upchurch, A. (2003) *Management Accounting, Principles and Practice*, 2nd edition, Financial Times/Prentice Hall, Harlow. See chapter 'Absorption of overheads'.

Weetman, P. (2002) *Management Accounting, an Introduction*, 3rd edition, Financial Times/Prentice Hall, Harlow. See chapter 'Accounting for materials, labour and overheads'.

Answers to self-assessment questions

S9.1. Macframe Limited

1 Picture frame moulding is a direct cost – identifiable and measurable.

2 Pay of assembly department's supervisor is an indirect cost – not specifically identifiable in product.

3 Heating oil used for cutting department is an indirect cost – not specifically identifiable in product.

4 Pay of employees assembling frames is a direct cost – identifiable and measurable.

5 Dab of glue put in each corner joint of frame is, in theory, a direct cost as it is identifiable and measurable. However, in practice, this would be treated as an indirect cost as the cost of measuring and valuing the dab of glue would be far greater than the value of the information gained. Accounting activities should always be carried out in a commercially sensible manner.

S9.2. Cayten Limited

	PA	PB	PC	SD	SE	Total
Indirect labour	80,850	87,750	36,600	45,900	42,400	293,500
Business rates (area)	3,000	2,000	1,250	750	1,000	8,000
Power (joules)	1,750	2,250	1,250	750	–	6,000
Light and heat (area)	1,800	1,200	750	450	600	4,800
Insurance (WDV)	600	1,200	750	150	–	2,700
Depreciation (orig. cost)	6,000	7,000	4,000	2,000	–	19,000
Sub-totals	**94,000**	**101,400**	**44,600**	**50,000**	**44,000**	**334,000**
Adj. SD	15,000	25,000	10,000	(50,000)	–	–
Adj. SE	11,000	17,600	15,400	–	(44,000)	–
Total overheads	**120,000**	**144,000**	**70,000**	**–**	**–**	**334,000**

PA	PB	PC
$\dfrac{120,000}{80,000}$	$\dfrac{144,000}{120,000}$	$\dfrac{70,000}{140,000} \times 100$
$= £1.50/\text{mh}$	$= £1.20/\text{dlh}$	$= 50\%$ of direct labour cost
$\times 7,000$ mh	$\times 9,800$ dlh	$\times £11,600$
$= £10,500$	$= £11,760$	$= £5,800$
Total absorbed $= £28,060$		$(10,500 + 11,760 + 5,800)$

Travelsound

Travelsound Ltd was started five years ago by three friends who had just graduated from university. They had lived in the same house for two years and were all passionate about music. During their many late-night discussions they talked much about music and, as two of them were electronic engineers, they often discussed the latest equipment for sound reproduction and how it could be improved. The third person had a joint degree in finance and marketing and saw the opportunity for a business venture involving state-of-the-art sound systems.

They started out in a garage at the home of one of their parents and soon found that ideas alone were not enough to run a business. Most of their work in the first two years consisted of upgrading and constructing personal computers and laptops. Through their contacts, they also gained from their old university several one-off contracts concerned with upgrading software and hardware (a perennial occupation for universities). At this stage in their development they employed five assistants.

Towards the end of their second year they bid for a contract to manufacture small quantities of an experimental mobile phone for a European electronics group. To their delight, they were awarded the contract and have produced several versions of this phone over the last few years. By the start of their fourth year they had 27 employees. In that year they gained the right to produce, under licence, mini-disc players for a Japanese company. This contract has gone very well despite the very tight profit margins involved. In fact, the sales price was slightly below the original estimated absorption production cost. They decided to go ahead on the assumption that they would be able to reduce their costs as they gained experience of manufacturing this product. (Although they were not aware of it, this was the reason they were awarded the contract, as other more established firms had turned it down as they believed it was not profitable.) Fortunately, Travelsound had made the right decision and this work currently has a positive net profit margin of around 3%.

However, in recent months, relations with this company have deteriorated, mainly due to a change in the pound/yen exchange rate. In fact, the three Travelsound directors believe that their licence will be revoked at the next renewal date in two months' time unless they are willing to trade in euros instead of UK pounds. They are apprehensive about this as the euro/pound exchange rate has been falling consistently for over a year. It would not be difficult for this work to be moved to mainland Europe where a significant amount of overcapacity exists.

Throughout their five-year history, they maintained an active interest in the improvement of sound systems. What little spare time the two engineering directors had was spent on developing a new method of sound reproduction. They are now at the point where, with the help of an agent, they have applied for a patent on their invention. They currently employ 88 people and made a net profit last year of £45,000. Their annual production rate is now 10,000 phones and 38,000 mini-disc players. They wish to grow in size and profitability but are unsure of how to do it. As an organisation, they are now approaching a crisis point. One alternative is for them to replace the mini-disc player production with a new product using their own new technology.

This product has been named the MNP, short for Music Net Phone. It combines a WAP phone with their own miniaturised sound reproduction system which is also able to play mini-discs. They have tentatively approached the European electronics group for whom they manufacture mobile phones, with a view to its marketing the MNP. The European company is very interested but needs some indication of price before taking the idea any further.

Travelsound now needs to cost the MNP using the absorption costing system. The directors decide to do this using next year's budget, which is based on continuing production of mobile phones and mini-disc players. They assume the overheads will be the same if the mini-disc player is replaced by the MNP. The following information comes from this budget.

Travelsound has three production cost centres and three service cost centres. The former are electronic components, plastic cases and assembly. The latter are the canteen, material stores and quality control. The quality controllers inspect goods received into the stores as well as the output of each production cost centre. The assembly shop uses the manufactured components, plastic cases and items from material stores to produce the finished items ready for delivery. The estimated cost for one MNP is £12.20 for materials and £9.80 for direct labour. A single materials store serves only the three production departments. The canteen is situated just inside the factory entrance.

The production overheads are shown as:

	£
Factory rent and rates	150,000
Depreciation of machinery (straight line)	89,250
Machinery insurance (like-for-like basis)	53,000
Cost centre managers' pay	80,000
Materials storekeepers' pay	19,125
Quality controller's pay	32,000
Heating and lighting	14,000
Canteen costs	29,920
Factory security	25,000
	492,295

The managers of the components, cases and assembly cost centres earn salaries of £30,000, £25,000 and £25,000 respectively. Factory security is provided by a local firm patrolling inside and outside the factory at intervals throughout the night. One quality controller earns £20,000 p.a., spending 30% of his time on stores materials and 70% on components. The other quality controller, who works part time, earns £12,000 p.a. and divides her time equally between cases and assembly. Any quality control costs other than pay should be considered proportional to the amounts of quality controllers' pay incurred by each cost centre. All employees eat in the canteen.

Other information:

	Canteen	Stores	Quality control	Assembly	Cases	Components
Area (sq. metres)	550	600	25	1,900	795	1,130
Employees	6	3	2	36	12	29
Number of stores issues	–	–	–	51,000	10,200	2,550
Direct labour hours	–	–	–	120,309	33,410	99,281
Direct labour cost (£)	–	–	–	611,404	148,596	450,000
Machine hours	–	–	–	100,973	51,236	453,791
Machinery cost (£000)	–	–	–	340	510	1,700
Machinery WDV (£000)	–	–	–	250	350	1,400

Tasks:

1 Calculate the overhead absorption rate (OAR) for each production cost centre. The bases used should be direct labour hours for assembly, machine hours for components and a percentage of direct labour cost for cases.

(40 marks)

2 Calculate the absorption production cost for one MNP if a batch of 100 MNPs takes 9,000 machine hours in the component shop, 667 direct labour hours in the assembly shop and has a direct labour cost of £1,100 in the case shop.

(10 marks)

3 **On no more than two sides of A4,** discuss the situation and advise Travelsound Ltd on its future course of action.

(50 marks)
(Total 100 marks)

Questions

An asterisk * on a question number indicates that the answer is given at the end of the book. Answers to the other questions are given in the Lecturer's Guide.

Q9.1* Lewington Limited

Lewington Ltd makes a variety of kitchen fittings and equipment. It uses a three-stage process involving cutting, assembly and finishing. The following figures are extracted from its budget for the current year:

	Cutting	Assembly	Finishing
Production overheads (£000)	1,600	2,000	1,400
Machine hours	40,000	25,000	14,000
Direct labour hours	10,000	40,000	20,000

The company uses an absorption costing system for calculating its costs.

A batch of 300 'DX' workstations has just been produced using £3,300 of materials, £4,500 of direct labour and the following quantities of time:

	Cutting	Assembly	Finishing
Machine hours	50	25	10
Direct labour hours	20	45	20

Tasks:

Calculate the unit production cost and the total production cost of the batch of 'DX' workstations using the following three alternative bases:

1 All overhead absorption rates are calculated on a machine hour basis.
2 All overhead absorption rates are calculated on a direct labour hour basis.
3 The Cutting overhead absorption rate is calculated on a machine hour basis but the Assembly and Finishing rates are calculated on a direct labour hour basis.

Comment on your findings.

Q9.2* Graham & Sara

Graham and Sara are partners in a clothes manufacturing firm. Graham manages menswear and Sara controls ladies fashions. They have just received last year's accounts which are summarised below.

	Mens £000	Womens £000	Total £000
Materials	78	26	104
Direct labour	18	30	48
Variable overheads	4	4	8
Variable production cost	100	60	160
Fixed production overheads	10	6	16
Total production cost	110	66	176
Increase in stock	2	1	3
Cost of sales	108	65	173
Marketing overheads	8	4	12
Administration overheads	4	4	8
Total cost	120	73	193
Sales revenue	118	78	196
Profit/(loss)	(2)	5	3

Naturally, Sara is pleased with the results but Graham is not so happy. On questioning their accountant he finds that the fixed production overheads have been apportioned on the basis of variable production costs. He wonders how the results would change if they were apportioned on different bases.

Tasks:

1 Redraft the above statement if the fixed production overheads were apportioned on the basis of:
   a) direct material cost
   b) direct labour cost
   c) variable overhead cost.
2 What do your answers tell you about the absorption costing system?

Q9.3* Stellar Showers

Stellar Showers Co. Ltd manufactures domestic electric showers. It moulds its own plastic casings but buys in the other components from a variety of sources. In addition to 54 production operatives, it employs two quality controllers and four stores operatives. The company's production facility consists of three production cost centres (moulding, assembly and packaging) and two service cost centres (quality control and material stores). Quality control inspects work in the three production centres as well as goods received into the materials store. The store services the three production centres only.

Stellar's annual budget lists the following production overheads:

	£
Electricity to run machines and equipment	40,000
Material stores running costs	80,000
Heating (oil-fired boiler)	13,000
Lighting	4,000
Supervision	65,000
Production manager	35,000
Business rates	16,000
Fire insurance	10,000
Quality controller's pay	30,000
Depreciation (straight line)	18,000

The supervision overhead consists of an assembly supervisor (£25,000 p.a.), a moulding supervisor (£20,000 p.a.) and a packaging supervisor (£20,000 p.a.).

The following information is also available:

	Moulding	Assembly	Packaging	Quality control	Stores
Head count	12	36	6	2	4
Machine wattage	4,500	1,200	300	–	–
Stores issue notes	2,000	14,500	3,500	–	–
Area (sq. metres)	300	800	500	50	350
Volume (cu. metres)	1,200	2,100	2,000	100	1,100
Fixed assets – cost	50,000	40,000	20,000	–	10,000
Fixed assets – WDV	22,000	18,000	9,000	–	1,000
Added value (£000)	800	5,700	500	–	–
Machine hours	34,967	24,080	3,944	–	–
Direct labour hours	20,016	63,986	10,998	–	–
Quality control hrs/wk	6	18	6	4	6

Tasks:

1 Calculate the most appropriate overhead absorption rate for each production cost centre.

2 Calculate the unit production cost of an SS40T shower if a batch of 800 uses the following resources:

Direct materials	£16,000
Direct labour	£8,800
Machine hours in moulding	1,500
Machine hours in assembly	900
Machine hours in packaging	170
Direct labour hours in moulding	1,200
Direct labour hours in assembly	3,500
Direct labour hours in packaging	1,000

Q9.4 Medley Limited

Medley Limited makes dishwashers. There are three production departments: machining, assembly and finishing; and two service departments: maintenance and stores.

Costs are as follows:

	Machining	Assembly	Finishing	Maintenance	Stores
Direct materials	£240,000	£160,000	£40,000	–	–
Direct wages	£200,000	£150,000	£100,000	–	–
Indirect wages	£9,000	£8,000	£8,000	£11,000	£8,000
Indirect materials	–	–	–	£4,000	–

Factory overheads are:

Business rates	£30,000
Factory manager's salary	£30,000
Heat and light	£20,000
Depreciation of machinery	£40,000

Production statistics are:

	Machining	Assembly	Finishing	Maintenance	Stores
Personnel	20	15	10	4	1
Area (sq. metres)	8,000	4,000	4,000	1,000	3,000
Kilowatt hours (000)	100	40	30	10	20
Machinery cost (£000)	100	50	50	–	–
Direct labour hours (000)	40	30	20	–	–
Machine maintenance hours	850	600	200	–	–
Material issue notes	1,800	1,000	500	100	–

Tasks:

1 Calculate an overhead absorption rate based on direct labour hours for each production department.
2 A standard dishwasher uses 4, 3 and 2 direct labour hours in machining, assembly and finishing respectively. If all direct labour is paid £5.00/hour and the cost of materials for one dishwasher is £48, what is the production cost of one dishwasher?

Q9.5 · Ugur Limited

Ugur Limited makes three different types of marine compass: Type A, Type D and Type N. Each compass passes through two production departments: assembling and finishing. Ugur absorbs its overheads on the basis of direct labour hours.

Production overheads for the next 12 months are expected to be

	£
Factory power	80,000
Depreciation	60,000
Fixed asset insurance	3,600
Supervisor's pay	40,000
Factory rent	70,400
	254,000

The following information for next year is also available:

	Assembly	Finishing
Number of direct operatives	30	20
Floor space (sq. metres)	16,000	9,000
Book value of fixed assets (£000)	60	30
Machine hours	15,000	30,000
Power (kilowatt hours used)	30,000	20,000
Supervisory staff	1	1

Times per product (hours):

	Assembly		Finishing	
	Labour	Machine	Labour	Machine
Type A	1.0	0.75	0.75	0.50
Type D	1.5	0.50	1.00	0.40
Type N	2.5	0.25	1.50	0.30

Each operative is expected to work 36 hours a week for 46 weeks a year.

Tasks:

1 Calculate the total overheads for each department.
2 Calculate the overhead absorption rate for each department (to three decimal places).
3 Calculate the overhead cost attached to each type of compass.
4 Recalculate your answers to 2. and 3. if overheads were absorbed on a machine hour basis and comment on your findings.

Product costs using activity-based costing

Chapter contents

Introduction

If we were to go back a few years into the last century and look at a typical manufacturing business, we would find that product costs consisted mainly of direct materials and direct labour. Indirect overhead costs would be only a small proportion of total product costs. If these overheads were attached to products in a way that was not very accurate, the consequences were not very serious. Product costs would be incorrect to a small extent, with some products slightly undercosted and others slightly overcosted.

In today's manufacturing environment, automated machinery and advanced technology often dominate the production process. At the time of writing, the British Automation and Robot Association announced record sales of robotic machinery in the UK to companies such as Toyota and BMW. The high cost of this advanced technology means high depreciation charges and high maintenance costs. As a result, the production overheads can be much larger than the direct costs. Errors in the way that overheads are attached to products are no longer insignificant. Indeed, traditional absorption costing in this high-technology environment can give grossly inaccurate product costs.

Before looking at activity-based costing (ABC) in detail, it is worth emphasising that it is not a universal panacea suitable for every organisation. Some businesses may be operating in stable environments, making much the same products as they were several years ago, with no sign of significant change. Here, direct costs are still much more important than the production overheads. These businesses may continue operating successfully using an absorption costing system.

However, it has to be said that this description applies to fewer and fewer companies in the twenty-first century. Tom Peters, the American management guru, expressed this well in his book *Thriving on Chaos*:

> *the times demand that flexibility and love of change replace our longstanding penchant for mass production and mass markets, based as it is upon a relatively predictable environment now vanished.*

The rate of change seems to increase incessantly in the business world, as it does in most other aspects of society. As firms customise their products more and more (smaller production batch sizes) and those products increase in complexity (compare modern computer games with older ones), absorption product costs become more and more inaccurate.

Absorption costing produces product costs which are **averages** between high- and low-volume products and between high- and low-complexity products. Figure 10.1 shows how product costs tend to be overstated for high-volume, low-complexity products but understated for low-volume, high-complexity ones. Neither can the costs represented by the other two quadrants be assumed to be accurate, due to compensating errors.

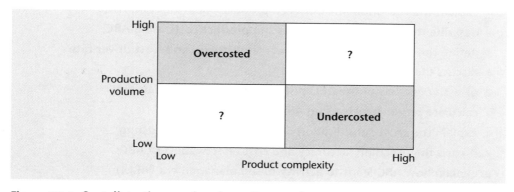

Figure 10.1 Cost distortions under absorption costing
Source: Based on R. S. Kaplan and R. Cooper (1998) *Cost and Effect: Using Integrated Cost Systems to Drive Profitability and Performance*, Harvard Business School Press, Boston, MA

It is easy to get carried away with the improved accuracy of ABC compared to traditional absorption costing and forget that it, too, uses estimates and approximations. The improvement in accuracy is significant, even for a basic ABC system. However, it does not give 100% accurate product costs. Figure 10.2 uses the analogy of an archery target to illustrate the comparative accuracy of the two systems.

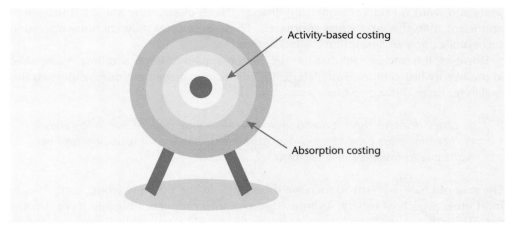

Figure 10.2 The product costing target
Source: Based on R. S. Kaplan and R. Cooper (1998) *Cost and Effect: Using Integrated Cost Systems to Drive Profitability and Performance*, Harvard Business School Press, Boston, MA

Learning objectives	Having worked through this chapter you should be able to:

- **explain the need for ABC;**
- **discuss how production volumes and product complexity can cause cost distortions;**
- **illustrate the difference in accuracy between absorption costing and ABC;**
- **explain the causation link between products, activities and costs;**
- **describe the procedure for calculating product costs using ABC;**
- **define the terms 'activity cost pool', 'cost driver' and 'cost driver rate';**
- **discuss the hierarchy of activities;**
- **give an overview of the ABC system in the form of a diagram;**
- **calculate product costs using ABC;**
- **explain the cross-subsidisation of costs in absorption costing;**
- **discuss the precision, accuracy and cost-effectiveness of ABC;**
- **explain how ABC leads to activity-based management (ABM);**
- **discuss the limitations of ABC.**

A new philosophy

Traditional absorption costing systems give product costs which enable production costs and stock valuations to be calculated. These valuations are an essential part of the audited financial accounts available to the public at large. The main objective is to ensure all production overheads are absorbed into the total annual production cost. This is achieved by identifying a factor whose behaviour **correlates** to the overhead costs. An

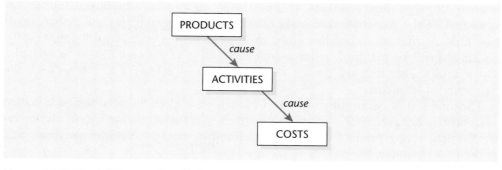

Figure 10.3 **The ABC causation link**

example of this is the use of direct labour hours as the factor for attaching the overheads of a production cost centre to its output. (Note that the direct labour is not the **cause** of all the overhead costs involved. Also note that the correlation does not have to be particularly strong – weakly correlated factors are often used.)

This ensures that the production costs are recovered, in total, by all the different types of product made by the business. As long as this broad objective is met, there is no requirement for individual product costs to be calculated as accurately as possible. In the past, it made little difference. Today, it can make a big difference. The costs of low-volume, complex products are usually subsidised by those of high-volume, simple products when absorption costing is used (see Figure 10.1).

ABC is different. Its **main** objective is to produce an accurate cost for each product in the range. The thinking behind ABC is that in order to control costs, it is necessary for them to be calculated **accurately**. A positive side-effect of this is that other important decisions, e.g. setting selling prices, will then be that much more effective.

ABC achieves this increase in accuracy through a simple logic:

- Products cause activities to happen.
- Activities cause costs to be incurred.

This *causation link* (see Figure 10.3) is fundamental to ABC. Note that it is **not** part of the absorption costing model.

The ABC process

ABC has the following five steps:

1 Identify the different activities performed by the business.
2 Calculate the total cost of each activity over the financial period (i.e. the cost pool).
3 Identify a cost driver (i.e. a causation factor) for each activity.
4 Calculate the cost driver rate (i.e. the average cost of one occurrence of the cost driver).
5 Assign part of the cost of each activity to different products based on the extent to which each product has caused the activity to occur (i.e. apply the cost driver rate).

For example, Storrit Ltd uses the same equipment to make two products, lever-arch files and box files. It has identified one of its activities as setting up the machinery to make a batch of one of these products. This particular activity has a budgeted annual cost of £9,000. In the year it plans to make 60 batches of lever-arch files and 30 batches of box files. A total of 90 batches gives an average set-up cost of £100 (£9,000/90). So £6,000 will be assigned to lever-arch files (60 × £100) and £3,000 to box files (30 × £100). This is based on the causation ratio of 2:1 = 60:30 = lever-arch file batches:box file batches.

The total cost of performing one type of activity in a given financial period is known as its *activity cost pool*. The mechanism for attaching accurate proportions of each activity cost pool to each product is by choosing a *cost driver* and calculating a *cost driver rate*. In the above example, Storrit Ltd:

1 The activity is setting up machinery.
2 The activity cost pool is £9,000.
3 The cost driver is the number of set-ups.
4 The cost driver rate is £100 a set-up (£9,000/(60 + 30)).
5 Lever-arch files are assigned £6,000 (60 set-ups @ £100/set-up).
  Box files are assigned £3,000 (30 set-ups @ £100/set-up).

Cost drivers are factors which CAUSE the activity cost pool to increase. Cost drivers are causation factors. For example, the greater the number of set-ups (cost driver), the greater the total cost of setting up the machinery (activity cost pool). Figure 10.4 lists some other examples of cost pools and their cost drivers.

Activity cost pool	Cost driver
Setting up machinery	Number of set-ups
Buying raw materials	Number of purchase orders
Controlling quality	Number of quality inspections
Operating machinery	Number of machine hours
Maintaining machinery	Number of maintenance hours

Figure 10.4 **Examples of activity cost pools and their cost drivers**

Sometimes, the organisation will have a choice of cost drivers and must choose the one it thinks most appropriate. In the case of setting up machinery, if this was much more complicated for some products than others, 'number of set-up hours' could be used instead of 'number of set-ups'.

Hierarchy of activities

It is important to understand that not all overheads increase in proportion to the number of units produced. (Traditional absorption costing assumes all overheads are volume related in this way, i.e. they all increase as output increases.)

Here are some of the categories into which activities can be analysed (examples of their cost drivers are shown in brackets):

● unit level, e.g. machining products (machine hours);
● batch level, e.g. purchasing materials (purchase orders);
● product level, e.g. maintenance of machinery (maintenance hours);
● facility level, e.g. site security (security hours).

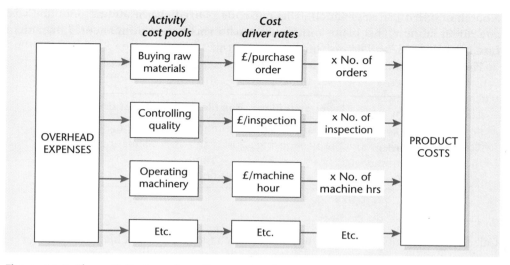

Figure 10.5 **The activity-based costing mechanism**

Process overview

Figure 10.5 gives an overview of the ABC process. (It is worth comparing this to Figure 9.2, the equivalent diagram for absorption costing in Chapter 9.)

(The following is a continuation of the Storrit Ltd example above.)

Storrit Ltd makes two products, lever-arch files and box files. The annual production overhead total of £38,000 has been analysed over four activities as shown below. The cost drivers have been defined and counted. Also, the cost driver rates have been calculated.

Activity	Activity cost pool (£)	Cost driver	No. of cost drivers/year	Cost driver rate
Setting up machinery	9,000	Machinery set-up	90	£100/set-up
Buying raw materials	10,000	Purchase order	50	£200/order
Controlling quality	4,000	Quality inspection	160	£25/inspection
Operating machinery	15,000	Machine hour	10,000	£1.50/machine hour
Total	£38,000			

In the year, Storrit plans to make 60 batches of lever-arch files and 30 batches of the more complicated box files. (The metal lever-arch mechanisms are bought in, ready to attach to the folded cardboard outer. The box files are made from large sheets of flat cardboard and are fitted with a holding clip and a box fastener.) Lever-arch files are produced in batches of 200 but box files are produced in batches of 150.

Direct cost	Lever-arch file (£)	Box file (£)
Raw materials	1.05	0.90
Direct labour	0.00	0.00
Total	1.05	0.90

Note that Storrit Ltd classifies all its labour costs as fixed overheads and does not have any **direct** labour. This is not unusual as most firms have a permanent, rather than casual, labour force and do not 'hire and fire' at will.

The annual number of cost drivers is split between the two products as follows:

Cost driver	Lever-arch files	Box files	No. of cost drivers/year
Machinery set-up	60	30	90
Purchase order	12	38	50
Quality inspection	60	100	160
Machine hours	6,000	4,000	10,000

Task:

Calculate the activity-based cost for one lever-arch file and one box file.

Solution:

Cost driver rate	Lever-arch files	Box files
£100/set-up	× 60 = 6,000	× 30 = 3,000
£200/order	× 12 = 2,400	× 38 = 7,600
£25/inspection	× 60 = 1,500	× 100 = 2,500
£1.50/machine hour	× 6,000 = 9,000	× 4,000 = 6,000
Total	18,900	19,100
Annual no. of files made	12,000	4,500
Production overhead per file	1.58	4.24
Direct cost per file	1.05	0.90
Production cost per file	**£2.63**	**£5.14**

Self-assessment question S10.1

Try the following question for yourself (answer at the end of the chapter).

Flatpack Industries Ltd makes many different items of household furniture in knock-down form. It has a budget for the current year which shows the total of production overheads to be £712,000. This has been analysed over five different activities as shown in the table below.

Flatpack Industries Ltd has been approached by P&Q plc to make 5,000 patio tables. The total cost of materials for this order is estimated at £70,000 and 2,000 hours of direct labour in the assembly department will be needed. The current rate of pay for assembly workers is £7.50 per hour. It is estimated that this order will cause the following production overhead activities to occur:

42 machinery set-ups   8 purchase orders raised   8,400 hours of machining
120 quality inspections   40 maintenance hours

Activity	Activity cost pool (£)	Cost driver	No. of cost drivers/year
Setting up machinery	220,000	Machinery set-up	2,750
Buying raw materials	32,000	Purchase order	250
Controlling quality	90,000	Quality inspection	4,500
Operating machinery	330,000	Machine hour	66,000
Maintaining machinery	40,000	Maintenance hour	800
Total	£712,000		

Task:

Calculate the activity-based production cost of this order (a) in total, and (b) per table.

Cross-subsidisation of costs

The introduction to this chapter points out that absorption costing tends to overstate some product costs and understate others (see Figure 10.1). This will now be examined in detail using the previous example of Storrit Ltd.

Let us assume that Storrit uses an absorption costing system based on machine hours.

Fixed overhead absorption rate = £38,000/10,000 machine hours = £3.80/mh

	Lever-arch files	Box files
Production overheads	3.80 × 6,000 mh = 22,800	3.80 × 4,000 mh = 15,200
Number of files produced	12,000	4,500
Production overheads/file	22,800/12,000 = 1.90	15,200/4,500 = 3.38
Direct costs/file	1.05	0.90
Absorption production cost/file	£2.95	£4.28
Compare:		
ABC production cost/file	£2.63	£5.14
Cross-subsidisation	£0.32	£(0.86)

This shows that when absorption costing is used, lever-arch files are overcosted and box files are undercosted. Lever-arch files are subsidising box files as they are bearing some of the costs caused by box files. For the whole annual production the errors compensate each other and the correct total of overheads is attached to production for the year. But, **at the level of individual products, significantly inaccurate production costs are being used and many important management decisions are based on them.**

Many firms use costs to help them set selling prices. Consider the implications of this. If Storrit Ltd sets its selling prices at twice the level of the absorption production cost, lever-arch files will be overpriced by £0.64 (2 × £0.32) and box files underpriced by £1.72 (2 × £0.86).

Now try the following question for yourself (answer at the end of the chapter).

Assuming Flatpack Industries Ltd (see S10.1 above) uses absorption costing based on a single, fixed overhead absorption rate per machine hour, calculate the production cost of the order for patio tables (a) in total, and (b) per table. Then compare your answers to those for S10.1 and comment on the cross-subsidisation of costs. Does your answer indicate that the patio table is more likely to be a complex, low-volume product line or a simple, high-volume one?

Precision, accuracy and cost-effectiveness

Absorption costing systems normally calculate their product costs to several decimal places, e.g. £8.9285. This gives the impression of a high degree of accuracy but it is really an example of mathematical precision. Because of the arbitrary correlations used by this traditional approach, it is quite possible that the first figure, i.e. the £8, is wrong (see Figure 10.2). If this is so, the calculation of several decimal places is a waste of resources, giving a misleading answer.

A traditional absorption costing system may be cheaper to operate than an ABC system but the cost of the errors resulting from its inaccuracies can be far greater. One important factor affecting the cost-effectiveness of ABC systems is the continuous fall in the price of information technology. The rapid evolution in information systems is greatly reducing their operating costs whilst, at the same time, greatly increasing their effectiveness.

ABC in service businesses

So far, this chapter has concentrated on production businesses and product costs. However, ABC is just as effective in service businesses such as banks, architecture, accountancy, driving schools, entertainment complexes, etc., as most of their costs are not volume related. The Co-op Bank is one example of a service provider which uses ABC.

The following example concerns the advertising agency Adage plc. Most of its work is the creation of advertising campaigns using print media such as newspapers and magazines. The agency sets its selling prices by adding 20% to total campaign costs. The following figures summarise the results for the last financial year:

	£000	£000
Sales revenue		6,600
Direct labour	2,000	
Overhead costs	3,500	
		5,500
Operating income		1,100

Adage is in the process of implementing its new ABC system but is still operating the absorption costing system it has used since its formation 30 years ago. Its old system absorbed overheads on the basis of the total cost of direct labour (e.g. copywriters, graphic artists and account managers) used for each campaign.

$$\text{Overhead absorption rate} = \frac{3,500,000}{2,000,000} = 175\% \text{ of direct labour cost}$$

During the recently ended financial year Adage completed a campaign for a product called Flamingo, a new range of bath soaps. The campaign costs were as follows using absorption costing:

	£
Direct labour	25,000
Overheads (£25,000 × 175%)	43,750
Campaign cost	68,750
Profit margin (@ 20%)	13,750
Price charged to customer	**82,500**

The new ABC system involved a detailed and time-consuming identification and analysis of Adage's activities. The result of this for the current year is summarised by the following table:

Activity	Cost driver	Annual cost pool (£)	Annual use of cost drivers	Cost driver rates
Clerical support	Clerical hours	1,500,000	375,000 hours	£4.00/clerical hour
Information systems	Computer hours	1,000,000	10,000 hours	£100.00/computer hour
General management	Management hours	600,000	30,000 hours	£20.00/management hour
Photocopying	Pages of copy	200,000	1,000,000 pages	£0.20/page
Telephone	Telephone calls	200,000	200,000 calls	£1.00/call
Total		3,500,000		

The ABC cost of the Flamingo campaign is calculated as follows:

Activity	Cost driver	Cost driver usage	Cost driver rate	Overhead attached (£)
Clerical support	Clerical hours	10,000 clerical hours	£4.00/clerical hour	40,000
Information systems	Computer hours	60 computer hours	£100.00/computer hour	6,000
General management	Management hours	800 management hours	£20.00/management hour	16,000
Photocopying	Pages of copy	2,500 pages	£0.20/page	500
Telephone	Telephone calls	1,500 calls	£1.00/call	1,500
			Total overhead	64,000
			Direct labour	25,000
			Total cost	89,000
			Profit (+20%)	17,800
			Selling price	106,800

Comparison	Campaign cost	Selling price
Absorption cost	68,750	82,500
Activity-based cost	89,000	106,800
Difference	(20,250)	(24,300)

Note that the activity-based cost is £6,500 greater than the absorption selling price! The Flamingo campaign must have been much more complex and demanding on resources than Adage's average campaign for that year as it has been significantly undercosted by the old system.

Try the following question for yourself (answer at the end of the chapter).

Gilmarsh is a large partnership of architects which currently operates an absorption costing system but is experimenting with an ABC system. The current annual budget shows the following:

	£000	£000
Sales revenue		3,120
Direct labour	1,600	
Overhead costs	800	
		2,400
Operating income		720

The architects absorb overheads as a percentage of the total cost of direct labour and their standard profit margin is 30% of total cost.

As part of their investigation into ABC, they wish to compare the two systems on a recently completed set of plans for a leisure centre. The cost of direct labour used on this job is £10,000. Their experimental ABC system is based on the following annual analysis:

Activity	Cost driver	Annual cost pool (£)	Annual use of cost drivers
Clerical support	Clerical hours	130,000	26,000 hours
Information systems	Computer hours	300,000	2,000 hours
General management	Management hours	50,000	5,000 hours
Printing and photocopying	Number of drawings	250,000	500,000 pages
Telephone	Telephone calls	70,000	35,000 calls
Total		800,000	

The leisure centre contract caused the following activities to happen:

Activity	Cost driver	Use of cost drivers
Clerical support	Clerical hours	400 hours
Information systems	Computer hours	30 hours
General management	Management hours	40 hours
Printing and photocopying	Number of drawings	3,500 pages
Telephone	Telephone calls	300 calls

Tasks:

For the leisure centre contract:

1 Calculate the absorption cost and selling price.
2 Calculate the activity-based cost and selling price.
3 Compare your findings and comment on them.

Activity-based management

In the light of this chapter so far, it is obvious that ABC can be a great help to managers in all sorts of organisations. Its major advantage is the increased accuracy in product costs, which means that costs can be controlled more effectively. It enables managers to get a better idea of the relative profitability of product lines. As a result, some products may be emphasised and others withdrawn or reduced in volume.

Marketing and administration overheads have not been discussed in this chapter but it is possible to use an ABC approach to find the relative costs of different customers and different administration procedures. This information helps managers to prioritise their time and effort. It may be that two customers, Jones Ltd and Smith & Co., buy the same value of items but Jones Ltd causes twice the amount of costs as Smith & Co. The former firm may require more visits from sales representatives, demand higher discounts and return 'unsuitable' goods more often. If this is so, an investigation into the conduct of Jones Ltd's account will probably reveal ways of reducing the cost of maintaining that particular customer. Without ABC, no one will know the extent to which this is happening.

ABC uses the causation link to measure accurately the resources used by product lines. The financial accounts, based on absorption costing, show the cost of resources provided by management. The total of resources supplied is almost always greater than the total of resources that should be consumed according to the ABC model. Financial accounting is a *resource supply* model but ABC is a *resource consumption* model. ABC identifies only the amount of resources that should be needed but absorption accounting uses the amount actually provided. The difference is the amount of resources that add no value to products.

Some of the resources supplied are used by activities not caused by product creation – for example, production machinery being used for a building maintenance job. Also, some 'legitimate' production activities may use more resources than they should – for example, storing raw material for three weeks instead of three days. Identification of these non-value-added resources and activities enables management to eliminate or reduce them. ABC makes this possible. This is what is meant by activity-based management (ABM).

Ultimately, in order to bring the amount of resources supplied into line with the amount consumed, the organisation needs to introduce activity-based budgeting (ABB). However, as stated earlier in the chapter, the successful implementation of ABC is a long process, measured in years rather than months. The second stage is the introduction of ABM, which usually follows automatically and is often the reason why ABC was introduced in the first place. However, switching to ABB is another huge change in corporate culture. Consequently, it also takes a number of years to implement successfully.

Absorption costing has been perfectly adequate for the best part of a hundred years, so is it really worth all the trouble of introducing ABC, ABM and ABB? The answer to that depends on two things. The first is the type of organisation you work for. The second is the degree of effectiveness you wish to achieve in controlling costs.

Limitations of ABC

Some costs, like heating and insurance, will apply to more than one activity cost pool. To divide them amongst all the appropriate cost pools, some subjective method of apportionment, as in absorption costing, has to be used. The causation link is lost at these points.

Sometimes, there is a choice of cost driver. For example, the 'setting-up machinery' cost pool could use the number of set-ups as the cost driver. Alternatively, it could use the number of set-up hours to differentiate between different types of set-up. Different cost drivers will probably give different product costs.

ABC systems are more complex than traditional absorption systems, consume more resources and cost more to operate. Also, they usually take a number of years to introduce properly. This is because they involve significant change throughout the company. For some companies, the costs of introducing ABC may outweigh the benefits.

The manager's point of view

This is a difficult and complex area, but a rewarding one. In most areas of life, the greater the effort put in, the better the results in the end. Activity-based costing is no different. It requires a major input from almost every area of the business – factory, maintenance, purchasing, warehousing, quality control, etc., as well as finance and IT. It is a company-wide project, which may involve cultural changes, with all the management angst that that is bound to bring. It will throw new light on the production processes, and lead to a clearer understanding of resource usage in the factory. And, at the end, it will probably bring you as close to the true product cost as it is possible to get. However, as in any costing system, there are still pitfalls to trap the unwary, as I think the experiences of my own company will serve to illustrate.

The company is a large international corporation, engaged in salt production and chemical manufacture of both traditional and specialised products. These encompass a diverse range of production processes: some simple, others complex, some highly capital-intensive and others mainly laboratory-based. ABC was first introduced into the salt division, an almost perfect environment for this type of system. There are no raw material costs; salt is available in the ground, effectively for free. It requires overheads to mine it and process it, until it becomes a package on a supermarket shelf. Since salt is the second-cheapest commodity in the world after water, the control of costs throughout the production and distribution processes is perhaps more critical than in any other business. ABC provided a yardstick against which to monitor the performance not only of each activity in the factory, but also of individual items of plant. It further allowed comparisons between similar activities in different factories, thereby constituting a form of benchmarking. But above all, it provided a reliable assessment of product cost, which enabled selling prices to be set with confidence.

In view of its success in the salt division, management decided to extend the use of ABC to all other areas of the company. In the traditional chemical divisions of the group, such as mine, the nature of the products is rather different from those in the salt division. Raw materials are a significant part of the cost build-up, perhaps amounting to around 50% in a typical product. Clearly, the value of ABC in this instance is of lesser significance, although it can still play a crucial role in shedding light on the true costs of production.

The installation of ABC into my division of the group proved to be a challenging, time-consuming, but ultimately very worthwhile experience. The first stage required the production managers to examine their processes and divide them up, as far as possible, into discrete activities. Then they determined the amount of resource consumed in running those activities. In a processing activity, for instance, the resources needed may have included the number of labour hours, supervisor hours, amount of electricity required to drive the machinery, steam to heat the process up, or ice to cool it down, and so on. Once costed, these figures would constitute the activity cost pool, which would be attributed to products by means of cost drivers, in the manner already described. The factory personnel carried out this analysis work with great diligence, so everyone felt confident that the results would be accurate.

When the consumption of resources in each activity had been calculated to everyone's satisfaction, we ran them against the production budget to find out how much of each resource would be needed to carry out our annual production programme. This is where the fun started! For a number of items, the amount of resource calculated by the system bore no relation whatsoever to the actual levels historically used in the factory. Electricity was the most marked example.

The system told us that we would need 2.5 million kWh to manufacture the production budget. Yet we knew our annual consumption of electricity, taken from the monthly invoices, was 6.5 million kWh! Where was the difference? 'Not in my area,' said each of the production managers, 'I know the electricity rating of each machine in my area, and the number of hours for which each of them is used, so I know that my numbers are right!' 'But,' I replied, 'the other 4 million kWh is definitely being used somewhere!' After a short impasse, an investigation was set in motion, and gradually the true situation started to emerge. The production managers had been correct in assessing the usage of their own production areas, but electricity was also being used in a whole host of other areas outside their specific control. These included the boilers, steam pumping, effluent plant, various cooling systems, air filtering, laboratory and maintenance equipment, space heating, lighting, air-conditioning, computers, offices, etc. The pattern of our electricity usage had never been seriously considered before. We had always assumed that the direct production areas were by far the largest users of electricity, but this exercise showed that, in fact, they used barely more than a third. In the light of this new knowledge, we were able to target our energy reduction programmes more effectively, and generate significant savings.

A similar experience occurred with direct labour. The system told us that we needed only 75% of the labour we were currently using. My suggestion that we could therefore make 25% of the workforce redundant had the production managers scurrying off to revise their figures! The managers had simply underestimated the true level of labour input actually used by many of their activities, and again, this new information enabled them to consider whether their labour usage was really as efficient as they had believed.

Once all these anomalies had been sorted out, we had a reasonably clear picture of how and where our resources were being used and the extent to which each individual product was responsible for consuming them. The system would require honing over a number of years, as further information about the processes came to light, but even our first attempt at an ABC system gave us an insight into the true nature of our costs that no other system would get anywhere near.

And at this point, of course, another series of problems presented themselves, this time throwing the sales departments into confusion. The cost of every single product had changed. The long-established, conventional, understanding of the profitability of each product, and therefore of the structure of the business itself, was suddenly on shaky ground. Some of our mainstay products were shown to be much less profitable than we had thought. Some, indeed, were now seen to be making a loss. Conversely, others which had never been competitive had suddenly become much cheaper, and could tolerate the price reductions necessary to make them sell.

However, this was not a time for rushed decisions. The installation of ABC had been a massive exercise. How accurate were these costs? Had we made any mistakes in the installation process, either in principle, or of a clerical nature? Were there any bugs in the new IT systems? Common sense decreed that we should proceed with caution, and refrain from taking any major decisions until the system had bedded down. Some errors were subsequently unearthed and corrected, but the original message remained largely the same, and gradually, selling prices were adjusted to restore the required levels of profitability.

But what should we do with those product lines which had now become unprofitable? Simply discontinue them? Here we run up against the recurring problem of all accounting systems, that of fixed costs. For all its increased accuracy in the direct costs centres, ABC still has the problem of general, non-specific fixed overhead (plant manager's costs, security, etc.). As in absorption costing, this is apportioned to products on some kind of semi-arbitrary basis, such as machine hours. We have already seen how these apportionments can distort reality. In most companies, this will still be a significant element of the final product cost. So, we have to ask ourselves some basic questions. Can we increase the price? (Always the first question!) Are the fixed cost apportionments reasonable? If we discontinue these products, can we eliminate these overheads, or will they simply devolve onto other products, making them unprofitable? Are these products in fact generating a high marginal income (sales revenue – variable costs) which is paying for a significant chunk of general fixed overhead, albeit not quite enough to return a profit? These may be difficult questions for management to resolve, but at least, thanks to ABC, the right questions are now being addressed.

The introduction of ABC had far-reaching effects on my chemical business. In addition to the clearer view of product costs, it also provided a set of standards against which our actual performance could be monitored. And this could be done in considerable detail. For instance, if one wanted to, one could monitor actual electricity usage by production batch, by activity, and compare it with the expected usage as determined in the ABC system. In practice, of course, the capture of the actual detail on a regular basis is likely to be excessively onerous, but it demonstrates what can be done. Management have to decide the level of detail at which the ABC system will operate, but simplicity in the initial stages is strongly recommended!

ABC worked extremely well in the salt division and also proved a valuable tool in the traditional chemical manufacturing companies. But it did not work so well for every business – in particular, those where the process machinery was fairly simple. Here, the raw material costs could exceed 70% of the total cost, so that ABC-controlled overheads amounted to no more than 30%. Moreover, in some cases, the various products and processes were sufficiently similar for management to feel that simple absorption costing techniques were perfectly adequate. Nevertheless, obliged to conform to the corporate policy of global installation of ABC, they chose to adopt a simplistic approach to ABC, by identifying only a few, broadly drawn activities, and treating a large proportion of their costs as general overhead. Thus, their version of ABC was only slightly more detailed than their existing absorption system. It continued to meet all management's needs and was effectively installed without major disruption to the business.

The point here is that ABC is not a panacea for all costing problems in all companies. It is a question of 'horses for courses'. Some businesses simply do not warrant it. Others will find it a lifesaver. And once the decision to install it has been taken, there remain some very critical choices about the level of detail to be used. Insufficient detail will waste the potential of the system, while excess detail runs the risk of overburdening the staff with initial set-up work, and then swamping them with operational data which may well hide the wood amongst the trees. Very careful, pragmatic planning is required to avoid these pitfalls, but if the company gets the balance right, there is no doubt that the benefits accruing are well worth the initial effort. In an increasingly competitive marketplace, a clear understanding of the nature of your company's costs becomes ever more critical. ABC, in the appropriate format for your company, is very likely to be the answer.

Summary

- Advanced technology means overheads are a large part of total cost.
- Absorption costing attaches overheads to products via arbitrary correlated factors.
- Absorption costing does not give accurate product costs.
- This applies particularly to low-volume, highly complex products.
- Activity-based costing (ABC) significantly improves the accuracy of product costs.
- ABC does not give 100% accurate product costs.
- The causation link between products, activities and costs is central to ABC.
- ABC product costs are calculated by a five-stage process.
- Overhead costs are attached to products via their causation factors, i.e. cost drivers.
- Not all activity costs operate at the unit level, i.e. increase directly with output.
- Activity costs also operate at the batch, product or facility level.
- Implementation of ABC systems reveals the previous cross-subsidisation of costs.
- ABC product costs are approximately right rather than precisely wrong.
- The falling price of information systems is making ABC ever more affordable.
- ABC can be equally effective in service businesses.
- ABC systems make activity-based management (ABM) possible.
- ABC and ABM make activity-based budgeting (ABB) possible.
- ABC has its limitations where accurate calculation of cost pools and choice of drivers are concerned.
- ABC systems use more resources than traditional absorption costing systems.
- ABC systems take several years to implement properly.
- ABC systems can be used alongside absorption systems.
- The main benefits are improved accuracy, cost control and management decisions.

Further reading

Atkinson, A., Banker, R., Kaplan, R. and Young, S. (2001) *Management Accounting*, 3rd edition, Prentice Hall, Harlow. See chapter 'Activity based cost management systems'.

Caplan, D., Melumad, N. D. and Ziv, A. (2005) 'Activity-based costing and cost interdependencies among products: the Denim Finishing Company', *Issues in Accounting Education*, Vol. 20, Issue 1, February.

Horngren, C., Bhimani, A., Datar, S. and Foster, G. (1999) *Management and Cost Accounting*, Prentice Hall Europe, Harlow. See Chapter 11, 'Activity based costing'.

Hughes, S. B. and Paulson Gjerde, K. A. (2003) 'Do different cost systems make a difference?', *Management Accounting Quarterly*, Vol. 5, Issue 1, Autumn.

Hussein, M. E. A. and Tam, K. (2004) 'Pilgrims Manufacturing, Inc.: activity-based costing versus volume-based costing', *Issues in Accounting Education*, Vol. 19, Issue 4, November.

Kaplan, R. and Cooper, R. (1998) *Cost & Effect: Using Integrated Cost Systems to Drive Profitability and Performance*, Harvard Business School Press, Boston, MA.

Kaplan, R. S. and Anderson, S. R. (2004) 'Time-driven activity-based costing', *Harvard Business Review*, Vol. 82, Issue 11, November.

Neumann, B. R., Gerlach, J. H., Moldauer, E., Finch, M. and Olson, C. (2004) 'Cost management using ABC for IT activities and services', *Management Accounting Quarterly*, Vol. 6, Issue 1, Autumn.

Upchurch, A. (2003) *Management Accounting, Principles and Practice*, 2nd edition, Financial Times/Prentice Hall, Harlow. See chapter 'Absorption of overheads', *sections* 'Activity based costing' *and* ' "Traditional" absorption costing and ABC compared'.

Weetman, P. (2002) *Management Accounting, an Introduction*, 3rd edition, Financial Times/Prentice Hall, Harlow. See chapter 'The frontiers of management accounting', *section* 'Activity based costing'.

Answers to self-assessment questions

S10.1. Flatpack Industries Ltd

Cost driver rate	Order for 5,000 tables
220,000/2750 = £80/set-up	× 42 = 3,360
32,000/250 = £128/purchase order	× 8 = 1,024
90,000/4,500 = £20/inspection	× 120 = 2,400
330,000/66,000 = £5/machine hour	× 8,400 = 42,000
40,000/800 = £50/maintenance hour	× 40 = 2,000
Total production overheads	50,784
Direct cost of materials	70,000
Direct labour cost	2,000 × 7.50 = 15,000
Total production cost	**£135,784**
Production cost per table	£135,784/5,000 = **£27.16**

S10.2. Flatpack Industries Ltd

Fixed overhead absorption rate = £712,000/66,000 machine hours = £10.79/mh

	Patio table
Production overheads	10.79 × 8,400 = 90,636
Materials	70,000
Direct labour	2,000 × 7.5 = 15,000
Total production cost	£175,636
Number of tables produced	5,000
Absorption production cost/table	£35.13
ABC production cost/table	£27.16
Cross-subsidisation	£7.97

This shows that when absorption costing is used, patio tables are overcosted. Patio tables are bearing some of the costs caused by the other products in the range. This indicates that they are more likely to be **high-volume and/or simple products** (see Figure 10.1).

S10.3. Gilmarsh Architectural Partnership

1   Overhead absorption rate = $\dfrac{800,000}{1,600,000}$ = 50% of direct labour cost

Absorption costing of leisure centre contract:	£
Direct labour	10,000
Overheads (£10,000 × 50%)	5,000
Absorption cost	15,000
Profit margin (@ 30%)	4,500
Price charged to customer	19,500

2   ABC of leisure centre contract:

Activity	Cost driver	Annual cost pool (£)	Annual use of cost drivers	Cost driver rates
Clerical support	Clerical hours	130,000	26,000 hours	£5.00/clerical hour
Information systems	Computer hours	300,000	2,000 hours	£150.00/computer hour
General management	Management hours	50,000	5,000 hours	£10.00/management hour
Printing and photocopying	Number of drawings	250,000	500,000 pages	£0.50/page
Telephone	Telephone calls	70,000	35,000 calls	£2.00/call
Total		800,000		

Activity	Cost driver	Contract's use of cost drivers	Cost driver rates	Overhead attached (£)
Clerical support	Clerical hours	400 hours	£5.00/clerical hour	2,000
Information systems	Computer hours	30 hours	£150.00/computer hour	4,500
General management	Management hours	40 hours	£10.00/management hour	400
Printing and photocopying	Number of drawings	3,500 pages	£0.50/page	1,750
Telephone	Telephone calls	300 calls	£2.00/call	600
			Total overhead	9,250
			Direct cost	10,000
			Activity-based cost	**19,250**
			Profit (@ 30%)	5,775
			Selling price	**25,025**

3 Comparison	Contract cost	Selling price
Absorption cost	15,000	19,500
Activity-based cost	19,250	25,025
Difference	(4,250)	(5,525)

Note that the activity-based cost is only £250 less than the absorption selling price.

The leisure centre contract appears to be more complex and demanding on resources than Gilmarsh's average contract as it has been significantly undercosted by the absorption system.

Danbake

Danbake Limited is a medium-sized bakery selling mainly to supermarket chains. It produces two types of pie: pork and game. Although both pies are the same size, the pork pie has a plain crust but the game pie has a lattice-work crust and more expensive ingredients. As the bakery is highly automated, its absorption costing system uses raw materials as the only direct cost. It attaches production overheads to both products equally per batch, using the number of batches baked in total as the absorption base. Each oven firing produces one batch of pies.

Dan, the owner–manager, has noticed that last year the sales of pork pies were significantly lower than expected but the sales of game pies were significantly higher. The selling prices are arrived at by doubling the total production cost prices. But Dan is wondering if he has got his pricing right. His accountant assures him that the costing system is working correctly but one of his work-experience students has questioned the way in which the system operates. It seems illogical to her that a game pie, which is more complicated to make, receives the same amount of overhead as a pork pie. She suggests that Dan should look at something called 'activity-based costing'.

The following figures are from this year's budget:

	Budgeted output (batches)	Cost of ingredients (per batch)	Weight of ingredients (per batch)	Preparation time (per batch)	Baking time (per batch)
Pork pie	700	£120	200 kg	1.80 hours	3.00 hours
Game pie	350	£180	250 kg	2.12 hours	2.57 hours

Together with his student, Dan investigates the current cost structure and produces the following information:

Overhead activity	Budgeted cost (£)	Cost driver
Pie preparation	316,200	Weight of ingredients
Oven preparation	16,674	Number of firings
Baking	24,000	Number of oven hours
Other	126,126	Batch preparation time
Total	**£483,000**	

Tasks:

1 Using the current absorption costing system, calculate the production cost and selling price for one batch of each type of pie.

(10 marks)

2 Using activity-based costing, calculate the production cost and selling price for one batch of each type of pie.

(50 marks)

3 Quantify the cross-subsidisation revealed by your results.

(10 marks)

4 Advise Dan whether or not he should replace his current absorption costing system with an activity-based costing system.

(30 marks)
(Total 100 marks)

Questions

An asterisk * on a question number indicates that the answer is given at the end of the book. Answers to the other questions are given in the Lecturer's Guide.

Q10.1* Hinj Limited

Hinj Limited manufactures and sells four products: arms, brackets, clips and D-rings. This year, for the first time, it is operating an activity-based costing system in parallel with its long-standing absorption costing system (which absorbs overheads on a machine hour basis).

The planned production activity cost pools and cost driver activity levels for all the output for the year are as follows:

Activity	Cost pool (£)	Activity level
Purchasing materials	41,500	1,000 purchase orders
Storing materials	41,600	650 issue notes
Setting up machinery	26,400	200 set-ups
Running machinery	73,000	7,300 machine hours
Total production overheads	182,500	

An analysis of actual annual production output for two of the products is as follows:

	Arms	Brackets
Units produced	1,000	500
Purchase orders	190	325
Stores issue notes	105	200
Set-ups	35	60
Machine hours	2,600	1,275
Direct materials	£8,250	£3,750
Direct labour	£46,000	£7,600

Tasks:

1 Calculate the production cost per unit for arms and brackets using the machine hour overhead absorption rate.
2 Calculate the production cost per unit for arms and brackets using the activity-based costing system.
3 Comment on your findings.

Q10.2* Numan Travel

Numan Travel plc started trading 10 years ago with its cheap airfare brand Flygo. Since then, it has expanded to offer three different types of holiday: Best Beaches, Cosy Cottages and Great Golfing. The following analysis was recently performed:

	No. of marketing staff	No. of reps per hotel	No. of hotels used	No. of customers	No. of reservations/ bookings
Best Beaches	30	1.0	192	950,000	375,000
Cosy Cottages	20	0.5	770	725,000	250,000
Great Golfing	18	0.5	192	150,000	25,000
Flygo	6	–	–	175,000	175,000
Total	74	–	1,154	2,000,000	825,000

Last year, the founder of the business relinquished the position of managing director and became executive chairman. His replacement as MD has suggested that the future of the company lies in the expanding golf sector. Also, because the cheap airfare market is becoming increasingly competitive, he suggests that the company withdraws from that sector. Further analysis reveals the following information:

(£000)	Best Beaches	Cosy Cottages	Great Golfing	Flygo	Total
Contribution	37,500	30,000	3,500	14,000	85,000
Advertising	15,000	15,000	2,000	3,500	35,500
Administration	18,000	12,000	1,200	8,400	39,600
Profit	4,500	3,000	300	2,100	9,900

The contribution is the sales revenue for each brand less the variable costs of operating that brand. Advertising costs are allocated directly to each brand but administration costs have been attached to brands on the basis of the number of reservations.

The chairman feels that the MD's strategy is mistaken but does not wish to appear to be heavy-handed on the basis of nothing more than an instinctive response. His last major act as MD was to instigate a pilot activity-based costing system to run in parallel with their existing absorption system. He wonders if this will provide him with a more convincing argument. So far, the pilot has produced the following activity analysis of the indirect administration costs:

	£000
Reservations/bookings	20,000
Holiday repping	10,000
Hotel liaison/contracting	6,000
Marketing	3,600
	39,600

Task:

Calculate the profit made by each brand using activity-based costing. Comment on the proposed strategy of the new MD.

Q10.3* Wilcock & Co.

Wilcock & Co. is a firm of solicitors which currently operates an absorption costing system but is experimenting with an activity-based costing system. The current annual budget shows the following:

	£000	£000
Sales revenue		2,422
Direct labour	1,384	
Overhead costs	346	
		1,730
Operating profit		692

Wilcock & Co. absorbs overheads as a percentage of the total cost of direct labour and its standard profit margin is 40% of total cost.

As part of the investigation into ABC, the solicitors wish to compare the two systems on a recently completed fraud case. The cost of solicitors' time used directly on this case is £15,000.

Their experimental ABC system is based on the following annual analysis:

Activity	Cost driver	Annual cost pool (£)	Annual use of cost drivers
Clerical support	Clerical hours	156,000	26,000 hours
General administration	Administration hours	60,000	3,000 hours
Photocopying	Number of photocopies	25,000	500,000 copies
Telephone	Telephone calls	105,000	70,000 calls
	Total	346,000	

The fraud case caused the following activities to happen:

Activity	Cost driver	Use of cost drivers
Clerical support	Clerical hours	500 hours
General administration	Administration hours	70 hours
Photocopying	Number of photocopies	1,500 copies
Telephone	Telephone calls	400 calls

Tasks:

For the fraud case:

1 Calculate the absorption cost and selling price.
2 Calculate the activity-based cost and selling price.
3 Compare your findings and comment on them.

Q10.4 Hoffman Ltd

Hoffman Ltd makes only two types of portable cooking stove, the Lightweight (LW) and the Megarange (MR). Last year it produced 4,500 LWs and 500 MRs. The direct materials cost £3.00 for one LW and £10.00 for one MR. The assembly workers who put the stoves together are all paid at the same rate of £6.30 an hour. When LWs are being produced each operative assembles nine stoves an hour and when MRs are being produced each operative assembles seven stoves an hour. This is the only labour that Hoffman classes as 'direct labour'. The factory uses automated machinery to manufacture the components which are common to both stoves. The other components are bought in. Each stove uses 15 machine hours in its construction.

For some time now, the company has been considering the introduction of activity-based costing. It has decided to recost last year's production using this method so it can compare costs to those under its current absorption costing system. The current overhead absorption rate is based on the number of machine hours. Last year's production activities have been analysed as follows:

Activity	Cost driver	Activity cost pool (£)
Purchasing	Purchase order	20,000
Training	Training hour	1,000
Setting up machines	No. of set-ups	2,250
Running machines	Machine hours	14,250
	Total	£37,500

The analysis also quantified the number of cost drivers caused by each stove:

Activity	No. of cost drivers caused by LWs	No. of cost drivers caused by MRs
Purchasing	360	40
Training	20	30
Setting up machines	60	30
Running machines	67,500	7,500

Tasks:

1 Calculate the absorption cost for each type of stove.
2 Calculate the activity-based cost for each type of stove.
3 Comment on your findings.

Q10.5 Pullman Products

Pullman Products manufactures ceramic discs for industrial use. It makes the discs in three sizes: small (S), medium (M) and large (L). Product costs are calculated using a simple absorption costing system which has only one overhead absorption rate (based on direct labour hours) for the whole manufacturing process. The following information is available:

	S	M	L
Material cost (£/disc)	6	20	72
Direct labour hours per disc	1.0	1.5	2.5
Weight of disc (kg)	1.0	3.0	11.0
Budgeted production (units)	10,000	2,000	4,000
Budgeted sales (units)	10,000	2,000	4,000

All direct labour is paid at £6/hour. The budgeted fixed production overheads total £1,380,000. Selling prices are calculated by adding 150% to the production cost.

Fierce competition from the Far East is forcing Pullman to review its selling prices, especially on its small disc. The recently appointed production manager has suggested that the use of activity-based costing may throw some light on this problem. To test the feasibility of this suggestion, a crude analysis of the firm's production overhead activities has been carried out and the results are shown below.

Activity	Cost driver	Activity cost pool (£)	Annual number of cost drivers
Clay preparation	Disc weight (kg)	180,000	60,000
Moulding	Disc weight (kg)	240,000	60,000
Firing	Kiln firing	912,000	50
Finishing	Number of discs	48,000	16,000
	Total	1,380,000	

In the budget period, there were 15 firings for small discs, 5 firings for medium discs and 30 firings for large discs.

Task:

For each disc, calculate the unit production cost and selling price using:

a) the absorption costing system;
b) the activity-based costing system.

Comment on your findings.

Q10.6 DFR

DFR operates a number of retail outlets selling a range of audio-visual products. These products range in size and value from small items such as portable radios that are easily displayed on shelves, to large and expensive equipment such as widescreen televisions. Some of these products take up considerable amounts of retail staff time advising customers at the point of sale.

DFR has a warehouse that it uses for storage of its products before they are delivered to its retail outlets using its own transport fleet. The warehouse and the retail outlets are all based in one country, but some of the outlets are significantly closer to the warehouse than others.

At present, warehousing costs are analysed between storage costs and distribution costs and these are then apportioned to retail outlets on the basis of the sales value of orders delivered. Retail outlet costs (including rent, heating and staff costs) are attributed to individual products based on their sales values.

For some time, the management of DFR has been considering the introduction of an Activity Based Costing (ABC) system. The management team has heard that this is a more accurate system of costing than that which is currently used, particularly since some of DFR's products require more involvement of staff in the retail outlets in advising customers of the meaning of the product specifications.

Required:

You have been appointed as a management accountant by DFR to introduce an ABC system. Prepare a report addressed to the Board of Directors of DFR that

a) Explains the weaknesses of the present method used by DFR when attributing costs to products and its implications for cost control and product profitability.

(9 marks)

b) States the principles of ABC.

(4 marks)

c) Explains, with suitable examples, how DFR's warehouse storage and distribution costs and retail outlet costs could be attributed to individual products using an ABC system.

(8 marks)

d) Explains how DFR will benefit from the introduction of an ABC system.

(4 marks)

(Total = 25 marks)

CIMA Intermediate: Management Accounting – Performance Management, November 2004

Q10.7 S & P Products plc

S & P Products plc purchases a range of good quality gift and household products from around the world; it then sells these products through 'mail order' or retail outlets. The company receives 'mail orders' by post, telephone and Internet. Retail outlets are either department stores or S & P Products plc's own small shops. The company started to set up its own shops after a recession in the early 1990s and regards them as the flagship of its business; sales revenue has gradually built up over the last 10 years. There are now 50 department stores and 10 shops.

The company has made good profits over the last few years but recently trading has been difficult. As a consequence, the management team has decided that a fundamental reappraisal of the business is now necessary if the company is to continue trading.

Meanwhile the budgeting process for the coming year is proceeding. S & P Products plc uses an activity-based costing (ABC) system and the following estimated cost information for the coming year is available:

Retail outlet costs:

Activity	Cost driver	Rate per cost driver	Number each year for department store	own shop
		£		
Telephone queries and requests to S & P	Calls	15	40	350
Sales visits to shops and stores by S & P sales staff	Visits	250	2	4
Shop orders	Orders	20	25	150
Packaging	Deliveries	100	28	150
Delivery to shops	Deliveries	150	28	150

Staffing, rental and service costs for each of S & P Products plc's own shops cost on average £300,000 a year.

Mail order costs:

Activity	Cost driver	Rate per cost driver Post	Telephone	Internet
		£	£	£
Processing 'mail orders'	Orders	5	6	3
Dealing with 'mail order' queries	Orders	4	4	1
		Number of packages per order		
Packaging and deliveries for 'mail orders' – cost per package £10	Packages	2	2	1

The total number of orders through the whole 'mail order' business for the coming year is expected to be 80,000. The maintenance of the Internet link is estimated to cost £80,000 for the coming year.

The following additional information for the coming year has been prepared:

	Department store	Own shop	Post	Telephone	Internet
Sales revenue per outlet	£50,000	£1,000,000			
Sales revenue per order			£150	£300	£100
Gross margin: mark-up on purchase cost	30%	40%	40%	40%	40%
Number of outlets	50	10			
Percentage of 'mail orders'			30%	60%	10%

Expected Head Office and warehousing costs for the coming year:

	£
Warehouse	2,750,000
IT	550,000
Administration	750,000
Personnel	300,000
	4,350,000

Required:

a) 1) Prepare calculations that will show the expected profitability of the different types of sales outlet for the coming year.

(13 marks)

2) Comment briefly on the results of the figures you have prepared.

(3 marks)

b) In relation to the company's fundamental reappraisal of its business,

1) discuss how helpful the information you have prepared in (a) is for this purpose and how it might be revised or expanded so that it is of more assistance;

(7 marks)

2) advise what other information is needed in order to make a more informed judgement.

(7 marks)

(Total = 30 marks)

CIMA Intermediate: Management Accounting – Decision Making, November 2001

CHAPTER 11

Comparison of profits under absorption and variable costing

Chapter contents

Introduction

Because the annual profit figure is such an important piece of information ('the bottom line') it is advisable to monitor profit throughout the year. Knowing how things are progressing enables you to take corrective action when necessary and avoid unpleasant surprises at the financial year-end. Most organisations do this by producing monthly or quarterly management accounts.

As the idea is to help meet the annual profit target, it seems sensible to use the same rules by which the annual profit is calculated. One of these is that fixed production overheads must be treated as **product** costs and not as **period** costs (see SSAP 9). In other words, annual accounts intended for public circulation are based on absorption costing. This works well for monthly accounting, provided that the pattern of trading is reasonably predictable over the year. However, for businesses whose trading pattern is difficult to predict, profits may be distorted. This also applies, to some extent, to seasonal businesses.

Distortions of profit do not help these businesses to monitor their real performance. So, it is not surprising that they sometimes decide to use a system which avoids this distortion. This alternative approach uses variable (also known as marginal) costing. Variable costing treats fixed production overheads as period costs rather than product costs. This is opposite to absorption costing used in the audited accounts **and will produce a different profit total**. However, at the end of the year, the internally reported 'variable profits' can be reconciled to the externally reported 'absorption profits'.

These two alternative financial models can be applied to a single set of commercial transactions, resulting in two different profit figures. This chapter shows you how to calculate the profits for a trading period in two different ways and how to reconcile them to each other.

Learning objectives

Having worked through this chapter you should be able to:
- **explain the difference between a product cost and a period cost;**
- **use budget information to predetermine an overhead absorption rate;**
- **explain why predetermined OARs are used in preference to actual OARs;**
- **explain how under- and overabsorption of overheads occurs;**
- **adjust profit and loss accounts for under- and overabsorption of overheads;**
- **calculate 'absorption' profit and 'variable' profit;**
- **reconcile 'absorption' profit to 'variable' profit;**
- **explain the limitations of both systems.**

Treatment of fixed production overheads

As stated above, absorption costing treats fixed production overheads as production costs and variable costing treats them as period costs. A production cost is the total direct cost (prime cost) plus absorbed production overhead (see Figure 11.1a). A period cost is one which relates to a time period rather than to the output of products or services (see Figure 11.1b).

Predetermination of overhead absorption rates

The previous chapter showed how overhead absorption rates (OARs) are calculated via allocation, apportionment and an appropriate choice of the base. These OARs are used to determine the production cost and stock valuations for period-end accounts. The practice is to use predetermined rates rather than actual rates. After all, the actual rates could only be determined after the period has ended, so selling prices could not be based on actual absorption costs. One possibility is to use the actual rates of the last-but-one month so that rates were fairly up to date. However, this would cause monthly fluctuations in the product cost figures (see below). If selling prices were based directly on costs, they would be changed every month. Prices going up and down at each month-end would give the impression of instability and incompetence in the eyes of customers.

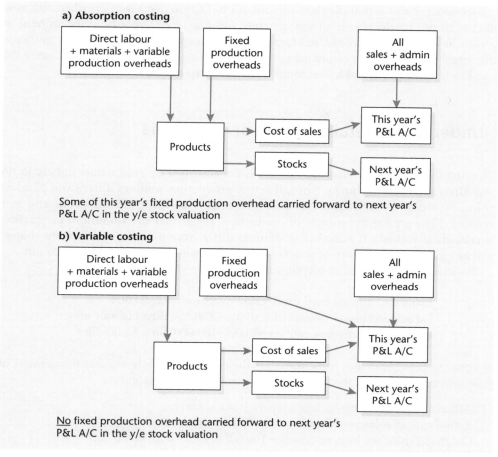

Figure 11.1 **Tracing overhead costs to the profit and loss account**

Annual basis:

> Estimated annual fixed production overheads = £36,000
> Estimated annual volume of activity = 12,000 machine hours
> Overhead absorption rate = £36,000/12,000 mh = £3.00/mh

Monthly basis:

	Month 1	**Month 2**	**Month 3**
Actual overheads incurred	3,000	3,520	2,500
Actual machine hours	1,000	1,100	909
Monthly actual OAR	£3.00/mh	£3.20/mh	£2.75/mh

For these reasons it is normal to calculate the OAR at the start of the year and apply it throughout. This means that the current year's production overhead cost and volume of activity used in the calculation are estimates rather than actual amounts. The major consequence of this is that the total amount of production overheads absorbed into product costs during the year is almost certainly going to be different from the amount of production overheads actually incurred. However, the profit and loss account must use the actual rather than the estimated figure. So an adjustment is necessary to change the overheads in the profit and loss account from estimated to actual amounts.

Under- and overabsorption of overheads

The first thing to note is that the overheads are absorbed by production and are in no way affected by sales volumes. Thus, if actual production volumes differ from planned volumes, either too much or too little overhead will end up in the profit and loss account. (The greater the volume of production, the greater the amount of production overheads absorbed.) If actual sales volumes differ from planned volumes, no change will be caused to the amount of production overheads in the profit and loss account.

Predetermined overhead absorption rate:

Estimated annual fixed production overheads = £500,000
Estimated annual volume of activity = 100,000 direct labour hours
Overhead absorption rate = £500,000/100,000 dlh = £5.00/dlh

If either of these estimates is incorrect (as they almost certainly will be) the amount of production overheads in the profit and loss account will be inaccurate.

i) Actual annual fixed production overheads = £525,000
    Actual annual volume of activity = 100,000 direct labour hours
    Overhead absorbed by production = 100,000 × £5.00 = £500,000
    Underabsorption of overheads = £25,000 (500,000 − 525,000)
    Unless this adjustment is made, profit will be overstated by £25,000.
ii) Actual annual fixed production overheads = £500,000
    Actual annual volume of activity = 112,000 direct labour hours
    Overhead absorbed by production = 112,000 × £5.00 = £560,000
    Overabsorption of overheads = £60,000 (560,000 − 500,000)
    Unless this adjustment is made, profit will be understated by £60,000.

Illustration – The Jinasy Umbrella Company

The Jinasy Umbrella Company makes an up-market all-purpose umbrella. It produces management accounts for internal use on a quarterly basis. Its fixed production overheads are budgeted at £20,000 a quarter (£80,000 a year) and its marketing and administration overheads at £19,000 a quarter (£76,000 a year). The production plan is for 4,000 umbrellas each quarter (16,000 a year). The selling price is £20 and the variable cost of each umbrella is £8. There are 1,000 umbrellas in stock at the start of the first quarter. The actual results for last year, expressed in numbers of umbrellas, are as follows:

	Q1	Q2	Q3	Q4	Year
Sales	4,000	2,000	1,000	8,000	15,000
Production	4,000	4,000	3,000	6,000	17,000

Calculate the quarterly and annual profits (i) using absorption costing and (ii) using variable costing. (iii) Explain why the profits differ. (Assume the total of actual overheads incurred were as forecast.)

Under both systems, stocks of finished umbrellas are valued at production cost.

	Variable costing	Absorption costing
Production cost:	variable cost	variable cost + fixed production overhead
	£8	£8 + (£20,000/4,000 units) = £13

Physical stock changes (number of umbrellas):

	Q1	Q2	Q3	Q4	Year
Opening stock	1,000	1,000	3,000	5,000	1,000
Actual production	4,000	4,000	3,000	6,000	17,000
Actual sales	4,000	2,000	1,000	8,000	15,000
Closing stock	1,000	3,000	5,000	3,000	3,000

i) Absorption costing (£000)

	Q1	Q2	Q3	Q4	Year
Opening stock	13	13	39	65	13
Add: Production cost	52	52	39	78	221
Less: Closing stock	(13)	(39)	(65)	(39)	(39)
Under-/(over)absorption	–	–	5	(10)	(5)
Cost of sales	52	26	18	94	190
Sales revenue	80	40	20	160	300
Gross profit	28	14	2	66	110
Non-production overhead	19	19	19	19	76
Net profit	9	(5)	(17)	47	34

ii) Variable costing (£000)

	Q1	Q2	Q3	Q4	Year
Opening stock	8	8	24	40	8
Add: Production cost	32	32	24	48	136
Less: Closing stock	(8)	(24)	(40)	(24)	(24)
Cost of sales	32	16	8	64	120
Sales revenue	80	40	20	160	300
Gross profit	48	24	12	96	180
Production overheads	20	20	20	20	80
Non-production overhead	19	19	19	19	76
Total fixed overheads	39	39	39	39	156
Net profit	9	(15)	(27)	57	24

iii) Reconciliation of profits (£000)

	Q1	Q2	Q3	Q4	Year
Absorption net profit	9	(5)	(17)	47	34
Variable net profit	9	(15)	(27)	57	24
Difference	–	10	10	(10)	10
Increase in stock (units)	–	2,000	2,000	(2,000)	2,000
Production overheads in					
stock increase (@ £5 a unit)	–	10	10	(10)	10

Annual results

The total of fixed production overheads charged in this year's 'variable' profit and loss account is the total incurred in this period, £80,000 (see Figure 11.1b). Variable profits are £24,000.

On the other hand, the net effect in this year's 'absorption' profit and loss account is that the amount of production overheads is reduced by £10,000, as follows:

> **Production overheads brought forward from last year
> (in opening stock) into this year = 1,000 units @ £5 = £5,000**
>
> **Production overheads carried forward from this year
> (in closing stock) into next year = 3,000 units @ £5 = £15,000**

The total of fixed production overheads charged in this year's 'absorption' profit and loss account is £70,000 (see Figure 11.2a).

The net reduction of £10,000 in production overhead charged will increase net profit from £24,000 (variable) to £34,000 (absorption).

Similar explanations and profit reconciliations can be made for each quarter (the process is summarised by Figure 11.3 below).

Self-assessment question S11.1

Try the following question for yourself (answer at the end of the chapter).

Hiphoptop Limited produces music CDs. Internal management accounts are drawn up on a quarterly basis. The company plans to produce and sell 12,000 CDs each quarter and have a stock of 2,000 CDs at the start of quarter 1. The selling price is £6 and the variable cost of each CD is £1. The production and non-production overheads are estimated at £24,000 and £30,000 a quarter respectively. The actual results for the year, expressed in numbers of CDs, are as follows:

	Q1	Q2	Q3	Q4	Year
Sales	9,000	16,000	6,000	13,000	44,000
Production	14,000	12,000	11,000	10,000	47,000

Calculate the quarterly and annual profits (a) using absorption costing and (b) using variable costing. (c) Explain why the profits differ. (Assume the total of actual overheads incurred was as forecast.)

a) Less overheads are brought into the current year in the value of opening stock than are carried forward into next year in the value of closing stock.

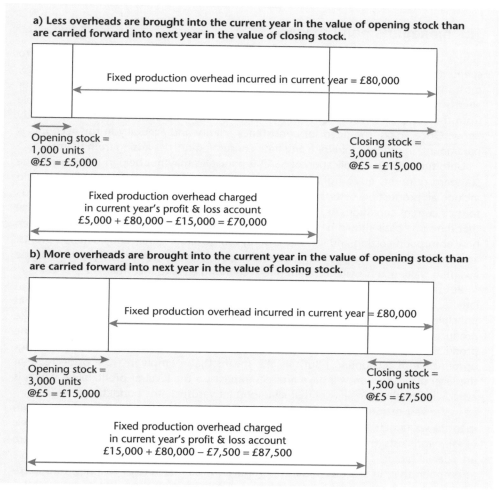

Figure 11.2 **Production overhead charged to the profit and loss account**

Limitations

Absorption profits make the realistic assumption that, in most years, most businesses will sell most of their stock. However, if the stock of finished goods brought forward into the current year proves to be unsaleable, absorption costing will bring forward overheads which should have been charged in last year's accounts.

When a seasonal business builds up stocks for next period's sales (as in quarter 3 for Jinasy) it can be argued that absorption profits avoid creating 'fictitious' losses for the build-up period. However, the greater the number of periods between production and sales (as in quarter 2 for Jinasy) the less convincing this argument becomes.

Absorption profits may be increased by producing extra units in order to increase stock levels rather than to enable sales. In certain cases, absorption profits may decrease even though the sales volume has increased. This creates some scope for the short-term manipulation of profits.

The manager's point of view

Senior managers tend to be busy people who, if not financially orientated, want to spend as little time as possible poring over interim statements of account. In practice, most managers will already have a gut feel about the current period's performance, or alternatively will have been able to obtain an indication of it from data readily available from the computer. Periodic accounts often serve only to confirm what they already know. Once again, the need for consistency, clarity and accuracy in the accounts is paramount, in order to minimise any time-consuming queries arising from them.

Unfortunately, the application of SSAP 9 principles may not help in this regard. The standard requires, quite rightly, that the valuation of products in inventory should include all production costs, including overheads incurred in bringing those products to their current condition. As this is the required basis for year-end accounts, it is logical that the same basis should be used for interim internal accounts. We have already seen how absorption costing and variable costing can generate significantly different profits, and the last thing management want to see is a substantial year-end adjustment as the inventory valuation is switched from one accounting basis to the other.

But the adoption of SSAP 9 in interim accounts can itself lead to confusion, particularly for periods as short as one month. Absorption costing may be precisely correct in principle, in that it matches costs to sales by transferring cost into inventory when the product goes into stock, and releasing it back into the profit and loss account when the product is sold. (This results directly from the application of the accruals or matching-up principle of accounting.) But this also means that a simple increase or decrease in the level of production will have a direct impact on the level of profitability, which is especially significant in view of that all-important yardstick, the budget.

In the vast majority of companies, the budget is the principal tool used by management to set targets and monitor performance. The budget predicts not only the levels of sales and costs, but also how these will be phased throughout the year. Unless there are special factors to consider, such as seasonal influences, it would be a reasonable assumption that, in any given month, production will match sales volumes, thus keeping inventory at a constant level. But life rarely turns out as planned. In some months, sales will exceed production, causing a net transfer of period cost out of inventory into the profit and loss account. Conversely, when production exceeds sales, there will be a net transfer of period costs out of the profit and loss account into inventory. And in an exceptionally poor sales month, profitability can apparently be improved by increasing production levels and transferring more overhead into inventory; this is probably the exact reverse of management's correct course of action, which should be to reduce production to reflect the lower demand. I stress that there is nothing wrong with these period cost transfers, which accurately reflect the movements of stock in and out of inventory. But when these movements take place against a fixed overhead monthly budget, the value of this budget as a control tool is diminished.

A solution to this problem is to use a combination of absorption and variable costing. The production overheads are fixed costs, incurred over a period of time, and it would be fair to argue that they should be written off in that period, in exactly the same way as non-production expenses such as marketing or administration. The marginal income generated by sales in the period (i.e. sales less variable costs) can then be set against the total period costs relating to that period, producing an easily understandable 'variable' net profit. The requirements of SSAP 9 can be satisfied by a 'below-the-line' adjustment, transferring the necessary amount to or from inventory, before striking a final reportable 'absorption' net profit for the month. In this way, we are structuring a set of figures which achieve all our objectives: they provide data of sufficient clarity for management purposes, meet the requirements of the standard, and also highlight separately the 'accountants' adjustment', which need concern only those who understand it!

The following example relates to The Jinasy Umbrella Company illustration earlier in the chapter.

Variable costing statement:

	Q1	Q2	Q3	Q4	Year
Opening stock	8	8	24	40	8
Add: Production cost	32	32	24	48	136
Less: Closing stock	(8)	(24)	(40)	(24)	(24)
Cost of sales	32	16	8	64	120
Sales revenue	80	40	20	160	300
Gross profit	48	24	12	96	180
Production overheads	20	20	20	20	80
Non-production overhead	19	19	19	19	76
Total fixed overheads	39	39	39	39	156
Variable net profit	9	(15)	(27)	57	24
'Below-the-line' adjustment:					
Adjustment for production					
overheads in stock increase	–	10	10	(10)	10
Absorption net profit	9	(5)	(17)	47	34

This monthly adjustment for period cost in inventory needs to be carefully monitored. In most systems, the use of budgeted expenditure and budgeted levels of production to calculate overhead recovery rates will be quite adequate for the purposes of internal monthly accounts. But for final audited accounts, the period costs held in inventory must be valued on actual experience, rather than budget. In a normal year, where expenditure and production run close to budget, the adjustment to actual may be minimal, but in an abnormal year, the company could be in for a nasty surprise. For instance, if the year had been going extremely well, and production had exceeded budget by 25%, the actual overhead rate would be recalculated at 20% (= 25/125) below the budgeted rate. If, at the same time, the production overhead budget was underspent by 10%, the overhead rate would decrease in total by nearly 30%. This would result in a substantial reduction of total overhead in inventory, and a corresponding increase in the charge written off in the profit and loss account. The accountants would not be popular unless this situation had been foreseen and communicated to management well in advance!

In practice, auditors will accept that the valuation of period costs in inventory should be based on normal levels of production and normal levels of expenditure. This will eliminate, or at least diminish, the impact of unusual or non-recurring events. For instance, if production had been halved in the last quarter as a result of serious plant failure, it would be wrong to double the period costs on products manufactured in that period as the situation was abnormal. The impact of such an event should be a write-off of any unrecovered overhead directly to the profit and loss account.

Acceptable norms can perhaps best be established by looking at production and expenditure over a longer period of time. In my company, we used the average production over the last three years, which had the effect of smoothing out any anomalies, without discarding them altogether. We also used actual expenditure in the year, as this was usually fairly constant. The most appropriate method of establishing norms is a matter for agreement with the auditors, and may vary from company to company. But, once agreed, it will be expected that this method will be applied consistently in future years.

There is one final point to mention in connection with period cost in inventory. As one moves across a year-end into a new financial year, the overhead absorption rates will be recalculated on the basis of the new budget. Unless your system is such that you can identify the overhead costs attributed to each individual item held in stock, you will have to revalue the whole of the inventory onto the new cost basis. Otherwise you will have some products going into stock at last year's cost, and coming out at this year's higher cost, resulting in an undervaluation of inventory. The revaluation of the period cost in inventory will produce a surplus (or deficit) which will have to be written off to future profit and loss accounts, complicating the period cost in inventory adjustment line still further. In my view, therefore, it is highly desirable to isolate the adjustment below the line, where it will not confuse non-financial users of the interim accounts.

Summary

- The choice between absorption profits and variable profits only exists for internal reporting (external reporting must use absorption profits).
- No change in stock level (P = S): absorption profit equals variable profit.
- Increase in stock level (P > S): absorption profit greater than variable profit.
- Decrease in stock level (P < S): absorption profit less than variable profit.

  (Where P = production volume and S = sales volume.)
- The more volatile the business, the more suitable are variable profits for internal reporting.
- The less volatile the business, the more suitable are absorption profits for internal reporting.

The process by which the absorption profit is reconciled to the variable profit is shown in Figure 11.3.

It is important to note that variable profit depends solely on sales volume, but absorption profit depends on both sales volume **and** production volume. The implication of this is that absorption profits can be improved by increasing production! The effect of increasing production is to increase closing stock. Remember that absorption profits are the ones that must be used for external reporting. In the short term, profits can be manipulated upwards by this strategy **without breaking any accounting rules**. In the medium/long term, high stock levels due to excess production will return to normal and the effect on profit will be downwards.

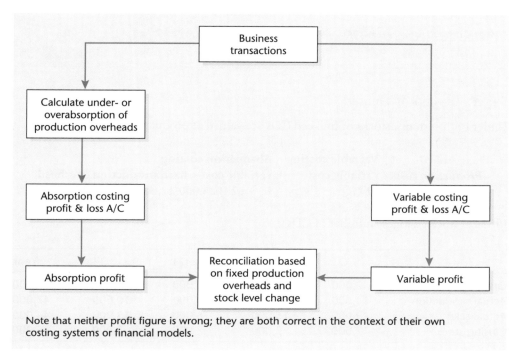

Note that neither profit figure is wrong; they are both correct in the context of their own costing systems or financial models.

Figure 11.3 **Reconciliation of absorption and variable costing profits**

Further reading

Baxter, W. T. (2005) 'Direct versus absorption costing: a comment', *Accounting, Business & Financial History*, Vol. 15, Issue 1, March.

Dugdale, D. and Jones, T. C. (2003) 'Battles in the costing war: UK debates, 1950–75', *Accounting, Business & Financial History*, Vol. 13, Issue 3, November.

Dugdale, D. and Jones, T. C. (2005) 'Direct versus absorption costing: a reply', *Accounting, Business & Financial History*, Vol. 15, Issue 1, March.

Horngren, C., Bhimani, A., Datar, S. and Foster, G. (2002) *Management and Cost Accounting*, 2nd edition, Prentice Hall Europe, Harlow. See Chapter 7, 'Income effects of alternative stock costing methods'.

Upchurch, A. (2003) *Management Accounting, Principles and Practice*, 2nd edition, Financial Times/Prentice Hall, Harlow. See chapter 'Absorption costing and marginal costing'.

Weetman, P. (2002) *Management Accounting, An Introduction*, 3rd edition, Financial Times/Prentice Hall, Harlow. See chapter 'Profit, performance and current developments', *section on* 'Absorption costing and variable costing'.

Answer to self-assessment question

S11.1. Hiphoptop Limited

Under both systems, stocks of finished CDs are valued at production cost.

	Variable costing	Absorption costing
Production cost:	variable cost	variable cost + fixed production overhead
	£1	£1 + £2 (£24,000/12,000 units) = £3

Physical stock changes (number of CDs):

	Q1	Q2	Q3	Q4	Year
Opening stock	2,000	7,000	3,000	8,000	2,000
Actual production	14,000	12,000	11,000	10,000	47,000
Actual sales	9,000	16,000	6,000	13,000	44,000
Closing stock	7,000	3,000	8,000	5,000	5,000

Under-/(over)absorption of overheads:

	Q1	Q2	Q3	Q4	Year
Planned production level	12,000	12,000	12,000	12,000	48,000
Actual production level	14,000	12,000	11,000	10,000	47,000
Under-/(over)absorption in units	(2,000)	0	1,000	2,000	1,000
Under-/(over)absorption @ £2/unit	(4,000)	0	2,000	4,000	2,000

a) Absorption costing (£000)

	Q1	Q2	Q3	Q4	Year
Opening stock	6,000	21,000	9,000	24,000	6,000
Add: Production cost	42,000	36,000	33,000	30,000	141,000
Less: Closing stock	(21,000)	(9,000)	(24,000)	(15,000)	(15,000)
Under-/(over)absorption	(4,000)	–	2,000	4,000	2,000
Cost of sales	23,000	48,000	20,000	43,000	134,000
Sales revenue	54,000	96,000	36,000	78,000	264,000
Gross profit	31,000	48,000	16,000	35,000	130,000
Non-production overhead	30,000	30,000	30,000	30,000	120,000
Net profit	1,000	18,000	(14,000)	5,000	10,000

b) Variable costing (£000)

	Q1	Q2	Q3	Q4	Year
Opening stock	2,000	7,000	3,000	8,000	2,000
Add: Production cost	14,000	12,000	11,000	10,000	47,000
Less: Closing stock	(7,000)	(3,000)	(8,000)	(5,000)	(5,000)
Cost of sales	9,000	16,000	6,000	13,000	44,000
Sales revenue	54,000	96,000	36,000	78,000	264,000
Gross profit	45,000	80,000	30,000	65,000	220,000
Production overheads	24,000	24,000	24,000	24,000	96,000
Non-production overhead	30,000	30,000	30,000	30,000	120,000
Total fixed overheads	54,000	54,000	54,000	54,000	216,000
Net profit	(9,000)	26,000	(24,000)	11,000	4,000

c) Reconciliation of profits (£000)

	Q1	Q2	Q3	Q4	Year
Absorption net profit	1,000	18,000	(14,000)	5,000	10,000
Variable net profit	(9,000)	26,000	(24,000)	11,000	4,000
Difference	**10,000**	**(8,000)**	**10,000**	**(6,000)**	**6,000**
Increase in stock (units)	5,000	(4,000)	5,000	(3,000)	3,000
Production overheads in stock increase (@ £2 a unit)	**10,000**	**(8,000)**	**10,000**	**(6,000)**	**6,000**

Canco Foods

Canco Foods specialises in the preparation and canning of three different products: new potatoes, mincemeat and ham. The company has three divisions (one for each product), each with its own production and sales facilities. It so happens that each division has the same cost structure for manufacturing and marketing its product. For each division, the annual fixed production overheads are £200,000 and the annual fixed administration and sales overheads combined are £80,000. These are incurred evenly over the year. Also, each division has an annual budget of 20,000 cases bought and sold; all stocks are zero on 1 January. The selling price is £50 a case and the delivery costs are £2.50 a case.

The preparation and canning of new potatoes starts in February and is completed by mid-June, but sales are evenly spread over the year. Mincemeat is produced at the same rate throughout the year but sales only occur between September and December, mainly for the Christmas mince pie market. Ham is produced and sold at a steady rate with very little variation from month to month. (Stocks of all three products are zero at 1 January.)

Costs per case for each product are:	£
Direct material and direct labour	21
Variable production overhead	3
Variable production cost	24

Activity (number of cases):

		January–June	July–December	Year
Potatoes	Production	20,000	–	20,000
	Sales	10,000	10,000	20,000
Mincemeat	Production	10,000	10,000	20,000
	Sales	–	20,000	20,000
Ham	Production	10,000	10,000	20,000
	Sales	10,000	10,000	20,000

Tasks:

1 Prepare summarised profit and loss accounts for each half-year and the whole year for each division using absorption costing.

(25 marks)

2 Prepare summarised profit and loss accounts for each half-year and the whole year for each division using variable costing.

(25 marks)

3 Reconcile the profits for each of the three periods by producing a statement involving a 'below-the-line' adjustment as shown in 'The manager's point of view' section of this chapter.

(10 marks)

4 **On no more than two sides of A4**, discuss the use of absorption costing and variable costing for the periodic, internal reporting of profitability.

(40 marks)

(Total 100 marks)

Questions

An asterisk * on a question number indicates that the answer is given at the end of the book. Answers to the other questions are given in the Lecturer's Guide.

Q11.1* Clamco

Clamco makes car clamps. The following information is from January's budget, which is based on a production volume of 6,000 clamps:

	£
Opening stock of clamps	0
Fixed manufacturing overhead	72,000
Variable manufacturing overhead	18,000
Selling and administrative expenses (all fixed)	25,000
Direct labour	120,000
Direct materials used	90,000
Selling price (per unit)	64

The actual production and sales volumes for the first three months of the year were as follows:

Number of clamps:	January	February	March	Quarter
Production level	6,000	5,000	7,000	18,000
Sales	4,000	6,000	7,000	17,000

Actual variable costs per unit and total fixed overheads incurred were exactly as forecast.

Tasks:

1 Calculate the profit for each month and for the quarter
   a) using absorption costing
   b) using variable costing.
2 Reconcile the profits for each month and for the quarter. Explain why they differ.

Q11.2* Rivilin plc

Rivilin is a uni-product firm with the following budgeted amounts:

	£
Unit selling price	60
Unit variable cost	20
Fixed production overhead per month	9,600

Rivilin's planned level of production is 800 units a month. However, actual activity was as follows:

	April	May	June
Units produced	800	750	820
Units sold	800	700	850

There was no opening stock at 1 April.

The actual fixed production overhead incurred was accurately predicted at £9,600 a month.

The non-production fixed overheads are £10,000 a month.

Required:

1 A variable costing profit statement for each month.
2 An absorption costing profit statement for each month.
3 An explanation of the difference in profits between the two statements.

Q11.3* The Valley Fireworks Corporation

The Valley Fireworks Corporation manufactures special firework display kits to sell to responsible organisations only. The following information is taken from its budget for 2002:

> **Opening stock of kits = closing stock of kits = 20 kits**
> **Annual production = annual sales = 1,200 kits**

	£ per unit	£ per year
Selling price	500	
Direct materials	60	
Direct labour	180	
Variable production overhead	10	
Variable distribution overhead	20	
Fixed production overhead		96,000
Fixed non-production overhead		144,000

The actual production and sales volumes for 2002 were:

(Units)	Q1	Q2	Q3	Q4	Year
Opening stock	10	290	550	690	10
Production	300	300	200	300	1,100
Sales	20	40	60	980	1,100
Closing stock	290	550	690	10	10

The variable costs per kit and the total fixed costs were as forecast.

Tasks:

1 Prepare profit statements for each of the four quarters and the year,
   a) using absorption costing
   b) using variable costing.

2 Reconcile the two profit figures for each quarter and prepare a summary statement in the following format:

	Qtr 1	Qtr 2	Qtr 3	Qtr 4	Year
Net profit using variable costing					
Adjustment for fixed production overheads in stock change					
Net profit using absorption costing					

3 Explain how both sets of profit figures can be useful to the management of The Valley Fireworks Corporation.

Q11.4 Nalpo Ltd

Nalpo Ltd manufactures and markets a small table that attaches to ladders. The following annual budget is based on 75,000 units made and sold:

	Per unit		Total	
	£	£	£	£
Sales revenue		5		375,000
Sales				
Production cost of sales:				
Variable	3		225,000	
Fixed	1		75,000	
		4		300,000
Gross profit		1		75,000
Selling and admin costs:				
Variable (10% of sales)		0.5	37,500	
Fixed			30,000	
				67,500
				7,500

Actual production figures for 2001 and 2002 were as follows:

	2001	2002
Opening stock	0	15,000
Production	85,000	70,000
Sales	70,000	80,000
Closing stock	15,000	5,000

Tasks:

You are required to:

1 Prepare budgeted statements of profitability on the basis of:
   a) absorption costing
   b) variable costing.
2 Reconcile the difference in profit in the two statements produced for part 1.

Q11.5 Brafire Ltd

Brafire manufactures small, portable electric fires. It has operated an absorption costing system since it started many years ago. However, the new managing director (who is studying part time for an MBA) has recently learned of the possibility of using a variable costing system as an alternative to the company's usual approach. He decides to investigate this further by applying both systems to next quarter's budget (shown below). To provide a good comparison, the output will be shown at both a constant level and a fluctuating one.

Budget for quarter 3 (units):

	July	August	September	Total
Sales volume	3,000	3,000	6,500	12,500
Constant output	4,500	4,500	4,500	13,500
Fluctuating output	4,500	4,000	5,000	13,500

There will be 500 fires in stock on 1 July. The selling price is £30 and the cost structure is as follows:

	£/unit
Direct materials	4.00
Direct labour	1.50
Variable production overheads	0.50
Fixed production overheads*	6.00
Fixed marketing overheads*	4.00
Total cost	16.00

* These figures are based on a constant monthly production level of 4,500 fires.

Tasks:

Produce a budgeted profit and loss account for internal management reporting using the following four bases:

1 Absorption costing and constant output levels.
2 Variable costing and constant output levels.
3 Absorption costing and fluctuating output levels.
4 Variable costing and fluctuating output levels.

Comment on your findings.

Q11.6 P Ltd

P Ltd manufactures a specialist photocopier. Increased competition from a new manufacturer has meant that P Ltd has been operating below full capacity for the last two years.

The *budgeted information* for the last two years was as follows:

	Year 1	Year 2
Annual sales demand (units)	70	70
Annual production (units)	70	70
Selling price (for each photocopier)	£50,000	£50,000
Direct costs (for each photocopier)	£20,000	£20,000
Variable production overheads (for each photocopier)	£11,000	£12,000
Fixed production overheads	£525,000	£525,000

Actual results for the last two years were as follows:

	Year 1	Year 2
Annual sales demand (units)	30	60
Annual production (units)	40	60
Selling price (for each photocopier)	£50,000	£50,000
Direct costs (for each photocopier)	£20,000	£20,000
Variable production overheads (for each photocopier)	£11,000	£12,000
Fixed production overheads	£500,000	£530,000

There was no opening stock at the beginning of year 1.

Required:

(a) Prepare the actual profit and loss statements for each of the two years using:
   - absorption costing
   - marginal costing

   (14 marks)

(b) Calculate the budgeted breakeven point in units and the budgeted margin of safety as a percentage of sales for year 1 and then again for year 2.

   (6 marks)

(c) Explain how the change in cost structure (as detailed in the budgeted information) has affected the values you have calculated in your answer to part (b).

   (5 marks)

   (Total = 25 marks)

CIMA Foundation: Management Accounting Fundamentals, November 2001

Pricing your products

Chapter contents

Introduction

One of the most important decisions that any business has to make is what prices to charge for its products and services. If it sets them too low, its profits may be insufficient for it to survive in the medium/long term. If it sets them too high, sales may be lost to competitors and profits may again be insufficient. In short, if it gets its pricing wrong it may go out of business!

So, how are selling prices calculated? Is there one best method? Or does it depend on each firm's business environment?

This chapter looks at three different points of view before attempting to integrate them into a practical pricing strategy. The viewpoints examined are those of the economist, the accountant and the marketer.

Having worked through this chapter you should be able to:

- explain the economist's pricing model;
- explain the accountant's pricing model;
- compare these by the use of charts;
- describe the optimum level of output;
- describe price elasticity of demand;
- explain cost-plus pricing;
- discuss the dangers of cost-plus pricing;
- discuss the marketer's view of pricing;
- explain the pricing strategies of skimming and penetration;
- explain target pricing as an integrating mechanism;
- discuss the limitations of pricing theory.

The economist's view

Optimum level of output

This is a simplified explanation based on economic theory. It is presented as an extension to breakeven analysis, which is covered in Chapter 5. Towards the end of that chapter there is a section detailing the limiting assumptions of that technique. Two of these limiting assumptions are that neither the variable cost, nor the selling price, change when the volume of output changes. This means that the total revenue and total cost lines on breakeven charts are **straight** and the total revenue line goes through the origin. The relationships between revenue, costs and volume are assumed to be linear (see Figures 12.1 and 12.3).

However, economists recognise that these simple relationships do not hold for all volumes of activity. Beyond a certain point, in order to increase the volume of sales, the

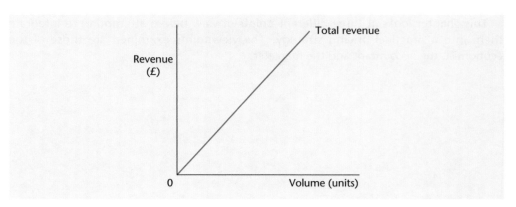

Figure 12.1 **Unit selling price remains the same for all volumes**

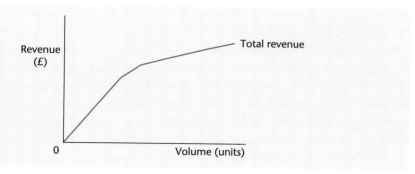

Figure 12.2 **Unit selling price reduces as volume increases**

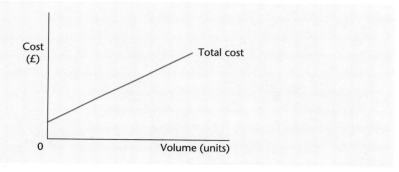

Figure 12.3 **Variable cost per unit remains the same for all volumes**

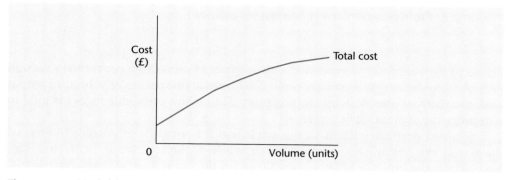

Figure 12.4 **Variable cost per unit reduces as volume increases**

unit selling price has to be reduced (see Figure 12.2). Economists quantify this relationship between price and quantity through the concept of price elasticity of demand. Also, beyond a certain point, the cost per unit should reduce due to bulk-buying discounts and other economies of scale (see Figure 12.4). The effect of these different assumptions is that the lines on the charts are now curved (at least beyond a certain volume).

Combining Figures 12.1 and 12.3 gives the familiar breakeven chart shown in Figure 12.5. Combining Figures 12.2 and 12.4 gives the economist's view of the same relationships. Note the implication for profit. The accountant's version (Figure 12.5)

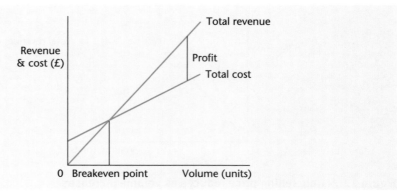

Figure 12.5 **Profit continues to increase with volume**

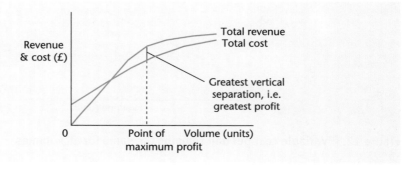

Figure 12.6 **Profit is maximised at one level of activity**

shows profit continuing to increase with volume. However, the economist's version (Figure 12.6) shows that maximum profit is achieved at one particular volume of output and, therefore, at one particular selling price. This is how economic theory is used to determine the optimum selling price.

The major problem with this approach is that it is virtually impossible to forecast accurately the revenue and cost curves shown in Figures 12.2 and 12.4. This is an unavoidable consequence of attempting to predict the future in an ever-changing world. Economic analysis can be insightful when applied to historical data but it is of limited practical use for setting future prices. Fortunately, there are several alternative ways of approaching this problem, as you will see later in this chapter.

Self-assessment question S12.1

Try the following question for yourself (answer at the end of the chapter).

Here is a profit–volume chart as used by accountants. Redraw it, showing how it might look from an economist's point of view.

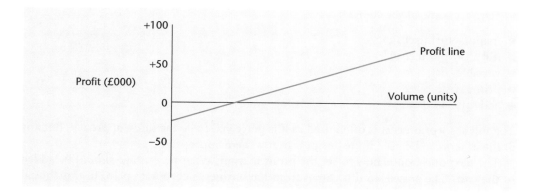

Price elasticity of demand

Another useful concept from the field of economics is that of *price elasticity of demand*. This concerns the rate at which the amount sold changes relative to the rate of change of the selling price. For products which are essentials or necessities, a large increase in price may only produce a small decrease in sales volume. For example, if petrol prices increased by 5%, the amount of petrol sold might decrease by only 2%. In this case, petrol can be described as having a 'low elasticity of demand' or being relatively 'price inelastic'. This reflects the small amount of change (or *stretching*) in demand relative to the amount of change in price. (Implicit in Figure 12.1 is the assumption that the price elasticity of demand is infinity.)

However, for other items, a small increase in price may produce a large decrease in sales volume. For example, a 5% increase in the price of coffee may produce a 10% decrease in the amount of coffee sold. In this case coffee could be described as having high elasticity of demand. The amount of coffee sold changes more than its price. One of the reasons for this is that coffee substitutes are more easily obtainable than petrol substitutes. It is easier to change from coffee to tea than to change your vehicle from petrol to diesel. When setting selling prices, it is very useful to have a reasonable idea of the product's price elasticity of demand as this will help to predict the revenue curve (see Figure 12.2). (Implicit in Figure 12.2 is the assumption that the price elasticity of demand is greater than 1.0 as total revenue continues to rise with output.)

The accountant's view

Cost-plus pricing

When setting the price of a product, the first thing an accountant usually thinks of is its cost. It is a fundamental rule of business that, in order to make a profit, prices have to be greater than costs. So, the product cost is first established and then a profit margin is added to give the selling price. But, as can be seen from earlier chapters, the concept of *product cost* is far from straightforward. There are at least three types of costing (variable, absorption and activity-based) and several specific costs within these types. So which is the best cost to use?

Here are some of the choices:

- manufacturing cost;
- full absorption cost;
- variable cost;
- prime cost;
- activity-based cost.

The full absorption cost is often used as it is perceived to be the safest approach, but any of the others can be used if the business thinks them appropriate.

The next question is how to set the profit margin. What percentage should be added to the cost? The answer to this comes from the business's corporate plan. In this should be stated the required *return on capital employed*. This enables the required annual profit to be estimated and from this the percentage profit margin can be calculated.

For example, if Kryptomatic Limited aims to achieve a 20% return on capital employed and its latest figure of total capital is £1 million, then its annual profit needs to be £200,000. If its budget for next year shows that its total costs will be £600,000, then its total sales revenue needs to be £800,000.

Below is an extract from Kryptomatic's budget for next year:

	£000
Direct materials	150
Direct labour	50
Prime cost	200
Variable production overheads	25
Fixed production overheads	75
Manufacturing cost	300
Administration overheads	120
Marketing overheads	180
Total cost	600
Required profit	200
Total revenue	800

If it adopted a **prime-cost-plus** approach, the 'plus' margin added would be

$$\frac{800 - 200}{200} = \frac{600}{200} = +300\%$$

If it adopted a **manufacturing-cost-plus** approach, the 'plus' margin added would be

$$\frac{800 - 300}{300} = \frac{500}{300} = +167\%$$

If it adopted a **full-cost-plus** approach, the 'plus' margin added would be

$$\frac{800 - 600}{600} = \frac{200}{600} = +33\%$$

Try the following question for yourself (answer at the end of the chapter).

Codex Limited has a target return on capital employed of 40% p.a. and its latest balance sheet shows its capital employed is £15 million. The following figures are from next year's budget. Calculate the cost-plus percentage Codex should use based on (a) prime cost, (b) manufacturing cost and (c) total cost.

	£m
Direct materials	8
Direct labour	12
Prime cost	20
Variable production overheads	1
Fixed production overheads	3
Manufacturing cost	24
Administration overheads	2
Marketing overheads	4
Total cost	30

The absorption cost suicide spiral

The main drawback of cost-plus pricing is that it ignores the demand aspects of a competitive environment. It assumes that all product demand is completely price inelastic. This is very unrealistic for the vast majority of products. Figure 12.7 illustrates the potential danger of blindly following the cost-plus approach.

The amount of fixed cost attached to each unit is calculated by dividing the total of fixed costs by the planned number of units. Every time the price is increased, the volume sold goes down, which causes an increase in fixed cost per unit and, consequently, a further price increase. If this downward spiral were allowed to happen, the company would very soon cease trading.

Here is a numerical example. Blinkered Limited produces a standard saddle. Its total annual fixed costs are £1 million and the variable cost of each saddle is £80. It prices the saddle by adding a 40% mark-up to its absorption cost.

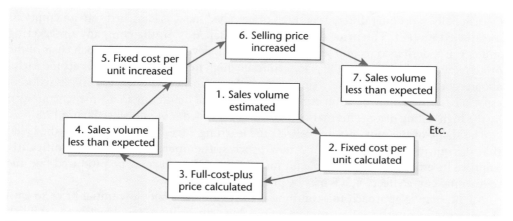

Figure 12.7 **The absorption cost suicide spiral**

1   Sales volume estimated at 50,000 units.
2   Fixed cost per unit = £20 (£1,000,000/50,000).
3   Absorption cost = £100 (£80 + £20); selling price = £140 (£100 + 40%).
4   Actual sales volume = 40,000 saddles.
5   Fixed cost per unit = £25 (£1,000,000/40,000).
6   Absorption cost = £105 (£80 + £25); selling price = £147 (£105 + 40%).
7   Sales volume falls to 33,000 saddles due to price increase.
8   Etc.

Blinkered Limited's profits diminish at an ever-increasing rate due to the downward spiral of sales volume. Before long, its losses will be unsustainable and it will have to cease trading.

The marketer's view

Existing products

No organisation functions in isolation. Trading takes place in the competitive environment of the marketplace, which means that firms cannot charge whatever they wish for their products. They have to set their prices in relation to those set by their competitors. This is particularly true for products that have been in existence for a while. The cost-plus method may suggest a selling price of £25 but if a competitor has a very similar product on the market for £19, it would be very risky to stick with the £25 price tag. Maybe the price should be reduced to £18 or £21; maybe the product should be discontinued. Maybe it should be altered in some way that clearly differentiates it from the competition, resulting in a perceived higher value in the eyes of the customer. If this is achieved, it may even be possible to set the selling price successfully above £25! This is an example of *product positioning* in which the selling price is an important factor. The point is that market considerations (not cost-plus calculations) should have the final say in the setting of the selling price.

New products

Occasionally, a product different enough to be called 'new' is launched into an empty or unsatisfied market. The price of new products depends on the company's marketing strategy. If it desires to recoup some of the research, development and launch costs of the product, it may decide to set the price artificially high to start with. This targets the **early-adopters** or **trend-setters** market segment. Once this segment is satisfied, the price is reduced, especially as there may be competitive products in the market by that time, encouraged by the high selling price. This marketing strategy is called *skimming* (see Figure 12.8).

The shape of the unit cost line reflects the **learning curve** concept based on the belief that during the initial period of a new process, the operatives usually significantly improve its efficiency. For example, in month one, 500 items may be produced but due to learning curve effects, 1,200 may be produced in month two.

An alternative approach to skimming is to set an artificially low initial price to gain the maximum number of customers as quickly as possible. The object is to establish brand loyalty so that profit foregone in the introductory stage is more than compensated for by profit from repeat sales after the price has been adjusted upwards sometime after

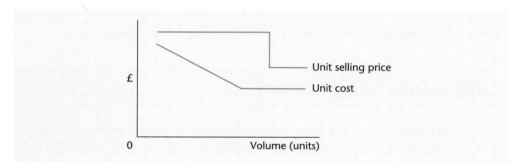

Figure 12.8 **Skimming pricing policy**

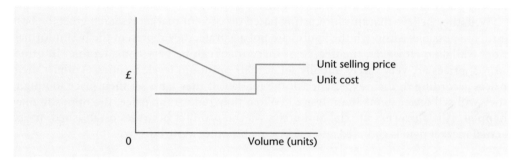

Figure 12.9 **Penetration pricing policy**

launch. The object of this approach is to build market share and discourage early competition. This marketing strategy is called *penetration* (see Figure 12.9).

Target pricing and costing: an integrated strategy

The traditional approach to price setting, which starts by establishing costs and ends with the selling price decision, is turned on its head by this new approach. The first thing to be done in target pricing is to set the selling price in the context of the marketplace and its constraints. This may well involve market research, trial selling in a small geographical area and consideration of the product life cycle. In other words, determine the highest price at which the product will sell the required volume. Next, calculate the desired profit margin and deduct this from the selling price. The resulting figure will be the maximum total cost allowable. The product designers then have to engineer the product so that its cost does not exceed the target cost.

This can be applied to the revamping of existing products as well as new ones. For example, cost savings may be achieved by replacing five components with one larger component, resulting in less labour assembly time even if there is no saving in material purchase costs. Savings may also be made in ordering and storage of components. The effects of production process learning curves are also taken into account when setting the target costs. (This may result in a contract which stipulates a **reduction** in selling price, rather than an increase, after a certain time has elapsed.) Target pricing is thought to have originated in Japan, where it is more commonly used than in other economies. However, its popularity in Europe and North America is gradually increasing.

Limitations of pricing theory

By now, you will appreciate how important it is to know the market price (i.e. the maximum price at which customers will buy the required number of items). Millions of pounds are spent every year on market research in pursuit of this information. Forecasting the quantities likely to be sold at different prices is an attempt to predict the future. It is as much an art as it is a science and is notoriously difficult to do accurately. So why do businesses spend so much on this each year?

Well, they believe that this forecasting based on current market research gives the best estimate possible. Although the figures are not accurate, they represent the best information available. However, the degree of inaccuracy can be very considerable. In other words, prices are very rarely initially set at their optimum level. Businesses adjust their prices according to their experience of the market. If they have set their price too high, they will sell fewer items than desired. When they reduce the price, the opposite may happen. It is a process of trial and error. As the product becomes established, more **actual** market data is gathered and the pricing becomes more effective.

The manager's point of view

Pricing is perhaps the single most crucial area in business management, and yet it is the one which is carried out amid the greatest number of unknowns. Almost every other aspect of the business can be managed from a position of knowledge. Costs, for instance, can be identified and controlled, new products developed and introduced, production processes improved, systems and procedures streamlined. But pricing is a gamble. Market intelligence will act as a guide, but in the end, the setting of prices will always be accompanied by a measure of risk. What will the customers' reaction be? Will they be driven to the competition? Will they be driven to adopt different technologies? What will the competition do? These questions are at the heart of every pricing decision, and make the process of running a business so exciting.

There are few rules to apply in the setting of prices. Of course the accountants must ensure that prices are sufficiently high to produce the expected returns, and one of the cost-plus bases (preferably ABC) will enable them to do this. However, in my view, this should be seen simply as a safety net against unacceptably low pricing, and should not play an active part in the price-setting procedure itself. The correct price for a product is the highest price that the market will accept. It is therefore primarily a decision for the marketing department. Profits are hard enough to come by at any time, so any pricing of products below their full potential is highly undesirable. Overpricing a product may be a mistake, but it is always much easier to reduce prices at a later stage than to increase them. The use of cost information in the initial formulation of prices may inhibit the imagination of the marketing department!

Pricing is influenced by many factors other than cost. Each business, and most likely each individual product within the business, will have a different set of circumstances affecting its market position. Is there anything about the product which distinguishes it from the competition, and which will allow us to charge a premium price? Perhaps it is easier to look at the situation from the point of view of purchasers. What factors will encourage them to pay the higher price?

Brand identity is clearly one such factor. A BMW and a Ford both have the necessary equipment to get buyers to their destination, but they will pay more for the BMW, either because they perceive that they are buying a higher-quality product, or because it panders to their ego. Whatever their motivation, their perception of the product will have an impact on the market price.

Product quality will usually allow a premium price to be charged. However, the right quality can be defined as that which meets, but does not exceed, the requirements of customers. They will not pay a premium price for a higher level of quality than they need. Also, it is worth remembering that the first priority for a purchasing officer is to ensure that there is material of the right quality available at the right time for use by the production or sales department. This is more important than shaving an extra per cent or two from the price. The loss of production or sales through stock shortages will normally far outweigh any cost-saving advantage.

The quality of the supplier is another key, but often underrated, element. Purchasers need to feel confident that the supplier will always meet their delivery requirements with consistent quality material. They may therefore feel more comfortable dealing with a solid, blue-chip company than with a small cut-price outfit which may be here today and gone tomorrow. In the chemical industry it has been possible for some time to source many raw materials from suppliers in India and China. Although prices are very competitive compared with the European competition, quality has not always been of a consistent standard. Moreover, the extended lead times involved inevitably limit flexibility where quick responsiveness to changing customer needs is paramount. The comfort factor of a local, reliable supplier may be worth paying extra for.

Patented products will clearly command a higher price, and can become significant profit generators if they are in the right market niche. But purchasers are always on the lookout for cheaper, unpatented alternatives, even if it means adopting different technologies or changing production processes. The higher the price, the greater the spur to customers to find cost-saving alternatives.

These are just a few of the many factors which influence the initial establishment of prices, and which will continue to cause price movements, perhaps even on a daily basis. The competition never stands still. It will react to every action taken and, as in a game of chess, the real skill in business is to anticipate the competitor's next move. The marketplace is constantly changing, and prices are being set in the light of the best information available at the time.

There are times when this feels like a leap in the dark. In the chemical industry, there has recently been a move towards global sourcing. Accordingly, one of our major customers notified us of their intention to source their worldwide requirements for a particular range of products from a single supplier. At the time, this business was split between several suppliers, and everyone was making good profits. We were asked to quote prices for each piece of business in each country. This was a daunting prospect. Business worth millions of dollars was at stake, so, at the end of this process, there were going to be some big losers and one big winner! At what level should we pitch the prices? How much of our existing profit should we give away in order to be sure of picking up the rest of the business? How aggressive would our competitors be as they stood to lose as much as we did? We arrived at a set of prices which we calculated would give us an acceptable return, and submitted them. It was with an enormous sense of relief that we heard we had been successful in picking up the entire contract.

But we were nevertheless left with a nagging doubt that perhaps we had pitched the prices too low and given away some profit unnecessarily.

As we basked in the success of this venture, we heard that another major customer was travelling down the same route, another worldwide tender, again with some very profitable business at stake. We went through the same agonising process, and made our submission. Unfortunately, on this occasion, we had underestimated the aggression of our competitors, who were still smarting from their failure in the previous tender, and we lost the business. Well, you win some, you lose some! Overall, we came out of it just ahead on profit, although at the cost of considerable anxiety.

For both tenders, we had set up a computer model which compared our proposed prices with the underlying costs, enabling us to monitor the overall profitability while we played with different pricing options. As this product range consisted mainly of high-margin-earning products, there was plenty of scope to reduce prices without jeopardising the minimum returns required. The underlying costs did not play a significant role in the establishment of our quoted prices; for us, the likely action of our competitors was the key factor. In this we were perhaps a good deal more fortunate than many other businesses, where costs are the overriding factor. At this latter end of the scale, I am aware of one company bidding to develop and supply automotive parts for a new range of vehicles due to come to market in five years' time. It quoted a price below today's total cost, on the assumption that advances in technology in the intervening period would generate sufficient cost savings to leave a profit. A high degree of entrepreneurship, as well as courage, is needed to do business on this basis.

You may feel that my comments in this chapter have strayed away from the main management accounting theme of this book. I make no apology for this. I wish to emphasise the point that the setting of prices is primarily a marketing, not an accounting, function. The accounting techniques described in the chapter are, of course, essential as a backdrop against which the marketing people can do their work, and it is the accountants who will monitor whether the pricing proposals will generate the overall returns required by management. But my guess is that, if the pricing of the automotive parts had been left to conservative accountants, the contract would have been lost. And if the worldwide tenders had been left to accountants, the subtle nuances in the marketplace would have been overlooked, and the bid weakened as a result. So, if there is any rule on pricing, it is 'leave it to the marketing people', whilst keeping a close eye on their decisions within the context of the company's overall financial objectives.

Summary

Economic theory helps us to understand the relationships between selling price, unit cost, profit and volume of activity. It tells us that there is an **optimum level of output and profit** rather than a range of continuously improving results. It also makes us aware that the demand for different products is affected by their selling prices to different extents. This is the *price elasticity of demand* concept.

The accounting approach is to establish the cost structure of products and then to increase this by a calculated percentage to give a profit margin. This is the *cost-plus* method with the amount of the 'plus' or mark-up being determined by the organisation's required return on capital employed. The full cost is probably used more than any other cost as it establishes a minimum price below which products cannot be sold profitably in the long term.

When finalising the selling price, it is critically important to consider the **competitive nature of the marketplace**. It is essential to know which products compete directly with yours and what their current prices are. Knowledge of your product's minimum price (equal to its full cost) and an understanding of its elasticity of demand enable you to decide intelligently on its selling price.

Target pricing is a strategy which integrates all three viewpoints discussed in this chapter. It starts by setting the price and then working backwards to establish the desired profit margin and the maximum allowable cost. If this cost cannot be achieved satisfactorily, the product is abandoned (unless there is good reason for its continuation). The result of this is that all the company's products should provide adequate profits, and cross-subsidisation of products should be avoided.

There is no getting away from the fact that, ultimately, the price-setting process is **subjective**. The selling price will be based upon the opinions, feelings and intuition of top managers who, hopefully, have their fingers on the pulse of the marketplace.

Further reading

Ahmed, M. N. and Scapens, R. W. (2003) 'The evolution of cost-based pricing rules in Britain: an institutionalist perspective', *Review of Political Economy*, Vol. 15, Issue 2, April.

Atkinson, A., Banker, R., Kaplan, R. and Young, S. (2001) *Management Accounting*, 3rd edition, Prentice Hall, Harlow. See chapter 'Using management accounting information for pricing and product planning'.

Cardinaels, E., Roodhooft, F. and Warlop, L. (2004) 'The value of activity-based costing in competitive pricing decisions', *Journal of Management Accounting Research*, Vol. 16.

Davila, A. (T.) and Wouters, M. (2004) 'Designing cost-competitive technology products through cost management', *Accounting Horizons*, Vol. 18, Issue 1, March.

Horngren, C., Bhimani, A., Datar, S. and Foster, G. (2002) *Management and Cost Accounting*, 2nd edition, Prentice Hall Europe, Harlow. See Chapter 12, 'Pricing decisions and customer profitability analysis'.

Ingenbleek, P., Debruyne, M., Frambach, R. T. and Verhallen, T. M. M. (2003) 'Successful new product pricing practices: a contingency approach', *Marketing Letters*, Vol. 14, Issue 4, December.

Matanovich, T. (2003) 'Pricing services vs. pricing products: don't buy into the duality myth. Focus on value to the customer', *Marketing Management*. Vol. 12, Issue 4, July/August.

Swenson, D., Shahid A., Bell, J. and Il-Woon Kim (2003) 'Best practices in target costing', *Management Accounting Quarterly*, Vol. 4, Issue 2, Winter.

Upchurch, A. (2003) *Management Accounting, Principles and Practice*, 2nd edition, Financial Times/Prentice Hall, Harlow. See Chapter 8, 'More decisions: price-setting and limiting factors', *section 5*, 'Price-setting'.

Answers to self-assessment questions

S12.1. Profit–volume chart based on economic theory

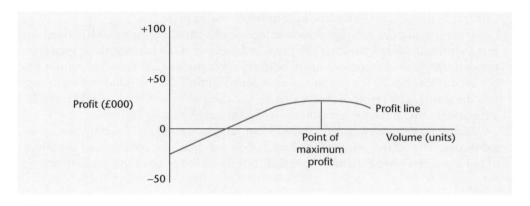

S12.2. Codex Limited

	£m	
Direct materials	8	
Direct labour	12	
Prime cost	20	
Variable production overheads	1	
Fixed production overheads	3	
Manufacturing cost	24	
Administration overheads	2	
Marketing overheads	4	
Total cost	30	
Required profit	6	(40% × £15m)
Total revenue	36	

a) If it adopted a **prime-cost-plus** approach, the 'plus' margin added would be

$$\frac{36 - 20}{20} = \frac{16}{20} = \textbf{+80\%}$$

b) If it adopted a **manufacturing-cost-plus** approach, the 'plus' margin added would be

$$\frac{36 - 24}{24} = \frac{12}{24} = \textbf{+50\%}$$

c) If it adopted a **full-cost-plus** approach, the 'plus' margin added would be

$$\frac{36 - 30}{30} = \frac{6}{30} = \textbf{+20\%}$$

The Electric Town Car Project

The primary objective of the recently formed Electric Town Car company is to manufacture and sell a small vehicle powered by electricity. This vehicle is code-named ETC. It will carry a minimum of two passengers and have luggage space adequate for a family shopping trip. The luggage space will be convertible into two child seats, greatly enhancing the flexibility of this urban vehicle. Its maximum speed will be 60 mph/100 kph and it will have a range of approximately 150 miles/240 km from a fully charged battery. Harmful emissions from the ETC will be negligible compared to petrol/diesel-engined cars. The ETC's fuel cost per mile will be about half that of existing equivalent-sized cars.

A comprehensive business plan has been produced to facilitate detailed discussion with potential investors. **After** these discussions had taken place, further independent market research was commissioned to produce a demand forecast at selling prices within £500 of their initial estimate.

Extracts from business plan

The competition has been identified as those petrol/diesel-engined cars which are the smallest in the current ranges of the global car manufacturers. The prices of these to the retail car dealers range from £5,000 to over £10,000, depending on specification. Initially, the ETC will be built to a single basic specification and the prices of the nearest competitors have been identified as follows:

Car 1 – £5,800
Car 2 – £5,650
Car 3 – £5,600
Car 4 – £5,350
Car 5 – £5,200

After much deliberation and discussion, the directors of ETC have decided that the equivalent selling price of their product should be £5,000. They also decided to adopt a profit margin of 20% of selling price (this is equivalent to 25% mark-up on total cost).

To enable the ETC company to produce and market its electric cars, it estimates that £500 million will need to be invested in buildings, machinery, office equipment, IT systems and other fixed assets. This would give a maximum operating capacity of 90,000 cars a year. In order to offer investors a reasonable return, ETC will have to generate a return on capital employed of 15%.

ETC's best estimate for the production cost of one car is as follows:

	£
Direct materials	1,133
Direct labour	200
Prime cost	**1,333**
Variable production overheads	167
Fixed production overheads	500
Manufacturing cost	**2,000**

Annual administration overheads are expected to be £15 million, research and development £45 million and marketing overheads £90 million. Advertising is responsible for about two-thirds of the marketing overheads. However, for a new vehicle in a very competitive market, ETC believes this is the very minimum it should spend. If possible, it would like to increase this by at least £10 million.

Extract from market research report

Demand forecast

Selling price £	Annual demand units
5,500	44,880
5,400	53,720
5,300	59,160
5,200	62,560
5,100	64,600
5,000	68,000
4,900	71,400
4,800	74,120
4,700	78,200
4,600	85,000
4,500	94,520

Task:

1 Advise ETC on its operating level and selling price. (Ignore taxation.)

(85 marks)

2 If ETC decided to spend an extra £10 million on advertising without reducing its target profit, how might it achieve this?

(15 marks)

(Total 100 marks)

Questions

An asterisk * on a question number indicates that the answer is given at the end of the book. Answers to the other questions are given in the Lecturer's Guide.

Q12.1* Demarco

Demarco makes miniature mobile generators and has a standard profit margin of 20% for all its products. Its annual budget includes marketing, administration and production overhead allowances of £60,000, £20,000 and £50,000 respectively. It also shows that the company intends to use £18,000 of materials and pay direct wages of £32,000. Marketing and administration overheads are all fixed but 10% of production overheads are considered to be variable. Demarco uses the cost-plus method of setting its selling prices.

Task:

Calculate the cost-plus percentage if the base was:

a) variable cost;
b) production cost;
c) full cost.

Q12.2* Wizkid

WSM Enterprises introduced the Wizkid in 1991 to compete with Action Man. Although the peak demand for these products occurred several years ago, sales have stabilised and WSM sells 15,000 Wizkids a year.

The recommended retail price is £24.99 and the current wholesale price is £10.00. However, the managing director wishes to increase the return on this product and has proposed a 100% mark-up on total variable costs.

WSM has an annual output of 15,000 Wizkids. The fixed costs related to this product are £40,000 and the variable (or marginal) costs are £6.00 per unit.

Tasks:

1 What is the breakeven volume of this product if a selling price of £10.00 is charged? What is the profit at this price?
2 What price would the MD like to charge? What would the resulting net profit be if there were no change in demand?
3 The marketing director has forecast a 10% drop in orders if the price is raised as suggested. What would WSM's profit be if this were to happen?
4 Discuss the other factors the MD should take into account when deciding on the selling price of Wizkids.

Q12.3* Ride-on Lawn Mowers

Ride-on makes and sells a mini-tractor lawn mower called the Luxon. The company is just about to start its new financial year for which the budget (recently approved by its holding company) shows the following:

	£000
Total capital employed	4,000
Total sales revenue	2,800
Total fixed costs	1,104
Net profit before tax	800
Return on capital employed (ROCE)	20%
Number of Luxons sold	1,120

Its holding company requires it to achieve a ROCE of at least 20% and Ride-on's directors are awarded annual bonuses if they succeed in this.

Yesterday, Ride-on's main competitor released details of a new product in direct competition to the mower. The Luxon has a selling price of £2,500 but its new rival has been priced approximately £300 below this. After a hastily convened meeting, Ride-on's top managers have decided to reduce the Luxon's price to £2,150 with immediate effect. They also feel that their forecast sales revenue now looks optimistic.

Tasks:

Advise them how they might maintain their forecast return on capital employed (ROCE) at 20% now that the Luxon's price has been reduced:

a) if total sales revenue is maintained at £2.8 million, and
b) if total sales revenue decreases to £2.5 million.

Q12.4 Theory questions

a) What is meant by 'price elasticity of demand'?
b) Create a numerical example of the 'absorption cost suicide spiral'.
c) Explain the differences between the accountant's and the economist's approach to pricing.
d) Why is pricing really a marketing function?
e) List the stages involved in target pricing.

Q12.5 Brightwell Shades

Brightwell Shades Limited has developed a new kind of sunglasses, the Shadewell, whose strength can be manually adjusted. The variable cost of one pair is £50 but the firm is unsure what the selling price should be. During a lengthy board meeting it was decided to commission some market research into the new product's price elasticity of demand. The results of the market research survey have just been received and are summarised as follows:

Sales price (£)	60	70	80	90	100
Sales volume (units)	16,000	13,000	10,000	7,000	4,000
Sales revenue (£)	960,000	910,000	800,000	630,000	400,000

It is estimated that when output is equal to, or greater than, 12,000 units the variable cost per unit will reduce to £45. Also, additional fixed costs of £50,000 will be incurred if production exceeds 8,800 units.

Task:

Advise the board on the selling price of the Shadewell.

Divisional performance and transfer pricing

Chapter contents

Introduction

At some time in your life you may find yourself working for a company that is actually a conglomeration of several companies, an amalgamation of separate 'strategic business units'. For example, Rolls-Royce Group plc has five separate business divisions; their performance for 2003 is shown in the extract from its annual review for that year (see Figure 13.1). Similarly, the BG Group plc (commonly known as British Gas) shows a segmental analysis in its annual review for 2003 (see Figure 13.2). Both these companies operate internationally but there are also many divisionalised firms which operate mainly within national boundaries.

If you worked for the group head office, you would be interested in knowing how each of your constituent divisions was performing. The answer to this seems very straightforward: why not simply list the divisions in the order of their profits? Unfortunately, there are several reasons why this is too simplistic and would give a

	Group turnover £m	Profit before interest £m
Civil Aerospace	2,694	82
Defence	1,398	132
Marine	927	32
Energy	584	30
Financial Services	42	(6)
	5,645	270

Figure 13.1 **The performance of Rolls-Royce Group plc for 2003**

	Group turnover £m	Total operating profit £m
Exploration & Production	1,794	959
Liquefied Natural Gas	945	77
Transmission and Distribution	678	116
Power Generation	184	129
Other activities	3	(30)
Less: Intra-group sales	(17)	
	3,587	1,251

Figure 13.2 **The performance of BG Group plc for 2003**

misleading picture. What about the amount of capital invested in each division? What return is it earning in percentage terms? The return on capital employed ratio may well order the divisions differently. Also, how much say does the division have about the amount of capital invested in it? And to what extent can each division influence the decisions on which assets are purchased?

What about the costs incurred by each division? Does it have complete control of all these or are some of them beyond its control? For instance, one division may be told by head office that it must operate from a certain site because the group cannot sell that site to any third party. This site may have outdated facilities or be in a location which is preventing the organisation from being competitive. The division may want to move to a different site with better transport links in order to reduce its costs. Is it wise to judge the division on its return on capital employed when it does not have control over the capital invested? Is this potentially misleading information worse than having no information at all?

All the divisions in a group benefit from the services provided by their head office and the cost of providing these services is usually significant. However, the head office does not create any sales revenue of its own against which these costs can be offset. It is logical for these costs to be divided amongst its operating divisions but what basis should be used for this distribution? The choice of bases includes sales revenue, contribution, operating profit, profit after interest, gross assets, net assets, book value of fixed assets, and so on. Or the head office may attempt to arrive at a 'fair' distribution of its costs based on the relative use of its services made by each division. Also, it may be that the amount of tax paid by the group as a whole can be reduced by the way in which head office costs are allocated to divisions.

This brings us to the related problem of 'transfer pricing', the amount for which goods and services are sold by one division to another division in the same group. If you look at the performance summary of the BG Group plc shown above, you will see the item 'intra-group sales' of £17 million. These sales must be deducted if the figure for the group turnover is to reflect accurately the amount of sales to customers outside the group. Again, this seems straightforward at first sight; a simple application of arithmetic should give us the true picture. However, a little thought will reveal the true complexity of the situation.

Should the transfer price charged by the selling division be the price it normally charges to outside customers? If it charges different prices to different customers, which one should be used? Will the buying division feel exploited because it knows that the selling division has not had to incur the normal amount of marketing expenses connected with third-party sales? Is it fair to expect a 'group' discount? Or should transfers be made at cost? After all, these divisions are all part of the same group and it is the group's combined results that matter in the end. If this approach is adopted, which cost should be used – variable cost or full cost? If variable cost is used, the selling division has no incentive whatsoever to make the sale. All it gets back is what it has had to pay out. What is the point of getting involved in activities for which you get no return? If full cost is used, the buying division may feel it is being asked unfairly to contribute to the overheads of the selling division. After all, these overheads tend to be fixed costs so they are not increased by internal transactions.

The measurement of divisional performance and the setting of transfer prices will now be discussed in detail.

Learning objectives	**Having worked through this chapter you should be able to:**

- **explain the different bases of divisionalisation;**
- **state the advantages of a divisional structure;**
- **list the roles played by head office;**
- **distinguish between the different types of responsibility centres;**
- **evaluate the use of different types of profit to measure performance;**
- **calculate a division's return on investment;**
- **calculate a division's residual income;**
- **compare and contrast return on investment with residual income;**
- **explain what a 'transfer price' is;**
- **explain how 'ideal' transfer prices are calculated;**
- **describe the four different approaches to 'practical' transfer pricing;**
- **calculate transfer prices using alternative methods;**
- **explain how 'international' transfer prices can be used to avoid paying tax;**
- **discuss the limitations of divisional performance measurement;**
- **discuss the limitations of transfer pricing.**

Region	2001	2002	2003
Europe/Rest of World	3,398	3,365	2,454
North America	1,664	1,287	(50)
S. America/S. Africa	(45)	(359)	(390)
Asia/Pacific	407	469	432
Total group	5,424	4,761	2,346

Figure 13.3 **Volkswagen GmbH's profit/(loss) by geographical area (€m)**

Bases of divisionalisation

The two annual review extracts shown at the beginning of this chapter both show an analysis of a company's activities according to its major product lines. However, some companies analyse their activities not by product but by geographical area; the Volkswagen group is one of these (see Figure 13.3).

Advantages of divisionalisation

As companies grow they tend to diversify their product range. Although this increased complexity consumes extra resources, it can be advantageous in an uncertain world. If one product line unexpectedly loses its popularity and its sales plummet, the company will be protected from the financial consequences by its other products. The organisation can be thought of as an investor holding a *portfolio* of products. So, in this way, it can minimise the risk posed by downturns in specific markets.

Another advantage of divisionalisation is that its inherent managerial autonomy increases the motivation of its managers. Of course, this depends on the degree of autonomy granted by the head office; the higher it is, the higher the motivation will be. It is generally accepted that most managers rise to the challenge of increased independence and responsibility.

Then there is the question of specialised knowledge. If all the decision making were retained by the head office of Rolls-Royce plc, its directors would have to be experts in such diverse markets as civil aircraft and marine power. The directors of British Gas would have to be experts in both exploration and power generation. The complexity of modern business dictates that it is unreasonable to expect such a wide degree of expertise in a very small number of people. Head office boards of directors realise that it is far more effective to concentrate specialised product and market knowledge in the top management of each division. This should result in better decisions which should translate into improved performance.

This also has the advantage of allowing the head office to get on with its own unique role of reviewing group strategy and co-ordinating inter-divisional activities. A useful side-effect of minimising head office involvement in operational activities is that there will be fewer opportunities for misunderstandings and wasted effort to arise. Communication should be more effective due to the avoidance of information overload and improved communication usually results in improved performance.

Role of head office

In addition to the co-ordinating role mentioned above, the head office should set corporate policies, goals and objectives. For example, it may decide that all divisions should be in the top three of their respective industry's league-table. Very often, the head office has the responsibility of raising the funds for capital investment in the divisions. After all, it is in a much better position to do this as the investors see the group as a single entity with pooled resources.

Also, in addition to setting long- or medium-term plans, it is standard practice for the head offices to set annual financial targets for divisions. For example, a return on capital employed of 18% a year may be required of one division but another division (considered to be more risky) may be required to produce 24%. Depending on the degree of autonomy, the head office may also set targets regarding sales revenues/volumes, market share, cash generation, etc.

Degrees of responsibility

The level of independent financial responsibility varies from group to group and sometimes within groups. The following are standard types of responsibility centres:

> **Cost centre** – responsible for costs only.
> **Revenue centre** – responsible for revenue only.
> **Profit centre** – responsible for costs and revenue, i.e. profit.
> **Investment centre** – responsible for capital investment and profit.

In reality, hybrids of these four standard types also exist. For example, a cost centre may be responsible for most, but not all, of its costs.

Profit centres

Consider the example in Figure 13.4 where four different profits are shown (in bold print). For which specific profit should a profit centre be responsible?

If *contribution* is used, managers may manipulate this by increasing operational gearing (increasing fixed costs and reducing variable costs, e.g. automation).

Controllable profit is a good measure of the **manager's** performance. However, to calculate this it is assumed that differentiation between controllable and non-controllable costs is possible. In reality, the distinction is sometimes blurred. Take petrol costs as an example: the amount of mileage covered is within the control of the division but the price of petrol is not. Is it worth splitting costs like this down into their controllable and non-controllable elements?

Profit before head office charges is a good measure of the **division's** performance rather than the manager's. It takes all the costs into account irrespective of whether they are controllable or not.

	£m
Sales revenue	1,100
Variable costs	695
Contribution	**405**
Controllable fixed costs	189
Controllable profit	**216**
Non-controllable fixed costs	44
Profit before head office charges	**172**
Head office charges	93
Divisional pre-tax profit	**79**

Figure 13.4 **The choice of profits**

Divisional pre-tax profit is not useful for measuring divisional performance as head office charges have been deducted. These charges can be calculated in any way the head office chooses and do not have to be logical or 'fair'.

Investment centres

Investment centres may simply decide which investments to make or they may also have the added responsibility of raising the funds. The performance of these profit centres with additional responsibility for capital investment is usually measured by either 'return on investment' or 'residual income'.

Return on investment (ROI)

The return on investment ratio is similar to the return on capital employed ratio; it is a relative measure, expressed as a percentage. Its objective is to give an idea of how well the investment has performed compared to other investments or its own pre-planned performance. Here are three versions of the ROI formula:

$$\frac{\text{Profit before interest and tax (PBIT)}}{\text{Capital employed in the division}}$$

$$or \quad \frac{\text{Profit before interest and tax (PBIT)}}{\text{Value of operational net assets}}$$

$$or \quad \frac{\text{Sales revenue}}{\text{Net assets}} \times \frac{\text{PBIT}}{\text{sales revenue}}$$

ROI depends in part on the measurement of profit and the valuation of operational assets. Unfortunately, profit can be relatively easily manipulated (legally or illegally) and if profit is unreliable, so is ROI. Also, in a divisional structure, sales and purchases between divisions tend to distort the profit measure. 'Transfer pricing' between divisions is the subject of the second part of this chapter. The basic problem is that transfer prices can be set in any way the head office decides; it does not have to be rational, logical or fair and may vary from division to division.

To complicate things further, there are several alternative ways in which the asset base can be measured. Should 'historical cost' be used? After all, it is objective and auditable. But this will distort the ROI ratio by ignoring depreciation, which reflects technical obsolescence and inefficiencies caused by age or wear and tear; the older the assets, the greater the distortion. Perhaps 'current cost' should be used. This gives an equitable basis for comparison but it is difficult to determine and is prone to subjectivity.

So, is 'net book value' (also known as 'written-down value') the answer? Well, this too has its drawbacks. If profit were to remain constant over two consecutive periods, ROI would increase due to the effect of depreciation; this would be misleading.

Residual income (RI)

This is an absolute measure expressed in monetary terms (not as a percentage). The formula used to calculate it is

$$RI = \text{profit before tax} - \text{notional interest charge}$$

This is an attempt to reflect the fact that if the division were not part of a group of companies, it would have to bear the cost of providing funds to buy its fixed assets. These funds are often provided by the head office without any specific charge to the division for them. The idea is to give a more realistic view of the division's performance as a 'stand-alone' unit.

The notional interest charge is partly determined by the division's cost of capital. This can be measured accurately on a historical basis but there is no guarantee that this will not change for the present year. The interest charge is also determined by the value of the asset base. Ideally, this should be calculated using the 'current cost' of assets but this is subjective. Alternatively, if 'net book value' or 'historical cost' is used, the residual income is distorted for the same reasons given above for ROI. So the residual income measure is also far from perfect.

Which measure should be used – ROI or RI?

Consider the example of Division C which, last year, produced £900 million controllable profit on capital invested of £6,000 million. This gave an ROI of 15% (900/6,000). This year, the division is considering a new capital project requiring an investment of £80 million. The estimated profit before head office charges is £10 million a year giving an ROI of 12.5% (10/80). The division is reluctant to go ahead with the project because, assuming an equivalent performance to last year on its existing assets, its average ROI will be reduced. Due to a relative downturn in the ROI percentage, the project will probably not go ahead.

But what will the RI calculation show for the same project? First of all, a 'notional income charge' must be calculated at a rate decided by the head office. If this rate were 10%, the interest would be £8 million (£80 million × 10%) and the RI £2 million (£10 – £8 million). This significant positive outcome indicates that the group would benefit from going ahead. Theoretically, it would be £2 million better off. To summarise the conflicting advice:

> ROI – reduced from 15.0% to 12.5% – **abandon project**
> RI – £2 million increase in wealth – **proceed with project**

Would you rather receive an extra £2 million or avoid a reduction in a percentage measurement? This is a very strong argument for recommending RI.

Of course, the two measures can, and often do, recommend the same course of action. For example, if the cost of capital had been 14% the notional interest charge would give a negative RI and both measures would recommend abandoning the project.

(If you have already studied capital investment appraisal, you will probably recognise a similarity in the comparison of net present value (NPV) and internal rate of return (IRR). NPV, which gives an absolute measure in money, is considered superior to IRR, which gives an answer in percentage terms.)

Try the following question for yourself (answer at the end of the chapter).

Self-assessment question S13.1

The Dominion Distillery Group is considering building a new industrial alcohol production facility in South West France at a cost of 30 million euros. The annual fixed costs are 20 million euros including 6 million which are not considered controllable by the division. Sales revenue is estimated at 156 million euros and variable costs at 134 million euros.

Using 'profit before head office charges' calculate

1 the return on investment;
2 the residual income using an interest rate of 5% a year;
3 the interest rate required to make RI = 0.

What justification might the group have for using profit **before** rather than **after** head office charges?

Transfer pricing

The *transfer price* is the monetary value for which goods and services are exchanged between different responsibility centres of the same organisation. If the responsibility centres are in different countries, the exchange value is referred to as the *international transfer price*.

Ideal transfer prices

About 50 years ago, an academic by the name of Hirschleifer produced an economic theory for establishing ideal transfer prices between divisions or fellow subsidiaries of a company. The value of this theoretically optimum price is found by calculating the *opportunity cost* to the supplier of the goods or services.

However, in practice, ideal transfer prices are not always used. Other considerations, such as the privacy of information and inter-division bargaining, encourage the use of non-ideal transfer prices. For example, sometimes the ideal price is the variable cost, but this means the supplying division earns zero contribution which is potentially demotivating as the division receives no reward for its effort.

Determination of transfer prices

The rules for determining transfer prices are drawn up by each organisation without reference to any external accounting-body guidelines. The extent to which the prices cover costs and contribute to internal profits is a matter of company policy. As these prices are internal to the company, it can set them in whatever way it chooses. The practical objective of setting transfer prices is to influence the behaviour of divisional managers – in particular, to avoid demotivating them.

We will now consider four alternative ways in which transfer prices can be set:

- Market-based.
- Cost-based.
- Negotiated.
- Administered.

Market-based transfer prices

Where identical products or services are being offered by other companies in the open market, it is possible to set the transfer price at the market price. This is the opportunity cost to the selling division (assuming it is operating at full capacity and can sell all it makes on the open market). By selling within the group, the division forgoes receiving the market price from an outside company. But if the transfer is made at market price, the selling division does not lose any income.

However, when inter-divisional transfers are made, these sales do not usually involve any marketing activity by the selling division. For this reason, the buying division may expect to pay less than the market price. This will increase the buying division's profits but will reduce those of the selling division. So, it is not unusual for inter-divisional conflict to arise as a result of transfer pricing policy, especially if the managers are remunerated, at least in part, by profit-related pay.

Cost-based transfer prices

When the selling division is operating at below full capacity it would be inappropriate to sell to another division at market price as it is not losing any profit on the transaction. In this situation the ideal transfer price is the *variable cost* (which is the opportunity cost to the selling division). But this gives no incentive to the selling division as its earnings are zero. Sometimes, to get round this, a nominal contribution margin is added. However, this could increase the selling price of the group's end product offered on the open market and may make it less competitive.

If *full cost* is used to determine the transfer price, the position is made worse. Sometimes a nominal profit margin is added on top of this to give an incentive to the selling division. The effect on the competitiveness of the final product on the open market will be aggravated.

It is worth noting that a cost-based approach does not give any incentive to the management of the selling division to control costs as these can be passed on to the buying division.

Negotiated transfer prices

Transfer prices can be set by negotiation between the managers of the selling and buying divisions. This works best where there is an active external market for the products as the external market price will significantly influence the transfer price by acting as a reference point.

Where there is no external market, negotiations usually lead to conflict. The 'selling' manager will want the price to be as high as possible but the 'buying' manager will want it to be as low as possible.

Administered transfer prices

Transfer prices can be set by an individual or committee of head office employees, none of whom are directly connected to the divisions involved. The head office administrator will follow corporate policy to determine the transfer prices. For example, the transfer price could be equal to variable cost plus X%, full cost plus Y% or market price less Z%.

There are two advantages of this approach: one is objective consistency and the other is the reduction of conflict. The disadvantages are the probable suboptimal economic performance of the group as a whole and the undermining of divisional autonomy and its consequent demotivating effect.

Example

Financial data for product X:

	£
Materials	11
Direct labour	2
Variable overhead	1
Variable cost	14
Fixed overhead	5
Full cost	19
Profit margin	8
Sales price	27

If operating at full capacity, the *ideal transfer price* is £27.

If operating at less than full capacity, the *ideal transfer price* is £14.

If operating at full capacity, the profit margin may be shared between supplying and buying divisions, so the *practical transfer price* may be £23 [19 + (50% × 8)].

If operating at less than full capacity, full cost may be used giving the supplying division a contribution to its fixed overheads. The *practical transfer price* would be £19 giving a positive contribution of £5.

Self-assessment question S13.2

Try the following question for yourself (answer at the end of the chapter).

Division S sells one of its products, an electric motor, to division B in the same group. One motor costs £36 in materials, £9 in direct labour, £5 in variable overhead and is assigned £15 of fixed overhead. The division sets its profit margin equal to 40% of its variable cost.

What is the ideal transfer price if the division is operating at (a) full capacity and (b) less than full capacity? Suggest practical transfer prices if the division is operating at (a) full capacity and (b) less than full capacity.

International transfer pricing

International transfer pricing is usually nothing more than a device to minimise the amount of tax paid in total by international organisations. Although divisional profitability may be distorted, this is normally perfectly legal. The group arranges its accounts so that most of its profits are declared by its divisions in low-tax areas. However, it is not difficult to see how losses and liabilities could be hidden by doing this. The tax avoidance possibilities encourage organisations to set up offshore subsidiaries in areas which demand little, if any, disclosure of corporate information.

Unfortunately, this secrecy can encourage false accounting and fraud as in the Parmalat scandal of late 2003 where billions of dollars of assets reported in a Caribbean subsidiary's accounts were found to be non-existent. Parmalat was based in Parma, Italy, and had extensive operational divisions in South America. But this sort of activity also happens much closer to home.

In 2004, company 'V' was being investigated by the UK tax authorities concerning transactions valued at hundreds of millions of dollars shown in the accounts of its Jersey-based subsidiary, 'J'. Company V buys coffee beans from growers in less developed countries and sells them to international coffee- and chocolate-making companies in developed ones. The difficulty seems to be that although the vast bulk of V's profits are shown in the accounts of its Jersey subsidiary, the coffee beans never physically pass through the island. The company paid no tax on its multi-million-dollar profits reported in the offshore tax haven of Jersey. Apparently, the subsidiary J does not exist in the normal sense of the word and is merely a 'postbox' operation with only a handful of administrative staff. This is very probably an example of transfer prices being used to avoid paying tax.

Limitations

Most of the limitations have already been discussed above. Measuring divisional performance involves choosing between alternative profits. The profits most often used are the 'profit before head office charges' and 'controllable profit'. The first is a good measure of the division's performance but the second is a better measure of the manager's performance. Also, profit is used rather than cash flow so RoI and RI are both subject to the distortions caused by creative accounting.

When determining inter-division transfer prices, some degree of behavioural psychology is usually involved. The objective is to avoid demotivating the divisional managers involved. But it is far from possible to please everybody all the time, especially when managers are remunerated by bonuses based on profit performance.

The manager's point of view

It makes obvious sense to divide up a company into manageable units and let each one operate with a measure of independence. There is nothing more energising for lower-level managers than to be given responsibility for a business area, provided they are granted sufficient authority and freedom of action. But how much autonomy should be devolved down to divisional managers? On one hand, 'interference' from Head Office can be seriously demotivating. On the other, senior managers do retain ultimate responsibility for the overall performance of the company, and would be negligent if they did not impose some level of supervision over the divisional activities.

The balance between Head Office control and freedom of action for divisional managers is a common point of debate. Head Office needs regular feedback from the divisions, so that they can spot any signs of underperformance at an early stage; but, with modern computer systems able to provide a wealth of information about the performance of every nook and cranny of the company, the temptation for senior management to micro-manage is very great. Divisional managers can find themselves spending ever more time responding to queries from Head Office, instead of concentrating their energies on managing the front end of the business.

Head Office may consider, and rightly so, that some elements of the company can be more effectively managed from the centre. An obvious example is IT, where it makes sense for all divisions to be using the same software, so that all data is produced on a comparable basis and further program developments need only be done once. Insurance is another area, where senior management must ensure that appropriate cover is in place to protect the company as a whole (and not least the senior management themselves). There is also a trend towards global purchasing agreements, where economies of scale across divisions can bring benefits to the company as a whole, even if individual divisions may feel they have lost out on more effective, local purchasing deals.

All of these elements serve to undermine the autonomy of the divisional manager. So how should his or her performance be judged? Should the profit calculations include a series of cost items over which the divisional manager has no control, or should they be excluded from the divisional accounts? How wise is it to contemplate the profitability of a business which has no IT or insurance costs charged to it? The elimination of 'uncontrollable' material purchasing costs could lead to some very peculiar, and possibly inappropriate, pricing decisions.

In my view, management is about running a business profitably, so managers should focus at all times on the true bottom line. Head Office charges are always unwelcome, but they do represent genuine costs. Divisional managers may have a legitimate grouse that the distance of Head Office departments from the front line means that there is less incentive for them to pare down costs. After all, at the sharp end, we tend to think about the number of sales needed to pay for a particular item of expenditure, an angle rarely considered by Head Office spending departments. But, in the end, the true costs, as far as one can ascertain them, should always be reflected against the sales revenue. Head Office costs will at least be budgeted. One of the tasks of management is to achieve the profit target in spite of uncontrollable factors affecting the business. If the cost of petrol rises unexpectedly, cover it by making savings elsewhere, or by generating more sales. 'Uncontrollable' costs have to be dealt with in just the same way as 'controllable' ones.

As discussed in the chapter on absorption costing, managers can attempt to increase the profitability of their own areas of responsibility at a stroke, by arguing for a reduction in overhead allocations. The same is true of Head Office charges. Another subtle way of increasing your profits is to argue for a change in the level of transfer prices. In all these cases, if you argue successfully, your division will benefit instantly at the expense of its rivals. These arguments can consume a large amount of time and energy, without generating a single extra cent for the company.

Transfer pricing is a can of worms. There is no right or wrong way to fix transfer prices, so the issue is always a bone of contention. Fortunately, within a UK group, transfer prices have no external effect, so management have a free rein to play whatever motivational games they like. UK companies are taxed on a group basis, so it does not matter where the profits are located. It is an entirely different matter in an international situation.

International companies have plenty of opportunity to divert profits into low-tax areas, thereby increasing their overall net income. Simply increasing or decreasing the transfer prices will have a direct impact on the bottom line. However, the tax authorities around the world are not stupid, and are well aware of this type of manipulation. In fact, they tend to assume that the principal objective of international companies is to rob them of their due, and as a result always pay very close attention to transfer pricing policies. There is a big risk to international companies here. For instance, if the UK tax authorities consider that the UK selling company is charging too low a transfer price for its goods to a French sister company, they will raise an assessment on the notional profit which they deem should have been earned. Meanwhile, the French authorities could come to the conclusion that the same transfer price had been too high, and similarly raise an assessment on the notional profit missed. The company could end up paying tax twice, on profit which never existed in the first place.

So how does a company avoid this situation? The tax authorities want to see a transfer pricing policy that is transparently objective and consistently applied. They take the simple view that intercompany sales should be carried out at arm's length. This may be fairly straightforward, if the product is also sold on the open market and a clear market price can be established. But this is not always the case. Market prices can vary considerably from one country to another, depending on a myriad of local factors, such as competition, exchange rates, local taxes, etc. The variation in the price of cars around Europe in recent times is a classic example of this. If the receiving company is simply selling on into the local market, the best option will be to allow it to make a profit equating to a commission, so a transfer price of ultimate selling price, less say 20%, is probably most appropriate.

But what if there is no market price? My company used to make a product in the UK which was shipped to Holland for incorporation into a different product, which was then shipped to our French company for onward sale to customers there. So where do we start? There were no real external market prices to refer to, either for the UK product, or for the Dutch product, and no real competition for this specialised product in France. In such cases, our policy was to use total cost plus 10% for each transfer, ensuring that each company in the line was receiving a fair reward for its contribution to the end product, and that the ultimate selling price did not become uncompetitive. Incidentally, in my view, fixed overhead should always be included in such cost calculations, as there is no reason why intercompany sales should not carry their full burden of cost.

Our total-cost-plus-10% policy was never applied blindly. We still had to make variations when it produced a clearly inequitable result. For instance, we manufactured a product for use in the cosmetics industry which had been very expensive to develop, but which now commanded a high price. There being no independent market for this, the cost-plus-10% basis would normally have been used, but this would have left considerably more profit in the receiving company than in the manufacturing company, which still had the developmental costs to recover. Similarly, we had another line of products which fell into the high-volume, low-price category, where the cost-plus-10% basis left insufficient profit in the receiving company. In these cases we had to move away from the standard policy in order to achieve an equitable split of profit. It was vitally important to document the reasons for this variation, so that the decision could be justified to the sceptical tax authorities.

So, for international companies, a transfer price based on market price remains the safest policy, but where this is not feasible, select another basis, and stick with it as far as you can. The overriding principle is that the transfer price should be demonstrably fair to all parties; the adopted policy should be consistently applied and any variations adequately documented. The tax authorities will certainly examine this area of your business, and you manipulate profit for tax avoidance purposes at your peril.

For companies operating solely within the UK, the issues are far less severe, but the principle of fairness still seems to me to be the overriding factor. There are far more productive uses for management time than the settling of internal disputes about transfer prices.

Summary

- Divisionalisation can be based on product type or geographical area.
- Divisionalisation reduces risk for the group.
- Divisionalisation encourages specialisation of management.
- Divisionalisation allows the head office to concentrate on strategy and fund raising.
- There are four types of responsibility centre: cost, revenue, profit and investment.
- There are four types of profit to measure divisional performance.
- Return on investment (ROI) is a relative percentage measure.
- Residual income (RI) is an absolute monetary measure.
- Transfer prices (TPs) are used for inter-division sales.
- The 'ideal' TP is the *opportunity cost* to the supplier of the goods or services.
- TPs can be determined in four ways: market-based, cost-based, negotiated and administered.
- Whether the division is working at full capacity or not can affect the TP.
- International TPs are often used to avoid tax.
- Divisional performance and transfer pricing have their limitations.

Further reading

Aggarwal, R. K. and Samwick, A. A. (2003) 'Performance incentives within firms: the effect of managerial responsibility', *Journal of Finance*, Vol. 58, Issue 4, August.

Arnold, J. and Turley, S. (1996) *Accounting for Management Decisions*, 3rd edition, Prentice Hall, Harlow. See Chapter 18.

Atrill, P. and McLaney, E. (2004) *Management Accounting for Decision Makers*, 4th edition, Financial Time/Prentice Hall, Harlow. See Chapter 10.

Drury, C. (2004) *Management and Cost Accounting*, 6th edition, Thomson Learning Business Press, London. See chapters on divisional profitability and transfer pricing.

Horngren, C., Foster, G. and Datar, S. (2002) *Cost Accounting*, 11th edition, Prentice Hall International, Harlow. See Chapter 22.

Przysuski, M., Lalapet, S. and Swaneveld, H. (2005) 'Multinational business strategies and transfer pricing in a global marketplace', *Corporate Business Taxation Monthly*, Vol. 6, Issue 5, February.

Vaysman, I. (1998) 'A model of negotiated transfer pricing', *Journal of Accounting & Economics*, Vol. 25, Issue 3, June.

Answers to self-assessment questions

S13.1. Dominion Distillery Group

	€m
Sales revenue	156
Variable costs	134
Contribution	**22**
Controllable fixed costs	14
Controllable profit	**8**
Non-controllable fixed costs	6
Profit before head office charges	**2**

1 $\text{ROI} = \dfrac{2}{30} = \mathbf{6.7\%}$

2 **RI:**   Notional interest charge $= 30 \times 5\% = 1.5$ million euros

Profit before head office charges – notional interest charge $= 2.0 - 1.5 = \mathbf{0.5}$ **million euros**

3 **New interest rate:**

Notional interest charge $= 2.0$

New interest rate $= 5\% \times (2.0/1.5) = \mathbf{6.7\%}$

The group may justify using profit **before** rather than **after** head office charges if the charges do not increase because of the new distillery. The same total head office cost would be distributed differently amongst the divisions with no increase to the group as a whole.

S13.2.

	£
Materials	36
Direct labour	9
Variable overhead	5
Variable cost	50
Fixed overhead	15
Full cost	65
Profit margin	20
Sales price	85

If operating at full capacity, the *ideal transfer price* is £85.

If operating at less than full capacity, the *ideal transfer price* is £50.

If operating at full capacity, the profit margin may be shared between supplying and buying divisions, so the *practical transfer price* may be £75 [65 + (50% × 20)].

If operating at less than full capacity, full cost may be used giving the supplying division a contribution to its fixed overheads. The *practical transfer price* would be £65 giving a positive contribution of £15.

VT Limited

VT Limited is one of several subsidiaries in the GP group of companies. It manufactures electronic control units and sells them both on the open market and to fellow subsidiaries. Recent market research has produced the following figures regarding the elasticity of demand of its TX9 controller:

Selling price	£6	£7	£8	£9	£10
Demand	30,000	25,000	21,000	16,000	13,000

The standard cost for the TX9 is as follows:

		£
Direct labour	0.20 hours @ £6/h	1.20
Direct materials:	1 multi-switch @ £2.50	2.50
	1 microchip @ £0.50	0.50
	Other components	0.20
Overhead	0.1 machine hours @ £4/mh	0.40
Total cost		4.80

Overheads are 90% fixed and 10% variable.

The multi-switches and microchips are supplied by fellow subsidiaries SGN Ltd and MLF Ltd respectively. All the other components are sourced outside the GP group. Cost and pricing data for these two components are as follows:

Unit costs	SGN Ltd Multi-switch	MLF Ltd Microchip
Direct labour	0.45	0.20
Direct materials	1.15	0.05
Overhead	0.40	0.10
Full cost	2.00	0.35
Internal transfer price	2.50	0.50
External market price	3.50	0.80

SGN is operating at full capacity and has a backlog of orders to fulfil. MLF is short of orders and, if more are not received soon, it may have to make some redundancies.

Tasks:

a) Based on the market research data, which price–volume combination will maximise the total **contribution** made by the TX9 controller for VT Limited?

(30 marks)

b) Assuming the proportion of fixed and variable overheads is the same for all GP's subsidiaries, determine the ideal transfer prices which will maximise profits for the **GP group** as a whole.

(20 marks)

c) **Based on your answers to part b**, determine the price–volume combination to maximise the total **contribution** to VT Ltd.

(20 marks)

d) Discuss the alternative ways that transfer prices can be calculated and comment briefly on the fact that 'ideal' transfer prices are not being used within the GP group.

(30 marks)

(Total 100 marks)

Review questions

The answers to these questions can be found in the text of the chapter.

R13.1 Divisionalisation

1 Explain what it is and the role played by the head office.
2 What are its advantages?

R13.2 Responsibility centres

1 Define four types of responsibility centre.
2 Discuss the alternative definitions of 'profit' that can be used to measure divisional performance (create an illustration of the figures involved).

R13.3 Transfer prices

1 Define the 'ideal' transfer price and explain why it is seldom used.
2 Discuss four ways in which transfer prices can be set.

Questions

An asterisk * on a question number indicates that the answer is given at the end of the book. Answers to the other questions are given in the Lecturer's Guide.

Q13.1* RI v ROI

The table below shows the annual results for the four divisions of a group company.

	(£000)			
Division	**A**	**B**	**C**	**D**
Sales revenue	156	445	3,014	2,036
Variable costs	134	400	2,642	1,781
Contribution	**22**	**45**	**372**	**255**
Controllable fixed costs	14	35	298	210
Controllable profit	**8**	**10**	**74**	**44**
Non-controllable fixed costs	6	7	50	30
Profit before head office charges	**2**	**3**	**24**	**14**
Head office charges	1	1	6	4
Divisional pre-tax profit	**1**	**2**	**18**	**10**
Capital employed	**30**	**60**	**450**	**240**

Tasks:

1 Calculate the return on capital employed for each of the four divisions and rank them accordingly.
2 Calculate the residual income for each of the four divisions using an interest rate of 5% and rank them accordingly.
3 Comment on your findings.

Q13.2* Gorgon Group plc

Gorgon Group plc is a manufacturer with a divisional structure. The Odeen division makes a single product which it sells outside the Gorgon Group as well as to the Trey division. Odeen's product has a variable cost of £17 a unit and its total annual fixed costs are £480,000. It sells 30,000 units externally at £40 each and 10,000 to Trey at £34 each. For its internal profit calculations, Odeen allocates 20% of total fixed costs to Trey and 80% to external sales.

Trey has been approached by an external supplier, Hexup Limited, which is offering a virtually identical product to that currently purchased from Odeen at a price of £30 each.

Tasks:

a) If Trey refuses Hexup's offer, calculate Odeen's annual profit and analyse it between intra-group and external activities.
b) If Trey buys its total requirement from Hexup and Odeen cannot replace the lost sales, what will be the effect on the profits of (1) Odeen, and (2) Gorgon?
c) If Odeen refuses to match Hexup's price and Trey buys its total requirement from Hexup, how many extra external sales would Odeen have to make to avoid any reduction in its profit?
d) If Trey decides to purchase half its requirement from Hexup, what effect will this have on Gorgon's profit?
e) If Odeen agrees to match Hexup's price of £30 provided Trey still buys 100% of its requirement from it, what effect will this have on Gorgon's profit?
f) Advise Gorgon Group regarding this situation.

Q13.3 MCP plc

MCP plc specialises in providing marketing, data collection, data processing and consulting services. The company is divided into divisions that provide services to each other and also to external clients. The performance of the Divisional Managers is measured against profit targets that are set by central management.

During October, the Consulting division undertook a project for AX plc. The agreed fee was £15,500 and the costs excluding data processing were £2,600. The data processing, which needed 200 hours of processing time, was carried out by the Data Processing (DP) division. An external agency could have been used to do the data processing, but the DP division had 200 chargeable skilled hours available in October.

The DP division provides data processing services to the other divisions and also to external customers. The budgeted costs of the DP division for the year ending 31 December 2002, which is divided into 12 equal monthly periods, are as follows:

	£
Variable costs:	
Skilled labour (6,000 hours worked)	120,000
Semi-skilled labour	96,000
Other processing costs	60,000
Fixed costs:	240,000

These costs are recovered on the basis of chargeable skilled labour hours (data processing hours) which are budgeted to be 90% of skilled labour hours worked. The DP division's external pricing policy is to add a 40% mark-up to its total budgeted cost per chargeable hour.

During October 2002, actual labour costs incurred by the DP division were 10% higher than expected, but other costs were 5% lower than expected.

Required:

a) Calculate the total transfer value that would have been charged by the DP division to the Consulting division for the 200 hours on its AX plc project, using the following bases:

   i)   actual variable cost;
   ii) standard variable cost + 40% mark-up;
   iii) market price.

(6 marks)

b) Prepare statements to show how the alternative values calculated in answer to requirement (a) above would be reflected in the performance measurement of the DP division **and** the Consulting division.

(12 marks)

c) Recommend, with supporting calculations, explanations and assumptions, the transfer value that should be used for the 200 hours of processing time in October. Your answer need not be one of those calculated in your answer to requirement (a) above.

(7 marks)
(Total = 25 marks)

CIMA Intermediate: Management Accounting – Performance Management, November 2002

Q13.4 CTD Ltd

CTD Ltd has two divisions – FD and TM. FD is an iron foundry division which produces mouldings that have a limited external market and are also transferred to TM division. TM division uses the mouldings to produce a piece of agricultural equipment called the 'TX' which is sold externally. Each TX requires one moulding. Both divisions produce only one type of product.

The performance of each Divisional Manager is evaluated individually on the basis of the residual income (RI) of his or her division. The company's average annual 12% cost of capital is used to calculate the finance charges. If their own target residual income is achieved, each Divisional Manager is awarded a bonus equal to 5% of his or her residual income. All bonuses are paid out of Head Office profits.

The following budgeted information is available for the forthcoming year:

	TM division	FD division
	TX per unit	Moulding per unit
	£	£
External selling price	500	80
Variable production cost	* 366	40
Fixed production overheads	60	20
Gross profit	74	20
Variable selling and distribution cost	25	** 4
Fixed administration overhead	25	4
Net profit	24	12
Normal capacity (units)	15,000	20,000
Maximum production capacity (units)	15,000	25,000
Sales to external customers (units)	15,000	5,000
Capital employed	£1,500,000	£750,000
Target RI	£105,000	£85,000

*   The variable production cost of the TX includes the cost of an FD moulding.

** External sales only of the mouldings incur a variable selling and distribution cost of £4 per unit.

FD division currently transfers 15,000 mouldings to TM division at a transfer price equal to the total production cost plus 10%.

Fixed costs are absorbed on the basis of normal capacity.

Required:

(a) Calculate the bonus each Divisional Manager would receive under the current transfer pricing policy and discuss any implications that the current performance evaluation system may have for each division and for the company as a whole.

(7 marks)

(b) Both Divisional Managers want to achieve their respective residual income targets. Based on the budgeted figures, calculate
(i)   the **maximum** transfer price per unit that the Divisional Manager of TM division would pay.
(ii) the **minimum** transfer price per unit that the Divisional Manager of FD division would accept.

(6 marks)

(c) Write a report to the management of CTD Ltd that explains, and recommends, the transfer prices which FD division should set in order to maximise group profits. Your report should also
● Consider the implications of actual external customer demand exceeding 5,000 units; and
● Explain how alternative transfer pricing systems could overcome any possible conflict that may arise as a result of your recommended transfer prices

Note: your answer must be related to CTD Ltd. You will not earn marks by just describing various methods for setting transfer prices.

(12 marks)
(Total = 25 marks)

CIMA Intermediate: Management Accounting – Decision Making, November 2002

Q13.5

M Ltd has two divisions, X and Y. Division X is a chip manufacturer and Division Y assembles mobile phones. Division X currently manufactures many different types of chip, one of which is used in the manufacture of the mobile phones. Division X has no external market for the chips that are used in the mobile phones and currently sets the transfer price on the basis of total cost plus 20% mark-up.

The budgeted profit and loss statement for Division Y for next year shows the following results:

Mobile phone range	P	Q	R
	£000	£000	£000
Sales	10,000	9,500	11,750
Less: Total costs	7,200	11,700	9,250
Profit/(loss)	2,800	(2,200)	2,500
Fixed costs	2,000	5,400	5,875

The total costs shown above include the cost of the chips.

Division Y uses a traditional absorption costing system based on labour hours.

M Ltd operates a performance measurement system based on divisional profits. In order to increase profit for the forthcoming year, Division Y has asked permission to buy chips from an external supplier.

The accountant of M Ltd has recently attended a conference on activity based costing (ABC) and has recommended that the divisions should implement an ABC system rather than continue to operate the traditional absorption costing system.

Required:

a) A presenter at the conference stated that 'ABC provides information that is more relevant for decision making than traditional forms of costing'. Discuss this statement, using Division Y when appropriate to explain the issues you raise.

(8 marks)

b) The management team of M Ltd has decided to implement ABC in all of the divisions. Discuss any difficulties which might be experienced when implementing ABC in the divisions.

(6 marks)

c) (i) Discuss the current transfer pricing system and explain alternative systems that might be more appropriate for the forthcoming year.

(7 marks)

(ii) Explain the impact that the introduction of an ABC system could have on the transfer price and on divisional profits.

(4 marks)
(Total 25 marks)

CIMA Intermediate: Management Accounting – Decision Making, May 2003

BUDGETARY CONTROL

Part 5 comprises:

'If you do not know where you want to go, you will probably end up somewhere else!' A foolish statement or a recommendation for planning? Budgets are a kind of route map: they detail a series of activities which will lead to a certain position at a certain time. Almost every organisation uses budgets to help it achieve its objectives.

The budgetary control process consists of two main activities. The first is the creation of the budget and the second is using the budget to control operations. Both of these activities take up large amounts of managers' time. If you are a manager, it is highly probable that you will be involved in the budgetary control process to a greater or lesser extent. This being so, you will benefit from an understanding of how budgets are constructed and how they are used. As a manager, you will be set targets; budgetary control can help you to meet them.

Budgets and their creation

Chapter contents

Introduction

If you were one of the top managers in an organisation, e.g. a director of a company, you would be expected to have a vision of where the organisation should be a few years from now. Knowing where you are going is one important aspect of leadership. However, although having a vision is very important, it is not sufficient in itself. You need to know how to go about realising that vision. First, you need to be able to **make the plans** which will get you to where you want to be. Second, you need to know the best way to **use those plans**. Armed with this knowledge you stand a fair chance of achieving your goals. Without it, you are much less likely to succeed. This chapter is all about how to make those plans, how to create a budget.

Note: Although budgets are just as important to service industries as they are to manufacturing industries, their preparation is illustrated in this chapter using examples of manufacturing. Budgets for service organisations are prepared in just the same way but, obviously, without the manufacturing schedules.

Having worked through this chapter you should be able to:

- explain what a budget is;
- explain how it fits into the corporate planning context;
- explain the basic theory of budgetary control systems;
- list the positive attributes of budgetary control systems;
- differentiate between fixed and flexible budgets;
- differentiate between incremental and zero-based budgeting;
- create functional budgets;
- create a budgeted profit and loss account, balance sheet and cash flow forecast;
- create flexible budgets;
- define standard cost;
- discuss the issues about the setting of standards;
- discuss the limitations of budgets.

Budgets and their context

A budget is a predictive model of organisational activity, quantitatively expressed, for a set time period. In plain English, a budget is a plan of operations and activities for the next year (or month etc.), stated in monetary values.

The organisation's strategic plan, not the annual budget, is the master plan of the organisation. This strategic plan should state the long-term organisational objectives and the policies through which these goals are to be achieved. The annual budget is created within the context of the strategic plan (see Figure 14.1).

The relationships between the various constituent budgets are illustrated in Figure 14.2.

STRATEGIC CORPORATE PLAN
– long-term organisational objectives
– policies through which goals are to be achieved

ANNUAL BUDGET
Master budget – profit and loss account, balance sheet and cash flow forecast,
Functional budgets – for departments or processes,
e.g. purchasing, marketing, material usage, etc.

Figure 14.1 **The budget in context**

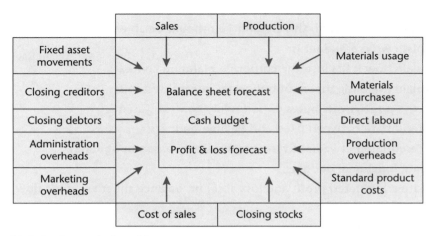

Figure 14.2 **Budget relationships**

Functional budgets

The primary budget

Where to start? Does it matter which budget is created first? The answer to this last question is yes. Start with the activity that determines all the other activities. In the vast majority of businesses this is sales. The amount of goods or services it is realistically considered can be sold in the budget period will influence all the other activities. This primary budget can be thought of as a limiting factor. (However, if titanium components were being manufactured for jet engines and there was a sudden unforeseen shortage of this material, then the limiting factor might be the availability of titanium. In this unusual case, the raw material budget would have to be the first one prepared.)

The sales forecast is the responsibility of the sales and marketing section and, because it is so crucial, it would have to be approved at the highest level in the organisation. The management accountant would have little, or no, input into this primary budget.

The production volume budget

To plan the production volume for a period it is necessary to know the stock levels of finished goods at the beginning and end of that period. These may be determined by a policy such as 'opening stock is to be equal to one-half of the next month's sales'. So, if it is planned to sell 100 items in March and 120 items in April, the stock will be 50 items on 1 March and 60 items on 1 April. As the sales volume is already known, the number of items to be made is determined by the following formula:

Production = sales + closing stock − opening stock

Self-assessment
question S14.1

Try the following question for yourself (answer at the end of the chapter).

The sales of Minnow Ltd are planned to be: April 100, May 140, June 120 and July 160 items. Stock levels are planned to be one-quarter of the next month's sales. What are the planned production budgets for April, May and June?

The raw material purchasing budget

To calculate this, it is necessary to know how much raw material will be used as well as knowing the policy on raw material stock levels. It may be that, due to the unreliability of supplies, the policy of a particular firm is to have sufficient stock at the start of a month for that month's production. The production volume budget will determine the amount of raw material usage and raw material purchases are therefore calculated as follows:

$$\text{Purchases} = \text{usage} + \text{closing stock} - \text{opening stock}$$

(This formula applies to both quantities and values.)

Self-assessment
question S14.2

Try the following question for yourself (answer at the end of the chapter).

Minnow Ltd plans to spread its production of 1,800 items evenly throughout the year. Each item uses five units of raw material. Minnow expects to start the year with 80 units of raw material in stock but to reduce this by 25% by the end of the year. If each unit of stock costs £6 to buy in, what is the company's raw material purchasing budget for the year?

The cost of sales budget

For a manufacturing organisation, the cost of sales is calculated by the following formula:

$$\text{Cost of sales} = \text{opening stock} + \text{production cost} - \text{closing stock}$$

(All the items in this equation relate to finished goods only.)

Self-assessment
question S14.3

Try the following question for yourself (answer at the end of the chapter).

If Minnow Ltd's stock of finished goods is valued at £30,000 on 1 January and £27,000 at 31 March and the cost of production is £20,000 a month, what is the cost of sales for the quarter?

The cash receipts budget

In order to prepare the cash budget, it is essential to know the amount of money planned to be received in each period. For sales made on 'cash terms' (i.e. transfer of goods and payment for them take place at the same time), the total receipts equal the total sales revenue. For sales made on 'credit terms' (i.e. payment takes place at a later time than the transfer of the goods), the picture is more complicated. The total of receipts in a period depends on the amount of debtors at the start and finish of the period as well as the amount sold on credit terms during that period.

$$\text{Receipts} = \text{opening debtors} + \text{credit sales} - \text{closing debtors}$$

Self-assessment question S14.4	*Try the following question for yourself (answer at the end of the chapter).*

Minnow Ltd plans to sell 2,400 items for £10 each evenly through the year, half on cash terms and half on credit terms of one month. If its opening debtors were £1,300, what would be the planned total of receipts from all sales during the year?
  (Assume all debtors pay on the due dates.)

The cash payments budget

In order to prepare the cash budget, it is also essential to know the amount of money planned to be paid out in each period. When goods and services are paid for immediately they are received, the total of payments equals the total of purchases. However, when purchases are made on credit terms, the total of purchases must be adjusted by the amount of creditors at the start and finish of the period to give the total amount of payments.

$$\text{Payments} = \text{opening creditors} + \text{credit purchases} - \text{closing creditors}$$

Self-assessment question S14.5	*Try the following question for yourself (answer at the end of the chapter).*

Minnow Ltd buys 1,600 items at £5 each evenly through the year, one-quarter on cash terms and three-quarters on two months' credit. If the company's opening creditors were £750, what would be the total of its payments for the year?
  (Assume all creditors are paid on the due dates.)

Master budgets

The cash budget or cash flow forecast

This budget is of particular importance to all organisations. If there is insufficient cash to pay all the bills due at a certain time, then the organisation may be forced out of business even though it is trading profitably (see Chapter 2).

The summary cash budget for the period is simply

Opening balance + receipts − payments = closing balance

However, it is normal to create a detailed cash budget for each month in order to monitor and control the organisation's cash resources. It is also useful to know the net result of monthly cash flows. Is more money coming in than going out (i.e. a net inflow) or is more going out than coming in (i.e. a net outflow)? Once this is known, the net cash flow can be combined with the opening balance to give the closing balance.

	Cash in
less:	**Cash out**
	Net cash flow
add:	**Opening balance**
	Closing balance

It is conventional to give net inflows a positive sign and net outflows a negative sign (shown below by the use of brackets).

The following is an example of a simple cash budget in summary terms:

		Jan	Feb	Mar	Total
	Cash in	45	49	54	148
less:	Cash out	37	53	41	131
	Net cash flow	8	(4)	13	17
add:	Opening balance	850	858	854	850
	Closing balance	858	854	867	867

Note that the opening balance for a month must be the same as the closing balance for the previous month. This is only to be expected as exactly the same money is being referred to by each of the two balances.

The illustration below shows these summary figures in bold type together with some of the detailed items that help to make them up.

	Jan	Feb	Mar	Quarter
Receipts:				
Credit sales	32	37	41	110
Cash sales	11	12	12	35
Other	2	–	1	3
Total	45	49	54	148

	Jan	Feb	Mar	Quarter
Payments:				
Purchases of materials	25	27	25	77
Wages	8	8	8	24
Expenses	4	4	5	13
Other	–	14	3	17
Total	37	53	41	131
Net in/(out)flow	8	(4)	13	17
Opening bank balance	850	858	854	*850*
Closing bank balance	858	854	867	*867*

Be careful of the two numbers (in italics) at the bottom right-hand corner. They are **not** found by adding across (like all those above them) but by **copying** the opening balance for the quarter (850) and then working down the 'Quarter' column. The resulting number (867) in the extreme bottom right-hand corner should be exactly the same as that on its immediate left. After all, they should both show the balance on 31 March.

The figures above show the months when the cash actually moves, i.e. comes in or goes out. For sales and purchases made on credit terms, this date will always be later than the point of sale or purchase. The cash budget may be dangerously misleading if these timing differences are not taken into account.

Note that the balances on the bottom two lines of the cash budget can be negative as well as positive. This shows that the organisation has a bank overdraft rather than a positive balance, a very common business situation.

When referring to cash budgets, use the terms *net inflow, net outflow, surplus* or *deficit* but **never** *profit* or *loss*.

The cash flow forecast is a very important management tool. It is used to:

- ensure that sufficient cash will be available to carry out planned activities;
- give a warning of the size of overdraft or loan needed;
- plan for investment of surplus cash.

Self-assessment question S14.6

Try the following question for yourself (answer at the end of the chapter).

Using the pro forma below, create (in pencil?) a cash budget from the following information: Opening balance is £150 *overdrawn*; credit receipts are £100 per month, cash receipts are £30 per month and other receipts are £70 in Feb.; Purchases are £100 per month, wages £25 per month, expenses £35 per month and other payments are £15 in Jan.

Cash budget for quarter ended 31 March

	Jan	Feb	Mar	Quarter
Receipts:				
Credit sales				
Cash sales				
Other				
Total				

	Jan	Feb	Mar	Quarter
Payments:				
Purchases of materials				
Wages				
Expenses				
Other				
Total				
Net in/(out)flow				
Opening bank balance				
Closing bank balance				

The budgeted profit and loss account and balance sheet

These budgets are compiled from information on the functional budgets or provided from elsewhere in the organisation. This is best appreciated by working through the case study at the end of this chapter.

Types of budget and budgeting methods

Fixed budget

This is a budget based on one predetermined level of activity. Its main function is to act as a master plan for the following year.

Flexible budget

This is a budget which, by recognising different cost behaviour patterns, is designed to change as the volume of activity changes. It can be thought of as several fixed budgets, each at a different level of activity, shown side by side.

Incremental budgeting

This approach to budget creation assumes that there will be little change in activity for next year compared to the current year. So the numerical amounts (known as *allowances*) are arrived at by taking last year's amount and adding an increment for any known changes and for inflation.

Zero-based budgeting

This is a method of budgeting which requires each cost element to be specifically justified, as though the activities were being undertaken for the first time. Without approval, the budget allowance is zero.

Flexible budgets

Shown below is a flexible budget for a firm which expects to sell about 1,400 items a year. However, its market tends to fluctuate year to year and so it also produces budgets for sales of 1,200 and 1,600 items. These are its estimates of the minimum and maximum annual sales.

Flexible budgeted profit and loss account for y/e 31 December

Sales (units)	1,200	1,400	1,600
Sales revenue (£000)	600	700	800
Materials	300	350	400
Labour	120	140	170
Factory overhead	20	21	27
Total	440	511	597
Gross profit	160	189	203
Marketing costs	16	18	20
Admin costs	30	30	30
Total	46	48	50
Net profit	114	141	153

This shows that net profit does not increase in direct proportion to sales volume. At maximum sales the net profit increases by only £12,000 for the extra 200 units sold over the expected number. But at minimum sales (200 units less than expected) net profit decreases by £27,000. This type of situation arises due to the way in which costs behave (see Chapter 2). Remember that many costs have both fixed and variable elements. For example, the marketing costs above have a fixed component of £4,000 and a variable component of £10 a unit. Sometimes, fixed costs step up. Weekend working had to be introduced to produce the extra 200 items needed for maximum sales. This caused extra labour costs at an overtime premium of 50% and additional factory overheads.

Understanding cost structures is essential for the creation of flexible budgets. If you are asked to create one involving stepped fixed costs you would have to be told both the activity level at which the step happened and the size of the step. But you would probably be expected to calculate the semi-variable costs (such as marketing in the above example) for yourself. One way of going about this is known as the 'high–low method' (also covered in Chapter 1, on cost behaviour).

Illustration using the semi-variable cost of water supplies

For the first six months of the year the monthly invoices for the use of water by the business were:

Month	Usage	Total cost (£)
1	520	12,080
2	570	12,310
3	600	12,400
4	510	12,040
5	540	12,160
6	500	12,000

Using only the highest- and lowest-usage months, the cost structure can be determined as follows:

Highest (month 3)	600 units	£12,400
Lowest (month 6)	500 units	£12,000
Difference	100 units	£400

Variable cost per unit produced = £400/100 = £4
Variable cost of 500 units = 500 × £4 = £2,000
Fixed cost (at 500 units) = total cost − variable cost
  = £12,000 − £2,000
  = £10,000

This can be checked by substituting these values in the other month. In month 3:

$$
\begin{aligned}
& £ \\
\text{Variable cost} &= 600 \times £4 = 2,400 \\
\text{Fixed cost} &= \underline{10,000} \\
\text{Total cost} &= \underline{12,400}
\end{aligned}
$$

When performing this check, be sure to use **only** the other occurrence used in the original calculation (month 3 in this case). Note that many costs do not behave as predictably as water bills.

As this method uses the two extreme values of the variable, it is advisable to check that these are representative of the normal cost behaviour. This can be done by sketching a scattergraph which will show up any 'outliers' or unrepresentative values.

Self-assessment question S14.7

Try the following question for yourself (answer at the end of the chapter).

The monthly costs of machine maintenance have been recorded during the past few months as follows. (During July the machine maintenance team were redeployed to assist on emergency repairs to the factory building.)

Month	Machine Maintenance hours	Total cost
October	155	2,013
September	122	1,723
August	135	1,902
July	69	280
June	157	2,073
May	149	1,937

If the machine maintenance hours for November are planned to be 180, estimate the machine maintenance cost for that month.

Standards and how they are set

A *standard* is the physical and financial plan for **one unit** of output.

> The standard cost *is the planned unit cost of the products, components or services produced in a period.*
> (*CIMA*, Management Accounting Official Terminology)

Example Standard cost data for one plastic wheel (type KR2)

Category	Item	Quantity	Price	Cost
Materials:	Plastic beads	1.2 kg	£2.00/kg	2.40
Labour:	Type A	0.25 h	£4.00/h	1.00
	Type D	0.10 h	£5.00/h	0.50
Variable overhead		0.35 h	£2.00/h	0.70
Variable cost				4.60
Fixed overhead (@ 900 wheels/week)		0.35 h	£4.60/h	1.61
Standard cost				£6.21

Bases for setting standards

There are three common sources for setting standards:

1 Performance levels of a prior period – these are based on recent experience.
2 Estimates of expected performance – these are based on recent experience and knowledge of any imminent changes.
3 Performance levels to meet organisational objectives – these are calculated from set targets; particularly useful if 'target costing' is used.

Approaches to standard setting

Standards are usually set at either *ideal* or *attainable* levels.

Ideal standards make no allowances for any inefficiencies. They are achievable only under the most favourable conditions and represent the theoretical maximum outcomes. It is not possible for actual performance to exceed ideal standards and their use may demotivate many employees.

Attainable standards are set at high but achievable levels; they represent a challenge. They make allowances for normal working conditions and are achievable by operating efficiently. They are capable of being exceeded and, therefore, can be used to motivate the workforce.

However, it is worth considering who decides what is the attainable level of performance. This decision is normally, at least partially, subjective. Top managers may have a different viewpoint from the budget holders charged with executing the budget.

This potential conflict of interests has led to *participative budgeting* where budget holders are involved in creating their own budgets. Management accounting staff help them to create their budgets, which then have to be agreed at a higher level of management. Two important points arise from this.

First, budget holders gain 'psychological ownership' from being involved in creating their own budget. It becomes 'their' budget rather than someone else's imposed upon them. They have a greater commitment to the success of their budget, which leads to improved performance. Non-involvement leads to a lack of interest in its success.

Second, as budget holders know they will ultimately be held responsible for meeting the budget, they have a natural tendency not to set their own targets too high. The technical term for these 'safety' or 'buffer' factors is *budgetary slack*. This is defined as 'the intentional overestimation of expenses and/or underestimation of revenues in the budgeting process' (CIMA *Management Accounting Official Terminology*).

The final decision on the contents of the budget belongs to senior management. However, this form of centralised control is potentially demotivating. To counteract this, the budget holder is usually given a high degree of responsibility for **how** the budget is achieved. He or she makes the day-to-day operating decisions and decides the tactics for meeting the corporate objectives. This bipartite approach effectively defuses the potential conflict between delegation and centralised control.

Importance of accurate standards

Badly set standards cause misleading variances whose investigation wastes both time and resources. Variances caused by poor standards are known as *planning variances*. One way to avoid these is by the systematic reviewing and updating of all standards.

Another aspect of accuracy is the question of how the budget allowance is arrived at for discretionary costs. How do you set the budget for items such as advertising or training? This type of cost may vary significantly from year to year. There is no easy answer to this question but managers should be aware of the problems posed by this type of cost.

Limitations of budgets as plans

In the 1970s, most large UK companies had a planning department employing a significant number of people. The wisdom of that era was that good planning for the next 5 to 10 years would enable the business to operate efficiently by anticipating and being prepared for future changes. Some also had outline plans for the next 15, 20 or 25 years. Many resources were tied up in the planning process. Thirty years later, at the beginning of the twenty-first century, the proportion of resources allocated to this process is far smaller.

The main reason is that the rate of change in the business environment has greatly accelerated during those years and shows no sign of slowing down. To plan in detail for the next 10 years is considered to be a waste of time. The organisation may be supplying different products and services in different markets by then. It may have been taken over or it may have acquired other organisations to take it in new directions. The stock markets of the world operate globally and faster than ever before. The amount of uncertainty in the business environment is much greater than it was before. Long-term planning is not seen as an effective use of resources. It is common to produce detailed plans only for the next year, and outline plans for the next three years only.

The manager's point of view

Almost every field of human endeavour can be improved by a little advance planning. This is particularly true of businesses, which are complicated operations consisting of numerous disparate activities and disciplines. Planning is crucial to ensure that all these disciplines are moving forward in the most efficient way for the enterprise as a whole.

In the vast majority of businesses, the most important driving force is the strategic sales plan. The sales department, with its close knowledge of the market in general and of individual customers' needs in particular, is best placed both to determine the growth potential of existing products, and to identify marketing opportunities for new products. Its view of what can be achieved, given the right products and supported by the right infrastructure, will provide the pattern of the company's direction for the foreseeable future.

The activities of all other departments in the company will be directed towards supporting the strategic sales plan. The technical department will develop new products to meet the customer requirements specified by the salesforce. Production will gear themselves up, through new equipment or plant modifications, to meet the sales forecast. Purchasing will identify reliable sources for any new materials required. Even Personnel and Administration will provide an infrastructure designed to support the overall plan.

It is then helpful to pull together the plans of all the departments into a long-range company plan. This should not be a detailed document, but should give an outline of the way the company might look over the next few years. In particular, it should ensure that the timing of any specific initiative is properly co-ordinated. For instance, is the development work for new products being started early enough? How long will it take to get approval for the capacity expansion project? Are we developing our people quickly enough to support the expanding business? All this will also lead to profit and cash forecasts, allowing the viability of the overall plan to be established at an early stage.

This should only be an outline document because the circumstances surrounding it will be constantly changing. Such is the pace of change in all fields now, in production and product technology, in IT and information flow, in increasing competition from all corners of the world, that plans can no longer be rigid. Ideally, they would change as every new circumstance emerged. It may not be practical to keep the company plan regularly updated, but the fact remains that managers must constantly be aware of the impact of external factors on their businesses, in both the short and long term.

The annual budget, however, is quite different. It is a working document, full of important detail, which enables the business to be controlled on a day-to-day basis. In my chemical company, the establishment of the budget was always the biggest exercise of the year. Although everyone traditionally complained about the amount of time it consumed, there is no doubt that the examination of the detail meant that all managers developed a profound understanding of the dynamics of the business. It was the only time in the year that the elements of the profit and loss account were closely examined, allowing cost/benefit issues to be questioned and cost-saving opportunities to be identified. For the rest of the year, the detailed budget became a yardstick against which actual performance could be confidently and easily measured.

If your company has a relatively stable customer base, it is highly desirable to set up a detailed sales budget by customer and product. A computerised sales reporting system will then be able to highlight with ease the areas where targets are not being met, so that early corrective action can be taken by the sales department. If your business consists of one-off contracts, it is clearly less easy to set up such a monitoring procedure, but it is still important to set up some appropriate measurement to provide an early warning of sales shortfalls.

The same principle applies to both direct costs of production and overheads. The budgeting process provides the opportunity to re-evaluate every aspect of cost. Are the standards used in product costing still accurate? Can we justify the level of expenditure we are proposing for, say, travel or advertising? Are there any new or one-off items we want to budget for in the current year? Or any items incurred last year which we do not expect to be repeated next year? This is why, in my view, zero-based budgeting should be used wherever possible.

In my company, managers were required to justify the whole of their budgeted expenditure each year. Travelling expenses, for instance, were always frighteningly large, as our salesforce used to travel all over the world, but by breaking this lump sum down into individual trips for each salesperson, it was possible to carry out a realistic review. Is it really necessary to have three trips to the Far East, or will two be enough? The sales manager has to provide a convincing justification. However, not all expense headings lend themselves easily to this type of analysis. Repairs to plant, for instance, was another large sum, which consisted of a mass of generally small items. The problem here is that, despite the use of sophisticated maintenance planning systems, there will always be a large number of unforeseeable repair costs. Moreover, the piece of equipment which incurred costly repairs last year is perhaps unlikely to break down again next year, so there is never an identifiable pattern to repairs. For this type of expense, therefore, we were obliged to adopt the incremental approach, taking average expenditure levels in recent years, and adding or subtracting amounts for known changes. In doing this, however, we accepted that we would be unable to exercise the same level of control as in many other areas of expenditure.

Incremental budgeting is a crude tool which allows inaccuracies and inefficiencies to be built into the system. Take salaries as an example. The actual salaries bill for last year is not the sum of the annual salaries of your employees. Staff turnover will inevitably mean that there are unfilled vacancies at times during the year. Replacement staff may have higher or lower salaries than the previous incumbents. There may have been promotions during the year, with accompanying salary increases. Temporary staff may also have been employed, at a much higher cost than permanent staff. Will overtime patterns be the same next year? As you can see, there are many occurrences which can have an impact on the total salary costs. When you come to budget for the following year, you have two options. You can assume that the same situations will occur again next year, so simply take last year's cost and add on a percentage for inflation. Alternatively, you can construct a detailed budget based on actual salaries and projected overtime levels, perhaps ignoring the impact of staff turnover, as it is impossible to forecast where in the company this will occur. Any savings arising from staff turnover can then be taken as favourable variances next year. My preference would always tend towards the latter option. If the managing director asks you why your department's salaries are over budget, you will be able to give a precise answer if you have a firm, detailed budget. If you have to answer 'Well, I think it's because we were understaffed last year', your credibility will undoubtedly suffer!

A detailed, well-constructed budget will also enable you to understand where there is some slack in the system. This is important for the inevitable moment when you receive an instruction from senior management to find more profit. It is a feature of budgeting that, when the proposals of all the departmental managers are put together, the resulting profit figure is never high enough! You will be asked to find more sales volumes, increase prices, or cut down costs, so it would be an unwise manager who did not leave a little slack in his or her initial numbers. If you work for a large corporation with multiple subsidiaries, the same phenomenon will occur at the higher level, when the budgets of all the businesses are added together. The profit is never high enough to meet the shareholders' expectations, and the instruction will come down to increase your local profit by a further factor. With a detailed budget, you can reflect these amendments by specific changes to your plans, e.g. by deferring the recruitment of new staff till later in the year. With a poorly constructed budget, however, this reiterative process will further distance your numbers from reality, and render the budget even less useful as a yardstick.

Summary

- Budgets are medium-term organisational plans expressed in monetary terms.
- They are intended to help the achievement of corporate, strategic long-term goals.
- Detailed functional or departmental budgets are prepared first.
- The summary master budget is prepared last; the process is bottom up.
- Budgets can be fixed or flexible.
- They are usually created incrementally, sometimes by a zero-based approach.
- Standards can be set in different ways and are subjective.
- Their main limitation is that they cannot be easily adjusted for unforeseen changes.

Further reading

Horngren, C., Bhimani, A., Datar, S. and Foster, G. (2002) *Management and Cost Accounting*, 2nd edition, Prentice Hall Europe, Harlow. See chapter 'Motivation, budgets and responsibility accounting'.

Langford, B. N. (2000) 'Production budgets, simplified', *Folio: The Magazine for Magazine Management*, Vol. 30, Issue 1, 1 January.

Otley, D. (1987) *Accounting Control and Organisational Behaviour*, Heinemann Professional Publishing, Oxford. See Chapter 7, 'Budgetary systems design'.

Upchurch, A. (2003) *Management Accounting, Principles and Practice*, 2nd edition, Financial Times/Prentice Hall, Harlow. See chapter 'Budgetary planning'.

Weetman, P. (2002) *Management Accounting, an Introduction*, 3rd edition, Financial Times/Prentice Hall, Harlow. See chapter 'Preparing a budget'.

Answers to self-assessment questions

S14.1

		April	May	June	July
	Sales	100	140	120	160
Add:	Closing stock	35	30	40	
Less:	Opening stock	25	35	30	40
	Production	**110**	**135**	**130**	

S14.2

Purchases = usage + closing stock − opening stock
= 9,000 + 60 − 80
= **8,980 units of raw material @ £6**
= **£53,880**

S14.3

		£
	Opening stock	30,000
Add:	Production	60,000
Less:	Closing stock	27,000
	Cost of sales	**63,000**

S14.4

		£	
	Opening debtors	1,300	
Add:	Credit sales	12,000	$(2,400 \times 10 \times 0.5)$
Less:	Closing debtors	1,000	

	£	
	£	
Receipts from debtors	12,300	
Receipts from cash sales	12,000	$(2,400 \times 10 \times 0.5)$
Total receipts for year	**24,300**	

S14.5

		£	
	Opening creditors	750	
Add:	Credit purchases	6,000	$(1,600 \times 0.75 \times £5)$
Less:	Closing creditors	1,000	$(200 @ £5)$
	Payments to creditors	5,750	
	Payments on cash terms	2,000	$(1,600 \times 0.25 \times £5)$
	Total payments for year	**7,750**	

S14.6

Cash budget for quarter ended 31 March

	Jan	Feb	Mar	Total
Receipts:				
Credit sales	100	100	100	300
Cash sales	30	30	30	90
Other	–	70	–	70
Total	130	200	130	460
Payments:				
Purchases of materials	100	100	100	300
Wages	25	25	25	75
Expenses	35	35	35	105
Other	15	–	–	15
Total	175	160	160	495
Net in/(out)flow	(45)	40	(30)	(35)
Opening bank balance	(150)	(195)	(155)	(150)
Closing bank balance	(195)	(155)	(185)	(185)

S14.7

It is obvious from the question that July is not a representative month and it should be excluded from your calculations. The scattergraph below confirms this:

High month:	June	157	2,073
Low month:	September	122	1,723
		35	350

Variable cost per hour = 350/35 = £10/hour

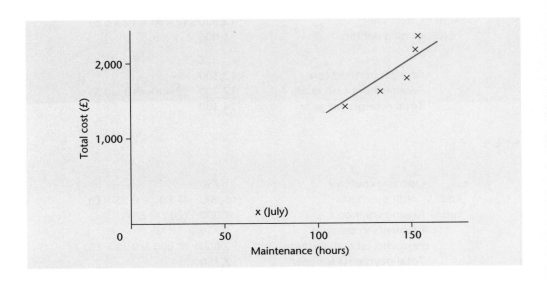

Calculate by using the highest month (June):

$$£$$

Total cost	$= 2{,}073$
Total variable cost $= 157\text{ h} \times £10/\text{h}$	$= \underline{1{,}570}$
Total fixed cost	$= \underline{503}$

Check by using the lowest month (September):

Total cost = total fixed cost + total variable cost
$$= 503 + (122 \times 10)$$
$$= \underline{£1{,}723}$$

So, the best estimate for maintenance expenditure in November is

Total cost = total fixed cost + total variable cost
$$= 503 + (180 \times 10)$$
$$= \underline{£2{,}303}$$

Omega is a long-established firm which used to make many different kinds of leather goods. However, in 2002 it made a loss for the first time in over 20 years. This was due to fierce competition, mainly from the Far East. In response to this, it has slashed its product range to its best-selling and most profitable items. It is hoping to benefit from economies of scale and now plans to make only two types of document case: the Delta and the Alpha.

Task:

From the following information, using the pro formas provided, you are required to create a budget for the year ending 31 December 2003.

Sales forecast

	Delta	Alpha
Number of cases sold	4,000	2,500
Selling price per case	£60	£55

Standard production data

Omega has only two production departments: Cutting and Stitching.
Unit costs:

Direct labour rates		Raw materials	
Cutting	Stitching	Leather	Zip fasteners
£6.00/h	£7.00/h	£3.00/unit	£1.00/unit

Product content

	Delta	Alpha
Leather	2 units	4 units
Zips	1 unit	2 units
Cutting dept. labour	2 hours	1.5 hours
Stitching dept. labour	1 hour	0.5 hour

Production overheads

	Cutting Department		Stitching Department	
	Fixed	**Variable**	**Fixed**	**Variable**
	£	**£**	**£**	**£**
Indirect labour	7,000	–	3,000	–
Indirect materials	–	3,000	–	9,000
Maintenance	2,000	1,000	500	500
Business rates	6,000	–	1,000	–
Depreciation	8,000	–	2,000	–
Electricity	1,000	2,000	500	1,000
	24,000	6,000	7,000	10,500

Marketing overheads

	£
Salaries	28,000
Advertising	24,000
Other	2,000
	54,000

Administration overheads

	£
Salaries	32,000
Bank charges	5,000
Other	4,150
	41,150

Stocks forecast

	Raw materials		Completed cases	
	Leather (units)	**Zips (units)**	**Delta (units)**	**Alpha (units)**
Opening stock	6,000	1,000	100	1,000
Closing stock	8,000	2,000	1,100	500

Debtors and creditors

Raw materials, labour, all overheads and debenture interest will be paid in full through the bank and cash accounts. Debtors and creditors at 31 December 2002 will pay and be paid during 2003. Debtors and creditors at 31 December 2003 are expected to be £25,000 and £10,000 respectively. One year's interest on the debenture is paid during the year.

Fixed assets

There are no disposals expected during 2003 but some new equipment will be acquired, on cash terms, for £20,000 just before the end of 2003.

Expected balance sheet as at 31 December 2002

	Cost	Depreciation provision	NBV
Fixed assets	£	£	£
Buildings	40,000	40,000	–
Machinery	200,000	50,000	150,000
	240,000	90,000	150,000
Current assets			
Raw material stock	19,000		
Finished goods stock	40,000		
Total stock		59,000	
Debtors		15,000	
Bank and cash		10,000	
		84,000	
Less: Current liabilities			
Creditors		8,000	
Net current assets			76,000
			226,000
Less: Long-term liabilities			
10% debenture 2006/08			120,000
			106,000
Financed by:			
Shareholders' capital			£
Ordinary shares			82,000
Retained profit			24,000
			106,000

Pro formas

1 Sales budget y/e 31 December 2003

	Units	Selling price £	Revenue £
Delta	....	....	....
Alpha	....	....	....
		Budget revenue	_____

2 Production budget y/e 31 December 2003

	Delta (units)	Alpha (units)
Planned sales	....	....
Desired closing stock finished goods	....	....
Total required	....	....
Less opening stock finished goods	....	....
Budgeted production	....	....

3　Direct materials usage budget y/e 31 December 2003

	Delta			Alpha		
	Material content (units/case)	Production (cases)	Usage (units)	Material content (units/case)	Production (cases)	Usage (units)
Leather	....	....	....	....	....	....
Zips	....	....	....	....	....	....

	Cost/unit £	Total usage	Cost of materials used £
Leather	....	....	....
Zips	....	....	....
		Budgeted material cost	_____

4　Direct materials purchases budget y/e 31 December 2003

	Leather	Zips
Desired closing stock	.... units	.... units
Units needed for production	.... units	.... units
Total required	.... units	.... units
Less opening stock	.... units	.... units
Purchases needed	.... units	.... units
Cost per unit	£...........	£...........
Budgeted purchases cost	£...........	£...........

5　Direct labour budget y/e 31 December 2003

	Labour content in product (hours)	Cases produced	Total labour hours	Rate per hour £	Total labour cost £
Cutting dept.					
Delta	....	....	....	....	....
Alpha	....	....	....	....	....
Stitching dept.					
Delta	....	....	....	....	....
Alpha	....	....	....	....	....
Budgeted labour hours and cost			_____		_____

6 **Production overheads budget y/e 31 December 2003**

	Cutting dept. (expected 13,000 direct labour hours)		Stitching dept. (expected 6,000 direct labour hours)	
	Fixed costs £	Variable costs £	Fixed costs £	Variable costs £
Indirect labour	....	....	....	....
Indirect materials	....	....	....	....
Maintenance	....	....	....	....
Business rates	....	....	....	....
Depreciation	....	....	....	....
Electricity	....	....	....	....
Budgeted overhead costs	_____	_____	_____	_____
Overhead absorption rate per direct labour hour	_____	_____	_____	_____

7 **Standard budgeted unit cost of manufacturing y/e 31 December 2003**

		Delta		Alpha	
	Unit cost £	Units in product	Cost £	Units in product	Cost £
Leather	....	....	....	....	....
Zips	....	....	....	....	....
Direct labour:					
Cutting	....	....	....	....	....
Stitching	....	....	....	....	....

		Delta		Alpha	
	Unit cost £	Units in product	Cost £	Units in product	Cost £
Production overheads:					
Cutting – Fixed	....	....	....	....	....
– Variable	....	....	....	....	....
Stitching – Fixed	....	....	....	....	....
– Variable	....	....	....	....	....
Standard cost of product			_____		_____

8 **Closing stock budget at 31 December 2003**

	Units	Unit cost £	Total cost £	£
Direct materials:				
Leather	....	....	....	
Zips	....	....	....	....
Finished products				
Delta	....	....	....	
Alpha	....	....	....	....
Budgeted closing stock				_____

9 Cost of sales budget y/e 31 December 2003

	£	£
Direct materials usage (3)	....	
Direct labour (5)	....	
Production overheads (6)	....	
Add: Opening stock finished products		....
Less: Closing stock finished products		....
Budgeted cost of sales		....

10 Marketing and administration expenses budget y/e 31 December 2003

	£	£
Marketing expenses:		
Salaries	....	
Advertising	....	
Other	....	....
Administrative expenses:		
Salaries	....	
Bank interest	....	
Other	....	....
Budgeted selling and administrative expenses		....

11 Budgeted profit statement y/e 31 December 2003

	£
Sales (1)	....
Less: Cost of sales (9)	....
Gross profit	....
Less: Marketing and admin. expenses (10)	....
Less: Interest on debenture	....
Budgeted net profit	

12 Cash budget y/e 31 December 2003 (summary form)

	£	£
Opening cash balance		....
Add receipts		....
Total cash available		....
Less payments:		
Purchases	....	
Direct labour (5)	....	
Factory overheads less depreciation (6)	....	
Marketing and admin. expenses (10)	....	
Debenture interest	....	
Fixed asset purchases	....	....
Budgeted closing cash balance		

13 Budgeted balance sheet of Omega Manufacturing as at 31 December 2003

	£ Cost	£ Depn provn	£ NBV
Fixed assets			
Buildings	....	....	....
Machinery	....	....	....
	....	....	....
Current assets			
Stocks:			
Finished goods	....		
Raw materials	....	....	
Debtors		....	
Bank and cash		....	
Less current liabilities			
Creditors		....	
Net current assets			....
			....
Less long-term liabilities			
10% Debenture 2006/08			....
			£_____
Financed by:			
Shareholders' capital			
Ordinary shares			....
Retained profits			....
			£_____

Questions

An asterisk * on a question number indicates that the answer is given at the end of the book. Answers to the other questions are given in the Lecturer's Guide.

Q14.1* Kellaway Limited

Kellaway Limited makes aluminium junction boxes for the electrical industry. It makes the boxes in three different sizes: small, medium and large. The following details are taken from next quarter's budget:

	Large	Medium	Small
Sales volume (units)	4,000	5,000	3,500
Direct labour:			
Fitters and turners (hours/unit)	1.25	0.90	0.80
Assemblers and packers (hours/unit)	0.40	0.25	0.20
Direct materials:			
Aluminium strips per unit	2.5	1.0	0.5
Packaging materials (metres)	1.25	0.75	0.5
Stocks:			
Finished goods opening stock (units)	300	400	200
Finished goods closing stock (units)	400	300	150

Rates of pay for fitters/turners and assemblers/packers are £10.00/hour and £6.00/hour respectively. Aluminium strips cost £3 each and packaging is £1/metre. Kellaway plans to have opening material stocks of 220 aluminium strips and 80 metres of packaging. The closing material stocks are 150 aluminium strips and 50 metres of packaging. The quarter's fixed production overheads of £31,700 are attached to product lines on a direct labour hour basis.

Tasks:

1 Create the production budget for the quarter.
2 Calculate the unit production cost of each type of junction box.
3 Create the materials usage budget in quantities and value.
4 Create the materials purchases budget in quantities and value.
5 Create the direct labour budget in hours and value.

Q14.2* Pierce Pommery

Pierce Pommery specialises in the manufacture of dry cider. The 1 litre bottles sell for £3.00 each, with 25% of sales on cash terms and 75% on one month's credit. The budget shows the following sales volumes:

Month	Litres
August	400,000
September	340,000
October	300,000
November	260,000
December	320,000
January	250,000

The company's policy is for opening stock of cider to equal one-fifth of each month's sales, but the stock of cider on 1 September was actually 80,000 litres. For stocks of apples, the policy is for opening stock to equal 50% of each month's usage. On 1 September, the stock of apples was actually 2,200 tonnes.

On average, 15 kilograms of apples are needed to produce 1 litre of cider (1 tonne = 1,000 kg). The cost price of apples is £50/tonne in September and October but £150/tonne in November and December as they have to be imported. Direct labour is paid in the month it is incurred and costs £0.20 a litre. Fixed overheads are £30,000 a month (including £5,000 for depreciation). Payment for apples is made two months after purchase but all other expenses are paid for one month after being incurred.

Tasks:

1 For the months of September, October, November and for the quarter as a whole, prepare the production budget (in litres) and the purchases budget (in tonnes and £).
2 For November only, prepare the cash budget. (Assume the bank balance on 1 November is £495,900 overdrawn.)

Q14.3* Norman Ropes

The sales budget for next year for a particular type of rope manufactured by Norman Ropes is as follows:

Period	Metres	Period	Metres
1	3,000	7	8,000
2	4,000	8	7,000
3	5,000	9	6,000
4	4,000	10	5,000
5	6,000	11	4,000
6	6,000	12	3,000

The stock of finished rope at the start of each period is to be equal to 25% of the sales estimate for the period. (Norman Rope's policy concerning finished product stock levels is to have a quantity of rope in stock approximately equal to one week's sales.) Exceptionally, at the beginning of period 1 there will be 1,500 metres of rope in stock. There is no work-in-progress at the end of any period.

This type of rope uses only one material, a nylon cord known as ARN. Many lengths of this cord are twisted together to form the rope. The budget assumes that each metre of rope uses 100 metres of ARN and that each metre of ARN will cost £0.04.

Materials equal to 25% of each period's usage are to be on hand at the start of the period. Exceptionally, the stock at the start of period 1 will be 125,000 metres of ARN. (Norman Rope's policy concerning raw material stock levels is to have a quantity of material in stock approximately equal to one week's usage.)

Tasks:

For the first **six** periods, prepare

a) the production budget (in metres of rope)
b) the materials usage cost budget
c) the materials purchases cost budget.

Q14.4 Bishop & Co.

Bishop & Co. manufactures vinyl pond lining for the water-garden industry. The company buys vinyl beads by the tonne and heats and rolls them into large sheets which are then cut to the required sizes. One tonne of beads produces 10,000 square metres of liner. Bishop & Co. is uncertain of demand for next year and decides to produce a flexible budget covering five activity levels from 400,000 square metres to 600,000 square metres in steps of 50,000 square metres.

The vinyl beads cost £800/tonne for purchases of up to and including 50 tonnes per year. Bishop & Co.'s supplier offers it the following bulk-purchase incentive. For annual purchases exceeding 50 tonnes the cost of every tonne in addition to the first 50 is £750.

The direct labour cost is made up of an annual lump sum of basic pay plus a volume-related bonus operative on all production output.

The present annual capacity of the manufacturing plant is 450,000 square metres. For production above this, a new machine will have to be purchased at a cost of £500,000. (No additional labour will be necessary to operate this highly automated machinery.) Bishop & Co.'s policy on depreciation is to write off machinery in equal instalments over 10 years, assuming a zero residual value.

The cost of insurance cover is a fixed amount up to a production level of 500,000 square metres. Beyond that, there is an additional cost per unit.

Bishop & Co. is currently one of the market leaders (in terms of sales volume) in the vinyl pond liner market although it is very competitive. Bishop & Co. sets its selling price per square metre on a cost-plus basis by adding a 300% mark-up to the total production cost. This covers marketing and administration expenses and leaves a little left over for profit.

Tasks:

1 Complete the following production department budget for next year:

(000 sqm)	400	450	500	550	600
	£	£	£	£	£
Vinyl beads	32,000				47,500
Direct labour	80,000				90,000
Electricity	8,000				10,000
Depreciation	22,000				34,000
Insurance	11,000				11,250
Other production costs	139,000				139,000
Total	292,000				331,750

2 If demand were to exceed 500,000 square metres and the new machinery was purchased, what effect might this have on Bishop's overall performance? What advice would you give regarding the purchase of the new machinery?

Q14.5 Chinkin Corporation

The Chinkin Corporation produces surfboards. Its sales have been 300 a month for the last few months but it is about to launch an expansion strategy aimed at increasing sales by 50% over the next four months, April to July. Sales in April are expected to be 300 boards but to increase by 50 units a month until 450 units are sold in July and each subsequent month.

The selling price of the boards is £50 and half the customers pay in the month following purchase. One-quarter take two months to pay and the other quarter pay cash-on-delivery, taking advantage of a 5% cash discount.

Chinkin has planned an advertising campaign for the months of April, May and June, costing a total of £40,000. Half this amount is payable in April and the remainder in two equal instalments in May and June.

To facilitate the increase in production, new plant and equipment costing £18,000 have been ordered for delivery in April, with payment in three equal monthly instalments, commencing in May. The cost of commissioning this machinery is estimated at £2,000 and will be paid to the outside contractors in April.

To lessen the impact of acquiring these fixed assets, Chinkin plans to arrange a three-month loan of £20,000 from its bank and expects to pay interest at the rate of 10% per annum. The interest will be paid in one amount on the same day as the capital sum is repaid. The money is to be transferred into its account on 3 April.

Raw materials cost £20 a unit and are paid for one month after purchase. Chinkin plans to have a monthly opening stock of raw materials equal to each month's production requirements. Similarly, its policy regarding stocks of finished boards is to have a monthly opening stock equal to each month's total sales.

Monthly fixed costs, including depreciation of £600, total £6,200 and are paid for in the month incurred.

The opening bank balance for April is expected to be £11,400 positive. Chinkin's current overdraft limit is £25,000.

Task:

Create Chinkin's monthly cash budget for the four-month period April to July and for the four-month period as a whole (work to the nearest £). Advise the corporation accordingly.

Q14.6 T Ltd

T Ltd is a newly-formed company that designs customised computer programs for its clients. The capital needed to fund the company will be provided by a venture capitalist who will invest £150,000 on 1 January 2002 in exchange for shares in T Ltd.

The Directors are currently gathering the information needed to help in the preparation of the cash budget for the first three months of 2002. The information that they have is given below.

Budget details

The budgeted sales (that is, the value of the contracts signed) for the first quarter of 2002 are expected to be £200,000. However, as the company will only just have commenced trading, it is thought that sales will need time to grow. It is therefore expected that 15% of the first quarter's sales will be achieved in January, 30% in February and the remainder in March. It is expected that sales for the year ending 31 December 2002 will reach £1,000,000.

Clients must pay a deposit of 5% of the value of the computer program when they sign the contract for the program to be designed. Payments of 45% and 50% of the value are then paid one and two months later respectively. No bad debts are anticipated in the first quarter.

There are six people employed by the company, each earning an annual gross salary of £45,000, payable in arrears on the last day of each month.

Computer hardware and software will be purchased for £100,000 in January. A deposit of 25% is payable on placing the order for the computer hardware and software, with the remaining balance being paid in equal amounts in February and March. The capital outlay will be depreciated on a straight-line basis over three years, assuming no residual value.

The company has decided to rent offices that will require an initial deposit of £13,000 and an ongoing cost of £6,500 per month payable in advance. These offices are fully serviced and the rent is inclusive of all fixed overhead costs.

Variable production costs are paid in the month in which they are incurred and are budgeted as follows:

January £1,200   *February* £4,200   *March* £8,000

A marketing and advertising campaign will be launched in January at a cost of £10,000 with a further campaign in March for £5,000, both amounts being payable as they are incurred.

Administration overhead is budgeted to be £500 each month: 60% to be paid in the month of usage and the balance one month later.

Tax and interest charges can be ignored.

Required:

(a) Prepare the cash budget by month and in total for the first quarter of 2002.

(15 marks)

(b) Identify and comment on those areas of the cash budget that you wish to draw to the attention of the Directors of T Ltd, and recommend action to improve cash flow.

(7 marks)

(c) Briefly explain three advantages for T Ltd of using a spreadsheet when preparing a cash budget.

(3 marks)

(Total = 25 marks)

CIMA Foundation: Management Accounting Fundamentals, November 2001

Q14.7 ST plc

ST plc produces three types of processed foods for a leading food retailer. The company has three processing departments (Preparation, Cooking and Packaging). After recognising that the overheads incurred in these departments varied in relation to the activities performed, the company switched from a traditional absorption costing system to a budgetary control system that is based on activity based costing.

The *foods* are processed in batches. The budgeted output for April was as follows:

	Output
Food A	100 batches
Food B	30 batches
Food C	200 batches

The number of activities and processing hours budgeted to process a batch of foods in each of the departments are as follows:

	Food A *Activities per* *batch:*	*Food B* *Activities per* *batch:*	*Food C* *Activities per* *batch:*
Preparation	5	9	12
Cooking	2	1	4
Packaging	15	2	6
Processing time	10 hours	375 hours	80 hours

The budgeted departmental overhead costs for April were:

	Overheads *$*
Preparation	100,000
Cooking	350,000
Packaging	50,000

Required:

(a) For food A ONLY, calculate the budgeted overhead cost per batch:
  (i) using traditional absorption costing, based on a factory-wide absorption rate per processing hour; and
  (ii) using activity based costing.

(6 marks)

(b) Comment briefly on the advantages of using an activity-based costing approach to determining the cost of each type of processed food compared to traditional absorption costing approaches. You should make reference to your answers to requirement (a) where appropriate.

(4 marks)

(c) The actual output for April was:

	Output
Food A	120 batches
Food B	45 batches
Food C	167 batches

Required:

Prepare a flexed budget for April using an activity based costing approach. Your statement must show the total budgeted overhead for each department and the total budgeted overhead absorbed by each food.

(10 marks)

(d) Discuss the advantages that ST plc should see from the activity based control system compared to the traditional absorption costing that it used previously.

(5 marks)
(Total = 25 marks)

CIMA Intermediate: Management Accounting – Performance Management, May 2004

CHAPTER 15 Using budgets to control operations

Chapter contents

Introduction

Having learned how to create a budget, you will have some idea of the complexity of this task. The budget in the case study at the end of the previous chapter comprised 13 schedules; a real organisation will probably have many more. Creating a budget uses a great deal of time, effort and money. So it is understandable for the people involved to heave a sigh of relief when the completed budget is accepted by top management. It must be tempting to file it away and get on with some other work. But if the budget is now forgotten about, all the resources that went into it will have been completely wasted!

The creation of the budget means that the plan is now ready to be put into action. This chapter is all about how budgets are **used** to control the activities of organisations, to take them towards their chosen destination.

Having worked through this chapter you should be able to:

- explain the basic theory of budgetary control systems;
- state the common formulae for cost variances and sub-variances;
- flex the budget to the actual level of production;
- calculate cost variances and their sub-variances;
- produce a profit reconciliation statement;
- illustrate the relationships between variances;
- discuss the additional benefits of budgetary control systems;
- manage the operating cost of budgetary control systems;
- comment on the problems of 'responsibility accounting';
- discuss the limitations of budgetary control systems;
- evaluate different management points of view concerning budgeting;
- list 10 points for good budgetary control.

Learning objectives

The budgetary control system

The basic principle of budgetary control systems is very simple and is best thought of as a cyclical four-step process (see Figure 15.1).

Although the budget is an annual statement, it is usually divided into 12 monthly periods. This is because if something starts to go wrong, an attempt to put it right needs to be made as soon as possible to minimise the negative effect. For example, if an underground water pipe cracked in month 2, causing the cost of the metered water supply

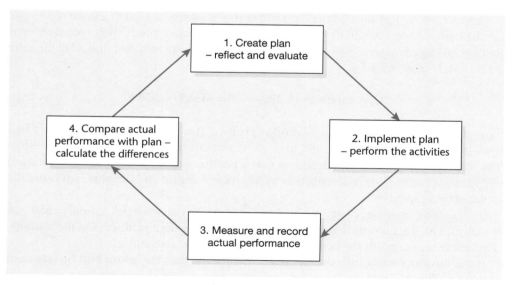

Figure 15.1 **The budgetary control loop**

unexpectedly to treble, a comparison of the actual and planned cost at the end of that month would reveal this and corrective action could be taken quickly. If the comparison was not made until the end of the year, the unnecessary extra cost would be much greater. The comparisons need to be made frequently if effective control is to be exercised.

Variances

Variances are the increases or decreases in profit which occur when things do not go according to plan. Variances are the differences referred to in step 4 of the budgetary control process (see Figure 15.1).

$$\text{Profit} = \text{sales revenue} - \text{total costs}$$

If sales revenue changes, then the profit will change. If total costs change, then profit will change.

A *variance* is a change in *profit* caused by changes in either sales revenue or costs from their budgeted levels.

Variance formulae and raw material variances

For every item of cost, e.g. raw material, the cost variance is calculated by the following formula:

$$\text{Cost variance} = \text{budgeted cost} - \text{actual cost}$$

Suppose the budget showed that 80 kg of material was to be used at a price of £15 per kg: the budgeted cost would be £1,200 (80 × 15). If the actual production record showed that only 65 kg of material had been used and that each kilogram cost only £10, then the actual cost is £650 (65 × 10).

$$\text{Cost variance} = 1,200 - 650 = +£550 = £550 \text{ F}$$

Note that the answer to this calculation is positive, it is **plus** £550. If the formula had been the other way round, it would have given a negative answer (650 − 1,200 = −550). The formulae are carefully designed so that a positive answer means that the variance will increase profit. This is described as a *favourable* variance and the plus sign is usually replaced by a capital 'F'.

In the above example, it was planned to spend £1,200 on material but only £650 was actually spent. This means that actual profit is £550 more than planned. On the assumption that the more profit the better, this result is 'good' or 'favourable'.

If the answer turns out to be negative, this means that the profit will be less than expected. This type of variance is 'bad' or '*adverse*' and the minus sign is usually replaced by a capital 'A'. (Sometimes 'U' for 'unfavourable' is used.)

Sub-variances

It is worth saying at this point that the words 'cost' and 'price' are often used to mean the same thing in colloquial English. However, in variance analysis these words are used in a precise sense to mean two different things. To avoid confusion in the calculation of variances it is a good idea to understand this clearly from the start.

'Price' refers to one item only. 'Cost' refers to the total expenditure for several items. For example, if 10 kilos of flour are bought at a *price* of £2 a kilo, the *cost* of the purchase is £20.

$$\text{Cost} = \text{price} \times \text{quantity}$$

Having got this distinction clear, the cost variance can now be analysed into its two component variances,

$$\text{Cost variance} = \text{price variance} + \text{quantity variance}$$

This enables us to find out how much of the profit change is due to a change in purchase **price** and how much is due to a change in the **quantity** used. This information may enable us to take corrective action to improve the profit or it may identify areas for further investigation.

Price variance

$$\text{Price variance} = (\text{budgeted price} - \text{actual price}) \times \text{actual quantity}$$
$$= (\text{BP} - \text{AP}) \times \text{AQ}$$

In the above example,

$$\text{Price variance} = (15 - 10) \times 65 = +325 = 325 \text{ F}$$

It is conventional always to calculate price variances at actual quantities used. This gives the difference in cost **due to price changes only**. (It is not distorted by any change in quantities used.)

Quantity variance

$$\text{Quantity variance} = (\text{budgeted quantity} - \text{actual quantity}) \times \text{budgeted price}$$
$$= (\text{BQ} - \text{AQ}) \times \text{BP}$$

In the above example,

$$\text{Quantity variance} = (80 - 65) \times 15 = +225 = 225 \text{ F}$$

It is conventional always to calculate quantity variances at budgeted prices. This gives the difference in cost **due to changes in quantity only**. (It is not distorted by any change in price.)

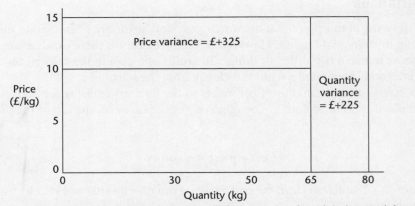

N.B. The budgeted cost is represented by the largest rectangle with its bottom left-hand corner at the origin. The actual cost is represented by the smaller rectangle with its bottom left-hand corner at the origin.

Figure 15.2 **Cost variance analysed into price and quantity elements**

Reconciliation of variances

	Price variance	325 F
Add:	Quantity variance	225 F
	Cost variance	550 F

These relationships are illustrated by Figure 15.2.

Terminology

There are two other types of variable cost: direct labour and variable overheads. They can also be analysed into their constituent price and quantity variances. However, these sub-variances are known by different names, as follows:

	Price variance **(BP – AP) AQ**	**Quantity variance** **(BQ – AQ) BP**
Raw materials	Price variance	Usage variance
Direct labour	Rate variance	Efficiency variance
Variable overheads	Expenditure variance	Efficiency variance

Observe that the same basic formulae are used for each of these cost types. It is possible to calculate all six variances named above if you can remember the two formulae shown at the top of the columns.

Note: In this context, the word 'standard' can be used instead of 'budget'.

So,

$$\text{standard price} = \text{budgeted price}$$

and

$$\text{standard quantity} = \text{budgeted quantity}$$

Try the following question for yourself (answer at the end of the chapter).

Roach Limited planned to use 100 kg of material at £5 per kg for last week's output. Although its production output was exactly as planned, it used 110 kg of material and paid only £4 per kg for it. Calculate the material cost, price and usage variances.

Direct labour variances

The price of labour is the rate at which it is paid, e.g. £9 per hour. The quantity of labour (the number of hours) needed to do a particular job is a measure of the efficiency of the workforce. This is why the sub-variances are known as the *rate variance* and the *efficiency variance*.

Here is an example. SUB Limited estimates that one particular order will need 30 hours of grade A labour, which is paid at the rate of £10 per hour. After the order has been completed, the records show that only 28 hours were taken, but these were paid at £11 per hour due to a new incentive bonus. What are the direct labour rate, efficiency and cost variances?

$$\text{Rate variance} = (\text{BP} - \text{AP}) \times \text{AQ}$$
$$= (\text{budgeted} - \text{actual rate}) \times \text{actual hours}$$
$$= (10 - 11) \times 28$$
$$= -28$$
$$= 28 \text{ A}$$

$$\text{Efficiency variance} = (\text{BQ} - \text{AQ}) \times \text{BP}$$
$$= (\text{budgeted hours} - \text{actual hours}) \times \text{budgeted rate}$$
$$= (30 - 28) \times 10$$
$$= +20$$
$$= 20 \text{ F}$$

$$\text{Cost variance} = \text{budgeted cost} - \text{actual cost}$$
$$= (30 \times 10) - (28 \times 11)$$
$$= 300 - 308$$
$$= -8$$
$$= 8 \text{ A}$$

Try the following question for yourself (answer at the end of the chapter).

Roach Limited has a small finishing department employing two people. The budget showed they were expected to work for a total of 4,000 hours during the year just ended. The standard rate of pay used was £6.50 per hour. The payroll shows they actually worked a total of 4,100 hours and were paid a total of £26,650 to produce the budgeted output. Calculate the direct labour cost, rate and efficiency variances.

Idle time variance

Consider the following situation:

$$\text{Budget} = 100 \text{ direct labour hours @ £5/h} = £500 \text{ cost}$$
$$\text{Actual} = 108 \text{ direct labour hours @ £4/h} = £432 \text{ cost}$$

Variance calculations:

$$
\begin{aligned}
&\textbf{Labour rate} &&= 108(5-4) &&= 108 \text{ F}\\
&\textbf{Labour efficiency} &&= 5(100-108) &&= \underline{(40)} \text{ A}\\
&\textbf{Labour cost variance} &&= 500-432 &&= \underline{\underline{68}} \text{ F}
\end{aligned}
$$

(Note that the £40 labour efficiency variance is shown in brackets as well as being followed by the capital 'A'. These brackets signify that this is a negative number.)

The analysis shows that the workforce were paid less than planned for each hour worked but that the number of hours needed to complete the work was eight more than planned. It indicates that the operatives were inefficient.

But what if the 108 hours included 10 hours that were paid normally but during which no work could be done? Suppose there had been a power cut, preventing operators from using their machines? This 10 hours of idle time means that only 98 hours were actually worked although 108 hours were paid. To get a better analysis of the situation, the variance caused by the idle time needs to be isolated and shown separately.

Amended variance calculations:

$$
\begin{aligned}
&\textbf{Labour rate} &&= 108(5-4) &&= 108 \text{ F}\\
&\textbf{Labour efficiency} &&= 5(100-98) &&= 10 \text{ F}\\
&\textbf{Idle time} &&= 5(98-108) &&= \underline{(50)} \text{ A}\\
&\textbf{Total labour variance} &&&&= \underline{\underline{68}} \text{ F}
\end{aligned}
$$

This more detailed analysis shows that far from being inefficient, the workforce were efficient. They took only 98 hours to complete work estimated to need 100 hours.

Idle time occurs only occasionally, but when it does, it is important for its effects to be separated from the other variances. Otherwise the operatives may be unnecessarily demotivated by being identified as inefficient when they are actually efficient. When idle time occurs, the variance formulae are modified as follows:

$$\textbf{Labour efficiency variance} = (\text{budgeted hours} - \text{actual hours } \textit{worked})$$
$$\times \textbf{budgeted rate}$$
$$\textbf{Idle time variance} \qquad = \text{idle hours} \times \textbf{budgeted rate}$$

Note that the idle time variance is always adverse and that the labour rate variance does not change.

Try the following question for yourself (answer at the end of the chapter).

Roach Limited has a direct labour budget for June's planned output of 2,000 hours at £10 per hour. Early in July it is found that the planned output for June was achieved but 2,100 hours were paid for at £11 per hour. However, no work could be done for 300 of the hours paid due to a failure in the just-in-time stock control system. Calculate the appropriate variances.

Variable overhead variances

Variable overheads are expenses indirectly associated with production activity. Two examples are lubricants for, and maintenance of, the production machinery. The more the machinery is used, the more these items cost. They increase or decrease as activity increases or decreases.

In Chapter 9, we saw that some mechanism is needed to include a 'fair' proportion of these indirect expenses in the product cost. One method often used is to spread these expenses out among products in the same proportion as they use direct labour hours. So, if each product A takes 8 dlh and each product B takes 4 dlh to complete, this means that not only will A have twice the labour cost of B, it will also have twice the variable overhead cost.

Using the example given above of SUB Limited, its variable overhead absorption rate is £3.00 per direct labour hour (dlh). This means that for the particular order involved, it planned to spend £90 (30 dlh × £3.00/dlh) on variable overheads. The order was actually completed in 28 dlh and the actual cost of the variable overheads was £79.80. Calculate the variable overhead cost, expenditure and efficiency variances.

$$\begin{aligned}
\text{Cost variance} &= \text{budgeted cost} - \text{actual cost} \\
&= 90.00 - 79.80 \\
&= +10.20 \\
&= \mathbf{10.20\ F}
\end{aligned}$$

$$\begin{aligned}
\text{Expenditure variance} &= (\text{budgeted absorption rate} - \text{actual absorption rate}) \\
&\quad \times \text{actual dlh} \\
&= (\text{budgeted abs. rate} \times \text{actual dlh}) \\
&\quad - (\text{actual abs. rate} \times \text{actual dlh}) \\
&= (£3.00 \times 28) - (£79.80) \\
&= 84.00 - 79.80 \\
&= +4.20 \\
&= \mathbf{4.20\ F}
\end{aligned}$$

$$\begin{aligned}
\text{Efficiency variance} &= (\text{BQ} - \text{AQ}) \times \text{BP} \\
&= (\text{budgeted dlh} - \text{actual dlh}) \times \text{budgeted absorption rate} \\
&= (30 - 28) \times 3.00 \\
&= +6.00 \\
&= \mathbf{6.00\ F}
\end{aligned}$$

Note that the combination of the expenditure and efficiency variances should give the cost variance.

Self-assessment question S15.4

Try the following question for yourself (answer at the end of the chapter).

Building on the example of Roach Limited in S15.1–3 above, it was planned to spend £4,400 on variable overheads giving a budgeted absorption rate of £1.10/dlh. At the end of the year it was found that the actual amount spent on variable overheads was £4,592. Calculate the variable overhead cost, expenditure and efficiency variances.

Fixed overhead variances

Fixed overheads are those indirect expenses which do **not** vary with output. In this book it is assumed that the organisations looked at operate a variable costing system as opposed to an absorption costing system. (In absorption systems, the analysis of fixed overhead variances is much more complex. This complexity tends to detract from the understanding of budgetary control systems as a whole. Therefore, fixed overhead variances in absorption costing systems will not be covered here. They are not essential for future managers unless you intend to specialise in accountancy.)

We will use a single cost variance (called 'expenditure') for fixed overheads as follows:

$$\text{Fixed overhead expenditure variance} = \text{budgeted fixed overhead} - \text{actual fixed overhead}$$

For example,	Budgeted fixed overhead	= £300,000
Less:	Actual fixed overhead	= £321,000
	Fixed overhead expenditure variance =	£(21,000) A

Self-assessment question S15.5

Try the following question for yourself (answer at the end of the chapter).

Roach Limited expects its total annual expenditure on fixed overheads to be £180,000 and decides to spread this evenly over its 12 accounting periods. If the amount actually spent on fixed overheads in month 8 is £16,100, what is the fixed overhead expenditure variance for that month?

The importance of the flexed budget

Suppose you were the manager responsible for a large production facility. For the year just ended, your budget for raw material costs was £9 million but your actual expenditure was only £8 million. Do you deserve a bonus?

It appears you have made a saving of £1 million, but this may not be so. There is not enough information to provide a clear answer. The £9 million budget was to achieve a certain level of production. If that level was achieved, then a bonus is probably deserved. But what if the production output was only half of what was planned? This means that only £4.5 million **should** have been spent on materials, not the £8 million actually spent! In this case, a bonus seems rather inappropriate.

To get meaningful answers when calculating the variances for the variable costs (materials, labour and variable overheads) the actual amounts must be compared to a budget which has been revised to the actual level of output. This revised budget is called the *flexed budget*; it is created **after** the actual figures are known. The effect of using the flexed budget instead of the original budget is that the variances will now show the differences between the actual costs and what those costs **should have been** for the output actually achieved. This is useful information. Variable cost variances based on the original budget will almost certainly be misleading.

Example

An illustration with raw materials (manufacturing wheels from raw plastic):

Original budget:	**10,000 wheels using 5 kg of plastic each @ £2.00/kg**
	Cost = 10,000 × 5 × 2 = £100,000
Actual expenditure:	**Total cost of plastic used in period was £74,880.**
	Thus, saving on budget £25,120

Is the production manager to be congratulated on this favourable variance? Yes – congratulations are in order **if** 10,000 wheels were actually produced.

But what if only 6,000 wheels were actually produced (each using 5.2 kg @ £2.40/kg = £74,880 cost)?

Flex the budget to the actual level of activity:

Flexed budget: 6,000 wheels using 5 kg plastic @ £2.00 = £60,000 cost
Material price variance = (2.0 − 2.4) × 31,200 = (12,480) A
Material usage variance = (30,000 − 31,200) × 2 = (2,400) A
Actual cost of materials = £74,880

Congratulations are not appropriate in this case.

As you can see from this example, flexed budgets use the same standard amounts as the original budget (1 wheel uses 5 kg of plastic costing £2/kg). The only thing that changes is the level of output or production volume. More often than not, the actual output differs from that planned. **When calculating variances, the first step is to create the flexed budget**.

This does not mean to say that the difference between the original and flexed budget is ignored. This difference is accounted for elsewhere by the sales volume variance (see below).

Try the following question for yourself (answer at the end of the chapter).

During week 32, Maykit Limited planned to produce 50 plastic boxes using 2 hours of direct labour for each box, paid at the standard rate of £10 per hour, giving a budgeted cost of £1,000. At the end of that week, it was found that 55 boxes had been produced, using 105 hours of labour paid at £10 per hour and costing £1,050. As there is no labour rate variance and the labour cost for the week was £50 greater than planned, is it accurate to say that the labour force must be working inefficiently?

Sales variances

As sales are concerned with income rather than cost, the sales price variance will differ from cost variances in the following way. If the actual sales price achieved is greater than the budgeted price then the profit will increase, giving a **favourable** variance. So the prices inside the brackets will be the opposite way round (**actual** – **budget**).

Sales price variance

Sales price variance = (actual price – budget price) × actual quantity

For example, Sales budget = 20,000 items @ £10; actual = 20,000 items @ £11
Sales price variance = (11 – 10) × 20,000 = 20,000 F

Sales volume variance

Sales volume variance = flexed budget profit – original budget profit

This is consistent with the only difference between the original and flexed budgets being the level of activity. The number of items produced is assumed to be the same as the number of items sold and the situation one of making to order and not for stock.

Try the following question for yourself (answer at the end of the chapter).

The following data refers to Pike Limited for the month of May. The original budget showed 400 items sold at £25 each, resulting in a profit of £2,000. The actual performance was 300 items sold at £26 each, resulting in a profit of £1,663. When the budget was flexed, it gave a revised profit of £1,650. Calculate the sales price variance and the sales volume variance.

The profit reconciliation statement

When the variance analysis exercise is complete, the original budget should be reconciled to the actual results to summarise the findings of the investigation. As the flexed budget is an important part of the analysis, it should be included in the reconciliation. An example of a profit reconciliation statement is shown below.

Pike Limited: profit reconciliation statement

		£	£
Original budget profit			**2,000**
Sales volume variance			(350) A
Flexed budget profit			**1,650**
Sales price variance			300 F
Material variances:	Usage	(140) A	
	Price	20 F	
	Cost		(120) A
Labour variances:	Efficiency	75 F	
	Rate	(25) A	
	Cost		50 F
Variable overhead variance:	Efficiency	56 F	
	Expenditure	(24) A	
	Cost		32 F
Fixed overhead expenditure variance			(249) A
Actual profit			**1,663**

Note that the adverse variances are shown in brackets. This is not compulsory but the author has found that it helps students to arrive at the correct answers, especially during exams. The capital 'A' or 'F' is compulsory.

Try the following question for yourself (answer at the end of the chapter).

Self-assessment question S15.8

From the following information (all figures in £000) produce a profit reconciliation statement. Fixed overheads cost 24 less than expected; variable overhead expenditure variance = 5 F and variable overhead efficiency variance = 1 A; labour variances are rate = 14 F and efficiency = 2 A; sales price variance = 18 A; material variances are usage = 39 F and price = 27 A; original budget profit = 400 and flexed budget profit = 431; there is also an idle time variance of 12.

Variance relationships

Figures 15.3 and 15.4 illustrate the interrelationships of variances.

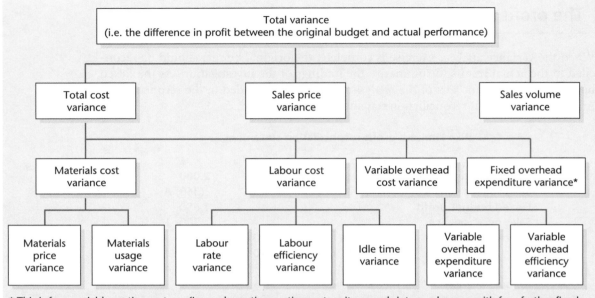

* This is for a variable costing system. (In an absorption costing system it expands into a subgroup with four further fixed overhead subvariances.)

Figure 15.3 **Variance family tree**

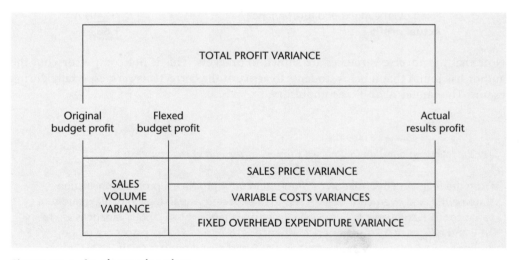

Figure 15.4 **An alternative view**

Additional benefits of the budgetary control system

As well as appropriately recording and evaluating performance, budgetary control systems have the following positive effects:

1 They **communicate** organisational aspirations. The annual organisational plan is distributed to budget holders who are then aware of what is expected of them.

2 They **co-ordinate** complex activities. For example, if there is no opening stock of finished goods and the company plans to sell 200,000 items next year, it must budget to produce at least 200,000 items.

3 They **authorise** budget holders. For example, if the purchasing budget shows that £1 million of materials are to be bought every month, the purchasing manager does not have to seek permission to spend this amount. The purchasing budget itself authorises this spending.

4 They **motivate** budget holders. Budgets can also be used as targets. The performance levels (known as *standards*) in a budget are often set **high but attainable** in order to encourage improvement.

Managing the cost of the system

The process of variance investigation is time consuming and has a cost of its own. Organisations need to control this activity. The usual approach is that of 'management by exception'. If operations are going more or less as planned and the variances are small, no follow-up activity takes place. However, where the variances are significant, they are investigated. But how do you know if a variance is significant or not?

This decision is inherently subjective and may vary from business to business. Someone has to decide **in advance** what the significance levels of their organisation are going to be. A percentage difference between budget and actual is determined in advance, subject to a minimum amount. For example, a given company may investigate all variances that are at least 5% different from budget provided they are at least £250 in amount. This approach is both relative and absolute. But another company may have a policy of 10% difference with a threshold of £10,000.

Responsibility accounting

Budgetary control works through people. Functional budgets are delegated to the lowest practical level, where an appropriate person is made the 'budget responsible manager'. For this to work effectively, the lines of authority must be clearly defined. This can be a problem, especially in those organisations operating a matrix approach to their management structure. Where two people are responsible for an item of income or cost, there is always room for dispute as to who should take the credit or accept the blame.

Responsibility accounting usually supports the payment of rewards, such as cash bonuses, to budget responsible officers for meeting their targets. The theory is that the company will benefit from their increased motivation and a 'win–win' situation will occur. For this to happen, the accounting mechanisms must be structured in the same way as the responsibilities. For example, if the regional sales managers are responsible for the value of sales in their areas, the budgets and reporting mechanisms must be analysed over these areas. A single set of aggregated figures for the whole country would not allow the individual responsibilities to be defined or monitored.

This allows companies to achieve their goals through 'management by objective' (MBO) as well as 'management by exception' (MBE). A good example of the latter is the investigation of variances only when they are significant. If actual performance is not very different to budget, things are considered to be going to plan, i.e. no exceptions have occurred.

Another aspect of responsibility accounting is that of **uncontrollable** costs. Not all costs are completely within the control of management. For example, the business rates for the factory may be one item on the production manager's budget. If the cost of these rates is completely outside that person's control, he or she is likely to be demotivated when held responsible for an adverse variance. To avoid this, either the situation should be made very clear in the variance analysis reports or the uncontrollable items should be extracted and isolated in a budget of their own. Unfortunately, problems still arise from some costs that are **partially** controllable. For instance, the cost of running the computerised management information system may be partly based on the manager's ability to retain experienced staff (temporary IT staff are expensive). But it is also based on the rates of pay in the marketplace. The manager may be responsible for the first but not for the second. In this case, it would be up to that manager to justify any adverse variances arising, if he or she can.

Limitations of the budgetary control process

For many, many years, most organisations have operated a budgetary control system. This management accounting technique has been enormously successful. Yet, during the last few years there have been signs of firms moving away from traditional budgeting. IKEA (furniture), Asea Brown Boveri (engineering), Svenska Handelbanken (banking) and Borealis (petrochemicals), all huge multinational organisations based in Europe, are examples of this trend. They believe that there is more to measuring and controlling business performance than can expressed by a traditional budget. The main influence on their thinking is the accelerating rate of change in the business environment. Many organisations are finding that their environment is not only constantly changing but changing faster and faster as time moves on.

Budgets tend to reinforce the 'old' way of doing things. Budget managers have many other responsibilities pressing on them when the budget creation deadline is imminent. To reflect changing circumstances changes may need to be made concerning which data is shown. Consequently, the layout of the form would need to be changed, but this would have to be approved at a high level, which would take considerable time and effort. The normal 'efficient' approach to this situation is to use the same form as last year, meet the deadline and get on with the next task. Over the years, the budget format becomes more and more divorced from reality and less effective in improving performance.

Having said this, budgets are still very effective and necessary instruments of control for the vast majority of organisations. If budgets were removed without something better being put in their place, the organisation would almost certainly start to deteriorate.

The manager's point of view

As discussed in the previous chapter, the first major objective of budgeting is to complete a detailed review of the business, and set up a budget framework which ensures that the company is progressing down its designated strategic path. The second objective is to monitor performance against that budget, but with the minimum amount of time and effort.

The main advantage of a detailed budget is that it provides a sound basis for management by exception. Once the budget is agreed, all departmental managers know exactly what is expected of them, in terms of the level of sales to be achieved, or the amount of cost they can incur. Subject to the normal safeguards, they are authorised to spend the amount budgeted in furtherance of their departmental objectives. Moreover, the managing director knows that he or she has nothing to worry about, providing managers are performing within the budgeted parameters. The MD simply reviews the numbers for any significant variances, and then gets on with the job of running the business.

The key to effective management by exception is the IT system. Information must be presented in such a way as to minimise any further analysis work. My company, for instance, used a simple but effective system for monitoring sales. This showed orders due out this month, by volume, sales value and marginal income (contribution), set against the budget for the month. Initially, it summarised these items for the whole company, but there was a feature which allowed the user to 'drill down' through the layers of product group and product line, to individual customer/product level. It took a matter of moments, therefore, on arriving at the office each morning, for me to update myself in detail on the progress of this month's sales. I knew exactly which customers and which products had so far failed to meet expectations. I was so familiar with our performance at all times that the monthly management accounts served merely to confirm what I already knew. Not only did this allow me to spend my time more productively, but also it gave me a detailed knowledge of our current situation from which to answer the regular stream of questions from our head office in the USA.

We had a similar 'drill down' system with which to interrogate previous months' results. By the simple expedient of ranking sales on the basis of variance from budget, an analysis of the causes of shortfalls and overachievements was the work of a few minutes. By presenting the information in the right format, all the traditional, painstaking sales analysis work was completely eliminated. It should be borne in mind that users at different levels in the company, e.g. managing director, sales manager or sales executive, may need the information in a different format, so a cleverly designed system should address the needs of all.

Analysis of manufacturing variances is another case in point. As we have seen above, each production batch will generate at least six variances. In any given month, the factory will produce hundreds of batches, so an enormous amount of variance information is produced. Each batch's variances will tell a slightly different story. In chemical manufacturing, no two batches are ever the same. The raw materials may have slight differences in specification, the chemical reactions might not work in precisely the same way, and even atmospheric temperatures and humidity might play their part. As a result, processes may need a further input of materials, or perhaps more reaction time or a longer cooling period. Each divergence from the standard generates manufacturing variances. How much time should be spent analysing it all? Whilst a manufacturing process is at the development stage, the production staff will clearly wish to examine all the information in detail, looking for clues which will help them to improve the efficiency of the processing. Once the process has stabilised, however, the production staff will, for the most part, ignore small variations on batches, and look for regular trends which indicate that a process change is required. They will only look at individual batches where there is either a significant variance or a complete batch failure.

Standards may sometimes be set as targets, in order to encourage greater efficiency in the factory. This can be a two-edged sword. The standards are incorporated in the product costs, so if they are drawn too tightly (showing low costs), there is a risk that the salespeople might be misled into thinking that they can reduce their selling prices. Production's failure to achieve the standards will emerge as adverse manufacturing variances on the profit and loss account, but will be seen as a local production problem, rather than an issue for the whole of the company. Conversely, if the standards are drawn too slackly (showing high costs), production will have a nice, comfortable time. However, the resultant higher costs might discourage salespeople from quoting more competitive prices and generating more business. In my view, standards should always be set at expected performance and not at 'target' levels. However, if there is still a requirement for a target, production can always be asked to produce at a specified level which will result in favourable variances. If they achieve this consistently, it can then be transferred into the product costs, and everyone is happy.

As in many areas of management accounting, the secret of success is to keep it simple but effective. When setting up new systems, there is a natural tendency to overelaborate. One wants to feel that a thorough and professional job has been done, and perhaps too little thought is directed at the practical aspects of managing the system when it is up and running. I have already described some of the benefits and pitfalls of the activity-based costing system, which my US head office decided to install throughout the organisation (see Chapter 10, on activity-based costing). One of the more complex aspects of this system was variance reporting. Normal standard costing principles were used, so the normal manufacturing variances described earlier in this chapter were generated. However, to make the product costs more accurate, and therefore of greater value to the salesforce, the standards were changed every three months. Actual performance was then monitored against the new standards, but as the original standards were still the basis of the budget, we had another set of variances capturing the difference between the original and revised standards. Somehow, for every batch produced, the number of variances had grown to 16! The monthly variance printout was three-quarters of an inch thick. We were swamped with information and, as a result, gave less attention to this area than we might otherwise have done.

A similar example of overkill occurred with our performance-monitoring reporting. We had developed a simple graphical representation of eight key measurements which we felt reflected our overall performance as a company on a monthly basis. These included the percentage of batches achieving specification without rework, the percentage of orders despatched on time, and the number of customer complaints received. By combining these eight measurements, we arrived at a single company performance indicator. It was crude, perhaps, but effective, as it helped to focus the minds of employees throughout the company on the need for high-quality performance. Our head office was quite taken with this concept, and decided to adopt it throughout the organisation. However, head office increased the number of measurements to 30, some of which were rather dubious as performance monitors. Purchase price variance was one example. Does a favourable PPV reflect a good performance by the purchasing department? Not necessarily. If the market price was coming down, perhaps the variance should have been twice the size. Conversely, a 10% adverse variance could be a fine performance if the market price had actually gone up by 20%. So the selection of performance monitors should be done with a great deal of care. Nevertheless, we duly submitted our data (a time-consuming exercise in itself), and the worldwide results were published in a vast monthly tome. This contained so much information, much of it flawed or inconsistent, that no one ever bothered to look at it, and the motivational impact was completely lost.

A really good information system, whether it is performance monitoring or budgetary control, will tell the users exactly what they need to know, nothing more, nothing less. And it will do so with the minimal amount of input from the users. Experience will help in deciding the right level, although even experienced managers can fall into the trap of immersing themselves in excessive amounts of data. It is one of the features of this technological age that there is more information available than the human mind can reasonably assimilate, and one of the most important business skills is the ability to specify exactly the information you want and the format in which you want it. Another significant business skill is obtaining the necessary programming time in the IT department, but that is another story!

Summary

- The budgetary control process is a continuous closed-loop system.
- It consists of planning, recording, comparing, evaluating and acting.
- The differences between budget and actual are known as variances.
- Cost variances can be analysed into their constituent price and quantity variances.
- The budget should be flexed before the cost variances are calculated.
- Sales volume variance is the difference in the original and flexed budget profits.
- Profit reconciliation statements give a complete summary of the variance analysis.
- Spin-offs include communication, co-ordination, authorisation and motivation.
- System operating costs are controlled by a 'management by exception' approach.
- Budget holders can be demotivated if held responsible for non-controllable costs.
- Budgetary control systems do not measure the effect of missed opportunities.
- A few large successful organisations claim to have recently abandoned budgeting.
- The vast majority of organisations still operate budgetary control systems.

Ten points for good budgetary control

1 Areas of responsibility are clearly defined.

2 Budgets are held at the lowest practical management level.

3 Non-controllable items are clearly identified.

4 Reporting system is routine/automatic.

5 Reporting periods are short.

6 Reports are produced soon after the period end.

7 Variance significance levels are pre-established.

8 Significant variances are always investigated.

9 Corrective action is taken where possible.

10 Senior management exemplify the importance of the budgetary control system.

Further reading

Atkinson, A., Banker, R., Kaplan, R. and Young, S. (2001) *Management Accounting*, 3rd edition, Prentice Hall, Harlow. See Chapter 11, 'Using budgets to achieve organisational objectives'.

Budding, G. T. (2004) 'Accountability, environmental uncertainty and government performance: evidence from Dutch municipalities', *Management Accounting Research*, Vol. 15, Issue 3, September.

'FA kicks off new budget control system' (2004) *Computer Weekly*, 30 November.

Horngren, C., Bhimani, A., Datar, S. and Foster, G. (2002) *Management and Cost Accounting*, 2nd edition, Prentice Hall Europe, Harlow. See chapters on 'Flexible budgets, variances and management control 1 & 2'.

Merchant, K. A. (1998) *Modern Management Control Systems: Text and Cases*, Prentice Hall, Englewood Cliffs, NJ.

Otley, D. (1987) *Accounting Control and Organisational Behaviour*, Heinemann Professional Publishing, Oxford. See Chapters 5 and 9, 'Performance appraisal' and 'Accounting for effective control'. (Other chapters concentrate on the 'human' aspects of budgetary control.)

Player, S. (2003) 'Beyond the budget games', *Intelligent Enterprise*, Vol. 6, Issue 16, 10 October Supplement.

Upchurch, A. (2003) *Management Accounting, Principles and Practice*, 2nd edition, Financial Times/Prentice Hall, Harlow. See chapters 'Budgetary control' and 'Analysis of variances'.

Weetman, P. (2002) *Management Accounting, an Introduction*, 3rd edition, Financial Times/Prentice Hall, Harlow. See chapters 'Standard costs' and 'Performance evaluation and feedback reporting'.

Answers to self-assessment questions

S15.1

Budget: 100 kg @ £5/kg = £500 cost
Actual: 110 kg @ £4/kg = £440 cost

Price variance $= (BP - AP) \times AQ$
$$= (5 - 4) \times 110 = \mathbf{110\ F}$$

Usage variance $= (BQ - AQ) \times BP$
$$= (100 - 110) \times 5 = \mathbf{(50)\ A}$$

Cost variance = budget cost − actual cost
$$= 500 - 440 = \mathbf{60\ F}$$

Note: The combined price and usage variances should equal the cost variance.

S15.2

Rate variance = (budgeted rate − actual rate) × actual hours
$$= (BR \times AH) - (AR \times AH)$$
$$= (6.50 \times 4,100) - 26,650$$
$$= 26,650 - 26,650$$
$$= \mathbf{zero}\ (\text{The actual rate paid must also} = £6.50/\text{hour.})$$

Efficiency variance = (budgeted hours − actual hours) × budgeted rate
$$= (4,000 - 4,100) \times 6.50$$
$$= (-100) \times 6.50$$
$$= -650$$
$$= \mathbf{650\ A}$$

Cost variance = budgeted cost − actual cost
$$= (4,000 \times 6.50) - 26,650$$
$$= 26,000 - 26,650$$
$$= -650$$
$$= \mathbf{650\ A}$$

Note: As the rate does not vary, the efficiency variance should equal the cost variance.

S15.3

Rate variance = (budgeted rate − actual rate) × actual hours paid
$$= (10 - 11) \times 2,100$$
$$= -2,100$$
$$= \mathbf{2,100\ A}$$

Efficiency variance = (budgeted hours − actual hours worked) × budgeted rate

$$= (2,000 - 1,800) \times 10$$
$$= +2,000$$
$$= 2,000 \text{ F}$$

Idle time variance = idle hours × budgeted rate

$$= 300 \times 10$$
$$= -3,000$$
$$= 3,000 \text{ A}$$

Labour cost variance = budgeted cost − actual cost

$$= (2,000 \times 10) - (2,100 \times 11)$$
$$= 20,000 - 23,100$$
$$= -3,100$$
$$= 3,100 \text{ A}$$

S15.4

Cost variance = budgeted cost − actual cost

$$= 4,400 - 4,592$$
$$= -192$$
$$= 192 \text{ A}$$

Expenditure variance = (budgeted absorption rate − actual absorption rate) × actual dlh

$$= (\text{Budgeted abs. rate} \times \text{actual dlh}) - (\text{actual abs. rate} \times \text{actual dlh})$$
$$= (1.10 \times 4,100) - (4,592)$$
$$= 4,510 - 4,592$$
$$= -82$$
$$= 82 \text{ A}$$

Efficiency variance = (BQ − AQ) × BP

$$= (\text{budgeted dlh} - \text{actual dlh}) \times \text{budgeted absorption rate}$$
$$= (4,000 - 4,100) \times 1.10$$
$$= -110$$
$$= 110 \text{ A}$$

Note: The combination of the expenditure and efficiency variances should give the cost variance.

S15.5

Fixed overhead monthly budget = 180,000/12 = 15,000
Less: Actual expenditure in month 8 = 16,100
Fixed overhead expenditure variance = −1,100
= 1,100 A

S15.6

As the actual output is different to that planned in the original budget, the first step is to **flex the budget** to the activity level of 110 items.
    Flexed budget (activity level = 55 items):

Cost = 55 units × 2 hours/unit × £10/hour = £1,100

Labour cost variance = budgeted cost − actual cost
= 1,100 − 1,050
= +50
= 50 F

Labour efficiency variance = (budgeted hours − actual hours) × budgeted rate
= (110 − 105) × 10
= +50
= 50 F

Labour rate variance = (budgeted rate − actual rate) × actual hours
= (10 − 10) × 105
= 0

These results show that the workforce are working **efficiently**; the statement made in the question is not accurate.

S15.7

Sales price variance = (actual price − budgeted price) × actual quantity sold
= (26 − 25) × 300
= +300
= 300 F

Sales volume variance = flexed budget profit − original budget profit
= 1,650 − 2,000
= −350
= 350 A

S15.8

Profit reconciliation statement

		£000	£000
Original budget profit			400
Sales volume variance			31 F
Flexed budget profit			431
Sales price variance			(18) A
Material variances:	Usage	39 F	
	Price	(27) A	
	Cost		12 F
Labour variances:	Efficiency	(2) A	
	Idle time	(12) A	
	Rate	14 F	
	Cost		0
Variable overhead variance:	Efficiency	(1) A	
	Expenditure	5 F	
	Cost		4 F
Fixed overhead expenditure variance			24 F
Actual profit			453

Anomira Ltd is a wholly owned subsidiary of an industrial conglomerate. It produces one standard size of sealing compound used in the motor vehicle industry. As the new management accountant of this company, you have been asked to explain why the actual results differed from the budget for the year just ended. You ascertain the following information.

The budget was for a volume of 100,000 units produced and sold, each using 2 kg of material at £3.00 per kg. The total of variable overheads was expected to be £100,000 and the fixed overheads £250,000. Total sales revenue was planned to be £1,500,000 and the 50,000 direct labour hours planned were expected to cost £250,000. The variable overhead absorption rate is £2.00 per direct labour hour.

The actual performance for last year showed production of 90,000 units and no change in stock levels over the year. Sales revenue was £1,440,000 and 196,000 kg of material was used, costing £529,200. Variable overheads were £94,500 and fixed overheads £255,000. The total cost of direct labour was £232,750 for 49,000 hours. However, 1,000 of these hours were completely non-productive due to a breakdown of the heating system during exceptionally bad winter weather causing the factory to be temporarily closed.

Tasks:

1 Perform a variance analysis (in as much detail as the information will allow) reconciling the actual profit to the budgeted profit.

(40 marks)

2 **On one side of A4 paper**, suggest possible explanations for any **significant** variances you have found.

(20 marks)

3 **On no more than two sides of A4 paper**, discuss budgetary control and responsibility accounting in organisations. Include comments on any dangers/limitations inherent in this technique.

(40 marks)
(Total 100 marks)

Questions

An asterisk * on a question number indicates that the answer is given at the end of the book. Answers to the other questions are given in the Lecturer's Guide.

Q15.1* Welco Ltd

Welco Ltd manufactures one type of hydraulic jack. The labour force, who are all paid at the same rate, assemble and finish two bought-in components. Each jack uses two metal castings and one rubber seal. The jacks are very popular and Welco sells all it can make. It budgets to make a profit of £4,400 each month.

The budget is as follows:

	Standard (1 item)		Budget (1,100 items)
		£	£
Rubber seals	(1 @ £2)	2	2,200
Metal castings	(2 @ £3)	6	6,600
Direct labour	(10 minutes)	1	1,100
Fixed overhead		7	7,700
		16	17,600
Sales revenue		20	22,000
Profit		4	4,400

The £7 fixed overhead consists of production, marketing and administration overheads. It is based on production and sales of 1,100 jacks (the budgeted activity level for each month).

Last month, the actual results were as follows:

Number of jacks made and sold	1,050
	£
Rubber seals (1,060 @ £1.95)	2,067
Metal castings (2,108 @ £3.25)	6,851
Direct labour (190 hours @ £5.90)	1,121
Fixed overhead incurred	7,600
	17,639
Sales revenue (1,050 @ £19)	19,950
Actual profit	2,311

Tasks:

1 Flex the budget to the actual level of activity.
2 Analyse the variances in as much detail as the figures will allow.
3 Create a profit reconciliation statement.

Q15.2* Stanley & Co.

Stanley & Co. manufactures door frames from a bought-in wooden moulding. The budget for one door frame has costs of £20 for materials and £6 for labour. Each frame has a standard usage of 5 metres of wooden moulding at a standard cost of £4.00 per metre. Each frame has a standard time of 0.50 hours and the standard rate of pay is £12.00 per hour.

The budget for April was for 2,200 frames with a material cost of £44,000 and a labour cost of £13,200.

However, 2,100 frames were actually produced in April, taking 1,000 hours to make at a total labour cost of £13,000. Also, 11,550 metres of wooden moulding were used at a total cost of £43,890.

Tasks:

1 Calculate the cost, quantity and price variances for materials and labour in April.
2 Suggest possible reasons for these variances.
3 If 50 of the 1,000 hours paid were during a power cut which prevented work continuing, what changes would you make to your answers to parts 1 and 2?

Q15.3* Ivanblast computer game

Bigcheque Ltd has created a new computer game called Ivanblast. It knows it will only have a five-week period from launch in order to market this successfully before pirating will reduce its sales to virtually zero. The budget for this period is

				£
Sales:	25,000 games	@ £50	=	1,250,000
Production materials:	25,000 blank CDs	@ £1.10	=	27,500
Variable overheads:	25,000 games	@ £0.50	=	12,500
Fixed overheads:			=	800,000
Net profit			=	410,000

(Note that, like many firms with highly automated production facilities, Bigcheque Ltd considers its production labour to be all fixed in nature. So, **all** labour costs are included in the fixed overheads.)

The actual results for the five-week period are shown below (no stocks of raw materials or finished computer games were left over at the end of the period).

				£
Sales:	30,000 games	@ £45	=	1,350,000
Production materials:	30,250 blank CDs	@ £1.00	=	30,250
Variable overheads:			=	15,000
Fixed overheads:			=	850,000
Net profit			=	454,750

Tasks:

1 Prepare a variance analysis for the period in as much detail as the figures allow.
2 Produce a statement reconciling the budgeted profit with the actual profit.
3 Comment on your findings.

Q15.4 Fripp Ltd

Variable costs	Standard costs (1 item)	Original budget (10,000 items)	Actual results (11,000 items)
		£	
Material A	5 kg @ £2.00/kg	100,000	66,000 kg @ £1.50/kg
Material B	10 kg @ £4.00/kg	400,000	99,000 kg @ £5.00/kg
Labour	2 hours @ £15.00/h	300,000	20,900 hours @ £16.00/h
Variable overhead	2 hours @ £3.00/h	60,000	20,900 hours @ £3.00/h

Task:

Calculate the variable cost variances of the above in as much detail as possible.

Q15.5 Elbo Ltd

Elbo Ltd makes roof tiles. It has two production departments: moulding and packing. It makes two different sizes of tile, the Handi and the Jiant. The following table shows the standard costs of labour per pallet of tiles (one pallet contains 144 tiles):

Department	Labour type	Standard hourly rate	Standard production hours per pallet	
		£	Handi	Jiant
Moulding	A	5.00	4	6
Moulding	C	4.00	5	8
Packing	A	5.00	1	2
Packing	B	4.50	2	3

During October, 400 pallets of Handis and 150 pallets of Jiants were actually produced and the following labour hours and costs were incurred:

Labour type	Moulding department		Packing department	
	Actual hours worked	Actual pay (£)	Actual hours worked	Actual pay (£)
A	2,600	12,480	695	3,336
B	–	–	1,250	5,875
C	3,180	12,720	–	–
Totals	5,780	25,200	1,945	9,211

Tasks:

For the month of October:

1 Create the labour budget (hours and £) for (a) Handis and (b) Jiants.
2 Calculate the budgeted direct labour cost of one pallet of Handis and one pallet of Jiants.
3 Calculate the budgeted total labour cost of each department and of the whole factory.

4 Calculate the direct labour cost variance for each department and for the factory.
5 For each department and labour type, analyse the cost variances into their rate and
   efficiency variances.
6 Comment on your findings.

Q15.6 JK plc

JK plc operates a chain of fast-food restaurants. The company uses a standard marginal
costing system to monitor the costs incurred in its outlets. The standard cost of one of
its most popular meals is as follows:

		£ per meal
Ingredients	(1.08 units)	1.18
Labour	(1.5 minutes)	0.15
Variable conversion costs	(1.5 minutes)	0.06
The standard price of this meal is		1.99

In one of its outlets, which has budgeted sales and production activity level of 50,000
such meals, the number of such meals that were produced and sold during April 2003
was 49,700. The actual cost data was as follows:

		£
Ingredients	(55,000 units)	58,450
Labour	(1,200 hours)	6,800
Variable conversion costs	(1,200 hours)	3,250
The actual revenue from the sale of the meals was		96,480

Required:

(a) Calculate
   (i) the total budgeted contribution for April 2003;
   (ii) the total actual contribution for April 2003.

(3 marks)

(b) Present a statement that reconciles the budgeted and actual contribution for April
   2003. Show all variances to the nearest £1 and in as much detail as possible.

(17 marks)

(c) Explain why a marginal costing approach to variance analysis is more appropriate in
   environments such as that of JK plc, where there are a number of different items
   being produced and sold.

(5 marks)
(Total = 25 marks)

CIMA Intermediate: Management Accounting – Performance Management, May 2003

Q15.7 TBS

TBS produces two products in a single factory. The following details have been extracted
from the standard marginal cost cards of the two products:

Product	S3 £/unit	S5 £/unit
Selling price	100	135
Variable costs:		
Material X (£3 per kg)	30	39
Liquid Z (£4.50 per litre)	27	45
Direct labour (£6 per hour)	18	24
Overheads	12	16

TBS uses a standard marginal costing system linked with budgets.

Budgeted data for the month of October included:

	S3	S5
Sales (units)	10,000	10,000
Production (units)	12,000	13,500
Fixed costs:		
Production		£51,000
Administration		£34,000

Actual data for the month of October was as follows:

	S3	S5
Sales (units)	12,200	8,350
Production (units)	13,000	9,400
Selling prices per unit	£96	£145
Variable costs:		
Material X	270,000 kgs costing	£786,400
Liquid Z	150,000 litres costing	£763,200
Direct labour	73,200 hours costing	£508,350
Overheads		£347,000
Fixed costs:		
Production		£47,550
Administration		£36,870

Required:

a) Calculate the budgeted profit/loss for October.

(2 marks)

b) Calculate the actual profit/loss for October.

(3 marks)

c) As a management accountant in TBS you will be attending the monthly management team meeting. In preparation for that meeting you are required to:

(i) Prepare a statement that reconciles the budgeted and actual profit/loss for October, showing the variances in as much detail as is possible from the data provided.

(15 marks)

(ii) State, and then briefly explain, the main issues in your profit reconciliation statement.

(5 marks)

(Total = 25 marks)

CIMA Intermediate: Management Accounting – Performance Management, November 2004

STRATEGY IMPLEMENTATION AND PERFORMANCE MANAGEMENT

Part 6

Part 6 comprises:

The discipline of management accounting is approximately 100 years old. Not surprisingly, it has changed and developed over its lifetime. It is currently going through its strategic management accounting phase. Managers are realising that management accounting techniques can be adapted to become agents for change. They can act as media through which organisations can achieve their objectives. New developments such as the 'balanced scorecard' (including non-financial performance indicators) and 'enterprise-wide systems' (integrating activity-based costing, activity-based accounting, activity-based budgeting and activity-based management) are modern strategic tools to tackle the managerial problems of the twenty-first century. Managerial accounting is no longer confined to the roles of costing, control and decision making. It is now part of the corporate strategy process.

But this is not the only change currently under way. Not-for-profit organisations, especially in the public sector, are adopting more and more management accounting techniques. There has been a significant increase in the degree of accountability to which they are subject. The many privatisations that occurred in the 1980s and 1990s encouraged these organisations to improve their accounting control systems and demonstrate management proficiency. Value for money has become a central tenet of public sector bodies and local authorities are now compelled to obtain several tenders before awarding contracts. A further manifestation of this change was the introduction of internal markets into the National Health Service. Thus, the rate of change is at least as fast in not-for-profit organisations as it is in commercial ones. For this reason, a chapter has been devoted to them to make explicit the additional degrees of social accountability to which they are exposed.

The book concludes with a discussion of issues currently being debated. Is budgeting being superseded by the balanced scorecard? Is activity-based costing really worth implementing and will it replace absorption costing? Is strategic management accounting appropriate for the public sector? At the time of writing, these are the 'hot' issues. Readers are invited to make up their own minds.

Strategic management accounting and performance indicators

Chapter contents

Introduction

In the previous chapters we have looked chiefly at product costing, decision making and budgetary control. It may surprise you to know that most of the techniques we have examined have been in use for 50 to 100 years. Figure 16.1 helps to put the development of management accounting into a historical perspective.

Early 20th century	Breakeven calculations and charts; Operating budgets and variance analysis; Job costing and overhead attachment.
Mid 20th century	Discounted cash flows for capital budgeting; Inter-divisional transfer pricing; Total quality management.
Late 20th century	Target costing; Activity-based costing; Activity-based management.

Figure 16.1 **Some major developments of management accounting**

The period since 1990 has not been another lull in theoretical development activity. Far from it – there has been a constant stream of new initiatives flowing from the wake-up call of Kaplan and colleagues in the mid-1980s. Johnson and Kaplan wrote the seminal text *Relevance Lost: The Rise and Fall of Management Accounting*, which was published in 1987 (by Harvard Business School Press, Boston). Their opening words are:

Today's management accounting information, driven by the procedures and cycles of the organization's financial reporting cycle, is too late, too aggregated and too distorted to be relevant for managers' planning and control decisions.

They describe how management accounting started out in the mid-nineteenth century as a service function providing information to managers in support of their various roles. Indeed, in those early days, much of it was done by managers rather than accountants. They go on to tell how, during the middle of the twentieth century, management accounting was hijacked by academics more interested in mathematical theory than practical usefulness to managers. They conclude by postulating the theory of activity-based costing as an aid to improving business performance. In other words, it was a turning point in the transference of emphasis from **accounting** back to **management**.

In the last 15 years or so, the emphasis of management accounting **has** moved away from ivory-tower academic theory towards practical business usefulness. The aim of **managerial** accounting is to improve managers' effectiveness and corporate performance. This movement is continuing and has further to go. It is interesting to note that, in the year 2000, the Chartered Institute of Management Accountants (CIMA) changed the name of its monthly magazine from *Management Accounting* to *Financial Management*. The dispensing of the word 'accounting' is symptomatic of this change of direction. The major field of activity of CIMA members is now seen as **management** (with a financial slant) rather than **accounting** (with a management slant).

This movement goes under the broad title of *strategic management accounting* and the objective of this chapter is to give a brief outline of some of the theories embraced by it. (A thorough investigation of them is outside the scope of this book but it is hoped that your appetite will be whetted and you will learn more about them in the near future.) Four techniques have been chosen from the many management activities in current use. The essential features of each will be described in turn. Then, a method of integrating these discrete techniques will be discussed. Finally, an integrated model of strategic management accounting will be given.

Having worked through this chapter you should be able to give a brief outline of:

- **total quality management;**
- **benchmarking;**
- **just-in-time;**
- **activity-based management;**
- **the balanced scorecard;**
- **strategic management accounting.**

Learning objectives

Total quality management

The aim of total quality management (TQM) is to improve continually the quality of the product. 'Quality' is a difficult concept to define and several definitions exist. However, the following is one of the most useful:

A quality product is one that meets the requirements of the customer.

This practical definition is useful in that it enables the degree of quality to be measured or estimated, provided the customer requirements are known. Of course, the operation of TQM has a cost. As much as they would like to, firms cannot spend endless amounts of money on improving quality. To help them decide how much they are prepared to spend on this, they need to understand the various cost elements involved.

The cost of quality is complex (see Figure 16.2) but, in simple terms, it consists of:

- the cost of preventing poor quality occurring in the first place;
- the cost of dealing with poor quality items after they have been produced.

There is a trade-off between the costs of **prevention** and those of **cure**. The more that is spent on prevention and appraisal, the less has to be spent on putting things right, and vice versa. Many firms believe that the cost of conformance is likely to be less than that of non-conformance. This is understandable when you consider some of the costs of external failure (i.e. failure occurring after the product has been received by the customer). These include the loss of customer goodwill and future orders. Although impossible to quantify precisely, these may be justifiably described as **potentially very significant**.

Cost of conformance	Cost of non-conformance
prevention costs	*internal failure costs*
– engineering and designing of product for quality	– cost of scrap
– engineering and designing of process for quality	– cost of reworking
– training of employees	– reinspection
– statistical process control	– failure investigation
– preventive maintenance	– cost of lost production
– etc.	– etc.
appraisal costs	*external failure costs*
– sample preparation	– loss of sales revenue
– sample testing	– warranty claims
– test reporting	– loss of future orders
– purchase and maintenance of test equipment	– loss of customer goodwill
– quality audits	– making good customer losses
– etc.	– product recalls
	– law suits
	– etc.

Figure 16.2 **The component costs of quality**

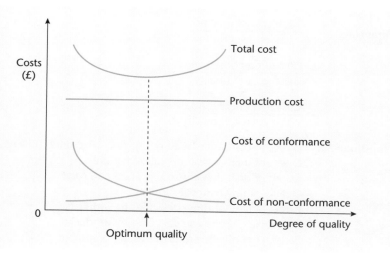

Figure 16.3 **Finding the optimum degree of quality (for a given activity level)**

Unfortunately, customers are not always explicit about their requirements. This being so, the providing firm will have to decide on how much to spend on quality. One way of going about this is to ascertain the combined cost of conformance and non-conformance for different degrees of quality (at a given level of production). The point at which the combined cost is at its minimum is the point of optimum quality, from a cost point of view, for the producing firm (see Figure 16.3). However, it should be recognised that some amount of rectification, internal and external, will probably arise when operating at this level of quality.

Of course, the curves drawn in Figure 16.3 are based on the assumption that all the costs are known. In reality, many of them are subjective and based on estimates. So how does a firm know if it is improving its quality? It needs to choose some performance criteria that will indicate whether or not this is so. Some of these performance indicators will be financial and others will be non-financial. Figure 16.4 lists a selection of them.

One of the principal aims of TQM in a mass-production environment is to achieve zero defects. Admittedly, this performance standard is a theoretical ideal but it does ensure that the search for quality improvement is ongoing even when significant milestones have been reached. When a firm achieves a failure rate of one item per million for its output it can be justifiably proud of its achievement. However, it should not rest on its laurels but strive for further improvement, say, one defect per 10 million. TQM is not just a technique, it is a managerial philosophy, attitude or 'way of life' embodying the idea of continuous improvement or *kaizen*.

Benchmarking

Benchmarking is all about performance measurement and review. Its fundamental aim is the achievement of competitive advantage by learning from the experience of others. The process involves several different organisations comparing certain aspects of

Financial: $\dfrac{\text{Total cost of quality}}{\text{Sales revenue}}$ %

$\dfrac{\text{Cost of conformance}}{\text{Total cost of quality}}$ %

$\dfrac{\text{Cost of non-conformance}}{\text{Total cost of quality}}$ %

Non-financial: Extent of computer-aided design/manufacturing (CAD/CAM)
Extent of built-in fault detection features
Extent of built-in automatic process controls
Quality of raw material supplies
Percentage of on-time deliveries by suppliers
Percentage of on-time deliveries by producer
Percentage of items returned as unacceptable
Number of customer complaints
Number of warranty claims

Figure 16.4 **Financial and non-financial indicators used in TQM**

their performance with each other. (It can also be used for independent divisions of one company.)

When considering this for the first time, firms are usually wary of participating for fear of competitors having access to confidential information, other participants benefiting more than themselves and company-specific factors reducing the usefulness of the exercise. However, it is possible to overcome these objections by using similar companies which are not direct competitors, concentrating on processes rather than results and looking at problems common to all the participants.

Examples of similar companies not in direct competition are illustrated by the following groups:

- *Retail consumables*: toiletries/household cleaning materials/home decorating supplies/ pet food.
- *Retail hardware*: cooking utensils/DIY tools/gardening equipment/car accessories.
- *Charities*: National Society for the Prevention of Cruelty to Children, Royal Society for the Prevention of Cruelty to Animals, Cancer Research, Royal British Legion, Royal National Institute for the Deaf, Royal Society for the Prevention of Accidents.

Topics for discussion and investigation may include the following:

- *Personnel*: roles, responsibilities, organisational structure.
- *Planning and control*: frequency and timeliness of budget reports, reporting level, thresholds for investigating variances, motivation mechanisms, committees, meetings.
- *Information systems*: user-friendliness, access levels, hardware, software, liveware, strategies for information management, e.g. using one company-wide database management system.
- *Communication channels*: briefing/cascading meetings, newsletters, appraisals, suggestion boxes, notice boards, intranet websites, publication of short-term results.

● *Financial management*: debtors collection period, creditors payment period, stock turnover period, gross profitability, overhead types to sales ratios.

The Xerox Corporation was an early adopter of this technique. Together with other members of its benchmarking group, it looked at research and development, factory layout, quality management, marketing, distribution channels, sales order processing and information systems.

The analysis of the information would be along the following lines:

● What things are we doing well?
● Which activities do we need to improve?
● What should we be doing that we are not doing now?

However, it is important that 'better' practices are not blindly followed without thought being given as to why they are successful in other firms. Good practices are not always directly transferable. Hopefully, different participants will obtain different benefits from this exercise. Some may gain insights into improving their information systems whilst others may become aware of possible improvements to their communication systems. Ideally, the benchmarking process will prove to be mutually beneficial. If nothing else, it usually provides the participants with a greater understanding of their external environment. Benchmarking is increasing in popularity and is not confined by national barriers.

Just-in-time

The common perception of just-in-time is that its main objective is the elimination of stocks. Those who operate it know that it embraces much more than this. A more complete list of its objectives includes the achievement of:

● zero defects;
● zero waste;
● zero inventory;
● zero lead times;
● continuous flow processes;
● flexible manufacturing.

The first four of these lend themselves to measurement by performance indicators.

Just-in-time systems are most suitable for high-volume, repetitive manufacturing, although they can be adapted for less repetitive manufacturing. They work best when the manufacturing schedule is stable for reasonably long periods of time (months rather than days). On the production line, the system operates by each workstation requesting materials to work on from the previous workstation. This is referred to as a 'pull' system and no workstation is allowed to 'push' its output down the line to the next operation. The mechanism by which this is achieved is the 'kanban' system. A kanban is simply a request for some output from the previous station. It is often in the form of a container **sent by** one station and used to transport the work-in-progress from the previous station to the requesting station. In this way, work is pulled down the line.

Just-in-time is active in the following four areas of manufacturing:

● product design;
● process design;
● human/organisation elements;
● manufacturing planning and control.

Product design uses value engineering to reduce the number of components used. It builds in achievable quality at appropriate levels. Where possible, it uses modular designs with parts common to other products and enables manufacturing to take place in flexible production cells with self-directed work teams.

Process design aims to make use of flexible manufacturing cells. It builds in preventative maintenance schedules and reduces machine set-up times to a minimum. In common with TQM, it uses computer-aided design/manufacturing (CAD/CAM), built-in fault-detection features and automatic process controls. Stock-holding areas are eliminated so that any unrequested work-in-progress is immediately seen as a problem demanding a solution. There is a famous saying, 'Inventory is like water in a river, it hides problems that are like rocks.' Get rid of the water and the rocks can no longer be ignored.

The human element is a holistic approach encouraging the use of **all** the employees' skills. This implies continuous training in new skills, including problem solving, and a flexible, multi-skilled labour force. The difference between direct and indirect labour is reduced – if not eliminated – and teamwork is encouraged. Employees are encouraged to use their brains as well as their bodies to achieve production goals. Computing power is made available to employees at the point of work to help them monitor their own performance and create solutions to their problems. This approach is sometimes known as *total employee involvement* or *empowerment*. Decision making is devolved to the people at the sharp end of the production process, leaving managers to tackle more strategic issues.

Manufacturing planning and control aims at continuous, rapid-flow, small-batch manufacturing but strictly within the confines of a 'pull' system. The use of kanbans encourages paperless, visual systems to control workflow. JIT software is commonly available to assist in the production planning process and this is usually interfaced with a materials resource planning (MRP) program. One advantage of this approach is that it reveals the costs of the 'hidden factory', i.e. those jobs and systems that are not really necessary and add no value to the products under a JIT environment. For example, in non-JIT manufacturing it is not unusual for 'progress chasers' to be employed to expedite specific orders for certain customers. This activity is unnecessary when production is planned and continuously monitored. Another very important aspect is the supplier relationship. The concept of the right-quality raw materials being delivered to the right place at the right time is central to JIT. It is common for raw materials not to be inspected on delivery. If defects do occur, the supplier is expected to rectify the situation immediately. If necessary, the manufacturer will send a team of its own employees to help with this process. It is no longer seen as essential to buy materials at the lowest possible price. The quality and reliability of supplies is more important. The two parties work together in a kind of partnership to their mutual benefit.

This has several implications for the management accounting information system. Traditional variance analysis can actually work against the successful operation of JIT. Purchasing the cheapest materials will give the most favourable price variance, but the low price may be due to the poor quality of the materials. Asset utilisation ratios can be positively misleading as they encourage continuous usage of machinery producing for stock. Direct labour hours are no longer an appropriate basis for the apportionment of overheads. New performance indicators are required to monitor and enforce the JIT system.

Activity-based management

Introduction

Activity-based management (ABM) can be thought of as a collection of actions performed by managers that are based on information provided by an activity-based costing (ABC) system. The aim is for the organisation to improve its performance by reducing its total costs whilst maintaining its sales revenue.

Kaplan and Cooper (*Cost and Effect: Using Integrated Cost Systems to Drive Profitability and Performance*, 1998, Harvard Business School Press, Boston, Chapter 8) divide these managerial activities into two categories: operational ABM and strategic ABM. Operational ABM is about **doing things right** and strategic ABM is about **doing the right things**. The objectives of operational ABM are to reduce the cost of activities and to increase capacity by improving efficiency. Note that capacity increases are only translated into improved performance if they are either eliminated (to reduce present costs) or used to facilitate expansion (to reduce future costs). If no action is taken, no improvement will materialise.

Operational ABM starts by identifying possible improvements to existing processes, prioritising them and allocating resources to carry them out. The next stage involves monitoring the results of these activities to identify the extent of the actual improvements achieved. The ABC system provides the information needed to verify the reduced spending on operational activities. The variances between planned and actual resource consumption should show clearly whether the anticipated benefits have or have not materialised.

The main objectives of strategic ABM are to increase the demand for high-profitability activities and to decrease the demand for low-profitability ones. The ABC system can give information about the profitability of individual products and individual customers. This enables marketing managers to concentrate on shifting the sales mix towards the most profitable products and the most profitable customers. At the other end of the supply chain, strategic ABM can inform decisions about new product development and supplier relationships by highlighting their demands on organisational activities and resources.

Value-added and non-value-added activities

Many authors encourage the practice of splitting activities into two types: value-added and non-value-added. They then advocate the elimination or reduction of the non-value-adding ones. This process is often put forward as the major objective of ABM. However attractive this may sound in theory, it is too simplistic to be universally

Activity categories

1 An activity required to produce the product or improve the process; the activity cannot, on a cost justification basis, be improved, simplified or reduced in scope at this time.

2 An activity required to produce the product or improve the process; the activity can be cost justifiably improved, simplified or reduced in scope.

3 An activity **not** required to produce the product or improve the process; the activity can be eventually eliminated by changing a process or company procedure.

4 An activity **not** required to produce the product or improve the process; the activity can be eliminated in the short run by changing a process or company procedure.

Figure 16.5 **Four categories concerning the value of activities**
Source: From R. S. Kaplan and R. Cooper (1998) *Cost and Effect: Using Integrated Cost Systems to Drive Profitability and Performance*, Harvard Business School Press, Boston, MA

beneficial. Implementing this basic dichotomy without careful consideration can be counter-productive.

Imagine yourself as a long-standing employee of a well-known organisation. The management have just announced, as part of their new ABM programme, that the job you have been doing for the last 12 years has been categorised as 'non-value-added'. How would you feel about that statement? Would it motivate you, demotivate you or have no effect? The vast majority of employees would be demotivated. The statement implies that the work **you have been instructed to do** for all those years has been a waste of time. Although you have always felt yourself to be a valued member of the workforce, the implication is that this may not be the case.

Of course, this may well not be true, but like most other people, this is probably how you would feel about it. As in many other situations, the way things are done can be more important than what is being done. In their book, Kaplan and Cooper tell how one company overcame this problem by extending the number of categories from two to four and wording each of their descriptions very carefully. The four categories are shown in Figure 16.5. Using these avoids the negative emotional overtones attached to the phrase 'non-value-added activity' and greatly reduces any demotivating effect on the employees. This analysis is more helpful than the two-category one as it helps managers to prioritise their actions. Obviously, category 4 activities should be given higher priority than category 3 ones, and so on.

Note that each of the four categories in Figure 16.5 refers to **improving the process** as well as producing the product. The earlier chapter on ABC concentrates on the causation link between products, activities and costs. It mentions **processes** very little. However, organisational performance can be improved by increasing the efficiency of its processes as well as reducing the costs of its products. The ABC model can support process drivers as well as cost drivers. Cost drivers relate to the quantity of activities caused by individual products but process drivers relate to the efficiency of carrying out those activities. The idea is to reduce the quantity of process drivers needed for the process to take place. For managers to know if their efforts at improving process efficiency are effective, appropriate performance indicators need to be built into the management accounting information system. A good way of doing this is through the 'balanced scorecard'.

The balanced scorecard

The balanced scorecard was first proposed by Kaplan and Norton in 1992. It is a device to aid managers in their efforts to improve corporate performance in line with corporate goals. To help managers avoid information overload it is recommended that four corporate goals or objectives are chosen for each of four 'perspectives' of organisational activity (16 items in total). Each goal is monitored by a different performance indicator and a specific target is set for each indicator. These indicators are sometimes referred to as *critical success factors (CSFs)* or *key performance indicators (KPIs)*. Figure 16.6 illustrates the balanced scorecard structure.

Specific targets are set for the desired performance level of each indicator. These should be stretch targets, high but achievable. If they are set either too low or too high, they will demotivate employees and performance will be suboptimal. So, the targets should be set very carefully. But even the careful setting of targets is not enough to ensure success. It is good practice for the people responsible for achieving targets to create 'action plans' setting out in detail how they are going to do this. A separate action plan should be created for each of the 16 objectives.

It is not imperative that each perspective has exactly four objectives; the idea is to keep the amount of monitored information small and, therefore, manageable. Also, if an organisation thinks it useful to have five perspectives, there is good reason to add an extra one. Balanced scorecards are essentially flexible and should always be tailored to the requirements of the organisation using them. However, as the number of items monitored is small, it is vital that the performance indicators are very carefully chosen. Duplication should be avoided; for example, no indicator should be used more than once on the scorecard. The goals listed should give a broad perspective of activities rather than a narrow one. In the past, it was not unusual for managers to be expected to monitor many more individual measurements, sometimes over 100. The pressing nature of their other duties meant that they could not do this effectively and strategy implementation was very difficult to achieve.

One of the perspectives concerns 'traditional' financial measures but the other three consist of non-financial items. Taken together, the financial, customer, internal business and innovation/learning indicators give a balanced view of corporate performance. Provided the non-financial performance indicators are carefully selected, improvement in them should automatically translate into improved financial performance. Accordingly, the non-financial factors are known as 'lead' indicators whereas the financial factors are 'lag' indicators.

The performance indicators often stem from the management techniques discussed earlier in the chapter. Most of the information will be available internally but sometimes it may have to be obtained via customer surveys, benchmarking, intercompany comparisons, etc. The number of indicators is limited on purpose in order to help management focus on their current priorities. The indicators included in the scorecard are not generic; they should be reviewed periodically to reflect changes of corporate strategy made in response to the external environment. This is facilitated by a flexible management information system, possibly based on a unified relational database used to warehouse both internal and external data. The balanced scorecard monitoring system is illustrated in Figure 16.7.

The financial perspective

Corporate goal	Performance indicator	Target
Survival	Liquid ratio	Increase to 0.8:1.0
Profitability	Return on capital employed	Improve by 5% over the year
Growth	Sales revenue	Increase by 4% a year above inflation
Self-funding	Interest cover ratio	Reduce interest to 10% of operating profit

The customer perspective

Corporate goal	Performance indicator	Target
Responsiveness	Sales order processing period	Reduce to 12 working days
Reliability	On-time deliveries	95% each month
Product quality	Complaints received	2% of goods delivered each month
Image	Ranking by customer	Customer's first or second choice in independent survey

The internal business perspective

Corporate goal	Performance indicator	Target
Satisfied employees	Staff turnover ratio	5% a year maximum
Production efficiency	Output per employee	Increase by 1% every 3 months
Working capital management	Cash cycle period	Reduce by 1 day every 2 months
Production quality	Value of defective production	Reduction of 2% every 3 months

The innovation and learning perspective

Corporate goal	Performance indicator	Target
Continuing introduction of new products	Proportion of sales from new products	15% of annual sales from products launched in current or previous financial year
Employee development	Number of training hours per employee	16 hours per year minimum for each employee
Product diversification	Number of new markets served	At least one new market entered each year
Product improvement	Spending on research and development	Minimum of 10% a year of after-tax profits

Figure 16.6 **The four perspectives of the balanced scorecard and examples of their application**

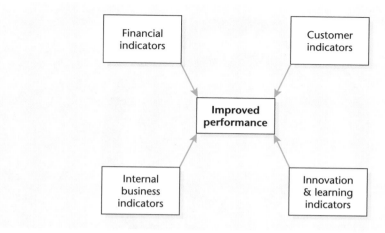

Figure 16.7 **The balanced scorecard**

In summary, the balanced scorecard is driven by organisational strategic objectives rather than a desire for operational control. It is not constrained by the financial year in the way that a budgetary control system is. Note that it is not a strategy in itself but a monitoring mechanism to help managers achieve the company's strategic goals.

Strategic management accounting

This term describes a broad management approach that makes use of external and non-financial information as well as internal financial information. It encompasses a variety of management techniques and is more of a philosophy than a technique in its own right. As such, there is no unique description of its contents. However, all strategic management accounting uses a wide variety of performance indicators in order to achieve the policy aims of the organisation.

For example, in order to achieve its strategic objectives, a company could adopt simultaneously the techniques of TQM, JIT, ABM and benchmarking. Key performance indicators from each of these techniques could be built into a balanced scorecard (the monitoring device) and the desired values of each of them, taken together, form a plan of management activity. The actual achieved values of the indicators give a measure of change in performance and management effectiveness. The ultimate goal of strategic management accounting is to increase competitive advantage via continuous improvement (see Figure 16.8). The model can easily be adapted for organisations using different management techniques by substituting them in the 'techniques' circle.

Limitations

Strategy is about doing the right things. Management accounting is fundamentally an information system. Strategic management accounting is about managers using an

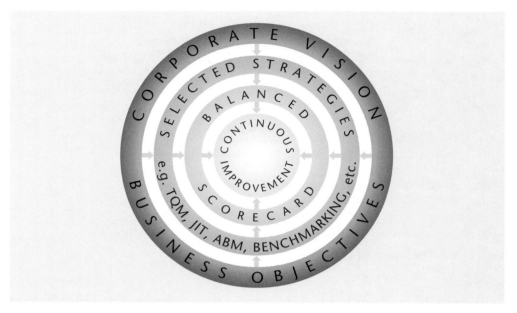

Figure 16.8 **Strategic management accounting**

effective information system to help them gain competitive advantage for their organisation by constantly improving performance.

This descriptive definition indicates two areas where this management model is vulnerable. The first is getting the strategy right: choosing the activities with the most potential and doing them in the most effective order. The second is the quality of the information system: choosing the best performance indicators and providing accurate, timely, summarised information in a flexible form.

Getting the strategy right is a perennial problem. Even when the indications are that you have got it right and results are improving, it is dangerous to sit back and become complacent. The business environment is constantly changing and your competitors are continually looking for ways of gaining competitive advantage over you. Strategy review and formulation should be a continuous activity of high-level managers. However, it is a fact of business life that they do not always get it right. The effectiveness of the strategic management accounting system depends on the quality of the organisational strategy.

It also depends on the quality of the information system. State-of-the-art systems are something of a movable feast. Is the information systems strategy to have one single, all-embracing database or two or three? Is the hardware network sufficient to support corporate needs? Is the data management system flexible enough to meet frequent changes in information requirements? Is the right data being collected? How reliable is the **external** data collected? Are systems maintenance and modification easy to achieve? The answers to these types of questions will indicate the effectiveness of the system.

In summary, the limitations of strategic management accounting are the difficulty of choosing the right strategy and the quality of the information system.

The manager's point of view

'Oh no, not another management initiative!' How often have we heard this cry as companies try to take advantage of the newest management theory? 'Oh dear, the managing director has read another book!' These typical reactions stem partly from the natural resistance to change, which is inherent in all organisations, and which, coincidentally, epitomises why such management initiatives are so important. It also suggests that previous initiatives may not have been properly managed, and eventually petered out, leaving a trail of cynicism throughout the workforce.

In my view, however, new management theories provide an effective catalyst for change, especially in companies whose hard-pressed managers are obliged to focus all their time on day-to-day issues. With pared-down staffing levels and an ever-increasing demand for information from parent companies, governments and regulatory bodies, let alone customers, there is already little enough time for managers to sit back and contemplate strategic issues. There is even less time to consider improvements in the internal organisation of the company. 'If the system works, leave well alone, and concentrate on generating more business' is the pragmatic approach adopted by many busy managers. As a result, the rate of change within the organisation declines, and the business finds itself falling behind its competitors.

Management theories, such as TQM and JIT, can provide the stimulus needed to engender change. The theories have been well thought through, documented and already put to the test in many companies. They are therefore easily accessible for a management which do not have time for philosophical thought about the nature of staff motivation or quality improvement. If someone else has already done all the original thinking, why not take advantage of it?

Each of the theories approaches the business of management from a different angle. TQM aims primarily at improving quality throughout the organisation. JIT tackles efficiency. Benchmarking looks at other organisations to see if there are any lessons to be learnt there. Each one provides managers with a different perspective on their business. The effect can be hugely stimulating. Anything which promises to raise the quality of the operation, cut down customer complaints, reduce stocks, increase the productivity of employees and plant, and much more, is bound to get a manager excited! But nevertheless, these theories should still be approached with care.

First of all, they require the overt commitment of the managing director and senior staff. I have seen such projects delegated to a lower-level manager, with the board of directors watching events from afar, and effectively acting as a barrier to change when anything remotely radical is proposed! Needless to say, these projects always fail. Any initiative designed to engender change needs to be driven from the top.

Secondly, the theory needs to be made relevant to the business in question. It is not uncommon for a company to adopt one of the theories, but somehow manage to keep it separate from the main thrust of the business. I have seen this happen in particular with the Quality Assurance standard, ISO 9000, where a company can carry out every one of the burdensome documentary procedures, but not improve quality by one jot. This is because the underlying concepts in the standard have not been absorbed into the culture of the workplace. The process of introducing these theories must be aimed at engendering change in the culture of the company, rather than simply setting up the bureaucratic procedures as stated in the manual.

Thirdly, these theories sometimes get a bad reputation within companies, because they are introduced with a major fanfare, then, a year or two later, they fade into obscurity. But a short-lived exercise like this is not necessarily a bad thing. All such radical new initiatives will make a big splash at the beginning, and if they are implemented in an effective way, the key principles will become part of the ethos of the company, in which case the initiative has done its job. It also makes way for the next one. A company which has extracted the maximum benefit from TQM, JIT, ABM and bench-marking should be in pretty good shape!

The process of introducing one of these systems into the company can have many beneficial influences, some of them anticipated, others coming as a surprise. Some years ago, my head office in the USA decided to introduce TQM throughout the organisation. This occurred just at the time that I took over as managing director of the UK subsidiary. TQM became a perfect vehicle for effecting a change of personality within the company, moving away from the hierarchical structure of my predecessors towards a more egalitarian organisation for the modern business environment. This is not the place to go into great detail about the mechanics of TQM, but it may be useful to identify one or two of the specific benefits which we derived from the process.

First of all, the entire workforce were put through a three-day TQM training programme. For this purpose, the employees were divided into small mixed groups from widely differing areas of the company. As a result, these groups threw together computer programmers with fork-lift truck drivers, sales managers with maintenance engineers, machine operators with accountants. It brought together people who would not come across each other in the normal course of their work, let alone sit down to discuss issues concerning the company. This process did much to break down the barriers between departments, as the objectives and the problems of each department became more widely understood. This simple fact possibly did more to change the culture of the company than all the benefits gained from the TQM process itself.

Another spin-off from this process was the mission statement. Most companies have a mission statement these days, and most of them are full of bland, standardised, buzzwords which are mostly meaningless. I regret that ours, too, fell into this trap, except in one respect. Included in our statement was the need to achieve a 'reputation for excellence', a concept which was directly related to a particular image problem which the subsidiary had somehow developed in previous years. This particular aim struck a chord with employees and positively affected their approach towards their daily tasks. The mission statement certainly added impetus to our search for quality, and a reputation for excellence was indeed quickly established in many of our areas of activity. A good mission statement is difficult to construct, and I believe that most of them fail to provide any real motivation to staff. However, it should be recognised that the mere discussion of company goals by ordinary members of the workforce is a hugely beneficial exercise in itself.

The main thrust of TQM, of course, is to improve the quality of every aspect of the company's operations, by adopting, among other things, an open and inclusive approach to employees. It is designed to release the power of the workforce, by delegating decision making down to the lowest practical level, by getting staff to work in multi-disciplinary teams to find solutions for joint problems, and by encouraging individual workers to consider the impact of their actions on people both up and down the line. One of the key vehicles for achieving this is to identify certain 'flagship' projects, and give as many people as possible the chance to serve on those teams. This worked well for a few years, but the novelty gradually wore off, and membership of a team eventually became a chore. The projects had become a burden on staff, separate from and additional to their normal daily responsibilities. At that point, we felt that the formal TQM process had run its course, so we discontinued it. However, by that time, the concepts were well and truly ingrained in the culture of the company and the staff continued to practise them, whether they were aware of it or not.

TQM, like the other techniques mentioned in this chapter, is sure to benefit your company to a greater or lesser extent. Whether you adopt these concepts wholeheartedly, or merely dabble with parts of them, the impact on your company will almost certainly be positive. Mistakes can easily be made during the process, and some employees will inevitably grumble, but there can be few better ways of effecting change in an organisation. Not only will you end up with a motivated and quality-conscious workforce, but your customers will get their orders delivered on time too!

Summary

All this is very interesting from a management point of view but is it really accounting? To answer this question, it is necessary to ask why management accounting exists. The fundamental reason is to provide managers with relevant, timely, accurate information to help them improve company performance. Strategic management accounting (as shown in Figure 16.8) precisely embodies this concept. Why, then, is it sometimes perceived to be not really directly concerned with **accounting**? To answer this I can do no better than to quote the last words of the seminal text *Relevance Lost: The Rise and Fall of Management Accounting* (Johnson and Kaplan, 1987, Harvard Business School Press, Boston):

> *For too many firms today, however, the management accounting system is seen as a system designed and run by accountants to satisfy the informational needs of accountants. This is clearly wrong. Accountants should not have the exclusive franchise to design management accounting systems. To paraphrase an old saying, the task is simply too important to be left to accountants. The active involvement of engineers and operating managers will be essential when designing new management accounting systems.*
>
> *Contemporary trends in competition, in technology, and in management demand major changes in the way organizations measure and manage costs and in the way they measure short- and long-term performance. Failure to make the modifications will inhibit the ability of firms to be effective and efficient global competitors.*

To finish, it is worth adding another quote to the above, this time from Charles Darwin, author of the famous theory in the *Origin of the Species*:

> *Those who respond quickly, thrive, those that do not, die.*

Further reading

Atkinson, A., Banker, R., Kaplan, R. and Young, S. (2001) *Management Accounting*, 3rd edition, Prentice Hall, Harlow. See chapter 'Management accounting and control systems for strategic purposes: assessing performance over the entire value chain'.

Bauer, K. (2005) 'KPIs: avoiding the threshold McGuffins', *DM Review*, Vol. 15, Issue 4, April.

Dilla, W. N. and Steinbart, P. J. (2005) 'Relative weighting of common and unique balanced scorecard measures by knowledgeable decision makers', *Behavioral Research in Accounting*, Vol. 17

Fanning, J. (1999) 'Budgeting in the 21st Century', *Management Accounting*, November.

Gering, M. and Rosmarin, K. (2000) 'Central beating: succeeding with the balanced scorecard means moving on from central planning', *Management Accounting*, June.

Horngren, C., Bhimani, A., Datar, S. and Foster, G. (2002) *Management and Cost Accounting*, 2nd edition, Prentice Hall Europe, Harlow. See Chapter 19, 'Control systems and performance measurements'.

Kaplan, R. and Norton, D. (1996) *The Balanced Scorecard*, Harvard Business School Press, Boston, MA.

Kaplan, R. and Norton, D. (2001) *The Strategy-focused Organisation: How Balanced Scorecard Companies Thrive in the New Business Environment*, Harvard Business School Press, Boston, MA.

Smith, M. (1999) *Management Accounting for Competitive Advantage*, LBC Information Services, Pyrmont, Australia.

Smith, M. (2000) 'Strategic management accounting: the public sector challenge', *Management Accounting*, January.

Ward, A. (2005) 'Implementing the balanced scorecard at Lloyds TSB', *Strategic HR Review*, Vol. 4, Issue 3, March/April.

Whittle, N. (2000) 'Older and wiser', *Management Accounting*, July/August.

Williams, K. (2004) 'What constitutes a successful balanced scorecard?', *Strategic Finance*, Vol. 86, Issue 5, November.

Questions

16.1 SG plc

SG plc is a long-established food manufacturer which produces semi-processed foods for fast food outlets. While for a number of years it has recognised the need to produce good quality products for its customers, it does not have a formalised quality management programme.

A director of the company has recently returned from a conference, where one of the speakers introduced the concept of Total Quality Management (TQM) and the need to recognise and classify quality costs.

Required:

(a) Explain what is meant by TQM and use examples to show how it may be introduced into different areas of SG's food production business.

(12 marks)

(b) Explain why the adoption of TQM is particularly important within a Just-in-Time (JIT) production environment.

(5 marks)

(c) Explain four quality cost classifications, using examples relevant to the business of SG plc.

(8 marks)
(Total = 25 marks)

CIMA Intermediate: Management Accounting – Performance Management, November 2002

16.2 HJL

HJL provides consultancy services to companies considering improving their telephone and communication systems, including those operated using computer technology. HJL employs a number of consultants and measures its performance based on profitability and the number of chargeable hours. Performance measures make comparisons between actual and budget performance using budgets that are developed on an incremental approach which adds 5% to the budget of the previous year.

The Managing Director has returned from a management training conference which provided her with a basic understanding of the use of alternative performance measures. Two of these were The Balanced Scorecard and Benchmarking. She has asked you, as a management accountant, to prepare a report to be discussed at the next meeting of the Board of Directors. The report should explain these terms and how the performance of the company may improve if HJL were to introduce these new performance measures.

Required:

Prepare a report, to be discussed at the next meeting of the Board of Directors, that:

a) Reviews the suitability of the existing performance measures used by HJL;

(7 marks)

b) Explains 'The Balanced Scorecard' and recommends, with reasons, performance measures that could be used if it were introduced in HJL;

(12 marks)

c) Explains 'Benchmarking' and the potential impact on operations within HJL if it were to be introduced.

(6 marks)
(Total = 25 marks)

CIMA Intermediate: Management Accounting – Performance Management, November 2004

16.3 Z Limited

Z Limited produces signs and labels for a number of businesses. Some of the signs are produced on vinyl and then fixed to vehicles and display panels whereas others are produced on metal and fixed to machinery and equipment to indicate how they are to be operated safely.

Presently Z Limited holds stocks of raw materials (vinyls, metals and inks) and controls the level of stock using a stock control system that involves the setting and monitoring of minimum, maximum and re-order stock levels for each stock item. There are also some specialist materials that are bought from suppliers as required.

Z Limited uses a number of suppliers, some of whom are based overseas. The Purchasing Manager of Z Limited is responsible for negotiating prices and contracts with suppliers for all of the materials used by the company. The performance of the manager is monitored as part of Z Limited's responsibility accounting system.

The Managing Director has recently returned from a conference on best practice where one of the speakers mentioned the use of Just-In-Time (JIT). The Managing Director seeks your advice, and has asked you to prepare a report that can be discussed at the next Board meeting.

Required:

(a) Prepare a report, addressed to the directors of Z Limited, that
   i)   describes the key features of a JIT system both for purchasing of raw materials and for their conversion into finished items for customers;

(3 marks)

   ii) identifies the advantages and disadvantages of operating a JIT system;

(4 marks)

   iii) explains the changes in working practices that would be necessary for a JIT system to succeed.

(6 marks)
(Total for requirement (a) = 13 marks)

(b) For some time the managers of Z Limited have complained that the responsibility accounting system is unfair. Managers are given targets that have been set by the Board of Directors and are expected to achieve the targets regardless of the level of actual activity and any changes that may have occurred since the targets were set.

Required:

i) Explain the meaning of responsibility accounting.

(3 marks)

ii) Discuss the implications of the scenario described in (b) and describe the changes that could be made to improve acceptance by managers of the responsibility accounting system.

(9 marks)
(Total = 25 marks)

CIMA Intermediate: Management Accounting – Performance Management, May 2004

CHAPTER 17 Business performance management

Chapter contents

Introduction

There are literally thousands and thousands of books and journal articles on the subject of managing businesses and improving their performance. Indeed, you are reading one of them now. The reason for this huge volume of advice is that the subject is universally important. No one starts a business with the intention that it should fail or perform in a mediocre fashion. Entrepreneurs create their businesses with the aim of being successful. Once they have achieved this, they can continue to run the business or sell it on, sometimes by floating it on the stock market. Whoever the owners are, you can be sure that they want the business to be managed so that it performs better and better.

Because entrepreneurs are both owners and managers, their control systems are very direct. In contrast, shareholders can only exert control **indirectly** through the directors they appoint to manage the business. The constant activity on the stock markets is evidence that shareholders are very interested in the performance of their investments. Shareholders sell their shares when they think the business is going to perform badly and they buy shares when they think it is going to perform well. When more shares are being sold than bought, the share price goes down; when more are bought than sold, the price goes up. In this way, shareholders communicate their opinions to the directors regarding their performance.

So company directors and managers should be encouraged to improve the performance of their businesses if they own shares in them. In this way, their rewards for managing the company come not only from their salaries and cash bonuses but also from the dividends and capital growth of their shareholdings. The direct link between business performance and the personal wealth of managers (based on the value of their shareholdings) is seen as an incentive to good management.

Some companies operate 'employee share purchase schemes' whereby employees are encouraged to invest, on favourable terms, in their own organisation. These 'share option schemes' are common in large companies. Management theory states that such ownership should bring about 'goal congruence' between owners and managers. In other words, they should both want the performance of the company to improve continuously.

Other businesses rely more on cash incentives to encourage their managers to improve performance. They believe that **cash today** is a better motivator than **share value tomorrow**. To achieve goal congruence, they usually offer cash bonuses based on targets directly linked to the budget. For example, a salesperson may be rewarded with a bonus equal to 5% of sales value for every £1 above the budgeted sales revenue.

However, a brief read of the financial press will show that some companies, many of which operate the type of incentive schemes described above, are getting worse rather than better. Also, those whose performance has improved in the past may now be exhibiting a decline. It seems that continuous improvement over long periods of time is very rarely achieved despite the common occurrence of personal incentive schemes. This chapter investigates why this is so.

Learning objectives	Having worked through this chapter you should be able to:

- discuss the weaknesses of traditional budgeting;
- explain how the various types of budget games are played;
- comment on the utility of budgetary control systems;
- describe the various mechanisms advocated by 'Beyond Budgeting';
- explain how people can be put at the heart of performance management;
- describe the factors of successful performance management initiatives;
- explain how NHS targets can lead to dysfunctional behaviour;
- discuss the effect of response times on service performance;
- describe the role of the balanced scorecard as a strategic management tool;
- understand the importance of continuous improvement.

The weaknesses of traditional budgeting

The 'tried-and-tested' method of controlling corporate performance is budgeting; it is used by almost every business in existence. (The creation and use of budgets is covered in previous chapters of this book.) In brief, it can be seen as a cyclical four-stage process (see Figure 15.1):

● Create plan.
● Implement plan.
● Measure performance.
● Compare plan to performance and evaluate differences.
● Create next plan, etc.

Of course, actual performance rarely, if ever, turns out to be identical to the original budget. Unforeseen events and unplanned internal changes occur at various times throughout the financial year. Managers respond to these deviations from plan as they arise and set new directions/objectives appropriate to the new situation. In this way, the annual performance of the business should at least resemble the last revision of the budget. So why does the traditional budgetary control system often produce disappointing results? What are its weaknesses?

First, unlike the business environment, budgets are difficult to change quickly. The rate of change in the environment is continuously increasing but the budgetary control system was designed almost a century ago when things changed much more slowly. For instance, in the 1920s, if you wanted to hold an important face-to-face meeting with a business associate in the USA, it would take you at least a week to travel there! It is now possible to travel there and back in the space of a day. The modern technological environment allows for vastly increased speeds of communication; video-conferencing is just one example.

Changing one line of a budget may have repercussions on many other lines and affect many other people. The introduction of a new product by a competitor may cause you to want to change your sales plan. But any such change will impact on purchasing, manufacturing, administration, marketing, etc. These areas are controlled by different budget-responsible officers who will need to agree the changes. This will involve them in extra work taking extra time which they probably have not got, so something will have to be postponed or lost in order to effect the budget change. Meetings will have to be arranged to discuss the proposed changes, then more meetings to 'sign off the changes'.

The natural reluctance of managers to take on additional tasks extends the amount of time taken to carry them out; it may even prevent them happening. That may be acceptable for the individuals involved but what about the company? Rival organisations may steal a competitive edge which will adversely affect the profit of the business. Also, the amount of work involved in continual changes may stifle innovation. In the cause of self-preservation, managers may learn to respond negatively to innovative ideas even though they may be good for the business.

Another major weakness stems from the widely adopted practice of giving cash bonuses to managers based on their performance measured against budget. These personal incentive schemes may be expressed in 'narrow' terms which ignore their effects on other parts of the business. Also, the achievement of their individual budget targets becomes more important to managers than acting in the best interests of the company **as a whole**. Budget-responsible officers often exhibit what is known as 'gaming behaviour'.

Budget games

There are several different types of budget game but the most common is where managers build 'slack' into their targets. The budget is constructed by negotiation between the budget holder and senior management (possibly with the technical support of a management accountant). The idea is that the budget holder is more likely to achieve his or her 'own' target than one imposed from above. But because the bonus depends on meeting his or her targets, the budget holder will be tempted to make them easier to achieve. So revenues tend to be underestimated and expenses overestimated.

Over the years, most executives have experienced their budget estimates of expenses being cut back in the name of efficiency. However, if they expect their estimates (known as 'allowances') to be cut back, they may well overestimate them in the first instance to avoid any reduction. If they expect an overall (or blanket) cutback of 10% they may inflate their suggested allowances by 11% (10% of 111 is 11) and end up with the number they originally wanted.

'Virement' is another game played as the year progresses. This is the recording of an expense under the wrong heading. For example, if the budget allowance for travel has already been reached before the end of a budget period, further travel expenses in that period may be incorrectly classed as training or some other item that has not used up all its allowance. This makes budget holders appear to be better at controlling expenditure than they actually are by hiding their overspending.

If, towards the end of a budget period, it looks as though an expense allowance will be underspent, it is common for the budget holder to go on a 'spending spree' buying items not strictly necessary at that time. These items would not have been bought had the budget expense allowance been lower. Note that this unnecessary spending behaviour may perpetuate the error in future years. In the eyes of the budget holder, it helps to avoid cutbacks in that particular expense budget in the next period; better to have the money available just in case it is needed than not to have the 'buffer' it creates.

Salespeople are often paid partly by commission on the sales they make. If the commission is triggered by sales reaching a certain value and the salespeople think they are not going to reach this threshold, they may attempt to bring forward 'regular' sales from the next period into the current one. Of course, these brought-forward sales will create a problem regarding the commission earned next period, but increased sales to other customers may more than compensate for these brought-forward sales. Most people prefer 'jam today' rather than 'jam tomorrow'.

On the other hand, in a good period, the salespeople may have sold well over estimate and reached the amount where the commission payments are capped at a maximum level (this is normal corporate practice). It may be that the salespeople could sell even more before the end of the period but why should they? They will not earn anything extra for doing so and these 'additional' sales will go towards next period's bonus. The effect of this on the business is that sales **and their resulting cash flow** will be delayed.

The effect of the budget games identified above is to feed misinformation into the budgetary control system. In turn, this will cause poor decisions to be made throughout the organisation resulting in suboptimal performance. As all budget schedules are interdependent, incorrect figures in one area will cause incorrect figures in other areas. Activities throughout the organisation will be based on misleading information!

This offers an insight as to why traditional budgetary control systems are not as successful as they should be. Their theoretical strength is almost always undermined to some extent by 'normal, selfish' human behaviour.

The effect of employee cash incentive schemes

Before looking at the last two games in more detail, we will look at how these employee incentive schemes operate, particularly those offering cash bonuses. First of all, employees are offered additional pay for reaching targets based on their budgets. However, companies acknowledge that the business environment may be better or worse than assumed for the creation of the original budget. To compensate for this, the threshold figure triggering the payment of a bonus is set below the budget allowance, say at 80% of that amount. From the company's point of view, this ensures a significant amount of the target is met before any bonus is paid.

Once the threshold has been reached, the activity will continue and the bonus will increase accordingly. However, companies like to keep their expenditure under control and will normally place an upper limit on the amount of bonus that can be earned in any period. This upper limit may be set at, say, 120% of the budget allowance.

To help understand the above, consider the example of a salesman whose budget states that he is to sell £50,000 of goods every month. He is on a bonus scheme which rewards him with 10% of sales value above £40,000 (80% of budget) subject to a sales cap of £60,000 (120% of budget). If he sells goods worth £40,000 or less in the period he earns zero bonus, if he sells £50,000 he earns £1,000 bonus, if he sells £60,000 he earns £2,000 bonus and if he sells £70,000 he still earns £2,000 bonus.

Imagine you are this salesman; it is approaching the end of the month and you have sold only £28,000 and you estimate that you will not sell more than £35,000. You realise it is most unlikely that you will earn any bonus this month. What effect do you think this will have on your motivation? What attitude will you adopt towards selling between now and the end of the month? Most people will stop making any effort to sell above the minimum and have a 'rest' before next month. After all, any sales that can be pushed forward into next month will help enhance the next bonus. This may lead to an active decision to stop selling this month.

Alternatively, if you have reached the bonus threshold before the month-end, you will be motivated to sell. You will want to take maximum advantage of this month's opportunity to earn as much as you possibly can. Every £1,000 of sales above £40,000 will earn you an extra £100. Suppose there is one week left before the month-end and it looks like you will sell a total of £57,000 in the period. Your bonus will be £1,700 (10% of 57,000−40,000). This is good but it could be better; you are missing out on £300 of bonus that will be lost to you for ever. Is there anything you can do to avoid this and maximise your earnings? What about next month's 'regular' sales? Is it possible to bring any of them forward into this month? This may cause a problem next month but it may be possible to make up for the 'missing' sales and at least you will have earned the maximum bonus this month.

On the other hand, with one week to go to the month-end, you may have just reached the £60,000 limit for which bonus is paid. How would this affect you? You have reached your maximum earnings for this month and have no incentive to sell for the remainder of the period. But you could help next month's bonus by postponing further sales to then. Why shouldn't you have a rest for a week – after all, you have earned it, haven't you?

This 'personal earnings/bonus management' behaviour may be advantageous to the employee but it can be counter-productive to the business. An obvious example of this, as mentioned above, is where sales are pushed into the future **together with the related cash inflow**. However, there are more subtle ways in which the company can be damaged. These will become apparent as we look in more detail at specific ways in which sales can be *pulled forward* and *pushed back*.

Pulling sales forward

One way of pulling sales forward from next month into the current one is to offer 'abnormal' discounts (assuming you have the authority to do so). These are discounts which are not justifiable from the company's point of view but offer an incentive to the customer to buy now rather than later. For example, offers 'only available for a limited period' could fall under this heading.

When selling to distributors/wholesalers ('intermediaries' in the supply chain) it may be possible to engage in 'channel stuffing'. This is where an excessive amount of goods are delivered to suppliers this month with the expectation that deliveries will be smaller next month or that some goods will be returned.

Alternatively, if customers are told by the salesman that he has heard 'on the grapevine' that a price increase is likely next month, it may encourage them to buy more than their normal amounts this month (and less next month). Of course, when no price increase occurs next month, they can be told the good news that this is due to the supplier's good management and that increases have been held off **for the time being**.

The ingenuity of employees to improve their bonuses can be very great. There is one documented case involving the export sale of a large, expensive machine where the trigger for the payment of the bonus to the sales team was its delivery to the customer. Because the machine was not completed in time for delivery in one month, arrangements were made for it to be shipped in kit form for later assembly. This did the trick as the technicality of the machine not being in workable order was not specified by the incentive system and the bonus was paid for the month of delivery. However, the supplier subsequently had to send an assembly team to the customer's premises involving much extra expenditure that it would not normally incur. This unnecessary cost had an adverse effect on company profits but the sales team got their bonuses earlier than they should have.

Pre-dating orders/invoices is another way of pulling sales forward. For example, if the goods are to be delivered on 1 August (the first day of the next period) but you can arrange for the invoice to be dated 31 July (the last day of the current period) then the associated bonus will be paid one month earlier than it should. However, it must be pointed out that this should not be possible if the company has adequate control systems in place. This is breaking the rules rather than bending them and if employees are caught, they should be subject to disciplinary measures. Having said that, it has certainly happened in the past and, where company control systems are poor, it could happen in the future.

Pushing sales back

On the other hand, if it is in the employees' personal interest to push sales back into the following period, they may arrange for delivery of the goods to be delayed until then. This may be possible by giving incorrect information to the despatch office. Alternatively, they may be able to arrange for the invoice to be post-dated to the next period. Again, corporate control systems should not allow this to happen but systems are rarely perfect.

A more subtle approach is for salespeople to voice to their customers the possibility of imminent price cuts. The spurious information is passed on under the guise of the salespeople's 'goodwill' towards their customers! Of course, the price cuts must never be guaranteed. The information is presented in the form of a rumour which may or may not turn out to be true. The 'get-out' clause is there to be used next month when no price decreases occur.

A less subtle approach is for a salesperson to avoid contact with a customer for a while. Orders normally occur when the salesperson and the customer's buyer communicate with each other. If, for any reason, communication cannot be established between them, the buyer may prefer to wait until it can. Of course, this ploy is usually only used on a very short-term basis. Any lengthy delay in making contact may result in the customer taking its business elsewhere. But towards the end of the month, it may be possible to utilise this tactic.

A more dangerous approach is for the salesperson to hint that there may be quality problems with the latest batch of manufactured goods and that it may be advisable for the customer to delay ordering until next month if possible. The customer would be asked to keep this information 'confidential', especially as the problem has now been sorted and the next batch out of the factory will be back to the normal standard of quality.

One further way of pushing sales into the future is for the salesperson to lie to the customer about stock availability. Again, this is a short-term ploy as the customer may give its business to a competitor to avoid serious delays.

The utility of budgetary control systems

There will also be other ways of moving sales backwards and forwards in time. People are nothing if not ingenious when it comes to increasing their earnings. Bonus schemes based on budget targets are very common and successful motivators of employees. Unfortunately, the resulting employee behaviour is not always in the best interests of the business. In fact, it can work seriously against them.

There is a significant body of evidence to show that traditional budgetary control systems are part of the current corporate performance problem rather than its solution. Much of this stems from personal incentive schemes being directly linked to budget targets. The 'gaming' behaviour which this encourages often causes businesses to perform less well than they would otherwise do.

The 'Beyond Budgeting' movement

Dissatisfaction with traditional budgeting has grown to the extent where opposition to it is mainly co-ordinated under a single umbrella movement that goes under the title of 'Beyond Budgeting'. This international movement operates a Beyond Budgeting Round Table with its own website (www.bbrt.org). It advocates the replacement of the traditional budgetary control system with an assortment of 'adaptive processes'. These are planning and decision-making processes which are not strictly part of the traditional budgetary control system. An example of these would be a 'rolling forecast' prepared every quarter for the following four quarters. It would not contain as much detail as a traditional budget but it would show summary figures of sales, costs, profits and cash flow. This enables managers to review the financial outlook of the business without being constrained by the corporate financial year used for the annual reporting cycle.

Two of the leading lights of this movement are Jeremy Hope and Robin Fraser. Their 1997 journal article 'Beyond Budgeting . . .' is reproduced in Chapter 19 of this book. However, since then, they have written a book entitled *Beyond Budgeting – How Managers Can Break Free from the Annual Performance Trap*, published by Harvard Business School Press in 2003. In their summary at the end of Chapter 4, they conclude that:

> By removing the budgeting process and fixed performance contract, firms are able to change the attitudes and behaviors of people at every level of the organization. In particular, they are likely to eradicate the undesirable behaviors that result from setting a fixed target that must be met even though the outcome is highly uncertain.

They also list six key principles that organisations should adhere to if they wish to manage without annual budgets:

1 *Base goals on external benchmarks rather than on internally negotiated targets.*
2 *Base evaluation and rewards on relative improvement contracts rather than on fixed performance contracts agreed upon in advance.*
3 *Make action planning a continuous and inclusive process rather than an annual and restrictive exercise.*
4 *Make resources available as required under KPI accountability rather than allocated in advance on the basis of annual budgets.*
5 *Coordinate cross-company actions dynamically according to prevailing customer demand rather than a predetermined annual master budget.*
6 *Base controls on effective governance and on a range of relative performance indicators rather than on fixed reviews against annual plans and budgets.*

There is not room in this book to discuss all aspects of the Beyond Budgeting methodology but I would recommend that you get hold of a copy of the book as it contains much of interest regarding business performance management (BPM). The six principles are summarised below.

1. Goals

It is a good idea for corporate goals to be based on external benchmarks and competitor performance. For example, one company might have goals of being number 1 in its industry in terms of sales revenue and achieving a return on shareholder funds of at least 20% a year. At the moment, the company may be fifth in its industry sales value league table and have a return on shareholder funds of only 13%, but instead of aiming to achieve the goals in one budget year, a longer period, say three years, could be allowed. This target aims at relative improvement rather than hitting a budget figure. This medium-term approach breaks the direct link with the budget year.

If work teams are empowered to set their own performance targets, they are likely to maximise their performance due to their psychological 'ownership' of them. Instead of creating targets based on budget figures, it is recommended that relative improvement should be the objective. An example would be setting a goal to improve the average time taken to complete the sales order processing cycle by at least 5% every quarter. When trust and empowerment are operating, it should be sufficient for senior management to know that teams have set their goals and are using action plans to pursue them.

2. Rewards

Setting the employee cash bonus threshold at 80% of the budget target is meant to combat a harsh environment such as a level of competition greater than that envisaged by the budget. But if the difficulties faced are such that it is not possible to reach the threshold, no bonus will be earned despite the strenuous efforts made by the employees.

On the other hand, if conditions are much more favourable than planned for, employees are able to earn significant bonuses without really trying. The illogicality of this is plain to see, yet this type of bonus incentive scheme is widespread. The effect of operating such schemes is to encourage employees to indulge in the dysfunctional behaviour of 'gaming' as discussed above. They give false and misleading information in order to increase the size of their bonuses. As subsequent business activities are based on this misinformation, it is no wonder that corporate performance suffers. **Financial incentives should not be based on predetermined budget targets.**

Hindsight should be used to help decide the amount of bonus payable. Bonuses are paid in arrears so why not take advantage of this and base the rewards more on the efforts made by employees than their achievements? After all, they are not responsible for changes in the business environment so why should they be punished for, or benefit from, them?

Team bonuses encourage co-ordination of activities which should result in improved performance. For optimal company performance, the bigger the team, the better. The formula for calculating the bonus should be based not on a budget target but on a set of key performance indicators (KPIs). These should be carefully chosen to reflect the appropriate corporate objectives. One of these objectives could be to respond faster to customer orders. If so, one of the KPIs could be the length of the sales order processing cycle. Another objective could be to offer at least one new or modified product every quarter. Using a set of KPIs enables these and other indicators to be included in the bonus formula; different weightings can be given to different indicators to reflect their relative importance.

3. Planning

The authority to create business plans and take decisions should be devolved to low-level work teams. All members of the team should be encouraged to participate in this and the plans should be reviewed systematically. For example, continuing the example in the 'goals' section above, a review could be performed every time the sales value league tables showed that the company had moved up one place in its industry table. (Note that the reviews may be dependent on events rather than time.) Teams should be encouraged to concentrate on the continuous creation of value rather than hitting fixed numerical targets.

4. Resources

Instead of resources being allocated a long time in advance, they could be made available as they are required. Project teams could request resources a little before they were needed; these requests would be based on up-to-date information rather than an out-of-date budget. Overall control can be exercised by a series of preset limits. For small projects, the authority to use resources could be devolved to the appropriate teams.

Central services, such as Information Systems or Personnel, should operate on an internal market basis at predetermined prices. This will ensure that they will only be used when necessary; if a service is freely available, it tends to be overused. This should also bring about an increase in the efficiency of central services as they respond to the demands made upon them. (This theory is also embodied in Charles Handy's *Doughnut Principle* of management.)

5. Co-ordination

Do not rely on annual budgets: plan more frequently by making periodic service-level agreements with other teams. Manage your short-term capacity in real time by adjusting it according to demand. The whole organisation will be more efficient if other teams are seen as internal customers or suppliers. Co-ordination will be improved if teams listen to their customers and respond accordingly. This is different to viewing customer demands as part of your predetermined budget plan. What customers want may not fit in with your budget and you may try to amend their requests to make them fit. How much better it is to respond to customer demands by giving customers what they want, when they want it, instead of being constrained by an out-of-date plan.

6. Controls

All companies should have good corporate governance policies in operation; the need for this has been highlighted by recent high-profile company scandals such as

Enron and WorldCom. These policies provide a framework in which effective internal control systems can be based. These systems are best expressed by clear, explicit sets of rules which are easily understood. For example, 'All debtors should be subject to the company credit control system; any exceptions to this must be authorised by the financial director.'

Actual results should be produced quickly and made available to all interested parties in the organisation. This information should be used to analyse trends and create moving averages rather than for variance analysis. Patterns and trends can be used to control performance by applying a 'management by exception' approach. Rolling forecasts and benchmarking/league tables should be encouraged and the actual performance of the KPI goals should be kept under review.

Abandoning the traditional budgetary control process is a bold step for any organisation. Indeed, many think it is a step too far. However, if you read the 'Beyond Budgeting' book you will come across real organisations which have had the courage to do this and replace the process with a variety of 'adaptive processes'. They include Ahlsell (a Swedish wholesaler with a turnover of about $1 billion), Leyland Trucks (part of the US-based PACCAR group) and Svenska Handelsbanken (a very large bank based in Sweden). These organisations have prospered rather than floundered since they took the decisive step of abandoning budgeting. Also, see the 'Sightsavers' charity story documented in Figure 18.2.

The counter point of view

Having read the above summary of the 'Beyond Budgeting' philosophy, you should now consider some of the arguments against abandoning the budget. The following paragraphs present a counter point of view to each of the six key 'Beyond Budgeting' principles stated above. They are the personal opinions of Nigel Burton who has written all the manager's point of view sections at the end of each chapter. During his career he has been the accountant, financial director and managing director in an international manufacturing company, and he speaks with the authority of many years' personal experience of these issues. It is fair to say that although he believes that the practice of budgeting needs to be continually improved, the total abandonment of budgeting would be detrimental to the vast majority of organisations.

1. Goals

If you want to be number 1 in the industry, the first thing to do is to establish the sales and profits of the current leader, and work out a strategy for achieving them yourself. This will give you a timescale and a required growth rate. You then need to go into the detail, to work out exactly how you are going to generate the increased sales/profits over the coming years, and how much you need to do each year. In other words, you need detailed annual budgets indicating what you need to do to achieve the long-term targets. In this way, budgets can be used as strategic tools rather than mere control mechanisms.

2. Rewards

The use of hindsight to determine cash bonuses sounds exemplary but is it possible to separate internal and external business environment factors from the efforts of individuals or discrete teams to produce a monetary formula for the calculation of bonuses? Is it possible to eliminate subjectivity from the bonus calculations? Maybe the bonus should be left entirely to the discretion of the manager, who is best placed to make such a judgement, but do you really want a significant part of your remuneration to be subject to the whim of your superior, whose own bonus might be enhanced if he or she can keep costs pared down to a minimum?

Basing a bonus formula on a small group of KPIs sounds fine at first hearing but it can be difficult to find ones which are objective, quantifiable and relevant. Also, KPIs can be manipulated in just the same way as budget targets by the playing of 'KPI games'.

3. Planning

A predetermined annual budget does not preclude any thought being given to the way the business is progressing, either long term or short term. For instance, consider an annual production budget containing details of capacity, labour requirements, material costs, etc. This does not prevent the actual monthly production plans being prepared on the basis of actual requirements at the time rather than the original production budget. The existence of a budget does not cause companies to ignore up-to-date information and stick with their original plans no matter what.

4. Resources

The annual budget acts as a **guide** to future requirements. Companies do not sanction expenditure on capital projects or additional personnel just because it was included in the original budget; all such expenditure needs to be justified at the time. Similarly, management are highly unlikely to turn down a profitable activity simply because it was not included in the budget. If a business thinks there is a good chance of making a profit by doing something outside its budgeted activities, it will find the necessary resources one way or another.

5. Co-ordination

Co-ordination is a normal management function. Short-term planning and capacity management are part of the day-to-day functions of management. Listening to internal and external customers' requirements is a TQM idea, and a very good one. It is in no way constrained by the existence of an annual budget. Obviously, managers have to react to the real world. The budget is simply a yardstick against which to assess the impact of their actions.

6. Controls

Trends and moving averages may be useful in some companies, but they can be very misleading, for instance, when a significant past event drops out of the moving average calculation. For other companies, variance analysis is perfectly suitable for assessing performance 'at a glance'.

The last chapter of this book, 'Current issues in management accounting', includes two journal papers on the usefulness of the budgetary control process, one from each perspective. The first, 'Beyond Budgeting', is Hope and Fraser's original paper on the subject which they developed into their book of the same title (discussed above). The other, 'Budgets hit back', claims that any plans to hold a funeral for the traditional budgeting process are very premature as most organisations still perceive budgets as very useful. Reading these papers will help you come to your own conclusions on this controversial subject.

Performance management and people

So far, this chapter has concentrated on the effects of personal incentive schemes on corporate performance. It now looks briefly at performance management from a human resources management perspective. The fact that this is an HRM perspective in no way invalidates its inclusion here in a chapter of a management accounting book dedicated to the management of business performance.

Performance management in this context has been described by Armstrong and Baron (1998) as 'a strategic and integrated approach to increasing the effectiveness of organisations by improving the performance of the people who work in them and by developing the capabilities of teams and individual contributors'. This is reinforced by Hartle (1995) who states that it is 'a process for establishing a shared understanding about what is to be achieved and how it is to be achieved and an approach to managing people which increases the probability of achieving job-related success'. He sets out a simple framework to support this – see Figure 17.1.

The alignment of personal goals with corporate objectives will enhance both the personal development of employees and the performance of the company. This will be achieved through training programmes and appraisal systems amongst other things. However, Hartle warns that the appraisal process should not be an isolated 'stand-alone' system divorced from other corporate systems. Rather, it should be 'integrated into the way the performance of the business is managed and it should link with other key processes such as business strategy, employee development and TQM'. This integration can be achieved by incorporating it within the performance management cycle (see Figure 17.2).

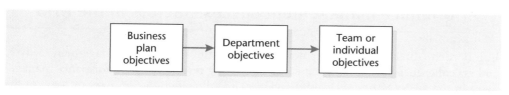

Figure 17.1 Setting objectives throughout the organisation
Source: From F. Hartle (1995) *Re-engineering the Performance Management Process*, Kogan Page, London

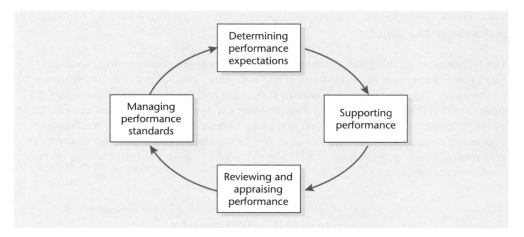

Figure 17.2 The performance management cycle
Source: From D. Torrington and L. Hall (2004) *Human Resource Management*, 6th edition, Prentice Hall, Harlow

Grote (2000) states that 'Organisations with world-class performance closely link their performance appraisal systems with their corporate strategy, mission statement, vision and values, since they recognise that the performance management system is the primary driver for ensuring that their mission, vision and strategy are achieved.' He goes on to say that they 'insist that all managers maintain consistent demanding standards for everyone, and they keep raising those standards. They work relentlessly to identify their highest potential managers and professionals and develop them quickly. They treat their HR departments as partners, staff them with the highest calibre talent available and insist they be active agents for change.'

Jack Welch, the revered former chief executive officer of GE in the USA, embraced this philosophy. He relates that he was constantly appraising GE employees everywhere he went, always setting high standards of performance. He did not believe in waiting for the annual round of appraisals to tell people what he thought of their work, good or bad.

Another very telling finding by Grote is that these world-class companies tend to keep their performance management systems secret because they believe them to be genuine sources of competitive advantage. This is corroborated by Ulrich (1996) who says, 'When employees are competent and committed, employee intellectual capital becomes a significant appreciable asset that is reflected in a firm's financial results.' These organisations do more than pay 'lip-service' to the old saying 'Employees are a company's most valuable assets.'

Performance management success factors in the NHS

Phil Barden (director of strategy development at the Harrogate Management Centre) and his colleagues have carried out some interesting research into performance management in the NHS (National Health Service). The following is a summary of some of the main points in his article 'Non-prescription remedy' (see 'Further reading' at the end of this chapter).

It appears that the main factor determining the success of BPM schemes in the NHS is not their degree of sophistication but the extent to which they are jointly designed by both senior managers and operational staff. He found that 'if staff were asked to set their own targets, these could be up to 20% more demanding than any that have been set for them. . . . It seems that employees are less worried about the toughness of targets and more concerned with their relevance.' More than anyone else, front-line staff know exactly what needs to be done to deliver the appropriate level of care and the areas where they are capable of making significant improvements. 'Senior managers . . . can contribute most by contextualising performance improvement. To do this, they need to explain to staff the aims of initiatives in terms of how – in whole system terms – such improvements will improve results.'

The research showed that executives who provided context, communication and resources were considered by staff to be good leaders. Performance management initiatives were most effective in establishments where the staff judged their top managers to be enabling and empowering rather than directive. In these organisations, BPM was something done **with** staff rather than **to** them. Where BPM systems had been imposed in a top-down fashion, the major changes sought did not materialise. The conclusions drawn by Barden's research include the following.

- Senior managers should acknowledge that front-line staff know more about how, and to what extent, processes can be improved.
- BPM systems/initiatives should be jointly designed by senior managers and front-line staff.
- Jointly negotiated targets are likely to be more demanding than imposed targets.
- Jointly negotiated targets are more likely to be achieved than imposed targets.
- The extent to which staff are involved in developing a BPM system is a better indicator of its future success than its degree of sophistication.

He concludes by emphasising that 'improved performance . . . comes from the recognition that senior managers do not have to know best, but do have to know who does know best – and in what areas'. He describes successful BPM initiatives as 'performance partnerships' to distinguish them from imposed schemes.

Targets, the NHS and 'target games'

To explore this theme further, it is worthwhile examining the target-based approach to NHS performance taken by the Labour government after coming to power in 1997. They set targets in a similar way to commercial organisations, awarding 'stars' to Primary Care and Hospital Trusts who achieve them. Two examples of these targets are (a) no patient should have to wait more than four hours in Accident & Emergency before being examined, and (b) patients should be able to see their family doctor within two working days of requesting an appointment. The more targets reached, the more stars are awarded and rewards and punishments are handed out on this basis. However, it is interesting to note that this target-based system encourages game-playing in the same way as the financial incentive schemes of commercial organisations do. Figure 17.3 reproduces an article by Gaby Hinsliff, chief political correspondent of the *Observer* newspaper, published on 1 August 2004. It provides a very good illustration of 'target games'.

Waiting-time figures 'rigged'

Health chiefs rigged the rules so that government targets for patients to see their GP in less than 48 hours could be met, according to a leaked memo passed to *The Observer*.

Ministers have trumpeted their success in slashing waiting times for a GP appointment, with official figures now showing that 98% of patients can see their family doctor within two working days of telephoning.

But serious questions emerge today with revelations that at least one local health trust not only tipped off its doctors as to the exact timing of the monthly survey of appointment availability, but also offered to draft in extra temporary doctors for those likely to miss it.

Southampton City Primary Care Trust emailed surgeries on 5 July, only two days before the survey was to be conducted, reminding them of the precise date and two-hour time slot when the call would come – and asking practices to contact them 'if you think you will have any problems hitting the GP 48-hours access target'. Doctors who did so were reportedly offered locums.

As local Lib Dem MP Sandra Gidley [was] accusing the health trust of 'fiddling' the figures, the British Medical Association denounced the tactics, arguing the survey should be 'reasonably random'.

'I am pretty sure I know why the trust has chosen to do it, because access targets are one of the things that go towards their star rating,' said Dr Hamish Meldrum, deputy chairman of the BMA's GP committee.

'But this is not something we would support. It just shows what happens when there are rather silly targets and a lot of importance is placed on them.'

The Department of Health yesterday insisted that using locums was 'consistent with our aim of ensuring that patients can see a GP or a nurse at a time convenient to them' and that it was routine for surgeries to know when the survey would happen.

However, Meldrum said his own practice was not forewarned of its survey. He had, however, heard 'tales of it being virtually as blatant as you are describing' in other areas.

Gidley, a former pharmacist whose Romsey constituency is covered by the trust, said such practices devalued the figures.

'If I were an NHS bureaucrat and wanted my pay rise, I would do everything I could think of to make sure that I hit my targets, so I can understand the pressures on them,' she said.

The row follows similar controversy over the government target that no patient should wait more than four hours in A&E. *The Observer* revealed in May that hospitals were warned that waits would be measured during one critical week of the year: some spent hundreds of thousands of pounds drafting extra medical staff for that week, or cancelled operations to free beds for casualty patients.

Figure 17.3 **'Waiting-time figures rigged'**
Source: Gaby Hinsliff, Chief Political Correspondent, the *Observer*, 1 August 2004

As users of the NHS, we all have an interest in its performance. Listeners to the *Today* programme on Radio 4 on 20 January 2005 would have heard the soundbite headline 'The average length of a consultation with a General Practitioner has risen from 9 to 14 minutes.' This was one of the conclusions drawn by a report published by the respected National Audit Office. The extra time available to patients appears to have increased by more than half, a significant improvement that invites our approval.

However, closer questioning revealed that the stated results came from a 'random survey', which is not a very reliable way of establishing the real situation. Several GPs responded by emailing the programme with information casting further doubt on the efficacy of the headline figures. They said that in many surgeries, appointments were organised on a 10-minute-slot basis. Taking into account the time needed for reading patient notes, physical changeover of patients, etc., GPs would probably spend no more than 7 minutes in a face-to-face meeting with the patient. This is only **half** the 14 minutes stated in the report!

They also pointed out that more use is being made of practice nurses for routine care treatment and that some surgeries may organise their appointments on 15-minute time slots. But anyone who heard the soundbite would be forgiven for thinking that the NHS had made a great stride forward in the length of time patients spent with their GPs.

Another example of the manipulation of target achievement came to light just a few days before the general election in May 2005. It appears that it was not uncommon for doctors' surgeries to refuse to give an appointment to any patient who asked for one more than 48 hours ahead. For example, a patient ringing on Monday for an appointment on Thursday or Friday of that week would be told to ring back the following day or the day after. Pre-planned 'appointments of convenience' were no longer available; all appointments had to made within 48 hours of the doctor's consultation. This certainly helped those surgeries doing this to meet their target.

But what about the patients trying to plan more than two days ahead? Apparently, if they phoned back in the morning to book their appointment, the lines were very busy and it was very difficult to get through. If they phoned back in the afternoon, there was no guarantee that there would be any appointments left, at least not with their usual doctor. This does little to improve patient care and causes worry and frustration, especially to elderly patients.

The outcome of all this was that official government figures showed that 99% of doctors' appointments were within 48 hours of asking and that 97% of patients in hospital Accident & Emergency departments were seen within four hours. The reality, from the point of view of patient care and giving priority to those most in need of medical attention, was significantly different.

In the period to May 2005, the government cut down the number of NHS targets from around 200 to about 60. This may be because they have worked; on the other hand, it may be because they have not. There is no doubt that many of the targets set have been crude, centrally imposed blunt instruments, diminishing the amount of clinical judgement required by those on the 'front line'. Has the meeting of targets been confused with effective healthcare?

However, in the mid-1990s, it was not unusual to have to wait for more than a week to see your doctor. So perhaps targets are not as 'bad' as indicated above; maybe they have helped to improve the service? Perhaps it is their headline-grabbing manipulation that brings them into disrepute? It does not seem appropriate to judge a complicated service like the NHS by the use of simplistic targets. An alternative approach is to refine the targets rather than scrap them but would the attendant complexity then make them unworkable? One thing is for sure, 'what you measure is what you get!'

Service performance and response times

The UK utility companies (e.g. electricity, gas, etc.) have adopted a 'specification-based' approach to their performance and quality of service. They specify maximum reaction times to customer requests; for example, upon requesting a service, customers may be guaranteed that someone will call them back within two working days to make an appointment to visit them. They may also be guaranteed that this visit will take place within five working days of them being called back. The company representative making the visit decides what work needs to be done and guarantees that this work will be carried out within the next five working days. In this way, it may take over two weeks for the company to provide the service requested by the customer.

On the surface, this seems reasonable. However, suppose the reason the customer rang in the first place was that her Internet connection over a telephone landline kept on cutting out, causing her to lose some orders for the business she runs from home. This intermittent fault is costing her money and she views the situation as an emergency to be fixed as soon as possible. But the phone company would see the situation more as a routine job that needed doing sometime in the near future.

The point is that the company performance (or service) required by the customer is to have her fault put right immediately. If it takes 10 days to achieve this, she will judge the performance to be unsatisfactory. But if the phone company has met or beaten its specified target response times, it will believe that it is providing good service. This situation has arisen due to the analysis of the service into its constituent parts, seeing it from a 'production' point of view. Unfortunately, this does not coincide with the customers' point of view; it ignores their view of the service as a single requirement and takes no account of the overall time taken to provide it.

But the utility companies are not entirely to blame for this state of affairs. The specification of maximum response times is often imposed on them by their industry regulator and if the regulator does not specify a maximum time in which the **whole** service must be performed, from start to finish, the company may not even bother to measure this, never mind attempt to meet it and satisfy the customer. If the company is meeting or beating the stipulated response times, it will believe it is providing good service and, if necessary, happily provide the statistics to prove it!

The role of the balanced scorecard

Introducing a balanced scorecard into an organisation often costs a lot more than expected. But although it consumes large amounts of resources it usually turns out to be well worth the cost and effort involved. After all, the basic objective of the balanced scorecard is to improve business performance. (Its mechanism and role are explained at the end of the chapter on strategic management accounting.)

Balanced scorecards use a small number of key performance indicators, mostly non-financial. But who decides which indicators are used? If the choice is imposed from above, the effectiveness of the initiative will be limited. On the other hand, if front-line operatives are involved in the choice of indicators, the balanced scorecard is more likely to bring about the desired improvements in corporate performance. As discussed above, it is these staff who know best where improvements can be made most efficiently. The performance indicators selected should come out of discussions between senior managers and front-line staff. Genuine consultation about these will pay handsome dividends.

The choice of balanced scorecard indicators is critical and deserves much thought (see Bourne and Neely's 'Cause and effect' article listed in further reading below). **Whatever a business decides to measure, it will strive to achieve**. Kaplan and Norton, the inventors of the balanced scorecard, express this succinctly as 'You get what you measure.' For example, suppose a company chooses 'average length of sales order processing' as one of its key performance indicators in the 'customer perspective' of its balanced scorecard. If this is currently taking 18 days and it finds out that its main competitor is taking only 16 days, it may decide to set itself a target of 14 days. If management seek to achieve this in isolation from other aspects of corporate performance the company may experience a significant increase in the number of complaints received concerning the quality of goods received by customers. It may be that a different method of delivery was adopted in order to achieve the new standard of 14 days but this caused a significant increase in damage to goods in transit. Instead of relying on its own delivery fleet, the firm may have hired outside contractors to move more goods in less time. Unfortunately, these contractors will not be as experienced as the firm's own staff and more damage will occur.

If the firm's own staff had been consulted, they may have been able to point out that the policy of having only one person per vehicle means that the driver also has to do all the unloading. If there were two employees per vehicle, one hour of unloading time a day could be saved and the number of deliveries increased by 15%. Alternatively, the vehicles could be modified somehow to speed up the unloading process. The drivers would be very aware of the possibilities but it is unlikely that senior managers would have any ideas in this respect due to their detachment from the unloading process.

The role of the balanced scorecard has developed over time. As well as being a mechanism for monitoring a broad range of performance indicators, it is now also seen as a strategic business tool, a mechanism for turning strategy into action. Because the performance indicators can be changed to suit an evolving environment or revised internal direction, the balanced scorecard can be used to implement new strategic objectives (see Figure 16.8). Where it is used throughout an organisation, it not only acts as a mechanism for including employees in the strategy process but also becomes a communication medium for new strategies. This applies just as much to not-for-profit organisations such as the Royal Navy as it does to profit-seeking businesses like Tesco (see Woodley's 'Ship shape' article in further reading below).

The way forward

It is in the interest of all organisations to re-examine and adapt their management systems continuously to ensure their effectiveness. Thoughtless repetition of business activities is no longer an option for successful organisations in the twenty-first century.

The management of business performance is a journey not a destination.

If you have not already done so, you will probably enjoy reading *The Goal* by Goldratt and Cox (2004). This is all about continuous improvement and is all the more interesting being written in the form of a novel.

Fundamentally, BPM is about continuous improvement and the best advice I can offer for achieving this is: **be open to new ideas.**

The manager's point of view

Academics are always trying to find the magic formula for business success. Many millions of words have been written by those who think they have found the Holy Grail, and read by those who are still searching. But the fact is that no such formula exists. There is no 'one-size-fits-all' method of management that will work for every organisation. This is because every business, every factory, every office and every employee are different. All the individual elements within each business contribute to a corporate culture which is unique to that business. Moreover, business conditions are constantly changing, not only as a result of actions taken within the company, but also through external factors far beyond the control of business managers. Everything is variable. The skill of management is to create a system which can control, or react quickly to, as many of the variables as possible. It will never be foolproof.

Because each company is unique, its performance measurement procedures must be tailored to suit its specific needs. The ideas put forward by management 'experts' are all worthy of consideration, but should never be followed blindly. They should be weighed in the light of your own company's strengths, weaknesses and strategies, to see if they have anything to contribute. Of the legion of suggestions on offer, some may be relevant to you and can be adapted for use, while others can simply be discarded.

For this reason, I would be hesitant to label annual budgeting as an outdated process which is detrimental to your company's development. It may be, of course, that a company undergoing a period of dramatic change may find a budget compiled many months ago to be of little use. However, if your company is one of the majority which is showing steady, unspectacular growth, the annual budget may exactly fit your requirements. At the same time, it would be a near-sighted manager who did not consider other ways to measure business performance. Goal setting, teamworking, specific improvement projects, personnel development, etc., are all essential elements of management, which cannot be specifically measured against the annual budget. There is no reason why one cannot use a variety of different types of measurement. The techniques are not mutually exclusive. Use any of them which you consider relevant and useful at any given time, and do not hesitate to change them when that usefulness ceases.

In my company, performance measurement operated on several levels. At the top was the long-range plan (LRP), already discussed in the chapter on budget creation. This was a financial document which pulled together the aspirations of all the individual departments in the company over the next five years, to see if it made a coherent whole. When it did not, those aspirations had to be changed in some way. Individual strategic plans were tailored, so that they fell more closely in line with company objectives for growth and profitability. Resources were directed towards those areas of the company which presented the best long-term growth prospects. Fundamental decisions could be taken concerning those elements of business which were worth backing, and those surplus to requirements.

The LRP is inevitably a broad-brush exercise, as no one can tell what will happen in five years' time, but it does provide a framework in which management can assess the overall impact on the company of every major decision they take. It is essential that management keep the long-term aspirations of the company in mind at all times. It is here that the corporate objectives of, say, becoming number 1 in the industry will be reflected. In order to become number 1, the company will have to achieve a certain level of turnover. The LRP will show if and when that target might be achieved.

The first year of the LRP can be worked up into a detailed annual budget. For my company, this was a revealing and constructive exercise, albeit time consuming and often tedious. But the result was a detailed yardstick against which to monitor the day-to-day operation of the business, with the minimum input from managers. The UK subsidiary had two businesses, one mature, profitable and slowly growing, the other much younger, faster growing and still struggling to reach the required levels of return. We found that the annual budget remained largely relevant for both businesses throughout the year. The budgeted profit was a commitment. When unexpected events occurred, as they always did, it was the task of management to find ways of redressing the situation. If the unexpected event was positive, the management could bask in overachievement, just until the next downside came round the corner.

In order to assess the real progress of the company during the year, we carried out regular forecasts for the remaining months, so we had a feel for how we would end up at the end of the year. This was similar to a rolling budget, except that we restricted it to the current year, in order to make the comparison with budget. The budgeted profit remained the target that corporate management required from us, in order to stay on track to achieve their own LRP objectives.

In addition to the formal budgeting process, we had a variety of other performance indicators, mostly in non-financial areas. These were targeted both at the strategic level, such as the regular introduction of new products, and at the practical level, such as the number of despatches made on time, or the number of batches made within specification without requiring any rework. We were able to target these to specific areas of concern in the company. They focused the minds of the employees very effectively, and encouraged improved performance quite independently of the budgeting system.

How should these performance-monitoring techniques be related to employee rewards and incentive schemes? To what extent do such schemes actually provide incentives to employees? To what extent do employees think about their potential bonuses as they carry out their allotted tasks, day by day, hour by hour? A salesmen working on a commission basis will see a clear relationship between the sales he has achieved and his pay packet at the end of the month, but for all other employees, the link is much more tenuous.

It is very difficult to make bonus schemes directly relevant. Games can be played with performance targets in just the same way as with budgets. The risk with individual targets is that a situation could conceivably arise where managers achieve all their targets for, say, reducing the order cycle time, eliminating lost-time accidents, etc., and so earn maximum bonuses, even though the company's profits have collapsed in an economic downturn! Running a company requires a team effort, so assessing an individual's performance in isolation could be misleading. The salesman achieved his target, but to what extent was this due to technical advances, which meant that the product more or less sold itself? Did the salesman who recorded 90% of his target fail, or did he actually produce a sterling performance in the light of adverse trading conditions? The factory missed most of its efficiency targets, but perhaps this was due to high and irregular demands from the salesforce which caused continuous changes to the production schedules? It makes much more sense to set targets for the whole team to achieve. Peer group pressure will operate on the weaker members of the team to improve their performance. And the best measurement of the team's performance is simply the achievement of the profit target. The annual profit is a representation of the efforts of the team, influenced by instances of good luck and bad luck, varying economic conditions and daily triumphs and disasters, and if all these, on balance, are favourable this year, then so be it.

As in most things a sense of balance is probably the best solution. My company's bonus scheme was weighted heavily towards financial results, with 75% attributed to profit achievement, and 25% allocated to projects specific to the individual. This recognised both team and individual efforts.

In general, incentive schemes tend to be aimed at managerial staff, people who are likely to be ambitious, professional and self-motivated. They will be driven by a desire to do a good job for their employers, enhance their career prospects and, more importantly, end the day with a feeling of a job well done. Job satisfaction is a powerful motivator and will normally provide incentive enough. Such people do not actually need a financial incentive to make them work hard. For them, a bonus represents a recognition of their value to the team and a pat on the back, which also happily enhances their bank balance.

Summary

- Budgets are out of date even before they are used.
- Budgets are very difficult to change quickly.
- Managers often see budgeting as a chore.
- Management by targets leads to dysfunctional 'gaming' behaviour.
- There are several different types of 'gaming' behaviour.
- Cash bonuses based on budget targets encourage 'gaming'.
- Personal objectives diverge from corporate objectives.
- Gaming has an adverse effect on the co-ordination of activities.
- 'Beyond Budgeting' advocates replacing budgeting with other processes.
- 'Beyond Budgeting' has six key principles to help achieve this.
- Counter-arguments can be made against the 'Beyond Budgeting' principles.
- 'Performance management' can describe a formal HRM system.
- Performance management in the NHS has its own success factors.
- The use of targets in the NHS produces gaming behaviour.
- Adhering to response times does not necessarily ensure good service.
- Balanced scorecards can be effective in improving business performance.
- Balanced scorecard performance indicators should be chosen very carefully.
- Managers need open minds to achieve continuous improvement.

Further reading

Armstrong, M. and Baron, A. (1998) *Performance Management: the New Realities*, Institute of Personnel and Development, London.

Barden, P. (2004) 'Non-prescription remedy', *Financial Management*, April.

Bishop, J. (2004) 'Beyond budgeting in practice', *Chartered Accountants Journal*, Vol. 83, Issue 11, December.

Bourne, M. and Neely, A. (2002) 'Cause and effect', *Financial Management*, September.

Brignall, S., Fitzgerald, L., Johnson, R. and Silvestro, R. (1991) 'Performance measurement in service businesses', *Management Accounting (UK)*, November.

Goldratt, E. and Cox, J. (2004) *The Goal*, North River Press, New York.

Grote, D. (2000) 'Creating a world class appraisal system', *Across the Board*, May.

Hartle, F. (1995) *Re-engineering the Performance Management Process*, Kogan Page, London.

Henschen, D. (2005) 'Amex ends budgeting as usual', *Intelligent Enterprise*, Vol. 8, Issue 4, 1 April.

Hope, J. and Fraser, R. (2003) *Beyond Budgeting – How Managers Can Break Free from the Annual Performance Trap*, Harvard Business School Press, Boston, MA.

Hope, J. and Fraser, R. (2003) 'New ways of setting rewards: the Beyond Budgeting model', *California Management Review*, Vol. 45, Issue 4, Summer.

Jensen, M. C. (2001) 'Corporate budgeting is broken – let's fix it', *Harvard Business Review*, November.

Lynch, R. and Cross, K. F. (1995) *Measure Up! Yardsticks for Continuous Improvement*, 2nd edition, Basil Blackwell, Oxford.

Prickett, R. (2003) 'Beyond budgeting case study 1, the private company', *Financial Management (CIMA)*, November.

Torrington, D. and Hall, L. (2004) *Human Resource Management*, 6th edition, Prentice Hall, Harlow.

Ulrich, D. (1996) *Human Resource Champions: The Next Agenda for Adding Value and Delivering Results*, Harvard Business School Press, Boston, MA.

Weiss, T. and Hartle, F. (1997) *Re-engineering Performance Management: Breakthroughs in Achieving Strategy Through People*, St Lucie Press, Boca Raton, FL.

Woodley, P. (2002) 'Ship shape', *Financial Management*, June.

Background

Medibed manufactures hospital beds. These are complicated mobile platforms with several moving parts. Medibed is located on the outskirts of Bromsgrove and has good connections to the motorway system. Bromsgrove is centrally situated in the UK and has a good-quality workforce. Medibed has never experienced any difficulty in finding appropriately trained staff during its expansion over the last 12 years.

The business started when George Wright was made redundant from a firm which is now one of its rivals. As a design engineer, George had some ideas about how the hospital beds he was helping to design could be improved. However, before he had the chance to develop these, his previous firm suffered a severe cash crisis and went into administration, emerging as a much smaller operation under new ownership. George invested his £30,000 redundancy pay into his new business, Medibed, and persuaded a local bank to invest a further £70,000 (secured against his domestic residence).

Starting with only three employees, Medibed has grown gradually over the years to become a well-established, medium-sized company specialising on a single product. George is now 57 years old and has decided to step back from the operational side of the business and cut down his input to one or two days a week. Instead of being both chairman and managing director, he has retained the chairmanship but has recently appointed a new managing director, Alex Medlev, from outside the business. Alex is 43 years old and was the production manager for six years of a firm producing office furniture.

It has been a difficult year for Medibed with competition becoming much more aggressive than in previous years. These difficulties can be seen from the following extracts from a recent management meeting chaired by the managing director:

Managing director:
You all know that the figures show that the labour force is working below standard. But I'm not sure I believe it. I walk round the factory every day and I don't see any slacking, the atmosphere is good and I have not seen any evidence of demotivation among the operatives. I'm not convinced our budgetary control system is telling us the whole truth.

Purchasing manager:
Well, it has served us well for many years. I'm not sure we can start to ignore it just because it is telling us something we would prefer was not happening.

Production director:

It's all very well for you to say that but I think Alex has a point. I realise we have to keep our costs down to remain competitive but I am not convinced sourcing a significant portion of our material components from Eastern Europe was a good idea. I reckon if we had stuck with our original UK suppliers in the first place we would have been better off all round, despite their higher prices. I suggest we reconsider our position on this as soon as possible.

Purchasing manager:

I don't agree. Just look at the figures and you will see how much money we have saved on our material costs. That is what I was asked to do and I've done it.

Production manager:

I admit the figures look good but we've all played budgetary games at some time or other. I think this is an area we really need to tighten up on.

Sales director:

I think we should remember that the bottom line is still positive. It has been difficult since we had that quality crisis in the first quarter of the year and had to cancel our attendance at the London Trade Show. But we have managed to stay in the black. Admittedly, our volume is well below the original budget but it could have been a lot worse; our past reputation has helped greatly but we can't rely on that any longer. I hope we will soon be in a position to increase our advertising spend up to previous levels but we must maintain the quality of our product. It is absolutely vital to our long-term success. I can't stress that enough.

Managing director:

I can't argue with that but I'm not convinced our traditional approach to performance and control is sufficient to help us do that and achieve our objectives in today's turbulent trading conditions. We are already facing a new wave of cheap imports from the Far East. We've got to be more pro-active in improving our performance. Some well-known firms are reputed to have given up budgets and seem to be doing all right without them, thank you very much. I know it is drastic but I think we have got to be prepared to be radical in our approach in order to survive. With the agreement of our chairman, I've just commissioned a report about controlling and improving our corporate performance from the management consulting branch of our auditors. I'm expecting to receive it in the near future, just after the end of the financial year.

Medibed's current budgetary control system

Medibed operates a traditional budgetary control system on a quarterly rather than a monthly basis. The financial reporting is also done quarterly. A significant part of the remuneration for the budget-responsible officers is dependent on them achieving their budgets.

The budget responsibilities are as follows:

Operational area	Budget responsible officer
Sales	Sales director
Materials budget	Purchasing manager
Labour budget	Production manager
Variable overhead budget	Production manager
Fixed overhead budget:	
Marketing	Sales director
Production	Production director
Administration	Managing director

The current financial year has just ended and the actual results for quarter 4 (Q4) are expected very soon. The results for the previous three quarters have been known since just before the management meeting two months ago.

Additional information

- All these budgets **have already been flexed** to the actual level of activity.
- The **original budget profit** (OBP) is £7,550,000.
- The budgeted selling price of one bed is £10,000.
- The actual selling price of one bed is £10,500.
- Variable overheads are absorbed on a labour hour basis.
- Labour operatives can earn bonuses dependent on their completing their tasks in less than the standard times allowed.

List of attached schedules

1 Summary budget for year and by quarter
2 Materials budget for year and by quarter
3 Labour budget for year and by quarter
4 Variable overheads budget for year and by quarter
5 Marketing fixed overheads budget for year and by quarter
6 Production fixed overheads budget for year and by quarter
7 Administration fixed overheads budget for year and by quarter
8 Sales volume budget for year and by quarter
9 Summary of actual results
10 Extracts from materials and labour flexed budgets for Q4
11 Extracts from materials and labour actual results for Q4
12 Variance analysis for the first three quarters.

1. Summary budget for year and by quarter

Item (£000)	Q1	Q2	Q3	Q4	Year
Materials	3,738	3,429	2,849	3,605	13,621
Labour	2,136	1,936	1,628	2,060	7,760
Variable ohds	534	460	407	515	1,916

Item (£000)	Q1	Q2	Q3	Q4	Year
Fixed ohds:					
Marketing	1,922	1,701	1,465	1,854	6,942
Production	1,602	1,453	1,221	1,545	5,821
Administration	748	645	570	721	2,684
Total costs	10,680	9,624	8,140	10,300	38,744
Sales revenue	11,890	10,990	9,100	11,550	43,530
Profit	1,210	1,366	960	1,250	4,786

2. Materials budget for year and by quarter

Item (£000)	Q1	Q2	Q3	Q4	Year
Frame	1,495	1,372	1,140	1,442	5,449
Mattress	1,121	1,028	855	1,082	4,086
Motors	523	480	399	504	1,906
Accessories	599	549	455	577	2,180
Total	3,738	3,429	2,849	3,605	13,621

3. Labour budget for year and by quarter

Item (£000)	Q1	Q2	Q3	Q4	Year
Grade A	1,142	904	843	1,090	3,979
Grade B	608	496	407	580	2,091
Grade C	386	536	378	390	1,690
Total	2,136	1,936	1,628	2,060	7,760

4. Variable overheads budget for year and by quarter

Item (£000)	Q1	Q2	Q3	Q4	Year
Assembly	232	201	187	235	855
Finishing	302	259	220	280	1,061
Total	534	460	407	515	1,916

5. Marketing fixed overheads budget for year and by quarter

Item (£000)	Q1	Q2	Q3	Q4	Year
Customer relations	495	412	340	480	1,727
Advertising	210	250	180	240	880
Salaries	910	900	945	920	3,675
Trade shows	307	139	0	214	660
Total	1,922	1,701	1,465	1,854	6,942

6. Production fixed overheads budget for year and by quarter

Item (£000)	Q1	Q2	Q3	Q4	Year
Assembly	492	476	405	506	1,879
Finishing	309	290	251	327	1,177
Materials handling	451	337	215	362	1,365
Salaries	350	350	350	350	1,400
Total	1,602	1,453	1,221	1,545	5,821

7. Administration fixed overheads budget for year and by quarter

Item (£000)	Q1	Q2	Q3	Q4	Year
Accounting	148	152	150	148	598
Heat & light	124	44	44	144	356
Site security	75	75	75	75	300
Directors' pay	200	200	200	200	800
General office	48	52	50	48	198
Other	153	122	51	106	432
Total	748	645	570	721	2,684

8. Sales volume budget for year and by quarter

	Q1	Q2	Q3	Q4	Year
Number of beds	1,189	1,099	910	1,155	4,353

9. Summary of actual results

Item (£000)	Q1+Q2+Q3	Q4	Year
Materials	9,540	3,659	13,199
Labour	6,070	2,072	8,142
Variable ohds	1,498	512	2,010
Fixed ohds:			
Marketing	4,806	1,909	6,715
Production	4,402	1,503	5,905
Administration	2,003	684	2,687
Total costs	28,319	10,339	38,658
Sales revenue	34,075	11,632	45,707
Profit	5,756	1,293	7,049

10. Extract from materials and labour flexed budgets for Q4

Materials: Motors	2,880 @ £175 each	= £504,000
Labour: Grade C	43,333 hours @ £9.00/h	= £389,997

11. Extract from materials and labour actual results for Q4

Materials: Motors	2,520 @ £200	= £504,000
Labour: Grade C	42,210 hours @ £9.50/h	= £400,995

Note: Due to a power failure, no work could be done during 1,155 of the 42,210 hours. The operatives used this time to generally tidy up their workplaces and then had to wait in the canteen until the power was restored.

12. Variance analysis for nine months (Q1 + Q2 + Q3)

Item (£000)	Budget for Q1+Q2+Q3	Actuals for Q1+Q2+Q3	Cost variances
Materials	10,016	9,540	476 F
Labour	5,700	6,070	370 A
Variable ohds	1,401	1,498	97 A
Fixed ohds:			
Marketing	5,088	4,806	282 F
Production	4,276	4,402	126 A
Administration	1,963	2,003	40 A
Total costs	28,444	28,319	125 F
Sales revenue	31,980	34,075	2,095 F
Profit	3,536	5,756	2,220 F

Tasks:

1 **Variance analysis**

Using the information provided to you in advance and the additional information provided below:

a) Perform a variance analysis on the materials (motors) budget extract for Q4.

(6 marks)

b) Perform a variance analysis on the labour (grade C) budget extract for Q4.

(8 marks)

c) Perform a variance analysis on all budget items for Q4 and present them in a table.

(4 marks)

d) Perform a variance analysis on all budget items for the year and present them in a table.

(4 marks)

e) Calculate the sales volume variance and the sales price variance for the year.

(4 marks)

f) Create a profit reconciliation statement for the year.

(4 marks)

g) Comment on Medibed's performance for the year.

(20 marks)

Note: Perform the variance analyses in as much detail as the information given will allow.

(Sub-total 50 marks)

2 **Budget games**
Define the term 'Budget Games', state 6 types of game and list four negative **effects** they have on companies.

(14 marks)

3 **'Beyond budgeting'**
Briefly state six measures you would recommend Medibed to take in order to manage its performance if it abandoned its traditional budgetary control system.

(12 marks)

4 **Balanced scorecard**
Design a Balanced Scorecard **for Medibed** with 3 items for each of the 4 'perspectives'.

(24 marks)

(Total 100 marks)

Question

Q17.1 W Limited

W Limited was formed five years ago by its current Managing Director to provide specialised holidays and tours. The company has grown rapidly over those years and now has offices in three different parts of the world and employs over 100 staff.

All of the managers are required to attend the company's annual conference. At the conference, the Managing Director presents the company's annual plan and gives each of the managers their financial targets for the forthcoming year.

A number of the managers are becoming dissatisfied with this approach to planning and budgeting within the company.

One manager commented, 'Just because we achieved a certain level of sales last year shouldn't mean that the target simply increases by 10%. We should be considering what's happening in the market place and planning accordingly.'

'I agree,' said another manager, 'these days we shouldn't be bound by financial targets.

Anyway, there are a number of quality issues that we ought to consider so that we can improve our business for the future.'

The managers decided to have a meeting with you as the company's Management Accountant. They asked for your help in providing a report that can be discussed at the next Management Team meeting which outlines their concerns over the present budgeting system and explains alternative techniques that could be used.

Required:

Prepare a report addressed to the Management Team that:

(i) explains the need for budgets;

(4 marks)

(ii) discusses the relevance of an incremental approach to budget setting for W Limited and suggests an alternative system;

(10 marks)

(iii) discusses the importance of quality, and explain how the balanced scorecard approach to performance management could be used by W Limited.

(11 marks)

(Total = 25 marks)

CIMA Intermediate: Management Accounting – Performance Management, May 2004

Not-for-profit organisations

Chapter contents

Introduction

There are many different types of organisation that exist for a purpose other than making a profit for the benefit of their owners. These not-for-profit organisations vary in size from large international groups to small local clubs. Their diversity is illustrated in Figure 18.1.

However, although it may seem paradoxical, not-for-profit organisations often **have** to make profits simply to ensure their own survival! Exceptions to this general rule are the single-purpose organisations that anticipate their own mortality by their implicit winding up once their specific purpose has been achieved. For example, The Millennium Commission was created to oversee the selection and application of public projects celebrating the end of the second millennium. It is envisaged that this body will cease to exist sometime in the next few years.

The fundamental difference between commercial and not-for-profit organisations is not that the latter do not make profits (often referred to as *surpluses*) but what is done with them. Commercial organisations almost always make a distribution of profits to their investors/owners every year, but not-for-profit organisations' surpluses are reinvested in themselves to help them meet their strategic objectives. People who invest in Vodaphone expect to receive annual dividends whereas people who put money into Oxfam do not.

Government
Local Government authorities
The Civil Service and national government departments

Health
Health Service trusts
Primary health care groups

Education
Higher Education Funding Council
Further Education Funding Council

Public service organisations
British Broadcasting Corporation
Citizens' Advice Bureau

International charities
Oxfam
Red Cross
World Wide Fund for Nature
Save the Children

National charities
St John's Ambulance
Royal National Institute for the Deaf
Samaritans
The British Museum
Tate Modern
The Earth Centre

Local charities
Pre-school toddler groups
Local football clubs
Local arts associations
Local gardening clubs
Village halls

Figure 18.1 **Different types of not-for-profit organisation**

Having worked through this chapter you should be able, for not-for-profit organisations, to:

- describe the variety of organisation types;
- discuss the appropriateness of different costing techniques;
- explain the extra dimensions of decision making;
- discuss the extra dimensions of breakeven analysis;
- compare the budgetary control process with that in the profit-making sector;
- discuss the extra dimensions of performance measurement;
- compare capital investment appraisal with that in the profit-making sector.

Learning objectives

Costing

The term 'not-for-profit organisation' encompasses a multitude of activities across the whole range of manufacturing, trading and service organisations. The costing technique used by them depends on the type of activity in which they are involved. Given this wide variety, it is not surprising that a contingency approach to costing exists. Different organisations choose the costing method which best suits them.

Typically, not-for-profit organisations in the public sector will be service based and may not benefit from the absorption costing techniques used in commercial manufacturing organisations. However, not-for-profit manufacturing organisations do exist. For example, the Remploy organisation employs disabled people to manufacture furniture.

The **allocation** of specific departmental costs and the **apportionment** of organisation-wide costs to individual departments **are** appropriate, in so far as charging the costs to the right place is concerned; indeed, much public sector budgeting is done in this way. However, the final stage of the absorption costing technique where costs are actually **absorbed** into products or specifically identifiable services will **not** be relevant unless a final discernible end product/service exists.

The choice of costing system is influenced by the proportion of overheads included in the total cost. If the overhead content is small, inaccuracies in their distribution will be much less important than if it was a large proportion. In a labour-intensive public sector service organisation, the application of elaborate techniques may not be a cost-effective method of producing accurate costs.

In addition to the usual cost considerations experienced by the profit-maximising businesses, public sector not-for-profit organisations have to consider the social costs and benefits involved. For example, the high financial cost of building new road schemes or public transport systems might be socially offset by a reduction in accident levels, so reducing hospital running costs as well as saving lives.

Pricing

Although 'profit' is not the key motive for many not-for-profit organisations, it will continue to be important in the maintenance of the real value of their net worth and hence, ultimately, their survival. In this regard, pricing is equally as important as controlling costs and will be influential in achieving the organisation's core objectives. As with any other entity, a not-for-profit organisation's reaction to its market environment will depend on whether it is a price-taker (in a highly competitive market) or a price-maker (in a non-competitive market). Setting prices in a non-competitive market is generally easier than in a competitive one. However, not-for-profit organisations, like any other, have to react to increases or decreases in costs passed on from their suppliers.

As in commercial companies, the pricing decisions in not-for-profit organisations are influenced by the price elasticity of demand of their products and services. However, public sensitivity will also play a part in determining the final prices set by public sector bodies. Not-for-profit organisations often lie squarely in the public eye and may well have an implicit extra sense of value for money placed upon them. For example, in many cases, the public expects the product or service to be completely free, such as with entry to museums. Not-for-profit organisations in the public sector have to overcome these additional psychological hurdles.

The not-for-profit organisation must first calculate its desired pricing level solely with regard to its market. It can then build upon this purely financial/economic base and consider the more political factors within its social, economic and environmental perspective. This threefold approach to accountability is encapsulated by the phrase 'the triple bottom line', which encapsulates business success in terms of 'people, profits and planet'.

- People – the organisation's most important resource; they create the success. Many organisations reward their employees by sharing their success with them.
- Profit – all organisations need a certain level of 'profit' to ensure survival and continuous development.
- Planet – many organisations are moving towards more sustainable industry practices. This is a consequence of organisations taking a genuine long-term view.

One example of putting this 'joined-up thinking' into practice is where a visitor attraction promotes its sustainable objectives by using differential pricing to offer a price reduction for visitors arriving by public transport rather than by car. Another example of how people, profit and planet are interlinked is when companies reverse the normal car mileage allowance structure so as to pay a higher rate for smaller, rather than larger, engine sizes.

Not-for-profit organisations may decide to buy or sell a product purely for profit-related reasons, but there are often wider environmental and social issues to consider, such as pollution or use of child labour. Different decisions may be made by commercial and not-for-profit organisations in the same circumstances. This is not to suggest that all commercial companies behave in an unethical manner; they do not. However, it is likely that not-for-profit organisations will have a greater in-built pressure to demonstrate an altruistic form of behaviour. Also, conforming to such additional social and environmental expectations usually results in extra cost and reduced profitability.

If you buy a packet of Cafédirect coffee, you will find the following explanation on the packet:

This coffee is bought directly from growers' co-operatives, not from middlemen. The price is never less than an agreed minimum – however low the world price falls. When the world price is above this minimum, Cafédirect pays an extra 10% social premium. Pre-payments, regular market price updates, and a business development programme help the growers continuously improve quality and negotiate better terms for all their coffee.

Cafédirect was founded by Equal Exchange, Oxfam Trading, Traidcraft and Twin Trading. It is hard to imagine commercial coffee suppliers operating in this way.

Another difficulty experienced by not-for-profit organisations is the adverse reaction in the marketplace to any proposed increase in their prices. This goes back to the public's expectation that a great deal of 'not-for-profit' or 'public domain' organisations should offer their goods or services below market price or even completely free of charge. When prescription charges are increased, there is usually a public outcry, accompanied by substantial press coverage. This contrasts with the fact that commercial companies rarely receive any public attention when increasing their prices.

Price levels are at least as important for not-for-profit organisations as they are for profit-seeking ones. Also, the extra dimensions involved make their calculation that much more difficult.

Decision making

Decision making tries to answer the questions '**What** should we do?', '**When** should we do it?', '**How** shall we do it?', '**Why** should we do it? What are the likely **consequences?**' and 'What are the **alternatives** (including doing nothing)?'

The public perception of most not-for-profit organisations is that their operations should be based on a long-term view. Such organisations are thought of as either perman-ent (such as local government organisations) or at least semi-permanent (such as local hospitals). This contrasts with the common perception of commercial organisations, which are deemed to operate on a short-term basis centred on the provision of annual returns to their owners. The fact that commercial companies almost always have medium- and long-term objectives built into their strategic plans is often overlooked.

In addition to the association with durability, these organisations are expected to provide a social service that may even be incorporated into their Memorandum of Association. The long-term time horizon augmented by social factors may well have an impact on the organisation's ability to fix its prices purely in accordance with an economic model.

As with all other operations, the use of both relevant costs and contribution analysis is crucial in arriving at the best decision for the not-for-profit organisation. It will also be faced with the occasional one-off decision which should be considered in the light of what is best for the business at that time. A series of accounting-based questions should first be answered; then a wider, managerial view sought, so as not to run the organisa-tion 'purely by numbers', which may result in valuable opportunities being missed.

The smaller the organisation, the more important it is for it to have an explicit policy for dealing with the more sporadic, one-off requests and opportunities. Without a well-defined process the organisation will not be able to make decisions on a consistent basis. Having a formal system will enable a price to be set which will at least exhibit some parity across the organisation, even if it may not be the optimum price in each case. The accountant's initial price calculation should be subject to wider management considerations, taking a longer-term view, which introduces a degree of stability into the market.

The political environment in which a not-for-profit organisation operates may cause the whole decision-making process to take longer. This may be because it has various layers of management, such as a series of committees, through which information must pass before a decision is reached. This lengthening of the decision process will often put the not-for-profit organisation at a disadvantage as opportunities may be missed.

Another factor within public sector organisations is that individuals' private political agendas may be introduced. This usually results in the organisation performing sub-optimally with regard to its strategic objectives. For example, a headteacher who wants her own children to receive free self-defence lessons may bring this about through her influence as a member of a local education authority committee on the school curriculum. The best way of counteracting this is to have transparent information systems and cross-departmental involvement in the decision-making process.

Breakeven analysis

Breakeven analysis determines **how much** of a particular event or activity we require to happen in order to cover the costs of achieving it. Quite often, the result of a breakeven analysis will indicate whether or not the activity under consideration is viable. However, this is more easily applied to profit-seeking companies than not-for profit organisations. The primary objective of the former is usually maximisation of their shareholders' investments, but the latter must consider wider social and environmental factors. Consequently, breakeven analysis is always going to be of less use to not-for-profit organisations than commercial ones.

It is important to remember that, in practice, the breakeven point is not necessarily 'fixed' once a decision is made. It may take only one input factor to change significantly for the original decision to be undermined. This works both ways – for example, the forced closure of a particular attraction at a visitor centre may well result in the breakeven entrance fee falling as operating overheads are reduced. Conversely, the provision of an extra salaried information officer in a Citizens' Advice Bureau will result in an increase in the breakeven point necessary to recover costs.

As not-for-profit organisations must still consider the concept of 'profit' to survive, even if it is not their *raison d'être*, they will often make the same evaluations of projects as their profit-seeking counterparts. This is especially true in the short term when considering, for example, whether to rent or buy a photocopier.

With regard to the longer term, the difference may be more apparent. For example, when setting admission charges, not-for-profit organisations will have to consider their principal objectives or corporate mission, in arriving at a suitable price. The question may be asked 'Should entry prices be reduced in order to increase visitor numbers and so promote the activities of the venture to a wider audience?' A profit-seeking venture, with shareholder wealth maximisation at the heart of its purpose, can base such a decision on the price elasticity of demand. The not-for-profit organisation has its non-financial 'primary purpose' to consider, whilst trying to ensure its own survival.

Budgets and control

The purpose of a budget within not-for-profit organisations is to promote the achievement of their wider, external goals through provision of an internal control mechanism. As such, the budget should be a means to an end and never cast in stone so that its rigidity precludes the furtherance of the organisation's primary purpose.

It is quite often difficult to get across the sheer importance of budgets and cost control to the employees of not-for-profit organisations, not to mention the wider public. This is because 'profit' is often seen as a dirty word in what is otherwise perceived as an altruistic project. A manifestation of this attitude is that the phrase 'profit and loss' is commonly replaced by the words 'surplus and deficit'. There will always be a cultural battle to be fought by financial managers to persuade others of the need for short-term surpluses to ensure long-term survival.

Control without vision may lead to stagnation but vision without control will almost certainly doom the organisation to failure. In reality you must have **both** to ensure that your organisation can continue to realise its purpose effectively.

The application of budgetary control techniques is very similar in all types of organisation. However, in the case of not-for-profit organisations, a wider context must always be considered in the light of the more extensive stakeholder mix concerned. For example, a project in receipt of public funds must take into account the requirements of all the different bodies providing these funds as well as the perceptions and reactions of the public itself.

For example, a not-for-profit arts association in a village I know decided to celebrate the millennium by creating a mosaic pavement depicting various aspects of village life. The bodies contributing funds to this £30,000 project included the arts association itself, the parish council, the local district council, the county council and the regional programme of the National Lottery. One condition imposed on the arts association was that the villagers themselves had to be consulted as to the design and content of the mosaic and that demonstrations and workshops must be held for them. The county council specified that a higher quality of paving than originally intended should be used if it was to contribute funds. It is very important that the public is consulted when public money is being spent. Public accountability is a fact of life for not-for-profit organisations and their budgets must reflect this.

It is just as true for not-for-profit organisations as it is for commercial profit-maximising ventures that, in the short to medium term, 'cash is king'. Over a longer timescale, funding can be arranged to suit the business requirements, but short-term cash control is paramount to ensure survival! Cash budgets are created and actual cash flows are monitored and compared to the budget. As a result of this, action can be taken to reverse any negative trends revealed.

Application of basic credit control techniques is, therefore, just as important in not-for-profit organisations as it is in profit-seeking ones. Indeed, in publicly accountable bodies, this may be even more critical as there may be little opportunity for private financial support. For example, National Health Service Trust budgets include an external financing limit statement showing the maximum the trusts are allowed to borrow from outside sources.

Capital expenditure budgeting remains important for not-for-profit organisations. (NHS Trust budgets include a capital expenditure/income statement.) Even so, not-for-profit organisations must ensure that capital projects do not detract from the fundamental objectives of the organisation. For example, a new art gallery must ensure it budgets for the purchase of appropriate art works. If it were to spend all its funds on the provision of a gallery building with insufficient left over for funding exhibits, it would not be able to meet its primary aim.

However, at the end of the day, no organisation is privy to unlimited resources and each will always have to 'cut its cloth' to suit its financial position. Inevitably, this leads to an adoption of capital rationing and hard choices over which projects to support and which to abandon.

In just the same way as in commercial profit-seeking organisations, the budget creation and control processes should be communicated clearly to the managers. Ideally, they should be encouraged to 'buy into' the figures by participating in their creation. When managers take an active part in setting their own budgets the plan becomes their own and not someone else's forced upon them. In this way, they have a vested interest in making the plan succeed.

Forecasting of potential revenue will be conducted along the same lines as in a profit-orientated business, with worst-, mid- and best-case scenarios and their associated flexed budgets being established when determining business plans etc. This will be useful in determining medium-term strategies for pursuing the long-term goals of the organisation.

As the not-for-profit venture grows, its budgetary control system needs to become more formal. This is necessary for the accurate measurement of its performance and control of its operations. Greater complexity necessitates greater formality. However, this is common to both profit-seeking and not-for-profit organisations, in both the public and private sectors.

Control without budgets?

Since the above section ('Budgets and control') was written for the first edition, the 'Beyond Budgeting' movement (discussed at length in the previous chapter on business performance management) has been severely critical of the traditional budgeting processes. So much so, in fact, that it has advocated their abolishment! However, it does recommend putting an array of 'adaptive practices' (such as balanced scorecards) in their place. Although there is tremendous opposition to abandoning budgets completely, it does seem as though it is possible to manage organisations well without them. Several international companies which have achieved this are named in the previous chapter.

There is no reason why this should not also apply to not-for-profit organisations. One example of this is SightSavers, a multi-million-pound international eyecare charity. It abandoned its traditional budgeting process because the demands of its medium-term projects (three to five years) were artificially constrained by the short-term (one year) requirements of its financial reporting and budgetary control systems. The mismatch in timescales caused the consumption of many of its resources without adding anything to the quality of its services or the achievement of its fundamental aims. The numbers were driving the activities when it should have been the other way round.

But as long as the budget existed, it was the basis for many decisions even though its contents were often out of date, having been overtaken by events in the regions in which the charity operates. Figure 18.2 tells what it has used to replace the budget and the benefits it has gained by doing so. Note that one side-effect is that misspending due to budgetary games has been eliminated. SightSavers believes that the quality of its operations has improved and it is now growing at the annual rate of 10%.

Break out of the budget cycle

How do you manage performance when the targets people have laboriously negotiated and committed to are made irrelevant at a stroke by floods in Bangladesh, the collapse of the Ghanaian currency or the wiping out of half their reserves in the equity crash? More generally, how do you manage multi-year investment programmes when you do not know what your income will be in the next twelve months?

These were the questions Adrian Poffley was asking himself in 1998 as he left Nairobi after an unhappy regional conference for SightSavers, a £20 million eyecare charity. As finance director, Poffley could see that the nub of the matter was a serious mismatch between the requirements of the three- to five-year timescales of the eyecare projects on the ground and the financial management system based on the formal accounting schedule. There must, he thought, be a better way. There was. SightSavers started by abolishing the budget.

The issues Poffley was wrestling with are among the biggest management headaches of the not-for-profit world. And not just for charities. Donors too are struggling to reconcile the requirement to account for their grants with growing pressure to maximise their impact. Too often the annual grant-giving round maps poorly onto the investment cycle of the charities. Just as bad, the larger the grant the more likely it is to be hedged with detailed controls that actually make the projects more difficult to manage flexibly on the ground.

One result of this emphasis on inputs is that much more is known about the amount of charitable spend than its quality. As a Cabinet Office review of the sector noted, credible information on impact is lacking. This is of increasing concern to institutional donors, from the lottery and government departments up to and including the biggest giver of all, the World Bank – of which more later.

Many organisations respond to uncertainty with increasingly detailed planning. The SightSavers budget consisted of 15,000 numbers and took six months to complete. 'We could tell you how many pencils we'd use in Ghana in the second week of February,' says Poffley.

But the greater the uncertainty the less useful the plan became. Even though its assumptions were out of date on day one, people continued to base decisions on it right until the day the next, equally flawed, plan was launched. The approaching financial year-end 'was like a brick wall no-one could see round'. If it wasn't in the budget it could not be done, or only with extreme difficulty – even if floods or the Iraq war had intervened.

After deep soul-searching, SightSavers decided to abandon the central plan and gear itself to events as they happened – to become event-rather than cycle-driven. It abolished the annual budget (with instant and enormous saving of man-hours) and for the two-inch-thick plan substituted a 12-page framework document which set out the themes and values within which its 250 employees were expected to operate.

Instead of battling to make the business fit the yearly numbers, managers now run the business around SightSavers' activities on the ground. Planning and forecasting have

Figure 18.2 **'Break out of the budget cycle'**
Source: Simon Caulkin, the *Observer*, 20 July 2003

become a continuous participatory activity – 'we expect ideas to be generated all the time and slotted into thinking as and when' says Poffley. Rolling 12-month forecasts (best estimates, not contracted outcomes) and, increasingly, trends and moving averages are used to track where the business is going – but no budget or variances.

The effects of making the figures fit the reality rather than vice versa are dramatic. At all levels, it's at last possible to see the wood from the trees. Instead of 40 pages of figures the trustees (i.e. the board) discuss activities according to a few key indicators: proportion of expenditure spent on charitable work, ratio of free reserves to commitments, and growth of fundraising – 'the appropriate level for governors to talk at'.

Resource allocation at corporate level operates in three directions only: charity work, fundraising and support. Below this, responsibility for resource management is devolved to operating units, where it should be – it's impossible to run local partnerships in 20 developing countries from headquarters.

Best of all, SightSavers has conjured funding certainty out of fundraising uncertainty. By judicious use of reserves, and better husbanding of its resources, it now feels able to guarantee minimum funding for programmes for the next 24 months (rather than one year at a time) and underwrites individual projects for their lifetime once agreement with the local partner has been signed. 'People can now plan ahead with confidence. We're at last running the organisation around its needs as a business, not for the accounting cycle,' says Poffley.

As for performance management, individuals still have fundraising targets, but these are aspirations, not contracts: performance measurement is carried out retrospectively in the light of events, and decouples achievement from targets. It's still tricky, but people no longer feel they are at the mercy of an arbitrary cycle and are being held to account for targets that events put beyond their control. Other benefits: an end to the spend-it-or-lose-it mindset (SightSavers always experienced mysterious spending peaks in December, although there is no seasonal aspect to blindness) and, less obviously, improved ability to spend money quickly and to good effect. Faced with a windfall, it wasn't paralysed by the iron cage of the budget. It can't be proved, but Poffley believes that investor confidence in SightSavers' efficient and effective resource allocation may be a factor in its steady 10 per cent annual growth rate.

Budgets? The last was in 2000. Half of the organisation's employees have never experienced one. No one would want to go back to the tyranny of the numbers, says Poffley, since this is manifestly a more appropriate way to run the business. The only way it would make a comeback is if conservative donors insisted on it.

The new system has survived several important changes of personnel, including the head of the trustees and the organisation's biggest spender, the director of programmes. Will it survive the loss of the chief executive or finance director?

It'll soon know. Poffley has been recruited by the World Bank to do the same job from the donor side that he has been carrying out for the charity: increase the impact of its $19.5 billion a year aid programme by fitting it to the needs of poor people on the ground rather than those of the accountants in Washington. It's too soon to call victory: but if it works, SightSaver's decision to end the tyranny of the budget may mark a turning point not only in development aid but in financial management in general.

Figure 18.2 (*cont'd*)

Performance measurement

Performance should not be evaluated in isolation. For example, what does a test score of 85 mean? Is it good or bad? We cannot say unless we know the desired level of attainment and the maximum number of marks available. If the maximum possible mark is 85 then a perfect score has been achieved. But if the maximum possible mark is 200, fewer than half the marks have been achieved. Also, it helps to know the minimum acceptable level, i.e. the pass mark. If this is 80 out of 200 (= 40%) then 85 is a successful attempt. However, if the minimum is 100 out of 200 (= 50%) a score of 85 represents an unsuccessful attempt. Predetermined performance targets enable the effectiveness of activities to be evaluated.

Various measurement criteria may be adopted, ranging from the traditional 'financial' viewpoint of bottom-line profit, to a more comprehensive 'balanced scorecard' approach encompassing a greater variety of strategic goals. The performance indicators chosen by organisations should encourage the achievement of their fundamental objectives. If being the first choice of its clients is one of an organisation's strategic objectives, it must have some device in place with which to measure the clients' opinions. In this way it can monitor its performance.

The core values of the organisation should be constantly borne in mind when choosing the performance criteria. Also, the monitoring and reporting mechanisms must be appropriately chosen to focus employee behaviour on the achievement of organisational objectives. The resulting common sense of direction encourages goal congruence between employee and employer. Well-chosen performance criteria have the advantage of aiding clear communication between organisation and worker.

As already mentioned in Chapter 15, on budgets and control, the use of variance analysis in performance appraisal is of great importance. The design of the reporting mechanism and the interpretation of resulting variances can be of tremendous significance in influencing the behaviour of individuals within the organisation. This behaviour will, in turn, have an effect on the organisation's ability to achieve its goals. However, it is important to remember that adverse variances can be a result of poor standard setting. To inform operatives that they have performed below standard when, in fact, they have done a good job is bad management. Great care should be exercised in the interpretation of variances. A frequent, systematic updating of standards is highly recommended. This is just as true for not-for-profit organisations as it is for profit-making ones.

To be effective, performance measurement must, like all 'good information', be timely, accurate, clearly communicated to the right people and relevant to their decision needs. In this age of advanced information systems, it is very important to scale down the amount of data to a manageable level to avoid so-called 'information overload'. Focusing on, say, half-a-dozen critical issues will help organisations achieve their strategic goals. If three measurements are chosen for each of these six issues, 18 'key performance indicators' will be regularly monitored. This is a reasonable load for a busy manager to cope with. Information systems may be able to cope easily with 10 times this amount but people cannot. Too much information is counter-productive.

In publicly accountable not-for-profit organisations, such as schools, there is likely to be a more externally based emphasis on performance. This arises as a result of either the public's general expectation of accountability and transparency on the part of these organisations (e.g. publication of hospital waiting-list times), or specifically due to the direct public funding of the entity (e.g. reporting of the achievements of Comic Relief's 'Red Nose Day' charity fund-raising efforts).

The emphasis on external reporting usually leads to a different set of key performance indicators from that of an inward-reporting entity. This is not to say that the more traditional measures of performance suddenly become obsolete, rather that there is an additional set of externally driven reporting requirements for organisations in the public domain.

Capital investment appraisal

The use of capital investment appraisal techniques in not-for-profit organisations will, as with more commercial enterprises, depend on the scale and complexity of their operations. Although the organisation should benefit from the application of these techniques, the costs associated with their application should be kept under consideration. The depth and number of evaluation techniques used will undoubtedly depend upon the level of resources available. It may well be impossible for a smaller body to ascertain whether capital expenditure, such as the purchase of a new till system in a local charity shop, ultimately adds any value to the operation. In many cases, such expenditure will be incurred purely as a result of the fear of the consequences of not doing so, and to analyse the decision formally would require resources of funding or skills that are simply not available.

For larger organisations involved in bigger investment decisions, greater emphasis will be placed on the formal methods of capital investment appraisal rather than 'rule of thumb' or 'gut-feeling' techniques. The reason for this is twofold: first, because there is usually greater accountability to a wider body of stakeholders in larger organisations and, second, because the higher level of funds involved means that larger sums are at risk.

Thus, there are many parallels in the use of appraisal techniques in not-for-profit and commercial organisations, the key similarity being one of scale. Where differences do occur is in the level of risk that is deemed acceptable to each type of organisation. By their very nature, profit-seeking entities are more likely to have a higher level of acceptable project risk as a trade-off for a higher level of potential reward.

Not-for-profit organisations will have a core *raison d'être* other than the maximisation of profit. As a result, they will be more limited in their choice of capital investment projects. Also, the level of acceptable risk is likely to be lower than that of a commercial organisation. Paradoxically, the converse could also be argued, as commercial organisations may well not be keen to invest in high-risk projects of a more social nature, such as the Millennium Dome at Greenwich. The risk may have to be reduced by the project being underwritten by national or local government to entice companies to become involved.

It may well be easier for a not-for-profit organisation to use tools such as benchmarking within its own and across alternative industries, as a means by which expensive investment mistakes can be minimised. For example, if one local government organisation has carried out extensive and conclusive research into a capital investment appraisal of a new police fingerprint database system, why should this not be made freely available to other local authorities in the promotion of greater crime prevention?

A further practical reason for applying comprehensive capital investment appraisal techniques may be that the not-for-profit entities are obliged to use them as a direct result of a funding condition. This ensures that the providers of grants are protected to some degree concerning the application of the funds provided. Where public funds are made available they usually come with many conditions to be met, to avoid potential clawback of any monies advanced. Various output indicators will have to be monitored and reported on. The grants themselves may well be released in stages, upon satisfaction of phased output targets.

Large public sector organisations may also use *cost–benefit analysis* to appraise major projects. This technique is wider than the capital investment appraisal techniques discussed earlier. It takes account of not only monetary costs and benefits but also non-monetary ones. It considers social factors in addition to economic ones. To do this it has to put monetary values on items not normally valued in this way.

Consider the problem of a Highways Authority deciding whether or not to build a new village bypass road. The quantitative costs, such as the total amount charged by the civil engineering contractor, pose no problem. But qualitative factors such as reduced congestion, reduced travelling time and the reduced number of accidents would also have a monetary value placed upon them. For example, based on the average costs of hospital treatment, one accident may be valued at £15,000. If it is estimated that the new road will prevent three accidents a year, the project would show a benefit of £45,000 a year. If it is estimated that two village businesses, dependent on passing trade, would close due to the new road, the loss in business rates to the local council would be estimated and shown as a cost.

Other less tangible factors, such as loss of local amenities and reduction of traffic pollution levels, may also have values placed upon them and be taken into account. (Note that although the Highways Authority would use cost–benefit analysis to ascertain the value of the project to society, the civil engineering contractor would not.) The obvious difficulty with this technique is that the valuations placed on qualitative factors are subjective rather than objective. Two people doing the same exercise would almost certainly produce two different numerical answers. Also, it is impossible to take all the implications of a project into account. The appraiser decides which factors to use and which to leave out, so adding a further degree of subjectivity to the exercise.

(Although very unusual, profit-seeking companies may also use cost–benefit analysis for their capital investment appraisals. For example, a company considering the intro-duction of a new human resources software system could place monetary values on items such as improved absence control, reduced cost of appointing new employees and the provision of real-time data to improve management decisions.)

Summary

- There are many different types of not-for-profit organisation.
- Costing systems are often adapted for not-for-profit organisations.
- Decision making is subject to the extra dimensions of social responsibility.
- Breakeven analysis is relevant to not-for-profit organisations.
- The budget should reflect the organisation's primary purpose.
- Managers should be willing to amend budgets to meet changed circumstances.
- Performance indicators should reflect the wide array of stakeholders.
- Capital investment appraisal techniques are relevant to not-for-profit organisations.
- Cost–benefit analysis allows for the social dimensions of capital investment.

Further reading

Allen, D. (2000) 'Management accountancy in the public sector', *Management Accounting*, February.

Allen, D. (2000) 'Prophets of dome', *Management Accounting*, December.

Ashton, D., Hopper, T. and Scapens, B. (1995) *Issues in Management Accounting*, 2nd edition, Financial Times/Prentice Hall, London. See Chapter 17, 'Caught in the act: public services disappearing in the world of accountable management'.

Jones, R. and Pendlebury, M. (2000) *Public Sector Accounting*, 4th edition, Financial Times Prentice Hall, Harlow. See chapter on public sector performance indicators and value-for-money audit.

Nyland, K. and Pettersen, I. J. (2004) 'The control gap: the role of budgets, accounting information and (non-)decisions in hospital settings', *Financial Accountability & Management*, Vol. 20, Issue 1, February.

Prickett, R. (2003) 'Beyond budgeting case study 2, the charity', *Financial Management (CIMA)*, November, p. 25.

Purdey, D. E. and Gago, S. (2002) 'Public sector managers handling accounting data: a UK framework validated in Spain', *Financial Accountability & Management*, Vol. 18, Issue 3, August.

http://www.sustainability.co.uk. This website gives an excellent introduction to the *triple bottom-line* concept.

http://www.isdesignet.com/Magazine/April'99/role.html. This article illustrates the *triple bottom-line* concept being put into practice in a floor-covering business. It is concerned with strategy rather than accounting (in a profit-making organisation).

Benshire Health Trust

In common with the rest of the National Health Service, Benshire Health Trust is having to cope with considerable constraints on resources. To address this, a new accountant was appointed two years ago to introduce a decentralised budgetary control system to make managers more accountable for their actions. The new system gave managers full responsibility for their costs. The central overhead support costs are devolved to the departments which buy in these central services.

However, the introduction of the new budgetary control system has not gone well. The chief executive, whose skills lie in the area of managing people rather than in financial control, is perplexed by the performance of the various departments. Last year's adverse variances produced by the orthopaedics department are typical of the situation (see below).

Actual outcome compared to fixed budget (orthopaedics)

	Actual	Budget	Variance
Annual patient days	10,000	9,000	1,000
Variable costs	£	£	£
Pharmacy	144,000	99,000	45,000 A
Laboratory	109,000	108,000	1,000 A
Meals	54,000	49,500	4,500 A
Laundry	40,000	36,000	4,000 A
Fixed costs			
Staff	300,000	300,000	–
Other	460,000	460,000	–
Total	**1,107,000**	**1,052,500**	**54,500** A

The chief executive is outraged that every variable cost variance is adverse and is, in his view, a demonstration of completely ineffective cost control. Moreover, he is becoming increasingly concerned, not only about the failure to keep within previous budgets, but also by the new budgets for next year which are being proposed by the department managers. Mindful of his lack of financial expertise, the chief executive has decided to bring in a new financial director. The latter has been recruited to investigate the problems with the newly decentralised system and to put forward some proposals on future development. In his initial meetings with senior staff the new financial director obtained the following quotes:

Chief executive:

I don't understand it. I didn't have these problems in my last organisation. People understood the system and its objectives. People didn't play games, they didn't build 'fudge factors' into their budgets. I don't see any budget reductions made in the light of our cost-saving information technology investment programme. As for the new budget reports, I never know if the variances are real or just a matter of poor phasing of expenditure across the year. I also need more warning of how the year is developing. I want realistic budget figures with a little to stretch people and we have got to have a budget which fits our corporate objectives. Or maybe we should scrap the budget altogether and put one of these new balanced scorecards in its place?

Department manager:

I'm not going to put another brave budget forward after last year. Last year they published a league table of performance against budget and I came bottom. This year I will be giving myself plenty of slack. Next year's budget is this year's plus 15 per cent. I am sure they will knock 5 per cent off straight away even without looking at the budget submission. As for the forms, reports and budget procedure, they just take too long. Every month I have to fill this massive form covering what I have spent and even what bills I am going to pay in the future. This is a system designed by accountants for accountants. I've got real work to do. In any case, I never get any feedback on the figures until months later.

Chief accountant:

We produce monthly reports with actual spend against budget and never get any credible responses explaining the variances. All we seem to get is complaints about the way we have phased the budgets. They don't understand it's not down to us that their budgets are cut – not that it makes any difference, they never know if they are overspent or not. All levels of management have poor budgetary discipline, the budget is there to be complied with. They're always being creative; it's amazing what gets classed as training when that line is underspent! How can I stop them from messing around with my accounts? Most managers aren't rigorous enough in defining their budget assumptions, especially the board, I keep telling them it's to protect them, especially when things go wrong.

A clinical director:

I am fed up with this budgetary control system, it just gives me a headache. Firstly, it's too complex. Secondly, I get the analysis of my expenditure five or six weeks after the month-end. Thirdly, I get no explanation of the variances! My staff have also become adept at beating the system. I found one spending her budget on non-essentials just so it wouldn't get cut next year. Another overspent manager negotiated with a local supplier to post-date an invoice into next year. Where will it end?

Tasks:

1 Is the chief executive correct in his view that the orthopaedics budget is indicative of a complete lack of control?

(25 marks)

2 What are the main functions of a budgetary control system? In what areas is Benshire Health Trust's budgetary control system failing to perform these?

(25 marks)

3 Comment on the practice of 'playing games' in budgetary control. How can this be stopped or at least kept to a minimum?

(25 marks)

4 Design a balanced scorecard for use by a hospital trust.

(25 marks)
(Total 100 marks)

Question

Q18.1 Medical practice

A medical practice had some unused space which it decided to use to expand the services provided to the local community. It has established a new specialist unit, which offers general health assessments and medical assessments for patients. The general health assessment involves a trained nurse assessing a patient's general health and if, for any reason, a patient requires a medical assessment, the nurse refers them to a doctor.

It is estimated that the standard times are 30 minutes for a general health assessment by the nurse, and an additional 60 minutes for a medical assessment by a doctor. The nurse and the doctor work independently of each other.

The medical practice employs the nurse and the doctor on a subcontract basis. The standard labour rates are as follows:

Nurse	£12 per hour
Doctor	£30 per hour

A total of 2,000 general health assessments and 250 medical assessments are budgeted for the forthcoming period.

Fixed overheads for the specialist unit are budgeted at £20,000 for the forthcoming period. These overheads are to be absorbed on an assessment-hour basis.

Although the medical practice is a non-profit making organisation, it is concerned that costs are controlled and that it offers a high-quality service.

Actual results:

The following actual results were recorded for the period:

- The nurse carried out 2,200 general health assessments and was paid £22,500 for working 1,500 hours.
- The doctor carried out 300 medical assessments and was paid £9,800 for working 350 hours.
- The fixed overheads amounted to £22,000.

Required:

a) Calculate the standard costs of:
   i) a general health assessment;
   ii) a medical assessment.

(5 marks)

b) Prepare an operating statement for the period using detailed variance analysis to reconcile the standard cost of the new specialist unit with the actual cost of the new specialist unit.

(10 marks)

c) Referring to your analysis in part (b):
   i)   for each of the variances you have calculated, state one possible reason why it may have occurred;

   (3 marks)

   ii) discuss the possible difficulties of using standard costing in this type of organisation.

   (7 marks)

   (Total = 25 marks)

CIMA Foundation: Management Accounting Fundamentals, May 2001

Current issues in management accounting

Chapter contents

Introduction

When the first edition of this book was published, stock markets around the world had just experienced dramatic falls in their values following the bursting of the 'dot.com' bubble. The two largest economies in the world, America and Japan, appeared to be on the edge of recession and the general outlook seemed rather gloomy after the preceding decade of relative prosperity. However, in the years since then, a downturn in trade rather than a full-blown recession has occurred. But this is only a partial picture.

The United Kingdom has experienced moderate consistent growth and has fared better than its European neighbours. The economies of China, and to a lesser extent, India have raced ahead. For example, China is now dominating the world textile market due to the joint advantages of cheap labour and an abundance of raw materials. India has benefited from the western boom in outsourcing services such as call centres, electronic transaction processing and software engineering.

Also, in the last few years, the importance of good corporate governance has come to the fore. Corporate fraud on a hitherto unprecedented scale by companies such as Enron, WorldCom and Parmalat has shaken the business world. (For this to happen, the corporate information systems must have been manipulated to a greater or lesser extent.) This has brought about further change in the way that business is regulated.

The point is that the business environment is changing rapidly and the way in which business is done has to change with it. As managerial accounting is a service function to management, it too must change. However, as anyone who has been involved with organisations knows, change is notoriously difficult to bring about smoothly. Consider the thoughts of the Italian scholar and diplomat Nicholas Machiavelli in his book, *The Prince*, written in 1513:

> *there is nothing more difficult to execute, nor more dubious of success, nor more dangerous to administer than to introduce a new order of things; for he who introduces it has all those who profit from the old order as his enemies, and he has only lukewarm allies in all those who might profit from the new.*

This is just as true today as it was 500 years ago. In their seminal text on continuous improvement, *The Goal*, published in 2004, Goldratt and Cox say:

> *Change is the hardest thing for an organisation to do. Did you ever stop to think that much of what we do as managers is actually directed against change? Management strives for control, predictability and certainty in the midst of all the variables. And it isn't just the managers who are against change, it's everybody.*

Note the implication that the exercise of control is contrary to the process of change (and remember that budgeting is fundamentally about control).

This chapter looks at two managerial accounting examples of this resistance to change, the inertia of the traditional budgetary control system and the reluctance to adopt activity-based costing, budgeting and management. Both these areas remain the cause of significant controversy and are likely to continue to do so for the foreseeable future. To enable you to examine them in more detail, some relevant articles from the journal of the Chartered Institute of Management Accountants are first summarised and then reproduced. These issues are still the major current issues in management accounting at the time of publication of this second edition: debating these controversial topics continues.

Should the traditional budgetary control process be discontinued?

The first article, 'Beyond Budgeting . . .', by Jeremy Hope and Robin Fraser, argues that traditional budgeting is no longer appropriate for companies that have most of their value represented by intellectual capital rather than tangible fixed assets. Microsoft Corporation is an obvious example, with well over 90% of its value in the form of human capital, i.e. the knowledge and skills of its employees. Budgets refer to tangible items and activities, so only a small proportion of its wealth is covered by its budget.

But not only service companies are in this position. Engineering and manufacturing firms such as Asea Brown Boveri (ABB) of Europe and GE of the USA both have over 80% of their value tied up in intellectual capital. These 'third-wave' organisations have embraced the information age and downgraded the importance of traditional budgetary control in order to operate effectively in the new business environment. They have successfully adopted strategic management accounting techniques in their drive for continuous improvement. However, many firms have been less successful in introducing the same techniques. The authors argue that this is due to their continuing use of traditional budgeting, which causes the corporate culture to 'snap-back' from empowerment to control. The ensuing mixed messages muddy communications and confuse employees, resulting in a lack of motivation and achievement.

Hope and Fraser say:

> *Traditional budgeting is clearly 'out of sync' with the emerging third-wave organisation. It strengthens the vertical chain of command and control rather than empowering the front line. It constrains rather than increases flexibility and responsiveness. It reinforces departmental barriers rather than encouraging knowledge-sharing across the organisation. It makes people feel undervalued – as 'costs to be minimised' rather than assets to be developed. And it is bureaucratic, internally focused and time-consuming. In short, its time is up.*

This sentiment is echoed by Jack Welch, chief executive officer of GE (currently the most admired firm in the USA). In *Fortune* magazine, 29 May 1995, he said:

> *The budget is the bane of corporate America. It never should have existed. A budget is this: if you make it, you generally get a pat on the back and a few bucks. If you miss it, you get a stick in the eye – or worse. . . . Making a budget is an exercise in minimalisation. You're always trying to get the lowest out of people, because everyone is negotiating to get the lowest number.*

It seems the CEO of one of the most successful companies of the modern era would like to see the demise of the traditional budgetary process.

The second article I reproduce is 'Budgets hit back' by Paul Prendergast. He begins by acknowledging that budgets encourage people to think short term and concentrate on operational detail, saying that: 'Our preoccupation with measuring and scorekeeping may cause us to miss the big picture needed in a rapidly changing business environment.' He also raises the problem of budgetary games, where 'senior management battle to set a challenging budget to "get the most out of staff", while their junior managers fight back to negotiate an easily achievable target'. He goes on to praise the balanced scorecard created by Kaplan and Norton and describes how this has been seen as a threat to traditional budgeting and control. However, he says that:

> *despite startling headings in some articles claiming that the budget was dead, a funeral would have been embarrassingly premature. Detailed reading of these cases indicates that where companies now had 'no budget', they instead had a plan, a rolling forecast, or some other yardstick which could be called, er . . . well, a budget.*

It seems that, for the vast majority of organisations, the budget is very much alive and well. Prendergast points out that the financial performance indicators included in the budget can be incorporated into the balanced scorecard approach, which also embraces non-financial key performance indicators such as customer satisfaction and company innovation. However, he acknowledges that 'budget games' have grown into 'scorecard games' and suggests that many managers find it easier to corrupt non-financial targets than financial ones. This may be because they often do not have a clear understanding of the effects of financial concepts such as 'accruals'. Budgets are here to stay, even if as only one part of a wider system embracing long-term strategic objectives.

Is activity-based costing/budgeting/management really worthwhile?

Activity-based costing is now over 10 years old, yet only a small minority of UK firms have adopted it. Given the acclaim with which it was greeted in the late 1980s, it could reasonably be expected to have been adopted by a majority of firms by now. Why has this not happened? The third article reproduced, 'The great debate', discusses the pros and cons of activity-based costing and compares it to absorption costing. It is in two parts, the first by Tom Kennedy and the second by Richard Bull.

Tom Kennedy confirms that management information needs have changed dramatically over the last decade or two and traditional systems have been criticised for not meeting these needs. He says that:

> *The practice of using volume-sensitive drivers to attach overhead costs to products may satisfy statutory and regulatory accounting requirements, but is not appropriate in today's competitive and dynamic business environment.*

He goes on to quote the chairman of General Motors complaining about the widespread inaccurate assignment of indirect costs to products.

Kennedy then describes activity-based costing as being primarily concerned with 'understanding causality and giving decision makers the potential to manage costs at the root' and claims that it better informs the decision-making process. Despite this, he reminds us that UK businesses have been urged to take an evolutionary, rather than a revolutionary, approach to this new system and points out that ABC is not always a good 'fit' for all organisations. Research has shown that the implementation of ABC systems has proved particularly difficult, often due to the inadequacy of the information systems on which they are run. He concludes with the words, 'Perhaps it is too early to write an obituary for traditional management accounting systems and to label ABC as the "holy grail".' Kennedy gives a cautious welcome to ABC in the UK.

In the second part of 'The great debate' Richard Bull states that 'ABC has become established as an essential tool of the management accountant'. He continues by clarifying the difference in approach between traditional absorption costing and ABC:

> *The traditional model starts with resources and seeks to allocate their costs to products. . . . In contrast, the ABC model starts with an enterprise's products and services. It then seeks to identify the activities required to produce or deliver them and, in turn, the resources required to carry out those activities.*

The difference in the level and nature of resources revealed by a comparison of the two systems identifies shortages/constraints and excesses/waste. Bull captures the essence of ABC by saying, 'it does not inevitably finish up with what there is; only with what there needs to be'. A contingency approach to costing systems is advised by advocating absorption costing for firms adopting a resource-based view and ABC for those with a market-led approach.

Where ABC is adopted, Bull says that its effectiveness depends on **how** it is used and stresses the importance of interpersonal relationships between managers. They should be encouraged to specify what each requires of the other in terms of activities rather than resources. For example, manager A may say 'I need a certain quantity of resource X' and manager B may reply 'I will provide you with a different quantity of resource Y which I think will satisfy your needs'. This dialogue leads to conflict and distrust. Alternatively, manager A may say 'To do my job, I need the following level of activities to be performed' and manager B may reply 'OK. Leave it with me and I will make sure this level of activities happens.' This dialogue leads to harmony and trust. In this way:

> *key activity drivers become apparent and this helps to distinguish those activities that add value from those that do not. . . . With the correct relationships and the appropriate management strategy the true potential of activity based costing has an opportunity to be realised.*

Bull encourages the adoption of ABC where it is appropriate but stresses the importance of how it is carried out.

The future of management accounting

The last article I reproduce, 'Existential crises', is written by David Allen, CBE, past president of CIMA and director of several companies. In it, he considers the changing role of management accountants. He starts by making explicit their dual roles of accounting and financial management. He then regrets the regularity with which academics/consultants produce new techniques to **measure** the 'real value' of intangible assets, deceiving their 'non-financial colleagues into buying the modern equivalent of the emperor's new clothes'.

The primary financial objective of commercial enterprises is stated as the maximisation of the net present value of future cash flows from company to shareholder. He bemoans the confusion between estimates of future cash flows and what they actually turn out to be. The former are predictions and projections based on beliefs and assumptions; they are made in the present and are yet to be realised. The latter can only be measured in arrears, after they have occurred and are in the past. But decisions have to be made before the event. If you wait until the items are measurable, it will be too late to change them. This reminds me of the Chinese proverb 'He who hesitates before taking a step will spend his entire life on one leg.' 'One-legged management' is not effective.

Allen concludes by saying:

> *The waning of accounting and the waxing of financial management amounts to a shift from hard to soft concepts, and is consistent with what is happening in other areas of management. . . . The problem is that, although there will always be a need for accounting, that part of the profession is shrinking. For a basis for decision support and monitoring, you need the financial management model, and you have to be comfortable with subjective judgements and unmeasurable values.*

The Chinese ideogram for 'crisis' is constructed from two other ideograms, one for 'opportunity' and the other for 'threat'. The threat outlined by Allen is that management accounting will become less relevant to the needs of today's managers; the opportunity is that its financial management role will make it **more** relevant.

As I said in my preface, 'Managerial accounting is about improving the future performance of organisations.'

The following four articles are reproduced by kind permission of The Chartered Institute of Management Accountants:

'Beyond Budgeting . . .'

Breaking through the barrier to 'the third wave'

Jeremy Hope and Robin Fraser

(First published in *Management Accounting* (*British*), Dec 1997. Full text: © 1997 The Chartered Institute of Management Accountants)

Jeremy Hope and Robin Fraser argue that the management accounting model that has served companies well in the second wave (the industrial age) must be changed if companies are to compete successfully in the third wave (the information age). They believe that the primary barrier to change is the budgeting system. They support their argument with evidence from highly successful Scandinavian companies that have completely abandoned budgeting. They also outline the further research that CAM-I is now undertaking internationally to develop a guide to help companies break through this barrier.

Much has already been said and written about how traditional management accounting fails to support hard-pressed managers in today's highly competitive world. But simply adopting new techniques such as activity-based costing and the balanced scorecard will not bring the expected benefits if they do not fit well with the chosen management structure and style. Accounting systems invariably mirror the existing management structure and, as this structure evolves, so should the accounting model. The problem is that, as firms try to adopt more flexible and responsive management approaches to focus on the customer, they often fail to support these changes by adapting the old accounting systems that were designed for a different competitive era. Indeed, many of these firms are finding (often too late) that the second wave economic model that stressed volume, scale and the recovery of fixed costs, doesn't sit well in the competitive climate of the third wave, where innovation, service, quality, speed and knowledge-sharing are the defining factors.

Moreover, the key competitive constraint is no longer land, labour or capital. It is, and will increasingly be, knowledge or intellectual capital (including competent managers, skilled knowledge workers, effective systems, loyal customers and strong brands). Financial capital is now a commodity bought and sold on the open market like apples and pears. You only have to consider the huge levels of share buybacks of recent years (even in persistent loss-makers like DEC) to realise that capital is now being 'laid off' in the same way that workers have been laid off over the past 20 years. Moreover, there is already strong evidence that those companies that have focused on building their

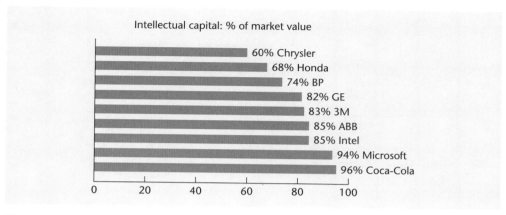

Figure 19.1

intellectual capital have provided excellent returns for their shareholders and have outperformed their competitors on every (financial) measure.

In most companies today, intellectual capital forms the greater part of their market value (see Figure 19.1). And this applies to manufacturing companies as well as high-tech and service businesses. In brand leaders like Coca-Cola, for example, intellectual capital forms an incredible 96% of market capitalisation leaving only 4% for the auditors to verify and report upon! But it is the two engineering giants of Europe and America – ABB (Asea Brown Boveri) and GE – that should really catch our eye. Both of these companies have over 80% of their value in intellectual capital, reflecting more than anything else the strength of their managerial capabilities.

Nor is this simply the result of high-flying stock markets. Many firms now recognise that the underlying source of future cashflows will increasingly come from the effective management of intellectual assets. Meeting the exact (and exacting) needs of the customer is what matters today, and this is more a function of leveraging knowledge to bid for contracts, solve problems, provide superior service and offer customised products, than simply investing, for example, in new productive capacity.

The implications for managers and accountants are obvious (see Figure 19.2). Maximising the value of intellectual assets has a far greater impact on shareholder value than maximising financial assets. This shift in emphasis demands new forms of organisation and new ways of managing and measuring performance.

Figure 19.2

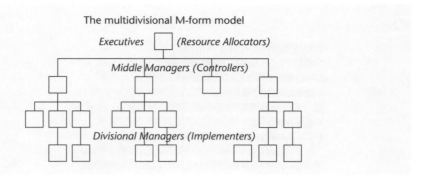

Figure 19.3

The emerging third wave organisation

Just as the multidivisional (M-form) structure set the standard for the industrial age, a new managerial model is now emerging that is likely to become the standard for the information age. In the M-form model (see Figure 19.3), pioneered in the 1920s by US giants like Du Pont and General Motors, top management is the fountain of knowledge, the strategist and the resource allocator; middle managers are the controllers; and the front-line managers are the implementers. These structures were established to support the rapid growth of second-wave companies as they expanded into new products and markets, and helped them to reduce the complexity of managing multiple strategies. These structures were created by devolving assets and accountability to departments and divisions, and they were supported by vertical information systems to enable top management to allocate resources and control their use. The so-called M-form was right for its time (1920s to 1970s) because capital was the key strategic resource. But in today's business environment the model is too bureaucratic, rigid and unresponsive, and it creates a culture that is risk-averse and gives a false sense of security.

Today we are operating in a highly competitive and rapidly changing business environment and, as we have already noted, the key resource is no longer financial, but intellectual capital. In the emerging model – let's call it the N-form (see Figure 19.4) – front-line managers are the entrepreneurs, strategists and decision makers, constantly

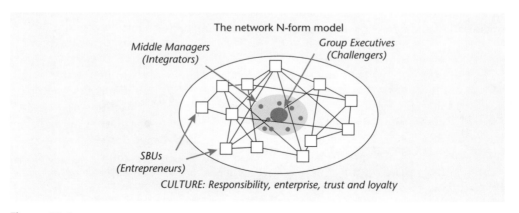

Figure 19.4

creating and responding to new opportunities for the business; middle managers are the horizontal integrators, building competencies across the organisation (and with external partners); and top managers provide inspiration and a sense of purpose while frequently challenging the status quo. In contrast to the M-form, this is a model that is in tune with the times. It has a softer, more organic form that is market-focused, lean and responsive.

ABB, recently voted by its peers as Europe's most admired company, has adopted many of the essential features of the N-form. With over 200,000 employees, it has created a federation of some 1,300 distinctive and separate businesses, each with multiple profit centres. It has a very lean HQ (about 150 people) and is highly decentralised. R&D, for example, is devolved to operating units, but it is leveraged horizontally. Each unit manages its own finances as if it were an independent company, but information across and up-and-down the group is open and fast. By adopting the N-form model, ABB has created a widely distributed network of entrepreneurs thus improving responsiveness while retaining the benefits of scale through mechanisms for horizontal integration.[1]

Another outstanding example of the N-form is ISS, a Danish contract cleaning company. The company's success is built on its respect for its people and the belief that, at whatever level in the organisation, people will make the right decision if they are properly informed. Cleaning supervisors are encouraged to run their operations as if they were independent businesses. Once thoroughly trained, supervisors receive financial reports by cleaning contract, and, because they are at the front line, treated as professionals and rewarded on team profitability, they exercise a control over costs that is far tighter than a financial controller could ever exercise remotely. With this philosophy, ISS has grown from a local office cleaning contractor to a multinational business with a $2bn turnover and 115,000 employees.

At the heart of the new model lie processes and teams. Indeed, many firms have already adopted a process-based approach to management in an attempt to align their operations with the needs of the customer. Driven by the TQM and re-engineering movements, processes offer managers a clearer view of which work should be done and, when new technology is applied, how such work can be done faster and more effectively.

The underlying philosophy in the N-form company is one of maximising value rather than minimising costs, and the focus of measurement systems is on strategic performance, value-adding processes and knowledge management. But, most important of all, it is a model based on trust between managers, workers, customers and partners. And, as many firms have discovered, this trust can be easily undermined when managers (typically when the 'going gets tough') are quickly driven back to 'managing by the numbers' – a path that invariably leads to arbitrary cost reductions, declining morale and falling profits.

Whether they recognise it or not, many firms have already adopted many of the elements of the new organisational model. TQM, BPR, decentralisation, empowerment, economic value added and the balanced scorecard are all pieces in this new jigsaw. However, studies show that for the vast majority of firms, these initiatives fail to bring the intended benefits. This failure is, more often than not, put down to poor communication or lack of top management commitment, but the real culprit is likely to be hidden within the accounting system itself. Indeed, many well planned changes and many attempts to shift the culture from one of compliance and control to enterprise and learning have foundered when management behaviour has been 'snapped back' into its old shape by the invisible power of the budgeting system (see Figure 19.5).

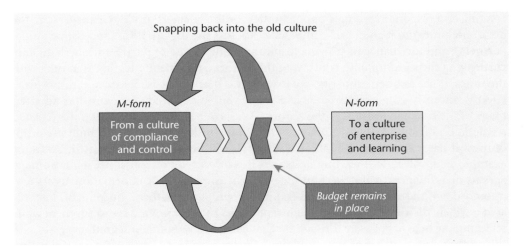

Figure 19.5

Scandinavians are dismantling budgeting

The extent of this power is all too obvious. Despite progress towards non-financial measures and the balanced scorecard, extensive surveys conducted by the leading accounting firms indicate that 99% of all companies in Europe (irrespective of country, industry or size) still operate with formal budgeting systems. While this is hardly surprising, a number of enterprising Scandinavian multinational companies have taken great strides down the path towards the N-form model and, in some cases, have dismantled their traditional budgeting systems altogether.

Svenska Handelsbanken abandoned traditional budgeting as long ago as 1979 and has since achieved dramatic success. It is now the largest bank in Scandinavia and the most efficient of the big banks in Europe. Chief executive Arne Martensson notes that a culture of thrift and improvement rather than imposed budgetary controls has enabled the bank to drive down costs to a level that is the envy of its competitors.

By operating each branch like an independent business, adopting a unique profit-sharing scheme based on performance relative to competitors, and developing a fast and open information system so that one branch can compare its performance against another, its cost/income ratio has been reduced to 45% (and falling). This compares with around 70% for many of its rivals such as NatWest, ABN-Amro and Deutschebank.[2]

IKEA, the world's largest furniture manufacturer and retailer, abandoned budgeting in 1992. Now its business managers merely have to keep costs within certain revenue ratios. Borealis, a Danish petrochemicals company with a turnover of £1.6bn, completely abandoned traditional budgeting in 1995 and its executives are delighted with the progress so far. Managers now use new mechanisms to steer the company, including scorecards, rolling financial forecasts, trend reporting and ABM. Several other Scandinavian companies (such as Volvo) are also at various stages of abandoning traditional budgets.

In all cases, these are large multinational corporations not prone to managerial experiments. They are making these changes for good business reasons that include improving competitiveness, enhancing the value of intellectual capital and ultimately increasing shareholders' wealth.

Budgeting – 'an unnecessary evil'

Some accountants may be alarmed at these radical changes and they will not be surprised to learn of the obstacles and objections faced by the early pioneers. One such pioneer was Dr Jan Wallander. When CEO of Svenska Handelsbanken, he encountered strong opposition when he decided to dismantle the entire budgeting system at a stroke. He called this opposition 'the budget bureaucratic complex'. To this, he says, belong all those people within companies who feel their position and their work is coupled to the budget system, as well as those professors, management consultants and other experts who write books, lecture and organise conferences about budgeting and its technical complications![3]

Why does Wallander (and others who have adopted the N-form philosophy) see budgeting as 'an unnecessary evil'? Let's look at the issue from the perspective of three N-form managers – those in charge of front-line business units, those in the middle, and those at the top of the organisation:

- *Front-line managers* become entrepreneurs and strategists in an organisation that is radically decentralised to meet the demands of a rapidly changing business environment. They see the budget as a commitment and therefore a constraint, as it is based on assumptions that are bound to be out of date as soon as the ink is dry. Instead of blindly following an approved financial plan (that may already be discredited), they need the freedom to operate within boundaries set by a clear corporate purpose and a measurement framework that will include challenging (but achievable) strategic targets.
- *Middle managers* become the 'horizontal integrators' and the hands-on coaches of front-line managers. They see budgets (especially if reinforced by rewards) as encouraging parochial behaviour that opposes their efforts to build competencies across the group. They also see budgets as a mechanism for top-down control and thus in conflict with their aim of developing the responsibility levels and enabling the self-regulation of front-line managers. They also know that, with a flattened hierarchy, there is no longer the resource available to fulfil their old tasks as controllers and administrators, and to revert back to this system would need many more people that would add cost but little value.
- *Top managers* become the creators and communicators of the group framework and values, challengers of the status quo, and leaders of renewal and improvement. They, like Jack Welch, CEO of the US giant GE, see budgeting as 'an exercise in minimalisation', rather than stretch. They also recognise that it is a poor mechanism for forecasting (because it is too inwardly focused) as well as being an inhibitor of enterprise and continuous improvement.

There are conflicts at every level. Traditional budgeting is clearly 'out of sync' with the emerging third-wave organisation. It strengthens the vertical chain of command and control rather than empowering the front line. It constrains rather than increases flexibility and responsiveness. It reinforces departmental barriers rather than encouraging knowledge-sharing across the organisation. It makes people feel undervalued – as 'costs to be minimised' rather than as assets to be developed. And it is bureaucratic, internally focused and time-consuming. In short, its time is up.

Alternative steering mechanisms

With all this talk of new organisational models and the inclusion of so-called 'soft' measures, the reader might be forgiven for wondering where this leaves financial management itself.

Let's try to understand how this will operate in practice by considering three of the purposes of traditional budgeting and how they might be achieved within the N-form model:

- *Forecasting and resource allocation* – In the N-form model, front-line units have direct access to capital and are encouraged to share productive capacity across the organisation. Managers prepare rolling plans (usually quarterly) and these are used for cash forecasting but not cost control. There is an important distinction here. While traditional budgets are forecasts, they are also commitments. In the traditional system, managers must participate in a bureaucratic and time-consuming process to build their understanding of and commitment to the figures against which they will be controlled. In the new model, forecasts are prepared quickly, updated when required, and need not be constrained by the annual planning cycle. They must also be as accurate and objective as possible. This requires good access to external data, fast and open information across the organisation and process-based models to understand the relationship between outputs and resources.
- *Measurement and control* – While performance responsibility and accountability is devolved to the lowest possible level, it is still vital that senior managers monitor cashflows and have up-to-the-minute information on profit performance. Aggressive performance targets will be agreed, but month-to-month measures will not be based on 'actual versus budget' reports, but on strategic milestones and relative measures. There will also be an emphasis on what some management writers have called 'double loop learning' or those 'how and why' performance questions that budget variance analyses so critically fail to answer. This can lead to important tactical changes in strategic direction through the year. The new measurement system is set within a framework of the balanced scorecard used not so much as a measurement system but as a strategic management system. Borealis, for example, uses market-independent ROCE target-setting and measurement, because the petrochemical business is very cyclical.
- *Cost management* – In the new model, effective cost management is achieved by creating a culture of thrift and continuous improvement, reinforced by a long-term organisation-wide reward system. Many firms, for example, are now educating their employees to understand such issues as which work adds value and thus helping them to identify and eliminate non-value-adding work (e.g. encouraging salespeople to spend more time with the customer). Once again, the emphasis is on managing value up rather than managing costs down. ABM and benchmarking are important weapons in the armoury of the N-form manager.

Surely, better budgeting is still possible?

The logic that we must change organisational form as we move from the industrial to the information age is compelling. But, given that nearly all companies today[4] still operate with traditional budgets, we must accept that there is some way to go before most of these companies will be convinced by the argument. Some will wish to continue, for the time being at least, to believe that better budgeting is possible and concentrate on improving their planning processes. Others will be looking for an evolutionary rather than a revolutionary approach to organisational change and the abandonment of budgeting.

The only significant attempt in the past 30 years to address the weaknesses of traditional budgeting has been the development of zero-base budgeting (ZBB). ZBB is a highly effective process for occasional reviews to improve resource reallocation and make significant cost reductions. Moreover, linking ZBB with BPR, activity-based budgeting and other improvement techniques can enhance its effectiveness for enterprise-wide cost reduction. But such one-off projects should not disguise the fact that ZBB is not suitable as an on-going budgeting system. It is too bureaucratic, internally focused and time-consuming. Moreover, it is just as 'out of sync' with the information age as traditional budgeting. Better budgeting is not the answer.

Many companies are already in the process of transition from M-form to N-form but failure to address the budgeting issue is likely to deny them long-term success. Nor is this problem obvious. Few researchers or practitioners have been flagging the budgeting issue as a major barrier to success and there are even fewer guidebooks to help the unwary manager.

What we have outlined in this article is a strong *prima facie* case for abandoning traditional budgeting and adopting a new form of organisation with alternative steering mechanisms. What companies now need are more comprehensive answers to these key questions:

- *Budgeting* – How in detail are those leading companies that have abandoned or significantly changed their budgeting systems now fulfilling the purposes for which budgeting has for so many years been used?
- *Context* – Is there really a coherent new form of organisation emerging that will provide a new context within which it will be clearer what steps should be taken and how they should link together?
- *Implementation* – What lessons have already been learned about how best to implement the necessary changes and what are the critical success factors?

CAM-I's sponsored research project

CAM-I, the international research consortium best known for its development of ABC, is now launching a sponsored research project (led by the authors), to find answers to these key questions.

The research programme, taking place throughout 1998, will be driven by the needs of a group of corporate sponsors. Our approach will be to build and test a working hypothesis concerning the role of budgeting within organisational change. With the help of the sponsors, we will select a number of target companies to visit and then use two main lines of enquiry:

- *'Inside out'* – How are these leading firms now fulfilling the purposes of the old budgeting process using new steering mechanisms or enhanced traditional methods?
- *'Outside in'* – How are they responding to the pressures of the information age through change in organisational form and management processes, and how do they now see their budgeting systems?

The deliverables from the project will include:

● *Case reports* – These detailed reports on the target company visits will provide a rich source of knowledge. We have little doubt that we will unearth a picture of trial and error, success and failure, feedback and learning.
● *Guidelines* – We expect to develop and enrich our understanding of the context for the changes required to meet the new business needs of the information age and will present guidelines and diagnostic tools that interested firms can follow, supported by practical examples.
● *Shared learning* – The opportunity for sponsors to steer and participate in the project will ensure that they receive far greater insights into its results than they would from just reading its conclusions when these are ultimately released.

> *The budget is the bane of corporate America. It never should have existed. A budget is this: if you make it, you generally get a pat on the back and a few bucks. If you miss it, you get a stick in the eye – or worse . . . Making a budget is an exercise in minimalisation. You're always trying to get the lowest out of people, because everyone is negotiating to get the lowest number.*
>
> (Jack Welch, CEO, GE, *Fortune*, 29 May 1995)

[1] The ABB case is based on a paper by Christopher A. Bartlett and Sumantra Ghoshal: 'Beyond the M-Form: toward a managerial theory of the firm', *http//lwww.gsia.cmu.deu/bosch/bart.html*
[2] *The Economist*, July 1997, 'Culture of thrift'.
[3] Dr Jan Wallander, Svenske Handelsbanken: *Budgeting – An Unnecessary Evil* (a summary in English of a recent book written in Swedish).
[4] Coopers & Lybrand 1996 and KPMG 1994: *Pan European financial management and budgeting surveys*.

(The authors are partners in Fraser Hope Associates and are working with CAM-I Inc, the US based international research consortium, on the Beyond Budgeting research project. Jeremy Hope is co-author of Transforming the Bottom Line *and* Competing in the Third Wave, *published by Harvard Business School Press. He was previously with 3i and subsequently spent ten years in business management. Tel: 01274 533012. Robin Fraser, formerly a management consulting partner in Coopers & Lybrand, led the development of C & L's Priority Base Budgeting and ABM practices and CAM-I's Advanced Budgeting study. He speaks on CIMA's Mastercourse 'Beyond Budgeting'. Tel: 01372 844942.)*

'Budgets hit back'

Paul Prendergast

(First published in *Management Accounting* (*British*), Jan 2000 v78. Full text: © 2000 The Chartered Institute of Management Accountants)

Paul Prendergast looks at the role of Budgets in this post-revolution age of balanced scorecards and activity-based management.

This article looks at the value of budgeting in a world of new management techniques. It also reports the author's research on the connection between an organisation's budget emphasis and managers' short-term orientation. Finally new control techniques are examined to see if they can help overcome the behavioural weaknesses of traditional control systems, or whether human nature will triumph again and corrupt the latest planning and control systems.

The problems

Luc Wilken once advised that, 'Accountants tend to see control as a solution; sociologists as a problem.' Our preoccupation with measuring and scorekeeping may cause us to miss the big picture needed in a rapidly changing business environment. Furthermore, the more control instituted by management (usually on the advice of management accountants), the more the divisional manager may feel a need to advance the division's performance even if this is to the detriment of the company as a whole.

Problems with budgeting as a planning and control technique fill lengthy chapters in many accounting books. A basic problem is that the budget is based on a lot of guess-work. As worldwide events have a more dynamic impact on companies, and as product life-cycles have shortened, budgets have become more inaccurate. Academics have suggested that actual performance be compared to a revised budget calculated in the light of full environmental knowledge after the period end. Accountants in the real world have responded with groans, feeling that they can just about juggle the original budget, forecasts and actuals without adding another complicating factor.

A second problem with budgets is the 'gaming' aspect which appears to have 'worsened' over the years. This is where senior management battle to set a challenging budget to 'get the most out of staff', while their junior managers fight back to negotiate an easily achievable target. Back in 1953, Chris Argyris wrote the seminal work *The Impact of Budgets on People*, which gave the upper hand to management as they managed/manipulated their subordinates to get improved performance. Since then everyone from shop floor worker to unit manager has learned how the game works. By 1970 when Schiff and Lewin wrote *The Impact of People on Budgets*, subordinates had hit back. Budgeting was no longer a technical issue but a time-consuming game for everyone. In the 1990s, sitcoms such as *Frasier* parody the 'radio shrink', while students consider individual sessions with the college counsellor an everyday part of life. Nowadays, where everyone is an amateur psychologist, dictatorial or manipulative budgets cause negative reactions, while getting unit managers to set their own budgets (for review) often leads to soft targets. The approval process becomes the end-game with both parties jockeying for position, having done much research to support their argument or to debunk the others' suggestions. Once the budget is set the game moves on to phase two. No longer is there a reward for the person who works hard for the company. Instead for those who understand the measurement system, the focus narrows to that of simply meeting the subjective and possibly corrupt budget.

The revolution

Based on the above it is no wonder that budgeting – along with traditional variance analysis, and traditional overhead absorption – was denigrated in the recent management accounting revolution. The issues raised by Kaplan, Brimson, Johnson and Kaplan *et al.* lit a fuse and, thanks to the development of ABC, ABM and the balanced scorecard, many consultants can finally enjoy early retirement in the Bahamas. More seriously, many large corporations have claimed great benefit from the introduction of the new techniques, leading to a better understanding of the business, better operational link to strategic goals, the dropping of uneconomic products and so on.

The balanced scorecard and drill-down software

Kaplan and Norton's balanced scorecard appeared to be a particular threat to the old style of budgeting and controlling. Kaplan and Norton's superb technique has taken the business world by storm. The idea is that companies should plan and monitor not just bottom-line profit or EPS figures, but the overall progress of the company in a balanced way. The company should, of course, measure financial performance, but also customer satisfaction, innovation and learning, and key performance indicators (KPIs) such as cycle time, yield, etc. Thus the company as a whole can get a favourable score when doing well on both short-term performance and indicators of future success. Prior to the balanced scorecard there was a belief that pressures to make short-term profits often obscured the need for continual internal improvement, new product development and the customer delight that would lead to repeat buys. Behavioural theorists certainly see merit in the balanced scorecard and Kaplan and others have developed the technique so that subsidiary objectives can be set down to operational level, helping employees understand how their contribution fits in with overall corporate strategy and success.

Software developed for the balanced scorecard includes Sapling's NetScore, where one can use the 'Strategic Traceability Chain' to ensure that objectives with measurable targets or KPIs are set, made up of many subtargets. The control pyramid is thus strategic at the top and yet detailed or operational for supervisors or employees further down the organisation. If supervisors and junior executives have appropriate targets and the information is fed correctly into the system the strategic performance can be easily monitored by senior management. Based on Kaplan's suggested image, the software's output resembles car or aircraft dials which show if the performance is empty/weak or all the way through to full/excellent. If one realises that a measure such as customer satisfaction is below the half-way or target mark, one can click on the measure to drill down and see what makes up the customer satisfaction score. It may be that there are four submeasures, of which one, say the company's percentage of sales returns, is the problem. Similarly, even if there are numerous levels to be drilled, the senior executive can get to the source of the issue which if left unchecked could have had a strategic impact on the company's future.

The attraction of these types of systems to the CEO and senior executives is clear. Senior management can think lofty strategic thoughts while simply keeping an eye on the balanced scorecard dials; only getting involved in the exceptional issues which (with excellent graphics) 'jump out' and call to him or her for action. Despite exaggerated hype the benefits of the balanced scorecard with its key performance indicators (KPIs) across various aspects of the business appear to be a winner.

The budget lives!

Despite startling headings in some articles claiming that the budget was dead, a funeral would have been embarrassingly premature. Detailed reading of these cases indicates that where companies now had 'no budget', they instead had a plan, a rolling forecast, or some other yardstick which could be called, er . . . well, a budget. Indeed Horngren *et al.* in 1997 could still claim that 'budgets are one of the most widely used tools for planning and controlling organisations'. Merchant, another giant of management information systems research, said in 1998, 'The issue is not whether to prepare a . . . budget, but rather how to do it.' Recent research such as that of Pierce and O'Dea in 1998 and that of Clarke and Toal in 1999 shows that the budget is still an essential part of most businesses.

Of course, the balanced scorecard has a financial section and stresses the determination of key performance indicators. Clearly a budget can still be a component part of the financial section of the balanced scorecard. Indeed, even in the early 1980s many monthly management reports contained not just budget and actual numbers, but also information such as Sales Returns, Orders and Efficiencies, which could also be considered part of any balanced scorecard. What has happened is that the old management information system has been integrated with measurements of new product development, customer delight, and continual improvement. The result, mirroring the development of ERP systems, is one businesswide planning and reporting technique.

They haven't gone away, you know

If older budgeting systems are still being used as part of newer control systems, the behavioural problems mentioned at the start of this article may resurface to corrupt the new system. Admittedly, if the budget is the only thing that unit managers are measured on, the temptation to corrupt the measure is greater than if there is a wider balanced scorecard, but the behavioural problems still remain. Leavins *et al.*, in a 1995 study, found evidence that in some circumstances budgetary pressure revealed 'a moderately positive relationship with slack'. This means that where unit managers 'must meet' certain targets or KPIs, they may well be inclined to corrupt the measure. In a balanced scorecard environment this may involve persuading the boss that times are hard and a sales target should be lower, or that a tougher efficiency target would only harm quality. It may involve manipulating cost estimates to ensure a padded budget (slack), or ensuring that a target for innovation in production is easily achievable given that new machines are on the way. Generally speaking the unit manager has much more technical information than the boss so that their influence on the standard setting is significant. Thus the unit manager's old game of 'arranging' an easy budget, has become a slightly more complicated game of 'fixing' the balanced scorecard's key performance indicators (KPIs).

The second problem area with budgeting is that managers may become more short-term orientated as a result of a budget (Hayes and Abernathy). As many budgeting systems are conducted on an annual cycle, and many managers change jobs (internally or externally) every few years, they may yield to short-term thinking for their decision making. My own research involving four companies in Ireland did not show a statistically significant relationship, but nonetheless the company with the highest degree of budget emphasis had the shortest time horizon, and the pattern continued with the other companies (see table).

COMPANIES' BUDGET EMPHASIS AND MANAGEMENT TIME ORIENTATION Rank of the four companies on the two measures The actual relationship shown below was as hypothesised		
	1 = least 4 = most	1 = shortest 4 = longest
COMPANY	BUDGET EMPHASIS	TIME ORIENTATION
Irish plc	4	1
Irish public sector	3	2
North American corp A	2	3
North American corp B	1	4
Note: Actual names of companies kept confidential as agreed with researchers.		

Clearly there is a danger that the financial section of the balanced scorecard with its short-term KPIs could encourage unit managers to meet the indicator but miss the big picture. For example, maintenance could be postponed to meet the annual cost target even though this might not make good business sense. Other KPIs could also cause problems. For example, a unit manager may report (or input!) that a slight improvement to the old product is in fact a new product. The manager thus meets the innovation measure and this feeds the top level system within the balanced scorecard, contributing towards a 'full tank'.

In fact many managers suggest that corrupting non-financial targets is a lot easier than corrupting financial targets. Many managers are unclear as to how the books are calculated, for example the effect of accruals; the non-financial measures are usually clearly understood. One example is where sales reps give a form to 'their' customer contacts to measure customer satisfaction, later collecting the completed form themselves. Often, as the purchaser has to face the sales rep on a continual basis, the soft option is taken and he or she claims to be very happy with the service. Thus a meaningless overestimate of satisfaction gets reported back up the organisation. This type of useless measurement is common, as the 100% customer satisfaction on the wall-chart of my local Ford Dealer demonstrates.

Corruption busters

There are a number of events which are helping to limit dysfunctional or non-congruent behaviour by managers. The first of these is the trend towards outsourcing. This has resulted in downsizing of the large corporations and the growth of a huge number of suppliers. The availability of a comparison to an outside price has helped many companies to avoid inflated cost standards. Managers, when contributing to budget-setting, know that the standard must be competitive with what an outside vendor would charge for the product or service. Another factor is the growth of benchmarking where a company's performance is compared against the average and best achieved in a group of companies. A third aspect in companies' favour is ironically the dynamism of today's businesses, with some companies going to the wall while their competitors head for the stars. Employees are more conscious of the need to be competitive and may be more amenable than before to a pitch emphasising the need to be lean and mean. Linked with the above is the growth of share options which, if not overly short-term focused, could also encourage a team approach to the setting of standards or KPIs.

Internal issues that management should work on include the need for senior management to genuinely understand their business, and thus ensure that good targets or KPIs are set. Traditionally, the information deficit is what gives the unit manager opportunity to pad his or her budget. Both balanced scorecard and ABC/B/M proponents claim that the new techniques help them to understand their business and its cost drivers better. If so the techniques could help deal with behavioural problems which have caused havoc with older information systems. One must admit, however, that similar claims were made for zero-base budgeting (ZBB), which has seen a fall in popularity.

Finally, I suggest that top-level reviews with associated rewards and pain take place. Many managers have happily corrupted budgets and acted to meet short-term unit rather than long-term company needs, knowing that, if caught, they would suffer no sanction. A typical scenario in an old-style budget environment would be that the line manager would get a verbal telling off from a finance executive, knowing that his or her own boss would not even hear about the incident. Budget variances were often seen as finance department problems rather than company problems. One hopes that in a balanced scorecard environment, reviews involve all top management and not just the budget manager, that the importance of system integrity is understood, and that there would be less tolerance of non-congruent behaviour.

Conclusion

Budgets have plenty of problems but their demise has been overhyped. New techniques such as the balanced scorecard and activity-based budgeting appear to help senior management understand their business success factors and cost drivers better. A balanced scorecard will contain more than just budgetary information, but the problems of bad targets, tunnel vision, and the manipulation of performance measures remain. By better understanding their business and by conducting regular reviews, top management could reduce non-optimal executive behaviour and make a success of the balanced scorecard. It would be nice if top management could also reward subordinates who acted in the company's long-term interest even though this made them miss their KPI targets. Unfortunately, human nature suggests that this might be a bridge too far. Senior management have behavioural issues too.

Argyris, C., *The Impact of Budgets on People*, The Controllership Foundation, 1952.
Brimson, J. A., *Cost Accounting, Robotics and the New Manufacturing Environment*, American Accounting Association, 1987.
Clarke, P. and Toal, I., 'Performance measurement in small firms in Ireland', *Irish Accounting Review*, Vol. 6, No. 1, Spring 1999.
Hayes, R. H. and Abernathy, W. J., 'Managing our way to economic decline', *Harvard Business Review*, pp. 67–77, July–August 1980.
Horngren, C. T., Foster, G. and Datar, S. M., *Cost Accounting: A Managerial Emphasis*, 9th edn, Int. edn, Prentice Hall, 1997, p. 176.

Johnson, H. T. and Kaplan, R. S., *Relevance Lost: The Rise and Fall of Management Accounting*, Harvard Business School Press, 1987.

Kaplan, R. S., 'Yesterday's accounting undermines performance', *Harvard Business Review*, July/August 1984, pp. 95–101.

Kaplan, R. S. and Norton, D., 'The balanced scorecard: measures that drive performance', *Harvard Business Review*, January/February 1992, pp. 71–79.

Leavins, J. R., Omer, K. and Vilutis, A., 'A comparative study of alternative indicators of budgetary slack', *Managerial Finance*, Vol. 21, (3), 1995, pp. 52–67.

Merchant, K. A., *Modern Management Control Systems: Text and Cases*, Int. edn, Prentice Hall, 1998, p. 332.

Pierce, B. and O'Dea, T., 'An empirical study of management accounting practices in Ireland', *Irish Accounting Review*, Vol. 5, No. 2, Autumn 1998, pp. 35–66.

Schiff, M. and Lewin, A. Y., 'The impact of people on budgets', *The Accounting Review*, April, 1970, pp. 259–268.

Wilken, L., *Accounting for the Human Factor*, p. 45, Parker, L. D., Ferris, K. R. and Otley, D., Prentice Hall, 1989.

(Paul Prendergast BComm, MComm, PCMA spent ten years in the computer industry in Ireland, the UK and the USA, and now lectures in AIT, Ireland. He conducts occasional behavioural evaluations of corporate decision making and control systems. E-mail pprendergast@ait.ie)

'The great debate'

Tom Kennedy and Richard Bull

(First published in *Management Accounting* (*British*) May 2000 v78. Full text: © 2000 The Chartered Institute of Management Accountants)

Much has been written about the demise of traditional management accounting systems and the revolutionary attributes of activity-based costing (ABC). Given the significant professional services that have been developed on the back of it, it is interesting that the system is not as popular in practice as its supporters would suggest.

ABC has been hailed as the answer to our prayers, but things are never that simple, argues Tom Kennedy.

Management accounting has undergone a renaissance since the mid-1980s. While much of this has been attributed to the pioneering work of Professor Robert Kaplan and his colleagues, opinion varies on the nature of these developments.

What is not in dispute is that the business environment and its management information needs have changed dramatically during that period. New models such as ABC have been hailed as the answer to our changing needs, and this has given rise to other applications such as activity-based management and shareholder-value analysis.

Traditional management accounting systems aimed to offer neutral, objective and calculable financial information. These systems were expected to bring to light the facts of costing, to enable the pursuit of efficiency and help better regulate management–labour relations. It was even suggested by some that they could translate the moral into the factual. However, they are criticised on the grounds that they do not provide the type of information required in today's highly competitive and global environment. They are accused of giving misleading signals about product costs and adopting a closed, historical and inward-looking focus. Critics say they do not accurately reveal the high costs of complexity caused by the proliferation of product lines, the globalisation of markets generally and the dramatic change in the cost profile of most organisations in the last thirty years or so.

The practice of using volume-sensitive drivers to attach overheads costs to products may satisfy statutory and regulatory accounting requirements, but is not appropriate in today's competitive and dynamic business environment.

The chairman of General Motors once remarked that 'Product cost numbers in American enterprises were often grossly inaccurate, particularly in the case of factories making multiple, differentiated products, because accounting technologies that would accurately assign indirect costs to products had often not been installed.' Tom Sheridan echoed these words ten years ago when he wrote: 'Tragically, many companies spend their time on the sheer mechanics and arithmetic of allocations, building up cost cascades that are a wonder to behold but which are not easily understood by the recipients and add little to the decision process.'

It was this perceived 'lost relevance' that triggered the development of ABC in the mid-1980s. It purports to undo many of the flaws of conventional management accounting by providing an organisation with strategic and operational, financial and non-financial information. It recognises business is a series of linked activities and processes that are undertaken to serve the customer and to deliver product attributes.

These processes and activities are where costs are happening. Managing their cause should improve the total cost figure and, ultimately, profitability and shareholder value. ABC is, therefore, the generic term to describe an alternative paradigm to traditional volume-based cost models. Its advocates claim that it is an accounting approach aimed primarily at understanding causality and giving decision-makers the potential to manage costs at the root, rather than a focus on product cost only.

This issue is not confined to the manufacturing industry. The service industry, despite its many different characteristics, has to contend with a large overheads cost base. By linking overheads to activity levels, it can utilise the activity-based concepts to better inform its decision-making processes.

But serious questions have been raised about the logic of the ABC model, and more research needs to be done to assess its impact on a firm's bottom line. The existence of two distinct views of contemporary management accounting practice only exacerbates the issue.

A number of US academics believe that traditional management accounting systems should be replaced by the revolutionary ABC. But in the UK, two scholars from the London School of Economics urge an evolutionary approach. They suggest that accountants should use their existing expertise to develop new and more flexible approaches to cost management and performance measurement systems.

Because ABC requires stringent pre-conditions, they are concerned that it would not be a good 'fit' in a number of organisations. They see no general crisis in the practice of management accounting as long as accountants respond positively to change and continue their search for innovative methods in a market-oriented context.

Current practice seems to support the evolutionary approach. Worldwide adoption rates for ABC have peaked at 20 per cent and a declining number of firms are giving it further consideration. This situation must be particularly disappointing for its advocates, despite the extensive high-profile marketing and consultancy services that have been developed. Anecdotal experience of problems associated with ABC implementation is supported by research documenting a high number of IT projects falling well short of their stated objectives.

CIMA-sponsored research found that there was significant management accounting change in the UK during the last decade. But the change took place primarily in the way management accounting is used and not necessarily in the introduction of new systems or techniques. This is also reflected in the 'decentring' of accounting knowledge and the accounting function generally.

Perhaps it is too early to write an obituary for traditional management accounting systems and to label ABC as the 'holy grail'. The real challenge is how to respond to the advent of pseudo accountants and take advantage of the emerging computer and communications technologies.

(Tom Kennedy is the head of the Department of Accounting & Finance at the University of Limerick.)

It's not just what you do with ABC – the way you do it is just as important, argues Richard Bull MA, ACMA, AMIMC.

ABC has become established as an essential tool of the management accountant. There is little dispute over the essential shape of the ABC model and many manuals explain its basic concepts. A number of software packages exist which facilitate the construction of a model for a particular enterprise and automate data entry and analysis.

Until now, attention in literature has primarily focused on the mechanics of ABC: how it works as a system and how it can be run most efficiently to improve the accuracy, meaning and timeliness of management information. But there is a danger in losing sight of the dynamics of the process. The true potential of any system, however good its routines and interfaces, largely depends on how it is used and applied. An appropriate management system is just as important as the information system. And this does not just mean in terms of organisation but goes to the very heart of the relationships within which the activity-based costing process is designed to operate.

There are two clear differences between the absorption costing model and ABC. These lie in the structure and direction of the two models. The traditional model starts with resources and seeks to allocate their costs to products. This gives a clue to the driving force behind this approach: a financial accountant's desire to 'balance the books' so that all costs can be fully accounted for.

In contrast, the ABC model starts with an enterprise's products and services. It then seeks to identify the activities required to produce or deliver them and, in turn, the resources required to carry out those activities.

ABC takes a completely different starting point to absorption costing. ABC establishes a separate 'stepping stone' and reaches the bedrock of resources by a reverse route. In doing so, it does not inevitably finish up with what there is; only with what there needs to be. When the actual level and nature of resources is found to be different, the 'balancing exercise' highlights excesses and shortages. This appeals to the management accountant's desire to identify waste and constraints.

These two contrasting features of the models, their direction and the components they use, often reflect the strategic focus of a business. If management adopts a 'resource-based' view then the absorption costing model would be more appropriate in its source and direction. However, if the company is to have a 'market-led' strategy, then it is more appropriate to adopt the structure and direction of the ABC model.

These different models require different system dynamics, but also different management and application. Take a company whose management system has been racked by inhouse competition and conflict between resource managers and product managers. The traditional model has only served to underpin the conflict. A service function, whether internal or external, may see its need for systems support in terms of the specific system configurations and program packages that it considers necessary to produce its results. Where resource costs are allocated directly to such services there is a temptation for the service group to express its requirements as resource specifications, which won't necessarily match the current resources or future budgets of the manager of those resources who is charged with providing them.

The ABC model allows a new relationship to be fostered. The supplier–customer relationship is given clear direction by placing the needs of the service function first. Requirements are expressed in terms of activities rather than resource, allowing sensible debate on common, yet neutral, ground. The key issue is what those activities need to achieve and the specification of how they can best be carried out. This provides the basis for negotiation rather than bartering.

Where the issue concerns IT, the IT manager may wish to develop those resources which he or she knows are most efficient. They may seek a way of achieving full use of them through proposing suitable applications for the service function to use. Already there is the basis for conflict of interests and competition over each other's 'patches', whether that be the technology and operators in IS or the products and services of the service function. Each 'side' can become entrenched in trying to manage the other, becoming distracted from their own core competencies.

ABC calls for the manager of the service function to express his or her needs in terms of activities. This may be in terms of the volume and nature of transactions, reports or processing of data, which need to be carried out to deliver the product or service from that group. In doing so, key activity drivers become apparent and this helps to distinguish those activities which add value from those that do not. It also provides a management tool to assess the level of activity for any given level of output. However, it also provides scope for the IS manager to determine the most efficient and effective way of resourcing this requirement, bearing in mind the capacity and processing power at his disposal or new methods of delivering the same result.

In both cases, departments are encouraged to apply their own area of expertise to the need. In many ways this is only reinforcing the widely accepted process of specifying and meeting requirements between internal customers and suppliers. But ABC imposes an additional discipline to ensure that such requirements are expressed as genuine requirements and not as solutions.

Your facilities manager may say, 'What we need is a building.' In reality, what they need is somewhere to carry out certain activities, whether they be manufacturing, administration, distribution or other activities. If this has to be done in a building, so be it. But the facilities manager, together with managers of other resource areas, may come up with a better solution using technology, production equipment or a distributive form of working which does not require centralisation of activities. The outcome may well be a building. But by involving the experts in logistics and physical facilities in arriving at the solution, the result is more likely to be an optimal one and one for which the facilities group will feel greater ownership.

It may be small wonder that the adoption of ABC does not always achieve what is expected of it. Perhaps this is because, at least in part, relationships have not adapted accordingly, with traditional rivalries and mistrust prevailing. With the correct relationships and the appropriate management strategy the true potential of activity-based costing has an opportunity to be realised.

Richardbull@bullr.fsnet.co.uk

'Existential crises'

David Allen

(First published in *Financial Management* (*British*), Nov 2000. Full text: © 2000 The Chartered Institute of Management Accountants)

As financial managers are called upon increasingly to provide the information firms need to support strategic decisions, David Allen ponders the mysteries of the concept of value.

Most CIMA members are acutely aware of the fundamental difference between the two principal aspects of their work: accounting and financial management. Nowhere is this seen more clearly than in the contrast between the former's focus on objectively verifiable costs, and the latter's focus on subjectively judgmental values.

It never ceases to amaze me, however, how few academics, analysts and consultants appreciate this difference. With depressing regularity, they produce tools that promise to measure the 'real value' of intangible assets, particular strategies, constituent businesses or even of total enterprises. These deceive non-financial colleagues into buying the modern equivalent of the emperor's new clothes.

The problem affects all sectors of the economy. For example, in the case of distributable profit-seeking enterprises, the first point to note is that the value of such enterprises to their shareholders in aggregate does not correlate with the totals of their respective balance sheets. And there is no reason why it should do. Arguments that balance sheets must include intangible assets (such as brands or knowledge) if they are to reflect the accurate and true value of a company can be excused only on the grounds of complete ignorance of the purpose of accounting statements.

Fortunately, if this comes to a dispute, accountants and non-financial experts can agree some common ground: the value of an enterprise to its shareholders is the net present value of future cash flows between the company and its shareholders (essentially dividends plus buybacks minus rights issues) discounted at the cost of capital. There is also general agreement that the financial objective of such enterprises should be to maximise this value.

If it were really possible to measure that value accurately and truly (as in the case of costs already incurred), future cash flows would be predetermined, so future decisions would be pre-empted and financial management would be a total waste of time. Once measured, value could be neither created nor destroyed. In fact, a large part of the role of strategic financial managers is to provide information on alternative options so managers can reach a decision. There cannot, therefore, ever be just one measurable value – there are many possible values, depending on the action chosen and the opportunities and problems that it creates.

Textbooks often describe the process of identifying the action that will have the best impact on the net present value of projected cash flows between firm and shareholders in aggregate as if the question is whether a particular project has a positive net present value or not. Practitioners, however, think in terms of increments and differentials: the question is which alternative has the greatest favourable impact on net present value. Seen this way, it is clear whether it can cope with uncertainty, risks, and contingent opportunities. The concept promulgated as 'real options' does not demand an alternative to the net present value approach; it can be accommodated within it.

But how do accountants support these decisions when they cannot see into the future? This depends on precise reading of the words used. In particular:

- Measurement is just one form of quantification, and is available only when something has already happened, or already exists. Since predictions are not measurements, neither are the values derived from them.
- Knowledge is just one form of information and, again, refers only to something that has already happened or already exists. Managers' beliefs about the future needs of customers, activities of competitors, capability of new facilities, etc. are vital information, but are not knowledge.
- The objective of an enterprise is expressed in terms of maximising the net present value of future cash flows, but the criterion against which decisions are made is the maximisation of the net present value of projected cash flows.

A distinguishing feature of strategic financial management is that the outcomes of decisions are monitored on the same terms as they were made, i.e. net present value. One of the main reasons for a variance is that earlier projections were not borne out by events. Had they been accurate and true measurements, they could not have been wrong.

The flip side of the coin is that anyone who insists on waiting for accurate measurements before they can make a decision will never make a decision – by the time things can be measured, it is too late to change them. Many people are surprised to find that the most important things in life cannot be measured even after the event. It is not possible to measure the benefit gained from past advertising, for example, because nobody knows what the sales would have been without it; but that does not rule out its quantification.

The waning of accounting and the waxing of financial management amounts to a shift from hard to soft concepts, and is consistent with what is happening in other areas of management (the moves from tangibles to intangibles, confrontation to teamwork, command and compliance to trust and commitment).

Many accountants find it hard to make this transition. 'If there are no facts about the future,' one recently asked me, 'can you blame me for spending my time looking backwards?' The problem is that, although there will always be a need for accounting, that part of the profession is shrinking. For a basis for decision support and monitoring, you need the financial management model, and you have to be comfortable with subjective judgements and unmeasurable values.

(*David Allen CBE is past president of CIMA and director of several companies.*)

Further reading

Ashton, D., Hopper, T. and Scapens, B. (1995) *Issues in Management Accounting*, 2nd edition, Financial Times/Prentice Hall, London. Many and various current issues discussed.

Goldratt, E. and Cox, J. (2004) *The Goal*, North River Press, New York.

Horngren, C., Bhimani, A., Datar, S. and Foster, G. (2002) *Management and Cost Accounting*, 2nd edition, Prentice Hall Europe, Harlow. See Chapter 20, 'Quality and throughput issues in managing costs', and Chapter 21, 'Time and strategy as emerging issues in cost management'.

Kaplan, R. and Norton, D. (2001) *The Strategy-focused Organisation: How Balanced Scorecard Companies Thrive in the New Business Environment*, Harvard Business School Press, Boston, MA.

Weetman, P. (2002) *Management Accounting, an Introduction*, 3rd edition, Financial Times/Prentice Hall, Harlow. See chapter 'The frontiers of management accounting'.

Glossary

This glossary is composed of definitions taken from *Management Accounting Official Terminology*, Revised 2000, published by the Chartered Institute of Management Accountants. I am most grateful to the CIMA for their permission to quote these definitions.

activity-based budgeting (ABB)
A method of budgeting based on an activity framework and utilising cost driver data in the budget-setting and variance feedback processes.

activity-based costing (ABC)
An approach to the costing and monitoring of activities which involves tracing resource consumption and costing final outputs. Resources are assigned to activities and activities to cost objects based on consumption estimates. The latter utilise cost drivers to attach activity costs to outputs.

activity-based management (ABM)
System of management which uses activity-based cost information for a variety of purposes including cost reduction, cost modelling and customer profitability analysis.

activity cost pool
A grouping of all cost elements associated with an activity (CAM-I)*.

allocate
To assign a whole item of cost, or of revenue, to a single cost unit, centre, account or time period.

apportion
To spread revenues or costs over two or more cost units, centres, accounts or time periods. This may also be referred to as 'indirect allocation'.

balanced scorecard approach
An approach to the provision of information to management to assist strategic policy formulation and achievement. It emphasises the need to provide the user with a set of information which addresses all relevant areas of performance in an objective and unbiased fashion. The information provided may include both financial and non-financial elements, and cover areas such as profitability, customer satisfaction, internal efficiency and innovation.

benchmarking
The establishment, through data gathering, of targets and comparators, through whose use relative levels of performance (and particularly areas of underperformance) can be identified. By the adoption of identified best practices it is hoped that performance will improve. Types of benchmarking include:

- *internal benchmarking*, a method of comparing one operating unit or function with another within the same industry;
- *functional benchmarking*, in which internal functions are compared with those of the best external practitioners of those functions, regardless of the industry they are in (also known as operational benchmarking or generic benchmarking);
- *competitive benchmarking*, in which information is gathered about direct competitors, through techniques such as reverse engineering;
- *strategic benchmarking*, a type of competitive benchmarking aimed at strategic action and organisational change.

budget
A quantitative statement, for a defined period of time, which may include planned revenues, expenses, assets, liabilities and cash flows. A budget provides a focus for the organisation, aids the co-ordination of activities, and facilitates control. Planning is achieved by means of a fixed *master budget*, whereas control is generally exercised through the comparison of actual costs with a *flexible budget*.

budget slack
The intentional overestimation of expenses and/or underestimation of revenues in the budgeting process.

budgetary control
The establishment of budgets relating the responsibilities of executives to the requirements of a policy, and the continuous comparison of actual with budgeted results, either to secure by individual action the objectives of that policy or to provide a basis for its revision.

capital investment appraisal
The application of a set of methodologies (generally based on the discounting of projected cash flows) whose purpose is to give guidance to managers with respect to decisions as to how best to commit long-term investment funds.

cost–benefit analysis
A comparison between the cost of the resources used, plus any other costs imposed by an activity (e.g. pollution, environmental damage) and the value of the financial and non-financial benefits derived.

cost driver
Any factor which causes a change in the cost of an activity, e.g. the quality of parts received by an activity is a determining factor in the work required by that activity and therefore affects the resources required. An activity may have multiple cost drivers associated with it (CAM-I)*.

direct cost
Expenditure which can be economically identified with and specifically measured in respect to a relevant cost object.

discount rate/cost of capital (as used in capital investment appraisal)
The percentage used to discount future cash flows generated by a capital project.

discretionary cost
A cost whose amount within a time period is determined by, and is easily altered by, a decision taken by the appropriate budget holder. Marketing, research and training are generally regarded as discretionary costs. Control of discretionary costs is through the budgeting process. Also known as *managed* or *policy* costs.

factoring

The sale of debts to a third party (the factor) at a discount, in return for prompt cash. A factoring service may be *with recourse*, in which case the supplier takes the risk of the debt not being paid, or *without recourse* when the factor takes the risk.

hurdle rate

A rate of return which a capital investment proposal must achieve if it is to be accepted. Set by reference to the cost of capital, the hurdle rate may be increased above the basic cost of capital to allow for different levels of risk.

internal rate of return (IRR)

The annual percentage return achieved by a project, at which the sum of the discounted cash inflows over the life of the project is equal to the sum of the discounted cash outflows.

invoice discounting

The sale of debts to a third party at a discount, in return for prompt cash. The administration is managed in such a way that the debtor is generally unaware of the discounter's involvement, and continues to pay the supplier.

just-in-time (JIT)

A system whose objective is to produce or to procure products or components as they are required by a customer or for use, rather than for stock. A just-in-time system is a 'pull' system, which responds to demand, in contrast to a 'push' system, in which stocks act as buffers between the different elements of the system, such as purchasing, production and sales.

just-in-time production

A production system which is driven by demand for finished products whereby each component on a production line is produced only when needed for the next stage.

just-in-time purchasing

A purchasing system in which material purchases are contracted so that the receipt and usage of material, to the maximum extent possible, coincide.

net present value (NPV)

The difference between the sum of the projected discounted cash inflows and outflows attributable to a capital investment or other long-term project.

opportunity cost

The value of the benefit sacrificed when one course of action is chosen, in preference to an alternative. The opportunity cost is represented by the forgone potential benefit from the best rejected course of action.

overhead absorption rate

A means of attributing overhead to a product or service, based for example on direct labour hours, direct labour cost or machine hours.

direct labour cost percentage rate

An overhead absorption rate based on direct labour cost.

direct labour hour rate

An overhead absorption rate based on direct labour hours.

machine hour rate

An overhead absorption rate based on machine hours.

The choice of overhead absorption base may be made with the objective of obtaining 'accurate' product costs, or of influencing managerial behaviour, as where overhead applied to (say) labour hours or part numbers appears to make the use of these resources more costly, thus discouraging their use.

overhead/indirect cost
Expenditure on labour, materials or services which cannot be economically identified with a specific saleable cost unit.

The synonymous term 'burden' is in common use in the USA and in subsidiaries of American companies in the UK.

payback
The time required for the cash inflows from a capital investment project to equal the cash outflows.

period cost
A cost which relates to a time period rather than to the output of products or services.

present value
The cash equivalent now of a sum receivable or payable at a future date.

pricing
The determination of a selling price for the product or service produced. A number of methodologies may be used, including:

competitive pricing
Setting a price by reference to the prices of competitive products.

cost-plus pricing
The determination of price by adding a mark-up, which may incorporate a desired return on investment, to a measure of the cost of the product/service.

dual pricing
A form of transfer pricing in which the two parties to a common transaction use different prices.

historical pricing
Basing current prices on prior period prices, perhaps uplifted by a factor such as inflation.

market-based pricing
Setting a price based on the value of the product in the perception of the customer. Also known as perceived value pricing.

penetration pricing
Setting a low selling price in order to gain market share.

predatory pricing
Setting a low selling price in order to damage competitors. This may involve dumping, which is selling a product in a foreign market at below cost, or below the domestic market price (subject to adjustments for taxation differences, transportation costs, specification differences, etc.).

premium pricing
The achievement of a price above the commodity level, due to a measure of product or service differentiation.

price skimming
Setting a high price in order to maximize short-term profitability, often on the introduction of a novel product.

range pricing
The pricing of individual products such that their prices fit logically within a range of connected products offered by one supplier, and differentiated by a factor such as weight of pack or number of product attributes offered.

selective pricing
Setting different prices for the same product or service in different markets. This practice can be broken down as follows:

- *category pricing* – cosmetically modifying a product such that the variations allow it to sell in a number of price categories, as where a range of 'brands' are based on a common product;
- *customer group pricing* – modifying the price of a product or service so that different groups of consumers pay different prices;
- *peak pricing* – setting a price which varies according to the level of demand;
- *service-level pricing* – setting a price based on the particular level of service chosen from a range.

time and material pricing
A form of cost-plus pricing in which price is determined by reference to the cost of the labour and material inputs to the product/service.

prime cost
The total cost of direct material, direct labour and direct expenses.

production cost
Prime cost plus absorbed production overhead.

relevant costs/revenues
Costs and revenues appropriate to a specific management decision. These are represented by future cash flows whose magnitude will vary depending upon the outcome of the management decision made. If stock is sold by a retailer, the relevant cost, used in the determination of the profitability of the transaction, would be the cost of replacing the stock, not its original purchase price, which is a sunk cost. *Abandonment analysis*, based on relevant cost and revenues, is the process of determining whether or not it is more profitable to discontinue a product or service than to continue it.

relevant range
The activity levels within which assumptions about cost behaviour in breakeven analysis remain valid.

rolling/continuous budget
A budget continuously updated by adding a further accounting period (month or quarter) when the earliest accounting period has expired. Its use is particularly beneficial where future costs and/or activities cannot be forecast accurately.

semi-variable cost/semi-fixed cost/mixed cost
A cost containing both fixed and variable components and which is thus partly affected by a change in the level of activity.

sensitivity analysis

A modelling and risk assessment procedure in which changes are made to significant variables in order to determine the effect of these changes on the planned outcome. Particular attention is thereafter paid to variables identified as being of special significance.

standard

A benchmark measurement of resource usage, set in defined conditions. Standards can be set on a number of bases:

a) on an *ex ante* estimate of expected performance
b) on an *ex post* estimate of attainable performance
c) on a prior period level of performance by the same organisation
d) on the level of performance achieved by comparable organisations
e) on the level of performance required to meet organisational objectives.

Standards may also be set at attainable levels which assume efficient levels of operation, but which include allowances for normal loss, waste and machine downtime, or at ideal levels, which make no allowance for the above losses, and are only attainable under the most favourable conditions.

standard cost

The planned unit cost of the products, components or services produced in a period. The standard cost may be determined on a number of bases (*see* standard). The main uses of standard costs are in performance measurement, control, stock valuation and in the establishment of selling prices.

strategic management accounting

A form of management accounting in which emphasis is placed on information which relates to factors external to the firm, as well as non-financial information and internally generated information.

strategic plan

A statement of long-term goals along with a definition of the strategies and policies which will ensure achievement of these goals.

sunk costs

Costs that have been irreversibly incurred or committed prior to a decision point and which cannot therefore be considered relevant to subsequent decisions. Sunk costs may also be termed *irrecoverable costs*.

target cost

A product cost estimate derived by subtracting a desired profit margin from a competitive market price. This may be less than the planned initial product cost, but will be expected to be achieved by the time the product reaches the mature production stage.

total quality management (TQM)

An integrated and comprehensive system of planning and controlling all business functions so that products or services are produced which meet or exceed customer expectations. TQM is a philosophy of business behaviour, embracing principles such as employee involvement, continuous improvement at all levels and customer focus, as well as being a collection of related techniques aimed at improving quality, such as full documentation of activities, clear goal-setting and performance measurement from the customer perspective.

transfer price

The price at which goods or services are transferred between different units of the same company. If those units are located within different countries, the term *international transfer pricing* is used.

The extent to which the transfer price covers costs and contributes to (internal) profit is a matter of policy. A transfer price may, for example, be based upon marginal cost, full cost, market price or negotiation. Where the transferred products cross national boundaries, the transfer prices used may have to be agreed with the governments of the countries concerned.

variance

The difference between a planned, budgeted or standard cost and the actual cost incurred. The same comparisons may be made for revenues.

variance analysis

The evaluation of performance by means of variances, whose timely reporting should maximise the opportunity for managerial action.

zero-based budgeting

A method of budgeting which requires each cost element to be specifically justified, as though the activities to which the budget relates were being undertaken for the first time. Without approval, the budget allowance is zero.

* CAM-I = Consortium for Advanced Manufacturing – International

Answers to end-of-chapter questions

The answers to those chapter-end questions marked with an asterisk are shown below. The answers to the other chapter-end questions are given in the Lecturer's Guide.

Q3.1 Panther plc – Solution

1. Profitability:

	2007	2006	2005
ROCE	$\dfrac{1,527}{6,046} = 25.3\%$	$\dfrac{837}{4,899} = 17.1\%$	$\dfrac{763}{4,570} = 16.7\%$
Asset utilisation	$\dfrac{23,093}{6,046} = 3.8$ times	$\dfrac{17,931}{4,899} = 3.7$ times	$\dfrac{14,345}{4,570} = 3.1$ times
Profit margin	$\dfrac{1,527}{23,093} = 6.6\%$	$\dfrac{837}{17,931} = 4.7\%$	$\dfrac{763}{14,345} = 5.3\%$
Gross profit margin	$\dfrac{5,699}{23,093} = 24.7\%$	$\dfrac{3,359}{17,931} = 18.7\%$	$\dfrac{2,987}{14,345} = 20.8\%$

2. Working capital:

	2007	2006	2005
Stock days	$\dfrac{2,850 \times 365}{17,394} = 65d$	$\dfrac{2,177 \times 365}{14,572} = 55d$	$\dfrac{1,790 \times 365}{11,358} = 58d$
Debtor days	$\dfrac{2,711 \times 365}{23,093} = 43d$	$\dfrac{2,260 \times 365}{17,931} = 46d$	$\dfrac{2,356 \times 365}{14,345} = 60d$
Purchases (CoS+CS−OS)	$17,394 + 2,850 - 2,177$ $= 18,067$	$14,572 + 2,177 - 1,790$ $= 14,959$	$11,358 + 1,790 - 1,689$ $= 11,459$
Creditor days	$\dfrac{3,216 \times 365}{18,067} = 65d$	$\dfrac{2,980 \times 365}{14,959} = 73d$	$\dfrac{2,474 \times 365}{11,459} = 79d$
Cash cycle	38 days	28 days	39 days

3. Liquidity:

	2007	2006	2005
Current ratio	$\dfrac{5,561}{4,615} = 1.2{:}1.0$	$\dfrac{4,437}{3,996} = 1.1{:}1.0$	$\dfrac{4,146}{4,254} = 1.0{:}1.0$
Liquid ratio	$\dfrac{2,711}{4,615} = 0.6{:}1.0$	$\dfrac{2,260}{3,996} = 0.6{:}1.0$	$\dfrac{2,356}{4,254} = 0.6{:}1.0$

4. Capital structure:

Gearing	$\dfrac{1,564}{6,046} = 25.9\%$	$\dfrac{964}{4,899} = 19.7\%$	$\dfrac{906}{4,570} = 19.8\%$
Interest cover	$\dfrac{1,527}{93} = 16.4$ times	$\dfrac{837}{59} = 14.2$ times	$\dfrac{763}{44} = 17.3$ times

5. Suggested scenario:

The only notable change in the first two years was the impressive reduction in the debtors collection period; it came down from 60 to 46 days, a 23% improvement. The company probably made a positive effort to improve its credit control in 2006. However, Panther plc improved its performance greatly in 2007.

Its ROCE went from 17.1% to 25.3% mainly due to its operating profit margin improving from 4.7% to 6.6%. The increase in gross profit margin from 18.7% to 24.7% appears to be responsible for this. But what caused these changes? Inspection of the balance sheet reveals a large increase in both debentures and fixed assets. Panther plc has raised £600 million in 2007 and invested it in new facilities (plant and equipment, buildings, etc.)

The increase in ROCE shows that the investment has been successful. It may be that the old and inefficient plant was replaced by up-to-date machinery. Or Panther may have introduced new product lines to replace its old ones which were showing signs of obsolescence.

The length of the cash cycle has deteriorated from 28 days to 38 days (almost back to where it was in 2005). This is due to a downturn in creditor days and stock days by 8 and 5 days respectively mitigated by an improvement of 3 debtor days. Profitability would be further improved if this trend could be reversed and 2006 levels re-established.

Liquidity has been remarkably stable over the period. Gearing has increased markedly from 19.7% to 25.9% due to the new debenture. (Due to this and the increase in profitability, the shareholders have seen a significant increase in their returns.) Interest continues to be well covered at over 16 times.

Q3.2 The Wholesale Textile Company Limited – Solution

1. Liquidity

	2005	2006
Current ratio		
$\dfrac{\text{Current assets}}{\text{Current liabilities}}$	$= \dfrac{240,000}{100,000} = 2.4{:}1.0$	$\dfrac{366,000}{152,000} = 2.4{:}1.0$
Acid test ratio		
$\dfrac{\text{Current assets} - \text{stock}}{\text{Current liabilities}}$	$= \dfrac{120,000}{100,000} = 1.2{:}1.0$	$\dfrac{178,000}{152,000} = 1.2{:}1.0$

There has been no significant change in these ratios. The liquidity of the company is more than adequate at present.

2. Profitability

	2005	2006
$\dfrac{\text{Gross profit}}{\text{Sales}}$	$= \dfrac{128{,}000}{600{,}000} \times 100 = \textbf{21.3\%}$	$\dfrac{152{,}000}{748{,}000} \times 100 = \textbf{20.3\%}$
$\dfrac{\text{Net profit}}{\text{Sales}}$	$= \dfrac{30{,}000}{600{,}000} \times 100 = \textbf{5.0\%}$	$\dfrac{34{,}000}{748{,}000} \times 100 = \textbf{4.5\%}$

Both gross and net profit have fallen as a percentage of sales. One possible explanation of this is that selling prices have been reduced, which may also account for the increase in sales volume (price elasticity of demand). This shortfall of £32,000 (£780,000 − £748,000) would affect the budgeted net profit margin on each item sold as each one would have to bear a greater amount of fixed costs than planned. On the other hand, the cost of sales may have increased, possibly due to stock deterioration, obsolescence or theft. Or it may have been a combination of both of these.

Note: It is impossible to produce meaningful ratios for 2006 using the budgeted sales figure of £780,000.

Also, it is worth noting that if the extra £60,000 had been provided by shareholders instead of debentures (thus eliminating the £4,000 interest charge) then:

For 2006

$$\frac{\text{Net profit before interest}}{\text{Sales}} = \frac{38{,}000}{748{,}000} \times 100 = 5.1\%$$

Thus, the decrease in net profitability (after interest) can be explained by the source of the extra capital. This is why the operating profit (profit before interest and tax, PBIT) should be used to evaluate management performance.

Return on capital employed (ROCE)

$\dfrac{\text{Operating profit}}{\text{Total operating assets}}$	$\dfrac{30{,}000}{200{,}000} \times 100 = 15.0\%$	$\dfrac{34{,}000 + 4{,}000}{294{,}000} = 12.9\%$

The new investment of £60,000 in 2006 is not yet making any improvement in profitability. Although apparently £20,000 had been spent on new fixed assets, the other £40,000 appears to be financing increased stock and debtors levels. This has resulted in the downward trend revealed by the above ratio.

3. Management effectiveness

Stock turnover period

	2005	2006
$\dfrac{\text{Year-end stock}}{\text{Cost of sales}}$	$\dfrac{120{,}000}{472{,}000} \times 100 = 25 \text{ days}$	$\dfrac{188{,}000}{596{,}000} \times 100 = 32 \text{ days}$

In order to compare 'like with like' (i.e. consistency) the year-end stock figure should be used instead of average stock.

The trend shown is disappointing. Possible explanations of this include stock levels being unnecessarily high at the end of 2006 due to deteriorating stock control. On the other hand, levels may have been purposefully increased for a good reason such as an impending strike at a manufacturing supplier.

Debtor collection period

2005   **2006**

$$\frac{\text{Year-end debtors}}{\text{Average daily credit sales}} = \frac{100,000}{540,000/365} = 68 \text{ days} \qquad \frac{164,000}{684,000/365} = 88 \text{ days}$$

Again, for consistency, year-end rather than average debtors should be used.

The possible reasons for this disappointing trend include a slackening of credit control at WTC Ltd. Alternatively, efforts in this department may have actually increased, but due to a worsening general economic climate, debts have become significantly more difficult to collect.

Note: Cash sales are not appropriate to this ratio.

To calculate the creditors payment period, the opening stock figure for 2005 would have to be known in order to calculate the average daily purchases. Sometimes, the cost-of-sales figure is used to approximate purchases but this assumes no change in stock value over the year.

The creditors payment period would enable the length of the cash cycle to be calculated. But even without this, the length of the operating cycle (stock days + debtor days) can be determined.

	2005	**2006**
Operating cycle	25 + 68 = 93 days	32 + 88 = 120 days

This shows a 29% deterioration in 2006. Management's effectiveness is worsening in both stock and debtor-control.

4. Capital structure

Gearing

$$\frac{\text{Long-term loans}}{\text{Capital employed}} = 0 \qquad \frac{60,000}{294,000} \times 100 = 20.4\%$$

This means that 20.4% of the funding of WTC Ltd is provided by third parties. It arises solely from the debenture issue.

$$\text{Interest cover} = \frac{\text{net profit + interest charges}}{\text{interest charges}} \qquad \frac{34,000 + 4,000}{4,000} = 9.5 \text{ times}$$

Enough net profit is earned to pay the debenture interest 9.5 times over in 2006.

Q3.3 Chonky Ltd – Solution

	2005	2006	2007	2008
Profitability ratios:				
Gross profit margin	$\frac{160}{400} = 40\%$	$\frac{195}{500} = 39\%$	$\frac{280}{800} = 35\%$	$\frac{320}{1,000} = 32\%$
ROCE	$\frac{30}{165} = 18.2\%$	$\frac{40}{180} = 22.2\%$	$\frac{58}{230} = 25.2\%$	$\frac{46}{272} = 16.9\%$
Asset utilisation	$\frac{400}{165} = 2.4$	$\frac{500}{180} = 2.8$	$\frac{800}{230} = 3.5$	$\frac{1,000}{272} = 3.7$
Net profit margin	$\frac{30}{400} = 7.5\%$	$\frac{40}{500} = 8.0\%$	$\frac{58}{800} = 7.25\%$	$\frac{46}{1,000} = 4.6\%$
Liquidity ratios:				
Current ratio	$\frac{57}{42} = 1.4{:}1.0$	$\frac{65}{51} = 1.3{:}1.0$	$\frac{111}{91} = 1.2{:}1.0$	$\frac{180}{140} = 1.3{:}1.0$
Liquid ratio	$\frac{33}{42} = 0.8{:}1.0$	$\frac{39}{51} = 0.8{:}1.0$	$\frac{37}{91} = 0.4{:}1.0$	$\frac{54}{140} = 0.4{:}1.0$
Working cap. management:				
Stock turnover period	$\frac{24 \times 365}{240} = 37\text{ d}$	$\frac{26 \times 365}{305} = 31\text{ d}$	$\frac{74 \times 365}{520} = 52\text{d}$	$\frac{126 \times 365}{680} = 68\text{ d}$
Debtors collection period	$\frac{11 \times 365}{120} = 34\text{ d}$	$\frac{15 \times 365}{160} = 34\text{ d}$	$\frac{35 \times 365}{350} = 37\text{d}$	$\frac{54 \times 365}{500} = 39\text{ d}$
Creditors payment period	$\frac{22 \times 365}{244} = 33\text{ d}$	$\frac{26 \times 365}{307} = 31\text{ d}$	$\frac{50 \times 365}{568} = 32\text{d}$	$\frac{92 \times 365}{732} = 46\text{ d}$
Cash cycle	38 days	34 days	57 days	62 days
Capital structure:				
Gearing	0	0	$\frac{30}{230} = 13\%$	$\frac{60}{272} = 22\%$
Interest cover	n/a	n/a	$\frac{58}{3} = 19\text{ times}$	$\frac{46}{6} = 8\text{ times}$

Q4.1 Worthy Limited – Solution

	2005	2006
1. ROCE		
$\dfrac{\text{PBIT}}{\text{TCE}}$	$\frac{350}{1,435} = 24\%$	$\frac{500}{1,770} = 28\%$
2. Gross profit %		
$\dfrac{\text{GP}}{\text{Sales}}$	$\frac{1,350}{3,000} = 45\%$	$\frac{1,900}{4,600} = 41\%$
3. Net profit %		
$\dfrac{\text{PBIT}}{\text{Sales}}$	$\frac{350}{3,000} = 12\%$	$\frac{500}{4,600} = 11\%$

4. Current ratio

$$\frac{\text{CA}}{\text{CL}} \qquad \frac{890}{1,505} = 0.6:1.0 \qquad \frac{2,150}{3,080} = 0.7:1.0$$

5. Liquid ratio

$$\frac{\text{CA} - \text{stock}}{\text{CL}} \qquad \frac{520}{1,505} = 0.3:1.0 \qquad \frac{950}{3,080} = 0.3:1.0$$

6. Stock turnover

$$\frac{\text{Y/E stock}}{\text{Av. daily CoS}} \qquad \frac{370}{1,650} \times 365 = 82 \text{ days} \qquad \frac{1,200}{2,700} \times 365 = 162 \text{ days}$$

7. Debtors collection period

$$\frac{\text{Y/E debtors}}{\text{Av. daily sales}} \qquad \frac{440}{3,000} \times 365 = 54 \text{ days} \qquad \frac{810}{4,600} \times 365 = 64 \text{ days}$$

8. Creditors payment period

$$\frac{\text{Y/E creditors}}{\text{Av. daily purch.}} \qquad \frac{450}{1,790} \times 365 = 92 \text{ days} \qquad \frac{950}{3,530} \times 365 = 98 \text{ days}$$

9. Cash cycle

Stock turnover period	82	162
Debtors collection period	54	64
Creditors payment period	(92)	(98)
Cash cycle	44 days	128 days

Note: Calculation of purchases

Cost of sales	1,650	2,700
+ Closing stock	370	1,200
– Opening stock	(230)	(370)
= Purchases	1,790	3,530

Comment

Although Worthy's net profit margin has decreased from 12% to 11% (caused by a decrease in gross profit margin from 45% to 41%), its ROCE has increased from 24% to 28% due to the increase in its asset utilisation from 2.1 times to 2.6 times.

However, its liquidity gives cause for concern. Both the current and liquid ratios are low and need careful monitoring. Although the current ratio has improved slightly, the liquid ratio appears very low for a manufacturer at 0.3:1.0. (Some businesses, such as Sainsbury's and Tesco, operate normally with very similar liquid ratios.)

The cause of the liquidity downturn can be identified by analysing the working capital ratios. The debtors collection period has worsened by 10 days but the creditors payment period has improved by 6 days; these changes, with a net effect of 4 days, are not the cause of the overdraft doubling from £0.9 to £1.95 million and the cash cycle increasing by 84 days from 44 to 128 days!

The major cause of concern is the stock turnover period which has doubled from 82 days to 162 days! The quantity of stock held at the year-end to support operations has increased by 200% in one year from £0.37 to £1.2 million whilst sales have only increased by 50% from £3.0 to £4.6 million. Why is so much extra stock needed compared to last year?

The reasons for this need further investigation; the increase **may be justifiable** but it is more likely to be due to a rapid deterioration in stock control. If stock levels are reduced so that they are proportional to the increase in sales, they would be £550,000 (£650,000 below the current level of £1.2 million). This change would reduce the overdraft on a £-for-£ basis to £1.3 million (£1,950,000 − £650,000), well within the original limit of £1.6 million.

However, as the sales expansion in 2006 was led by price reductions, this correction strategy may be a tall order as sales volumes will have risen by more than 50% to achieve this increase in sales revenue. Even so, it would be a good strategy to pursue; aiming high will hopefully achieve a significant improvement in stock control. At the same time, targets should also be set for improving the debtors collection period and the creditors payment period. This will further reduce the amount of overdraft needed.

Q4.2 BKZ Limited – Solution

1. Cash budget (£000)

Month	April	May	June	July	August	September
Rev. 30%	6	12	18	30	30	30
50%	0	10	20	30	50	50
15%	0	0	3	6	9	15
Total IN	6	22	41	66	89	95
Expenses	63	53	57	63	63	63
Deprec'n	13	13	13	13	13	13
Total OUT	50	40	44	50	50	50
Net IN/(OUT)	(44)	(18)	(3)	16	39	45
Op. balance	2	(42)	(60)	(63)	(47)	(8)
Cl. balance	(42)	(60)	(63)	(47)	(8)	37

Comment: The predicted overdraft exceeds the limit imposed by the bank for each of the first four months; the worst position shows the need for an overdraft of £63,000 at the end of June. The original plan is not viable unless there is a cash injection of at least £23,000.

2. Cash budget (£000)

Month	April	May	June	July	August	September
Rev. (60−6)%	10.8	21.6	32.4	54.0	54.0	54.0
20%	0	4	8	12	20	20
15%	0	0	3	6	9	15
Total IN	10.8	25.6	43.4	72.0	83.0	89.0
Expenses	63	53	57	63	63	63
Deprec'n	13	13	13	13	13	13
Total OUT	50	40	44	50	50	50
Net IN/(OUT)	(39.2)	(14.4)	(0.6)	22.0	33.0	39.0
Op. balance	2	(37.2)	(51.6)	(52.2)	(30.2)	2.8
Cl. balance	(37.2)	(51.6)	(52.2)	(30.2)	2.8	41.8

Advice: The cash discount has improved the cash flow but the overdraft still exceeds the bank's limit in May and June by over £10,000. Also, £25,200 of profit will be lost in the period due to the cash discount [(420,000 × 60%) × 10%].

One alternative to offering a cash discount is to pay the expenses (excluding depreciation) one month after they have been incurred. The original budgeted profit would be unaffected and the cash budget would then be as follows:

A. Cash budget (£000)

Month	April	May	June	July	August	September
Rev. 30%	6	12	18	30	30	30
50%	0	10	20	30	50	50
15%	0	0	3	6	9	15
Total IN	6	22	41	66	89	95
Expenses		63	53	57	63	63
Deprec'n		13	13	13	13	13
Total OUT	0	50	40	44	50	50
Net IN/(OUT)	6	(28)	1	22	39	45
Op. balance	2	8	(20)	(19)	3	42
Cl. balance	8	(20)	(19)	3	42	97

If this were achievable, only half of the overdraft facility would be needed. But, it is very unlikely that a new company would be able to purchase its supplies on credit terms. A more realistic target may be for BKZ to source half its supplies on one month's credit. In this case, the cash budget would be as follows:

B. Cash budget (£000)

Month	April	May	June	July	August	September
Rev. 30%	6	12	18	30	30	30
50%	0	10	20	30	50	50
15%	0	0	3	6	9	15
Total IN	6	22	41	66	89	95
(Exps–Depn) 50%	25	20	22	25	25	25
(Exps–Depn) 50%	0	25	20	22	25	25
Total OUT	25	45	42	47	50	50
Net IN/(OUT)	(19)	(23)	(1)	19	39	45
Op. balance	2	(17)	(40)	(41)	(22)	17
Cl. balance	(17)	(40)	(41)	(22)	17	62

This shows that the bank's limit will only be exceeded by £1,000 at the end of June. By careful management of payments to creditors in June, it should be possible to postpone at least £1,000 of payments into July so that the overdraft at the end of June is no more than £40,000. Alternatively, or in addition, the bank could be asked for a temporary overdraft limit extension of £1,000 for the month of June. Also, there would be no loss of profit as there would be no need to introduce a cash discount.

Q4.3 Rogers Motor Parts – Solution

1. Calculations

	2005	2004
Mark-up	$\dfrac{50,000}{150,000} \times 100$	$\dfrac{40,000}{80,000}$
	= **33%**	= **50%**
Gross profit/sales	$\dfrac{50,000}{200,000} \times 100$	$\dfrac{40,000}{120,000}$
	= **25%**	= **33%**
Return on capital employed	$\dfrac{35,000}{50,000} \times 100$	$\dfrac{30,000}{38,000}$
	= **70%**	= **79%**
Debtor period	$\dfrac{36,000}{200,000} \times 365$	$\dfrac{12,000}{120,000} \times 365$
	= **66 days**	= **37 days**
Stock turnover days	$\dfrac{18,000}{150,000} \times 365$	$\dfrac{7,000}{80,000} \times 365$
	= **44 days**	= **32 days**
Purchases (CoGS + Cl. stk – Op. stk)	$150,000 + 18,000 - 7,000$ $= 161,000$	$80,000 + 7,000 - 5,000$ $= 82,000$
Creditor payment period	$\dfrac{37,000}{161,000} \times 365$	$\dfrac{15,000}{82,000} \times 365$
	= **84 days**	= **67 days**
Cash cycle	$66 + 44 - 84$ $= $ **26 days**	$37 + 32 - 67$ $= $ **2 days**
Current ratio	$\dfrac{54,000}{47,000}$	$\dfrac{20,000}{15,000}$
	= **1.1:1.0**	= **1.3:1.0**
Liquid ratio	$\dfrac{54,000 - 18,000}{47,000}$	$\dfrac{20,000 - 7,000}{15,000}$
	= **0.8:1.0**	= **0.9:1.0**

2. Discussion

The following points appear to be due to the reduction in selling prices:

- Sales have increased by £80,000 (67%).
- Gross profit increased by £10,000 (25%) and net profit by £5,000 (16.7%).
- Mark-up has fallen steeply (50% to 33%) as has the gross profit percentage (33% to 25%).

- Return on capital employed (based on year-end balances) is still high despite a fall from 79% to 70%.
- Increased sales may also be due to the near doubling of the credit period allowed to customers (37 to 66 days).
- This would also explain the cash balance changing from £1,000 positive to £10,000 negative.

The liquidity position at the end of 2005, as measured by both current and liquid ratios, appears satisfactory although slightly worse than 2004. However, the cash flow position is alarming. This is a classic case of 'overtrading' where the necessary additional working capital to facilitate the rapid trading expansion was not anticipated. The overdraft is right on the limit and cheques are likely to 'bounce', destroying suppliers' confidence and causing them to insist on cash terms for future purchases. This is particularly so as creditor days have increased from 67 to 84 days resulting in more chasing by suppliers and a reduction in their confidence. Once cheques are dishonoured, word will soon get round the industry and a vicious downward spiral will follow, possibly leading to insolvency. Although Vic's strategy has increased his net profit by 17%, his business is in danger of collapsing; he is 'walking on a knife-edge' at the moment.

Vic would be well advised to tighten up his debt collection which seems to have slipped out of control. By collecting his debts earlier he will be able to return to paying his suppliers two months after delivery and reduce the threat of their withdrawing his credit. He should also take steps to reduce the number of days stock spends on his premises; this will also improve his cash position. These two actions should also enable him to reduce the amount of the overdraft used; this is essential to help prevent the vicious spiral referred to above. Vic was probably so busy due to the 67% expansion in sales that he forgot about the importance of controlling his working capital. If he does not give this his immediate attention, he may well find himself out of business!

He should also seriously reconsider his strategy of cutting prices to achieve more volume. Apart from the increased working capital requirement, he has probably doubled his sales volume. But all the extra work this involves is generating only a very modest increase in net profit. Many of his new sales probably make him no money at all!

Q5.1 Bodgit Ltd – Solution

		£	Workings	£
1 a)	Materials	15	Sales price	50
	Direct labour	8	Less: Variable cost	30
	Variable overheads	7	Unit contribution	20
	Variable cost	30		

b) BEP = fixed costs/unit contribution = 3,000/20 = **150 chairs**

c) Total contribution = fixed costs + profit

$\quad$ 200 × 20 = 3,000 + profit

$\quad\quad$ **Profit = £1,000**

d) Total contribution = fixed costs + profit

$\quad$ N × 20 = 3,000 + 4,000

$\quad\quad$ N = 7,000/20

$\quad\quad\quad$ = **350 chairs**

2 a) BEP = fixed costs/unit contribution

Workings	£
Materials	18 (15 × 1.20)
Direct labour	8
Variable overheads	7
Variable cost	33
Sales price	48
Unit contribution	15

$$= (3{,}000 + 1{,}000)/15$$
$$= \mathbf{267\ chairs}$$

b) Total contribution = fixed costs + profit
$$350 \times 15 = 4{,}000 + \text{profit}$$
$$\text{Profit} = 5{,}250 - 4{,}000$$
$$\mathbf{Profit = \pounds1{,}250}$$

c) Margin of safety = (actual − BEP)/actual
$$= (350 - 267)/350$$
$$= 83/350$$
$$= \mathbf{24\%\ of\ sales}$$

d) Total contribution = fixed costs + profit
$$N \times 15 = 4{,}000 + 4{,}000$$
$$N = 8{,}000/15$$
$$N = \mathbf{533\ chairs}$$

3 The answers to these questions should be viewed as estimates because the variable costing financial model is based on several assumptions and approximations. For example, total revenue and total cost are shown as straight lines on the breakeven chart. In reality, they are curved as the selling price and total cost *per unit* tend to decrease as the volume of activity increases.

Also, breakeven charts are applicable only to single products (or constant sales mixes of several products). In reality, almost all manufacturers make more than one product. For breakeven purposes this necessitates a theoretical apportionment of the firm's fixed assets between different products. Some degree of approximation and subjectivity is unavoidable in this process.

Q5.2 Concord Toy Company – Solution

Operating Unit 1

Workings

Unit contribution = sales price − variable cost = 2.00 − 1.50 = £0.50
Sales forecast = £800,000/£2 = 400,000 pens

1 $$\text{BEP} = \frac{\text{fixed costs}}{\text{contribution/Unit}} = \frac{\pounds150{,}000}{\pounds0.5} = \mathbf{300{,}000\ units}$$

Breakeven point in £ sales = 300,000 × £2/pen = **£600,000**

2 $$\text{Margin of safety} = \frac{\text{planned sales} - \text{breakeven sales}}{\text{planned sales}} = \frac{\pounds800{,}000 - \pounds600{,}000}{\pounds800{,}000} = \mathbf{25\%}$$

3 ROCE at 400,000 pens: Profit = total contribution − total fixed cost

$$= (400,000 \times £0.50) - 150,000 = 50,000$$

$$\text{ROCE} = \frac{50,000}{300,000} = 16.7\%$$

4 For 450,000 pens: Total contribution = 450,000 × £0.50 = £225,000

less total fixed cost   = £150,000

equals net profit   = £ 75,000

When a firm operates at maximum capacity, problems usually occur due to the lack of 'leeway' or safety margin if anything goes wrong. These problems affect through-put and profitability adversely.

5 Total contribution   = total fixed cost + profit

$N \times$ unit contribution = total fixed cost + profit

$$N = \frac{\text{total fixed cost} + \text{profit}}{\text{unit contribution}}$$

$$N = \frac{150,000 + 60,000}{£0.50}$$

$$N = \textbf{420,000 pens}$$

6 Possible actions to increase profitability:
  ● Review selling prices in the light of the effects on sales volume of the price elasticity of demand. Price reductions can lead to increased profitability if elasticity is relatively high and price increases can have the opposite effect.
  ● Review the potential for cost reduction in fixed overheads.
  ● Review the potential for cost reduction in variable costs.

Operating Unit 2

1 $\text{ROCE} = \dfrac{700,000}{3,600,000} \times 100 = \textbf{19.4 \%}$

2

	Buggy	**Scooter**	**Personal stereo**
Selling price	20	10	10
Variable cost	6	2	4
Unit contribution	14	8	6

Working in 'bundles' of 1 buggy + 1 scooter + 1 personal stereo, the contribution of one 'bundle' = 14 + 8 + 6 = 28

$$\text{BEP} = \frac{\text{total fixed cost}}{\text{unit contribution}} = \frac{2,100,000}{28} = 75,000 \text{ bundles}$$

		(£000)	
BEP occurs at	75,000 buggies	@ £20 =	1,500
	75,000 scooters	@ £10 =	750
	75,000 personal stereos	@ £10 =	750
	225,000 products		**= 3,000 sales**

3	Forecast	−10%	−20%	Breakeven
	£000	£000	£000	£000
Sales	4,000	3,600	3,200	3,000
Variable costs	1,200	1,080	960	900
Contribution	2,800	2,520	2,240	2,100
Fixed costs	2,100	2,100	2,100	2,100
Profit	700	420	140	Nil

4 Unit 2 should not drop the personal stereo immediately as it has a positive contribution. If the company does drop the personal stereo, does not use the spare capacity released and fixed costs remain unchanged, its profit will be

	£
Sales	3,000
Variable costs	800
Contribution	2,200
Fixed costs	2,100
Profit	100

i.e. it will be worse off than it is at present. The personal stereo should not be discontinued unless it can be replaced by a product or products that provide at least £600,000 contribution or unless, by dropping the product, fixed costs can be reduced by at least £600,000. For example, if the personal stereo was dropped 75,000 more scooters would have to be produced and sold to maintain profits at £700,000.

5 The danger is that this 20% price increase will cause a fall in sales volume.
New unit contribution = 12 − 4 = 8   Current total contribution = £600,000
No. of units needed = 600,000/8 = 75,000 units
If the price of the personal stereo was raised to £12, it must sell at least 75,000 units (current volume = 100,000 units) to prevent the company's profit falling below £700,000.

6 Additional information required on the new product would be:
- the selling price per unit
- the variable cost per unit
- the contribution per unit
- the expected unit sales per year
- the length of the contract
- the cost of the new plant
- the residual value of the new plant
- the life of the new plant
- the annual depreciation charge of the new plant
- the rate of interest on the bank loan.

Q5.3 Rover's 'last chance saloon' – Solution

1 Retail price   = 22,000
  Trade price   = 16,500   (22,000 × 75%)
  Rover's total cost price = 13,200   (16,500 × 80%)

At BEP, total contribution   = total fixed costs
(Unit contribution × 140,000) = total fixed costs

a) Variable cost   = 6,600   (13,200 × 50%)
    Selling price   = 16,500
    Unit contribution   = 9,900
    Total fixed costs   = **£1,386,000,000**   (140,000 × 9,900)
                           = **£3,800,000/day**

b) Variable cost   = 8,580   (13,200 × 65%)
    Selling price   = 16,500
    Unit contribution   = 7,920
    Total fixed costs   = **£1,109,000,000**   (140,000 × 7,920)
                           = **£3,000,000/day**

c) Variable cost   = 10,560   (13,200 × 80%)
    Selling price   = 16,500
    Unit contribution   = 5,940
    Total fixed costs   = **£832,000,000**   (140,000 × 5,940)
                           = **£2,300,000/day**

2 Total contribution = total fixed cost + profit
$$N \times 7,920 = 1,109,000,000 + 100,000,000$$
$$N = 1,209,000,000/7,920$$
$$N = \textbf{152,652 cars}$$

3   £
Total contribution   = 200,000 × £7,920 = 1,584,000,000
Less: Total fixed cost   = 1,109,000,000
Profit   = **£475,000,000**

4 Profit = £10,000,000,000 × 20% = £2,000,000,000
Total contribution = total fixed cost + profit
$$N \times 7,920 = 1,109,000,000 + 2,000,000,000$$
$$N = 3,109,000,000/7,920$$
$$N = \textbf{392,551 cars}$$

Q6.1 Burgabar Corporation – Solution

(£000)	West Ham	Hackney	Forest Gate	Mile End	Total
Sales	100	120	120	140	480
Variable costs	20	24	24	28	96
Contribution	80	96	96	112	384
Salaries & wages	32	32	34	34	132
Fixed costs	30	30	32	34	126
Head office	20	24	24	28	96
Total fixed costs	82	86	90	96	354
Profit	(2)	10	6	16	30

If West Ham is closed and fixed costs remain unchanged (except as stated in question):

For Burgabar Group:	£000	£000
Total contribution (96 + 96 + 112)		304
Total fixed costs	354	
Less West Ham's salaries & wages	(32)	
Less reduction in head office costs	(10)	
Add redundancy pay	8	
Revised total fixed cost		320
Revised group loss for next year		(16)

Advice

The immediate closure of the West Ham branch would lose the group £46,000 in the next year. It would turn a group profit of £30,000 into a loss of £16,000.

If head office costs could be reduced by £10,000 without closing West Ham, all the branches would show a profit if sales remained the basis of apportionment for head office charges.

A positive strategy would be to aim to increase West Ham's annual sales from £100,000 to £105,000. This 5% increase would increase West Ham's contribution to £84,000 and turn its £2,000 loss into a £2,000 profit. Also, group profit would increase from £30,000 to £34,000.

The best option is to pursue a sales drive at West Ham (and possibly at the other branches at the same time) aimed at a minimum 5% improvement. The worst thing Burgabar could do is to close the West Ham branch immediately.

Q6.2 Profoot Ltd – Solution

1. Current year

	P1	P2	
Variable costs per pair:	£	£	
Materials	15.00	15.00	
Labour – Machining (£8/hour)	2.00	2.00	
– Assembly (£7/hour)	3.50	3.50	
– Packing (£6/hour)	0.50	0.50	
Total unit variable cost	21.00	21.00	
Selling price	40.00	40.00	
Unit contribution	19.00	19.00	
Annual sales demand (pairs)	14,000	10,000	
Total contribution	£266,000	£190,000	£456,000
Less: Total fixed costs			£300,000
Net profit			**£156,000**

2. Next year – full demand met

	P1	P2	PDL
	£	£	£
Variable costs per pair:			
Materials	15.00	20.00	32.50
Labour – Machining (£8/hour)	2.00	4.00	4.00
– Assembly (£7/hour)	3.50	3.50	7.00
– Packing (£6/hour)	0.50	0.50	0.50
Total unit variable cost	21.00	28.00	44.00
Selling price	40.00	50.00	65.00
Unit contribution	19.00	22.00	21.00
Order of preference	*3*	*1*	*2*
Annual sales demand (pairs)	14,000	7,000	5,000
Total contribution – per type	£266,000	£154,000	£105,000
– per total			£525,000
Less: Total fixed costs (£300,000 × 1.02)			£306,000
Net profit			**£219,000**

3. Next year – maximum of 8,500 machine hours

	P1	P2	PDL
Unit contribution	19.00	22.00	21.00
Machine hours/pair	0.25	0.50	0.50
Unit contribution/machine hour	76.00	44.00	42.00
Order of preference	*1*	*2*	*3*
Production*	**14,000**	**7,000**	**3,000**
Total contribution – per type	£266,000	£154,000	£63,000
– total			£483,000
Less: Total fixed costs (£300,000 × 1.02)			£306,000
Net profit			**£177,000**

* Production workings:

Preference	Model	Demand	Mh/pair	Total mh	Cum. mh
1	P1	14,000	0.25	3,500	3,500
2	P2	7,000	0.50	3,500	7,000
3	PDL	3,000	0.50	1,500	8,500

4. Additional machine

Shortfall in production of PDLs = 5,000 – 3,000 = 2,000 pairs
Shortfall in machine hours   = 2,000 × 0.50 = 1,000 mh

This is within the capacity of the new machine. So purchasing the machine will allow the shortfall to be eliminated.

Total extra contribution from machine = 2,000 pairs × £21 = £42,000
But, additional fixed cost depreciation = 420,000/10 = £42,000
Thus, net effect on profit   = nil

Q6.3 King & Co. – Solution

Budget

	Total cost (£000)	Fixed cost (£000)	Variable cost (£000)
Manufacturing	3,000	2,000	1,000
Sales & admin	1,500	1,000	500
Total	4,500	3,000	1,500

	Total (£000)	Unit (£)
Sales commission (@ 5%)	250	0.25
Other variable costs	1,250	1.25
All variable costs	1,500	1.50
Sales revenue	5,000	5.00
Contribution	3,500	3.50

Contract

	Unit (£)	Total (£000)
Other variable cost	1.25	62.5
Badge	0.50	25.0
All variable costs	1.75	87.5
Sales revenue	4.00	200.0
Contribution	2.25	112.5

Comment

As all fixed overheads will be recovered by the budgeted sales, the contribution from this one-off contract will translate directly into profit. The managing director's rejection of this contract will lose the company £112,500.

    The breakeven price would be the variable cost of £87,500 (£1.75 a cap). So King & Co. would make a healthy profit even at a price of half the amount offered. The managing director should think again.

Q7.1 Burton Brothers – Solution

Assuming the machine is sold to Bridge & Co.

Item	Cash	Avoidable	Future	Note	Amount	Relevant in/(out)
Owing by Wey	Y	Y	N	1	(590 – 180 – 150) = 260	–
Costs to date	Y	N	N	2	£273,480	–
Completion: direct labour	Y	Y	Y	3	2,000 × (10 – 4)	(12,000)
Completion: contracted materials	Y	Y	Y	4	24,000 – 6,000	(18,000)
Completion: regularly used materials	Y	Y	Y	5	204,000/4	(51,000)
Completion: materials not regularly used	Y	Y	Y	3	204 – 24 – 51	(129,000)

Item	Cash	Avoidable	Future	Note	Amount	Relevant in/(out)
Completion: production overheads	N	N	Y	6	2,000 × £88	–
Additions: materials	Y	Y	Y	5	45,000 – 13,500	(31,500)
Additions: substitute materials	Y	Y	Y	7		(12,000)
Additions: direct labour	Y	Y	Y	3	400 × (10 – 4)	(2,400)
Additions: production overheads	N	N	Y	6	400 × £88	–
Scrap value of machine as it stands	Y	Y	Y	7		(6,000)
Selling price to Bridge & Co.	Y	Y	Y	3		400,000
Net relevant cash flow in/(out)						**£138,100**

Notes
1   This income will not now happen; it is not a future item.
2   Sunk cost.
3   Avoidable.
4   Committed cost, effectively of £6,000; other £18,000 is avoidable.
5   Replacement cost.
6   Non-cash item.
7   Opportunity cost.

Advice

Although Bridge & Co.'s offer of £400,000 is much less than the £590,000 agreed by Wey Ltd, despite the extra modifications, Burton Brothers will be £138,100 better off in cash terms if it accepts it.

Q7.2 Eezikum – Solution

Item	Cash	Avoidable	Future	Note	Amount	Relevant in/(out)
UK cancellation fees	Y	Y	Y	1	11 × £10,000	(110,000)
UK lost fees	Y	Y	Y	1	11 × £15,000	(165,000)
UK out-of-pocket expenses	Y	Y	Y	2	11 × £2,500	27,500
New equipment	Y	Y	Y	1	100,000 – 40,000	(60,000)
Lost interest on deposit a/c	Y	Y	Y	3	100,000 × 9/12 × 12%	(9,000)
US fees	Y	Y	Y	2	125 × £10,000	1,250,000
US out-of-pocket expenses	Y	Y	Y	1	125 × 2,000	(250,000)
Airfares	Y	Y	Y	1	2 × £14,500	(29,000)
Health insurance	Y	Y	Y	1		(6,000)
Travel insurance	Y	N	Y	4		–
Net cash flow in/(out)						**£648,500**

Notes
1   Avoidable cost.
2   Avoidable income.
3   Opportunity cost.
4   Sunk cost.

The net benefit of accepting the US tour is £648,500.

Q7.3 Carbotest Corporation – Solution

Item	Cash	Avoidable	Future	Note	Amount	Relevant in /(out)
Contract price	Y	Y	Y			152,000
Components – 35,000	Y	Y	Y	1	35,000 × £3	(105,000)
– 5,000	Y	Y	Y	2	5,000 × £1	(5,000)
– scrap value	Y	Y	Y	3		(1,000)
Harness	Y	Y	Y	4	1,000 × £9	(9,000)
Skilled labour – pay	Y	N	Y	5		–
– abandoned work	Y	Y	Y	6	60,000 – 48,000	(12,000)
Supervision	Y	N	Y	7		–
Machines – depreciation	N	N	Y	8		–
– resale value	Y	Y	Y	9		(5,000)
– lease costs	Y	Y	Y	10	6 × £500	(3,000)
Accommodation – planning permission	Y	N	N	11		–
Temporary building	Y	Y	Y	12	£8,000 + £2,000	(10,000)
Car park – construction cost	Y	N	Y	13		–
Fixed overheads	N	N	Y	14		–
Net cash flow						**£2,000**

Notes
1 Replacement cost.
2 Modification cost.
3 Opportunity cost.
4 All at replacement cost as harness is already in regular use.
5 Unavoidable cost, will be paid irrespective of decision.
6 Lost cash contribution = opportunity cost.
7 Unavoidable, permanent employee.
8 Non-cash expense.
9 Opportunity cost.
10 Replacement cost.
11 Committed cost.
12 Construction and demolition costs.
13 Postponed, not avoided.
14 Non-cash, unavoidable.

Note: Net cash inflow of £2,000 is very close to breakeven. Are the effort and risk involved worth it? Suppose unforeseen difficulties appear? To what extent will the postponement of the car park demotivate employees? On balance, I would **not** recommend acceptance of the contract.

Q8.1 Frynas & Co. – Solution

1 Straight-line depreciation charge $= \dfrac{\text{original cost} - \text{residual value}}{\text{fixed asset lifetime}}$

$$= \frac{£(620,000 - 20,000)}{4 \text{ years}}$$

$$= £150,000/\text{year}$$

$$ARR = \frac{\text{average annual profit}}{\text{initial investment}} = \frac{(200/4)}{620} \times 100 = \frac{50}{620} \times 100 = 8.1\%$$

If this project is carried out, it will lower the company's ROCE which is currently 11.1%. The size of the effect depends on the size of the investment compared to the total of all its investments.

2

Year	Trading profit/(loss)	Depreciation charge	Cash in/ (out)	Cumulative cash in/(out)
1	(50,000)	150,000	100,000	100,000
2	50,000	150,000	200,000	300,000
3	150,000	150,000	300,000	600,000
4	50,000	150,000	200,000	800,000
	200,000	600,000	800,000	

$$\text{Payback period} = 3 + \frac{(620,000 - 600,000)}{200,000} = 3 + \frac{20,000}{200,000} = 3.1 \text{ years}$$

3 and 4 (£000)

Year	Cash in/ (out)	10% factors	Present value	11% factors	Present value
0	(620)	1.000	(620)	1.000	(620)
1	100	0.909	91	0.901	90
2	200	0.826	165	0.812	162
3	300	0.751	225	0.731	219
4	200	0.683	137	0.659	132
5	20	0.683	14	0.659	13
			NPV = +12		NPV = (4)

$$\text{NPV at } 10\% = £12,000$$
$$IRR = 10 + (12/16 \times 1\%) = 10.75\%$$

5 The ARR of 8.1% compares badly with Frynas's ROCE of 11.1%. This project will probably reduce the company's overall ROCE to below 11.0%. The payback period is just over 3/4 of the project's life span. This is not encouraging. Bearing in mind the assumptions and limitations of the technique, a positive £12,000 NPV on a £620,000 project should be viewed as a breakeven position. The IRR of 10.75% does not tell us anything as it is a relative measure and we do not know what Frynas's 'hurdle' rate is, although it is most unlikely to be less than its ROCE of 11.1%. This means that the IRR calculation advises against the project going ahead.

Q8.2 Binley Blades Limited – Solution

Year	0	1	2	3	4	5
Cash in/(out) (£000)						
Plant & equipment	–2,000	0	0	0	0	500
Research & development	0	0	0	0	0	0
Materials usage	0	–500	–500	–500	–500	–500
Direct labour	0	–200	–200	–200	–200	–200
Indirect labour	0	–10	–10	–10	–10	–10
Working capital	–150	0	0	0	0	150
Depreciation	0	0	0	0	0	0
Production overheads	0	–5	–5	–5	–5	–5
Sales & admin overheads	0	0	0	0	0	0
Finance overhead	0	0	0	0	0	0
Sales revenue	0	1,450	1,450	1,450	1,450	1,450
Net cash in/(out)	–2,150	735	735	735	735	1,385
10% discount factors	1	0.9090	0.8264	0.7513	0.6830	0.6209
Present values	–2150	668.18	607.43	552.21	502.01	859.97

Net present value = £1,040,000

Notes
1 Only relevant cash flows should be used for NPV calculations. Non-cash items should be excluded.
2 The disposal of plant and equipment at the end of five years gives rise to a cash inflow of £500,000. The written-down value of £1,000,000 in Binley's accounts is irrelevant.
3 Research and development costs are 'sunk' costs already incurred and not relevant.
4 Material usage and direct labour cause equivalent cash flows to occur.
5 Only half the indirect labour attached to the project is actually caused by it.
6 The working capital is released at the end of the project, equivalent to a cash inflow.
7 Depreciation is a non-cash expense and not relevant to this project.
8 Only 12.5% of the production overheads attached to the project are caused by it.
9 No additional sales and administration overheads are caused by the project.
10 Interest on the loan must not be included as it is already built into the discount rate.
11 The discount factors used were incorrect.

Comment

The corrected NPV is just over £1 million positive, strongly indicating that the project should go ahead.

Q8.3 Stobo plc – Solution

1. Payback periods

Stobo plc Payback periods

	Project SR		Project OHC		Project PF	
Year	In/(out)	Cumulative	In/(out)	Cumulative	In/(out)	Cumulative
0	–44	–44	–40	–40	–44	–44
1	16	–28	8	–32	12	–32
2	14	–14	10	–22	12	–20
3	12	–2	12	–10	12	–8
4	10	8	14	4	12	4
5	8	16	16	20	12	16
Payback period:						
	3.2 years		3.7 years		3.7 years	

2. Net present values

Project SR (£000)

Year	Cash in/(out)	Discount rate 10%	Present value
0	−44	1.000000	−44.000000
1	16	0.909091	14.545455
2	14	0.826446	11.570248
3	12	0.751315	9.015778
4	10	0.683013	6.830135
5	8	0.620921	4.967371

NPV = £2,929,000

5-year IRR = 13%

NPV = 2.928985

Project OHC (£000)

Year	Cash in/(out)	Discount rate 10%	Present value
0	−40	1.000000	−40.000000
1	8	0.909091	7.272727
2	10	0.826446	8.264463
3	12	0.751315	9.015778
4	14	0.683013	9.562188
5	16	0.620921	9.934741

NPV = £4,050,000

5-year IRR = 13%

NPV = 4.049897

Project PF (£000)

Year	Cash in/(out)	Discount rate 10%	Present value
0	−44	1.000000	−44.000000
1	12	0.909091	10.909091
2	12	0.826446	9.917355
3	12	0.751315	9.015778
4	12	0.683013	8.196161
5	12	0.620921	7.451056

NPV = £1,489,000

5-year IRR = 11%

NPV = 1.489441

3. *Advice:* Summary of results

	SR	OHC	PF
PBP	3.2 years	3.7 years	3.7 years
NPV (£000)	2,929	4,050	1,489
IRR	13%	13%	11%

Although stress relief (SR) has the shortest payback period, the best option is oral hygiene and chiropody (OHC) as it has the highest net present value and internal rate of return.

Q9.1 Lewington Limited – Solution

Workings

	Cutting	Assembly	Finishing
OAR/mh	$\dfrac{1,600,000}{40,000}$	$\dfrac{2,000,000}{25,000}$	$\dfrac{1,400,000}{14,000}$
	= £40/mh	= £80/mh	= £100/mh
OAR/dlh	$\dfrac{1,600,000}{10,000}$	$\dfrac{2,000,000}{40,000}$	$\dfrac{1,400,000}{20,000}$
	= £160/dlh	= £50/dlh	= £70/dlh

1 Machine hour rates   £
Direct materials   3,300
Direct labour   4,500
Prime cost   7,800
Production overheads:
    Cutting   50 mh × £40/mh = 2,000
    Assembly   25 mh × £80/mh = 2,000
    Finishing   10 mh × £100/mh = 1,000
                                              5,000
Production cost   **12,800**   Cost/unit = £42.67

2 Direct labour hour rates   £
Direct materials   3,300
Direct labour   4,500
Prime cost   7,800
Production overheads:
    Cutting   20 dlh × £160/dlh = 3,200
    Assembly   45 dlh × £50/dlh = 2,250
    Finishing   20 dlh × £70/dlh = 1,400
                                              6,850
Production cost   **14,650**   Cost/unit = £48.83

3 Mixed rates   £
Direct materials   3,300
Direct labour   4,500
Prime cost   7,800
Production overheads:
    Cutting   50 mh × £40/mh = 2,000
    Assembly   45 dlh × £50/dlh = 2,250
    Finishing   20 dlh × £70/dlh = 1,400
                                              5,650
Production cost   **13,450**   Cost/unit = £44.83

4 *Comment:* The choice of OAR makes a significant difference to the production cost (over 10% in this case). This illustrates the approximate nature of absorption costing.

Q9.2 Graham & Sara – Solution

1 a) **Direct material cost**

	Men's £000	Women's £000	Total £000
Materials	78	26	104
Direct labour	18	30	48
Variable overheads	4	4	8
Variable production cost	100	60	160
Fixed production overheads	12	4	16
Total production cost	112	64	176
Increase in stock	2	1	3
Cost of sales	110	63	173
Marketing overheads	8	4	12
Administration overheads	4	4	8
Total cost	122	71	193
Sales revenue	118	78	196
Profit/(loss)	(4)	7	3

b) **Direct labour cost**

	Men's £000	Women's £000	Total £000
Materials	78	26	104
Direct labour	18	30	48
Variable overheads	4	4	8
Variable production cost	100	60	160
Fixed production overheads	6	10	16
Total production cost	106	70	176
Increase in stock	2	1	3
Cost of sales	104	69	173
Marketing overheads	8	4	12
Administration overheads	4	4	8
Total cost	116	77	193
Sales revenue	118	78	196
Profit/(loss)	2	1	3

c) **Variable overhead cost**

	Men's £000	Women's £000	Total £000
Materials	78	26	104
Direct labour	18	30	48
Variable overheads	4	4	8
Variable production cost	100	60	160
Fixed production overheads	8	8	16
Total production cost	108	68	176
Increase in stock	2	1	3
Cost of sales	106	67	173
Marketing overheads	8	4	12
Administration overheads	4	4	8
Total cost	118	75	193
Sales revenue	118	78	196
Profit/(loss)	–	3	3

2 Summary of alternative profit/(loss) (£000)

	Men's	Women's	Total
Variable production cost	(2)	5	3
Direct material cost	(4)	7	3
Direct labour cost	2	1	3
Variable overhead cost	–	3	3

These results show the arbitrary nature of the absorption costing system regarding the internal distribution of overheads between departments/products. Note that the overall total figure is not affected.

The objective of the absorption costing system is to ensure all the production overheads are absorbed. It is **not** primarily concerned with 'accurate' (in the sense of 'caused by') product or departmental costs.

Q9.3 Stellar Showers – Solution

Table showing apportionments and allocations

	Moulding	Assembly	Packaging	Q. control	Stores	Total
M/c electr.	30,000	8,000	2,000	–	–	40,000
Stores	–	–	–	–	80,000	80,000
Heating	2,400	4,200	4,000	200	2,200	13,000
Lighting	600	1,600	1,000	100	700	4,000
Superv'n*	20,000	25,000	20,000	–	–	65,000
Prod. mgr	4,000	28,500	2,500	–	–	35,000
Bus. rates	2,400	6,400	4,000	400	2,800	16,000
Fire ins.	4,400	3,600	1,800	–	200	10,000
QC pay	–	–	–	30,000	–	30,000
Depr'n	7,500	6,000	3,000	–	1,500	18,000
Total	71,300	83,300	38,300	30,700	87,400	311,000
Qual. con.	5,117	15,350	5,117	(30,700)	5,116	–
Total	76,417	98,650	43,417	–	92,516	311,000
Stores	9,252	67,074	16,190	–	(92,516)	–
Total	85,669	165,724	59,607	–	–	311,000

* Allocated

1

	Moulding	Assembly	Packaging
Overhead absorption rate	$\dfrac{85,669}{34,967}$	$\dfrac{165,724}{63,986}$	$\dfrac{59,607}{10,998}$
	£2.45/mh	£2.59/dlh	£5.42/dlh

2 Batch of 800 SS40Ts:

Moulding	$1,500 \times 2.45 =$	3,675
Assembly	$3,500 \times 2.59 =$	9,065
Packaging	$1,000 \times 5.42 =$	5,420
Direct materials	$=$	16,000
Direct labour	$=$	8,800
		42,960

Unit production cost $= £42,960/800 = £53.70$

Workings

Apportionment of machine electricity (total cost £40,000):
Most **rational** basis of apportionment is 'wattage'. Total wattage $= 6,000$

	Moulding	Assembly	Packaging	Q. con.	Stores	Total
Proportion	$\dfrac{4,500}{6,000}$	$\dfrac{1,200}{6,000}$	$\dfrac{300}{6,000}$	–	–	$\dfrac{6,000}{6,000}$
	15/20	4/20	1/20	–	–	20/20
Overhead cost	£40,000	£40,000	£40,000	–	–	£40,000
Apportionment	**£30,000**	**£8,000**	**£2,000**	–	–	**£40,000**

Apportionment of production manager's pay (total cost £35,000):
Most **rational** basis of apportionment is 'added value'. Total added value $= £7.0$ million

	Moulding	Assembly	Packaging	Q. con.	Stores	Total
Proportion	$\dfrac{0.8}{7.0}$	$\dfrac{5.7}{7.0}$	$\dfrac{0.5}{7.0}$	–	–	$\dfrac{7.0}{7.0}$
	8/70	57/70	5/70	–	–	70/70
Overhead cost	£35,000	£35,000	£35,000	–	–	£35,000
Apportionment	**£4,000**	**£28,500**	**£2,500**	–	–	**£35,000**

Apportionment of business rates (total cost £16,000):
Most **rational** basis of apportionment is 'area'. Total area $= 2,000$ sq. m

	Moulding	Assembly	Packaging	Q. con.	Stores	Total
Proportion	$\dfrac{300}{2,000}$	$\dfrac{800}{2,000}$	$\dfrac{500}{2,000}$	$\dfrac{50}{2,000}$	$\dfrac{350}{2,000}$	$\dfrac{2,000}{2,000}$
	6/40	16/40	10/40	1/40	7/40	40/40
Overhead cost	£16,000	£16,000	£16,000	£16,000	£16,000	£16,000
Apportionment	**£2,400**	**£6,400**	**£4,000**	**£400**	**£2,800**	**£16,000**

Apportionment of lighting (total cost £4,000):
Most **rational** basis of apportionment is 'area'. Total area = 2,000 sq. m

	Moulding	Assembly	Packaging	Q. con.	Stores	Total
Proportion	$\dfrac{300}{2,000}$	$\dfrac{800}{2,000}$	$\dfrac{500}{2,000}$	$\dfrac{50}{2,000}$	$\dfrac{350}{2,000}$	$\dfrac{2,000}{2,000}$
	6/40	16/40	10/40	1/40	7/40	40/40
Overhead cost	£4,000	£4,000	£4,000	£4,000	£4,000	£4,000
Apportionment	**£600**	**£1,600**	**£1,000**	**£100**	**£700**	**£4,000**

Apportionment of heating oil (total cost £13,000):
Most **rational** basis of apportionment is 'volume'. Total volume = 6,500 cu. m

	Moulding	Assembly	Packaging	Q. con.	Stores	Total
Proportion	$\dfrac{1,200}{6,500}$	$\dfrac{2,100}{6,500}$	$\dfrac{2,000}{6,500}$	$\dfrac{100}{6,500}$	$\dfrac{1,100}{6,500}$	$\dfrac{6,500}{6,500}$
	12/65	21/65	20/65	1/65	11/65	65/65
Overhead cost	£13,000	£13,000	£13,000	£13,000	£13,000	£13,000
Apportionment	**£2,400**	**£4,200**	**£4,000**	**£200**	**£2,200**	**£13,000**

Apportionment of fire insurance (total cost £10,000):
Most **rational** basis of apportionment is 'WDV'. Total WDV = £50,000

	Moulding	Assembly	Packaging	Q. con.	Stores	Total
Proportion	$\dfrac{22,000}{50,000}$	$\dfrac{18,000}{50,000}$	$\dfrac{9,000}{50,000}$	–	$\dfrac{1,000}{50,000}$	$\dfrac{50,000}{50,000}$
	22/50	18/50	9/50	–	1/50	50/50
Overhead cost	£10,000	£10,000	£10,000	–	£10,000	£10,000
Apportionment	**£4,400**	**£3,600**	**£1,800**	–	**£200**	**£10,000**

Apportionment of depreciation (total cost £18,000):
Most **rational** basis of apportionment is 'fixed asset cost'. Total FA cost = £120,000

	Moulding	Assembly	Packaging	Q. con.	Stores	Total
Proportion	$\dfrac{50}{120}$	$\dfrac{40}{120}$	$\dfrac{20}{120}$	–	$\dfrac{10}{120}$	$\dfrac{120}{120}$
	5/12	4/12	2/12	–	1/12	12/12
Overhead cost	£18,000	£18,000	£18,000	–	£18,000	£18,000
Apportionment	**£7,500**	**£6,000**	**£3,000**	–	**£1,500**	**£18,000**

Apportionment of quality control (total cost £30,700):
Most **rational** basis of apportionment is 'QC work hours'. Total hours = (40 − 4) = 36

	Moulding	Assembly	Packaging	Q. con.	Stores	Total
Proportion	$\dfrac{6}{36}$	$\dfrac{18}{36}$	$\dfrac{6}{36}$	–	$\dfrac{6}{36}$	$\dfrac{36}{36}$
	1/6	3/6	1/6	–	1/6	6/6
Overhead cost	£30,700	£30,700	£30,700	–	£30,700	£30,700
Apportionment	**£5,117**	**£15,350**	**£5,117**	–	**£5,116**	**£30,700**

Apportionment of stores costs (total cost £92,516):
Most **rational** basis of apportionment is 'issues'. Total issues = 20,000

	Moulding	Assembly	Packaging	Q. con.	Stores	Total
Proportion	$\dfrac{2,000}{20,000}$	$\dfrac{14,500}{20,000}$	$\dfrac{3,500}{20,000}$	–	–	$\dfrac{20,000}{20,000}$
	4/40	29/40	7/40	–	–	40/40
Overhead cost	£92,516	£92,516	£92,516	–	–	£92,516
Apportionment	**£9,252**	**£67,074**	**£16,190**	–	–	**£92,516**

Q10.1 Hinj Limited – Solution

1 Absorption costing

$$\text{OAR} = \frac{\text{total overheads}}{\text{total machine hours}} = \frac{182,500}{7,300} = £25 \text{ mh}$$

		Arms		Brackets
Direct materials		8,250		3,750
Direct labour		46,000		7,600
Overheads	(2,600 @ £25)	65,000	(1,275 @ £25)	31,875
		£119,250		£43,225
Per unit	[1,000]	£119.25	[500]	£86.45

2 Activity-based costing

	Cost pool (£)	Activity level	Cost driver rate
Purchasing	41,500	1,000 purch. orders	£41.50/order
Stores	41,600	650 issue notes	£64.00/issue
Set-ups	26,400	200 set-ups	£132.00/set-up
Machine running costs	73,000	7,300 machine hours	£10.00/mh

		Arms		Brackets
Direct materials		8,250		3,750
Direct labour		46,000		7,600
Purchasing	(190 × £41.5)	7,885	(325 × £41.5)	13,487.5
Stores	(105 × £64)	6,720	(200 × £64)	12,800
Set-ups	(35 × £132)	4,620	(60 × £132)	7,920
Machining	(2,600 × £10)	26,000	(1,275 × £10)	12,750
		£99,475		£58,307.5
Per unit	[1000]	£99.475	[500]	£116.615

3 Comment

The above shows that, under absorption costing, 'Arms' have been overcosted and 'Brackets' undercosted. One possible effect of this cross-subsidy is that 'Arms' have been overpriced and 'Brackets' underpriced. This, in turn, will affect their sales volumes in the market place.

Q10.2 Numan Travel – Solution

		Best Beaches		Cosy Cottages		Great Golfing
No. of reps:		(192×1)	+	(770×0.5)	+	(192×0.5)
	=	192	+	385	+	96
	=	673				

Admin. activity	Cost £000	Cost driver	Annual no. of cost drivers	Cost driver rate
Booking	20,000	Reservation	825,000	£24.2424/reservation
Holiday repping	10,000	Representative	673	£14,858.84/rep
Hotel contracting	6,000	Hotel	1,154	£5,199.31/hotel
Marketing	3,600	Marketing employee	74	£48,648.65/marketing employee

ABC attachment of administration overheads

£000	Best Beaches	Cosy Cottages	Great Golfing	Flygo	Total
Booking @ £24.2424	9,091	6,061	606	4,242	20,000
Repping @ £14,858.84	2,852.9	5,720.7	1,426.4	–	10,000
Hotel contracting @ £5,199.31	998.3	4,003.5	998.3	–	6,000
Marketing @ £48,648.65	1,459.5	973.0	875.7	291.9	3,600
Totals	14,402	16,758	3,906	4,534	39,600

£000	Best Beaches	Cosy Cottages	Great Golfing	Flygo	Total
Contribution	37,500	30,000	3,500	14,000	85,000
Advertising	15,000	15,000	2,000	3,500	35,500
Contribution less advertising	22,500	15,000	1,500	10,500	49,500
Admin overheads	14,402	16,758	3,906	4,534	39,600
Profit	**8,098**	**(1,758)**	**(2,406)**	**5,966**	**9,900**
Preference	1	3?	4?	2	

Comment

ABC shows that, on a cost-causation base, Flygo makes the second-highest profit of the four brands and Great Golfing makes the largest loss. This shows the new MD's strategy to be very high risk.

Q10.3 Wilcock & Co. – Solution

1 Overhead absorption rate $= \dfrac{346,000}{1,384,000} = 25\%$ of direct labour cost

Absorption costing of fraud case:	£
Direct labour	15,000
Overheads (£15,000 × 25%)	3,750
Absorption cost	**18,750**
Profit margin (40% × £18,750)	7,500
Price charged to customer	**26,250**

2 Activity-based costing of fraud case:

Activity	Cost driver	Annual cost pool (£)	Annual use of cost drivers	Cost driver rates
Clerical support	Clerical hours	156,000	26,000 hours	£6.00/clerical hour
General administration	Admin. hours	60,000	3,000 hours	£20.00/admin hour
Photocopying	Number of copies	25,000	500,000 copies	£0.05/copy
Telephone	Telephone calls	105,000	70,000 calls	£1.50/call
		346,000		

Activity	Cost driver	Contract's use of cost drivers	Cost driver rates	Overhead attached (£)
Clerical support	Clerical hours	500 hours	£6.00/clerical hour	3,000
General administration	Admin. hours	70 hours	£20.00/admin hour	1,400
Photocopying	Number of copies	1,500 copies	£0.05/copy	75
Telephone	Telephone calls	400 calls	£1.50/call	600
			Total overhead	5,075
			Direct cost	15,000
			AB cost	**20,075**
			Profit (@ 40%)	8,030
			Selling price	**28,105**

3 **Comparison:**

	Cost	Selling price
Absorption cost	18,750	26,250
Activity-based cost	20,075	28,105
Difference	(1,325)	(1,855)

The current absorption costing system is undercosting this case by £1,325, which results in a shortfall in sales revenue of £1,855. This case is being subsidised by other cases, which will be overcosted and overpriced.

Q11.1 Clamco – Solution

Workings

	January
Direct labour	120,000
Direct materials	90,000
Variable production overhead	18,000
Variable cost	228,000
Fixed production overhead	72,000
Absorption cost	300,000

Variable cost/unit = £228,000/6,000 units = £38/unit
Absorption cost/unit = £300,000/6,000 units = £50/unit
Fixed production overhead/unit = £72,000/6,000 units = £12/unit

Physical stock changes (number of units)

	Jan	Feb	Mar	Qtr
Opening stock	0	2,000	1,000	0
Actual production	6,000	5,000	7,000	18,000
Actual sales	4,000	6,000	7,000	17,000
Closing stock	2,000	1,000	1,000	1,000

1. a) Absorption costing (£000) (abs. prod. cost = £50/unit)

	Jan	Feb	Mar	Qtr
Opening stock	0	100	50	0
Add: Production cost	300	250	350	900
Less: Closing stock	100	50	50	50
Under/(over)absorption	0	12	(12)	0
Cost of sales	200	312	338	850
Sales revenue	256	384	448	1,088
Gross profit	56	72	110	238
Non-production overhead	25	25	25	75
Net profit	**31**	**47**	**85**	**163**

b) Variable costing (£000) (var. prod. cost = £38/unit)

	Jan	Feb	Mar	Qtr
Opening stock	0	76	38	0
Add: Production cost	228	190	266	684
Less: Closing stock	76	38	38	38
Cost of sales	152	228	266	646
Sales revenue	256	384	448	1,088
Gross profit	104	156	182	442
Production overheads	72	72	72	216
Non-production overhead	25	25	25	75
Total fixed overheads	97	97	97	291
Net profit	**7**	**59**	**85**	**151**

2. Reconciliation of profits (£000)

	Jan	Feb	Mar	Qtr
Absorption net profit	31	47	85	163
Variable net profit	7	59	85	151
Difference	**24**	**(12)**	**–**	**12**
Increase in stock (units)	2,000	(1,000)	–	1,000
Production overheads in stock increase (@ £12 a unit)	**24**	**(12)**	**–**	**12**

Q11.2 Rivilin plc – Solution

Workings

	£/unit	
Variable production cost	20	– variable costing production and stock value
Fixed production cost	12	– £9,600/800 units – planned absorption rate
Absorption production cost	32	– absorption costing production and stock value

Stock movements (units)

	April	May	June
Opening stock	–	–	50
Production	800	750	820
Sales	(800)	(700)	(850)
Closing stock	–	50	20
Change in level	–	+50	−30

1. Variable costing profit statement (£)

	April	May	June
Opening stock	–	–	1,000
Production (@ £20)	16,000	15,000	16,400
Less: Closing stock	–	1,000	400
Cost of sales	16,000	14,000	17,000
Sales (@ £60)	48,000	42,000	51,000
Gross profit	32,000	28,000	34,000
Less: Production overheads	9,600	9,600	9,600
Less: Non-production overheads	10,000	10,000	10,000
Net profit	12,400	8,400	14,400

2. Absorption costing profit statement (£)

	April	May		June	
Opening stock	–		–		1,600
Production (@ £32)	25,600		24,000		26,240
Less: Closing stock	–		1,600		640
Cost of sales	25,600		22,400		27,200
Under/(over)recovery of fixed production overheads	–	(50 × £12)	600	(20 × £12)	(240)
Adjusted cost of sales	25,600		23,000		26,960
Sales (@ £60)	48,000		42,000		51,000
Gross profit	22,400		19,000		24,040
Less: Non-production overheads	10,000		10,000		10,000
Net profit	12,400		9,000		14,040

3. Explanation of profit differences

April – no stock movement – identical profits

May – stock increase – absorption profits higher by £600 (50 × £12)

June – stock decrease – absorption profits lower by £360 (30 × £12)

Q11.3 The Valley Fireworks Corporation – Solution

Workings

Direct labour	180
Direct materials	60
Variable production overhead	10
Variable cost	250
Fixed production overhead	80
Absorption cost	330

Fixed production overhead/unit = £96,000/1,200 units = £80/unit

Underabsorption = (1,200 – 1,100) units × £80/unit fixed overhead = £8,000

Physical stock changes (number of units)

	Q1	Q2	Q3	Q4	Year
Opening stock	10	290	550	690	10
Actual production	300	300	200	300	1,100
Actual sales	20	40	60	980	1,100
Closing stock	290	550	690	10	10

1. a) Absorption costing (£000) (abs. prod. cost = £330/unit)

	Q1	Q2	Q3	Q4	Year
Opening stock	3,300	95,700	181,500	227,700	3,300
Add: Production cost	99,000	99,000	66,000	99,000	363,000
Less: Closing stock	95,700	181,500	227,700	3,300	3,300
Under/(over)absorption	–	–	8,000	–	8,000
Cost of sales	6,600	13,200	27,800	323,400	371,000
Sales revenue	10,000	20,000	30,000	490,000	550,000
Gross profit	3,400	6,800	2,200	166,600	179,000
Non-production overhead – fixed	36,000	36,000	36,000	36,000	144,000
– variable @ £20	400	800	1,200	19,600	22,000
Net profit	(33,000)	(30,000)	(35,000)	111,000	13,000

b) Variable costing (£000) (var. prod. cost = £250/unit)

	Q1	Q2	Q3	Q4	Year
Opening stock	2,500	72,500	137,500	172,500	2,500
Add: Production cost	75,000	75,000	50,000	75,000	275,000
Less: Closing stock	72,500	137,500	172,500	2,500	2,500
Cost of sales	5,000	10,000	15,000	245,000	275,000
Sales revenue	10,000	20,000	30,000	490,000	550,000
Gross profit	5,000	10,000	15,000	245,000	275,000
Production overheads – fixed	24,000	24,000	24,000	24,000	96,000
Variable non-production overhead	400	800	1,200	19,600	22,000
Fixed non-production overhead	36,000	36,000	36,000	36,000	144,000
Net profit	(55,400)	(50,800)	(46,200)	165,400	13,000

2. Reconciliation of profits (£000)

	Q1	Q2	Q3	Q4	Year
Absorption net profit	(33,000)	(30,000)	(35,000)	111,000	13,000
Variable net profit	(55,400)	(50,800)	(46,200)	165,400	13,000
Difference	**22,400**	**20,800**	**11,200**	**(54,400)**	–
Increase in stock (units)	280	260	140	(680)	–
Production overhead in stock increase (@ £80/unit)	**22,400**	**20,800**	**11,200**	**(54,400)**	–

	Q1	Q2	Q3	Q4	Year
Net profit using variable costing	(55,400)	(50,800)	(46,200)	165,400	13,000
Adjustment for fixed production overheads in stock change	22,400	20,800	11,200	(54,400)	–
Net profit using absorption costing	(33,000)	(30,000)	(35,000)	111,000	13,000

3. The profit figures derived from variable costing give a realistic view of performance for each period as they do not carry forward any fixed production overheads incurred in one period to the next. This enables managers to monitor performance and to create useful internal reports.

The profit figures derived from absorption costing are created using the basic rule for the treatment of fixed production overheads which has to be followed for external reporting purposes. It enables managers to monitor the cumulative profits which will ultimately be used by the owners of the business to judge the performance of its managers.

Q12.1 Demarco – Solution

	£000
Direct materials	18
Direct labour	32
Variable production overheads	5
Variable cost	**55**
Fixed production overheads	45
Production cost	**100**
Admin overheads	20
Marketing overheads	60
Full cost	**180**
Margin @ 20%	45
Sales revenue	**225**

a) Variable cost = 55:

$$\frac{225 - 55}{55} \times 100 = \frac{170}{55} \times 100 = 309\%$$

Variable cost plus 309%

b) Production cost = 100:

$$\frac{225 - 100}{100} \times 100 = \frac{125}{100} \times 100 = 125\%$$

Production cost plus 125%

c) Full cost = 180:

$$\frac{225 - 180}{180} \times 100 = \frac{45}{180} \times 100 = 25\%$$

Full cost plus 25%

Q12.2 Wizkid – Solution

	£
Selling price	10.00
Variable cost	6.00
Unit contribution	4.00

1 At BEP (say at N units)
  Total contribution = total fixed costs
      $N \times 4.00 = 40,000$
          $N = 10,000$
  Thus, BEP is 10,000 units

	£
Total contribution = $15,000 \times 4.00 = 60,000$	
Total fixed costs =	40,000
Profit =	20,000

2

	£
Variable cost	6.00
100% mark-up	6.00
Selling price	**12.00**

	£
Total contribution $(15,000 \times 6.00)$	90,000
Less: Total fixed costs	40,000
Net profit	**50,000**

3 $(15,000 - 10\%) \times$ unit contribution

	£
$13,500 \times 6.00$	= 81,000
Less: Total fixed costs	= 40,000
Net profit	= **41,000**

4 Other factors to be taken into account include:
  – competitors' prices
  – corporate objectives
  – pricing strategy
  – product life cycle stage
  – effect on profit of lowering prices and increasing demand.

Q12.3 Ride-on Lawn Mowers – Solution

Workings

Original budget = 1,120 units

	£
Total sales revenue	2,800,000
Total profit	800,000
Total full cost	2,000,000
Total fixed cost	1,104,000
Total variable cost	896,000
Variable cost/unit = 896,000/1,120 = £800/unit	

a) Total sales revenue is £2.8 million and sales price reduced to £2,150.
Assume no change in fixed costs.

No. of units sold = £2,800,000/2,150 = 1,302

For ROCE to stay at 20%, profit must stay at £800,000.

Total sales revenue	2,800,000
Required profit	800,000
Total costs	2,000,000
Total fixed cost	1,104,000
Total variable cost	896,000

Revised variable cost/unit = 896,000/1,302 = £688/unit
Original variable cost/unit = £800/unit
Required reduction in variable cost = **£112/unit**

112/800 = **14%**

b) Total sales revenue reduces to £2.5 million and sales price reduced to £2,150.
Assume no change in fixed costs.

No. of units sold = £2,500,000/2,150 = 1,163

Profit must stay at £800,000 for ROCE to stay at 20%.

Total sales revenue	2,500,000
Required profit	800,000
Total costs	1,700,000
Total fixed cost	1,104,000
Total variable cost	596,000

Revised variable cost/unit = 596,000/1,163 = £512/unit
Original variable cost/unit = £800/unit
Required reduction in var. cost = **£288/unit**

288/800 = **36%**

Advice

As shown above, the budgeted full cost of the Luxon is £1,800. But as the selling price has been significantly decreased, a greater number will have to be sold to achieve the £800,000 forecast profit which is needed to maintain ROCE at 20%.

- If total sales revenue can be maintained at £2.8 million (despite the price reduction to £2,150) and fixed costs cannot be reduced, the variable costs will have to be reduced by 14% to £688 per unit. This is a challenging target but may well be achievable.
- If total sales revenue decreases to £2.5 million in this very competitive market and fixed costs cannot be reduced, the variable costs will have to be reduced by 36% to £512 per unit. This is a huge task and is probably unachievable.

The variable costs need to be re-examined with a view to their reduction. The mower should be re-engineered. For example, is it possible to use less costly components which still meet specifications? Is it possible to replace several parts with just one that will do the job? If so, resources will be saved in ordering, inspection, storage and fitting. Even if the full amount of savings cannot be made, the greater they are, the less will be the fall in their ROCE.

The company would be well advised also to scrutinise its fixed overheads to see if any of these could be reduced. It is likely that some saving will be found, but less than the total amount needed. However, this would mean that the variable cost reduction target would diminish and so become more achievable.

The best chance of receiving an annual bonus next year is to employ the technique of *target costing/pricing* to reduce variable costs by at least 14%. Also, the selling price reduction needs to be sufficient to increase volume by 16.25% $[(1,302 - 1,120)/1,120]$. This will maintain sales revenue, net profit, ROCE and the annual bonus!

Q13.1 RI v ROI – Solution

Division	A	B	C	D
Profit before head office charges	2	3	24	14
Capital employed	30	60	450	240
ROCE	6.7%	5.0%	5.3%	5.8%
ROCE preferences	1	4	3	2
Notional interest @ 5%	1.5	3.0	22.5	12.0
RI (profit before HO charges – interest)	0.5	0.0	1.5	2.0
RI preferences	3	4	2	1

Comment

'Profit before head office charges' has been used to calculate ROCE as this is the most appropriate measure of divisional performance. Note that the two sets of rankings give different answers as to which divisions have performed better than others. Both answers are correct; which one is used depends entirely on head office.

Q13.2 Gorgon Group plc – Solution

A. **Odeen Division**

	External	Trey	Total
Quantity	30,000	10,000	40,000
Sales price	40	34	
Variable cost	17	17	
Unit contribution	23	17	
Total contribution	690,000	170,000	860,000
Fixed costs	384,000	96,000	480,000
Profit	**306,000**	**74,000**	**380,000**

B. **1. Odeen division**

Total contribution	690,000
Total fixed cost	480,000
Profit	210,000
Compare	380,000
Reduction	170,000 (45%)

2. Gorgon Group

Trey saves 10,000 @ £4	40,000
Odeen loses	(170,000)
Gorgon's net loss	**(130,000)**

C. Odeen loses   (170,000)
   External unit contribution   23
   Extra sales = 170,000/23 = 7,391   (25% of 30,000)

D. Effect on total contribution and profit:
   Trey's increase = 5,000 @ £4 = 20,000
   Odeen's decrease = 5,000 @ £17 = (85,000)
   Gorgon Group's decrease   **(65,000)**

E. Odeen loses 10,000 @ £4   = 40,000
   Trey gains 10,000 @ £4   = 40,000
   Net effect on Gorgon Group = Nil

F. *Advice*: The group should encourage Odeen to lower its transfer price to £30 to match Hexup's offer. Odeen will still be making a healthy £13 contribution a unit on intra-group sales so any demotivation caused should be minimal.

Q14.1 Kellaway Limited – Solution

1. Production budget

Production = sales + closing stock – opening stock

	Large	Medium	Small
Sales	4,000	5,000	3,500
+ Closing stock	400	300	150
– Opening stock	(300)	(400)	(200)
= Production	**4,100**	**4,900**	**3,450**

2. Unit production costs

	Large	Medium	Small
Direct labour:			
Fitters/turners	$1.25 \times 10 = 12.50$	$0.90 \times 10 = 9.00$	$0.80 \times 10 = 8.00$
Assemblers/packers	$0.40 \times 6 = 2.40$	$0.25 \times 6 = 1.50$	$0.20 \times 6 = 1.20$
Direct materials:			
Aluminium	$2.5 \times 3 = 7.50$	$1.0 \times 3 = 3.00$	$0.5 \times 3 = 1.50$
Packaging	$1.25 \times 1 = 1.25$	$0.75 \times 1 = 0.75$	$0.5 \times 1 = 0.50$
Production overhead*	$1.65 \times 2.00 = 3.30$	$1.15 \times 2.00 = 2.30$	$1.00 \times 2.00 = 2.00$
Unit production cost	**£26.95**	**£16.55**	**£13.20**

Total DLH = 4,100(1.25 + 0.40) + 4,900(0.90 + 0.25) + 3,450(0.80 + 0.20)
        = 6,765 + 5,635 + 3,450
        = 15,850
* Overhead absorption rate = £31,700/15,850 = £2.00/dlh

3. Materials usage quantity budget

	Large	Medium	Small	Total
Aluminium	2.5 × 4,100 = 10,250	1.0 × 4,900 = 4,900	0.5 × 3,450 = 1,725	16,875 strips
Packaging	1.25 × 4,100 = 5,125	0.75 × 4,900 = 3,675	0.50 × 3,450 = 1,725	10,525 metres

Materials usage cost budget
Aluminium = 16,875 strips @ £3 = £50,625
Packaging = 10,525 metres @ £1 = £10,525

4. Materials purchases budget

	Aluminium (strips)	Packaging (metres)
Usage	16,875	10,525
+ Closing stock	150	50
− Opening stock	(220)	(80)
= Purchases	16,805	10,495
	@ £3	@ £1
Purchases	£50,415	£10,495

5. Direct labour budget

F/T = Fitters/Turners
A/P = Assemblers/Packers

	Large	Medium	Small	Total
F/T	4,100 × 1.25 = 5,125	4,900 × 0.9 = 4,410	3,450 × 0.8 = 2,760	12,295 dlh
A/P	4,100 × 0.4 = 1,640	4,900 × 0.25 = 1,225	3,450 × 0.2 = 690	3,555 dlh

F/T 12,295 @ £10.00 = £122,950
A/P 3,555 @ £6.00   = £21,330

Q14.2 Pierce Pommery – Solution

1. Production budget

Production = sales + closing stock − opening stock

(000 litres)	Sept	Oct	Nov	Qtr	Dec
Sales	340	300	260	900	320
Closing stock	60	52	64	64	50
Opening stock	80	60	52	80	64
Production	**320**	**292**	**272**	**884**	**306**

Purchases budget

Purchases = usage + closing stock − opening stock

(tonnes)	Sept	Oct	Nov	Qtr	Dec
Usage	4,800	4,380	4,080	13,260	4,590
Closing stock	2,190	2,040	2,295	2,295	
Opening stock	2,200	2,190	2,040	2,200	
Purchases	4,790	4,230	4,335	13,355	
Cost/tonne	£50	£50	£150		£150
Purchases (£)	239,500	211,500	650,250	1,101,250	

2. Cash budget

	Workings	November
Cash sales	Nov 260,000 × £3 × 25%	195,000
Credit sales	Oct 300,000 × £3 × 75%	675,000
Total in		870,000
Apple purchases	from September	239,500
Direct labour	272,000 × £0.20	54,400
Overheads (excl. depreciation)	from October	25,000
Total out		318,900
Cash in/(out)		551,100
Opening balance		(495,900)
Closing balance		55,200

Q14.3 Norman Ropes – Solution

Norman Ropes – Model answer

Period	1	2	3	4	5	6	7
a) Production budget (metres of rope)							
Add: Sales	3,000	4,000	5,000	4,000	6,000	6,000	8,000
Less: Opening stock	1,500	1,000	1,250	1,000	1,500	1,500	2,000
Add: Closing stock	1,000	1,250	1,000	1,500	1,500	2,000	1,750
Production (metres)	2,500	4,250	4,750	4,500	6,000	6,500	7,750
b) Materials usage cost budget							
Usage (metres of ARN)	250,000	425,000	475,000	450,000	600,000	650,000	775,000
Cost (£)	10,000	17,000	19,000	18,000	24,000	26,000	31,000
c) Materials purchases cost budget							
Add: Cost of materials used	10,000	17,000	19,000	18,000	24,000	26,000	31,000
Less: Opening stock	5,000	4,250	4,750	4,500	6,000	6,500	7,750
Add: Closing stock	4,250	4,750	4,500	6,000	6,500	7,750	
Purchases (£)	9,250	17,500	18,750	19,500	24,500	27,250	

Q15.1 Welco Ltd – Solution

1. Flexed budget (1,050 units)

	£
Seals (1,050 @ £2)	2,100
Castings (2,100 @ £3)	6,300
Labour ([1,050/6] h @ £6)	1,050
Fixed overheads	7,700
Total costs	17,150
Revenue (1,050 @ 20)	21,000
Profit	3,850

2. Materials variances

	Seals		**Castings**	
Usage:	$(BQ - AQ)BP$		$(BQ - AQ)BP$	
	$(1,050 - 1,060)2$		$(2,100 - 2,108)3$	
	-20	$= \mathbf{20\ A}$	-24	$= \mathbf{24\ A}$
Price:	$(BP - AP)AQ$		$(BP - AP)AQ$	
	$(2.00 - 1.95)1,060$		$(3.00 - 3.25)2,108$	
	$+53$	$= \mathbf{53\ F}$	-527	$= \mathbf{527\ A}$
Cost:	Budget cost – actual cost		Budget cost – actual cost	
	$2,100 - 2,067$		$6,300 - 6,851$	
	$+33$	$= \mathbf{33\ F}$	-551	$= \mathbf{551\ A}$

Direct labour variances
Efficiency: $(BQ - AQ)BP = (175 - 190)6 = -90 = \mathbf{90\ A}$
Rate: $(BP - AP)AQ = (6.00 - 5.90)190 = +19 = \mathbf{19\ F}$
Cost: Budget cost – actual cost $= 1,050 - 1,121 = -71 = \mathbf{71\ A}$

Fixed overhead variance
Cost: Budget FO – actual FO $= 7,700 - 7,600 = +100 = \mathbf{100\ F}$

Sales variances
Price: $(AP - BP)AQ = (19 - 20)1,050 = -1,050 = \mathbf{1,050\ A}$
Volume: Flexed budget profit – original budget profit
$3,850 - 4,400 = -550 = \mathbf{550\ A}$

3. Profit reconciliation statement

Original budget profit				**4,400**
Sales volume variance				550 A
Flexed budget profit				**3,850**
Sales price variance				1,050 A
Materials:	Seals:	Usage	20 A	
		Price	53 F	
		Cost		33 F
	Castings:	Usage	24 A	
		Price	527 A	
		Cost		551 A
Direct labour:		Efficiency	90 A	
		Rate	19 F	
		Cost		71 A
Fixed overhead expenditure				100 F
Actual profit				**2,311**

Q15.2 Stanley & Co. – Solution

Workings

Flexed budget (for 2,100 frames)

£

Materials: 2,100 × 5.0 m × £4.00/m = 10,500 m × £4.00/m = 42,000
Labour: 2,100 × 0.50 h × £12.00/h = 1,050 h × £12.00/h = 12,600
Total = 54,600

Actual performance (for 2,100 frames)

Materials: 11,550 m × £3.80/m = 43,890
Labour: 1,000 h × £13.00/h = 13,000
Total = 56,890

1. Variance calculations

Materials usage: (BQ – AQ)BP
(10,500 – 11,550)4.00 = **(4,200) A**

Materials price: (BP – AP)AQ
(4.00 – 3.80)11,550 = **2,310 F**

Materials cost: Budgeted cost – actual cost
42,000 – 43,890 = **(1,890) A**

Labour efficiency: (BQ – AQ)BP
(1,050 – 1,000)12.00 = **600 F**

Labour rate: (BP – AP)AQ
(12.00 – 13.00)1,000 = **(1,000) A**

Labour cost: Budgeted cost – actual cost
12,600 – 13,000 = **(400) A**

2. Possible explanations for variances

Materials usage = (4,200)A
- wastage from poorer-quality materials
- wastage due to demotivated workforce
- out-of-date standards

Materials price = 2,310 F
- lower-priced substitute material used
- unexpected discounts achieved
- lower prices from new supplier
- out-of-date standards

Labour efficiency = 600 F
- motivated workforce due to pay rise
- more highly skilled type of labour used
- out-of-date standards

Labour rate = (1,000) A
- recent pay rise
- some overtime at premium rates may have occurred
- out-of-date standards

3. Amendments

The payment of 'idle time' during the power cut affects the labour efficiency variance only.

Labour efficiency: (BQ – AQ *worked*)BP
                    (1,050 – 950)12.00   = 1,200 F
Idle time: Idle hours × budgeted rate
                    –50 × 12.00   = (600) A
                    Combined (as previous) = 600 F

It was originally thought that the operatives had worked efficiently by saving 50 hours at £12 = £600 (50/1,050 = 4.8% improvement on standard). It is now clear that they were twice as efficient as originally thought as they saved 100 hours at £12 = £1,200 (100/1,050 = 9.5% improvement on standard).

Q15.3 Ivanblast – Solution

Flexed budget: £
Sales: 30,000 games   @ £50   = 1,500,000
Production materials: 30,000 blank CDs   @ £1.10 =   33,000
Variable overheads: 30,000 games   @ £0.50 =   15,000
Fixed overheads: =   800,000
Net profit   =   652,000

1. Variance analysis

Sales volume variance
= flexed budget profit – original budget profit
= 652,000 – 410,000
= +242,000
= **242,000 F**

Sales price variance = (AP – BP)AQ
= (45 – 50)30,000
= –150,000
= **150,000 A**

Material quantity variance	$= (BQ - AQ)BP$ $= (30,000 - 30,250)1.10$ $= -275$ $= \underline{\underline{275\ A}}$
Material price variance	$= (BP - AP)AQ$ $= (1.10 - 1.00)30,250$ $= +3,025$ $= \underline{\underline{3,025\ F}}$
Material cost variance	$=$ budgeted cost – actual cost $= 33,000 - 30,250$ $= +2,750$ $= \underline{\underline{2,750\ F}}$
Variable overhead cost variance	$=$ budgeted variable overhead – actual variable overhead $= 15,000 - 15,000$ $= \underline{\underline{0}}$
Fixed overhead expenditure variance	$=$ budgeted fixed overhead – actual fixed overhead $= 800,000 - 850,000$ $= -50,000$ $= \underline{\underline{50,000\ A}}$

2. Budget reconciliation statement

	£	£
Original budget profit		**410,000**
Sales volume variance		242,000 F
Flexed budget profit		**652,000**
Sales price variance		150,000 A
Material quantity variance	275 A	
Material price variance	3,025 F	
Material cost variance		2,750 F
Var. ohd cost variance		–
Fix. ohd expenditure variance		50,000 A
Actual profit		**454,750**

3. The 10% reduction in sales price seems to have paid off as the number of games sold increased by 20%. The net effect of the sales volume and sales price variances is £92,000 favourable.

A total of 275 CDs were wasted. This could have been caused by deciding to purchase slightly inferior CDs than originally planned at the slightly cheaper price of £1.00 as opposed to £1.10. However, the favourable material price variance of £3,025 shows this was a good idea. On the other hand, the material quantity variance may be the result of simply not building normal production wastage into the budget, If so, this planning error has now been revealed and should not be repeated in future.

The adverse fixed overhead expenditure variance of £50,000 should not have occurred and should be investigated.

The net result of the period's activities is that the actual profit is £44,750 (11%) greater than originally planned.

Index